INPUT-OUTPUT ANALYSIS:

FOUNDATIONS
AND EXTENSIONS

Ronald E. Miller
Peter D. Blair

University of Pennsylvania

INPUT-OUTPUT ANALYSIS:

FOUNDATIONS
AND EXTENSIONS

Prentice-Hall, Inc., Englewood Cliffs, New Jersey 07632

Library of Congress Cataloging in Publication Data

MILLER, RONALD E.
    Input-output analysis.

    Includes bibliographies and index.
    1. Input-output analysis.   I. Blair, Peter D.
II. Title.
HB142.M55   1985   339.2′3   84-17975
ISBN   0-13-466715-8

Editorial/production supervision and
    interior design: *Pamela Wilder*
Cover design: *Edsal Enterprises*
Manufacturing buyer: *Ed O'Dougherty*

Printed in the United States of America

10   9   8   7   6   5   4   3   2   1

ISBN 0-13-466715-8   01

Prentice-Hall International, Inc., *London*
Prentice-Hall of Australia Pty. Limited, *Sydney*
Editora Prentice-Hall do Brasil, Ltda., *Rio de Janeiro*
Prentice-Hall Hispanoamericana, S.A., *Mexico*
Prentice-Hall Canada Inc., *Toronto*
Prentice-Hall of India Private Limited, *New Delhi*
Prentice-Hall of Japan, Inc., *Tokyo*
Prentice-Hall of Southeast Asia Pte. Ltd., *Singapore*
Whitehall Books Limited, *Wellington, New Zealand*

Contents

4 Multipliers in the Input-Output Model *100*

5 Organization of Basic Data for Input-Output Models *149*

9 Selected Topics *317*

A Mathematical Background: Matrix Algebra and Solutions to Systems of Linear Equations *366*

B The U.S. National Input-Output Tables (1947–1977) *405*

Preface

Our object in this text is to present the fundamentals of the input-output model and to sketch some of the areas into which it has been extended in recent years. Judging by publications in scholarly journals as well as reports and monographs from government agencies and private consulting groups, there is a great deal of work being done with and use being made of input-output models throughout the world. This is partly a reflection of technological advances that make possible the collection, processing, and manipulation of very large data sets of the sort that are required in real-world applications of the input-output model. It is also a reflection of the fact that much progress has been made in the direction of generating reasonably accurate sets of input-output data from other than primary, direct-survey sources; thus the often-heard complaint, some years ago, that input-output tables are completely unavailable or are out of date (and, hence, of questionable usefulness) by the time they are available is now becoming less true. Finally, the current level of active applications of input-output models reflects the simple real-world fact that there is increasing need for quantitative analyses of impacts—economic, energy, environmental—of various actual or contemplated exogenous factors, such as changes in government policies.

It is therefore particularly ironic that there is no complete, up-to-date and accessible book on the subject. The well-known text by Miernyk (William H. Miernyk, *The Elements of Input-Output Analysis*, 1965) is now out of date, and a more recent book by Richardson (Harry W. Richardson, *Input-Output and Regional Economics*, 1972), also widely read, is out of print, and has been for some time. It is our hope that this book will fill that void as well as introduce some contemporary extensions of input-output not covered in those texts, and that it will be of use and appeal to both students and researchers. We very recently became aware of Bulmer-Thomas's book (*Input-Output Analysis in Developing Countries*, 1982), which also has some of the same motivation. Its concentration is on construction of input-output tables and their use in addressing problems that are of concern to less-developed countries.

We have used versions of most of the chapters in our classes in the Regional Science Department at the University of Pennsylvania, both under-graduate and graduate, attended primarily by students in regional science, economics, and city and regional planning. As usual, we have learned a great deal from their comments and questions. We are indebted to Karen Polenske and an anonymous reader for incisive comments and most particularly to Andrew Isserman for his extraordinarily thorough reading and thoughtful suggestions. Production of the several manuscript versions of this text was possible, in the early stages, primarily through the remarkable efforts of Kelly Herb. Later in the process, Kathy Klingler and Donna Tart corrected and rearranged text with an alacrity for which word processing equipment can only be partly responsible. All this (often frenzied) activity was overseen and orchestrated with unusual calm and capability by Helen Neff. We are grateful to all. It is also a pleasure to acknowledge the role played by our colleagues in providing a congenial atmosphere in which to work.

RONALD E. MILLER
PETER D. BLAIR

INPUT-OUTPUT ANALYSIS:
FOUNDATIONS
AND EXTENSIONS

chapter

1

Introduction

Input-output analysis is the name given to an analytical framework developed by Professor Wassily Leontief in the late 1930s, work for which he received the Nobel Prize in Economic Science in 1973 (Leontief 1936, 1941). One often speaks of a Leontief model when referring to input-output. The term *interindustry analysis* is also used, since the fundamental purpose of the input-output framework is to analyze the interdependence of industries in an economy. We will see shortly that an input-output model in its most basic form consists of a system of linear equations, each one of which describes the distribution of an industry's product throughout the economy.

Actually, the original idea of developing a detailed accounting of interindustry activity is much older than Leontief's model. In fact, input-output can be thought of as a formalization of concepts set forth many years earlier by the French economist François Quesnay. In 1758, Quesnay published a "Tableau Économique," which was a diagrammatic representation of how expenditures can be traced through an economy in a systematic way. He illustrated his thinking by describing how a landowner who receives a sum of money as rent spends half of this sum on agricultural products and half on products of artisans. In turn, farmers buy industrial products, artisans buy food and raw materials, and so on. In Quesnay's later work (discussed in Phillips 1955), he placed observations such as those just described in the form of a table that resembles the "transactions table" developed much later by Leontief. In fact, Leontief (1941, p. 9) introduces his own empirical work by stating that "this work may be best described as an attempt to construct a Tableau Économique of the United States." There were mixed reactions to Quesnay's work after it appeared in the mid-1700s, ranging from "genius" (Marx, trans. 1952, and Mirabeau 1766) to the opinion that "it should be reduced to an embarrassed footnote" (Gray 1931). Today, input-output analysis is one of the most widely applied methods in economics.

More than a century after Quesnay, another Frenchman, Léon Walras, applied notions of Newtonian mechanics in developing a theory of general equilibrium in economics. In this work Walras (1874) utilized a set of production coefficients that related the quantities of factors required to produce a unit of a particular product to levels of total production of that product. We shall see very similar coefficients in Leontief models. As it turns out, Leontief's model is really an approximation of the Walrasian model, with several important simplifications that allowed a theory of general equilibrium to be applied. Leontief presented the theoretical framework and U.S. tables for 1919 and 1929 in 1936 (Leontief 1936), followed somewhat later by his first book on the input-output structure of the U.S. economy (Leontief 1941). This book was revised in 1951 in an enlarged and expanded edition that presented the U.S. input-output table for 1939. Additional developments in Leontief's model are presented in, among others, Leontief et al. (1953), Leontief (1966), Leontief (1974), and in volumes of proceedings of several international conferences on input-output techniques. A more detailed historical account of the early development of input-output is given in Chapter 1 of Polenske and Skolka (1976).

The availability of high-speed digital computers has made input-output a very useful tool; prior to the appearance of such machines, the computational requirements of input-output models made them very difficult and impractical to implement. Today, in the U.S. alone, input-output is routinely applied in national economic analysis by the U.S. Department of Commerce, and in regional economic planning and analysis by states, industry, and the research community. The model is widely applied throughout the world; the United Nations has promoted input-output as a practical planning tool for less-developed countries and has sponsored a standardized system of economic accounts for developing input-output models.

In recent years the input-output framework has been extended to deal more explicitly with such topics as interregional flows of products and accounting for energy consumption, environmental pollution, and employment associated with industrial production. In this text we present the foundations of the input-output model as originally developed by Leontief, as well as the evolution of these extensions to the basic framework. In addition, we illustrate many of the applications of input-output and its usefulness for practical policy questions.

The basic Leontief input-output model is generally constructed from observed economic data for a specific geographic region (nation, state, county, etc.). One is concerned about the activity of a group of industries that both produce goods (outputs) and consume goods from other industries (inputs) in the process of producing each industry's own output. In practice, the number of industries considered may vary from only a few to hundreds or even thousands. For instance, an industrial sector title might read "oil refineries," or that same sector might be broken down into a number of specific petroleum products.

The fundamental information with which one deals in input-output analysis concerns the flows of products from each industrial sector considered as a producer to each of the sectors considered as consumers. This basic information from which an input-output model is developed is contained in an interindustry transactions table. The rows of such a table describe the distribution of a producer's output throughout the economy. The columns describe the composi-

TABLE 1-1 INPUT-OUTPUT TRANSACTIONS TABLE

		PRODUCERS								FINAL DEMAND			
		Agriculture	Mining	Construction	Manufacturing	Trade	Transportation	Services	Other	Personal Consumption Expenditures	Gross Private Domestic Investment	Net Exports of Goods and Services	Government Purchases of Goods and Services
PRODUCERS	Agriculture												
	Mining												
	Construction												
	Manufacturing												
	Trade												
	Transportation												
	Services												
	Other												
VALUE ADDED	Employees	Employee compensation								GROSS NATIONAL PRODUCT			
	Owners of Business and Capital	Profit-type income and capital consumption allowances											
	Government	Indirect business taxes											

Source: U.S. Department of Commerce, Bureau of Economic Analysis (February, 1979).

3

tion of inputs required by a particular industry to produce its output. These interindustry exchanges of goods constitute the shaded portion of Table 1-1. The additional columns, labeled *Final Demand*, record the sales by each sector to final markets for their production, such as personal consumption purchases and sales to the federal government. (For example, electricity is sold to other sectors as an input to production [an interindustry transaction] and also to consumers [a final-demand sale].) The additional rows, labeled *Value Added*, account for the other (nonindustrial) inputs to production, such as labor. In Chapter 2 we will explore how to develop Leontief's input-output model from this basic transactions table.

Next, we turn to the extremely important issue of analysis at the regional level in Chapter 3. Input-output multipliers, which are widely employed in real-world applications, are discussed in Chapter 4. Chapter 5 deals with the construction of input-output tables from a system of economic accounts and the impact of aggregation on the behavior of input-output models. Two of the most important problem areas into which the input-output model has been extended in recent years are energy analysis and ecologic/environmental analysis. These form the subject matter of Chapters 6 and 7. In Chapter 8 we discuss partial-survey and nonsurvey approaches designed to attempt to deal with the problem that the kinds of surveys needed to collect input-output data for an economy can be expensive and very time consuming, resulting in tables of input-output coefficients that are old before they are born. Finally, in Chapter 9, we mention several newer and less-developed directions in which the input-output approach may be extended: supply-side models, linkage analysis, along with dynamic, price, and mixed models. While other writers have felt differently, it is our belief that the time invested in recalling (or indeed learning, if for the first time) a relatively modest amount of matrix algebra is more than rewarded in the way that it facilitates an understanding of both the basic input-output model and, perhaps more importantly, the newer extensions. Hence Appendix A presents the rudiments of matrix algebra and linear equation systems. In Appendix B we present input-output information for the U.S. economy for a series of years. We will have occasion to refer to these often in the following chapters.

REFERENCES

Gray, Alexander. *The Development of Economic Doctrine*. New York: John Wiley and Sons, Inc., 1931.

Leontief, Wassily. *Input-Output Economics*. New York: Oxford University Press, 1966.

———. "Quantitative Input-Output Relations in the Economic System of the United States." *Review of Economics and Statistics* 18, no. 3 (August 1936): 105–25.

———. "Structure of the World Economy." *American Economic Review* 64, no. 6 (December 1974): 823–34.

———. *The Structure of American Economy: 1919–1929*. New York: Oxford University Press, 1941. 2nd ed., rev. and enl., 1951. Reprint. White Plains: International Arts and Sciences Press, 1976.

Leontief, Wassily et al. *Studies in the Structure of the American Economy*. New York: Oxford University Press, 1953. Reprint. White Plains: International Arts and Sciences Press, 1976.

MARX, KARL. *A History of Economic Theories*. Edited by Karl Kautsky. Translated by Terence McCarthy. New York: The Langland Press, 1952.

MIRABEAU, M. *Philosophie Rurale ou Economic Generale et Politique de L'agriculture Pour Servir à L'ami Des Hommes*. Amsterdam, 1766.

PHILLIPS, ALMARIN. "The Tableau Economique as a Simple Leontief Model." *Quarterly Journal of Economics* 69, no. 1 (February 1955): 137–44.

POLENSKE, KAREN R., and JIRI V. SKOLKA, eds. *Advances in Input-Output Analysis*. Proceedings of the Sixth International Conference on Input-Output Techniques, Vienna, April 1974. Cambridge, Mass.: Ballinger Publishing Co., 1976.

WALRAS, LEON. *Elements of Pure Economics*, 1874. Translated by W. Jaffé. Homewood, Illinois: Richard Irwin, Inc., 1954.

U.S. DEPARTMENT OF COMMERCE. Bureau of Economic Analysis. "The Input-Output Structure of the U.S. Economy, 1972." (Reprinted from P. Ritz. "The Input-Output Structure of the U.S. Economy." *Survey of Current Business* 59, no. 2 (February 1979): 34–72, and P. Ritz, E. Roberts, and P. Young. "Dollar Value Tables for the 1972 Input-Output Study." *Survey of Current Business* 59, no. 4 (April 1979): 51–72.)

chapter 2

Foundations of Input-Output Analysis

2-1 | INTRODUCTION

In this chapter we begin to investigate the fundamental structure of the input-output model, the assumptions behind it, and also some of the simplest kinds of problems to which it is applied. Basic references, to which the interested reader is referred, are Bulmer-Thomas (1982), Miernyk (1965), Richardson (1972), and Yan (1969). Chenery and Clark (1959), Isard et al. (1960, ch. 8), Stone (1961), and Yamada (1961) are also useful, although older. Later chapters will explore the special features that are associated with regional models and some of the extensions that are necessary for particular kinds of problems—for example, in energy or environmental studies. In addition to introductory texts of the sort noted above, there are numerous books dealing with the underlying mathematical structure of the input-output model (e.g., Morgenstern, ed., 1954) and with underlying economic assumptions and practical difficulties in implementation of input-output analyses (e.g., National Bureau of Economic Research 1955). In addition to Leontief's original work (cited in Chapter 1), Leontief (1966) contains a collection of articles on particular aspects of the input-output model; there are several sets of volumes made up of papers from international conferences on input-output techniques and applications (e.g., Carter and Bródy, eds., 1970; Bródy and Carter, eds., 1972; and Polenske and Skolka, eds., 1976).

The mathematical structure of an input-output system consists of a set of n linear equations with n unknowns; therefore, matrix representations can be utilized, and the kinds of analysis discussed in Appendix A on matrix algebra are applicable. While solutions to the input-output equation system, via an inverse matrix, are straightforward mathematically, we will discover that there are interesting economic interpretations to some of the algebraic results. We will also find that certain special properties of diagonal matrices are especially useful in representing some of the relationships in an input-output model.

2-2 | NOTATION AND FUNDAMENTAL RELATIONSHIPS

An input-output model is constructed from observed data for a particular economic area—a nation, a region (however defined), a state, etc. In the beginning, we will assume (for reasons that will become clear in the next chapter) that the economic area is a country. The economic activity in the area must be divisible into a number of segments or producing sectors. These may be industries in the usual sense (e.g., steel) or they may be much smaller categories (e.g., steel nails and spikes) or much larger ones (e.g., manufacturing). The necessary data are the flows of products from each of the sectors (as a producer) to each of the sectors (as a purchaser); these *interindustry* flows (or *intersectoral* flows—the terms *industry* and *sector* are generally used interchangeably in input-output analysis) are measured for a particular time period (usually a year) and in monetary terms—for example, the dollar value of steel sold to automobile manufacturers last year.

The exchanges of goods between sectors are, ultimately, sales and purchases of physical goods—tons of steel bought by automobile manufacturers last year. In accounting for transactions between and among all sectors, it is possible in principle to record all exchanges either in physical or in monetary terms. While the physical measure is perhaps a better reflection of one sector's use of another sector's product, there are enormous measurement problems when sectors actually sell more than one good (a Cadillac and a Chevrolet Citation are distinctly different products with different prices; in physical units, however, both are cars). For these and other reasons, then, accounts are generally kept in monetary terms, even though this introduces problems due to changes in prices which do not reflect changes in the use of physical inputs.

Denote the observed monetary value of the flow from sector i to sector j by z_{ij}. Sector j's demand for inputs from other sectors during the year will have been related to the amount of goods produced by sector j over that same period. For example, the demand from the automobile sector for the output of the steel sector is very closely related to the output of automobiles, the demand for leather by the shoe-producing sector depends on the number of shoes being produced, etc.

In addition, in any country there are sales to purchasers who are more external or exogenous to the industrial sectors that constitute the producers in the economy—for example, households, government, and foreign trade. The demands of these units—and hence the magnitudes of their purchases from each of the industrial sectors—are generally determined by considerations that are relatively unrelated to the amount being produced in each of the units. For example, government demand for aircraft is related to broad changes in national policy, budget levels, or defense needs; consumer demand for small cars is related to gasoline availability, and so on. The demand of these external units, since it tends to be much more for goods to be used as such and not to be used as an input to an industrial production process, is generally referred to as *final demand*.

Thus, if the economy is divided into n sectors, and if we denote by X_i the total output (production) of sector i and by Y_i the total final demand for sector

i's product, we may write

$$X_i = z_{i1} + z_{i2} + \cdots + z_{ii} + \cdots + z_{in} + Y_i \qquad (2\text{-}1)$$

The z terms on the right-hand side represent the interindustry sales by sector i, thus the entire right-hand side is the sum of all sector i's interindustry sales and its sales to final demand. Equation (2-1) represents the distribution of sector i's *output*. There will be an equation like this reflecting sales of the output of each of the n sectors.

$$
\begin{aligned}
X_1 &= z_{11} + z_{12} + \cdots + z_{1i} + \cdots + z_{1n} + Y_1 \\
X_2 &= z_{21} + z_{22} + \cdots + z_{2i} + \cdots + z_{2n} + Y_2 \\
&\;\;\vdots \\
X_i &= z_{i1} + z_{i2} + \cdots + z_{ii} + \cdots + z_{in} + Y_i \\
&\;\;\vdots \\
X_n &= z_{n1} + z_{n2} + \cdots + z_{ni} + \cdots + z_{nn} + Y_n
\end{aligned}
\qquad (2\text{-}2)
$$

Consider the information in the ith column of z's on the right-hand side, that is,

$$
\begin{bmatrix}
z_{1i} \\
z_{2i} \\
\vdots \\
z_{ii} \\
\vdots \\
z_{ni}
\end{bmatrix}
$$

These elements are the sales to sector i, that is, i's purchases of the products of the various producing sectors in the country; the column thus represents the sources and magnitudes of sector i's *inputs*. Clearly, in engaging in production, a sector also pays for other items—for example, labor and capital—and uses other inputs as well, such as inventoried items. All of these together are termed the *value added* in sector i. In addition, imported goods may be purchased as inputs by sector i. All of these inputs (value added and imports) are often lumped together as purchases from what is called the *payments* sector, whereas the z's on the right-hand side of Eq. (2-2) serve to record the purchases from the *processing* sector, the so-called *interindustry inputs*. (Since each equation in [2-2] includes the possibility of purchases by a sector of its own output as an input to production, these *inter*industry inputs include *intra*industry flows as well.)

The magnitudes of these interindustry flows can be recorded in a table, with sectors of origin (i.e., sellers) listed on the left and the same sectors, now destinations (i.e., purchasers), listed across the top. From the column point of view, these show each sector's inputs; from the row point of view the figures are each sector's outputs; hence the name *input-output table*. These figures are the core of input-output analysis.

TABLE 2-1 INPUT-OUTPUT TABLE OF INTERINDUSTRY FLOWS OF GOODS

		Purchasing Sector					
		1	2	$\cdots$	i	$\cdots$	n
Selling Sector	1	z_{11}	z_{12}		z_{1i}		z_{1n}
	2	z_{21}	z_{22}		z_{2i}		z_{2n}
	$\vdots$	$\vdots$	$\vdots$				
	i	z_{i1}	z_{i2}		z_{ii}		z_{in}
	$\vdots$	$\vdots$	$\vdots$				
	n	z_{n1}	z_{n2}		z_{ni}		z_{nn}

Input-Output Transactions and National Accounts

As was suggested by Table 1-1, an input-output transactions (flows) table, such as that shown in Table 2-1, constitutes part of a complete set of income and product accounts for an economy. To emphasize the other elements in a full set of accounts, we consider a small, two-sector economy. We present an expanded flow table for this extremely simple economy in Table 2-2.

The component parts of the final demand vector for sectors 1 and 2 represent, respectively, consumer (household) purchases, purchases for (private) investment purposes, government (federal, state, and local) purchases, and sales abroad (exports). These are often grouped into *domestic* final demand ($C + I + G$) and *foreign* final demand (exports, E). Then $Y_1 = C_1 + I_1 + G_1 + E_1$, and similarly $Y_2 = C_2 + I_2 + G_2 + E_2$. The component parts of the payments sector represent payments by sectors 1 and 2 for employee compensation (labor services, L_1 and L_2) and for all other value-added items—for example, government services (paid for in taxes), capital (interest payments), land (rental payments), entrepreneurship (profit), and so on. Denote these other value-added payments by N_1 and N_2; then total value-added payments are $W_1 = L_1 + N_1$ and $W_2 = L_2 + N_2$, for the two sectors. In addition, purchases of imported inputs are recorded in the payments sector; these are denoted M_1 and M_2. Finally, then, total expenditures in the payments sector by sectors 1 and 2 are $\overline{W}_1 = W_1 + M_1$ and $\overline{W}_2 = W_2 + M_2$, respectively. If the exports part of the final demand column is *net* exports, then all the elements in the imports row will have been

TABLE 2-2 EXPANDED FLOW TABLE FOR TWO-SECTOR ECONOMY

		Processing Sectors		Final Demand (Y)				Total Output (X)
		1	2					
Processing Sectors	1	z_{11}	z_{12}	C_1	I_1	G_1	E_1	X_1
	2	z_{21}	z_{22}	C_2	I_2	G_2	E_2	X_2
Payments Sector ($\overline{W}$)	Value Added (W) $\Big\{$	L_1 N_1 M_1	L_2 N_2 M_2	L_C N_C M_C	L_I N_I M_I	L_G N_G M_G	L_E N_E M_E	L N M
Total Outlays (X)		X_1	X_2	C	I	G	E	X

netted out of the appropriate elements in a *gross* exports column, in which case $W_i = \overline{W_i}$ for all i, since there will no longer be an imports row. It is thus possible for one or more elements in the net export column to be negative, if the value of imports of those goods exceeds the value of exports. Also, if the federal government *sells* more of a stockpiled item (e.g., wheat) than it buys, a negative entry in the government column of the final demand part of the table could result. If the negative number is large enough, it can swamp the other (positive) final demand purchases of that good, leaving a negative total final demand figure. (This phenomenon can be observed in the seven-sector versions of the U.S. tables for 1972 and 1977; see Tables B-19 and B-20 in Appendix B.)

The elements in the intersection of the value-added rows and the final demand columns represent payments by final consumers for labor services (for example, L_C includes household payments for, say, domestic help; L_G represents payments to government workers) and for other value added (for example, N_C includes interest payments by households). In the imports row and final demand columns are, for example, M_G, which represents government purchases of imported items, and M_E, which represents imported items that are reexported.

Summing down the total output column, total gross output throughout the economy, X, is

$$X = X_1 + X_2 + L + N + M$$

This same value can be found by summing across the bottom row; namely

$$X = X_1 + X_2 + C + I + G + E$$

In national income and product accounting, it is the value of total *final* product that is of interest—goods available for consumption, export, and so on. Equating the two expressions for X and subtracting X_1 and X_2 from both sides leaves

$$L + N + M = C + I + G + E$$

or

$$L + N = C + I + G + (E - M)$$

The left-hand side represents gross national income—the total factor payments in the economy—and the right-hand side represents gross national product—the total spent on consumption and investment goods, total government purchases, and the total value of net exports from the economy.

With respect to the composition of final demand in the U.S. economy, consumption is by far the largest individual component. In 1982 the percentages of total final demand were as follows: personal consumption expenditures, 65 percent; gross private domestic investment (including producers' durable equipment, plant construction, residential construction, and net inventory change), 13 percent; state and local government purchases, 13 percent, and federal government purchases, 8 percent; net foreign exports, 1 percent.[1]

---

[1] From U.S. Department of Commerce, Bureau of the Census (1983, p. 449).

Production Functions and the Input-Output Model

In input-output work, a fundamental assumption is that the interindustry flows from i to j—recall that these are for a given period, say a year—depend entirely and exclusively on the total output of sector j for that same time period. Clearly, no one would argue against the idea that the more cars produced in a year, the more steel will be needed during that year by automobile producers. Where argument *does* arise is over the exact nature of this relationship. In input-output analysis it is as follows: After observing z_{ij}, the flow of input from i to j, and X_j, the total (gross) output of j, form the ratio of input to output, z_{ij}/X_j, denoted a_{ij}:

$$a_{ij} = \frac{z_{ij}}{X_j} \tag{2-3}$$

This ratio is termed a technical coefficient; the terms input-output coefficient and (direct) input coefficient are also often used. For example, if $z_{14} = \$300$ and $X_4 = \$15,000$, $a_{14} = \$300/\$15,000 = 0.02$. Since this is actually $\$0.02/\$1$, the 0.02 would be interpreted as the "dollar's worth of inputs from sector 1 per dollar's worth of output of sector 4." From Eq. (2-3), $a_{ij}X_j = z_{ij}$. This is trivial algebra, but it presents the operational form in which the technical coefficients are used. In input-output analysis, once a set of observations has given us the result $a_{14} = 0.02$, this technical coefficient is assumed to be unchanging in the sense that if one asked how much sector 4 would buy from sector 1 *if* sector 4 were to produce a total output (X_4) of $\$45,000$, the input-output answer would be $z_{14} = (0.02)(\$45,000) = \$900$. That is, when output of sector 4 is tripled, the input from sector 1 is tripled. The a_{ij}'s are viewed as measuring *fixed* relationships between a sector's output and its inputs. Economies of scale in production are thus ignored; production in a Leontief system operates under what is known as constant returns to scale.

In addition, input-output analysis requires that a sector use inputs in *fixed proportions*. Suppose, to continue the previous example, that sector 4 also buys inputs from sector 2, and that, for the period of observation, $z_{24} = \$750$. Therefore, $a_{24} = z_{24}/X_4 = \$750/\$15,000 = 0.05$. For $X_4 = \$15,000$, inputs from sector 1 and from sector 2 were used in the proportion $P_{12} = z_{14}/z_{24} = \$300/\$750 = 0.4$. If X_4 were $\$45,000$, z_{24} would be $(0.05)(\$45,000) = \$2250$; since $z_{14} = \$900$ for $X_4 = \$45,000$, the proportion between inputs from sector 1 and from sector 2 is $\$900/\$2250 = 0.4$, as before. This is simply a reflection of the fact that $P_{12} = z_{14}/z_{24} = a_{14}X_4/a_{24}X_4 = a_{14}/a_{24} = 0.02/0.05 = 0.4$; the proportion is the ratio of the technical coefficients, and since the coefficients are fixed, then the input proportion is fixed.

For the reader with some background in basic microeconomics, we can identify the form of production function inherent in the input-output system and compare it with that in the general neoclassical microeconomic approach. Production functions relate the amounts of inputs used by a sector to the maximum amount of output that could be produced by that sector with those inputs. An illustration is

$$X_j = f(z_{1j}, z_{2j}, \cdots, z_{nj}, W_j, M_j)$$

Using the definition of the technical coefficients in Eq. (2-3), we can see that in the Leontief model this becomes

$$X_j = \frac{z_{1j}}{a_{1j}} = \frac{z_{2j}}{a_{2j}} = \cdots = \frac{z_{nj}}{a_{nj}}$$

(This ignores, for the moment, the contributions of W_j and M_j.)

A problem with this extremely simple formulation is that it is meaningless if a particular input i is not used in production of j, since then $a_{ij} = 0$ and hence z_{ij}/a_{ij} is infinitely large. Thus, the more usual specification of the kind of production function that is embodied in the input-output model is

$$X_j = \min\left(\frac{z_{1j}}{a_{1j}}, \frac{z_{2j}}{a_{2j}}, \cdots, \frac{z_{nj}}{a_{nj}} \right)$$

where the notation $\min(x, y, z)$ denotes the smallest of the numbers x, y, and z. In the input-output model, for those a_{ij} coefficients that are not zero, these ratios will all be the same, and equal to X_j—from the fundamental definition of a_{ij} in Eq. (2-3). For those a_{ij} coefficients that are zero, the ratio z_{ij}/a_{ij} will be infinitely large and hence will be overlooked in the process of searching for the smallest among the ratios. This specification of the production function in the input-output model clearly reflects the assumption of constant returns to scale; multiplication of $z_{1j}, z_{2j}, \cdots, z_{nj}$ by any constant will multiply X_j by the same constant. (Tripling all inputs will triple output, cutting inputs in half will halve output, etc.)

For the reader who is acquainted with the economist's production function geometry, we examine the usual representation in input space for a two-sector economy with a set of isoquants (constant output curves) depicting higher and higher levels of output, as in Fig. 2-1(a). (For a given value of z_{1j} in Fig. 2-1[a], increasing z_{2j} leads to increases in X_j—intersections with higher-value isoquants.) Input substitution is possible, as indicated by the isoquants showing alternative input combinations that generate the same level of output. (For example, moving rightward along a particular isoquant in Fig. 2-1[a] can be accomplished by reducing the amount of input 2 and increasing the amount of input 1, or leftward by reducing z_{1j} and increasing z_{2j}.)

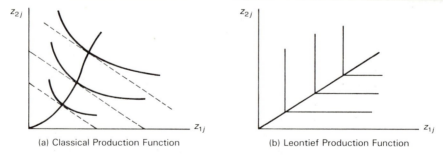

(a) Classical Production Function   (b) Leontief Production Function

FIGURE 2-1   Production functions in input space.

The shape of the isoquants in Fig. 2-1(a) reflects two specific classical assumptions about how inputs are combined to produce outputs. The negative slopes of the isoquants represent the fact that as the amount of one input is decreased, the amount of the other input must be increased in order to maintain the level of production indicated by a specific isoquant. The fact that the curves bulge toward the origin (mathematically, their convexity) reflects the economist's law of diminishing marginal productivity.[2] The "expansion path" representing input combinations that are used for various levels of output is a curve from the origin through the points of tangency between isocost (constant cost) lines (dashed in Fig. 2-1[a]) and the isoquants.

In the Leontief model, the isoquant "curves" of constant output appear as in Fig. 2-1(b). Once the observed proportion of inputs 2 and 1 is known, as $P_{12} = z_{1j}/z_{2j}$, then additional amounts of *either* input 1 or input 2 alone are useless from the point of view of increasing the output of j. Only when availabilities of *both* input 1 and input 2 are increased can X_j increase; and only if the amounts of increase of 1 and 2 are in the proportion P_{12} will all the available amounts of both be used up. Of course, the "true" geometric representation should be in n-dimensional input space, with a separate axis for each of the n possible inputs; the principles are the same, however, when only two inputs are considered. From the Leontief production function, if $z_{1j}, z_{2j}, \cdots, z_{(n-1)j}$ were all doubled but z_{nj} were only increased by 50 percent (multiplied by 1.5), then the minimum of the new ratios would be z_{nj}/a_{nj} and the new output of sector j would be 50 percent larger. There would be excess and unused amounts of inputs from sectors $1, 2, \cdots, (n-1)$. But since inputs are not free goods, sector j will not buy more from any sector than is needed for its production, and thus the input combinations chosen by sector j will lie along the ray as represented in Fig. 2-1(b).

Once the notion of a set of fixed technical coefficients is accepted, Eqs. (2-2) can be rewritten, replacing each z_{ij} on the right by $a_{ij}X_j$.

$$X_1 = a_{11}X_1 + a_{12}X_2 + \cdots + a_{1i}X_i + \cdots + a_{1n}X_n + Y_1$$

$$X_2 = a_{21}X_1 + a_{22}X_2 + \cdots + a_{2i}X_i + \cdots + a_{2n}X_n + Y_2$$

$$\vdots$$

$$X_i = a_{i1}X_1 + a_{i2}X_2 + \cdots + a_{ii}X_i + \cdots + a_{in}X_n + Y_i \qquad \textbf{(2-4)}$$

$$\vdots$$

$$X_n = a_{n1}X_1 + a_{n2}X_2 + \cdots + a_{ni}X_i + \cdots + a_{nn}X_n + Y_n$$

These equations serve to make explicit the dependence of interindustry flows on the total outputs of each sector. They also bring us closer to the form needed in

[2] From basic microeconomics concepts, recall that the slope of an isoquant (assuming that these are smooth functions) at any point is the ratio of the marginal productivities of inputs 1 and 2. These marginal productivities, in turn, are the partial derivatives of the production function (also assumed smooth) with respect to each of the inputs. Thus, the slope is f_1/f_2. As we move rightward along an isoquant, the amount of input 2 used decreases and the amount of input 1 used increases. By diminishing marginal productivity, then f_1 decreases and f_2 increases; hence the slope decreases, as is true for the isoquants in Fig. 2-1(a).

input-output *analysis*, in which the following kind of question is asked: If the demands of the exogenous sectors were forecast to be some specific amounts next year, how much output from each of the sectors would be necessary to supply these final demands? From the point of view of this equation, the $Y_1, Y_2, \cdots, Y_n$ are known numbers, the a_{ij} are known coefficients, and the $X_1, X_2, \cdots, X_n$ are to be found. Therefore, bringing all X terms to the left,

$$X_1 - a_{11}X_1 - a_{12}X_2 - \cdots - a_{1i}X_i - \cdots - a_{1n}X_n = Y_1$$
$$X_2 - a_{21}X_1 - a_{22}X_2 - \cdots - a_{2i}X_i - \cdots - a_{2n}X_n = Y_2$$
$$\vdots$$
$$X_i - a_{i1}X_1 - a_{i2}X_2 - \cdots - a_{ii}X_i - \cdots - a_{in}X_n = Y_i$$
$$\vdots$$
$$X_n - a_{n1}X_1 - a_{n2}X_2 - \cdots - a_{ni}X_i - \cdots - a_{nn}X_n = Y_n$$

and, grouping the X_1's together in the first equation, the X_2's in the second, and so on,

$$\left(1 - a_{11}\right)X_1 - a_{12}X_2 - \cdots - a_{1i}X_i - \cdots - a_{1n}X_n = Y_1$$
$$- a_{21}X_1 + \left(1 - a_{22}\right)X_2 - \cdots - a_{2i}X_i - \cdots - a_{2n}X_n = Y_2$$
$$\vdots$$
$$- a_{i1}X_1 - a_{i2}X_2 - \cdots + \left(1 - a_{ii}\right)X_i - \cdots - a_{in}X_n = Y_i \qquad (2\text{-}5)$$
$$\vdots$$
$$- a_{n1}X_1 - a_{n2}X_2 - \cdots - a_{ni}X_i - \cdots + \left(1 - a_{nn}\right)X_n = Y_n$$

For a given set of Y's, this is simply a set of linear equations in the n unknowns, $X_1, X_2, \cdots, X_n$, and hence, as discussed in Appendix A, it may or may not be possible to find a unique solution. In matrix terms, define

$$A = \begin{bmatrix} a_{11} & a_{12} & \cdots & a_{1i} & \cdots & a_{1n} \\ a_{21} & a_{22} & \cdots & a_{2i} & \cdots & a_{2n} \\ \vdots & \vdots & & \vdots & & \vdots \\ a_{n1} & a_{n2} & \cdots & a_{ni} & \cdots & a_{nn} \end{bmatrix}, \quad X = \begin{bmatrix} X_1 \\ X_2 \\ \vdots \\ X_n \end{bmatrix}, \quad Y = \begin{bmatrix} Y_1 \\ Y_2 \\ \vdots \\ Y_n \end{bmatrix}$$

and let I be the $n \times n$ identity matrix. Notice that the matrix $(I - A)$ will have $(1 - a_{11}), (1 - a_{22}), \cdots, (1 - a_{ii}), \cdots, (1 - a_{nn})$ on its main diagonal and, since the identity matrix contains zeros everywhere else, $(I - A)$ will simply contain $- a_{ij}$ terms elsewhere. Then the complete $n \times n$ system shown in Eq. (2-5) is just[3]

$$(I - A)X = Y \qquad (2\text{-}6)$$

---

[3]This is parallel to the form $AX = B$ that is usually used to denote a set of linear equations (as in Appendix A). The difference is purely notational; since it is standard in input-output analysis to define the technical coefficients matrix as A, then the matrix of coefficients in the input-output equation system becomes $(I - A)$. Similarly, convention is responsible for denoting the right-hand sides of the input-output equations by Y instead of B.

and whether or not there is a unique solution thus depends on whether or not $(I - A)$ is singular; that is, it depends on whether or not $(I - A)^{-1}$ exists. The matrix A is known as the matrix of technical, input-output, or direct input coefficients. If $|I - A| \neq 0$, then $(I - A)^{-1}$ can be found and the unique solution is given by

$$X = (I - A)^{-1}Y \qquad (2\text{-}7)$$

where $(I - A)^{-1}$ is often referred to as the *Leontief inverse*.

If the elements in $(I - A)^{-1}$ are denoted by α_{ij}, then the equations summarized in Eq. (2-7) are

$$X_1 = \alpha_{11}Y_1 + \alpha_{12}Y_2 + \cdots + \alpha_{1j}Y_j + \cdots + \alpha_{1n}Y_n$$
$$\vdots$$
$$X_i = \alpha_{i1}Y_1 + \alpha_{i2}Y_2 + \cdots + \alpha_{ij}Y_j + \cdots + \alpha_{in}Y_n \qquad (2\text{-}8)$$
$$\vdots$$
$$X_n = \alpha_{n1}Y_1 + \alpha_{n2}Y_2 + \cdots + \alpha_{nj}Y_j + \cdots + \alpha_{nn}Y_n$$

This makes clear the dependence of each of the gross outputs on the values of each of the final demands. (For readers who are familiar with differential calculus and partial derivatives, note that $\partial X_i / \partial Y_j = \alpha_{ij}$.)

2-3 | AN ILLUSTRATION OF INPUT-OUTPUT CALCULATIONS

Numerical Example: Hypothetical Figures — Approach I

We now turn to a small numerical example, as presented in Table 2-3. For the moment, the final demand elements and the value-added elements have not been disaggregated into their component parts.

The corresponding table of input-output coefficients, a_{ij}, is found by dividing each flow in a particular column of the processing sectors in Table 2-3 by the total output of the sector represented by that column. Thus: $a_{11} = 150/1000 = 0.15$; $a_{21} = 200/1000 = 0.2$; $a_{12} = 500/2000 = 0.25$; $a_{22} = 100/2000 = 0.05$. In matrix notation, using the "hat" to produce a diagonal

TABLE 2-3 Flows (z_{ij}) for Hypothetical Example

	To	Processing Sectors 1	2	Final Demand (Y_i)	Total Output (X_i)
From Processing Sectors	1	150	500	350	1000
	2	200	100	1700	2000
Payments Sector ($\overline{W}_i$)		650	1400	1100	3150
Total Outlays (X_i)		1000	2000	3150	6150

TABLE 2-4 TECHNICAL COEFFICIENTS
(THE A MATRIX) FOR HYPOTHETICAL
EXAMPLE

		Sectors	
		1	2
Sectors	1	.15	.25
	2	.20	.05

matrix from a vector, and recalling the special properties of the inverse to a diagonal matrix (Section A-6 in Appendix A),

$$A = Z(\hat{X})^{-1} = \begin{bmatrix} 150 & 500 \\ 200 & 100 \end{bmatrix} \begin{bmatrix} 1/1000 & 0 \\ 0 & 1/2000 \end{bmatrix}$$

The A matrix is shown in Table 2-4.

The principal way in which input-output coefficients are used for *analysis* is as follows. We assume that the numbers in Table 2-4 represent the structure of production in the economy; the columns are, in effect, the production recipes for each of the sectors, in terms of inputs from all the sectors. To produce one dollar's worth of good 2, for example, one needs as interindustry ingredients 25 cents' worth of good 1 and 5 cents' worth of good 2. These are, of course, only the inputs needed from other productive sectors; there will be inputs of a more "nonproduced" nature as well, such as labor, from the payments sectors. For an analysis of interrelationships among productive sectors, these are not of major importance.

We can now ask the question: If *final demand* for sector 1's output were to increase to $600 next year and that for sector 2's output were to decrease to $1500—for example, because of changes in government spending, consumers' tastes, and so on—how much total output from the two sectors would be necessary in order to meet this demand? In the year of observation, when $Y = \begin{bmatrix} 350 \\ 1700 \end{bmatrix}$, we saw that $X = \begin{bmatrix} 1000 \\ 2000 \end{bmatrix}$, precisely because, in producing to satisfy final demands, each sector must also produce to satisfy the *interindustry* demands for inputs into the processes of production themselves. Now we are asking, for $Y_1 = 600$ and $Y_2 = 1500$, what must X_1 and X_2 be; clearly X_1 can be no less than $600 and X_2 no less than $1500. These would be the necessary outputs if neither product were used in production and all output were directly available for final demand. But since both products serve as inputs, in a manner that is reflected in the technical coefficients of Table 2-4, it seems clear that in the end, more than $600 worth of sector 1's output and more than $1500 worth of sector 2's output will have to have been produced in order to meet the new final demands.

Using the fundamental relationships expressed in Eqs. (2-6) and (2-7), we find for this particular numerical example that $(I - A) = \begin{bmatrix} .85 & -.25 \\ -.20 & .95 \end{bmatrix}$ and hence $|I - A| = 0.7575 \neq 0$, so we know that $(I - A)^{-1}$, the Leontief inverse, can be found. In this example, using the straightforward definition of the inverse, namely $(I - A)^{-1} = (1/|I - A|)$ $[\mathrm{adj}(I - A)]$ gives $(I - A)^{-1} =$ $(1/0.7575)\begin{bmatrix} .95 & .25 \\ .20 & .85 \end{bmatrix} = \begin{bmatrix} 1.2541 & .3300 \\ .2640 & 1.1221 \end{bmatrix}$. The needed total outputs are then found from Eq. (2-7) as

$$X = \begin{bmatrix} 1.2541 & .3300 \\ .2640 & 1.1221 \end{bmatrix}\begin{bmatrix} 600 \\ 1500 \end{bmatrix} = \begin{bmatrix} 1247.46 \\ 1841.55 \end{bmatrix} \tag{2-9}$$

These values of X_1 and X_2 are one measure of the *impact* on the economy of the new (forecast) final demands.[4]

In many cases, the dollar value of sectoral gross output may not ultimately be the most important measure of the economic impact following a change in exogenous demands. Gross output requirements could be translated into employment coefficients (in either dollar or physical—for example, person-years—terms) per dollar of sectoral output. Let these coefficients be denoted

$$E = \begin{bmatrix} e_1 & e_2 \end{bmatrix}$$

Then $\mathscr{E} = \hat{E}X = \hat{E}[(I - A)^{-1}Y]$ produces a vector whose elements are the total amount of employment in each sector that accompanies the new exogenous final demand. That is,

$$\mathscr{E} = \begin{bmatrix} e_1 & 0 \\ 0 & e_2 \end{bmatrix}\begin{bmatrix} X_1 \\ X_2 \end{bmatrix} = \begin{bmatrix} e_1 X_1 \\ e_2 X_2 \end{bmatrix}$$

If, additionally, it is possible to produce an occupation-by-industry matrix, P, where p_{ij} is the *proportion* of sector j's employment that is in occupation i, then $N = P\hat{\mathscr{E}}$ gives a matrix of employment by sector by occupation type. With k occupation types and two sectors,

$$P = \begin{bmatrix} p_{11} & p_{12} \\ \vdots & \vdots \\ p_{k1} & p_{k2} \end{bmatrix}$$

and

$$N = P\hat{\mathscr{E}} = \begin{bmatrix} p_{11}e_1 X_1 & p_{12}e_2 X_2 \\ \vdots & \vdots \\ p_{k1}e_1 X_1 & p_{k2}e_2 X_2 \end{bmatrix}$$

Column sums would give total labor use by the sector represented by that column; row sums give total employment of a particular occupational category across all sectors. (The vector $P\mathscr{E}$ shows employment by occupational category, aggregated across all sectors.)

---

[4] Here X_1 and X_2 have been shown to two decimals for later comparison. In any actual analysis, such detail would hardly be warranted because of the much less accurate data from which the technical coefficients are derived (compare the figures in Table 2-3).

To continue with the numerical example, we have $X = \begin{bmatrix} 1247.46 \\ 1841.55 \end{bmatrix}$. Suppose that $e_1 = 0.30$ and $e_2 = 0.25$ give the dollars' worth of labor inputs per dollar's worth of output of the two sectors. (We will examine the role of labor inputs and household consumption in an input-output model in some detail in Section 2-5, below.) Then

$$\mathscr{E} = \hat{E}X = \begin{bmatrix} 0.30 & 0 \\ 0 & 0.25 \end{bmatrix} \begin{bmatrix} 1247.46 \\ 1841.55 \end{bmatrix} = \begin{bmatrix} 374.24 \\ 460.39 \end{bmatrix}$$

Consider an economy with three occupational groups: (1) carpenters, (2) engineers, and (3) miners. Suppose that

$$P = \begin{bmatrix} 0 & 0.8 \\ 0.6 & 0.2 \\ 0.4 & 0 \end{bmatrix}$$

(For example, this says that 60 percent of sector 1's labor force is engineers; 80 percent of sector 2's labor force is made up of carpenters, etc.) Then

$$N = P\hat{\mathscr{E}} = \begin{bmatrix} 0 & 0.8 \\ 0.6 & 0.2 \\ 0.4 & 0 \end{bmatrix} \begin{bmatrix} 374.24 & 0 \\ 0 & 460.39 \end{bmatrix} = \begin{bmatrix} 0 & 368.31 \\ 224.54 & 92.08 \\ 149.70 & 0 \end{bmatrix}$$

Column sums of N give 374.24 and 460.39, as expected. Row sums give the economywide (across both sectors) employment of carpenters, engineers, and miners, respectively. If sectoral disaggregation is not necessary, then

$$P\mathscr{E} = \begin{bmatrix} 0 & 0.8 \\ 0.6 & 0.2 \\ 0.4 & 0 \end{bmatrix} \begin{bmatrix} 374.24 \\ 460.39 \end{bmatrix} = \begin{bmatrix} 368.31 \\ 316.62 \\ 149.70 \end{bmatrix}$$

gives employment by occupational type, across sectors.

A wide variety of such conversion vectors (as in E) or matrices (as in P) is possible. In arid regions, water-use coefficients, $W = [w_1 \quad w_2]$ could be used, as $\hat{W}X$, to assess the water consumption associated with new outputs generated by new final demands. Indeed, the new outputs can be translated into impacts on (use of) any number of exogenous "scarce resources." This conversion of gross outputs into scarce resource impacts is explored more fully in Chapter 7.

Numerical Example: Hypothetical Figures — Approach II

Consider the same economy, whose 2×2 technical coefficients matrix is given in Table 2-4 and for which the projected Y vector was $\begin{bmatrix} 600 \\ 1500 \end{bmatrix}$. We can examine the question of outputs necessary to satisfy this final demand in a more intuitive way that is less mechanical than finding elements in an inverse matrix.

1   Initially, it is clear that sector 1 needs to produce \$600 and sector 2, \$1500. If the sectors are going to meet the new final demands, they could not get away with producing *less* than these amounts.

2   However, to produce \$600, sector 1 needs, as inputs to that productive process, $(0.15)(\$600) = \$90$ from itself and $(0.20)(\$600) = \$120$ from sector 2.

These figures come from the coefficients in column 1 of the A matrix—the production recipe for sector 1. Similarly, to produce its $1500, sector 2 will have to buy $(0.25)($1500) = 375 from sector 1 and $(0.05)($1500) = 75 from itself. Thus sector 1 must, in fact, produce the $600 noted in 1, above, plus another $$(90 + 375) = 465 more, to satisfy the needs for inputs that it has itself and also that come from sector 2. Similarly, sector 2 will have to produce an additional $$(120 + 75) = 195 to satisfy its own need plus that of sector 1 for inputs to produce the "original" $600 and $1500.

3   In 2, above, we found the interindustry needs that resulted from production of $600 in sector 1 and $1500 in sector 2. These were $465 and $195, for sectors 1 and 2, respectively. But now we realize that this "extra" production, above the $600 and $1500, will also generate interindustry needs. That is, in order to engage in the production of $465, sector 1 will need $(0.15)($465) = 69.75 from itself and $(0.20)($465) = 93 from sector 2. Similarly, sector 2 will now also need $(0.25)($195) = 48.75 from sector 1 and $(0.05)($195) = 9.75 from itself. The total new demands for sector 1 and sector 2 output are thus $$(69.75 + 48.75) = 118.50 and $$(93 + 9.75) = 102.75, respectively.

4   At this point we realize that it is necessary to treat the additional $118.50 for sector 1 and $102.75 for sector 2 in the same fashion as the $465 and $195 in 3. Hence we find additional required outputs of $43.46 and $28.84 from sectors 1 and 2, respectively.

5   Continuing in this way, we find that eventually the numbers become so small that they can be ignored (less than $0.005).

Looking at the total impact of a particular set of final demands this way is often described as looking at the "round-by-round" effects. The initial demands generate a need for inputs from the productive sectors; this is the "first round" of effects, as found in 2, above. But these outputs themselves generate a need for additional inputs—"second round" effects—as found in 3, above; and so forth. For the present example, these figures have been collected in Table 2-5.

For sector 1, the sum of these round-by-round effects, $647.53, plus the original demand of $600, is $1247.53; for sector 2, the total is $341.57 + $1500 = $1841.57. These total outputs (except for small rounding errors) are the same as those found by using the Leontief inverse, where $X_1 = 1247.46 and $X_2 = 1841.55. (It was for this particular comparison that the two-decimal accuracy was kept in the Leontief-inverse approach to this example.)

In this second view of the numerical example we have developed something of a feeling for the way in which external (final) demands are transmitted through the productive sectors of the economic system in the input-output model of that system. In fact, we see that the elements of $(I - A)^{-1}$ are really very

TABLE 2-5   ROUND-BY-ROUND IMPACTS (IN DOLLARS) OF $Y_1 = 600 AND $Y_2 = 1500

Round	1	2	3	4	5	6	7	8 + 9 + 10 + 11
Sector								
1	465	118.50	43.46	13.73	4.60	1.50	.50	.24
2	195	102.75	28.84	10.13	3.25	1.08	.35	.17

useful and important numbers. Each captures, in a single *number*, an entire *series* of direct and indirect effects. (The equivalence between Approaches I and II is examined for the general case in Appendix 2-1.)

Numerical Example: Mathematical Observations

The inverse in this small example, $(I - A)^{-1} = \begin{bmatrix} 1.2541 & .3300 \\ .2640 & 1.1221 \end{bmatrix}$, illustrates a general feature of Leontief inverses for input-output models of any size; the diagonal elements are larger than 1. This is entirely consistent with the economic logic of the round-by-round approach. From Eq. (2-9)

$$X_1 = (1.2541)(600) + (.3300)(1500)$$

Looking at the first product on the right, the new final demand of $600 for the output of sector 1 is multiplied by the coefficient (1.2541). This can be thought of as $(1 + 0.2541)(600)$. The (1)(600) reflects the fact that the $600 new demand for sector 1 output must be met by producing $600 more of that output. The additional (0.2541)(600) captures the additional sector 1 output required because this output is also used as an input to production activity in sectors 1 and 2. Similarly, from Eq. (2-9),

$$X_2 = (.2640)(600) + (1.1221)(1500)$$

and the same logic explains why the coefficient (1.1221) relating sector 2 total output to new final demand for sector 2 goods, $1500, must be greater than 1.

For the two-sector case, it is not difficult to see that both of the diagonal elements in $(I - A)^{-1}$ will be greater than 1. (A more complicated derivation can be used for the general n-sector input-output model.) From the definition of the adjoint and the determinant of $(I - A)$,

$$\alpha_{11} = \frac{(1 - a_{22})}{(1 - a_{22})\left[(1 - a_{11}) - \dfrac{a_{12}a_{21}}{(1 - a_{22})}\right]} = \frac{1}{1 - a_{11} - \dfrac{a_{12}a_{21}}{(1 - a_{22})}}$$

which is always greater than 1 when $a_{11} > 0$ and/or $a_{12}a_{21} > 0$—since $(1 - a_{22})$ is never negative. Similar reasoning shows that $(1 - a_{11})/|I - A| > 1$ also.

Whether or not the off-diagonal elements are larger than 1 depends entirely on the sizes of a_{12} and a_{21}, relative to $|I - A|$. In most actual input-output tables, with a rather detailed breakdown of sectors, the off-diagonal elements in $(I - A)^{-1}$ will be less than 1, as in Eq. (2-9). However, for example, if a_{21} in Table 2-4 had been 0.80 instead of 0.20, so that the coefficients matrix had been

$$A = \begin{bmatrix} .15 & .25 \\ .80 & .05 \end{bmatrix}$$

then

$$(I - A)^{-1} = \begin{bmatrix} 1.5638 & 0.4115 \\ 1.3169 & 1.3992 \end{bmatrix}$$

Notice that a coefficient as large as $a_{21} = 0.8$—which says that there is 80 cents' worth of sector 2 output in a dollar's worth of sector 1 output—is not likely to be seen often in real tables. The sizes of the between-sector technical coefficients, a_{ij} ($i \neq j$), and of the off-diagonal elements in $(I - A)^{-1}$ are related to the level of sectoral detail (that is, the number of sectors) in the model. We will return to this topic in Chapter 5, when we consider the effects of aggregating (combining) sectors in an input-output model. (In Appendix 2-2 we examine the conditions under which a Leontief inverse matrix will always contain only nonnegative elements, as logic suggests should always be the case.)

Numerical Example: The U.S. 1967 Data

We present a highly aggregated, seven-sector version of the 1967 U.S. input-output coefficients matrix and its associated Leontief inverse in Tables 2-6 and 2-7. (Appendix B contains a series of such tables for the U.S. economy for several years, at both the 23- and 7-sector levels of aggregation.) The effects of various final-demand vectors can be easily quantified. Notice that all on-diagonal elements in the inverse in Table 2-7 are larger than 1 and all off-diagonal elements are smaller than 1.

For example, suppose that there were increased foreign demand (the export component of the final-demand vector) for agricultural and manufactured items of \$1.2 million and \$6.8 million, respectively. Using ΔY for the vector of changes in final demands, then ΔX, the vector of resulting changes in outputs, is found as $\Delta X = (I - A)^{-1} \Delta Y$. Here (in millions of dollars)

$$\Delta Y = \begin{bmatrix} 1.2 \\ 0 \\ 0 \\ 6.8 \\ 0 \\ 0 \\ 0 \end{bmatrix}$$

and we find from $(I - A)^{-1}$ in Table 2-7 that (in millions of dollars)

$$\Delta X = \begin{bmatrix} 2.605 \\ 0.387 \\ 0.149 \\ 12.074 \\ 0.938 \\ 1.628 \\ 0.127 \end{bmatrix}$$

Clearly, as would be expected, the greatest effect, \$12.074 million, is on the manufacturing sector, and the next-greatest effect, \$2.605 million, is felt in the agricultural sector. However, the services sector also would need to increase its economic activity by \$1.628 million. Effects on all other sectors are less than \$1 million. Notice that the total new output effect throughout the country, obtained by summing the elements in ΔX, is \$17.91 million; this is generated by a total

TABLE 2-6 THE 1967 U.S. TECHNICAL COEFFICIENTS MATRIX (A)

		1	2	3	4	5	6	7
1	Agriculture	.2939	.0000	.0025	.0516	.0009	.0081	.0203
2	Mining	.0022	.0504	.0090	.0284	.0002	.0099	.0075
3	Construction	.0096	.0229	.0003	.0042	.0085	.0277	.0916
4	Manufacturing	.1376	.0940	.3637	.3815	.0634	.0896	.1003
5	Trade & Transportation	.0657	.0296	.1049	.0509	.0530	.0404	.0775
6	Services	.0878	.1708	.0765	.0734	.1546	.1676	.1382
7	Other	.0001	.0054	.0008	.0055	.0183	.0250	.0012

new exogenous demand of $8 million. This again illustrates the multiplicative effect in an economy of an exogenous stimulus such as an increase in one or more components of final demand. These multiplier effects will be discussed in further detail in Chapter 4.

2-4 | THE POWER SERIES APPROXIMATION OF $(I - A)^{-1}$

In preparing input-output coefficients tables for many real-world applications of the model, in which one wants to maintain a reasonable distinction between sectors (e.g., so that sectors producing aluminum storm windows and women's apparel are not lumped together as a single sector labeled "manufacturing"), at least 40 sectors are not unusual. The amount of computer capacity needed to invert a 40×40 ($I - A$) matrix will vary with the particular inversion program that is used, but it is not likely at present that facilities in all the regions throughout the world where input-output studies are being carried out would necessarily have the capacity to generate directly inverses to matrices of this size. One approach is then to aggregate the data into a smaller number of sectors. We will say more about such sectoral aggregation later, but clearly industrial (sectoral) detail is lost in the process. Secondly, the inversion calculations themselves can be carried out sequentially on a series of submatrices of $(I - A)$. (This is illustrated in Appendix A on matrix algebra.) However, a rather straightforward matrix algebra result for the $(I - A)$ matrix makes possible an approximation to $(I - A)^{-1}$ that requires no inverses at all.

By definition, we know that A is a nonnegative matrix, meaning that $a_{ij} \geq 0$ for all i and j. (This characteristic is written $A \geq 0$.) The sum of the

TABLE 2-7 THE 1967 U.S. LEONTIEF INVERSE MATRIX ($[I - A]^{-1}$)

		1	2	3	4	5	6	7
1	Agriculture	1.4474	.0206	.0546	.1277	.0167	.0323	.0531
2	Mining	.0175	1.0632	.0316	.0538	.0079	.0206	.0201
3	Construction	.0240	.0346	1.0122	.0177	.0188	.0402	.1024
4	Manufacturing	.3860	.2328	.6592	1.7075	.1635	.2288	.2858
5	Trade & Transportation	.1345	.0632	.1617	.1142	1.0799	.0758	.1238
6	Services	.2192	.2582	.1955	.2007	.2245	1.2525	.2352
7	Other	.0104	.0147	.0125	.0169	.0263	.0341	1.0111

elements in the jth column of A indicates the dollars' worth of inputs from other sectors that are used in making a dollar's worth of output of sector j. In an open model, given the economically reasonable assumption that each sector uses some inputs from the payments sector (labor, other value added, etc.), then each of these column sums will be less than one. (That is, $\sum_{i=1}^{n} a_{ij} < 1$ for all j.) For input-output coefficients matrices with these two characteristics, it is possible to approximate the gross output vector X associated with any final demand vector Y without finding $(I - A)^{-1}$.

Consider the matrix product

$$(I - A)(I + A + A^2 + A^3 + \cdots + A^n)$$

where, for square matrices, A^2 denotes AA, $A^3 = AAA = AA^2$, and so on. Premultiplication of the series in parentheses by $(I - A)$ can be accomplished by first multiplying all terms in the right-hand parentheses by I and then multiplying all terms by $(-A)$. This leaves only $(I - A^{n+1})$; all other terms cancel—for A^2 there is a $-A^2$, for A^3 there is a $-A^3$, and so on. Thus

$$(I - A)(I + A + A^2 + A^3 + \cdots + A^n) = (I - A^{n+1}) \qquad (2\text{-}10)$$

If it were true that for large n (or, more formally, as $n \to \infty$), the elements in A^{n+1} all become zero, or close to zero (i.e., $A^{n+1} \to 0$), then the right-hand side of Eq. (2-10) would be simply I, and the matrix series postmultiplying $(I - A)$ on the left-hand side of Eq. (2-10) would constitute the inverse to $(I - A)$, from the fundamental defining property of an inverse, that a matrix times its inverse generates the identity matrix.

For any matrix, M, if we sum the absolute values of the elements in each column, the largest sum is termed the *norm* of M—denoted $N(M)$ or $\|M\|$.[5] For example, for the coefficient matrix A given in Table 2-4 above, $N(A) = 0.35$, which is the sum of the elements in the first column. (The sum of the elements in column 2 is 0.30, which is less than 0.35.) There is a theorem which states that for a pair of matrices, A and B, that are conformable for the multiplication AB, the product of the norms of A and B is no smaller than the norm of the product AB, that is, that $N(A)N(B) \geq N(AB)$. By replacing B with A, it follows that $N(A)N(A) \geq N(A^2)$ or $[N(A)]^2 \geq N(A^2)$ and finally, continuing similarly,

$$[N(A)]^n \geq N(A^n) \qquad (2\text{-}11)$$

As was noted above, all column sums of an open and "reasonable" A matrix will be less than one, so we know that $N(A) < 1$. Moreover, since $a_{ij} \geq 0$, we also know that $a_{ij} \leq N(A)$; no element in a nonnegative matrix can be larger than the largest column sum. Thus: (1) since $N(A) < 1$, $[N(A)]^n \to 0$ as $n \to \infty$; (2)

[5]*A norm* is just a measure of the general size of the elements in a matrix. (It is not a measure of the size of the matrix itself; this is given by the dimensions of the matrix.) For example, a nonnegative $m \times n$ matrix that has all elements smaller than 0.1 will have a smaller norm than one that has all elements larger than 10. There are actually many possible definitions of the norm of a matrix. The one used here (maximum column sum) is probably the simplest.

from Eq. (2-11), this means that $N(A^n) \to 0$ also as $n \to \infty$; (3) finally, then, all elements in A^n must approach zero, since no single element in a nonnegative matrix can be larger than the norm of that matrix. This is the result that we are interested in. The right-hand side of Eq. (2-10) becomes simply I as n gets large and so

$$(I - A)^{-1} = (I + A + A^2 + A^3 + \cdots) \tag{2-12}$$

(This is analogous to the series result in ordinary algebra that $1/(1 - a) = 1 + a + a^2 + a^3 + \cdots$, for $|a| < 1$.) Then $X = (I - A)^{-1}Y$ can be found as

$$X = (I + A + A^2 + A^3 + \cdots)Y \tag{2-13}$$

Removing parentheses, this is

$$X = Y + AY + A^2Y + A^3Y + \cdots = Y + AY + A(AY) + A(A^2Y) + \cdots \tag{2-14}$$

That is, each term after the first can be found as the preceding term premultiplied by A. (In many applications it has been found that after about A^7 or A^8, the terms multiplying Y become insignificantly different from zero.)

Returning to the original A matrix and the Y vector of the example in Section 2-3—$A = \begin{bmatrix} .15 & .25 \\ .20 & .05 \end{bmatrix}$ and $Y = \begin{bmatrix} 600 \\ 1500 \end{bmatrix}$—we have

$$AY = \begin{bmatrix} 465 \\ 195 \end{bmatrix}, \qquad A^2Y = \begin{bmatrix} .0725 & .0500 \\ .0400 & .0525 \end{bmatrix}\begin{bmatrix} 600 \\ 1500 \end{bmatrix} = \begin{bmatrix} 118.50 \\ 102.75 \end{bmatrix},$$

$$A^3Y = \begin{bmatrix} .0209 & .0206 \\ .0165 & .0126 \end{bmatrix}\begin{bmatrix} 600 \\ 1500 \end{bmatrix} = \begin{bmatrix} 43.44 \\ 28.80 \end{bmatrix},$$

$$A^4Y = \begin{bmatrix} .0073 & .0063 \\ .0050 & .0048 \end{bmatrix}\begin{bmatrix} 600 \\ 1500 \end{bmatrix} = \begin{bmatrix} 13.83 \\ 10.20 \end{bmatrix},$$

$$A^5Y = \begin{bmatrix} .0024 & .0021 \\ .0017 & .0015 \end{bmatrix}\begin{bmatrix} 600 \\ 1500 \end{bmatrix} = \begin{bmatrix} 4.59 \\ 3.27 \end{bmatrix},$$

$$A^6Y = \begin{bmatrix} .0008 & .0007 \\ .0006 & .0005 \end{bmatrix}\begin{bmatrix} 600 \\ 1500 \end{bmatrix} = \begin{bmatrix} 1.53 \\ 1.11 \end{bmatrix},$$

$$A^7Y = \begin{bmatrix} .0003 & .0002 \\ .0002 & .0002 \end{bmatrix}\begin{bmatrix} 600 \\ 1500 \end{bmatrix} = \begin{bmatrix} .48 \\ .42 \end{bmatrix}.$$

Hence the individual terms in the power series approximation (except for rounding errors) simply represent the magnitudes of the round-by-round effects, as were recorded in Table 2-5. (The reader should reconsider the algebra of the round-by-round calculations to be convinced that, in fact, they were equivalent to premultiplication of Y by a series of powers of the A matrix.) Thus it is possible that one may capture "most" of the effects associated with a given final demand by using the first few terms in the power series. This is, generally, a much simpler computational procedure than finding the Leontief inverse.

2-5 | OPEN MODELS AND CLOSED MODELS

The model that we have dealt with thus far, $(I - A)X = Y$, depends on the existence of an exogenous sector, disconnected from the technologically interrelated productive sectors, since it is here that the important final demands for outputs originate. The basic kinds of transactions that constitute the activity of this sector, as we have seen, are consumption purchases by households, sales to government, gross private domestic investment, and shipments in foreign trade (either gross exports or net exports—exports from a sector less the value of imports of the same goods). In the case of households, especially, this "exogenous" categorization is something of a strain on basic economic theory. Households (consumers) earn incomes in payment for their labor inputs to production processes, and, as consumers, they spend their income in rather well patterned ways. And in particular, a *change* in the amount of labor needed for production in one or more sectors—say an increase in labor inputs due to increased output —will lead to a change (here an increase) in the amounts spent by households as a group for consumption. In other words, although households tend to purchase goods for "final" consumption, the amount of their purchases is related to their income, which depends on the outputs of each of the sectors. Also, as we have seen, consumption expenditures constitute possibly the largest single element of final demand; at least in the U.S. economy they are approximately two thirds of the total final-demand figure.

Thus one could move the household sector from the final-demand column and place it inside the technically interrelated table, that is, make it one of the "endogenous" sectors. This is known as closing the model with respect to households. This requires a row and a column for the new household sector—the former showing how its output (labor services) is used as an input by the various sectors and the latter showing the structure of its purchases (consumption) distributed among the sectors. It is customary to add the household row and column at the bottom and to the right of the coefficient table. Dollar flows *to* consumers, representing wages and salaries received by households from the n sectors in payment for their labor services, would fill an $(n + 1)$st row—$[z_{n+1,1} \, z_{n+1,2} \cdots z_{n+1,n}]$. Dollar flows *from* consumers, representing the values of household purchases of the goods of the n sectors, would fill an $(n + 1)$st

column—$\begin{bmatrix} z_{1, n+1} \\ z_{2, n+1} \\ \vdots \\ z_{n, n+1} \end{bmatrix}$. Finally, an element in the $(n + 1)$st row and the $(n + 1)$st

column, $z_{n+1, n+1}$, would represent household purchases of labor services. Thus Table 2-1 would have one new row, at the bottom, and one new column, at the right.

The ith equation, as shown in (2-1), would now be modified to

$$X_i = z_{i1} + z_{i2} + \cdots + z_{ii} + \cdots + z_{in} + z_{i, n+1} + Y_i^* \qquad (2\text{-}15)$$

where Y_i^* is understood to represent the remaining final demand for sector i's output—exclusive of that from households, which is now captured in $z_{i, n+1}$. In addition to this kind of modification on each of the equations in set (2-2), there would be one new equation for the total "output" of the household sector, which is defined to be the total value of its sale of labor services to the various sectors, that is, total earnings. Thus

$$X_{n+1} = z_{n+1,1} + z_{n+1,2} + \cdots + z_{n+1,i} + \cdots + z_{n+1,n} + z_{n+1,n+1} + Y_{n+1}^*$$

$$(2\text{-}16)$$

The last term on the right in Eq. (2-16) would include, for example, payments to government employees.

Household input coefficients are found in the same manner as any other element in an input-output coefficients table: The value of sector j's purchases of labor (for a given period), $z_{n+1,j}$, divided by the value of total output of sector j (for the same period), X_j, gives the value of household services (labor) used per dollar's worth of j's output; $a_{n+1,j} = z_{n+1,j}/X_j$. For the elements of the household purchases (consumption) column, the value of sector i's sales to households (for a given period), $z_{i,n+1}$, is divided by the total output of the household sector, X_{n+1}. Thus household "consumption coefficients" are $a_{i,n+1} = z_{i,n+1}/X_{n+1}$.

The ith equation in the fundamental set given in (2-4), above, becomes

$$X_i = a_{i1}X_1 + a_{i2}X_2 + \cdots + a_{in}X_n + a_{i,n+1}X_{n+1} + Y_i^* \qquad (2\text{-}17)$$

and the added equation which relates household output to output of all of the sectors is

$$X_{n+1} = a_{n+1,1}X_1 + a_{n+1,2}X_2 + \cdots + a_{n+1,n}X_n + a_{n+1,n+1}X_{n+1} + Y_{n+1}^*$$

$$(2\text{-}18)$$

Similarly, parallel to the equations in (2-5), we now have, for the ith equation, rewriting Eq. (2-17)

$$-a_{i1}X_1 - a_{i2}X_2 - \cdots + (1 - a_{ii})X_i - \cdots - a_{in}X_n - a_{i,n+1}X_{n+1} = Y_i^*$$

and, for the household equation, rewriting Eq. (2-18)

$$-a_{n+1,1}X_1 - a_{n+1,2}X_2 - \cdots - a_{n+1,n}X_n + (1 - a_{n+1,n+1})X_{n+1} = Y_{n+1}^*$$

Denote the n-element row vector of household input coefficients to the original n sectors, $a_{n+1,j}$ $(j = 1, \cdots, n)$, by H_R (for household row), the n-element column vector of consumption coefficients from the original n sectors, $a_{i,n+1}$ $(i = 1, \cdots, n)$, by H_C (for household column), and $a_{n+1,n+1}$ by h. Denote by $\bar{A}$ the $(n+1) \times (n+1)$ technical coefficients matrix with households included. Using partitioning (Section A-7 of Appendix A) to separate the old A matrix from the new sector,

$$\bar{A} = \left[\begin{array}{c|c} A & H_C \\ \hline H_R & h \end{array} \right]$$

Let $\overline{X}$ denote the $(n + 1)$-element column vector of gross outputs

$$\overline{X} = \begin{bmatrix} X_1 \\ \vdots \\ X_n \\ X_{n+1} \end{bmatrix} = \begin{bmatrix} X \\ \hline X_{n+1} \end{bmatrix}$$

Also, let Y^* be the n-element vector of remaining final demands for output of the original n sectors and $\overline{Y}$ the $(n + 1)$-element vector of final demands, including that for the output of households

$$\overline{Y} = \begin{bmatrix} Y_1^* \\ \vdots \\ Y_n^* \\ Y_{n+1}^* \end{bmatrix} = \begin{bmatrix} Y^* \\ \hline Y_{n+1}^* \end{bmatrix}$$

Then the new system of $n + 1$ equations, with households endogenous, can be represented as

$$(I - \overline{A})\overline{X} = \overline{Y} \tag{2-19}$$

or

$$\begin{bmatrix} I - A & -H_C \\ \hline -H_R & (1 - h) \end{bmatrix} \begin{bmatrix} X \\ \hline X_{n+1} \end{bmatrix} = \begin{bmatrix} Y^* \\ \hline Y_{n+1}^* \end{bmatrix} \tag{2-20}$$

That is, we have the set of n equations

$$(I - A)X - H_C X_{n+1} = Y^*$$

and the added one for households

$$-H_R X + (1 - h)X_{n+1} = Y_{n+1}^*$$

Together these determine the values of outputs for the n original sectors— $X_1, \cdots, X_n$—and the value of household services used (wages paid) to produce those outputs—X_{n+1}. If the $(n + 1) \times (n + 1)$ coefficient matrix is nonsingular, the unique solution can be found using an inverse matrix in the usual way

$$\begin{bmatrix} X \\ \hline X_{n+1} \end{bmatrix} = \begin{bmatrix} I - A & -H_C \\ \hline -H_R & (1 - h) \end{bmatrix}^{-1} \begin{bmatrix} Y^* \\ \hline Y_{n+1}^* \end{bmatrix} \tag{2-21}$$

or

$$\overline{X} = (I - \overline{A})^{-1}\overline{Y}$$

Consider again the information given in Table 2-3. Suppose that the household consumption part of final demand and the household labor input part of the payments sector are as shown in Table 2-8.

That is, of the $650 bought by sector 1 from the payments sectors (Table 2-3), $300 was for labor services; of the $1400 bought by sector 2, $500 was for labor inputs. Also, of the $1100 which represented purchases of final-demand sectors from the payments sectors, $50 was paid out by households for labor

TABLE 2-8 FLOWS (z_{ij}) FOR HYPOTHETICAL EXAMPLE, WITH HOUSEHOLDS EXPLICIT

From	To	Processing Sectors 1	Processing Sectors 2	Household Consumption (C)	Other Final Demand (Y*)	Total Output (X)
Processing	1	150	500	50	300	1000
Sectors	2	200	100	400	1300	2000
Labor Services (L)		300	500	50	150	1000
Other Payments (N + M)		350	900	500	400	2150
Total Outlays (X)		1000	2000	1000	2150	6150

services (e.g., domestic help); government purchases of labor would be included (and perhaps the only element) in the $150. The $500 would include such items as household payments to government (taxes) and household purchases of imported goods, and included in the $400 would be government purchases of imports.

The total output of the household sector, as in Eq. (2-16), is (here $n + 1 = 3$), $X_3 = z_{31} + z_{32} + z_{33} + Y_3^* = 300 + 500 + 50 + 150 = 1000$. The household input coefficients, $a_{n+1,j} = z_{n+1,j}/X_j$, are: $a_{31} = 300/1000 = 0.3$, $a_{32} = 500/2000 = 0.25$ and $a_{33} = 50/1000 = 0.05$. That is, $H_R = [0.3 \quad 0.25]$ and $h = 0.05$. Similarly, household consumption coefficients, $a_{i,n+1} = z_{i,n+1}/X_{n+1}$, are $a_{13} = 50/1000 = 0.05$ and $a_{23} = 400/1000 = 0.4$; thus $H_C = \begin{bmatrix} 0.05 \\ 0.4 \end{bmatrix}$. Therefore,

$$(I - \bar{A}) = \begin{bmatrix} .85 & -.25 & -.05 \\ -.20 & .95 & -.40 \\ -.30 & -.25 & .95 \end{bmatrix}$$

Finally, as the reader can check from basic definitions

$$(I - \bar{A})^{-1} = \begin{bmatrix} 1.3651 & 0.4253 & 0.2509 \\ 0.5273 & 1.3481 & 0.5954 \\ 0.5698 & 0.4890 & 1.2885 \end{bmatrix} \qquad (2\text{-}22)$$

Consider again the numerical example in Section 2-3. There we assumed a change in the final demand vector such that Y_1 went from 350 to 600 and Y_2 from 1700 to 1500. Referring now to Table 2-8, simply for illustration, suppose that this entire final-demand change was concentrated in the Other Final Demand sector. In fact, let it represent a change in the demands of the federal government (which are a part of the Other Final Demand (Y_i^*) column in Table 2-8). These new demands of $600 and $1500 represent increases in both cases, from the current levels of $300 and $1300 for all nonhousehold final-demand categories.

The most straightforward comparison is now to use the 3×3 Leontief inverse $(I - \bar{A})^{-1}$ in Eq. (2-22) in conjunction with a

$$\bar{Y} = \begin{bmatrix} 600 \\ 1500 \\ 0 \end{bmatrix}$$

to find the impact of these changes in the final demands for the outputs of sectors 1 and 2 on the two original sectors plus the added impact due to closure of the model with respect to households. That is,

$$\begin{bmatrix} X_1 \\ X_2 \\ X_3 \end{bmatrix} = \overline{X} = \begin{bmatrix} 1.3651 & 0.4253 & 0.2509 \\ 0.5273 & 1.3481 & 0.5954 \\ 0.5698 & 0.4890 & 1.2885 \end{bmatrix} \begin{bmatrix} 600 \\ 1500 \\ 0 \end{bmatrix} = \begin{bmatrix} 1456.94 \\ 2338.51 \\ 1075.48 \end{bmatrix}$$

Recall that in the earlier example of Section 2-3, with households exogenous to the model, the new necessary gross outputs were $X_1 = \$1247.46$ and $X_2 = \$1841.55$. The new (larger) values of $\$1456.94$ and $\$2338.51$, respectively, reflect the fact that *additional* outputs are necessary to satisfy the anticipated increase in consumer spending, as reflected in the household consumption coefficients column, expected because of the increased household earnings due to increased outputs from sectors 1 and 2 and hence increased wage payments. Using the labor input coefficients $a_{31} = 0.3$ and $a_{32} = 0.25$, the necessary household inputs for the original gross outputs (when households were exogenous) would be

$$a_{31} X_1 + a_{32} X_2 = (0.3)(1247.46) + (0.25)(1841.55) = 834.63$$

Thus, as would be expected, outputs are increased for all three sectors, due to the introduction of a formerly exogenous sector (households) into the model. The example serves to illustrate an expected outcome—namely that when the added impact of more household consumption spending due to increased wage income is explicitly taken into consideration in the model, the outputs of the original sectors in the interindustry model (here sectors 1 and 2) are larger than when consumer spending is ignored.

In this section we have introduced the basic considerations involved in moving households from final demand into the model as an endogenous sector—that is, in closing the model with respect to households. Similar kinds of data and algebraic extensions would be needed if other exogenous sectors—for example, federal, or state and/or local government activities—were to be made endogenous in the model. However, because the value of consumption tends to be by far the largest component of final demand (as noted earlier, 65 percent for the United States in 1982) and because of the direct linkage between earned income and consumption and between consumption and output, the household sector is the one final-demand sector that is most often moved inside the model.

In practice, however, the issue is more subtle and the procedure is more complicated than might be suggested by the discussion in this section. All of the previous reservations about the a_{ij}'s apply here as well, if not with greater force. For *each* additional dollar of received earnings, households are assumed to spend 5 cents on the output of sector 1, 40 cents on the output of sector 2, and so on. Those coefficients, which reflect *average* behavior during the observation period when household income was $\$1000$ ($a_{31} = 50/1000$ and $a_{32} = 400/1000$), are assumed to hold for the additional, or *marginal*, amounts of household earnings associated with the new outputs of sectors 1 and 2. One approach, particularly at the regional level, is to try to divide consumers into two groups: established residents, for whom the new income associated with new production would represent an addition to current earnings, and new residents (in-migrants), who may have moved in search of employment and for whom the new income represents total earnings. For the former group, a set of marginal consumption coefficients might be appropriate, while for the latter group average consumption coefficients would be relevant.

In addition, spending patterns of consumers, especially out of additions to (or reductions in) disposable income will depend on the income category in which a particular consumer is located. An addition of $100 to the spendable income of a worker earning $10,000 per year is likely to be spent differently from an additional $100 in the hands of an engineer with an annual income of $45,000, and both will no doubt differ from the way in which the $100 would be spent by a previously unemployed person. In effect, this is simply noting that inputs to the household sector (consumption) per dollar of output (household income) will not be independent of the level of that output. Yet such independence is assumed in the way that the direct input coefficients are used in an input-output model; each sector's production function (column of direct input coefficients) is assumed to represent inputs per dollar's worth of output, regardless of the amount (level) of that output.

Another approach, then, is to disaggregate "the" household sector into several sectors, distinguished by total income. For example, $0–$10,000, $10,000–$20,000, $20,000–$30,000; over $30,000. Consumption coefficients, by sector, could then be derived for each income class. We will return to this issue in a regional context in Chapter 3 and again in Chapter 4, where multipliers are discussed and where the nature of the "closure" of the model with respect to households plays an important role. (A very thorough discussion of an approach for incorporating a disaggregated household sector into the endogenous part of an input-output model, using a good deal of matrix algebra, can be found in Miyazawa 1976.)

One could imagine a process of moving, one by one, each of the remaining sectors from the final-demand vector into the interindustry coefficient matrix, constructing rows of input coefficients and columns of purchase coefficients until there were no exogenous sectors at all. This is termed a *completely closed model*. However, the economic logic behind fixed coefficients in the case, say, of a government sector is less easy to accept than for the productive sectors, and completely closed models are less frequently implemented in practice.[6]

---

[6]The original work done by Leontief, however, was in the framework of a completely closed model of the United States for 1919. See Leontief (1951). Note that a completely closed input-output model will be a set of *homogeneous* linear equations (Appendix A, section A-9). The interested reader may wish to examine why it is the case that the rows of the $(I - A)$ matrix in a completely closed model will be linearly dependent and hence the model will always have nontrivial but multiple solutions. Actual output will then be determined by considerations external to the model, such as boundaries fixed by resource constraints and sectoral capacities.

2-6 | SUMMARY

We have introduced the basic structure of the input-output model in this chapter. After investigating the special features of sectoral production functions that are assumed in the Leontief system, we examined its mathematical features. Importantly, the model is expressed in a set of linear equations, and we have tried to indicate the connection between the purely algebraic solution to the input-output equations, using the Leontief inverse matrix, and the logical, economic content of the round-by-round view of production interrelationships in an economy. Both the algebraic details as well as the economic assumptions needed to close the model with respect to households were discussed. Some of the special problems associated with the concept of household consumption coefficients have been addressed in applications, especially at the regional level. We therefore turn to regional input-output models in the next chapter.

It is important to add the regional dimension; many if not most important policy questions are not purely national in scope. Rather, analysts (even at the national level) are interested in differential regional effects of, say, a change in national government policy regarding exports. It is important to know not only the total magnitudes of the new outputs, by sector, that come about because of stimulation of exports, but also to know something of their geographical incidence—is a particularly depressed area helped by such export stimulation, or does the increased output occur largely in regions that are economically more healthy? Extensions of the basic model to deal with issues of this sort will occupy us in Chapter 3.

APPENDIX 2-1
THE RELATIONSHIP BETWEEN APPROACHES I AND II

To examine the connection between the two alternative approaches to the numerical example in Section 2-3, we consider a general two-sector economy, of which the illustration in Section 2-3 was a particular example. Thus, let $A = \begin{bmatrix} a_{11} & a_{12} \\ a_{21} & a_{22} \end{bmatrix}$, and suppose that Y_1 and Y_2 represent forecasted values of new final demands. First of all, using the Leontief-inverse approach, we find

$$(I - A) = \begin{bmatrix} (1 - a_{11}) & -a_{12} \\ -a_{21} & (1 - a_{22}) \end{bmatrix}$$

and, provided that $|I - A| \neq 0$, that is, provided that $(1 - a_{11})(1 - a_{22}) - (-a_{12})(-a_{21}) \neq 0$,

$$(I - A)^{-1} = \begin{bmatrix} \dfrac{(1 - a_{22})}{|I - A|} & \dfrac{a_{12}}{|I - A|} \\ \dfrac{a_{21}}{|I - A|} & \dfrac{(1 - a_{11})}{|I - A|} \end{bmatrix} \tag{2-1-1}$$

Thus, since $X = (I - A)^{-1}Y$, the necessary gross outputs will be

$$X_1 = \left[\frac{(1 - a_{22})}{|I - A|}\right] Y_1 + \left[\frac{a_{12}}{|I - A|}\right] Y_2$$

$$X_2 = \left[\frac{a_{21}}{|I - A|}\right] Y_1 + \left[\frac{(1 - a_{11})}{|I - A|}\right] Y_2 \qquad (2\text{-}1\text{-}2)$$

The round-by-round calculation of total impacts requires only the elements of the A matrix. Thus, the first-round impact on sector 1—in terms of what it must produce to satisfy its own and sector 2's needs for inputs—is $a_{11}Y_1 + a_{12}Y_2$. For sector 2, it is $a_{21}Y_1 + a_{22}Y_2$. (These were \$465 and \$195 in the numerical example.) The second-round impact results from production that is necessary to take care of first-round needs. For sector 1, this is

$$a_{11}\underbrace{(a_{11}Y_1 + a_{12}Y_2)}_{\substack{\text{Sector 1} \\ \text{Round 1}}} + a_{12}\underbrace{(a_{21}Y_1 + a_{22}Y_2)}_{\substack{\text{Sector 2} \\ \text{Round 1}}}$$

For sector 2, the second-round effect is given by

$$a_{21}\underbrace{(a_{11}Y_1 + a_{12}Y_2)}_{\substack{\text{Sector 1} \\ \text{Round 1}}} + a_{22}\underbrace{(a_{21}Y_1 + a_{22}Y_2)}_{\substack{\text{Sector 2} \\ \text{Round 1}}}$$

(These were \$118.50 and \$102.75 in the numerical example.) The nature of the expansion is now clear. For sector 1 in round 3, we will have

$$a_{11}\underbrace{\left[a_{11}(a_{11}Y_1 + a_{12}Y_2) + a_{12}(a_{21}Y_1 + a_{22}Y_2)\right]}_{\text{Sector 1, Round 2}}$$

$$+ a_{12}\underbrace{\left[a_{21}(a_{11}Y_1 + a_{12}Y_2) + a_{22}(a_{21}Y_1 + a_{22}Y_2)\right]}_{\text{Sector 2, Round 2}}$$

and for sector 2 in round 3:

$$a_{21}\underbrace{\left[a_{11}(a_{11}Y_1 + a_{12}Y_2) + a_{12}(a_{21}Y_1 + a_{22}Y_2)\right]}_{\text{Sector 1, Round 2}}$$

$$+ a_{22}\underbrace{\left[a_{21}(a_{11}Y_1 + a_{12}Y_2) + a_{22}(a_{21}Y_1 + a_{22}Y_2)\right]}_{\text{Sector 2, Round 2}}$$

(These were \$43.46 and \$28.84 in the numerical example.) Without going further, we can develop an expression for an approximation to X_1, on the basis of only three rounds of effects, in terms of Y_1 and Y_2, the exogenous demands, and the technical coefficients. Collecting the terms for round-by-round effects on sector 1, we have

$$X_1 \cong Y_1 + a_{11}Y_1 + a_{11}^2 Y_1 + a_{12}a_{21}Y_1 + a_{11}^3 Y_1 + a_{11}a_{12}a_{21}Y_1$$
$$+ a_{12}a_{21}a_{11}Y_1 + a_{12}Y_2 + a_{11}a_{12}Y_2 + a_{12}a_{22}Y_2 + a_{11}a_{11}a_{12}Y_2$$
$$+ a_{11}a_{12}a_{22}Y_2 + a_{12}a_{21}a_{12}Y_2 + a_{12}a_{22}a_{22}Y_2$$

or

$$X_1 \cong \left(1 + a_{11} + a_{11}^2 + a_{11}a_{21} + a_{11}^3 + a_{11}a_{12}a_{21} + a_{12}a_{21}a_{11} \right)Y_1$$
$$+ \left(a_{12} + a_{11}a_{12} + a_{12}a_{22} + a_{11}a_{11}a_{12} + a_{11}a_{12}a_{22} \right. \qquad \textbf{(2-1-3)}$$
$$\left. + a_{12}a_{21}a_{12} + a_{12}a_{22}a_{22} \right)Y_2$$

A similar expression could be derived for X_2. The object of this algebra is to make clear that in round 2, the effect comes through *pairs* of coefficients being multiplied together (e.g., a_{11}^2 and $a_{11}a_{12}$); in round 3, the effect comes by way of the product of *triples* of coefficients (e.g., a_{11}^3 and $a_{11}a_{12}a_{21}$). Similarly, in round 4, sets of four coefficients will be multiplied together, and in round n, sets of n coefficients will be multiplied. All $a_{ii} < 1$ and $a_{ij} < 1$ since producer j must buy, from each supplier i, less than one dollar's worth of inputs per dollar's worth of output. Therefore it is clear that eventually the effects in the "next" round will be essentially negligible. Yet mathematically, the true expression for X_1 would have the form

$$X_1 = (1 + \text{infinite series of terms involving}$$
$$\text{products of pairs, triples,} \cdots \text{ of } a_{ij}\text{'s})Y_1 \qquad \textbf{(2-1-4)}$$
$$+ (\text{similar infinite series})Y_2$$

There would be a parallel expression for X_2. If we denote these two parenthetical series terms by s_{11} and s_{12}, and in the similar expression for X_2 by s_{21} and s_{22}, we have gross outputs related to final demands by

$$X_1 = s_{11}Y_1 + s_{12}Y_2$$
$$X_2 = s_{21}Y_1 + s_{22}Y_2 \qquad \textbf{(2-1-5)}$$

Clearly, evaluation of the s terms as four different infinite series would be a difficult and tedious task.

Alternatively, we could think of the new total output X_1 as composed of two parts: (1) the forecasted final demands for sector 1's output, Y_1, and (2) all of the direct and indirect effects on sector 1 generated by Y_1 and Y_2. (This approach was suggested in Dorfman, Samuelson, and Solow 1958, section 9.3.) That is, define $F_1 = a_{11}Y_1 + a_{12}Y_2$, the first-round response from sector 1 due to the forecasted final demands, and, similarly, let $F_2 = a_{21}Y_1 + a_{22}Y_2$. These first-round outputs will similarly generate second-round outputs, and so on, exactly as did Y_1 and Y_2 above. In fact, we are simply suggesting that the final outputs can be looked at as a series of round-by-round effects on Y_1 and Y_2 *or* as Y_1 and Y_2, plus a series of round-by-round effects on F_1 and F_2, respectively. In this alternative view, a complete derivation similar to that preceding Eq. (2-1-5) would lead to

$$X_1 = Y_1 + s_{11}F_1 + s_{12}F_2$$
$$X_2 = Y_2 + s_{21}F_1 + s_{22}F_2$$

(2-1-6)

or, substituting $F_1 = a_{11}Y_1 + a_{12}Y_2$ and $F_2 = a_{21}Y_1 + a_{22}Y_2$ into Eq. (2-1-6) and collecting terms, we have

$$X_1 = (1 + s_{11}a_{11} + s_{12}a_{21})Y_1 + (s_{11}a_{12} + s_{12}a_{22})Y_2$$
$$X_2 = (s_{21}a_{11} + s_{22}a_{21})Y_1 + (1 + s_{21}a_{12} + s_{22}a_{22})Y_2$$

(2-1-7)

Since Eqs. (2-1-5) and (2-1-7) both show X_1 and X_2 as linear functions of Y_1 and Y_2, the coefficients in corresponding positions must be equal. That is,

$$s_{11} = 1 + s_{11}a_{11} + s_{12}a_{21} \qquad s_{12} = s_{11}a_{12} + s_{12}a_{22}$$
$$s_{21} = s_{21}a_{11} + s_{22}a_{21} \qquad s_{22} = 1 + s_{21}a_{12} + s_{22}a_{22}$$

Since the a_{ij}'s are known—they are the observed elements of the technical coefficients matrix, A—we can rearrange these four equations to generate one pair in s_{11} and s_{12} and a second pair in s_{21} and s_{22}.

$$s_{11} = 1 + s_{11}a_{11} + s_{12}a_{21}$$
$$s_{12} = s_{11}a_{12} + s_{12}a_{22}$$
$$s_{21} = s_{21}a_{11} + s_{22}a_{21}$$
$$s_{22} = 1 + s_{21}a_{12} + s_{22}a_{22}$$

or, rearranging to emphasize that the s's are unknowns and the a's are known coefficients

$$(1 - a_{11})s_{11} - a_{21}s_{12} = 1$$
$$- a_{12}s_{11} + (1 - a_{22})s_{12} = 0$$
$$(1 - a_{11})s_{21} - a_{21}s_{22} = 0$$
$$- a_{12}s_{21} + (1 - a_{22})s_{22} = 1$$

or

$$\begin{bmatrix} (1 - a_{11}) & -a_{21} \\ -a_{12} & (1 - a_{22}) \end{bmatrix} \begin{bmatrix} s_{11} \\ s_{12} \end{bmatrix} = \begin{bmatrix} 1 \\ 0 \end{bmatrix}$$

(2-1-8a)

$$\begin{bmatrix} (1 - a_{11}) & -a_{21} \\ -a_{12} & (1 - a_{22}) \end{bmatrix} \begin{bmatrix} s_{21} \\ s_{22} \end{bmatrix} = \begin{bmatrix} 0 \\ 1 \end{bmatrix}$$

(2-1-8b)

Both sets of equations have the same coefficient matrix. Since

$$\begin{bmatrix} (1 - a_{11}) & -a_{21} \\ -a_{12} & (1 - a_{22}) \end{bmatrix}^{-1} = \frac{1}{(1 - a_{11})(1 - a_{22}) - a_{12}a_{21}} \begin{bmatrix} (1 - a_{22}) & a_{21} \\ a_{12} & (1 - a_{11}) \end{bmatrix}$$

and since $(1 - a_{11})(1 - a_{22}) - a_{12}a_{21}$ is the same as $|I - A|$ in Eqs. (2-1-1) and

(2-1-2), the solutions to the pairs of linear equations in Eq. (2-1-8) are

$$\begin{bmatrix} s_{11} \\ s_{12} \end{bmatrix} = \begin{bmatrix} \dfrac{(1 - a_{22})}{|I - A|} & \dfrac{a_{21}}{|I - A|} \\[3mm] \dfrac{a_{12}}{|I - A|} & \dfrac{(1 - a_{11})}{|I - A|} \end{bmatrix} \begin{bmatrix} 1 \\ 0 \end{bmatrix}$$

$$\begin{bmatrix} s_{21} \\ s_{22} \end{bmatrix} = \begin{bmatrix} \dfrac{(1 - a_{22})}{|I - A|} & \dfrac{a_{21}}{|I - A|} \\[3mm] \dfrac{a_{12}}{|I - A|} & \dfrac{(1 - a_{11})}{|I - A|} \end{bmatrix} \begin{bmatrix} 0 \\ 1 \end{bmatrix}$$

That is,

$$s_{11} = \frac{(1 - a_{22})}{|I - A|}$$

$$s_{12} = \frac{a_{12}}{|I - A|}$$

$$s_{21} = \frac{a_{21}}{|I - A|}$$

$$s_{22} = \frac{(1 - a_{11})}{|I - A|}$$

These algebraic expressions equate the four infinite series terms, whose complex form was suggested in Eqs. (2-1-3) and (2-1-4), to extremely simple functions of the elements a_{ij} of A. Moreover, these four simple functions are precisely the four elements of the Leontief inverse, as found in Eq. (2-1-1). That is, in economic terms, the $(I - A)^{-1}$ matrix captures in each of its elements all of the infinite series of round-by-round direct and indirect effects that the new final demands have on the outputs of the two sectors. The elements of this matrix are often therefore termed *multipliers*. We use α_{ij}'s to denote the elements of the Leontief inverse. For the two-sector case, for example, given a forecast for Y_1 and Y_2 for next period, the total effect on X_1 is given by $\alpha_{11}Y_1 + \alpha_{12}Y_2$, the sum of the multiplied effects of each of the individual final demands. Multipliers will be discussed extensively in Chapter 4.

APPENDIX 2-2
THE HAWKINS-SIMON CONDITIONS

No matter how many terms we use in the series approximation to $(I - A)^{-1}$ in Eq. (2-12), it is clear that each of the terms contains only nonnegative elements, since all $a_{ij} \geq 0$. That is, not only is $A \geq 0$, but also $A^2 \geq 0, \cdots, A^n \geq 0$; therefore, $(I + A + A^2 + \cdots)$ is a matrix of nonnegative terms. If the elements of Y are all nonnegative, then the associated X will contain nonnegative elements also. This is what one would expect; when faced with a set of nonnegative final demands, Y, it would be meaningless in an economy to find that one or more of the necessary gross outputs, the elements in X, were negative.[7] For a Leontief system with $A \geq 0$ and $N(A) < 1$ (so that the results in Eq. [2-12] hold), we know that negative outputs will never be required from any sector to satisfy nonnegative final demands.

One could also explore conditions under which, given $Y \geq 0$, a nonnegative X would always result by examining the general definition of $(I - A)^{-1}$, namely

$$(I - A)^{-1} = \left(\frac{1}{|I - A|} \right) [\mathrm{adj}(I - A)]$$

For example, for the simplest, two-sector case,

$$(I - A)^{-1} = \begin{bmatrix} \dfrac{(1 - a_{22})}{|I - A|} & \dfrac{a_{12}}{|I - A|} \\[2mm] \dfrac{a_{21}}{|I - A|} & \dfrac{(1 - a_{11})}{|I - A|} \end{bmatrix}$$

In order that any nonnegative Y generate a nonnegative X, all of the elements in the Leontief inverse must be nonnegative. This means that the numerators must all be nonnegative and the denominator must be positive (that is, the denominator must not be zero, either). Or, all numerators could be nonpositive and the denominator negative, since the ratio of two negative numbers is, of course, positive.

We have already noted that $a_{ij} \geq 0$ and that $N(A) < 1$. Thus (and also by their definition) all $a_{ij} < 1$. This means that all numerators in $(I - A)^{-1}$ are nonnegative. Therefore, if $|I - A| > 0$, all elements in the 2×2 Leontief inverse will be nonnegative.

Hawkins and Simon (1949) investigated the issue of nonnegative solutions to more general equation systems. For a system in which $A \geq 0$ (as in the input-output case) but in which no restriction is placed on the column sums of A, they found for the 2×2 case that necessary and sufficient conditions to assure $X \geq 0$ are[8]

(a) $(1 - a_{11}) > 0$ and $(1 - a_{22}) > 0$

(b) $|I - A| > 0$ (2-2-1)

These conditions have a straightforward geometrical interpretation. We examine the solution-space representation. The fundamental relations

(a) $(1 - a_{11})X_1 - a_{12}X_2 = Y_1$

(b) $-a_{21}X_1 + (1 - a_{22})X_2 = Y_2$ (2-2-2)

[7]In some models, negative values could have meaning. If both X's and Y's were defined as changes (for example, next year minus this year) then a result like $X_3 = -400$ could be interpreted as a *decrease* of $400 in sector 3's output next year.

[8]From Appendix A we learn that the requirement for a unique solution to $(I - A)X = Y$ is that $|I - A| \neq 0$. Now we are further restricting this determinant to only positive values.

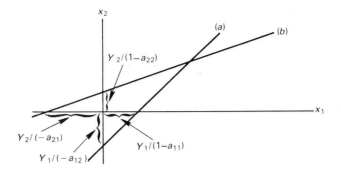

FIGURE 2-2-1(a) Solution space representation of Eqs. (2-2-2); $a_{12} > 0$ and $a_{21} > 0$.

define a pair of linear equations in $X_1 X_2$ space. By setting one variable at a time equal to zero in each equation, it is easy to find the intercepts of each line on each axis. These are shown in Fig. 2-2-1(a), for an arbitrary (but positive) set of final-demand values, Y_1 and Y_2. (Assume that both a_{12} and a_{21} are strictly positive, i.e., that each sector sells some inputs to the other. In a highly aggregated model this is virtually certain to be the case.)

As long as $(1 - a_{11}) > 0$ and $(1 - a_{22}) > 0$—the first Hawkins-Simon condition in the 2×2 case—for $Y_1 > 0$ and $Y_2 > 0$, the intercept of Eq. (2-2-2)(a) on the X_1-axis will be to the right of the origin and the intercept of Eq. (2-2-2)(b) on the X_2-axis will be above the origin. Therefore, for nonnegative total outputs, it is required that these two equations intersect in the first quadrant, which means that the slope of equation (a) must be greater than the slope of equation (b). These slopes are:

For equation (a)
$$\frac{\dfrac{Y_1}{a_{12}}}{\dfrac{Y_1}{(1 - a_{11})}} = \frac{(1 - a_{11})}{a_{12}}$$

For equation (b)
$$\frac{\dfrac{Y_2}{(1 - a_{22})}}{\dfrac{Y_2}{a_{21}}} = \frac{a_{21}}{(1 - a_{22})}$$

and thus the slope requirement is $(1 - a_{11})/a_{12} > a_{21}/(1 - a_{22})$. Multiplying both sides of the inequality by $(1 - a_{22})$ and by a_{12}—both of which are assumed to be strictly positive—does not alter the direction of the inequality, giving $(1 - a_{11})(1 - a_{22}) > a_{12} a_{21}$ or $(1 - a_{11})(1 - a_{22}) - a_{12} a_{21} > 0$, which is just $|I - A| > 0$, the second Hawkins-Simon condition in the 2×2 case.

The effects of less interdependence in the two-sector economy are illustrated in Figs. 2-2-1(b) and 2-2-1(c). If $a_{21} = 0$, meaning that $z_{21} = 0$ (sector 1

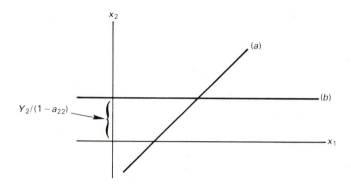

FIGURE 2-2-1(b)   Solution space representation of Eqs. (2-2-2);
$a_{21} = 0$.

uses no inputs from sector 2), then the slope of the line labeled (b) is zero. It is simply a horizontal line intersecting the X_2-axis at the height $Y_2/(1 - a_{22})$. This is to be expected; the gross output necessary from sector 2 depends only on final demand for the output of sector 2, Y_2, and the amount of *intra*industry input that sector 2 buys from itself, a_{22} (Fig. 2-2-1[b]). Similarly, if $a_{12} = 0$—sector 2 buys no inputs from sector 1—line (a) in the figure will have an infinite slope; that is, it will be vertical through the point $Y_1/(1 - a_{11})$ on the X_1-axis (Fig. 2-2-1[c]).

As discussed in Appendix A, the minor of an element a_{ij} in an $n \times n$ square matrix, A, is defined as the determinant of the $(n - 1) \times (n - 1)$ matrix remaining when row i and column j are removed from A. Another kind of minor that is associated with a matrix (not with a particular element in a matrix) is a *principal minor*. If one or more rows and the same columns are removed from A, the determinant of the remaining square matrix is a principal minor of A. For a 3×3 matrix A, removal of row and column 1, *or* row and column 2, *or* row

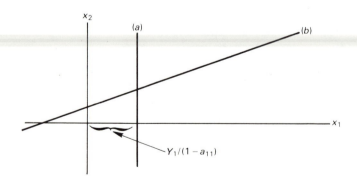

FIGURE 2-2-1(c)   Solution space representation of Eqs. (2-2-2);
$a_{12} = 0$.

and column 3 leaves, in each case, a square 2×2 matrix. The determinants of those three matrices are all principal minors of A (sometimes called second-order principal minors, because they are determinants of 2×2 matrices). Moreover, removal of rows and columns 1 and 2, *or* rows and columns 1 and 3, *or* rows and columns 2 and 3 leaves, in each case, a square 1×1 matrix (recall that the determinant of a 1×1 matrix is defined simply as the value of the element itself); these are the three first-order principal minors of A. By extension, the third-order principal minor in this case is just the determinant of the entire 3×3 matrix. Using the concept of principal minors of a square matrix, notice that the Hawkins-Simon conditions for the 2×2 case in Eq. (2-2-1) can be expressed simply as the requirement that *all principal minors* of $(I - A)$ be strictly positive. Generalization from the results in Eq. (2-2-1) to conditions for an $n \times n$ system is not completely straightforward; however, the definition of principal minors of a matrix presents a simple way of expressing the rule for the $n \times n$ case. Namely, regardless of the size of n, the parallel to Eq. (2-2-1) is that all principal minors of $(I - A)$ should be positive. Thus the general condition is

(a) $(1 - a_{ii}) > 0$, for $i = 1, \cdots, n$ (positivity of all first-order principal minors in $[I - A]$)

(b)   All second-order principal minors in $(I - A)$ must be strictly positive

(c)   All third-order principal minors in $(I - A)$ must be strictly positive   (2-2-3)

$$\vdots$$

(n − 1)   All $(n - 1)$st-order principal minors in $(I - A)$ must be strictly positive

(n) $|I - A| > 0$ (positivity of the nth-order principal minor)

Since even the 3×3 case can be misleading, the interested reader may wish to write out the elements of adj$(I - A)$ in the 3×3 and 4×4 cases—with 9 and 16 cofactors in the adjoints, respectively—to get at least a general idea of the way in which the complexity of these rules increases with the number of sectors in the input-output model.

| PROBLEMS*

2-1   Dollar values of last year's interindustry transactions and total outputs for a two-sector economy (agriculture and manufacturing) are as shown below:

$$Z = \begin{bmatrix} 500 & 350 \\ 320 & 360 \end{bmatrix}, \qquad X = \begin{bmatrix} 1000 \\ 800 \end{bmatrix}$$

a   What are the two elements in the final-demand vector?
b   Suppose that Y_1 increases by \$50 and Y_2 decreases by \$20. What new gross outputs would be necessary to satisfy the new final demands?

---

*Problems marked with an asterisk are to be done on a computer.

(1) Find an approximation to the answer by using the first five terms in the power series.

(2) Find the exact answer using the Leontief inverse.

2-2 Interindustry sales and total outputs in a small three-sector national economy for year t are given in the following table, where values are shown in thousands of dollars. (S_1, S_2, and S_3 represent the three sectors.)

| | *Interindustry Sales* | | | |
	S_1	S_2	S_3	*Total Output*
S_1	350	0	0	1000
S_2	50	250	150	500
S_3	200	150	550	1000

a Find the technical coefficients matrix, A, and the Leontief inverse matrix, $(I - A)^{-1}$, for this economy.

b Suppose that because of government tax policy changes, final demands for the outputs of sectors 1, 2, and 3 are projected for next year (year $t + 1$) to be 1300, 100, and 200, respectively (also measured in thousands of dollars). Find the total outputs that would be necessary from the three sectors to meet this projected demand, assuming that there is no change in the technological structure of the economy (that is, assuming that the A matrix does not change from year t to year $t + 1$).

c Find the original (year t) final demands from the information in the table of data. Compare with the projected (year $t + 1$) final demands. Also, compare the original total outputs with the outputs found in part **b**. What basic feature of the input-output model do these two comparisons illustrate?

2-3 Using the data of Problem 2-1, above, suppose that the household (consumption) expenditures part of final demand is $90 from sector 1 and $50 from sector 2. Suppose, further, that payments from sectors 1 and 2 for household labor services were $100 and $60, respectively; that total household (labor) income in the economy was $300; and that household purchases of labor services were $40. Close the model with respect to households and find the impacts on sectors 1 and 2 of the new final demands in part **b** of Problem 2-1, above, using the Leontief inverse for the new 3 × 3 coefficient matrix. Compare the outputs of sectors 1 and 2 with those obtained in Problem 2-1 using the same final demands. How do you explain the differences?

2-4 Consider an economy organized into three industries: lumber and wood products, paper and allied products, and machinery and transportation equipment. A consulting firm estimates that last year the lumber industry had an output valued at $50 (assume all monetary values are in units of $100,000), 5 percent of which it consumed itself; 70 percent was consumed by final demand; 20 percent by the paper and allied products industry; and 5 percent by the equipment industry. The equipment industry consumed 15 percent of its own products, out of a total of $100; 25 percent went to final demand; 30 percent to the lumber industry; 30 percent to the paper and allied products industry. Finally, the paper and allied products industry produced $50, of which it consumed 10 percent; 80 percent went to final demand; and 5 percent went to the lumber industry, 5 percent to the equipment industry.

a Construct the input-output transactions matrix for this economy on the basis of these estimates from last year's data. Find the corresponding matrix of technical coefficients, and show that the Hawkins-Simon conditions are satisfied.

b Find the Leontief inverse for this economy.

c A recession in the economy this year is reflected in decreased final demands. In particular,

Industry	% Decrease in Final Demand
Lumber & Wood Products	25
Machinery & Transportation Equipment	10
Paper & Allied Products	5

What would be the total production of all industries required to supply this year's decreased final demand?

d Compute the value-added and intermediate output vectors for the new transactions table.

2-5 Consider a simple two-sector economy containing industries A and B. Industry A requires \$2 million worth of its own product and \$6 million worth of Industry B's output in the process of supplying \$20 million worth of its own product to final consumers. Similarly, Industry B requires \$4 million worth of its own product and \$8 million worth of Industry A's output in the process of supplying \$20 million worth of its own product to final consumers.

a Construct the input-output transactions table describing economic activity in this economy.

b Find the corresponding matrix of technical coefficients and show that the Hawkins-Simon conditions are satisfied.

c If in the year following the one in which the data for this model was compiled there were no changes expected in the patterns of industry consumption, and if a final demand of \$15 million worth of good A and \$18 million worth of good B were presented to the economy, what would be the total production of all industries required to supply this final demand as well as the interindustry activity involved in supporting deliveries to this final demand?

2-6 Consider the following transactions table, Z, and total outputs vector, X, for two sectors, A and B:

$$Z = \begin{bmatrix} 6 & 2 \\ 4 & 2 \end{bmatrix}, \qquad X = \begin{bmatrix} 20 \\ 15 \end{bmatrix}$$

a Compute the value-added and final-demand vectors. Show that the Hawkins-Simon conditions are satisfied.

b Consider the r-order round-by-round approximation of $X = (I - A)^{-1}Y$ to be:

$$\tilde{X} = \sum_{i=0}^{r} A^i Y \qquad (\text{remember that } A^0 = I)$$

For what value of r do all the elements of $\tilde{X}$ come within 0.2 of the actual values of X?

c Assume that the cost of performing impact analysis on the computer using the round-by-round method is given by:

$$C_r = c_1 r + c_2(r - 1)$$

where r is the order of the approximation (c_1 is the cost of an addition operation and c_2 is the cost of a multiplication operation). Also, assume that $c_1 = 0.5c_2$ and that the cost of computing $(I - A)^{-1}$ exactly is given by:

$$C_e = 20c_2$$

and the cost of using this inverse in impact analysis (multiplying it by a final-demand vector) is given by:

$$C_f = c_2$$

If we wish to compute the impacts (total outputs) of a particular (arbitrary) final-demand vector to within at least 0.2 of the actual values of $X = (I - A)^{-1}Y_a$, where Y_a is an arbitrary final-demand vector, should we use the round-by-round method or should we compute the exact inverse and then perform impact analysis? Assume that the same order approximation that you found in **b** would suffice for the round-by-round method. The idea is to find the least-cost method for computing the solution.

d   Suppose we had four arbitrary final-demand vectors whose impact we wanted to assess. How would you now answer **c**?

e   For what number of final-demand vectors does it not make any difference which method we use (in answer to the question in **c**)?

2-7 Assume that you have a very limited computer (e.g., yourself) that can directly determine the inverse of matrices no larger than 2×2. Given this limited computer, explain how you could go about determining the Leontief inverse of the following matrix of technical coefficients:

$$A = \begin{bmatrix} 0 & .1 & .3 & .2 & .2 \\ .1 & .1 & .1 & 0 & 0 \\ .2 & 0 & .1 & .3 & .1 \\ .3 & 0 & 0 & .1 & .3 \\ .3 & .2 & .1 & .1 & .2 \end{bmatrix}$$

a   Compute the inverse in this manner.

b   What implications does such a procedure have for the computation of very large matrices (e.g., $n > 1000$)?

2-8 You have assembled the following facts about the two sectors that make up the economy of a small country that you want to study (data pertain to the most recent quarter). Total interindustry inputs were $50 and $100, respectively, for Sectors 1 and 2. Sector 1's sales to final demand were $60 and Sector 1's total output was $100. Sector 2's sales to Sector 1 were $30 and this represented 10 percent of Sector 2's total output.

a   You also know that government purchases constitute 70 percent of the final demand of both sectors. You are asked to assess, using input-output analysis, the effect on total national output $(X_1 + X_2)$ of a contemplated 25 percent across-the-board cutback in government spending (assume that spending in the other final-demand categories remains unchanged). Decide whether or not you have enough information. If you do, find the impact of this government action; if you do not have enough information, explain exactly why not (i.e., what is lacking?).

b   An alternative being considered by the government is maintenance of the spending level in conjunction with imposition of a value-added tax, as is common now in Europe, on firms in the country. If the contemplated tax were 12 percent and 14 percent for Sectors 1 and 2, respectively, would the revenue gained by this policy be more or less than the government money saved by decreased spending in part **a**? (Assume that neither sector uses any imported inputs.)

2-9 You are in charge of a project to generate an input-output table for a small country and then assess the impact of anticipated changes in final demands in that country. Preliminary work has indicated that a two-sector classification will be adequate, at least initially. One team of your investigators is responsible for collecting data for Sector 1. They discover that there are only two firms, A and B, in Sector 1, but the two firms keep differing and incomplete records. The data gathered (all for last year) are: A sold \$40 to itself, \$80 to B, and \$170 to final-demand sectors. Firm B's records are less complete: It sold nothing to A and kept \$20 worth of its own output; further, its sales to final demand were twice its total interindustry sales. The team responsible for Sector 2 data also has incomplete success. They learn that Sector 2 buys \$.20 worth of input from A per dollar's worth of Sector 2 output, and \$.05 worth of input from itself per dollar's worth of output. Also, total intermediate inputs bought by Sector 2 last year were \$400, and Sector 2's total output was \$1000. Sales from Sector 2 to Firms A and B combined were 80 percent of total Sector 2 output last year. This exhausts the available data (and also the two research teams).

a   Given these data, it is your job to try to build a two-sector input-output technical coefficients matrix for the country. Do it.

b   To convince yourself that the figures are not wildly wrong, check to see whether or not the Hawkins-Simon conditions are satisfied.

c   What will be the effect on regional gross outputs if final demands for the output of Firm A and Sector 2 increase by \$30 and \$50, respectively, but the demand for Firm B's output drops to \$200?

d   How do you explain the drop in X_2 in part c (from its original value of \$1000) when final demand for Sector 2's output increased by more than 30 percent?

2-10*   Given the following transactions table for industries a, b, and c, and the total output as shown, compute the final-demand vectors and show that the inverse of $(I - A)$ exists.

	Transactions			
	a	b	c	Total Output
a	3	8	6	22
b	2	4	5	18
c	7	3	9	31

Use the power series to approximate X to within 0.1 of the actual output values shown above. What was the highest power of A required?

2-11*   Consider the following transactions and total output data for an eight-sector economy.

$$Z = \begin{bmatrix} 8565 & 8069 & 8843 & 3045 & 1124 & 276 & 230 & 3464 \\ 1505 & 6996 & 6895 & 3530 & 3383 & 365 & 219 & 2946 \\ 98 & 39 & 5 & 429 & 5694 & 7 & 376 & 327 \\ 999 & 1048 & 120 & 9143 & 4460 & 228 & 210 & 2226 \\ 4373 & 4488 & 8325 & 2729 & 29671 & 1733 & 5757 & 14756 \\ 2150 & 36 & 640 & 1234 & 165 & 821 & 90 & 6717 \\ 506 & 7 & 180 & 0 & 2352 & 0 & 18091 & 26529 \\ 5315 & 1895 & 2993 & 1071 & 13941 & 434 & 6096 & 46338 \end{bmatrix}$$

$$X' = \begin{bmatrix} 37610 & 45108 & 46323 & 41059 & 209403 & 11200 & 55992 & 161079 \end{bmatrix}$$

a   Compute A and $(I - A)^{-1}$.

b   If final demands in sectors 1 and 2 increase by 30 percent while that in sector 5 decreases by 20 percent (while all other final demands are unchanged), what new total outputs will be necessary from each of the eight sectors in this economy?

| *REFERENCES*

BRÓDY, ANDREW, and ANNE P. CARTER, eds. *Input-Output Techniques*. Proceedings of the Fifth International Conference on Input-Output Techniques, Geneva, 1971. Amsterdam: North-Holland, 1972.

BULMER-THOMAS, V. *Input-Output Analysis in Developing Countries*. New York: John Wiley and Sons, Inc., 1982.

CARTER, ANNE P., and ANDREW BRÓDY, eds. *Input-Output Techniques*. Vol. 1, *Contributions to Input-Output Analysis*. Vol. 2, *Applications of Input-Output Analysis*. Proceedings of the Fourth International Conference on Input-Output Techniques, Geneva, January 1968. Amsterdam: North-Holland, 1970.

CHENERY, HOLLIS B., and PAUL G. CLARK. *Interindustry Economics*. New York: John Wiley and Sons, Inc., 1959.

DORFMAN, ROBERT, PAUL A. SAMUELSON, and ROBERT SOLOW. *Linear Programming and Economic Analysis*. New York: McGraw-Hill, 1958.

HAWKINS, DAVID, and HERBERT A. SIMON. "Note: Some Conditions of Macroeconomic Stability." *Econometrica* 17, no. 3–4 (July–October 1949): 245–48.

ISARD, WALTER et al. *Methods of Regional Analysis: An Introduction to Regional Science*. New York: The Technology Press of MIT and John Wiley and Sons, Inc., 1960.

LEONTIEF, WASSILY. *Input-Output Economics*. New York: Oxford University Press, 1966.

———. *The Structure of American Economy, 1919–1939*. New York: Oxford University Press, 1951.

MIERNYK, WILLIAM H. *The Elements of Input-Output Analysis*. New York: Random House, 1965.

MIYAZAWA, KENICHI. *Input-Output Analysis and the Structure of Income Distribution*. Berlin: Springer-Verlag, 1976.

MORGENSTERN, OSKAR, ed. *Economic Activity Analysis*. New York: John Wiley and Sons, Inc., 1954.

NATIONAL BUREAU OF ECONOMIC RESEARCH. *Input-Output Analysis: An Appraisal*. Vol. 18, *Studies in Income and Wealth*. Princeton: Princeton University Press, 1955.

POLENSKE, KAREN R., and JIRI V. SKOLKA, eds. *Advances in Input-Output Analysis*. Proceedings of the Sixth International Conference on Input-Output Techniques, Vienna, April 1974. Cambridge, Mass.: Ballinger Publishing Co., 1976.

RICHARDSON, HARRY W. *Input-Output and Regional Economics*. New York: John Wiley and Sons (Halsted Press), 1972.

STONE, RICHARD. *Input-Output and National Accounts*. Paris: Organization for European Economic Cooperation, 1961.

U.S. DEPARTMENT OF COMMERCE, BUREAU OF THE CENSUS. *Statistical Abstract of the United States: 1984*. Washington, D.C.: U.S. Government Printing Office, 1983.

YAMADA, ISAMU. *Theory and Application of Interindustry Analysis*. Tokyo: Konokuniya Bookstore Co., Ltd., 1961.

YAN, C. S. *Introduction to Input-Output Economics*. New York: Holt, Rinehart and Winston, 1969.

chapter 3

Input-Output Models at the Regional Level

3-1 | INTRODUCTION

Originally, applications of the input-output model were carried out at national levels—for example, to assess the impact on the individual sectors of the U.S. economy of a change from war to peacetime production as the end of World War II approached. More recently, interest in economic analysis at the regional level—whether for a group of states (as in a federal reserve district), an individual state, a county, or a metropolitan area—has led to modifications of the input-output model which attempt to reflect the peculiarities of a regional (subnational) problem. There are two basic features of a regional economy that influence the characteristics of a regional input-output study.

First, although the data in a national input-output coefficient table are obviously some kind of averages of data from individual producers who are located in specific regions, the structure of production in a particular region may be identical to or it may differ markedly from that recorded in the national input-output table. Soft drinks of a particular brand that are bottled in Boston probably incorporate basically the same ingredients in the same proportions as are present in that brand of soft drink produced in Kansas City or Atlanta or in any other bottling plant in the United States. On the other hand, electricity produced in eastern Washington by water power (Coulee Dam) represents quite a different mix of inputs from electricity that is produced from coal in the greater Philadelphia area or by means of nuclear power elsewhere. For these reasons, the early methodology for regional input-output applications—which used a "modified" national table—has given way to coefficient tables that are actually constructed for a particular region on the basis of data specific to that region.

Secondly, it is generally true that the smaller the economic area, the more dependent that area's economy is on trade with "outside" areas—exports and imports across the region's borders—both for sales of regional outputs and purchases of inputs needed for production. That is, one of the elements that contributed to the exogenous final-demand sector in the model described in Chapter 2—exports—now will generally be relatively much more important; similarly, a higher proportion of inputs will be imported from producers who are located outside of the region. To exaggerate, a one-world economy would have no "foreign trade" (exports and imports), since all sales and purchases would be internal to the worldwide "region," whereas an urban area depends to a great degree on imports and exports (for example, imports of leather to the shoe industry in Boston, exports of Boeing commercial aircraft from Seattle).

In this chapter we will explore some of the attempts that have been made to incorporate these features of a regional economy into an input-output framework; that is, we will look at frameworks for *regional* input-output analysis. Such regional input-output models may deal with a single region or with two or more regions and their interconnections. The several-region case is termed *interregional input-output analysis* (in one version) or *multiregional input-output analysis* (in another version). We will examine each of these kinds of regionalized input-output models, as well as the balanced regional model.

There is an enormous amount of input-output work at the regional level. Examples of some of the earliest regional applications are found in Moore and Petersen (1955), Isard and Kuenne (1953), Miller (1957), and Hirsch (1959). Two bibliographies of regional work are Bourque and Cox (1970) and Giarratani, Maddy, and Socher (1976). The reader is referred particularly to the latter and to the annual indexes in such journals as *Journal of Regional Science, International Regional Science Review, Annals of Regional Science*, and *Environment and Planning, A*, for additional references. (Additional possible journals include *Regional Studies, Growth and Change, Urban Studies, Land Economics, Regional Science and Urban Economics, Regional Science Perspectives*, and *Economic Geography*.) In addition, many regional input-output tables and studies using these tables are published by the appropriate departments of state and local governments for whom the analysis was done, or by universities where the work was done. Examples of these kinds of publications are State of California (1980), Emerson (1969, 1971) for Kansas, Lamphear and Roesler (n.d.) for Nebraska, Loviscek et al. (1979) for West Virginia, Mullendore et al. (1972) for North Central Texas and University of New Mexico, Bureau of Business Research (1965). This listing is in absolutely no way exhaustive; the intention is only to indicate the wide variety of sources. A very thorough discussion of the details involved in producing a regional input-output table is provided by Isard and Langford (1971)—the region involved was the Philadelphia Standard Metropolitan Statistical Area—and in Miernyk et al. (1967) for Boulder, Colorado, and Miernyk et al. (1970) for West Virginia. Overviews of regional input-output models are to be found in Polenske (1980, Chapter 3) and in Miernyk (1982).

3-2 | SINGLE-REGION MODELS

National Coefficients

Generally, regional input-output studies attempt to quantify the impacts on the producing sectors located in a particular region that are caused by new final demands for products made in the region. Early regional studies (Isard and

Kuenne 1953; Miller 1957) used a national table of technical coefficients in conjunction with an adjustment procedure that was designed to capture some of the characteristics of the regional economies, since specific coefficient tables for the particular regions did not exist.[1]

We use a superscript R to designate "region R" in the same way that subscript i denoted "sector i" in the discussion in Chapter 2. Thus, just as X_i was used to denote the gross output of sector i, we let Y^R denote the (vector of) new exogenous demand for goods made in region R. If R denotes Washington State, one element of Y^R could be an order from a foreign airline for commercial aircraft from the Boeing Company in the state of Washington. Similarly, X^R will denote the (vector of) outputs of the various sectors in region R. The problem in these early regional studies was that a national technical coefficients matrix, A, was available, but what was needed, essentially, was a matrix showing inputs from firms *in the region* to production *in that region*. Denote this matrix (for the moment) by A^R and assume, in the absence of evidence to the contrary, that local producers use the same production recipes of inputs as are shown in the national coefficients table. That is, assume that the technology of production in each sector in region R is the same as in the nation as a whole. Nonetheless, in order to translate new regional final demands, Y^R, into new outputs of *regional* firms, X^R, the national coefficients matrix must be modified to A^R so as to indicate only the inputs of locally produced (region R) goods in local (region R) production.

Early studies carried out this modification through the use of estimated regional supply percentages, one for each sector in the regional economy, designed to show the percentage of the total required outputs from each sector that could be expected to originate within the region. One straightforward way to estimate these percentages, using data that may often be obtainable at the regional level, requires (1) total regional output of sector j, X_j^R, (2) exports of good j from region R, E_j^R, and (3) imports into region R of good j, M_j^R. Then, one can form

$$p_j^R = \frac{\left(X_j^R - E_j^R \right)}{\left(X_j^R - E_j^R + M_j^R \right)}$$

The numerator is the *locally produced* amount of good j that is available to purchasers in region R; the denominator is the *total* amount of good j that is available in region R, either produced locally or imported. (Thus $p_j^R \times 100$ will produce an estimate of the regional supply percentage for sector j in region R—the percentage of good j available in R that is produced there.)

Examples of these percentages from the Delaware Valley study (Isard and Kuenne 1953) are: agriculture and fisheries (sector 1), 0; food and kindred products (sector 2), 60; business services (sector 38) or personal and repair services (sector 39), 95 (which is the maximum percentage ever used, to allow for the possibility that there may always be *some* importation of the goods or services of any sector). Examples of the regional supply percentages in the Pacific

---

[1]The "regions" were the Greater New York–Philadelphia urban-industrial region (consisting of 2 counties in Connecticut, 11 in New York, 19 in New Jersey, and 5 in Pennsylvania) in the first case and the states of Washington, Oregon, and Idaho in the second.

Northwest study (Miller 1957), for the same sectors, are: agriculture and fisheries, 27; food and kindred products, 66; business services or personal and repair services, 95. Both the Delaware Valley and the Pacific Northwest studies utilized the same 1947 U.S. input-output table with 44 sectors (plus households, sector 45).

Assuming that we have such proportions, p_i^R, for each sector in the economy ($i = 1, \cdots, n$), each element in the ith row of the national coefficients matrix, A, could be multiplied by p_i^R to generate a row of locally produced inputs of good i to all local producers. If we arrange the proportions in an n-element column vector, P, then our working estimate of the regional matrix will be $A^R = \hat{P}A$. Given any Y^R, we could then find X^R as $X^R = (I - \hat{P}A)^{-1}Y^R$. Recall that a hat over a vector indicates the diagonal matrix created from that vector, and premultiplication by a diagonal matrix uniformly alters the rows of the matrix being premultiplied—the elements in the ith row of A are each multiplied by p_i^R. This uniform modification of the elements in a row of A is a strong assumption. It means, for example, that if the aircraft, kitchen equipment, and pleasure boat sectors in Washington all use aluminum (sector i) as an input, the A^R matrix embodies the assumption that all three sectors buy the same percentage, p_i^R, of their total aluminum needs from firms located within the state.

Using the two-sector example from Chapter 2, $A = \begin{bmatrix} .15 & .25 \\ .20 & .05 \end{bmatrix}$. Assume that this is a national table, and that we want to use it for region R; that is, there is no evidence that the basic structure of production in the sectors in the region differs from the national average structure, as reflected in A. The unique features of the region, however, are reflected in the regional supply percentages, representing proportions of inputs that are expected to be supplied by firms within the region. Suppose we estimate that 80 percent of any output from sector 1 will come from firms in sector 1 within the region, but only 60 percent of sector 2 output can be expected to be supplied by firms in sector 2 within the region. Thus $P = \begin{bmatrix} .8 \\ .6 \end{bmatrix}$. Suppose that the projected final demand in the region is $Y^R = \begin{bmatrix} 600 \\ 1500 \end{bmatrix}$ (this is the final-demand vector that was used for some of the numerical examples in Chapter 2). Since

$$\hat{P} = \begin{bmatrix} .8 & 0 \\ 0 & .6 \end{bmatrix}, \quad A^R = \hat{P}A = \begin{bmatrix} .8 & 0 \\ 0 & .6 \end{bmatrix}\begin{bmatrix} .15 & .25 \\ .20 & .05 \end{bmatrix} = \begin{bmatrix} .12 & .20 \\ .12 & .03 \end{bmatrix},$$

$$(I - A^R)^{-1} = \begin{bmatrix} 1.169 & .241 \\ .145 & 1.061 \end{bmatrix}$$

and, using this regional inverse directly,

$$X^R = (I - A^R)^{-1}Y^R = \begin{bmatrix} 1.169 & .241 \\ .145 & 1.061 \end{bmatrix}\begin{bmatrix} 600 \\ 1500 \end{bmatrix} = \begin{bmatrix} 1062.90 \\ 1678.50 \end{bmatrix} \qquad \text{(3-1)}$$

Since the assumption made is that the technological structure of production in the region is the same as the nation—but that not all the necessary inputs can be supplied completely by firms within the region—the *total* necessary outputs to meet the new final demand of 600 for sector 1 and 1500 for sector 2 in region R

will be

$$X = (I - A)^{-1} Y^R = \begin{bmatrix} 1.254 & .330 \\ .264 & 1.122 \end{bmatrix} \begin{bmatrix} 600 \\ 1500 \end{bmatrix} = \begin{bmatrix} 1247.40 \\ 1841.40 \end{bmatrix} \qquad (3\text{-}2)$$

This is a result that we have already seen in Chapter 2. The difference between the outputs found in Eqs. (3-2) and (3-1) will be new outputs from firms located outside of the region in which the final demand change has occurred. Here this is

$$X - X^R = \begin{bmatrix} 184.50 \\ 162.90 \end{bmatrix}$$

which represents the dollar value of outputs from firms in sectors 1 and 2 that will have to be imported into region R as inputs to sector 1 and sector 2 production there.

The result for X^R is *not* what would be obtained by premultiplying the total outputs, in X, by 0.80 and 0.60, respectively. In fact,

$$\hat{P}X = \hat{P}\left[(I - A)^{-1} Y^R\right] = \begin{bmatrix} 0.8 & 0 \\ 0 & 0.6 \end{bmatrix} \begin{bmatrix} 1247.40 \\ 1841.40 \end{bmatrix} = \begin{bmatrix} 997.92 \\ 1104.84 \end{bmatrix}$$

Since early regional input-output studies used the power-series approximation to the Leontief inverse, Appendix 3-1 explores the use of the regional supply percentages in the power series, for the interested reader. The error in using $\hat{P}X$, as above, also becomes apparent.

In more recent regional input-output analyses, attempts have been made to model the characteristics of the regional economy more precisely. We examine these briefly in the following subsection, and we return to the "regionalization" problem in Chapter 8.

Regional Coefficients

We noted above that electricity produced in Washington will have a different production recipe (column of technical coefficients) from electricity made in Pennsylvania. These regionally produced electricities are really two different products—"hydroelectric power" and "coal-fired electrical power." As another example, consider the aircraft sector. In a national table, this would include the manufacture of a mix of commercial, business, and personal aircraft. One input to this sector would be the huge jet engines used on 747 and DC-10 commercial airliners. On the other hand, the aircraft sector in a regional table for the state of Pennsylvania would reflect the manufacture of Piper airplanes only, for which the jumbo jet engines are not an input at all; in a Washington table, however, jet engines are an extremely important input.

Sectors in even very disaggregated national input-output tables will be made up of a variety of products—as in the aircraft sector example. And firms within that sector, located in various regions of the country, will generally produce only a small number of those products—Boeing in Washington does not produce private propeller-driven airplanes; Piper in Pennsylvania does not produce jet airliners. This illustrates the so-called product-mix problem in input-output; namely, that firms classified in the same sector actually produce different sets of products. The most straightforward way to avoid this problem is to survey firms in the region and construct what is called a survey-based regional input-output table. In conducting such a survey, one can pose essentially two variants of the basic question. In asking firms in sector j in a particular region about their use of various inputs, the question can be: How much of sector i's product did you buy last year in making your output? (For example, how much aluminum did aircraft manufacturing in Washington State buy last year?) Alternatively, the question can be the more exacting one: How much of sector i's product produced by firms located in the region did you buy last year—and how much from firms in sector i located outside of the region? (For example, how much of the total aluminum used by aircraft producers in Washington State was supplied by aluminum producers located within the state, and how much came from firms located outside the state?)

In the former case (the less exacting question), a truly *regional technical coefficients* table would be produced; this would better reflect production practices in the region than does the national table—it would eliminate the input of large jet engines into the manufacture of Piper private airplanes in Pennsylvania, for example. But it would not address the question of how much of each required input came from within the region and how much was imported; hence, an additional set of regional supply percentages would still be required for any specific kind of *regional* impact analysis. On the other hand, a set of coefficients based on inputs supplied from firms within the region for outputs of firms in the region would reflect both regional production technology and the input amounts to be expected from inside the region. These might be termed *regional input coefficients*. They are to be distinguished from regional technical coefficients since they do not describe accurately the technology of regional firms, but rather only the way in which those firms use local inputs. (*Intraregional input coefficients* would be an even more precise description, but it may be unnecessarily cumbersome.[2])

To simplify the notation when we generalize in later sections to many-region models, we now use the superscript L (instead of R, for "region") for the region in question, and let M denote the rest of the nation. Then let z_{ij}^{LL} denote the dollar flow of goods from sector i in region L to sector j in region L. Similarly, z_{ij}^{ML} represents dollars' worth of inputs from sector i located in region M (i.e., outside of region L) to sector j in region L. Just as the order of subscripts is "from-to" with respect to sectors, the order of superscripts indicates "from-to" with respect to geographic locations. If one had a complete set of data on z_{ij}^{LL} for all sectors in the regional economy ($i, j = 1, \cdots, n$), and also data on gross outputs of each sector in the region, X_j^L ($j = 1, \cdots, n$), the set of regional input coefficients of the following sort could be derived.

$$a_{ij}^{LL} = \frac{z_{ij}^{LL}}{X_j^L} \tag{3-3}$$

Using the notation of Chapter 2, let Z^{LL} be the $n \times n$ matrix of these intraregional flows and $\hat{X}^L$ the $n \times n$ diagonal matrix of regional gross outputs;

---

[2]Tiebout (1969, 335) used "direct intraregional interindustry coefficient," which is completely precise but also rather cumbersome.

then the $n \times n$ matrix of regional input coefficients can be represented as

$$A^{LL} = Z^{LL} (\hat{X}^L)^{-1} \qquad (3\text{-}4)$$

Similarly, if one had a complete set of data on Z_{ij}^{ML}, then dividing each z_{ij}^{ML} by X_j^L gives *trade coefficients*, showing the dollar's worth of input i produced by firms in region M that is used per dollar's worth of output of sector j in region L. (*Interregional input coefficient* would also serve as an accurate description, but it too is cumbersome.) That is,

$$a_{ij}^{ML} = \frac{z_{ij}^{ML}}{X_j^L} \qquad (3\text{-}5)$$

Given the trade flows from region M to region L, Z^{ML}, and again, using $\hat{X}^L$, we represent the matrix of trade coefficients as

$$A^{ML} = Z^{ML} (\hat{X}^L)^{-1} \qquad (3\text{-}6)$$

One way to assess the *regional* impact of a final-demand change in region L, Y^L, would be as

$$X^L = (I - A^{LL})^{-1} Y^L \qquad (3\text{-}7)$$

Notice that this regional input coefficients matrix, A^{LL}, is what was being approximated in the early regional input-output studies described above by $A^R = \hat{P}A$, since the regional supply percentages times a set of national coefficients was used as an estimate of the amounts of needed inputs that would be supplied by firms within the region.[3]

In the case of the less-detailed survey questions (how much aluminum was used by aircraft manufacturers in Washington State, irrespective of where the aluminum came from), the flows are sometimes denoted $z_{ij}^{\cdot L}$, where the dot indicates that all possible geographical locations for sector i are lumped together. (Sometimes a small o is used instead of a dot, primarily because it is easier to read.) In the present two-region example, this means either within the region, z_{ij}^{LL}, or outside of it, z_{ij}^{ML}, since M designates "everywhere but L." Mathematically, in this example, $z_{ij}^{\cdot L} = z_{ij}^{LL} + z_{ij}^{ML}$; the point is that information on the various $z_{ij}^{\cdot L}$ is found from a less-detailed survey than would be required for the component parts, z_{ij}^{LL} and z_{ij}^{ML}.

Thus, regional technical coefficients are defined as

$$a_{ij}^L = \frac{z_{ij}^{\cdot L}}{X_j^L} \qquad (3\text{-}8)$$

(For consistency, this should properly be denoted $a_{ij}^{\cdot L}$, but for notational simplic-

---

[3]The elements in A^R are truly only an approximation to the elements in A^{LL} since, as we saw earlier, $A^R = \hat{P}A$; that is, A^R embodies both the assumptions of national technology at the regional level and the same imported proportion of good i to all regional sectors that use i as an input. There is no relationship of this sort among the elements in row i of a survey-based A^{LL} matrix.

ity we will understand this to be represented by the single regional superscript.) In this two-region situation, $a_{ij}^L = z_{ij}^{\cdot L}/X_j^L = (z_{ij}^{LL} + z_{ij}^{ML})/X_j^L$, or $a_{ij}^L = a_{ij}^{LL} + a_{ij}^{ML}$—from Eqs. (3-3) and (3-5). That is, the regional technical coefficient is the sum of the regional input coefficient and the trade coefficient (showing imports to L from M). Again, the point is that one may choose to estimate the a_{ij}^L directly, through a regional survey. In such a case, the two component parts (region L inputs and inputs imported from region M) will not usually be estimated individually.

Letting $Z^L = [z_{ij}^{\cdot L}]$ be the $n \times n$ matrix of these inputs, the set of regional technical coefficients can be represented as

$$A^L = Z^L (\hat{X}^L)^{-1} \qquad (3\text{-}9)$$

(This is, in particular, to be contrasted with A^{LL} in Eq. (3-4).) Given a set of regional technical coefficients of this sort, the impact on the output of sectors *throughout the national economy* of a change in demand in region L, Y^L, could be found as

$$X = (I - A^L)^{-1} Y^L \qquad (3\text{-}10)$$

To assess the *regional* impacts, one would still need some kind of regional information, such as a set of regional supply percentages, P, so as to estimate A^{LL} by $\hat{P}A^L$. Then the impact in region L would be found as

$$X^L = (I - \hat{P}A^L)^{-1} Y^L \qquad (3\text{-}11)$$

This is to be compared with Eq. (3-7), where a set of survey-based regional input coefficients was used.

Closing a Regional Model with Respect to Households

One suggestion that has been made for closing an input-output model with respect to households, for analysis at the regional level, is that not one but two rows and columns should be added to the direct-input coefficients matrix. Suppose that the impacts of projected increases in final demand are sought. Sectoral outputs will increase and there will consequently be increased payments for labor services. The basic idea is that a distinction should be made between consumption habits of established residents of the region, who may experience an increase in their incomes (for example, through overtime) and the consumption patterns of new residents, who may move into the region in anticipation of employment.

One argument is that the current residents will spend each dollar of new income according to a set of *marginal* consumption coefficients, while new residents will distribute their purchases according to a set of *average* consumption coefficients. If sales, by sector, could be broken down into those to new residents and those to existing residents, and if labor payments, by sector, could be similarly disaggregated, then marginal and average household consumption coefficients could be derived. Similarly, given sectoral outputs, "old" and "new" labor inputs per dollar's worth of output could be found.

In practice, such data are not so conveniently available. Tiebout (1969) describes in general (that is, without specific figures) the derivation of these kinds of coefficients for the regional economy of the state of Washington. Miernyk et al. (1967) investigate essentially the same issue for their Boulder, Colorado, input-output study.[4] In addition, however, an attempt was made in the Boulder study to disaggregate the income increases to existing residents by income class, with lower marginal consumption propensities in higher income classes. (See Miernyk et al. 1967, esp. Chapter V.)

Instead of disaggregating households into "old" and "new" residents, Blackwell (1978) proposes a tripartite division into intensive and extensive (current residents and new residents, respectively) and also redistributive, which is that portion of any new income that goes to previously unemployed local residents. The distinction between currently employed and currently unemployed workers is also explored in some detail by Madden and Batey (1983).[5] The importance of capturing local spending by households in regional input-output analyses is emphasized in Hewings and Romanos (1981). Work continues on improving the manner in which a regional input-output table is closed with respect to households.

3-3 | MANY-REGION MODELS—THE INTERREGIONAL APPROACH

Single-region models of the sort described in the previous section represent one approach to modeling a regional economy in input-output terms. What they fail to do, however, is to recognize in any operational way the interconnections between regions. The one region of interest (in the above, this was region L) was "disconnected" from the rest of the country within which it is located, either through a survey-based intraregional matrix, A^{LL}, or through an approximation of that matrix given by a set of estimated regional supply percentages, $\hat{P}$, and a regional matrix, A^L.

For a country made up of several regions, a number of important questions have several-region implications. Next year's national defense budget might include a large order for a certain type of aircraft built in California, the overhaul of a fleet of ships in Virginia, and expansion of a missile-detection facility in North Dakota. Each of these new demands will probably have ramifications not only within the region (state, in this example) where the work is done, but also in other states. The total economic effect is therefore likely to be larger than the sum of the regional effects in California, Virginia, and North Dakota. Firms outside California will produce goods that will be imported to California for aircraft production; those firms, in turn, may import goods from other states for *their* production. Materials for ship overhaul will come to

---

[4] The contribution of Tiebout in formulating this distinction between spending patterns of established and new residents in a region is acknowledged by Miernyk et al. (1967, 104, n. 9). It should be noted that a draft of Tiebout's paper was completed by 1967; it was published posthumously in 1969, following his death in January of 1968.

[5] The work of Madden and Batey is representative of a growing body of research linking population and economic models. Other examples (by no means an exhaustive list) include Schinnar (1976), Beyers (1980), Madden and Batey (1980), Batey and Madden (1981), Gordon and Ledent (1981), Ledent and Gordon (1981), and Joun and Conway (1983). These combined models are often referred to as *demoeconomic—* or *ecodemographic*.

Virginia from suppliers outside that state. Electronic parts for the missile-detection facility in North Dakota will be imported from elsewhere and the electronics firms, in turn, will need both local (wherever they are located) and imported inputs, and so on.

We will examine in this section the first of two types of many-region input-output models that attempt to capture these important kinds of interregional linkages as well as the regional aspects of production. This is the interregional input-output (IRIO) model. The first presentation of this model is in Isard (1951). For this reason, it is sometimes termed the "Isard" model. A complete reference is Isard et al. (1960, Chapter 8.) In the next section we will examine an alternative approach, the multiregional input-output (MRIO) model. As will be seen, the interregional input-output model requires a large amount of detailed data. Probably the most ambitious attempt to implement the model in a real-world situation is the series of Japanese survey-based interregional tables, beginning with 1960 data and updated every five years. (See Japanese government 1964, 1969, 1974.) Also, there has been work in Holland implementing a Dutch three-region interregional model. (See, for example, Oosterhaven 1981.) The main difficulty with implementation of many-region input-output models is that data on shipments of goods between sectors *and* between regions are not readily available. This has generated a great deal of work in mathematical approaches to estimating interregional commodity flows. These methods are often relatively complex; some are discussed in Chapter 8, where various kinds of nonsurvey or partial-survey methods for estimating input-output information are introduced.

Basic Structure of Two-Region Interregional Input-Output Models

For purposes of illustration, consider a two-region economy (for example, in Italy, northern Italy and southern Italy; or, in the United States, New England and the rest of the United States). Using L and M, as before, for the two regions, let there be three producing sectors in region L and two in region M. Suppose, as in section 3-2, that one has information on the flows z_{ij}^{ML} and z_{ij}^{LL}. There will be six of the former, since, in region M, i and $j = 1, 2$, and in region L, i and $j = 1, 2, 3$. There will be nine of the latter. Suppose, further, that the same kind of information is available (perhaps through a survey) on the use of inputs by firms located in region M; z_{ij}^{LM} and z_{ij}^{MM}. Table 3-1 indicates the full set of data. (To be more consistent with the already-familiar subscript notation, one could denote the regions by 1 and 2, respectively. Then an element such as z_{13}^{ML} would be denoted z_{13}^{21}. However, for purposes of exposition it seems clearer to use uppercase letters to designate specific regions; for example, so as to avoid having z's with four different numbers attached to them.) Using the same notation as earlier, this complete table of intraregional and interregional data can be represented as

$$Z = \left[\begin{array}{c|c} Z^{LL} & Z^{LM} \\ \hline Z^{ML} & Z^{MM} \end{array} \right]$$

In the regional models of section 3-2, we utilized *intra*regional information only

TABLE 3-1 INTERINDUSTRY, INTERREGIONAL FLOWS OF GOODS

	Selling Sector	Purchasing Sector	Region L			Region M	
			1	2	3	1	2
Region L	1		z_{11}^{LL}	z_{12}^{LL}	z_{13}^{LL}	z_{11}^{LM}	z_{12}^{LM}
	2		z_{21}^{LL}	z_{22}^{LL}	z_{23}^{LL}	z_{21}^{LM}	z_{22}^{LM}
	3		z_{31}^{LL}	z_{32}^{LL}	z_{33}^{LL}	z_{31}^{LM}	z_{32}^{LM}
Region M	1		z_{11}^{ML}	z_{12}^{ML}	z_{13}^{ML}	z_{11}^{MM}	z_{12}^{MM}
	2		z_{21}^{ML}	z_{22}^{ML}	z_{23}^{ML}	z_{21}^{MM}	z_{22}^{MM}

—as in Eqs. (3-3), (3-4), and (3-7). We now want to incorporate much more explicitly the *inter*regional linkages, as presented by the information in the Z^{LM} and Z^{ML} matrices.

These off-diagonal matrices—Z^{LM} and Z^{ML}—need not be square. Here Z^{LM} has dimensions 3×2 and Z^{ML} is a 2×3 matrix. The on-diagonal matrices, Z^{LL} and Z^{MM}, are always square; for this example the dimensions are 3×3 and 2×2, respectively. While the elements in Z^{LM} represent "exports" from region L and simultaneously "imports" to region M, it is usual in input-output work to refer to these as *interregional trade*, or simply *trade*, flows and to use the terms *export* and *import* when dealing with foreign trade that crosses national, not just regional, boundaries.

By surveying firms in both regions on the amount of locally produced inputs and the amount of inputs from the other region that they used, one would accumulate the data shown in the various *columns* of Table 3-1. On the other hand, the figures in Table 3-1 could also be gathered by asking firms in each region how much they sold to each of the sectors in their region and how much they sold to sectors in the other region. This would generate the figures shown in the various *rows* of Table 3-1.[6]

Consider again the basic equation from the general input-output model, as given in Eq. (2-1) of Chapter 2, namely

$$X_i = z_{i1} + z_{i2} + \cdots + z_{ii} + \cdots + z_{in} + Y_i$$

Recall that one of the components in the final demand term, Y_i, was exports of sector i's goods. In the two-region interregional input-output model, that part of Y_i that represents sales of sector i's product to the productive sectors in the other region (but not to consumers—households—in the other region) is removed from the final demand category, Y_i, and specified explicitly. For the two-region case, with three sectors in region L and two sectors in region M, for example, the output of sector 1 in region L would be expressed as

$$X_1^L = z_{11}^{LL} + z_{12}^{LL} + z_{13}^{LL} + z_{11}^{LM} + z_{12}^{LM} + Y_1^L \qquad (3\text{-}12)$$

The first three terms on the right-hand side represent the sales from sector 1 in

---

[6]Usually, one has some (not complete) information on purchases and also some (not complete) information on sales. The problem then is to produce a table from possibly inconsistent data. This reconciliation problem is discussed in section 8-6 of Chapter 8.

region L to the three sectors (itself and two others) within the region; the next two terms are the interregional trade flows from sector 1 in region L to the two sectors that are in region M. The last term, Y_1^L, represents sales to final demand for the output of sector 1 in region L. This would include household consumption in L, exports from the region *except* those sales to productive sectors in region M, government demand for products made by firms in sector 1 in region L, and so on.

There will be similar equations for X_2^L and X_3^L, and also for X_1^M and X_2^M. The regional input coefficients for region L—$a_{ij}^{LL} = z_{ij}^{LL}/X_j^L$—were given in Eq. (3-3). There will also be a set for region M, namely

$$a_{ij}^{MM} = \frac{z_{ij}^{MM}}{X_j^M} \tag{3-13}$$

The interregional trade coefficients are found similarly, where the denominators are gross outputs of sectors in the *receiving* region. We saw a_{ij}^{ML} in Eq. (3-5); similarly,

$$a_{ij}^{LM} = \frac{z_{ij}^{LM}}{X_j^M} \tag{3-14}$$

Using these regional input and trade coefficients to replace z_{ij}^{LL} by $a_{ij}^{LL}X_j^L$ and z_{ij}^{LM} by $a_{ij}^{LM}X_j^M$, Eq. (3-12) can be reexpressed as

$$X_1^L = a_{11}^{LL}X_1^L + a_{12}^{LL}X_2^L + a_{13}^{LL}X_3^L + a_{11}^{LM}X_1^M + a_{12}^{LM}X_2^M + Y_1^L \tag{3-15}$$

Again, there will be similar expressions for X_2^L, X_3^L, X_1^M and X_2^M. (Compare the equations in (2-4) in Chapter 2, where there was no regional dimension—no superscripts L and M—and where there were n sectors.) Following the same development as in Chapter 2, if we move all terms involving X^L or X^M to the left, Eq. (3-15) becomes

$$\left(1 - a_{11}^{LL}\right)X_1^L - a_{12}^{LL}X_2^L - a_{13}^{LL}X_3^L - a_{11}^{LM}X_1^M - a_{12}^{LM}X_2^M = Y_1^L \tag{3-16}$$

There are similar equations that have Y_2^L, Y_3^L, Y_1^M, and Y_2^M on the right-hand sides.

For the present example, in which region L has three sectors, A^{LL} as given in Eq. (3-4) is

$$A^{LL} = \begin{bmatrix} a_{11}^{LL} & a_{12}^{LL} & a_{13}^{LL} \\ a_{21}^{LL} & a_{22}^{LL} & a_{23}^{LL} \\ a_{31}^{LL} & a_{32}^{LL} & a_{33}^{LL} \end{bmatrix}$$

Also, for this example, the 2×2 matrix for region M is given by $A^{MM} = Z^{MM}(\hat{X}^M)^{-1}$, and the two trade coefficient matrices are represented by $A^{LM} = Z^{LM}(\hat{X}^M)^{-1}$ and $A^{ML} = Z^{ML}(\hat{X}^L)^{-1}$; these are 3×2 and 2×3, respectively. Using these four matrices, the five equations of which Eq. (3-16) is the first can be represented compactly as

$$(I - A^{LL})X^L - A^{LM}X^M = Y^L$$
$$- A^{ML}X^L + (I - A^{MM})X^M = Y^M$$

(3-17)

where Y^L is the three-element vector of final demands for region L goods, and Y^M is the two-element vector of final demands for region M goods.

We can define the complete coefficient matrix for a two-region interregional model as consisting of the four submatrices

$$A = \begin{bmatrix} A^{LL} & A^{LM} \\ A^{ML} & A^{MM} \end{bmatrix}$$

For the current example, this will be a 5×5 matrix. By similarly defining a five-element gross-output vector containing X^L and X^M, the outputs in the two regions, respectively

$$X = \begin{bmatrix} X^L \\ X^M \end{bmatrix}$$

and a five-element final-demand vector made up of the two regional final demand vectors Y^L and Y^M

$$Y = \begin{bmatrix} Y^L \\ Y^M \end{bmatrix}$$

then the complete two-region interregional input-output system is still representable as

$$(I - A)X = Y$$

as in Eq. (2-6) in Chapter 2. A solution will be given (as usual) by

$$X = (I - A)^{-1}Y$$

(3-18)

Less compactly, Eq. (3-17) is

$$\left\{ \begin{bmatrix} I & 0 \\ 0 & I \end{bmatrix} - \begin{bmatrix} A^{LL} & A^{LM} \\ A^{ML} & A^{MM} \end{bmatrix} \right\} \begin{bmatrix} X^L \\ X^M \end{bmatrix} = \begin{bmatrix} Y^L \\ Y^M \end{bmatrix}$$

(3-19)

(The reader should be clear that, when multiplied out, this gives exactly the set of equations in [3-17].)

Note that in using an interregional model of this kind for analysis, not only is stability of the regional input coefficients necessary (the elements of A^{LL} and A^{MM}), but also the trade coefficients are assumed unvarying over time (the elements of A^{LM} and A^{ML}). Thus both the structure of production in each region and trade patterns between regions are "frozen" in the model. For a given level of final demands in either or both regions, the necessary gross outputs in both regions can be found in the usual input-output fashion, by premultiplying Y by the inverse of the $(I - A)$ matrix, that is, the inverse of the matrix in curly brackets on the left of Eq. (3-19). Clearly this complete $(I - A)$ matrix will be larger than that for the single-region model—if both regions are divided into n sectors, the single-region matrix would be of size $n \times n$ and the full two-region interregional model would be of size $2n \times 2n$, which means four times as many (possible) elements (many of which may be zero, of course). However, aside from these dimensionality effects, the analysis proceeds along similar lines.

The advantage is that the model captures the magnitude of effects on each sector in each region; interregional linkages are made specific by sector in the supplying region and by sector in the receiving region. The accompanying disadvantages are primarily the greatly increased data needs and the necessary associated assumptions on constancy of trading relationships. If it is not always easy to accept the idea of constant input coefficients in general, in the national input-output model, it may be even more difficult to believe that imports of good i per dollar's worth of sector j output in a specific region remain constant, no matter how much sector j's output changes.

Interregional Feedbacks in the Two-Region Model

Consider an increase in the demand by a foreign airline for commercial aircraft produced by a manufacturer located in Washington State. Certain subassemblies and parts will be purchased from sectors outside the region (for example, jet engines from Connecticut). This stimulus of new output in Connecticut because of new output in Washington is often termed an interregional spillover effect. The increased demand for aircraft will increase the demand for engines and consequently for all of the direct and indirect inputs to the manufacture of jet engines, one of which might be extruded aluminum shapes made in the state of Washington. This idea is illustrated in Figure 3-1.

The arrow connecting Washington output to Connecticut output represents an interregional spillover effect. The loop (two arrows) connecting Washington output to itself, via Connecticut output, represents an interregional feedback effect; in other words, Washington needs more inputs from Connecticut and therefore Connecticut needs more inputs from everywhere, including Washington. The interregional model in its two-matrix-equation form, Eq. (3-17), allows one to isolate exactly the magnitude of such interregional feedbacks.

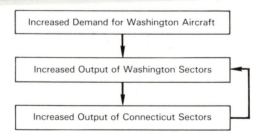

FIGURE 3-1 Increases in Washington final demands affecting Washington outputs via Connecticut.

Suppose, in Eq. (3-17), that we read X^L, X^M, Y^L, and Y^M as "changes in," that is, as if they were ΔX^L, ΔX^M, ΔY^L, and ΔY^M. Thus, given a vector of changes in final demands in the two regions, we can find the consequent changes in gross outputs in both regions. Assume, for simplicity, that $Y^M = 0$—that is, we are assessing the impacts in both regions of a change in final demands in region L only. Under these conditions, solving the second equation in (3-17) for X^M gives

$$X^M = (I - A^{MM})^{-1} A^{ML} X^L$$

and putting this into the first equation, we have

$$(I - A^{LL}) X^L - A^{LM}(I - A^{MM})^{-1} A^{ML} X^L = Y^L \qquad (3\text{-}20)$$

Note that a single-region model (for region L), as in Eq. (3-7), would be $(I - A^{LL}) X^L = Y^L$. The "extra" term on the left in Eq. (3-20), which is

$$A^{LM}(I - A^{MM})^{-1} A^{ML} X^L \qquad (3\text{-}21)$$

represents exactly the added demands made on the output of region L because of interregional trade linkages; it is the interregional feedback. Consider the various parts of this term, starting at the right: (a) $A^{ML} X^L$ represents the magnitude of flows from M to L because of increased output in L (engines shipped from Connecticut to Washington), (b) $(I - A^{MM})^{-1} A^{ML} X^L$ translates these flows into total direct and indirect needs in M to produce the required shipments from M (Connecticut production needed to supply the engines for shipment to Washington), (c) $A^{LM}(I - A^{MM})^{-1} A^{ML} X^L$ indicates the magnitude of the additional sales from L to M that will be necessary to sustain the total M-based production found in (b) (Washington sales to Connecticut as inputs to the total Connecticut production).

Thus the strength and importance of interregional linkages depend not only, as one would expect, on the elements of the trade coefficient matrices—A^{LM} and A^{ML}, in this example—but also on the full set of regional input coefficients in the other region, as represented by the Leontief inverse for that region—$(I - A^{MM})^{-1}$ in the example. It is precisely these kinds of spatial linkages that distinguish complete interregional models from single-region models. Since the feedback term is subtracted from $(I - A^{LL}) X^L$, or $X^L - A^{LL} X^L$, in Eq. (3-20), it is clear that for a given value of Y^L, X^L will necessarily have to be *larger* than in the single-region analysis in order that the required shipments to region M can be met, as well as the usual intraregional shipments, $A^{LL} X^L$.

Numerical Example: Hypothetical Two-Region Interregional Case

To illustrate for the two-region case, suppose that the following figures, in Table 3-2, represent the data in Table 3-1.

Also, let $Y^L = \begin{bmatrix} 200 \\ 1000 \\ 50 \end{bmatrix}$ and $Y^M = \begin{bmatrix} 515 \\ 450 \end{bmatrix}$, so that $Y = \begin{bmatrix} Y^L \\ \hline Y^M \end{bmatrix} = \begin{bmatrix} 200 \\ 1000 \\ 50 \\ \hline 515 \\ 450 \end{bmatrix}$;

TABLE 3-2 FLOW DATA FOR A HYPOTHETICAL TWO-REGION INTERREGIONAL CASE

Selling Sector	Purchasing Sector	Region L			Region M	
		1	*2*	*3*	*1*	*2*
Region L *1*		150	500	50	25	75
2		200	100	400	200	100
3		300	500	50	60	40
Region M *1*		75	100	60	200	250
2		50	25	25	150	100

thus

$$X^L = \begin{bmatrix} 1000 \\ 2000 \\ 1000 \end{bmatrix}, \quad X^M = \begin{bmatrix} 1200 \\ 800 \end{bmatrix}, \quad \text{and} \quad X = \begin{bmatrix} X^L \\ \hline X^M \end{bmatrix} = \begin{bmatrix} 1000 \\ 2000 \\ 1000 \\ 1200 \\ 800 \end{bmatrix}.$$

Then $A^{LL} = Z^{LL}(\hat{X}^L)^{-1}$ is found to be

$$A^{LL} = \begin{bmatrix} .15 & .25 & .05 \\ .20 & .05 & .40 \\ .30 & .25 & .05 \end{bmatrix}$$

Similarly, A^{MM}, A^{LM}, and A^{ML} can be found. They are

$$A^{MM} = \begin{bmatrix} .167 & .313 \\ .125 & .125 \end{bmatrix}$$

$$A^{LM} = \begin{bmatrix} .021 & .094 \\ .167 & .125 \\ .050 & .050 \end{bmatrix}$$

$$A^{ML} = \begin{bmatrix} .075 & .050 & .060 \\ .050 & .013 & .025 \end{bmatrix}$$

and thus

$$A = \begin{bmatrix} A^{LL} & A^{LM} \\ \hline A^{ML} & A^{MM} \end{bmatrix} = \begin{bmatrix} .150 & .250 & .050 & .021 & .094 \\ .200 & .050 & .400 & .167 & .125 \\ .300 & .250 & .050 & .050 & .050 \\ \hline .075 & .050 & .060 & .167 & .313 \\ .050 & .013 & .025 & .125 & .125 \end{bmatrix}$$

and

$$(I - A)^{-1} = \begin{bmatrix} 1.424 & .466 & .291 & .192 & .305 \\ .635 & 1.424 & .671 & .410 & .457 \\ .639 & .537 & 1.336 & .251 & .311 \\ \hline .268 & .201 & .198 & 1.342 & .549 \\ .147 & .092 & .093 & .216 & 1.254 \end{bmatrix}$$

Impacts on the sectors in both regions of various new final-demand vectors in either or both regions can now be found. For example, with new demand of 100 for the output of sector 1 in each region, $Y' = [100 \quad 0 \quad 0 \mid 100 \quad 0]$, and, using $(I - A)^{-1}$ given above,

$$X = \begin{bmatrix} 161.60 \\ 104.50 \\ 89.00 \\ \hline 161.00 \\ 36.30 \end{bmatrix}$$

Any other mix of new final demand in two regions could also be examined. If demand were 100 for the output of each sector in each region, then

$$X = \begin{bmatrix} 267.80 \\ 359.70 \\ 307.40 \\ \hline 255.80 \\ 180.20 \end{bmatrix}$$

and if the new final demand were 100 for the output of sector 1 in region L only, the consequent new vector of total outputs in both regions would be

$$X = \begin{bmatrix} 142.40 \\ 63.50 \\ 63.90 \\ \hline 26.80 \\ 14.70 \end{bmatrix}$$

It is to be emphasized that the final demands in the interregional input-output model are for outputs produced in a particular region. That is, $Y_1^L = 100$ means that there is a final demand of 100 for sector 1 goods that are produced in region L. If sector 1 were aircraft production and region L were Washington, new orders from a foreign airline for Boeing commercial airliners would be represented in the value for Y_1^L. This region-specific orientation of final demands in the interregional model is to be contrasted with the situation in the multiregional input-output model, as we will see in section 3-4, below.

Using these hypothetical data, we can illustrate the differences between the results from a single-region model for region L alone and the results from this two-region interregional model. From the information on A^{LL} alone, we find

$$(I - A^{LL})^{-1} = \begin{bmatrix} 1.365 & .425 & .251 \\ .527 & 1.348 & .595 \\ .570 & .489 & 1.289 \end{bmatrix}$$

Suppose that the new final demands for sectors 1 and 2 in region L are 600 and 1500, respectively. Using this single-region model and ignoring interregional linkages, as in Eq. (3-7), we have

$$X_S^L = (I - A^{LL})^{-1} Y^L = \begin{bmatrix} 1.365 & .425 & .251 \\ .527 & 1.348 & .595 \\ .570 & .489 & 1.289 \end{bmatrix} \begin{bmatrix} 600 \\ 1500 \\ 0 \end{bmatrix} = \begin{bmatrix} 1456.50 \\ 2338.20 \\ 1075.50 \end{bmatrix}$$

(We use X_S^L to make clear that these are outputs in the single-region model.) However, if we use the full two-region interregional model, with $Y' = [600 \quad 1500 \quad 0 \mid 0 \quad 0]$, we find

$$X = \begin{bmatrix} 1551.30 \\ 2517.00 \\ 1188.30 \\ \hline 460.20 \\ 224.70 \end{bmatrix}$$

Note, in particular, that the first three elements in X are the outputs of the sectors in region L; that is, $X_T^L = \begin{bmatrix} 1551.30 \\ 2517.00 \\ 1188.30 \end{bmatrix}$. (Here, X_T^L reminds us that these are outputs in the two-region interregional model.)

As is expected from the discussion above, each of the region L outputs is larger in the interregional model because the interregional feedbacks are captured in that model. One measure of the "error" that would be involved in ignoring these feedbacks—that is, in using a single-region model as opposed to an interregional model—would be given by the percentage of total output in region L that one fails to capture when using a single-region model only. Total output over all sectors in region L in the two-region model is the sum of the dollar values of the three outputs in X_T^L, namely $i'X_T^L$; here this is 5256.60. Total output estimated in the single-region model (the sum of the elements in X_S^L—$i'X_S^L$) is 4870.20. Thus the underestimate that occurs in using the single-region model is 386.40, which is $(386.40/5256.60) \times 100 = 7.4$ percent of the total true (two-region model) output. Formally, this overall percentage error (OPE) is found as $[(i'X_T^L - i'X_S^L)/i'X_T^L] \times 100$ or, equivalently, $[i'(X_T^L - X_S^L)/i'X_T^L] \times 100$. In addition, of course, in the single-region model, there is no output in region M (since there is no region M) caused by the new demands for region L goods; in this example, however, we see that a total of 684.90 was required in new region M production.

It thus becomes an interesting empirical question to try to assess the importance of interregional feedbacks in real-world regional input-output models. If it turned out that the error caused by ignoring interregional linkages when assessing the impact of new region L final demands on region L outputs was quite small, then one might argue that (at least for such questions) the apparatus of an interregional model would be unnecessary. The answer will depend, in part, upon the relative strengths of the interregional linkages; in the two-region model this means on the magnitudes of the elements in A^{LM} and A^{ML}, as in Eq. (3-21). Precisely this question has been investigated; however, the results are inconclusive. In a rather early set of experiments, the conclusion was reached that such interregional feedback effects were likely to be very small (less than one half of one percent, using the overall percentage error measure presented above for illustration). (See Miller 1966, 1969.) Other studies have tended to confirm the relative smallness of interregional feedback effects by comparing output multipliers from single- and many-region input-output models. We will examine these results in Chapter 4, where multipliers are discussed. More recently there has been some work on derivation of upper limits on the percentage error that could be expected in certain interregional input-output models when the interregional feedbacks are ignored (Gillen and Guccione 1980).

As is to be expected, the error is strongly influenced by the level of self-sufficiency in region L—that is, by whether or not region L is relatively dependent on imports from region M. Higher dependence is reflected in larger coefficients in A^{ML} which, again as in Eq. (3-21), generate a larger feedback term. It is also apparent that self-sufficiency is a function of the geographic size of the region. In a two-region model with Nebraska (region L) and the rest of the United States (region M), the average element in A^{ML} will be larger than in a two-region model in which region L is the United States west of the Mississippi and region M is the United States east of the Mississippi. However, in the Nebraska (L)/rest-of-the-United States (M) example, the elements in A^{LM} (reflecting rest-of-the-United States dependence on inputs from Nebraska) will be generally much smaller than in the United States West (L)/United States East (M) example. Thus it is not easy to generalize on how the geographical size of the respective regions influences the size of the interregional feedbacks.

In any case, a single-region model, by definition, cannot capture effects outside of that region, and there are many kinds of economic impact questions that have important ramifications in more than one region of a national economy. In these cases, some kind of connected-region model is essential. The interregional input-output framework provides one such approach.

Interregional Models with More Than Two Regions

In a three-region model, let the regions be denoted by superscripts L, M, and N. Then the complete coefficient matrix can be defined as

$$A = \begin{bmatrix} A^{LL} & A^{LM} & A^{LN} \\ A^{ML} & A^{MM} & A^{MN} \\ A^{NL} & A^{NM} & A^{NN} \end{bmatrix} \tag{3-22}$$

With $X = \begin{bmatrix} X^L \\ X^M \\ X^N \end{bmatrix}$ and $Y = \begin{bmatrix} Y^L \\ Y^M \\ Y^N \end{bmatrix}$, the complete three-region interregional input-output model is still representable as

$$(I - A)X = Y$$

This is the compact statement for the following set of matrix equations

$$(I - A^{LL})X^L - A^{LM}X^M - A^{LN}X^N = Y^L$$
$$- A^{ML}X^L + (I - A^{MM})X^M - A^{MN}X^N = Y^M \tag{3-23}$$
$$- A^{NL}X^L - A^{NM}X^M + (I - A^{NN})X^N = Y^N$$

(Compare Eq. [3-17] for the two-region model.) The underlying logic is the same as that for the two-region model, and the Eqs. (3-23) can be built up in the same way as were those in (3-17). Also, the magnitudes of the interregional feedback effects can be made specific.

To sketch the general case of many regions, we resort to numbering regions (instead of using uppercase letters) as well as sectors. For a p-region model, the complete coefficient matrix will be

$$A = \begin{bmatrix} A^{11} & A^{12} & \cdots & A^{1p} \\ A^{21} & A^{22} & \cdots & A^{2p} \\ \vdots & \vdots & & \\ A^{p1} & A^{p2} & \cdots & A^{pp} \end{bmatrix}$$

Letting $X = \begin{bmatrix} X^1 \\ \vdots \\ X^p \end{bmatrix}$ and $Y = \begin{bmatrix} Y^1 \\ \vdots \\ Y^p \end{bmatrix}$, the complete model is still

$$(I - A)X = Y$$

representing a set of p matrix equations similar to those shown in Eq. (3-23), namely

$$(I - A^{11})X^1 - A^{12}X^2 - \cdots - A^{1p}X^p = Y^1$$
$$\vdots \qquad\qquad\qquad\qquad\qquad\qquad (3\text{-}24)$$
$$-A^{p1}X^1 - A^{p2}X^2 - \cdots + (I - A^{pp})X^p = Y^p$$

It is easy to see that Eq. (3-17), above, is just the special case where $p = 2$ and where L replaces 1 and M replaces 2. Similarly, Eq. (3-23) is the case for $p = 3$, with L instead of 1, M instead of 2, and N instead of 3.

The data requirements increase quickly with the number of regions. Assuming that all regions are divided into n sectors (not a necessary requirement at all—each region could have a different number of sectors), a complete two-region interregional model requires data for four coefficient matrices of size $n \times n$, a three-region model contains nine $n \times n$ matrices, a four-region model has sixteen such matrices, and a p-region model has p^2 such $n \times n$ matrices. However, interregional models with a relatively small number of regions may be useful, since one region can always be defined as the "rest of the world." A three-region model might concentrate on a particular county, region 2 could be the "rest of the state," and region 3 the "rest of the nation" (outside the state).

Numerical Example: The Japanese Interregional Model

The nine regions in the Japanese interregional system are shown below, in Fig. 3-2. Data have been assembled for both 25 and 10 sectors in each region. In Table 3-3 we present the input coefficient matrix for a version of the model for 1965 that has been aggregated both spatially, to three regions,[7] and sectorally, to five sectors in each region. The Leontief inverse matrix for this three-region interregional model is shown in Table 3-4. Notice that two off-diagonal elements

[7]The regions are: Central (Kanto), North (Hokkaido, Tohoku, and Hokuriko), and South (Kyushu, Shikoku, Chugoku, Kinki and Tokai).

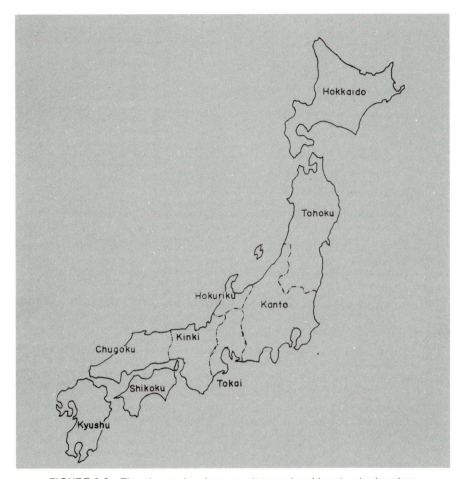

FIGURE 3-2   The nine-region Japanese interregional input-output system.

in this 15×15 inverse (in row 3, column 2, and in row 13, column 12) are greater than 1. As with the small example in section 2-3 of Chapter 2, this reflects the fact that the elements in corresponding positions in the input coefficients matrix (Table 3-3) were unusually large. And this, in turn, is related to the fact that sector 3 (construction and manufacturing) is very large—that is, an aggregate of a great many individual sectors.

We consider the differential effects of a $100,000 increase in export demand for manufactured goods (sector 3), first assuming that the demand is for goods from the Central region, then assuming that it is for goods made in the North, and finally that it is for goods produced in the South. Using ΔY^C, ΔY^N, and ΔY^S, respectively, letting 0 represent a five-element row vector of all zeros, where appropriate, and transposing to obtain row vectors, which are easier to

TABLE 3-3 Input Coefficients in the Five-Sector, Three-Region Japanese Interregional System (1965)

Industry	Central Industry					North Industry					South Industry				
	1	2	3	4	5	1	2	3	4	5	1	2	3	4	5
Central															
1 Agriculture	.053	.000	.009	.011	.009	.001	.000	.007	.000	.001	.001	.000	.001	.000	.010
2 Mining	.000	.001	.001	.001	.002	.000	.000	.001	.000	.000	.000	.000	.000	.000	.000
3 Construction and Manufacturing	.428	.723	.250	.240	.180	.012	.004	.052	.001	.013	.017	.005	.044	.000	.014
4 Transportation	.000	.001	.010	.090	.012	.000	.000	.002	.015	.001	.000	.000	.001	.007	.001
5 Other	.012	.029	.042	.117	.125	.000	.001	.015	.001	.010	.000	.000	.007	.001	.014
North															
1 Agriculture	.004	.000	.000	.000	.000	.089	.001	.017	.039	.021	.002	.000	.000	.000	.000
2 Mining	.000	.000	.000	.000	.000	.002	.005	.002	.007	.011	.000	.000	.000	.000	.000
3 Construction and Manufacturing	.068	.041	.020	.000	.002	.362	.521	.160	.233	.129	.034	.028	.012	.000	.001
4 Transportation	.000	.002	.000	.014	.000	.000	.008	.010	.025	.011	.000	.000	.000	.023	.000
5 Other	.003	.034	.001	.000	.001	.010	.033	.027	.095	.103	.002	.008	.000	.000	.001
South															
1 Agriculture	.002	.000	.002	.000	.000	.002	.000	.006	.000	.000	.072	.000	.011	.016	.010
2 Mining	.000	.000	.000	.000	.000	.000	.000	.001	.000	.000	.001	.004	.001	.002	.004
3 Construction and Manufacturing	.036	.021	.082	.000	.013	.012	.012	.056	.000	.007	.473	.719	.303	.264	.196
4 Transportation	.000	.000	.001	.024	.000	.000	.000	.001	.022	.000	.000	.003	.009	.068	.012
5 Other	.001	.005	.006	.000	.003	.000	.001	.009	.000	.003	.012	.050	.037	.112	.110

TABLE 3-4 LEONTIEF INVERSE MATRIX FOR THE FIVE-SECTOR, THREE-REGION JAPANESE INTERREGIONAL SYSTEM (1965)

Industry	Central (Industry)					North (Industry)					South (Industry)				
	1	2	3	4	5	1	2	3	4	5	1	2	3	4	5
Central															
1 Agriculture	1.064	.012	.015	.019	.014	.005	.006	.011	.004	.003	.003	.003	.004	.002	.002
2 Mining	.001	1.002	.001	.002	.003	.001	.001	.002	.001	.001	.000	.000	.000	.000	.000
3 Construction and Manufacturing	.639	1.016	1.380	.413	.299	.064	.067	.110	.043	.045	.082	.085	.099	.041	.051
4 Transportation	.008	.013	.016	1.107	.019	.002	.003	.005	.019	.003	.002	.002	.003	.010	.002
5 Other	.050	.088	.072	.170	1.161	.013	.017	.029	.014	.019	.013	.016	.019	.011	.025
North															
1 Agriculture	.007	.003	.001	.001	.001	1.108	.015	.024	.053	.030	.003	.002	.001	.002	.000
2 Mining	.000	.001	.000	.000	.000	.003	1.008	.003	.010	.013	.000	.000	.000	.000	.000
3 Construction and Manufacturing	.108	.087	.038	.019	.012	.488	.648	1.218	.335	.200	.059	.055	.025	.018	.009
4 Transportation	.001	.004	.001	.017	.001	.005	.015	.013	1.031	.014	.001	.001	.001	.026	.001
5 Other	.008	.042	.003	.004	.002	.028	.059	.038	.121	1.124	.004	.011	.002	.004	.002
South															
1 Agriculture	.006	.005	.005	.003	.002	.006	.006	.010	.004	.002	1.089	.016	.020	.026	.017
2 Mining	.000	.001	.001	.000	.000	.001	.001	.001	.000	.000	.002	1.006	.002	.004	.005
3 Construction and Manufacturing	.150	.173	.179	.072	.064	.075	.089	.128	.051	.038	.773	1.099	1.488	.481	.352
4 Transportation	.003	.005	.005	.031	.002	.002	.003	.004	.026	.002	.009	.016	.016	1.081	.018
5 Other	.013	.021	.017	.011	.009	.009	.012	.020	.010	.007	.049	.105	.065	.156	1.141

present, we have

$$(\Delta Y^C)' = \begin{bmatrix} 0 & 0 & 100 & 0 & 0 & \vdots & 0 & \vdots & 0 \end{bmatrix}$$

$$(\Delta Y^N)' = \begin{bmatrix} 0 & \vdots & 0 & 0 & 100 & 0 & 0 & \vdots & 0 \end{bmatrix}$$

$$(\Delta Y^S)' = \begin{bmatrix} 0 & \vdots & 0 & \vdots & 0 & 0 & 100 & 0 & 0 \end{bmatrix}$$

Premultiplying first ΔY^C, then ΔY^N, and finally ΔY^S by the Leontief inverse in Table 3-4 generates the results presented in Table 3-5. The new export demand of $100,000 generates differing total economic effects, depending on the regional location of the sector experiencing the new demand. When the demand is for manufactured goods made in the Central region, the total output of all sectors in that region increases by $148,400. If the demand is for manufactured goods from the North, the total value of new outputs in that region is $129,600; and when the $100,000 of new demand is for manufactured goods made in the South, total southern-region output increases by $159,100. Adding across the three regions in each case, the total new national output necessary to satisfy the new final (export) demand for manufactured goods is $173,400 when the demand is for goods from the Central region, $161,600 when the demand is for northern goods, and $174,500 when it is for southern goods.

With respect to economic connections between regions, Table 3-5 clearly reflects the predominant importance of manufacturing activity in the southern region of Japan. The amounts produced in the region whose manufactured goods experience the new demand represent the following percentages of total new national output: Central, 86 (that is, $(148.4/173.4) \times 100$); North, 80; South, 91. When the $100,000 of new demand is for central goods, the stimulation of southern production is in the amount of $20,700 while there is only $4,300 worth of new northern production. Similarly, with $100,000 of new demand for northern goods, southern production is $16,300, and that in the Central region is $15,700. Finally, new demand for southern goods generates the largest within-region effects ($159,100); while new output from Central region

TABLE 3-5 REGION- AND SECTOR-SPECIFIC EFFECTS (IN $1000) OF A $100,000 INCREASE IN FINAL DEMAND FOR SECTOR 3 GOODS (JAPANESE INTERREGIONAL MODEL)

Sector	Produced in the Central Region (ΔY^C)			Produced in the Northern Region (ΔY^N)			Produced in the Southern Region (ΔY^S)		
	Central	North	South	Central	North	South	Central	North	South
1	1.5	.1	.5	1.1	2.4	1.0	.4	.1	2.0
2	.1	0	.1	.2	.3	.1	0	0	.2
3	138.0	3.8	17.9	11.0	121.8	12.8	9.9	2.5	148.8
4	1.6	.1	.5	.5	1.3	.4	.3	.1	1.6
5	7.2	.3	1.7	2.9	3.8	2.0	1.9	.2	6.5
Total	148.4	4.3	20.7	15.7	129.6	16.3	12.5	2.9	159.1

TABLE 3-6 Average Values of the Leontief Inverse Coefficients in Each Submatrix of Table 3-4

	Central	North	South
Central	.343	.020	.019
North	.014	.304	.009
South	.031	.020	.361

sectors is next largest, at $12,500; in the North the effect is only a $2,900 increase in outputs.

One very general view of the economic importance of each of the regions in this three-region interregional economy comes from an inspection of the average values of the coefficients in each of the nine submatrices in $(I - A)^{-1}$ in Table 3-4. These average Leontief inverse coefficients are shown in Table 3-6.

Averaging across the rows of Table 3-6 gives a very general measure of the magnitude of total economic activity *in that region* needed to supply required inputs to satisfy a dollar's worth of new final demand anywhere in the three-region economy. These row averages are: Central .127; North, .109; South .137. By the row-averages measure, the rankings of the regions—in terms of overall importance as suppliers of inputs for production throughout the national economy—are: South, Central, North. Alternatively, one can investigate the role of each region as a supplier of inputs to other regions, ignoring inputs that are used internally within the region in which they are produced. That is, we can find the row averages in Table 3-6, ignoring the diagonal elements. These are: Central .020; North, .012; South, .026. Ranked by this measure also (in terms of importance as a supplier of inputs for production in *other* regions), we have: South, Central, North.

Note that column sums in Table 3-6 are: Central, .388; North, .344; and South, .389. This simply suggests that when we average over all sectors and when we include inputs to production in a region that are (1) supplied by producers in that region or (2) imported from other regions in the national economy, we have hidden most of the regional economic differences. Hence average total inputs per dollar's worth of (average) output are very similar across regions.

3-4 | MANY-REGION MODELS—THE MULTIREGIONAL APPROACH

While a complete interregional model of the sort described in section 3-3 is thus far generally beyond possibility for very many regions and/or sectors because of the problems of data availability (Japan and Holland providing exceptions), the framework has inspired modifications and simplifications in the direction of operationality. One very ambitious attempt in this direction is the U.S. multiregional input-output (MRIO) model that was initiated at the Harvard Economic Research Project (HERP) and has since been developed primarily by Professor Polenske and her associates at MIT. In its most detailed form, this is a 51-region model (the 50 states and Washington, D.C.) with 79 sectors in each region. The U.S. MRIO model is an extremely ambitious empirical application of the framework suggested (independently) by Chenery (1953) and Moses (1955). For this reason, it is sometimes classified as the "Chenery-Moses" model. (An early comparison of this and the Isard IRIO model is provided in Hartwick 1971.) A description of the model and its construction is provided in Polenske (1980). One detailed application of the U.S. MRIO model is in Golladay and Haveman (1977), where potential increases in consumer incomes resulting from alternative tax policies are distributed among sectors and across regions, using the multiregional input-output framework.

The multiregional model contains counterparts to the regional input coefficients matrices—for example, A^{LL}—and the trade coefficients matrices—for example, A^{LM}. In both cases the attempt has been to specify a model in which the data are more easily obtained. We examine these two modifications in turn.

The Regional Tables

The multiregional input-output model uses a regional *technical* coefficients matrix, A^L, in place of the regional *input* coefficients matrix, A^{LL}. These regional technical coefficients, a_{ij}^L, were described in section 3-2, where they were contrasted with the regional input coefficients, a_{ij}^{LL}. They were defined in Eqs. (3-8) and (3-3), respectively, and the corresponding matrices were given in Eqs. (3-9) and (3-4). Recall that for the regional technical coefficients, information regarding the region of origin of a given input is ignored; one only needs information on shipments of the sort $z_{ij}^{\cdot L}$, the dollars' worth of input from sector i used by sector j in region L.

In practice, when actual regional data on technology are not available, estimates of regional technical coefficients matrices are sometimes made using what is known as the product-mix approach. The basic assumption is that input requirements per unit of output are constant from region to region at a very fine level of industrial classification, but that a distinguishing characteristic of production at the regional level is the composition of sector outputs, when one is dealing with more aggregate sectors. To return to our earlier illustration of the product-mix problem, when three-engine commercial jets are made in Washington or California (or anywhere else), they use, among other things, three jet engines as inputs; when single-engine propeller-driven private aircraft are made in Pennsylvania or in any other state, they use one propeller engine as one of the inputs to production. But the important fact to capture is that the output of the sector designated "aircraft" in a Washington table is composed of a vastly different mix of products (commercial jets) than the "aircraft" sector in Pennsylvania (private airplanes).

To illustrate, assume that sector 2 is food and kindred products, and that it contains only three subsectors, which can be designated by their outputs: tomato soup (sector 2.1), chocolate bars (sector 2.2), and guava jelly (sector 2.3). Assume that the *national* technical coefficients from sector 8, paper and allied products, to each of these subsectors are: 0.005, 0.009, and 0.003. (These represent labels, wrappers, etc.) Suppose that we want to derive coefficients for inputs from sector

8 to sector 2, a_{82}, for New Jersey (region J) and for Florida (region F). The data that we would need are shown in Table 3-7, where N designates *national* data. That is, the food and kindred products sector was composed of only tomato soup (\$700) and chocolate bars (\$300) output (no guava jelly) in New Jersey; in Florida it was made up of tomato soup (\$80) and guava jelly (\$420)—no chocolate bars.

Purchases of paper and allied products as inputs to New Jersey food and kindred products production over the period covered by the output figures in Table 3-7 are then assumed to be the sum of

$$a_{8,2.1}^N X_{2.1}^J = (.005)(700) = 3.50$$

$$a_{8,2.2}^N X_{2.2}^J = (.009)(300) = 2.70$$

$$a_{8,2.3}^N X_{2.3}^J = (.003)(0) \quad = 0$$

for a total of \$6.20 in necessary inputs from sector 8 to production in sector 2 in New Jersey. Thus, since $X_2^J = X_{2.1}^J + X_{2.2}^J + X_{2.3}^J = 1000$,

$$a_{82}^J = 6.20/1000 = .0062$$

Similarly, for Florida,

$$a_{8,2.1}^N X_{2.1}^F = (.005)(80) \quad = 0.40$$

$$a_{8,2.2}^N X_{2.2}^F = (.009)(0) \quad = 0$$

$$a_{8,2.3}^N X_{2.3}^F = (.003)(420) = 1.26$$

The total Florida inputs from sector 8 thus would be estimated as \$1.66. Since $X_2^F = 80 + 0 + 420 = 500$, we have

$$a_{82}^F = 1.66/500 = .0033$$

TABLE 3-7 DATA NEEDED FOR CONVERSION OF NATIONAL TO REGIONAL COEFFICIENTS VIA THE PRODUCT-MIX APPROACH

National Data		
To sector 2: Food and Kindred Products		
Subsectors 2.1	2.2	2.3
(tomato soup)	(chocolate bars)	(guava jelly)
From sector 8: Paper and Applied Products		
$a_{8,2.1}^N = .005$	$a_{8,2.2}^N = .009$	$a_{8,2.3}^N = .003$
Regional Data		
Outputs (in dollars) by subsector of sector 2		
(New Jersey)	(Florida)	
$X_{2.1}^J = 700$	$X_{2.1}^F = 80$	
$X_{2.2}^J = 300$	$X_{2.2}^F = 0$	
$X_{2.3}^J = 0$	$X_{2.3}^F = 420$	
Total Outputs (Sector 2)		
$X_2^J = 1000$	$X_2^F = 500$	

TABLE 3-8 INTERREGIONAL SHIPMENTS OF COMMODITY i

Shipping Region	Receiving Region					
	1	2	$\cdots$	M	$\cdots$	p
1	z_i^{11}	z_i^{12}	$\cdots$	z_i^{1M}	$\cdots$	z_i^{1p}
2	z_i^{21}	z_i^{22}	$\cdots$	z_i^{2M}	$\cdots$	z_i^{2p}
$\vdots$	$\vdots$					
L	z_i^{L1}	z_i^{L2}	$\cdots$	z_i^{LM}	$\cdots$	z_i^{Lp}
$\vdots$	$\vdots$					
p	z_i^{p1}	z_i^{p2}	$\cdots$	z_i^{pM}	$\cdots$	z_i^{pp}

Formally,

$$a_{82}^{J} = \frac{\left(a_{8,2.1}^{N} X_{2.1}^{J} + a_{8,2.2}^{N} X_{2.2}^{J} + a_{8,2.3}^{N} X_{2.3}^{J} \right)}{X_2^{J}}$$

$$a_{82}^{F} = \frac{\left(a_{8,2.1}^{N} X_{2.1}^{F} + a_{8,2.2}^{N} X_{2.2}^{F} + a_{8,2.3}^{N} X_{2.3}^{F} \right)}{X_2^{F}}$$

That is,

$$a_{82}^{J} = a_{8,2.1}^{N} \left(\frac{X_{2.1}^{J}}{X_2^{J}} \right) + a_{8,2.2}^{N} \left(\frac{X_{2.2}^{J}}{X_2^{J}} \right) + a_{8,2.3}^{N} \left(\frac{X_{2.3}^{J}}{X_2^{J}} \right)$$

and

$$a_{82}^{F} = a_{8,2.1}^{N} \left(\frac{X_{2.1}^{F}}{X_2^{F}} \right) + a_{8,2.2}^{N} \left(\frac{X_{2.2}^{F}}{X_2^{F}} \right) + a_{8,2.3}^{N} \left(\frac{X_{2.3}^{F}}{X_3^{F}} \right)$$

and we see that the *regional* coefficients derived in this way are *weighted averages* of the national detailed coefficients, where the weights are the proportions of subsector outputs to total output of the sector (e.g., $X_{2.1}^{J}/X_2^{J}$) in each state.

The Trade Tables

The interconnections among regions in the multiregional input-output model are captured in the trade coefficient tables in an entirely different way from the interregional input-output framework. Trade flows in the multiregional model are estimated by sector, again to take advantage of the kinds of data likely to be available. For sector i, data are gathered on the flows of i from a particular region to all others. Let z_i^{LM} denote the dollar flow of good i from region L to region M, irrespective of the sector of destination in the receiving region.[8] These flows will include shipments to the producing sectors in region M

---

[8]To be consistent with the notation $z_{ij}^{\cdot L}$ or $z_{ij}^{\circ L}$, above, this should properly be $z_{i\cdot}^{LM}$ or $z_{i\circ}^{LM}$. However, when the blank space is in the second subscript position, it is easier to distinguish than when it is in the first superscript position.

as well as to final demand in M. Thus there is, for each sector, a shipments matrix of the sort shown in Table 3-8. (In the HERP model, $p = 51$.)

Note that each of the column sums in this table represents the total shipments of good i into that region from all of the regions in the model; denote this total, for column M in the table for good i, by T_i^M. That is,

$$T_i^M = z_i^{1M} + z_i^{2M} + \cdots + z_i^{LM} + \cdots + z_i^{pM} \tag{3-25}$$

If each element in column M is divided by this total, we have coefficients denoting the *proportion* of all of good i used in M that comes from each region L ($L = 1, \cdots, p$). These are defined to be the interregional trade coefficients and are denoted c_i^{LM}; that is

$$c_i^{LM} = \frac{z_i^{LM}}{T_i^M}$$

(Since there are 79 sectors in the HERP model, there will be 79 such tables; each table has 51×51 possible entries, many of which may be zero.)

For later use, these coefficients are rearranged as follows. For each possible origin-destination pair of regions, denote by C^{LM} the n-element column vector

$$C^{LM} = \begin{bmatrix} c_1^{LM} \\ \vdots \\ c_n^{LM} \end{bmatrix}$$

These elements show, for region M, the proportion of the total amount of each good used in M that comes from region L. Finally, construct $\hat{C}^{LM}$ (where, as usual, the hat means that a vector has been turned into a diagonal matrix)

$$\hat{C}^{LM} = \begin{bmatrix} c_1^{LM} & 0 & \cdots & 0 \\ 0 & c_2^{LM} & \cdots & 0 \\ \vdots & & & \\ 0 & 0 & \cdots & c_n^{LM} \end{bmatrix} \tag{3-26}$$

for L, $M = 1, \cdots, p$. Note that there will be *intra*regional "trade" matrices in this set. For example, there will be a matrix $\hat{C}^{MM}$ with elements $c_i^{MM} = z_i^{MM}/T_i^M$—indicating the proportion of good i used in region M that came from within region M. That is,

$$\hat{C}^{MM} = \begin{bmatrix} c_1^{MM} & 0 & \cdots & 0 \\ 0 & c_2^{MM} & \cdots & 0 \\ \vdots & & & \\ 0 & 0 & \cdots & c_n^{MM} \end{bmatrix} \tag{3-27}$$

The Multiregional Model[9]

Consider a small two-sector, two-region example. Let

$$A^L = \begin{bmatrix} a_{11}^L & a_{12}^L \\ a_{21}^L & a_{22}^L \end{bmatrix}, \qquad A^M = \begin{bmatrix} a_{11}^M & a_{12}^M \\ a_{21}^M & a_{22}^M \end{bmatrix},$$

$$\hat{C}^{LM} = \begin{bmatrix} c_1^{LM} & 0 \\ 0 & c_2^{LM} \end{bmatrix}, \quad \text{and} \quad \hat{C}^{MM} = \begin{bmatrix} c_1^{MM} & 0 \\ 0 & c_2^{MM} \end{bmatrix}$$

Then the multiregional input-output model uses the matrix

$$\hat{C}^{LM}A^M = \begin{bmatrix} c_1^{LM}a_{11}^M & c_1^{LM}a_{12}^M \\ c_2^{LM}a_{21}^M & c_2^{LM}a_{22}^M \end{bmatrix}$$

where the interregional input-output model uses A^{LM}. Similarly,

$$\hat{C}^{MM}A^M = \begin{bmatrix} c_1^{MM}a_{11}^M & c_1^{MM}a_{12}^M \\ c_2^{MM}a_{21}^M & c_2^{MM}a_{22}^M \end{bmatrix}$$

is used in the multiregional model in place of A^{MM} in the interregional model. Therefore the multiregional input-output model embodies the same assumption as was used in the earlier regional models with estimated supply percentages. Looking at the top rows of the $\hat{C}^{LM}A^M$ and $\hat{C}^{MM}A^M$ matrices, note that both sectors 1 and 2 in region M are assumed to have the same proportion of their total use of commodity 1 supplied from region L—that is, c_1^{LM}—and the same proportion supplied from within region M—c_1^{MM}.

For example, if sector 1 in both regions L and M is electricity production and sector 2 in region M is automobile production, then if $c_1^{LM} = 0.6$, this means that 60 percent of all electricity used in making electricity in region M comes from region L and 60 percent of all electricity used in automobile manufacture in region M *also* comes from region L. And similarly, since in this two-region model it would be true that $c_1^{MM} = 0.4$, 40 percent of the electricity used in both electricity production and automobile production in M comes from within the region.

Since the interregional shipments that are recorded in Table 3-8 include sales to both producing sectors and final-demand users in the receiving region, the final demands in region M are met in part by firms within the region ($\hat{C}^{MM}Y^M$) and in part by direct purchases from firms in region L ($\hat{C}^{LM}Y^M$). To continue the illustration with $c_1^{LM} = 0.6$, where sector 1 is electricity production, 60 percent of the final demand for electricity in region M will *also* be satisfied by producers in region L.

---

[9]In this section we emphasize the structural parallels between the multiregional model and the interregional model. In Appendix 3-2 to this chapter the basic relationships in the multiregional model are derived from standard economic and input-output theory.

The multiregional input-output counterpart to Eqs. (3-17) for the two-region interregional model is therefore

$$(I - \hat{C}^{LL}A^L)X^L - \hat{C}^{LM}A^M X^M = \hat{C}^{LL}Y^L + \hat{C}^{LM}Y^M$$
$$- \hat{C}^{ML}A^L X^L + (I - \hat{C}^{MM}A^M)X^M = \hat{C}^{ML}Y^L + \hat{C}^{MM}Y^M \tag{3-28}$$

Letting

$$A = \left[\begin{array}{c|c} A^L & 0 \\ \hline 0 & A^M \end{array}\right], \qquad C = \left[\begin{array}{c|c} \hat{C}^{LL} & \hat{C}^{LM} \\ \hline \hat{C}^{ML} & \hat{C}^{MM} \end{array}\right], \qquad X = \left[\begin{array}{c} X^L \\ \hline X^M \end{array}\right], \quad \text{and} \quad Y = \left[\begin{array}{c} Y^L \\ \hline Y^M \end{array}\right],$$

Eqs. (3-28) can be represented as

$$(I - CA)X = CY \tag{3-29}$$

for which a solution will be given by

$$X = (I - CA)^{-1}CY \tag{3-30}$$

The extension to more than two regions is straightforward. Equations for the three-region model would be

$$(I - \hat{C}^{LL}A^L)X^L - \hat{C}^{LM}A^M X^M - \hat{C}^{LN}A^N X^N = \hat{C}^{LL}Y^L + \hat{C}^{LM}Y^M + \hat{C}^{LN}Y^N$$

$$- \hat{C}^{ML}A^L X^L + (I - \hat{C}^{MM}A^M)X^M - \hat{C}^{MN}A^N X^N = \hat{C}^{ML}Y^L + \hat{C}^{MM}Y^M + \hat{C}^{MN}Y^N$$

$$- \hat{C}^{NL}A^L X^L - \hat{C}^{NM}A^M X^M + (I - \hat{C}^{NN}A^N)X^N = \hat{C}^{NL}Y^L + \hat{C}^{NM}Y^M + \hat{C}^{NN}Y^N$$

(Compare Eq. [3-23], for the three-region interregional model.) By appropriate extension of matrices A, C, X, and Y to incorporate three regions, the fundamental model is still $(I - CA)X = CY$, as in Eq. (3-29), with solution $X = (I - CA)^{-1}CY$, as in Eq. (3-30).

Finally, for the general many-region case, we number the regions, as before. When there are p regions, let

$$A = \begin{bmatrix} A^1 & 0 & \cdots & 0 \\ 0 & A^2 & \cdots & 0 \\ \vdots & \vdots & & \\ 0 & 0 & \cdots & A^p \end{bmatrix}, \qquad C = \begin{bmatrix} \hat{C}^{11} & \cdots & \hat{C}^{1p} \\ \hat{C}^{21} & \cdots & \hat{C}^{2p} \\ \vdots & & \\ \hat{C}^{p1} & \cdots & \hat{C}^{pp} \end{bmatrix},$$

$$X = \begin{bmatrix} X^1 \\ X^2 \\ \vdots \\ X^p \end{bmatrix}, \quad \text{and} \quad Y = \begin{bmatrix} Y^1 \\ Y^2 \\ \vdots \\ Y^p \end{bmatrix}.$$

Then $(I - CA)X = CY$ still represents the system; only the dimensions of the matrices have changed.

Numerical Example: Hypothetical Two-Region Multiregional Case

Assume that we have the flow data in Table 3-9, representing total inputs purchased by producing sectors in each region, regardless of whether these are locally produced or imported from the other region. These are the $Z^L = [z_{ij}^{\cdot L}]$

TABLE 3-9 FLOW DATA FOR A HYPOTHETICAL TWO-REGION MULTIREGIONAL CASE

Purchasing Sector	Region L			Region M		
	1	2	3	1	2	3
Selling Sector 1	225	600	110	225	325	125
2	250	125	425	350	200	270
3	325	700	150	360	240	200

and $Z^M = [z_{ij}^{\cdot M}]$ data.

Suppose, further, that $X^L = \begin{bmatrix} 1000 \\ 2000 \\ 1000 \end{bmatrix}$ and $X^M = \begin{bmatrix} 1200 \\ 800 \\ 1500 \end{bmatrix}$, so that the regional technical coefficient matrices, as in Eq. (3-9), are

$$A^L = \begin{bmatrix} .225 & .300 & .110 \\ .250 & .063 & .425 \\ .325 & .350 & .150 \end{bmatrix}, \qquad A^M = \begin{bmatrix} .188 & .406 & .083 \\ .292 & .250 & .180 \\ .300 & .300 & .133 \end{bmatrix}$$

For the trade tables, we need measures of T_i^L and T_i^M, as given in Eq. (3-25)—the total amount of each good, i, that is available in each region. Table 3-10 provides an example of these data. (Note that the row sums for each sector in each region must be the total output for that sector in that region, as recorded in the appropriate X vector.) The interregional trade coefficients—$c_i^{LM} = z_i^{LM}/T_i^M$—are easily found. Here

$$C^{LL} = \begin{bmatrix} .721 \\ .812 \\ .735 \end{bmatrix} \qquad C^{LM} = \begin{bmatrix} .183 \\ .583 \\ .078 \end{bmatrix} \qquad C^{ML} = \begin{bmatrix} .279 \\ .188 \\ .265 \end{bmatrix} \qquad C^{MM} = \begin{bmatrix} .817 \\ .417 \\ .922 \end{bmatrix}$$

As in Eqs. (3-26) and (3-27), we therefore have

$$\hat{C}^{LL} = \begin{bmatrix} .721 & 0 & 0 \\ 0 & .812 & 0 \\ 0 & 0 & .735 \end{bmatrix} \qquad \hat{C}^{LM} = \begin{bmatrix} .183 & 0 & 0 \\ 0 & .583 & 0 \\ 0 & 0 & .078 \end{bmatrix}$$

$$\hat{C}^{ML} = \begin{bmatrix} .279 & 0 & 0 \\ 0 & .188 & 0 \\ 0 & 0 & .265 \end{bmatrix} \qquad \hat{C}^{MM} = \begin{bmatrix} .817 & 0 & 0 \\ 0 & .417 & 0 \\ 0 & 0 & .922 \end{bmatrix}$$

TABLE 3-10 INTERREGIONAL COMMODITY SHIPMENTS FOR THE HYPOTHETICAL TWO-REGION MULTIREGIONAL CASE

	Commodity 1		Commodity 2		Commodity 3	
	L	M	L	M	L	M
L	800	200	1300	700	900	100
M	310	890	300	500	325	1175

Thus the building blocks in this example for the two-region multiregional input-output model are

$$A = \begin{bmatrix} A^L & 0 \\ \hline 0 & A^M \end{bmatrix} = \begin{bmatrix} .225 & .300 & .110 & 0 & 0 & 0 \\ .250 & .063 & .425 & 0 & 0 & 0 \\ .325 & .350 & .150 & 0 & 0 & 0 \\ \hline 0 & 0 & 0 & .188 & .406 & .083 \\ 0 & 0 & 0 & .292 & .250 & .180 \\ 0 & 0 & 0 & .300 & .300 & .133 \end{bmatrix}$$

$$C = \begin{bmatrix} \hat{C}^{LL} & \hat{C}^{LM} \\ \hline \hat{C}^{ML} & \hat{C}^{MM} \end{bmatrix} = \begin{bmatrix} .721 & 0 & 0 & .183 & 0 & 0 \\ 0 & .812 & 0 & 0 & .583 & 0 \\ 0 & 0 & .735 & 0 & 0 & .078 \\ \hline .279 & 0 & 0 & .817 & 0 & 0 \\ 0 & .188 & 0 & 0 & .417 & 0 \\ 0 & 0 & .265 & 0 & 0 & .922 \end{bmatrix}$$

Therefore

$$(I - CA)^{-1}C = \begin{bmatrix} 1.127 & .447 & .300 & .478 & .418 & .153 \\ .628 & 1.317 & .606 & .552 & 1.115 & .323 \\ .512 & .526 & 1.101 & .335 & .470 & .247 \\ \hline .625 & .369 & .250 & 1.224 & .456 & .216 \\ .238 & .385 & .205 & .278 & .650 & .167 \\ .472 & .445 & .589 & .594 & .529 & 1.232 \end{bmatrix} \qquad (3\text{-}31)$$

and, for example, the impacts of new final demands of 100 for sector 1 outputs by consumers in each region—that is, with $Y' = [100 \quad 0 \quad 0 \mid 100 \quad 0 \quad 0]$—are found, as in Eq. (3-30), as

$$X = (I - CA)^{-1}CY = \begin{bmatrix} 160.50 \\ 118.00 \\ 84.70 \\ \hline 184.90 \\ 51.60 \\ 106.60 \end{bmatrix}$$

That is, $X^L = \begin{bmatrix} 160.50 \\ 118.00 \\ 84.70 \end{bmatrix}$ and $X^M = \begin{bmatrix} 184.90 \\ 51.60 \\ 106.60 \end{bmatrix}$. Similarly, if $Y' = [100 \quad 0 \quad 0 \mid 0 \quad 0 \quad 0]$, which represents new final demands of 100 for sector 1 output by consumers in region L, we find

$$X = \begin{bmatrix} 112.70 \\ 62.80 \\ 51.20 \\ \hline 62.50 \\ 23.80 \\ 47.20 \end{bmatrix}$$

It is important to bear in mind, from the general statement of the multiregional input-output model in Eqs. (3-29) or (3-30), that both intermediate demands, AX, and final demand, Y, are premultiplied by the matrix C, which distributes these demands to supplying sectors across regions. Thus Y^L and Y^M represent demands by the final-demand sectors in regions L and M respectively, *not* final demands for the products of regions L and M (as in the interregional input-output model). The operation CY converts these demands into a set of shipments by each region to contribute toward satisfaction of the final demands. In the two-region model here, Y^L is satisfied in part by shipments from sectors in region L, $\hat{C}^{LL}Y^L$ (as in Eq. [3-28]), and in part by shipments from sectors in region M, $\hat{C}^{ML}Y^L$ (again, as in Eq. [3-28]). An example of a typical element in Y^L might be new energy demands by a state government resulting from a new state office building in region L in that state. Depending upon the particular region, some or all of that energy demand will be met from within region L, the rest from outside the region. This is reflected in the appropriate elements in $\hat{C}^{LL}$ and $\hat{C}^{ML}$.

Thus, if one wants to assess the impacts of new *region-specific* final demands (such as from a foreign airline for Boeing airliners, as in the interregional example in section 3-3) it is necessary to replace CY by, say, Y^*, which represents the new final demands *already distributed* appropriately to the region or regions of interest, and then to find

$$X = (I - CA)^{-1}Y^* \qquad (3-32)$$

This is to be contrasted with Eq. (3-30). Continuing with the data for this example, if $(Y^*)_1^L = 100$ represents the value of new foreign airline orders for aircraft produced in region L, we would find

$$(I - CA)^{-1} = \begin{bmatrix} 1.463 & .471 & .359 & .258 & .345 & .135 \\ .668 & 1.483 & .720 & .526 & .600 & .290 \\ .604 & .572 & 1.445 & .274 & .327 & .145 \\ \hline .314 & .298 & .263 & 1.428 & .676 & .212 \\ .216 & .167 & .221 & .292 & 1.326 & .162 \\ .409 & .376 & .329 & .636 & .743 & 1.308 \end{bmatrix} \qquad (3-33)$$

(Compare Eq. [3-31].) Hence, for this region-specific new final demand, using Eq. (3-32),

$$X = \begin{bmatrix} 146.30 \\ 66.80 \\ 60.40 \\ \hline 31.40 \\ 21.60 \\ 40.90 \end{bmatrix}$$

Numerical Example: The U.S. Multiregional Model

We present an aggregated version of the 1963 U.S. multiregional input-output model that was mentioned at the beginning of this section (Polenske

1980).[10] For the sake of simplicity of exposition, we have aggregated spatially to three regions[11] and sectorally to five sectors in each region. The A, C, $(I - CA)^{-1}C$, and $(I - CA)^{-1}$ matrices (each 15×15) are presented in Tables 3-11, 3-12, 3-13, and 3-16.

We consider the differential effects of a \$100,000 increase in household final demand for manufactured goods (sector 3). We first assume that this demand is from households in the East, then from households in the Central region, and finally from households in the West. Thus, our Y vectors, which will be premultiplied by the inverse in Table 3-13, are

$$(\Delta Y^E)' = \begin{bmatrix} 0 & 0 & 100 & 0 & 0 \vdots & 0 \vdots & 0 \end{bmatrix}$$

$$(\Delta Y^C)' = \begin{bmatrix} 0 \vdots & 0 & 0 & 100 & 0 & 0 \vdots & 0 \end{bmatrix}$$

$$(\Delta Y^W)' = \begin{bmatrix} 0 \vdots & 0 \vdots & 0 & 0 & 100 & 0 & 0 \end{bmatrix}$$

Results are presented in Table 3-14.

The differing regional economic effects of the \$100,000 in new household demand are apparent from the table. When the new demand is located in the East, sectors in the East must produce a total of \$128,000 in new output. When the demand is located in the Central region, new output from sectors in that region totals \$154,700; and if the \$100,000 is new demand in the West, the total new western sector outputs will be \$117,200. Adding across the three regions in each of these cases, total new U.S. national output that would be necessary to satisfy the hypothetical new \$100,000 in household demand for sector 3 is \$206,600, \$211,200, or \$202,500, depending on whether the demand is located in the East, Central region, or West.

In the U.S. multiregional model, the importance of manufacturing activity in the Central region is reflected in Table 3-14. The amounts produced in the region in which the new household demand originates represent the following percentages of total new U.S. output: East, 62 (that is, $(128.0/206.6) \times 100$); Central 73; West, 58. When the new demand is from households in the East, the stimulation of central and western production is in the amounts of \$70,000 and \$8,600, respectively. With new western household demand for manufactured goods, the economic stimulation in other regions is in the amounts of \$54,500 in the Central region and \$30,800 in the East. Finally, new central household demand for manufactured goods requires \$43,600 and \$12,900 in new outputs from sectors in the East and West, respectively.

As in the Japanese interregional case, we get a very general view of the economic importance of each of the regions in this three-region multiregional economy from the average values of the coefficients in each of the nine submatrices in $(I - CA)^{-1}C$ in Table 3-13. These averages are shown in Table 3-15. Averaging across the rows in Table 3-15 gives a very general measure of

[10]An updated set of U.S. multiregional data became available in early 1984. (See U.S. Department of Health and Human Services, 1983.)

[11]The regions, defined in terms of the census regions they encompass, are: East (New England, Middle Atlantic, South Atlantic), Central (East North Central, West North Central, East South Central, West South Central), and West (Mountain, Pacific).

TABLE 3-11 Input Coefficients, A, in the Five-Sector, Three-Region U.S. Multiregional System (1963)

	East Industry					Central Industry					West Industry				
Industry	1	2	3	4	5	1	2	3	4	5	1	2	3	4	5
East															
1 Agriculture	.082	.003	.012	.005	.061	.000	.000	.000	.000	.000	.000	.000	.000	.000	.000
2 Mining	.000	.196	.043	.000	.000	.000	.000	.000	.000	.000	.000	.000	.000	.000	.000
3 Construction and Manufacturing	.156	.211	.302	.076	.110	.000	.000	.000	.000	.000	.000	.000	.000	.000	.000
4 Services	.096	.133	.131	.220	.101	.000	.000	.000	.000	.000	.000	.000	.000	.000	.000
5 Transportation and Utilities	.012	.001	.061	.002	.234	.000	.000	.000	.000	.000	.000	.000	.000	.000	.000
Central															
1 Agriculture	.000	.000	.000	.000	.000	.039	.002	.031	.008	.068	.000	.000	.000	.000	.000
2 Mining	.000	.000	.000	.000	.000	.000	.304	.060	.001	.000	.000	.000	.000	.000	.000
3 Construction and Manufacturing	.000	.000	.000	.000	.000	.100	.145	.291	.075	.117	.000	.000	.000	.000	.000
4 Services	.000	.000	.000	.000	.000	.213	.150	.123	.212	.102	.000	.000	.000	.000	.000
5 Transportation and Utilities	.000	.000	.000	.000	.000	.010	.001	.077	.002	.229	.000	.000	.000	.000	.000
West															
1 Agriculture	.000	.000	.000	.000	.000	.000	.000	.000	.000	.000	.068	.000	.026	.005	.107
2 Mining	.000	.000	.000	.000	.000	.000	.000	.000	.000	.000	.000	.299	.047	.001	.000
3 Construction and Manufacturing	.000	.000	.000	.000	.000	.000	.000	.000	.000	.000	.110	.136	.251	.076	.107
4 Services	.000	.000	.000	.000	.000	.000	.000	.000	.000	.000	.190	.156	.138	.223	.100
5 Transportation and Utilities	.000	.000	.000	.000	.000	.000	.000	.000	.000	.000	.012	.000	.069	.002	.232

TABLE 3-12 Trade Coefficients, C, in the Five-Sector, Three-Region U.S. Multiregional System (1963)

Industry	East Industry 1	2	3	4	5	Central Industry 1	2	3	4	5	West Industry 1	2	3	4	5
East															
1 Agriculture	.621	.000	.000	.000	.000	.055	.000	.000	.000	.000	.019	.000	.000	.000	.000
2 Mining	.000	.586	.000	.000	.000	.000	.063	.000	.000	.000	.000	.021	.000	.000	.000
3 Construction and Manufacturing	.000	.000	.738	.000	.000	.000	.000	.156	.000	.000	.000	.000	.105	.000	.000
4 Services	.000	.000	.000	.824	.000	.000	.000	.000	.141	.000	.000	.000	.000	.069	.000
5 Transportation and Utilities	.000	.000	.000	.000	.721	.000	.000	.000	.000	.165	.000	.000	.000	.000	.126
Central															
1 Agriculture	.345	.000	.000	.000	.000	.865	.000	.000	.000	.000	.198	.000	.000	.000	.000
2 Mining	.000	.375	.000	.000	.000	.000	.851	.000	.000	.000	.000	.258	.000	.000	.000
3 Construction and Manufacturing	.000	.000	.239	.000	.000	.000	.000	.805	.000	.000	.000	.000	.177	.000	.000
4 Services	.000	.000	.000	.156	.000	.000	.000	.000	.826	.000	.000	.000	.000	.114	.000
5 Transportation and Utilities	.000	.000	.000	.000	.257	.000	.000	.000	.000	.794	.000	.000	.000	.000	.204
West															
1 Agriculture	.033	.000	.000	.000	.000	.080	.000	.000	.000	.000	.783	.000	.000	.000	.000
2 Mining	.000	.039	.000	.000	.000	.000	.086	.000	.000	.000	.000	.720	.000	.000	.000
3 Construction and Manufacturing	.000	.000	.023	.000	.000	.000	.000	.039	.000	.000	.000	.000	.718	.000	.000
4 Services	.000	.000	.000	.020	.000	.000	.000	.000	.033	.000	.000	.000	.000	.817	.000
5 Transportation and Utilities	.000	.000	.000	.000	.022	.000	.000	.000	.000	.041	.000	.000	.000	.000	.670

TABLE 3-13 Inverse Matrix, $(I - CA)^{-1}C$, for the Five-Sector, Three-Region U.S. Multiregional System (1963)

Industry	East					Central					West				
	Industry					Industry					Industry				
	1	2	3	4	5	1	2	3	4	5	1	2	3	4	5
East															
1 Agriculture	.658	.005	.012	.005	.039	.062	.002	.007	.002	.016	.022	.002	.004	.001	.012
2 Mining	.004	.681	.032	.003	.005	.002	.101	.015	.002	.003	.002	.043	.010	.001	.003
3 Construction and Manufacturing	.125	.182	1.009	.085	.130	.047	.084	.292	.040	.074	.035	.061	.204	.028	.060
4 Services	.105	.144	.163	1.032	.128	.060	.074	.083	.220	.069	.039	.052	.060	.117	.054
5 Transportation and Utilities	.017	.015	.064	.008	.896	.009	.010	.039	.005	.254	.007	.008	.030	.004	.201
Central															
1 Agriculture	.383	.011	.024	.006	.050	.905	.013	.042	.011	.075	.222	.008	.021	.005	.047
2 Mining	.011	.598	.058	.007	.012	.011	1.192	.088	.009	.014	.008	.463	.048	.006	.011
3 Construction and Manufacturing	.103	.177	.448	.056	.114	.131	.229	1.134	.096	.168	.070	.134	.335	.045	.097
4 Services	.120	.147	.111	.245	.095	.222	.225	.187	1.031	.154	.091	.123	.091	.186	.083
5 Transportation and Utilities	.018	.020	.059	.008	.394	.021	.022	.096	.011	1.008	.014	.015	.050	.007	.322
West															
1 Agriculture	.039	.002	.004	.001	.009	.089	.003	.007	.002	.013	.832	.005	.026	.006	.077
2 Mining	.002	.079	.009	.001	.002	.002	.154	.014	.002	.003	.005	.941	.043	.004	.006
3 Construction and Manufacturing	.013	.025	.048	.007	.014	.019	.036	.073	.010	.019	.097	.131	.905	.071	.096
4 Services	.017	.026	.018	.034	.015	.031	.041	.025	.053	.020	.177	.172	.146	1.014	.113
5 Transportation and Utilities	.002	.003	.007	.001	.038	.003	.003	.010	.001	.063	.014	.009	.052	.006	.804

TABLE 3-14 Region- and Sector-Specific Effects (in $1000) of a $100,000 Increase in Final Demand for Sector 3 Goods from Households Located in One of the Regions (U.S. Multiregional Model)

	From Households in the Eastern Region (ΔY^E)			From Households in the Central Region (ΔY^C)			From Households in the Western Region (ΔY^W)		
Sector	East	Central	West	East	Central	West	East	Central	West
1	1.2	2.4	.4	.7	4.2	.7	.4	2.1	2.6
2	3.2	5.8	.9	1.5	8.8	1.4	1.0	4.8	4.3
3	100.9	44.8	4.8	29.2	113.4	7.3	20.4	33.5	90.5
4	16.3	11.1	1.8	8.3	18.7	2.5	6.0	9.1	14.6
5	6.4	5.9	.7	3.9	9.6	1.0	3.0	5.0	5.2
Total	128.0	70.0	8.6	43.6	154.7	12.9	30.8	54.5	117.2

the magnitude of total economic activity in that region needed to satisfy a dollar's worth of new household demand located anywhere in the three-region economy. These averages are: East, .109; Central, .172; West, .092. By these measures, the ranking of regions in terms of overall importance as suppliers of inputs for production throughout the U.S. economy are: Central, East, West. Alternatively, ignoring intraregional inputs, the averages of the off-diagonal elements in each row are: East, .053; Central, .116; West, .023. Ranked by this measure also (that is, importance of a region as a supplier of inputs for production in *other* regions), we have: Central, East, West.

As in the Japanese interregional case, column sums can be found. Here these sums are: East, .370; Central, .375; West, .372. Again, averaging over all sectors and including all regions, we find that average total inputs per dollar's worth of (average) output are very similar across U.S. regions. Recall that in the Japanese case these column sums were between .360 and .377. Thus in both of these developed countries, the proportion of the value of interindustry inputs to the value of total output is around .37. That is, on average about 63 percent of the value of outputs in these countries consists of payments for value-added inputs.

Recall that in the MRIO model, as in Eq. (3-29), the Y vector represents exogenous final demands located in specific regions and that the operation CY translates those demands into shipments from within the region or from outside the region to satisfy the demands. If we want to assess the sectoral and spatial impacts of, say, new export demands for goods produced in a particular region,

TABLE 3-15 Average Values of Inverse Coefficients in Each Submatrix of Table 3-13

	East	Central	West
East	.222	.063	.042
Central	.131	.284	.100
West	.017	.028	.230

TABLE 3-16 Inverse Matrix, $(I - CA)^{-1}$, for the Five-Sector, Three-Region U.S. Multiregional System (1963)

	East (Industry)					Central (Industry)					West (Industry)				
Industry	1	2	3	4	5	1	2	3	4	5	1	2	3	4	5
East															
1 Agriculture	1.057	.006	.015	.005	.051	.004	.002	.005	.001	.009	.002	.001	.003	.001	.006
2 Mining	.006	1.141	.040	.003	.005	.002	.033	.011	.002	.003	.001	.014	.005	.001	.002
3 Construction and Manufacturing	.177	.261	1.333	.096	.158	.040	.074	.102	.031	.059	.031	.050	.063	.022	.042
4 Services	.135	.200	.199	1.240	.158	.058	.068	.063	.054	.052	.032	.042	.038	.031	.035
5 Transportation and Utilities	.023	.019	.075	.008	1.218	.008	.010	.032	.005	.064	.007	.007	.022	.004	.051
Central															
1 Agriculture	.036	.009	.016	.005	.039	1.043	.014	.049	.013	.085	.019	.006	.015	.004	.038
2 Mining	.011	.131	.045	.006	.011	.011	1.376	.099	.009	.015	.007	.146	.036	.005	.009
3 Construction and Manufacturing	.085	.137	.158	.047	.088	.141	.249	1.372	.107	.190	.051	.093	.105	.036	.070
4 Services	.052	.085	.079	.063	.066	.248	.251	.213	1.235	.177	.052	.078	.062	.049	.057
5 Transportation and Utilities	.016	.018	.044	.007	.101	.023	.023	.109	.012	1.245	.012	.013	.037	.006	.082
West															
1 Agriculture	.004	.002	.002	.001	.005	.005	.002	.006	.002	.010	1.061	.006	.034	.007	.111
2 Mining	.002	.018	.007	.001	.002	.002	.049	.014	.002	.003	.006	1.288	.056	.005	.007
3 Construction and Manufacturing	.010	.016	.018	.005	.010	.010	.023	.027	.008	.015	.120	.174	1.252	.085	.136
4 Services	.008	.014	.012	.009	.010	.015	.024	.019	.013	.015	.222	.230	.198	1.239	.162
5 Transportation and Utilities	.002	.002	.005	.001	.010	.002	.003	.008	.001	.016	.018	.011	.070	.007	1.194

TABLE 3-17   Region- and Sector-Specific Effects (in $1000) of a $100,000 Increase in Export Demand for Sector 3 Goods Produced in One of the Regions (U.S. Multiregional Model)

Sector	Goods Produced in the Eastern Region $[(\Delta Y*)^E]$			Goods Produced in the Central Region $[(\Delta Y*)^C]$			Goods Produced in the Western Region $[(\Delta Y*)^W]$		
	East	Central	West	East	Central	West	East	Central	West
1	1.5	1.6	.2	.5	4.9	.6	.3	1.5	3.4
2	4.0	4.5	.7	1.1	9.9	1.4	.5	3.6	5.6
3	133.3	15.8	1.8	10.2	137.2	2.7	6.3	10.5	125.2
4	19.9	7.9	1.2	6.3	21.3	1.9	3.8	6.2	19.7
5	7.5	4.4	.5	3.2	10.9	.8	2.2	3.7	7.0
Total	166.2	34.2	4.4	21.3	184.2	7.4	13.1	25.5	160.9

we denote the final-demand vector by $Y*$ and find X as in Eq. (3-31). If our three hypothetical new final demands were for manufactured goods (sector 3) produced in the eastern, central, or western regions, respectively, we would have

$$\left[(\Delta Y*)^E\right]' = \begin{bmatrix} 0 & 0 & 100 & 0 & 0 & \vdots & 0 & \vdots & 0 \end{bmatrix}$$

$$\left[(\Delta Y*)^C\right]' = \begin{bmatrix} 0 & \vdots & 0 & 0 & 100 & 0 & 0 & \vdots & 0 \end{bmatrix}$$

$$\left[(\Delta Y*)^W\right]' = \begin{bmatrix} 0 & \vdots & 0 & \vdots & 0 & 0 & 100 & 0 & 0 \end{bmatrix}$$

In conjunction with $(I - CA)^{-1}$, in Table 3-16, we find new outputs as in Eq. (3-32); results are shown in Table 3-17.

As with the results in Table 3-14, observations on differing regional effects of the new export demand for goods produced in a specific region can be made here. Averages of elements in $(I - CA)^{-1}$ in Table 3-16 would now be used to generate information such as that in Table 3-15, which came from $(I - CA)^{-1}C$. This is left as an exercise for the interested reader.

3-5 | THE "BALANCED REGIONAL" MODEL

Structure of the Balanced Regional Model

A model that has a particular kind of regional dimension was proposed by Leontief (1953, Ch. 4) and has been implemented in specific applications, including an analysis of the effects in the U.S. economy, on both sectors and regions, of a diversion of production away from military goods and to nonmilitary consumer goods (Leontief et al. 1965). This has been termed the *balanced regional model*. The basic mathematical structure of this model is identical to that of the interregional input-output model above, but the interpretation of each of the pieces of the model is rather different. The entire analytical structure is based on the observation that in any national economy there are goods with different kinds of market areas. There are some goods for which production and consumption balance at the national level. These are goods that have essentially a national market area; sectors such as automobiles, aircraft, furniture, and agriculture would be representative. On the other hand, there are other sectors for which production and consumption tend to balance at a lower geographical level, i.e., which serve a regional or local rather than a national market. Examples might be electricity, real estate, warehousing, and personal and repair services. Clearly there is in actuality an entire spectrum of possibilities, from sectors that serve extremely small local markets (shoe repair) to large national and international markets (aircraft). For illustration, however, we suppose that all sectors can be assigned to either a national (N) or a regional (R) category. (One possible criterion for classification of sectors would be the percentage of interregional as opposed to intraregional shipments of the products of that sector.)

Then, from a table of national input coefficients, one can rearrange the sectors so that, for example, all the regional sectors are listed first and all of the national sectors follow. Let sectors $1, 2, \cdots, r$ represent the regionally balanced sectors and let sectors $r + 1, \cdots, n$ represent nationally balanced sectors. Then, let the rearranged table of national input coefficients be

$$A = \left[\begin{array}{c|c} A^{RR} & A^{RN} \\ \hline A^{NR} & A^{NN} \end{array} \right] \tag{3-34}$$

Let X^R and Y^R, which are r-element column vectors, represent total output and final demand for the regional sectors, and X^N and Y^N, which are $(n - r)$-element column vectors, represent output and final demand for each of the national sectors. Define

$$X = \left[\begin{array}{c} X^R \\ \hline X^N \end{array} \right] \quad \text{and} \quad Y = \left[\begin{array}{c} Y^R \\ \hline Y^N \end{array} \right]$$

Then, in exactly the same spirit as the two-region interregional input-output model, we have

$$(I - A)X = Y$$

That is, in the present case

$$\begin{aligned} (I - A^{RR})X^R - A^{RN}X^N &= Y^R \\ -A^{NR}X^R + (I - A^{NN})X^N &= Y^N \end{aligned} \tag{3-35}$$

It is important to notice that the R and N superscripts do not refer here to specific geographic locations of sectors, as in the interregional model. Rather, they serve to partition the sectors into two types—those designated national and those designated regional.[12]

---

[12] Partitioning of this sort can be done for a wide variety of purposes. For example, if one is particularly interested in energy-producing sectors, one might want to divide all sectors into two groups—those that produce energy and those that do not produce energy. Partitionings of this kind will be discussed again in Chapters 6 and 7.

More compactly

$$\left[\begin{array}{c|c} (I - A^{RR}) & -A^{RN} \\ \hline -A^{NR} & (I - A^{NN}) \end{array}\right]\left[\begin{array}{c} X^R \\ \hline X^N \end{array}\right] = \left[\begin{array}{c} Y^R \\ \hline Y^N \end{array}\right]$$

and so

$$\left[\begin{array}{c} X^R \\ \hline X^N \end{array}\right] = \left[\begin{array}{c|c} (I - A^{RR}) & -A^{RN} \\ \hline -A^{NR} & (I - A^{NN}) \end{array}\right]^{-1}\left[\begin{array}{c} Y^R \\ \hline Y^N \end{array}\right] \tag{3-36}$$

Using regular solution procedures, we find the total outputs of each sector in each of the two categories, due to an exogenous change in final demand for the outputs of one or more national sectors and/or one or more regional sectors. Using $\left[\begin{array}{c|c} S & T \\ \hline U & V \end{array}\right]$ to represent the elements of the inverse on the right-hand side of Eq. (3-36), we have

$$\begin{aligned} X^R &= SY^R + TY^N \\ X^N &= UY^R + VY^N \end{aligned} \tag{3-37}$$

For example, in the arms-reduction study, there was assumed to be a 20 percent across-the-board decrease in government demand for the output of military-related goods, some of which were produced by national sectors (e.g., aircraft) and some of which were produced by regional sectors (e.g., warehousing), and an assumed across-the-board increase in nonmilitary final demands. Hence, elements in both Y^R and Y^N experience change.

Thus far, there is nothing explicitly *spatial* in the model. The categorization of either nationally balanced or regionally balanced sectors deals only with the size of the market areas involved. For regional sectors, we need to have the new final demands, Y^R, distributed across regions. That is, we need to have $Y^{R(L)}$, the final demand for regionally balanced goods in region L, where $\sum_L Y^{R(L)} = Y^R$. In addition, we need, for each region L, an estimate of the proportion of the total output of each nationally balanced sector that is produced in region L. That is, we need

$$P^L = \left[\begin{array}{c} p_{r+1}^L \\ \vdots \\ p_n^L \end{array}\right]$$

Of the total new output of national goods, X^N, sectors $r + 1$ through n in region L will therefore have to produce $\hat{P}^L X^N$, respectively. Since the elements of P^L are the proportions of total national output that occur in region L, it must be true that $\sum_L p_i^L = 1$ for $i = r + 1, \cdots, n$; that is $\sum_L \hat{P}^L = I$.

Thus the total output in region L, $X^{(L)}$ is an n-element vector

$$X^{(L)} = \left[\begin{array}{c} X^{R(L)} \\ \hline X^{N(L)} \end{array}\right] \tag{3-38}$$

made up of $X^{R(L)}$, the outputs of the r regionally balanced goods that are made in region L, and $X^{N(L)}$, the production of nationally balanced goods that occurs in region L. This latter is just $\hat{P}^L X^N$.

The $X^{R(L)}$ term involves essentially two components: (1) production in region L to meet region-specific final demand for regionally balanced goods, $Y^{R(L)}$ (e.g., Michigan production because of new final demand in Michigan for electricity produced in that state) and (2) production in region L to turn out that region's share of nationally balanced goods, $X^{N(L)}$ (e.g., Michigan electricity used as an input to Michigan production of automobiles to satisfy part of the new nationwide demand for automobiles). That is,

$$
\begin{aligned}
X^{R(L)} &= \left(I - A^{RR} \right)^{-1} Y^{R(L)} + \left(I - A^{RR} \right)^{-1} A^{RN} X^{N(L)} \\
&= \left(I - A^{RR} \right)^{-1} Y^{R(L)} + \left(I - A^{RR} \right)^{-1} A^{RN} \hat{P}^L X^N
\end{aligned}
\tag{3-39}
$$

Appendix 3-3 derives these results directly from observations on the inverse of the partitioned matrix in Eq. (3-36). For the allocation of region L's share of production of nationally balanced goods, as noted above, we have

$$
X^{N(L)} = \hat{P}^L X^N
\tag{3-40}
$$

In this way, then, the balanced regional model allocates the impacts of new Y^R and Y^N demand to the various sectors in each region.

Numerical Example

Consider the following hypothetical data. Let

$$
A = \left[\begin{array}{c|c} A^{RR} & A^{RN} \\ \hline A^{NR} & A^{NN} \end{array} \right] = \left[\begin{array}{cc|cc} .10 & .15 & .05 & .03 \\ .03 & .10 & .02 & .10 \\ \hline .12 & .03 & .20 & .10 \\ .10 & .02 & .25 & .15 \end{array} \right]
\tag{3-41}
$$

and

$$
Y = \left[\begin{array}{c} Y^R \\ \hline Y^N \end{array} \right] = \left[\begin{array}{c} 100 \\ 100 \\ \hline 200 \\ 200 \end{array} \right]
$$

Then X is found as in Eq. (3-36)

$$
X = \left[\begin{array}{c} X^R \\ \hline X^N \end{array} \right] = \left[\begin{array}{c} 168.30 \\ 163.40 \\ \hline 325.70 \\ 354.70 \end{array} \right]
\tag{3-42}
$$

These figures represent total outputs, throughout the nation, of the four sectors.

Assume that there are three regions in the country and that the region-specific distribution of final demands Y^R was

$$
Y^{R(1)} = \left[\begin{array}{c} 40 \\ 30 \end{array} \right], \qquad Y^{R(2)} = \left[\begin{array}{c} 50 \\ 30 \end{array} \right], \qquad Y^{R(3)} = \left[\begin{array}{c} 10 \\ 40 \end{array} \right]
$$

and that $P^1 = \begin{bmatrix} 0.6 \\ 0.3 \end{bmatrix}$, $P^2 = \begin{bmatrix} 0.2 \\ 0.4 \end{bmatrix}$, and $P^3 = \begin{bmatrix} 0.2 \\ 0.3 \end{bmatrix}$. We find $(I - A^{RR})^{-1}$ from the data in A

$$(I - A^{RR})^{-1} = \begin{bmatrix} 1.117 & 0.186 \\ 0.037 & 1.117 \end{bmatrix}$$

Finally, then, using Eq. (3-39) we find

$$X^{R(1)} = \begin{bmatrix} 67.47 \\ 51.75 \end{bmatrix}, \qquad X^{R(2)} = \begin{bmatrix} 72.73 \\ 52.97 \end{bmatrix}, \qquad X^{R(3)} = \begin{bmatrix} 28.05 \\ 58.65 \end{bmatrix} \qquad \textbf{(3-43)}$$

(Note, as must be the case in a consistent model, that X^R, as found above in Eq. [3-42], is indeed $X^{R(1)} + X^{R(2)} + X^{R(3)}$.) Using $\hat{P}^1$, $\hat{P}^2$, and $\hat{P}^3$, the distribution of nationally balanced goods across regions is

$$X^{N(1)} = \hat{P}^1 X^N = \begin{bmatrix} 195.40 \\ 106.40 \end{bmatrix}, \qquad X^{N(2)} = \hat{P}^2 X^N = \begin{bmatrix} 65.14 \\ 141.90 \end{bmatrix},$$

$$X^{N(3)} = \hat{P}^3 X^N = \begin{bmatrix} 65.14 \\ 106.40 \end{bmatrix} \qquad \textbf{(3-44)}$$

where, as we have seen, the values in X^N must equal $X^{N(1)} + X^{N(2)} + X^{N(3)}$, because of the way in which the P's are defined.

Putting the results in Eqs. (3-43) and (3-44) together, as in Eq. (3-38), we have

$$X^{(1)} = \begin{bmatrix} 67.47 \\ 51.75 \\ \hline 195.40 \\ 106.40 \end{bmatrix} \qquad X^{(2)} = \begin{bmatrix} 72.73 \\ 52.97 \\ \hline 65.14 \\ 141.90 \end{bmatrix} \qquad X^{(3)} = \begin{bmatrix} 28.05 \\ 58.65 \\ \hline 65.14 \\ 106.40 \end{bmatrix} \qquad \textbf{(3-45)}$$

and the entire outputs in Eq. (3-42) have been allocated across the three regions. In the balanced regional model, then, production in each region is assumed to utilize the same technology, as reflected in the $(I - A^{RR})$ matrix and its inverse. But the model does recognize that production, whether of goods with a national market area or with a subnational market area, occurs in geographically specific locations, and the information in the distribution of the Y^N elements and in the P^L vectors reflects this spatial distribution of production.

3-6 | SUMMARY

In this chapter we have explored some of the most important modifications that need to be made to the basic input-output model (Chapter 2) when analysis is to be carried out at the regional level. We have seen that the input-output framework can be used either to study one single region in isolation, or it can be employed in studying one or more regions whose economic connections are made explicit in the model. While the representations of these connected regional models appear quite complicated, we have seen that the models are logical extensions of the basic input-output structure that are designed to (1) reflect possibly differing production practices for the same sectors in different regions and (2) capture the trade relationships between sectors in different regions. Much of Leontief's recent work has been with an input-output model in which "region" is replaced by "nation" in the preceding sentence. That is, the entire world economy is composed of a set of interconnected national economies, just as a nation is made up of a set of interconnected regions. In this kind of global model, impacts of alternative development policies in less-developed countries can be studied. (See, for example, Leontief 1974 or Leontief et al. 1977.)

In the next chapter, we will examine multiplier analysis in the input-output model. This is one of the most common input-output applications. We will view multipliers in the context of both the nonregional model and the regional models, in their interregional and multiregional versions.

APPENDIX 3-1
The Power Series Approximation and Regional Supply Percentages

Recall from Chapter 2 that

$$X = (I - A)^{-1}Y = (I + A + A^2 + A^3 \dots)Y$$
$$= Y + AY + A^2Y + A^3Y + \cdots$$
$$= Y + AY + A(AY) + A(A^2Y) + \cdots$$

Given a national technical coefficients matrix, A, we want to quantify the regional output impacts, X^R, resulting from some new regional final demand, Y^R. Proceeding in round-by-round fashion, the initial impact *in the region* is just Y^R. (In the example of a new order for aircraft from Boeing in the state of Washington, this vector will contain all zeros except for the aircraft manufacturing row, which will contain the dollar value of the commercial aircraft order.) The next term would be AY^R, the first-round impacts of the new regional demand multiplied by the *national* technical coefficients matrix. (In the same example, this will capture *all* first-round inputs, regardless of whether they are supplied by producers within or outside of Washington.) To convert this first-round effect to a regional effect, each element in the vector AY^R is multiplied by the associated regional percentage; this "regionalization" of the first-round effects can be represented as $\hat{P}AY^R$. (These are the first-round inputs supplied by Washington producers.) It is then *these* regional first-round impacts that lead to a second-round effect, $A(\hat{P}AY^R)$, which in turn must be "regionalized" through multiplication by the regional percentages, that is, by $\hat{P}A(\hat{P}A)Y^R$, which is just $(\hat{P}A)^2Y^R$. Further rounds, each converted in the same way to regional effects, would lead finally to

$$X^R = Y^R + (\hat{P}A)Y^R + (\hat{P}A)^2Y^R + (\hat{P}A)^3Y^R + \cdots$$
$$= \left[I + (\hat{P}A) + (\hat{P}A)^2 + (\hat{P}A)^3 + \cdots \right] Y^R \tag{3-1-1}$$

The bracketed expression is seen to be just the power series approximation to $(I - \hat{P}A)^{-1}$; hence this procedure is equivalent to estimating a regional technical coefficients matrix, A^R, by $\hat{P}A$, as we did in section 3-2.

Using the same illustration as in that section, we have

$$Y^R = \begin{bmatrix} 600 \\ 1500 \end{bmatrix}$$

$$\hat{P}AY^R = \begin{bmatrix} .12 & .20 \\ .12 & .03 \end{bmatrix} \begin{bmatrix} 600 \\ 1500 \end{bmatrix} = \begin{bmatrix} 372 \\ 117 \end{bmatrix}$$

$$(\hat{P}A)^2 Y^R = (\hat{P}A)(\hat{P}A)Y^R = \begin{bmatrix} .12 & .20 \\ .12 & .03 \end{bmatrix} \begin{bmatrix} 372 \\ 117 \end{bmatrix} = \begin{bmatrix} 68.04 \\ 48.15 \end{bmatrix}$$

$$(\hat{P}A)^3 Y^R = (\hat{P}A)(\hat{P}A)^2 Y^R = \begin{bmatrix} .12 & .20 \\ .12 & .03 \end{bmatrix} \begin{bmatrix} 68.04 \\ 48.15 \end{bmatrix} = \begin{bmatrix} 17.79 \\ 9.61 \end{bmatrix}$$

$$(\hat{P}A)^4 Y^R = (\hat{P}A)(\hat{P}A)^3 Y^R = \begin{bmatrix} .12 & .20 \\ .12 & .03 \end{bmatrix} \begin{bmatrix} 17.79 \\ 9.61 \end{bmatrix} = \begin{bmatrix} 4.06 \\ 2.42 \end{bmatrix}$$

$$(\hat{P}A)^5 Y^R = (\hat{P}A)(\hat{P}A)^4 Y^R = \begin{bmatrix} .12 & .20 \\ .12 & .03 \end{bmatrix} \begin{bmatrix} 4.06 \\ 2.42 \end{bmatrix} = \begin{bmatrix} 0.97 \\ 0.56 \end{bmatrix}$$

Summing these six terms gives

$$X^R \cong \begin{bmatrix} 1062.86 \\ 1677.74 \end{bmatrix}$$

Recall from Eq. (3-1) in the text that $X^R = (I - \hat{P}A)^{-1}Y^R = \begin{bmatrix} 1062.90 \\ 1678.50 \end{bmatrix}$. Additional terms in the power series would have made the approximation even closer.

Using (incorrectly) $\hat{P}[(I - A)^{-1}Y^R]$ in power-series form, we have

$$\hat{P}[(I + A + A^2 + A^3 + \cdots)Y^R] = (\hat{P} + \hat{P}A + \hat{P}A^2 + \hat{P}A^3 + \cdots)Y^R$$

Not only do the squared, cubed, $\cdots$ terms differ from their (correct) counterparts in Eq. (3-1-1), but we also see that the original new regional final demand, Y^R, is (incorrectly) reduced to $\hat{P}Y^R$.

From the example in section 3-2, we found that $X = (I - A)^{-1}Y^R$, which represents total output from both within and outside of region R, was $X = \begin{bmatrix} 1247.40 \\ 1841.40 \end{bmatrix}$. The difference, $X - X^R$, is equal to $[(I - A)^{-1} - (I - \hat{P}A)^{-1}]Y$. Using the power-series approximations to these two inverses, the interested reader may wish to work out that $X - X^R = (AY - \hat{P}AY) + (A^2Y - (\hat{P}A)^2Y) + (A^3Y - (\hat{P}A)^3Y) + \cdots$ and note that each term represents the amount that has to be imported to the region to make up the difference in that particular round between the total output needed and the amount that is forthcoming from within the region for that round.

APPENDIX 3-2
BASIC RELATIONSHIPS IN THE MULTIREGIONAL INPUT-OUTPUT MODEL

In standard input-output fashion, the total demand for commodity i in region M is given by

$$\sum_{j=1}^{n} a_{ij}^{M} X_j^{M} + Y_i^{M} \tag{3-2-1}$$

The total supply of commodity i in region M is the total that is shipped in from other regions,

$$\sum_{L=1}^{p} z_i^{LM} \qquad (L \neq M)$$

plus the amount that is supplied from within the region, z_i^{MM}. This is just T_i^{M}, the sum of the elements in column M in Table 3-8, as defined in Eq. (3-25). Since shipments (supplies) occur only to satisfy needs (demands), we have, for each commodity i

$$T_i^{M} = \sum_{j=1}^{n} a_{ij}^{M} X_j^{M} + Y_i^{M} \tag{3-2-2}$$

Total production of i in region L is equivalent to the total amount of i shipped from L, including that kept within the region

$$X_i^{L} = \sum_{M=1}^{p} z_i^{LM} \tag{3-2-3}$$

From the definition of the interregional trade coefficients in section 3-4—$c_i^{LM} = z_i^{LM}/T_i^{M}$—Eq. (3-2-3) can be rewritten as

$$X_i^{L} = \sum_{M=1}^{p} c_i^{LM} T_i^{M} \tag{3-2-4}$$

Putting T_i^{M}, as defined in Eq. (3-2-2), into Eq. (3-2-4)

$$X^{L} = \sum_{M=1}^{p} c_i^{LM} \left(\sum_{j=1}^{n} a_{ij}^{M} X_j^{M} + Y_i^{M} \right) \tag{3-2-5}$$

for $i = 1, \cdots, n$.

Using familiar matrix notation, let

$$X^{L} = \begin{bmatrix} X_1^{L} \\ \vdots \\ X_n^{L} \end{bmatrix}, \qquad X^{M} = \begin{bmatrix} X_1^{M} \\ \vdots \\ X_n^{M} \end{bmatrix}, \qquad Y^{M} = \begin{bmatrix} Y_1^{M} \\ \vdots \\ Y_n^{M} \end{bmatrix},$$

$$A^{M} = \begin{bmatrix} a_{11}^{M} & \cdots & a_{1n}^{M} \\ \vdots & & \vdots \\ a_{n1}^{M} & & a_{nn}^{M} \end{bmatrix}, \quad \text{and} \quad \hat{C}^{LM} = \begin{bmatrix} c_1^{LM} & 0 & \cdots & 0 \\ 0 & c_2^{LM} & & \\ \vdots & & & \vdots \\ 0 & & & c_n^{LM} \end{bmatrix}.$$

The reader should be convinced that the entire set of n equations for outputs of goods in region L can be expressed as

$$X^{L} = \sum_{M=1}^{p} \hat{C}^{LM} (A^{M} X^{M} + Y^{M}) = \sum_{M=1}^{p} \hat{C}^{LM} A^{M} X^{M} + \sum_{M=1}^{p} \hat{C}^{LM} Y^{M} \tag{3-2-6}$$

There will be p such matrix equations, one for each region L $(L = 1, \cdots, p)$. Again using matrix notation, as in section 3-4, we can construct the "super" matrices

$$X = \begin{bmatrix} X^1 \\ \vdots \\ X^M \\ \vdots \\ X^p \end{bmatrix}, \qquad Y = \begin{bmatrix} Y^1 \\ \vdots \\ Y^M \\ \vdots \\ Y^p \end{bmatrix}, \qquad A = \begin{bmatrix} A^1 & \cdots & 0 & \cdots & 0 \\ \vdots & \ddots & & & \vdots \\ 0 & & A^M & & 0 \\ \vdots & & & \ddots & \vdots \\ 0 & \cdots & 0 & \cdots & A^p \end{bmatrix},$$

and

$$C = \begin{bmatrix} \hat{C}^{11} & \cdots & \hat{C}^{1M} & \cdots & \hat{C}^{1p} \\ \vdots & & \vdots & & \vdots \\ \hat{C}^{L1} & \cdots & \hat{C}^{LM} & \cdots & \hat{C}^{Lp} \\ \vdots & & \vdots & & \vdots \\ \hat{C}^{p1} & \cdots & \hat{C}^{pM} & \cdots & \hat{C}^{pp} \end{bmatrix}$$

Then the p matrix equations in (3-2-6) can be compactly expressed as

$$X = C(AX + Y) = CAX + CY \tag{3-2-7}$$

from which

$$(I - CA)X = CY \tag{3-2-8}$$

and

$$X = (I - CA)^{-1}CY \tag{3-2-9}$$

as in Eqs. (3-29) and (3-30) in the text.

APPENDIX 3-3
The Inverse of a Partitioned $(I - A)$ Matrix

Let

$$(I - A) = \begin{bmatrix} (I - A^{RR}) & -A^{RN} \\ \hline -A^{NR} & (I - A^{NN}) \end{bmatrix} = \begin{bmatrix} E & F \\ \hline G & H \end{bmatrix} \quad \text{and} \quad (I - A)^{-1} = \begin{bmatrix} S & T \\ \hline U & V \end{bmatrix}.$$

Using the results on the inverse of a partitioned matrix, as shown in section A-7 of Appendix A, we find

$$\begin{aligned} S &= (I - A^{RR})^{-1}(I + A^{RN}U) & T &= (I - A^{RR})^{-1}A^{RN}V \\ U &= VA^{NR}(I - A^{RR})^{-1} & V &= \left[(I - A^{NN}) - A^{NR}(I - A^{RR})^{-1}A^{RN} \right]^{-1} \end{aligned}$$

$$\tag{3-3-1}$$

Thus, since $X = (I - A)^{-1}Y$, we have

$$X^R = SY^R + TY^N$$
$$X^N = UY^R + VY^N \qquad \text{(3-3-2)}$$

This generates total output throughout the nation of both regionally balanced goods (X^R) and nationally balanced goods (X^N). Further, substituting for S and T in Eq. (3-3-2), from Eq. (3-3-1), we find

$$X^R = (I - A^{RR})^{-1}Y^R + (I - A^{RR})^{-1}A^{RN}[UY^R + VY^N] \qquad \text{(3-3-3)}$$

But X^N, as in Eq. (3-3-2), is just the bracketed term on the right-hand side of Eq. (3-3-3). That is,

$$X^R = (I - A^{RR})^{-1}Y^R + (I - A^{RR})^{-1}A^{RN}X^N \qquad \text{(3-3-4)}$$

To distribute both X^R and X^N production to individual regions, we need the regional distribution of final demands for regional goods—$Y^{R(L)}$, for each region L—and we need the regional distribution of production of each of the nationally balanced goods—P^L—for each region. Then, to add the spatial dimension, for a specific region L, Y^R becomes $Y^{R(L)}$ and X^N becomes $X^{N(L)}$, which is $\hat{P}^L X^N$. Therefore

$$X^{R(L)} = (I - A^{RR})^{-1}Y^{R(L)} + (I - A^{RR})^{-1}A^{RN}\hat{P}^L X^N \qquad \text{(3-3-5)}$$

as in Eq. (3-39) in the text.

❘ PROBLEMS

3-1   The data in problem 2-2 were for a small national economy. Consider a region within that national economy that contains firms producing in each of the three sectors. Suppose that the technological structure of production of firms within the region is estimated to be the same as that reflected in the national data, but that there is need to import into the region (from producers elsewhere in the country) some of the inputs used in production in each of the regional sectors. In particular, the percentages of required inputs from sectors 1, 2, and 3 that come from within the region are 60, 90, and 75, respectively. If new final demands for the outputs of the regional producers are projected to be 1300, 100, and 200, what total outputs of the three regional sectors will be needed in order to meet this demand?

3-2   The following data represent sales (in dollars) between and among two sectors in regions L and M.

$$
\begin{array}{cc}
 & \begin{array}{cccc} L & & M & \end{array} \\
\begin{array}{c} L \\ \\ M \end{array} &
\left[
\begin{array}{cc|cc}
40 & 50 & 30 & 45 \\
60 & 10 & 70 & 45 \\
\hline
50 & 60 & 50 & 80 \\
70 & 70 & 50 & 50
\end{array}
\right]
\end{array}
$$

In addition, sales to final demand purchasers were $Y^L = \begin{bmatrix} 200 \\ 200 \end{bmatrix}$ and $Y^M = \begin{bmatrix} 300 \\ 400 \end{bmatrix}$. These data are sufficient to create a two-region interregional input-output model connecting regions L and M. If, because of a stimulated economy, household demand increased by \$280 for the output of sector 1 in region L and by \$360 for the output of sector 2 in region L, what are the new necessary gross outputs from each of the sectors in each of the two regions to satisfy this new final demand? That is, find $\Delta X = \begin{bmatrix} \Delta X^L \\ \Delta X^M \end{bmatrix}$ associated with ΔY.

3-3 Suppose that you have assembled the following information on the dollar values of purchases of each of two goods in each of two regions, and also on the shipments of each of the two goods between regions:

Purchases in Region L		Purchases in Region M	
$z_{11}^{\cdot L} = 40$	$z_{12}^{\cdot L} = 50$	$z_{11}^{\cdot M} = 30$	$z_{12}^{\cdot M} = 45$
$z_{21}^{\cdot L} = 60$	$z_{22}^{\cdot L} = 10$	$z_{21}^{\cdot M} = 70$	$z_{22}^{\cdot M} = 45$

Shipments of Good 1		Shipments of Good 2	
$z_1^{LL} = 50$	$z_1^{LM} = 60$	$z_2^{LL} = 50$	$z_2^{LM} = 80$
$z_1^{ML} = 70$	$z_1^{MM} = 70$	$z_2^{ML} = 50$	$z_2^{MM} = 50$

These data are sufficient to generate the necessary matrices for a two-region multiregional input-output model connecting regions L and M. There will be six necessary matrices—A^L, A^M, $\hat{C}^{LL}$, $\hat{C}^{LM}$, $\hat{C}^{ML}$, and $\hat{C}^{MM}$. All of these will be 2×2 matrices. If the projected demands for the coming period are $Y^L = \begin{bmatrix} 50 \\ 50 \end{bmatrix}$ and $Y^M = \begin{bmatrix} 40 \\ 60 \end{bmatrix}$, find the gross outputs for each sector in each region necessary to satisfy this new final demand; that is, find X^L and X^M.

3-4 A federal agency for a three-region country has collected the following data on input purchases for two sectors, (1) manufacturing and (2) agriculture, for last year, in dollars. These flows are not specific with respect to region of origin; that is, they are of the $z_{ij}^{\cdot L}$ sort. Denote the three regions by A, B, and C.

	Region A		Region B		Region C	
	1	2	1	2	1	2
1	200	100	700	400	100	0
2	100	100	100	200	50	0

Also, gross outputs for each of the two sectors in each of the three regions are known. They are:

$$ X^A = \begin{bmatrix} 600 \\ 300 \end{bmatrix} \qquad X^B = \begin{bmatrix} 1200 \\ 700 \end{bmatrix} \qquad X^C = \begin{bmatrix} 200 \\ 0 \end{bmatrix} $$

The agency hires you to advise them on potential uses for this information.

a Your first thought is to produce a *regional* technical coefficients table for each region. Is it possible to construct such tables? If so, do it; if not, why not?

b You also consider putting the data together to generate a national technical coefficients table. Is this possible? If so, do it; if not, why not?

c Why is it not possible to construct from the given data a three-region multiregional input-output model?

d   If the federal government is considering spending $5000 on manufactured goods and $4500 on agricultural products next year, what would you estimate as the national gross outputs necessary to satisfy this government demand?

e   Compare the national gross outputs for sectors 1 and 2 found in **d**, above, with the original gross outputs, given in the data set from last year. What feature of the input-output model does this comparison illustrate?

3-5*   Consider the following two-region interregional input-output transactions table:

	North			South			
	(1)	(2)	(3)	(1)	(2)	(3)	
	Agriculture	Mining	Construction & Manufacturing	Agriculture	Mining	Construction & Manufacturing	Total Output
North							
Agriculture (1)	277757	3654	1710816	8293	26	179483	3633382
Mining (2)	319	2412	598591	15	112	30921	743965
Construction & Manufacturing (3)	342956	39593	6762703	45770	3499	1550298	10931024
South							
Agriculture (1)	7085	39	98386	255023	3821	1669107	3697202
Mining (2)	177	92	15966	365	3766	669710	766751
Construction & Manufacturing (3)	71798	7957	2017905	316256	36789	8386751	14449941

a   Find the final-demand vectors and the technical coefficients matrices for each region.

b   Assume that the rising price of imported oil (upon which the economy is 99 percent dependent) has forced the construction and manufacturing industry (sector 3) to reduce *total output* by 10 percent in the South and 5 percent in the North. What are the corresponding amounts of output available for final demand? (Assume interindustry relationships remain the same, that is, the technical coefficients matrix is unchanged.)

c   Assume that tough import quotas imposed in Western Europe and the U.S. on this country's goods have reduced the final demand for output from the country's construction and manufacturing industries by 15 percent in the North. What is the impact on the output vector for the North region? Use a full two-region interregional model.

d   Answer the question in part **c**, above, ignoring interregional linkages, that is, using the Leontief inverse for the North region only. What do you conclude about the importance of interregional linkages in this aggregated version of this economy?

3-6*   Consider the three-region, five-sector version of the U.S. MRIO model given in Tables 3-11, 3-12, and 3-13. Suppose that a new government military project is initiated in the western United States which stimulates new final demand in that region of (in millions of dollars)

$$\Delta Y^W = \begin{bmatrix} 0 \\ 0 \\ 100 \\ 40 \\ 25 \end{bmatrix}$$

What is the impact on total production of all sectors in all three regions of the United States economy stimulated by this final demand in the West?

3-7 *   Suppose the same final-demand vector given in problem 3-6 is placed on goods and services produced in the South of the Japanese IRIO model given in Tables 3-3 and 3-4. What is the impact on total production of all sectors in all three regions of Japan of this final demand in the South?

REFERENCES

BATEY, PETER W. J., and MOSS MADDEN. "Demographic-Economic Forecasting Within an Activity-Commodity Framework: Some Theoretical Considerations and Empirical Results." *Environment and Planning, A* 13, no. 9 (September 1981): 1067–83.

BEYERS, WILLIAM B. "Migration and the Development of Multiregional Economic Systems." *Economic Geography* 56, no. 4 (October 1980): 320–34.

BLACKWELL, JON. "Disaggregation of the Household Sector in Regional Input-Output Analysis: Some Models Specifying Previous Residence of Worker." *Regional Studies* 12, no. 3 (September 1978): 367–77.

BOURQUE, PHILIP J., and MILICENT COX. *An Inventory of Regional Input-Output Studies in the United States.* Seattle: University of Washington, Graduate School of Business Administration, 1970.

California, State of, Department of Water Resources. *Measuring Economic Impacts. The Application of Input-Output Analysis to California Water Resources Problems.* Bulletin 210. Sacramento: Department of Water Resources, 1980.

CHENERY, HOLLIS B. "Regional Analysis." In *The Structure and Growth of the Italian Economy,* edited by Hollis B. Chenery, Paul G. Clark, and Vera Cao Pinna, 97–129. Rome: U.S. Mutual Security Agency, 1953.

EMERSON, M. JARVIN. "The Interindustry Structure of the Kansas Economy." Topeka: Kansas Office of Economic Analysis and Planning Division, Kansas Department of Economic Development, January 1969.

———. "The 1969 Kansas Input-Output Study." Topeka: Kansas Office of Economic Analysis and Planning Division, Kansas Department of Economic Development, 1971.

GIARRATANI, FRANK, JAMES D. MADDY, and CHARLES F. SOCHER. *Regional and Interregional Input-Output Analysis: An Annotated Bibliography.* Morgantown, W.Va.: West Virginia University Library, 1976.

GILLEN, WILLIAM J., and ANTONIO GUCCIONE. "Interregional Feedbacks in Input-Output Models: Some Formal Results." *Journal of Regional Science* 20, no. 4 (November 1980): 477–82.

GOLLADAY, FREDERICK, and ROBERT H. HAVEMAN. *The Economic Impacts of Tax-Transfer Policy: Regional and Distributional Effects.* New York: Academic Press, 1977.

GORDON, PETER, and JACQUES LEDENT. "Towards an Interregional Demoeconomic Model." *Journal of Regional Science* 21, no. 1 (February 1981): 79–87.

HARTWICK, JOHN M. "Notes on the Isard and Chenery-Moses Interregional Input-Output Models." *Journal of Regional Science* 11, no. 1 (April 1971): 73–86.

HEWINGS, GEOFFREY J. D., and MICHAEL C. ROMANOS. "Simulating Less-Developed Regional Economies Under Conditions of Limited Information." *Geographical Analysis* 13, no. 4 (October 1981): 373–90.

HIRSCH, WERNER Z. "Interindustry Relations of a Metropolitan Area." *Review of Economics and Statistics* 41, no. 4 (November 1959): 360–69.

ISARD, WALTER. "Interregional and Regional Input-Output Analysis: A Model of a Space Economy." *Review of Economics and Statistics* 33, no. 4 (November 1951): 318–28.

ISARD, WALTER, et al. *Methods of Regional Analysis: An Introduction to Regional Science.* New York: The Technology Press of MIT and John Wiley and Sons, Inc., 1960.

ISARD, WALTER, and ROBERT E. KUENNE. "The Impact of Steel upon the Greater New York–Philadelphia Industrial Region." *Review of Economics and Statistics* 35, no. 4 (November 1953): 289–301.

ISARD, WALTER, and THOMAS LANGFORD. *Regional Input-Output Study: Recollections, Reflections, and Diverse Notes on the Philadelphia Experience.* Cambridge, Mass.: The MIT Press, 1971.

JAPANESE GOVERNMENT, ADMINISTRATIVE MANAGEMENT AGENCY et al. "The 1960 Input-Output Table of Japan." Tokyo, 1964.

———. "The 1965 Input-Output Table of Japan." Tokyo, 1969.

———. "The 1970 Input-Output Table of Japan." Tokyo, 1974.

JOUN, RICHARD Y. P., and RICHARD S. CONWAY, JR. "Regional Economic-Demographic Forecasting Models: A Case Study of the Washington and Hawaii Models." *Socio-Economic Planning Sciences* 17, no. 5–6 (October–December 1983): 345–53.

LAMPHEAR, F. CHARLES, and THEODORE W. ROESLER. "1967 Nebraska Input-Output Tables," University of Nebraska—Lincoln, Bureau of Business Research, Lincoln, Nebraska, n.d.

———. "1970 Nebraska Input-Output Tables," University of Nebraska—Lincoln, Bureau of Business Research, Lincoln, Nebraska, n.d.

LEDENT, JACQUES, and PETER GORDON. "A Framework for Modeling Interregional Population Distribution and Economic Growth." *International Regional Science Review* 6, no. 1 (Fall 1981): 85–90.

LEONTIEF, WASSILY. "Structure of the World Economy: Outline of a Simple Input-Output Formulation." *American Economic Review* 64, no. 6 (December 1974): 823–34.

LEONTIEF, WASSILY, ANNE P. CARTER, and PETER A. PETRI. *The Future of the World Economy.* New York: Oxford University Press, 1977.

LEONTIEF, WASSILY, et al. *Studies in the Structure of the American Economy.* New York: Oxford University Press, 1953.

———. "The Economic Impact—Industrial and Regional—of an Arms Cut." *Review of Economics and Statistics* 47, no. 3 (August 1965): 217–41.

LOVISCEK, ANTHONY L., et al. *The 1975 West Virginia Input-Output Study: Modeling a Regional Economy.* Morgantown, W.Va.: West Virginia University Library, 1979.

MADDEN, MOSS, and PETER W. J. BATEY. "Achieving Consistency in Demographic-Economic Forecasting," *Papers, Regional Science Association* 44 (1980): 91–106.

———. "Linked Population and Economic Models: Some Methodological Issues in Forecasting, Analysis, and Policy Optimization," *Journal of Regional Science* 23, no. 2 (May 1983): 141–64.

MIERNYK, WILLIAM H. *Regional Analysis and Regional Policy.* Cambridge, Mass.: Oelgeschlager, Gunn & Hain, Publishers, Inc., 1982.

MIERNYK, WILLIAM H., et al. *Impact of the Space Program on a Local Economy: An Input-Output Analysis.* Morgantown, W.Va.: West Virginia University Library, 1967.

———. *Simulating Regional Economic Development.* Lexington, Mass.: D.C. Heath and Co., 1970.

MILLER, RONALD E. "The Impact of the Aluminum Industry on the Pacific Northwest: A Regional Input-Output Analysis." *Review of Economics and Statistics* 39, no. 2 (May 1957): 200–209.

———. "Interregional Feedback Effects in Input-Output Models: Some Preliminary Results." *Papers, Regional Science Association* 17 (1966): 105–25.

———. "Interregional Feedbacks in Input-Output Models: Some Experimental Results." *Western Economic Journal* 7, no. 1 (March 1969): 41–50.

MOORE, FREDERICK T., and JAMES W. PETERSEN. "Regional Analysis: An Interindustry Model of Utah." *Review of Economics and Statistics* 37, no. 4 (November 1955): 368–83.

MOSES, LEON N. "The Stability of Interregional Trading Patterns and Input-Output Analysis." *American Economic Review* 45, no. 5 (December 1955): 803–32.

MULLENDORE, WALTER E., ARTHUR L. EKHOLM, and PAUL M. HAYASHI. *An Input-Output Model of the North Central Region of Texas*. Arlington, Tex.: University of Texas at Arlington, 1972.

OOSTERHAVEN, JAN. *Interregional Input-Output Analysis and Dutch Regional Policy Problems*. Aldershot, Hampshire (U.K.): Gower Publishing Co., 1981.

POLENSKE, KAREN R. *The U.S. Multiregional Input-Output Accounts and Model*. Lexington, Mass.: Lexington Books, 1980.

SCHINNAR, ARIE P. "A Multi-Dimensional Accounting Model for Demographic and Economic Planning Interactions." *Environment and Planning, A* 8, no. 4 (June 1976): 455–75.

TIEBOUT, CHARLES M. "An Empirical Regional Input-Output Projection Model: The State of Washington 1980." *Review of Economics and Statistics* 51, no. 3 (August 1969): 334–40.

U.S. DEPARTMENT OF HEALTH AND HUMAN SERVICES, OFFICE OF THE ASSISTANT SECRETARY FOR PLANNING AND EVALUATION. *The Multiregional Input-Output Accounts*, 1977. Washington, D.C.: U.S. Government Printing Office, 1983.

UNIVERSITY OF NEW MEXICO, BUREAU OF BUSINESS RESEARCH. "A Preview of the Input-Output Study." *New Mexico Business* (October 1965): 1–23.

4

Multipliers in the Input-Output Model

4-1 | INTRODUCTION

One of the major uses of input-output information, in the format of an input-output model, is to assess the effect on an economy of changes in elements that are exogenous to the model of that economy. In Chapters 2 and 3 we presented several numerical illustrations of the ways in which assumed changes in final-demand elements (e.g., federal government spending) were translated, via the appropriate Leontief inverse, to corresponding changes that would be needed in the outputs of the industrial sectors of a national or regional economy. When the exogenous changes occur because of the actions of only one "impacting agent" (or a small number of such agents) and when the changes are expected to occur in the short run (e.g., next year), the term *impact analysis* is usually employed. Examples are a change in federal government demand for aircraft or in consumer demand for recreation vehicles.

On the other hand, when longer-term and broader changes are examined, then we are dealing with projections and forecasting. If we project the levels of final demand for outputs of all sectors in a regional economy five years hence, and estimate, using the Leontief inverse, the outputs from all regional sectors that will be needed to satisfy this demand, this is an exercise in regional forecasting. As the period of projection gets longer, the accuracy of such an exercise tends to decrease, both because our ability to forecast the new final demands (the elements of Y) accurately will diminish and also because the coefficient matrix (the elements of A and hence $[I - A]^{-1}$) may tend to get out of date. We will investigate the issue of temporal stability of input-output coefficients in Chapter 8.

Whether using the input-output model for impact analysis or for forecasting, the general form is $X = (I - A)^{-1}Y$. Thus the usefulness of the result, X, will depend on the "correctness" of both $(I - A)^{-1}$ and Y. Our concern in this chapter (and elsewhere throughout this book) is with the elements a_{ij} and hence with the Leontief inverse matrix, $(I - A)^{-1}$. The Y vector incorporates the assumed or projected behavior of one or more final-demand elements. Thus, accuracy in the estimation of these elements is also of paramount importance to generating an accurate result. When the question is one of impact, then the final-demand value or values are usually completely specified—for example, what is the impact, by sector, of a new order for $2.5 million worth of sector j output by the federal government? Then Y contains 2.5 (million) in the jth row and zeros elsewhere. On the other hand, to find X for some future year requires a projection of the A matrix and the final-demand vector to that year. We will investigate some of the approaches for changing A over time in Chapter 8. The projection of Y is a problem that is often approached via econometric models. (There is a growing literature on this issue of the interactions between input-output models and econometric models, particularly at the regional level. For representative examples, see L'Esperance et al. 1977, Conway 1979, Stevens et al. 1981, or Kushnirsky 1982.) The input-output forecasts of 1985 industrial outputs (and employment) for the U.S. economy in Almon et al. (1974, Chapters 8 and 9) depend on detailed and painstaking projections of each of the components of final demand—personal consumption expenditures, investment in capital equipment, construction, inventories, imports and exports, and government expenditures (1974, Chapters 2 through 7, respectively). In some but by no means all "joined" input-output and econometric models, the econometric model provides a forecast of the final demands, which then "drive" the input-output model.

Several summary measures, derived from the elements of $(I - A)^{-1}$, are often employed in impact analysis; these are what are known as input-output multipliers. We examine these multipliers, in both national and regional contexts, in this chapter. Introductory discussions on multipliers in the input-output model can be found in, among others, Miernyk (1965, ch. 3), Richardson (1972, ch. 3), and Schaffer (1976, ch. 5). More recent discussions on problems with some conventional definitions of multipliers, and possible inconsistencies, can be found in much of the work in which Jensen has played a role—for example, Jensen (1978), West and Jensen (1980), and Jensen and West (1980). In a regional context, DiPasquale and Polenske (1980) discuss multipliers thoroughly in the multiregional input-output model.

4-2 | GENERAL STRUCTURE OF MULTIPLIER ANALYSIS

Three of the most frequently used types of multipliers are those that estimate the effects of the exogenous changes on (a) outputs of the sectors in the economy, (b) income earned by households because of the new outputs, and (c) employment (in physical terms) that is expected to be generated because of the new outputs. We examine these in turn, in this section, for the general input-output model. In Appendix 4-1 we have collected the results in compact matrix notation. Then, in Section 4-3, we will examine the particular characteristics that these multipliers have in interregional and multiregional input-output models.

The notion of multipliers rests upon the difference between the *initial* effect of an exogenous (final demand) change and the *total* effects of that change. The total effects can be defined in either of two ways—as the *direct and indirect* effects (which means that they would be found via elements in the Leontief inverse of a model that is open with respect to households) or as *direct, indirect, and induced* effects (which means that they would be found via elements of the Leontief inverse of a model that is closed with respect to households).[1] The multipliers that are found by using direct and indirect effects are also known as *simple* multipliers. When direct, indirect, and induced effects are used, they are called *total* multipliers.

Output Multipliers

An output multiplier for sector j is defined as the total value of production in all sectors of the economy that is necessary in order to satisfy a dollar's worth of final demand for sector j's output. For the simple output multiplier, this total production is the direct and indirect output effect, obtained from a model in which households are exogenous. The initial output effect on the economy is defined to be simply the initial dollar's worth of sector j output needed to satisfy the additional final demand. Then, formally, the output multiplier is the *ratio* of the direct and indirect effect to the initial effect alone.

We continue with the small example of section 2-3 in Chapter 2, in which we had a coefficients matrix (with households exogenous) of

$$A = \begin{bmatrix} .15 & .25 \\ .20 & .05 \end{bmatrix} \tag{4-1}$$

and a Leontief inverse of

$$(I - A)^{-1} = \begin{bmatrix} 1.254 & .330 \\ .264 & 1.122 \end{bmatrix} \tag{4-2}$$

(For most of the numerical examples in the remainder of this book we will keep, at most, three figures to the right of the decimal point.) Using ΔY and ΔX to represent *changes in* final demand and gross outputs, respectively, $\Delta Y(1) = \begin{bmatrix} 1 \\ 0 \end{bmatrix}$ indicates an additional dollar's worth of final demand for the output of sector 1 only, and $\Delta Y(2) = \begin{bmatrix} 0 \\ 1 \end{bmatrix}$ indicates, similarly, an additional dollar's worth of final demand for the output of sector 2 only. Thus, for example, the implications for all (here both) sectors in the economy of an additional dollar's worth of final

---

[1] In some discussions of multipliers in an input-output model, what we have called the *initial* effect is termed the *direct* effect. For later exposition—for example, in looking at shortcut methods for finding multipliers—when the power series approximation

$$(I - A)^{-1} = I + A + A^2 + A^3 + \cdots$$

will be used, it seems to us preferable to associate "initial" with the I term, "direct" with A, and "indirect" with the remaining terms, $A^2 + A^3 + \cdots$.

demand for sector 1 output is found as $(I - A)^{-1}\Delta Y(1)$. Denote this total effect on both sectors by $\Delta X(1)$.

$$\Delta X(1) = \begin{bmatrix} 1.254 & .330 \\ .264 & 1.122 \end{bmatrix} \begin{bmatrix} 1 \\ 0 \end{bmatrix} = \begin{bmatrix} 1.254 \\ .264 \end{bmatrix} \tag{4-3}$$

This is, of course, just the first column of the Leontief inverse. If we represent the elements of $(I - A)^{-1}$ as α_{ij}'s, then $\Delta X(1) = \begin{bmatrix} \alpha_{11} \\ \alpha_{21} \end{bmatrix}$.

Note that additional outputs of \$1.254 from sector 1 and \$0.264 from sector 2 are required for a dollar of new final demand for the output of sector 1 *only*. The \$1.254 from sector 1 represents \$1.00 to satisfy the original new dollar of final demand plus an additional \$0.254 for intra- and interindustry use. The \$0.264 from sector 2 is for intra- and interindustry use only. The sector 1 output multiplier, O_1, is defined as the sum of the elements in the $\Delta X(1)$ column, namely \$1.518, divided by \$1. That is, $O_1 = \$1.518/\$1 = 1.518$, a dimensionless number. The \$1 in the denominator is the *initial* effect on sector 1 output of the new dollar's worth of final demand for sector 1's product. That is, the dollar's worth of final demand becomes an additional dollar's worth of sector 1 output as the first term in the series assessment of total direct and indirect effects on sector 1 production. Formally, utilizing the unity row notation to generate column sums

$$O_1 = i'\Delta X(1) = \sum_{i=1}^{n} \alpha_{i1} \tag{4-4}$$

where $n = 2$ in this example.

Similarly,

$$\Delta X(2) = \begin{bmatrix} 1.254 & .330 \\ .264 & 1.122 \end{bmatrix} \begin{bmatrix} 0 \\ 1 \end{bmatrix} = \begin{bmatrix} .330 \\ 1.122 \end{bmatrix} = \begin{bmatrix} \alpha_{12} \\ \alpha_{22} \end{bmatrix}$$

and

$$O_2 = i'\Delta X(2) = \sum_{i=1}^{n} \alpha_{i2} \tag{4-5}$$

In this example, $O_2 = 1.452$. In general, the simple output multiplier for sector j, O_j, is given by

$$O_j = \sum_{i=1}^{n} \alpha_{ij} \tag{4-6}$$

Thus, for example, if a government agency were trying to determine in which sector of the economy to spend an additional dollar (or \$100, or \$100,000, or whatever amount), comparison of output multipliers would show where this spending would have the greatest impact in terms of total dollar value of output generated throughout the economy. Note that when maximum total output effects are the exclusive goal of government spending, it would always be rational to spend all the money in the sector whose output multiplier was the largest (here, the larger, since there are only two sectors). Even with anticipated expenditures of \$100,000, there would be no reason, on the basis of output multipliers alone, to divide that spending between the sectors.

Of course, there might well be other reasons—taking into account strategic factors, equity, capacity constraints for sectoral production, and so on—for using some of the new final-demand dollars on the output of the other sector (or sectors, when $n > 2$). Note also that multipliers of this sort may overstate the effect on the economy in question if some sectors are operating at or near capacity and hence some of the needed new inputs would have to be imported to the economy and/or outputs from some sectors would be shifted from exports and kept in the economy for use as inputs. Phenomena such as these will assume even more importance in regional models.

If we consider the input coefficient matrix closed with respect to households (as described in section 2-5 of Chapter 2), then we capture in the model the additional *induced* effects of household income generation through payments for labor services and the associated consumer expenditures on goods produced by the various sectors. Continuing with the example from section 2-5, recall that the augmented coefficients matrix, with an added household row and column, was

$$\bar{A} = \begin{bmatrix} .15 & .25 & .05 \\ .20 & .05 & .40 \\ .30 & .25 & .05 \end{bmatrix} \tag{4-7}$$

and the Leontief inverse, with elements $\bar{\alpha}_{ij}$, was

$$(I - \bar{A})^{-1} = \begin{bmatrix} 1.365 & 0.425 & 0.251 \\ 0.527 & 1.348 & 0.595 \\ 0.570 & 0.489 & 1.289 \end{bmatrix} \tag{4-8}$$

as in Eq. (2-22) in Chapter 2, but rounding to three decimals. Clearly, the elements in $(I - \bar{A})^{-1}$ also relate final-demand changes to sectoral outputs, only now these are in a model with households endogenous, and hence the effects tend to be larger.

To assess the impact of a new dollar's worth of final demand for sector 1 output, we would now form the three-element vector $\Delta \bar{Y}(1) = \begin{bmatrix} 1 \\ 0 \\ 0 \end{bmatrix}$ (meaning no exogenous change in demand for sector 2 output or for labor services), and find

$$\Delta \bar{X}(1) = (I - \bar{A})^{-1} \Delta \bar{Y}(1) = \begin{bmatrix} 1.365 \\ 0.527 \\ 0.570 \end{bmatrix}$$

(Compare Eq. [4-3] above.) Adding these elements would give, parallel to Eq. (4-4), above,

$$\bar{O}_1 = i' \Delta \bar{X}(1) = \sum_{i=1}^{n+1} \bar{\alpha}_{i1} \tag{4-9}$$

with $n = 2$, as before. For this example, $\bar{O}_1 = 2.462$. (If one were interested in the total output effect over the original n sectors only, not including the new household sector, one would sum the $\bar{\alpha}_{i1}$ from $i = 1$ to $i = n$ only, i.e., omit the last element in the first column of $[I - \bar{A}]^{-1}$ from the summation. We can denote these *truncated* total output multipliers by $\overline{O}(t)_j$. Here $\overline{O}(t)_1 = 1.892$.) The total output multiplier for sector 2 is thus

$$\overline{O}_2 = \sum_{i=1}^{n+1} \overline{\alpha}_{i2} \tag{4-10}$$

(Compare Eq. [4-5], above, for the simple output multiplier.) For this example, $\overline{O}_2 = 2.262$ and $\overline{O}(t)_2 = 1.773$. In general, for sector j, the total output multiplier is given by

$$\overline{O}_j = \sum_{i=1}^{n+1} \overline{\alpha}_{ij} \tag{4-11}$$

and the truncated total output multiplier is $\overline{O}(t)_j = \sum_{i=1}^{n} \overline{\alpha}_{ij}$.

Example: The U.S. Input-Output Model for 1967   We again use the seven-sector 1967 U.S. model. The Leontief inverse was shown as Table 2-7 in Chapter 2; it is also part of Table B-18 in Appendix B, and it is not repeated here. The simple output multipliers, arranged in a row vector, O, are easily found to be

$$O = \begin{bmatrix} 2.2390 & 1.6873 & 2.1273 & 2.2385 & 1.5376 & 1.6843 & 1.8315 \end{bmatrix}$$

That is, the largest multipliers are those associated with agriculture and with manufacturing. The multiplier is also relatively large for sector 3, construction. In this model, small multipliers are associated with sectors 2, 5, and 6.

Income Multipliers

As the name implies, income multipliers attempt to translate, in one way or another, the impacts of final-demand spending changes into changes in income received by households (labor supply), rather than translating the final-demand changes into total value of sectoral output. There are basically two ways in which this can be done.

Income Effects or Household Income Multipliers   One straightforward approach is simply to convert each element in a particular column of $(I - A)^{-1}$, which measures the value of direct plus indirect output effects, into dollars' worth of household income via household input coefficients. These are the coefficients that make up the $(n + 1)$st (household) row, H_R, that is used in closing the model with respect to households, and which indicate household income received per dollar's worth of sectoral output. In the current example, these coefficients are the first two elements in the bottom row of $\overline{A}$ in Eq. (4-7). Thus the direct plus indirect effects for sector j would be in terms of dollars' worth of new household income, and the initial effect is in terms of (one) dollar's worth of final demand, and hence output, for sector j. Unlike output multipliers, then, they do not "blow up" or multiply one (initial) estimate of *output* to another (larger) estimate of *output*. Rather they translate an initial $1.00 output estimate (which comes from an initial \$1.00 final-demand change) into an expanded (direct plus indirect) estimate of the value of resulting employment (household income). In general, then, using H_j for the simple household income multiplier for sector j,

$$H_j = \sum_{i=1}^{n} a_{n+1,i} \alpha_{ij} \tag{4-12}$$

Again, "simple" refers to the fact that these multipliers are found using elements in the $(I - A)^{-1}$ matrix, with households exogenous.

Continuing the same example, in $\bar{A}$ in Eq. (4-7), we have $a_{n+1,1} = 0.3$ and $a_{n+1,2} = 0.25$. Thus, for sector 1, we multiply the elements of $\Delta X(1)$ by $a_{n+1,1}$ and $a_{n+1,2}$, respectively; $H_1 = [a_{n+1,1} \quad a_{n+1,2}] \Delta X(1) = [a_{n+1,1} \quad a_{n+1,2}] \begin{bmatrix} \alpha_{11} \\ \alpha_{21} \end{bmatrix}$

$= \sum_{i=1}^{n} a_{n+1,i} \alpha_{i1}$ (here $n = 2$). In particular, for this example

$$H_1 = (0.3)(1.254) + (0.25)(0.264) = 0.376 + 0.066 = 0.442$$

This figure, 0.442, says that an additional dollar of final demand for the output of sector 1, when all of the direct and indirect effects are converted into dollar estimates of income, would generate \$0.442 of new household income; of this total, \$0.376 would be earned by employees in sector 1 and \$0.066 would be earned by sector 2 employees.

Similarly, for sector 2 the direct and indirect income effect is found as

$$H_2 = [a_{n+1,1} \quad a_{n+1,2}] \Delta X(2) = [a_{n+1,1} \quad a_{n+1,2}] \begin{bmatrix} \alpha_{12} \\ \alpha_{22} \end{bmatrix} = \sum_{i=1}^{n} a_{n+1,i} \alpha_{i2}$$

(here $n = 2$). That is,

$$H_2 = (0.3)(0.33) + (0.25)(1.122) = 0.099 + 0.281 = 0.380$$

for the present example. Interpreted in the same way, this says that a dollar's worth of final demand for the output of sector 2 becomes \$0.38 worth of new household income, when all direct and indirect effects are taken into account, via the Leontief inverse. Employees in sector 1 would receive \$0.099 in new income; those in sector 2 would earn \$0.281. From this example, using this measure of effectiveness, dollars of final demand—for example, new government purchases—generate more dollars of new household income when they are spent on the output of sector 1 than when they are spent on the output of sector 2.

If the elements in $(I - \bar{A})^{-1}$ are weighted similarly, *total* (direct plus indirect plus induced) income effects or *total* household income multipliers are obtained. As before, using an overbar to denote the multiplier derived from $\bar{A}$, in which households have been included in the matrix, the parallel to H_j in Eq. (4-12) is

$$\bar{H}_j = \sum_{i=1}^{n+1} a_{n+1,i} \bar{\alpha}_{ij} \tag{4-13}$$

For our numerical example,

$$\bar{H}_1 = (0.3)(1.365) + (0.25)(0.527) + (0.05)(0.570) = .570$$

and

$$\bar{H}_2 = (0.3)(0.425) + (0.25)(1.348) + (0.05)(0.489) = .489$$

Note that these total household income multipliers for sectors 1 and 2 are precisely equal to the first two elements in the bottom row of $(I - \bar{A})^{-1}$ in Eq. (4-8); that is, $\bar{\alpha}_{n+1,1}$ and $\bar{\alpha}_{n+1,2}$. Recall the interpretation of any element, $\bar{\alpha}_{ij}$, in $(I - \bar{A})^{-1}$; it measures the total (direct, indirect, and induced) effect on sector i output of a dollar's worth of new demand for sector j output. Thus $\bar{\alpha}_{n+1,j}$ is the total effect on the output of the household sector, which is the total value of labor services needed, when there is a dollar's worth of new final demand for goods of sector j. This is precisely what we mean by the total household income effect or total household income multiplier. So

$$\bar{H}_j = \bar{\alpha}_{n+1,j} \tag{4-14}$$

In Appendix 4-2, the relationship between the total household income multipliers and the bottom-row elements of $(I - \bar{A})^{-1}$ is shown exactly, using matrix algebra results on the inverse of a partitioned matrix. If we are only interested in household income-generating effects originating in the n original sectors, we would calculate a truncated total household income multiplier, $\bar{H}(t)_j$, by summing over $i = 1$ to $i = n$ only in Eq. (4-13). For the example, $\bar{H}(t)_1 = 0.541$ and $\bar{H}(t)_2 = 0.465$.

Type I and Type II Income Multipliers   With household income multipliers, one has some choice regarding what should logically be termed the initial effect of new final demand. With output multipliers it was fairly clear that the initial effect of a new dollar's worth of final demand for sector j output is that sector j production must increase by one dollar (and eventually, of course, by more than one dollar). With income effects, the same dollar's worth of new demand for sector j becomes, initially, the same dollar's worth of new output by sector j; this is what we considered the initial effect in developing the household income multipliers, above. However, the initial dollar's worth of new output from sector j means an initial additional income payment of $a_{n+1,j}$ to workers in sector j. Hence $a_{n+1,j}$ could be viewed as the initial *income* effect of the new demand for sector j output.

Thus there is a second kind of simple income multiplier, the type I income multiplier, for any sector j. This has the direct and indirect income effect, or the simple household income multiplier, as in Eq. (4-12), as a numerator, and uses as a denominator not the initial dollar's worth of output but rather its initial labor income effect, $a_{n+1,j}$. As is common in economics, we can use Y to denote income, and let Y_j represent this type of income multiplier for sector j. (Recall that Y_j is also used to denote final demand for sector j output; the meaning will always be clear from the context in which it is used.) Then

$$Y_j = \sum_{i=1}^{n} \frac{a_{n+1,i}\alpha_{ij}}{a_{n+1,j}} = \frac{H_j}{a_{n+1,j}} \tag{4-15}$$

In our example,

$$Y_1 = \frac{(a_{31}\alpha_{11} + a_{32}\alpha_{21})}{a_{31}} = 0.442/0.3 = 1.47$$

$$Y_2 = \frac{(a_{31}\alpha_{12} + a_{32}\alpha_{22})}{a_{32}} = 0.380/0.25 = 1.52$$

Again, if one closes the coefficients matrix with respect to households, income effects similar to these type I multipliers can be calculated; these are termed type II income multipliers.[2] As usual, using the overbar to denote a measure that is calculated from the Leontief inverse of the matrix with households endogenous,

$$\overline{Y}_j = \sum_{i=1}^{n+1} \frac{a_{n+1,i}\overline{\alpha}_{ij}}{a_{n+1,j}} = \frac{\overline{H}_j}{a_{n+1,j}} \tag{4-16}$$

The parallel between this measure and the type I effect in Eq. (4-15) is the same as that between the total $(\overline{H}_j)$ and simple (H_j) household income multipliers in Eqs. (4-13) and (4-12). The numerator for Y_j is H_j from Eq. (4-12); the numerator for $\overline{Y}_j$ is $\overline{H}_j$ from Eq. (4-13) or from Eq. (4-14). Thus, for exactly the same reasons as in the case of $\overline{H}_j$, we can alternatively define $\overline{Y}_j$ as

$$\overline{Y}_j = \overline{\alpha}_{n+1,j}/a_{n+1,j} \tag{4-17}$$

Continuing with the same example, we have

$$\overline{Y}_1 = \frac{\overline{H}_1}{a_{31}} = \frac{\overline{\alpha}_{31}}{a_{31}} = \frac{0.570}{0.3} = 1.90$$

$$\overline{Y}_2 = \frac{\overline{H}_2}{a_{32}} = \frac{\overline{\alpha}_{32}}{a_{32}} = \frac{0.489}{0.25} = 1.96$$

These multipliers, 1.90 and 1.96, show by how much the initial income effects (0.3 and 0.25) are blown up, or multiplied, when direct, indirect, and induced effects (due to household spending because of increased household income) are taken into account, via the Leontief inverse of $\overline{A}$, in which households are an endogenous sector. Truncated type II income multipliers would, as usual, be

[2]The designations "type I" and "type II" seem to have originated with Moore (1955). Calculation of these quantities (albeit in a regional setting) was pioneered by Moore and Petersen (1955) for Utah and later by Hirsch (1959) for St. Louis. Moses (1955) questions the logic of using the initial income change, $\$a_{n+1,j}$, instead of the initial expenditure change, $\$1.00$, as the denominator, as is done in household income multipliers.

found by summing over $i = 1$ to $i = n$ in Eq. (4-16); that is, as

$$\bar{Y}(t)_j = \frac{\bar{H}(t)_j}{a_{n+1,j}}.$$

For our example, $\bar{Y}(t)_1 = 1.803$ and $\bar{Y}(t)_2 = 1.860$.

Relationship Between Simple and Total Household Income Multipliers or Between Type I and Type II Income Multipliers   To the extent that the results of an input-output analysis in which households remain exogenous tend to under-estimate total effects, total or type II multipliers may be more useful than simple or type I multipliers in estimating potential impacts. However, if one is primarily interested in ranking or ordering the sectors—for example, which sector has the largest multiplier, which has the next largest, and so on—then simple or type I multipliers are just as useful as total or type II (and usually easier to obtain), because the ratio of total to simple household multipliers or type II to type I income multipliers can be shown to be a constant across all sectors. Since $\bar{Y}_j = \bar{H}_j/a_{n+1,j}$ and $Y_j = H_j/a_{n+1,j}$, it follows that $\bar{Y}_j/Y_j = \bar{H}_j/H_j$. What is now claimed is that $\bar{Y}_j/Y_j = k$ (a constant) for all j. Moreover, the constant k can be easily found without any need for $(I - A)^{-1}$, the Leontief inverse for the system with households endogenous. This represents a computational advantage. To show that this ratio is a constant requires that we apply some facts on the inverse of a partitioned matrix (see Appendix A) to the partitioned $(I - A)$ matrix, with an $(n + 1)$st household row and column. This is done in Appendix 4-3 to this chapter, for the interested reader. Note that in our illustrative example we found $H_1 = 0.442$, $\bar{H}_1 = 0.570$, $H_2 = 0.380$, $\bar{H}_2 = 0.489$, $Y_1 = 1.47$, $\bar{Y}_1 = 1.90$, $Y_2 = 1.52$, and $\bar{Y}_2 = 1.96$. Therefore, $\bar{H}_1/H_1 = 0.570/0.442 = 1.29$, $\bar{Y}_1/Y_1 = 1.90/1.47 = 1.29$, and the same values can be found for $\bar{H}_2/H_2$ and $\bar{Y}_2/Y_2$; thus, $k = 1.29$ for this example.

Which Multiplier to Use   As a practical matter, the choice between multi-plier effects as measured by H_j (and $\bar{H}_j$) or as measured by Y_j (and $\bar{Y}_j$) depends on the nature of the exogenous change whose impact is being studied. If that change is, for example, an increase in federal government spending on output of the aircraft sector, then the most useful figures may be those that convert the total dollar value of new government spending into total new income earned by households in the economy—the household income multipliers H_j and $\bar{H}_j$. The impacts of decreases can also be assessed. Using $H_1 = 0.442$ and $H_2 = 0.380$ from the example, we would estimate that a tariff policy that would increase foreign demand for sector 1 goods by $100,000 would ultimately lead to an increase of $(0.442)(\$100,000) = \$44,200$ in new income earned, while a policy that increased export demand for sector 2 goods by $100,000 would generate $(0.380)(\$100,000) = \$38,000$ in new household income earned. If we attempt to capture the consumer spending that is associated with income earned, via a model that is closed with respect to households, we would use $\bar{H}_1$ and $\bar{H}_2$ and our estimates would be $(0.570)(\$100,000) = \$57,000$ and $(0.489)(\$100,000) = \$48,900$, respectively. In either case, we find that stimulation of export demand for sector 1 output generates the larger effect.

On the other hand, suppose that management teams in two different industries, i and j, were considering moving a large assembly plant out of the country because of lower labor costs abroad. If these plants had annual payrolls to labor of $\$p_i$ and $\$p_j$, respectively, then a measure of the total household income lost throughout the national economy because of the contemplated relocations would be given by $Y_i p_i$ and $Y_j p_j$—or by $\overline{Y}_i p_i$ and $\overline{Y}_j p_j$, if one wants to include induced effects with households endogenous. For example, using $Y_1 = 1.47$ and $Y_2 = 1.52$ from our example, if a plant in industry 1 with an annual payroll of \$100,000 were to move out of the country, we would estimate a total income loss of $(1.47)(\$100,000) = \$147,000$ throughout the economy. Similarly, if a new plant in industry 2, with an annual payroll of \$250,000, were to move into the economy, we could estimate the total stimulation to household income throughout the economy because of this new industrial activity as $(1.52)(\$250,000) = \$380,000$. Again, if we capture consumer spending using a model that is closed with respect to households, our estimates, using $\overline{Y}_1 = 1.90$ and $\overline{Y}_2 = 1.96$, would be a $(1.90)(\$100,000) = \$190,000$ income loss from the out-movement of the plant in industry 1 and a $(1.96)(\$250,000) = \$490,000$ increase in income earned caused by the in-movement of a plant in industry 2.

Even More Income Multipliers   In the Boulder study (Miernyk et al. 1967), income multipliers were calculated from a regional input-output model that had been closed with respect to households according to whether the new income went to new residents or current residents, and the current residents were divided into four income classes. These have been termed type III income multipliers, and they are smaller, sector by sector, than the type II income multipliers. This is to be expected, since marginal consumption coefficients, which are associated with current residents' consumption habits, tend to be smaller than average consumption coefficients, which are associated with new residents' consumption habits and which are the exclusive basis of the type II multipliers.[3]

Although the ratio of type III to type II income multipliers is not constant across sectors, the range was only 0.84–0.91, with an average of 0.88. Since the (constant) ratio of type II to type I income multipliers in this study was 1.34, this means that the ratio of type III to type I income multipliers averaged 1.18. If a similar narrow range of ratios of type III to type II income multipliers were found in other regional studies in which households were similarly disaggregated, it would be possible to approximate type III income multipliers across all sectors by appropriate "inflation" of the type I multiplier. In the Boulder study, the inflating factor would be 1.18.

Further, Madden and Batey (1983) derive what they term type IV income multipliers. Like the type III multipliers, these are (generally) larger than type I

---

[3]In the Boulder study, the *average* household consumption coefficient, for the products of all 31 sectors of the local economy, is 0.4005; the *marginal* household consumption coefficient for the products of the same 31 sectors, averaged over the four income classes used in that study, is 0.1730. (Calculated from Tables IV-2 and V-4a, respectively, in Miernyk et al. [1967].) The type III multipliers in the Boulder study were found not from the Leontief inverse of a model that had been closed with respect to households in this disaggregated way but rather in an iterative, round-by-round fashion.

but smaller than type II income multipliers. The distinction here is between the spending patterns of currently employed local residents and the spending patterns of currently unemployed local residents.[4]

Employment Multipliers

If it is possible to estimate relationships between the value of output of a sector and employment in that sector (in *physical*, not monetary, terms), then one can calculate employment multipliers, rather than income multipliers, for each sector. For example, recall from section 2-5 of Chapter 2 that in our closed model we had total outputs of $X_1 = \$1000$, $X_2 = \$2000$, and, for the household sector, $X_3 = \$1000$. Denote by e_i the number of employees in sector i. Assume, for the example, that $e_1 = 3$ (clearly, the number is unrealistically small, but it is in line with our assumption that the output of sector 1 was only $1000; if X_1 had been assumed to be $1,000,000, we could have assumed that e_1 was 3000). Similarly, let $e_2 = 4$. Then the *physical* labor input coefficients are found as $w_{n+1,i} = e_i/X_i$; for this example, with $n = 2$, $w_{31} = 0.003$ and $w_{32} = 0.002$. These are employees per dollar's worth of output. In general, for an n-sector input-output model, one could find

$$W_R = [w_{n+1,1}, w_{n+1,2}, \cdots, w_{n+1,n}]$$

as a parallel to the n-element row vector $H_R = [a_{n+1,1}, a_{n+1,2}, \cdots, a_{n+1,n}]$ that represented the dollar value of labor inputs to each of the n sectors per dollar's worth of sectoral output. Assume also that $e_3 = 1$. Note that e_3 represents the number of workers employed by the household sector as, for example, domestic help. Then $w_{33} = 0.001$.

Recall from the dollar flows in Table 2-8 of Chapter 2 that $z_{31} = \$300$, $z_{32} = \$500$, and $z_{33} = \$50$; these were the payments from sectors 1, 2, and households (3) for labor services. Thus, payments per employee were $100, $125, and $50, respectively. That is, using the physical input coefficients, as in W_R, makes explicit the differing wage rates in different sectors.

Employment Effects or Household Employment Multipliers   These measures parallel the income effects and household income multipliers described above. The major difference is that the physical labor input coefficients, $w_{n+1,j}$, are used instead of the monetary labor input coefficients, $a_{n+1,j}$. That is, the elements in W_R are used in place of the elements in H_R. Using E_j for the simple employment effect or simple household employment multiplier for sector j, the measure analogous to H_j in Eq. (4-12) is

$$E_j = \sum_{i=1}^{n} w_{n+1,i}\alpha_{ij} \tag{4-18}$$

[4]Conway (1977) has proposed to apply the terms "type A" and "type B" multipliers to the numerators of "type I" and "type II" multipliers. The motivation is to facilitate studies of changes in multiplier values over time. When the multiplier is a ratio in which both numerator and denominator elements change over time, a change in a multiplier value can reflect changes in either the numerator or in the denominator or in both. Notice that for income multipliers, Conway's type A and type B multipliers, for sector j, are what we have denoted H_j and $\overline{H}_j$.

Continuing the previous example, now with $w_{31} = 0.003$ and $w_{32} = 0.002$, we have

$$E_1 = (0.003)(1.254) + (0.002)(0.264) = 0.00429$$
$$E_2 = (0.003)(0.33) \ + (0.002)(1.122) = 0.00323$$

These multipliers appear to be very small, but that is simply because they represent jobs created *per dollar* of new sectoral output (which, as usual, arises because of an additional dollar's worth of final demand for the sector). If they were multiplied by 1000, to 4.29 and 3.23, these multipliers would represent new jobs created *per $1000* of new output.

If $(I - \bar{A})^{-1}$ is used instead of $(I - A)^{-1}$, then we have the total employment effect or total household employment multiplier, analogous to $\bar{H}_j$ in (4-13), of

$$\bar{E}_j = \sum_{i=1}^{n+1} w_{n+1,i}\bar{\alpha}_{ij} \qquad (4\text{-}19)$$

Continuing with our example,

$$\bar{E}_1 = (0.003)(1.365) + (0.002)(0.527) + (0.001)(0.570) = 0.00572$$
$$\bar{E}_2 = (0.003)(0.425) + (0.002)(1.348) + (0.001)(0.489) = 0.00446$$

(Again, if we were interested only in the total employment effect on the original n sectors, not including the household sector, we would sum on the right-hand side of $\bar{E}_j$ in Eq. [4-19] from $i = 1$ to $i = n$ only, omitting the last element in the jth column of $[I - \bar{A}]^{-1}$—along with its associated $w_{n+1,n+1}$—from the summation. That is, the truncated total employment effect or truncated total household employment multiplier for sector j is $\bar{E}[t]_j = \sum_{i=1}^{n} w_{n+1,i}\bar{\alpha}_{ij}$. For the example, $\bar{E}[t]_1 = 0.00515$ and $\bar{E}[t]_2 = 0.00397$.)

Type I and Type II Employment Multipliers Following the same argument as was presented for types I and II income multipliers, one may wish to relate the simple or total employment effect to an initial change in *employment*, not final demand (and output) in monetary terms. That is, a dollar's worth of new output by sector j means additional jobs in sector j in the amount $w_{n+1,j}$. The type I employment multiplier uses E_j as a numerator and $w_{n+1,j}$ (not $1) as the denominator. We denote this multiplier by W_j for sector j; in Chapter 2 we used W_j for the value added in sector j—this is another place where a particular notation will have to serve more than one purpose but, again, it will always be clear from the context which meaning is appropriate. Thus

$$W_j = \frac{E_j}{w_{n+1,j}} = \sum_{i=1}^{n} \frac{w_{n+1,i}\alpha_{ij}}{w_{n+1,j}} \qquad (4\text{-}20)$$

For our example,

$$W_1 = 0.00429/0.003 = 1.430$$
$$W_2 = 0.00323/0.002 = 1.615$$

That is, for each new job created in sector 2, for example, there is a total of 1.615 jobs created in all sectors throughout the economy.

Finally, using $(I - \bar{A})^{-1}$ rather than $(I - A)^{-1}$ allows us to measure type II employment multipliers, $\bar{W}_j$. Parallel to the types I and II income multipliers, we have

$$\bar{W}_j = \frac{\bar{E}_j}{w_{n+1,j}} = \sum_{i=1}^{n+1} \frac{w_{n+1,i}\bar{\alpha}_{ij}}{w_{n+1,j}} \tag{4-21}$$

For the example,

$$\bar{W}_1 = \frac{0.00572}{0.003} = 1.907$$

$$\bar{W}_2 = \frac{0.00446}{0.002} = 2.230$$

(Truncated versions, which result from summing $i = 1$ to $i = n$ only on the right-hand side of [4-21] are again possible. Here $\bar{W}[t]_1 = 1.717$ and $\bar{W}[t]_2 = 1.985$.)

Relationship Between Simple and Total Household Employment Multipliers or Between Type I and Type II Employment Multipliers While it is not possible to establish a constant relationship between type II and type I employment multipliers, as was the case for total and simple or for type II and type I income multipliers, there is an expression for the *differences* in value between $\bar{E}(t)$ and E, the truncated total and the simple household employment multiplier. Appendix 4-4 shows that the n-element row vector of these differences, D, is

$$D = (1/g)W_R(I - A)^{-1}H_C H_R(I - A)^{-1}$$

Since the denominators of the type I and type II employment multipliers are the same, the information in D allows one to construct type II truncated employment multipliers using the inverse of $(I - A)$ only, in conjunction with the known elements in W_R, H_C (the column vector of household consumption coefficients), and H_R (and g, as defined in Eq. [4-3-3] in Appendix 4-3).

The interested reader might wish to check that for the two-sector example we have been using, $D = [0.00086 \quad 0.00074]$. These are exactly the amounts by which $\bar{E}(t)_1$ and E_1 differ and by which $\bar{E}(t)_2$ and E_2 differ, namely $0.00515 - 0.00429 = 0.00086$ and $0.00397 - 0.00323 = 0.00074$.

Summary

In Table 4-1, we collect together the various measures of initial, direct plus indirect, and direct plus indirect plus induced effects as they relate to output, income, and employment in an economy. In particular, we try to sort out the elements that constitute the numerators and the denominators of the various multipliers. As Table 4-1 illustrates, there are two quite different measures of what is considered to be the initial effect in calculating income and employment multipliers. Clearly, the measures given in H (or $\bar{H}$) and E (or $\bar{E}$) are

TABLE 4-1 Initial, Direct plus Indirect, and Direct plus Indirect plus Induced Effects for Output, Income, and Employment Multipliers

	Output Effects	Income Effects	
Exogenous Change	$\Delta Y_j = \$1.00$	$\Delta Y_j = \$1.00$	
	Change in sector j output $= \Delta X_j = 1$	Change in sector j output $= \Delta X_j = 1$	Change in sector j payments to labor $= a_{n+1,j}$
Initial Effect (N) (Sector j)			
Direct + Indirect Effect (D + I) (All Sectors) (Model open with respect to households)	$\displaystyle\sum_{i=1}^{n}\alpha_{ij}$	$\displaystyle\sum_{i=1}^{n} a_{n+1,i}\alpha_{ij}$	
Simple Multiplier $[(D+I)/N]$	$O_j = \displaystyle\sum_{i=1}^{n}\alpha_{ij}/\Delta X_j = \sum_{i=1}^{n}\alpha_{ij}/1 = \sum_{i=1}^{n}\alpha_{ij}$	$H_j = \displaystyle\sum_{i=1}^{n} a_{n+1,i}\alpha_{ij}/\Delta X_j = \sum_{i=1}^{n} a_{n+1,i}\alpha_{ij}/1 = \sum_{i=1}^{n} a_{n+1,i}\alpha_{ij}$	$Y_j = \displaystyle\sum_{i=1}^{n} a_{n+1,i}\alpha_{ij}/a_{n+1,j}$ (also called type I income multiplier)
Direct + Indirect + Induced Effect (D + I + I) (All Sectors) (Model closed with respect to households)	$\displaystyle\sum_{i=1}^{n+1}\bar\alpha_{ij}$	$\displaystyle\sum_{i=1}^{n+1} a_{n+1,i}\bar\alpha_{ij}$	
Total Multiplier $[(D+I+I)/N]$	$\bar O_j = \displaystyle\sum_{i=1}^{n+1}\bar\alpha_{ij}/\Delta X_j = \sum_{i=1}^{n+1}\bar\alpha_{ij}/1 = \sum_{i=1}^{n+1}\bar\alpha_{ij}$	$\bar H_j = \displaystyle\sum_{i=1}^{n+1} a_{n+1,i}\bar\alpha_{ij}/\Delta X_j = \sum_{i=1}^{n+1} a_{n+1,i}\bar\alpha_{ij}/1 = \sum_{i=1}^{n+1} a_{n+1,i}\bar\alpha_{ij}$	$\bar Y_j = \displaystyle\sum_{i=1}^{n+1} a_{n+1,i}\bar\alpha_{ij}/a_{n+1,j}$ (also called type II income multiplier)

TABLE 4-1 CONTINUED

Exogenous Change	Employment Effects $\Delta Y_j = \$1.00$	
	Change in sector j output $= \Delta X_j = 1$	Change in sector j employment $= w_{n+1,j}$
Initial Effect (N) (Sector j)		
Direct + Indirect Effect ($D+I$) (All Sectors) (Model open with respect to households)	$\displaystyle\sum_{i=1}^{n} w_{n+1,i}\,\alpha_{ij}$	
Simple Multiplier $[(D+I)/N]$	$\displaystyle E_j = \sum_{i=1}^{n} w_{n+1,i}\,\alpha_{ij}/\Delta X_j$ $\displaystyle = \sum_{i=1}^{n} w_{n+1,i}\,\alpha_{ij}/1 = \sum_{i=1}^{n} w_{n+1,i}\,\alpha_{ij}$	$\displaystyle W_j = \sum_{i=1}^{n} w_{n+1,i}\,\alpha_{ij}\Big/ w_{n+1,j}$ (also called type I employment multiplier)
Direct + Indirect + Induced Effect ($D+I+I$) (All Sectors) (Model closed with respect to households)	$\displaystyle\sum_{i=1}^{n+1} w_{n+1,i}\,\bar\alpha_{ij}$	
Total Multiplier $[(D+I+I)/N]$	$\displaystyle \bar E_j = \sum_{i=1}^{n+1} w_{n+1,i}\,\bar\alpha_{ij}/\Delta X_j$ $\displaystyle = \sum_{i=1}^{n+1} w_{n+1,i}\,\bar\alpha_{ij}/1 = \sum_{i=1}^{n+1} w_{n+1,i}\,\bar\alpha_{ij}$	$\displaystyle \bar W_j = \sum_{i=1}^{n+1} w_{n+1,i}\,\bar\alpha_{ij}\Big/ w_{n+1,j}$ (also called type II employment multiplier)

TABLE 4-2 SUMMARY OF GENERAL MULTIPLIER FORMULAS AND VALUES
FOR THE NUMERICAL EXAMPLES

Multiplier	Equation Number	Algebraic Definition	Values for Numerical Examples Sector 1	Sector 2
Output				
Simple	(4-6)	$O_j = \sum_{i=1}^{n} \alpha_{ij}$	1.518	1.452
Total	(4-11)	$\bar{O}_j = \sum_{i=1}^{n+1} \bar{\alpha}_{ij}$	2.462	2.262
Income				
Simple Household	(4-12)	$H_j = \sum_{i=1}^{n} a_{n+1,i}\alpha_{ij}$	.442	.380
Total Household	(4-13)	$\bar{H}_j = \sum_{i=1}^{n+1} a_{n+1,i}\bar{\alpha}_{ij}$	.570	.489
Type I	(4-15)	$Y_j = H_j / a_{n+1,j}$	1.470	1.520
Type II	(4-16)	$\bar{Y}_j = \bar{H}_j / a_{n+1,j}$	1.900	1.960
Employment				
Simple Household	(4-18)	$E_j = \sum_{i=1}^{n} w_{n+1,i}\alpha_{ij}$	.00429	.00323
Total Household	(4-19)	$\bar{E}_j = \sum_{i=1}^{n+1} w_{n+1,i}\bar{\alpha}_{ij}$	.00572	.00446
Type I	(4-20)	$W_j = E_j / w_{n+1,j}$	1.430	1.615
Type II	(4-21)	$\bar{W}_j = \bar{E}_j / w_{n+1,j}$	1.907	2.230

appropriate for different kinds of questions than are the measures given in Y (or $\bar{Y}$) and W (or $\bar{W}$). Moreover, one might also consider alternative definitions of the initial effect in output terms—for example, $\sum_{i=1}^{n} a_{ij}$, which is the total initial input requirement across all sectors in the economy needed for one dollar's worth of output from sector j. (On this and other issues regarding definitions of multipliers, the reader is referred to West and Jensen 1980.) We have presented here what appear to us to be the most widely used definitions.

In Table 4-2 we present the multiplier formulas, along with equation numbers and the values of the multipliers from our two-sector numerical example. Table 4-1-1 in Appendix 4-1 contains these multiplier formulas in matrix form.

4-3 | MULTIPLIERS IN REGIONAL MODELS

In Section 4-2 we presented the basic concepts of output, income, and employment multipliers. Given an input-output coefficients matrix, A, output multipliers quantify effects in terms of output in all sectors of the economy in response to an external stimulus in final demand. With estimates of household inputs to each sector in monetary terms, $a_{n+1,j}$, and household consumption coefficients, $a_{i,n+1}$, one can close the model with respect to households and derive total as compared to simple output multipliers. Using the $a_{n+1,j}$ as weights, one can also derive income multipliers. Finally, with estimates of labor inputs to each sector in physical terms, $w_{n+1,j}$, one can derive employment multipliers. All of these measures, which quantify impacts on the economy under study, rely on the fact that the A matrix (as well as the $a_{n+1,j}$, $a_{i,n+1}$, and $w_{n+1,j}$) must represent interindustry relationships *within that economy*. In particular, if sector i is agriculture and sector j is food processing, a_{ij} must represent the value of inputs of agricultural products *produced within the economy* (not imported) per dollar's worth of output of the food-processing sector in the same economy.

Regional Multipliers

Actually, it is very often the case that we are interested in impacts at the regional level. For example, the federal government may be trying to decide where to award a new military contract and have as one of its concerns the stimulation of economic development in one or more less-developed states. A state government may wish to allocate funds for labor skill training in one or more industries among several counties with currently above-average levels of unemployment, and so on. In a single-region input-output model, as in section 3-2 of Chapter 3, the $A^R = \hat{P}A$ matrix represented one way of trying to capture regional interrelationships among sectors, and the various kinds of multipliers discussed above would acquire a spatial dimension by using the elements of A^R and its Leontief inverse.

For example, recall the example of Chapter 3 in which the national table, $A = \begin{bmatrix} .15 & .25 \\ .20 & .05 \end{bmatrix}$, was modified because of the assumption that in region R the basic technology of production in sectors 1 and 2 was essentially the same as that reflected in the two columns of A, but the *proportions* of inputs required from sectors 1 and 2 that could be expected to come from within the region were $p_1 = 0.8$ and $p_2 = 0.6$. Forming $P = \begin{bmatrix} 0.8 \\ 0.6 \end{bmatrix}$, $A^R = \hat{P}A$, and for this example

$$A^R = \begin{bmatrix} .12 & .20 \\ .12 & .03 \end{bmatrix} \quad \text{and} \quad (I - A^R)^{-1} = \begin{bmatrix} 1.169 & 0.241 \\ 0.145 & 1.061 \end{bmatrix}$$

Hence the regional simple output multipliers, as in Eq. (4-6), are $O_1^R = 1.314$ and $O_2^R = 1.302$. Recall from section 4-2, above, that the output multipliers in the original A matrix were $O_1 = 1.518$ and $O_2 = 1.452$. The difference, of course, is due to the fact that the elements of A have been reduced, using the regional percentages in P, to reflect the need for imports to supply some of the necessary production. Similarly, external (not regional, denoted $\tilde{R}$) output multipliers are $O_1^{\tilde{R}} = 1.518 - 1.314 = 0.204$ for sector 1 and $O_2^{\tilde{R}} = 1.452 - 1.302 = 0.150$ for sector 2. The interpretation of these is similar to that for other output multipliers: For each dollar's worth of final demand in the region for sector 1 output, 20.4 cents' worth of output will be needed from firms in all sectors outside of the region. And for each dollar's worth of final demand in the region for sector 2 output, this figure is 15 cents.

If we have estimates of household inputs, household consumption, and income earned in the region, the model can be closed with respect to households, allowing calculation of regional total output multipliers. If we assume that the household input coefficients in the region are the same as those for the nation as a whole and that these represent labor supplied by workers living in the region, then $a_{31}^R = 0.30$, $a_{32}^R = 0.25$, and $a_{33}^R = 0.05$. Also, if we assume that sectors 1 and 2 supply 80 percent and 60 percent, respectively, of consumer needs (the same percentages as they supply of the needs for production), then $a_{13}^R = (0.8)(0.05) = 0.04$ and $a_{23}^R = (0.6)(0.40) = 0.24$ and

$$\bar{A}^R = \begin{bmatrix} .12 & .20 & .04 \\ .12 & .03 & .24 \\ .30 & .25 & .05 \end{bmatrix} \quad \text{and} \quad (I - \bar{A}^R)^{-1} = \begin{bmatrix} 1.217 & 0.282 & 0.123 \\ 0.263 & 1.164 & 0.305 \\ 0.453 & 0.395 & 1.172 \end{bmatrix}$$

Therefore, the regional total output multipliers, as in Eq. (4-11) for sectors 1 and 2, are $\bar{O}_1 = 1.933$ and $\bar{O}_2 = 1.841$.

Similarly, with the information on regional labor inputs (in monetary terms) and household consumption coefficients, various income multipliers can be found for the region. Here, the regional simple household income multipliers, as in Eq. (4-12), are

$$H_1^R = (0.3)(1.169) + (0.25)(0.145) = 0.387$$

$$H_2^R = (0.3)(0.241) + (0.25)(1.061) = 0.338$$

and the regional total income multipliers, as in Eq. (4-13), are

$$\bar{H}_1^R = (0.3)(1.217) + (0.25)(0.263) + (0.05)(0.453) = 0.453$$

$$\bar{H}_2^R = (0.3)(0.282) + (0.25)(1.164) + (0.05)(0.395) = 0.395$$

These total multipliers are, as we have seen in section 4-2, the first two elements in the bottom row of $(I - \bar{A}^R)^{-1}$.

Similarly, the type I and type II income multipliers for the region are found, as in Eqs. (4-15) and (4-16), as

$$Y_1^R = \frac{H_1^R}{a_{31}^R} = \frac{0.387}{0.3} = 1.290$$

$$Y_2^R = \frac{H_2^R}{a_{32}^R} = \frac{0.338}{0.25} = 1.352$$

and

$$\bar{Y}_1^R = \frac{\bar{H}_1^R}{a_{31}^R} = \frac{0.4535}{0.3} = 1.512$$

$$\bar{Y}_2^R = \frac{\bar{H}_2^R}{a_{32}^R} = \frac{0.3954}{0.25} = 1.582$$

With estimates of regional employment (in physical terms) per dollar's worth of output of the two local sectors, we could also calculate various regional employment multipliers. Assume that the physical regional employment coefficients are the same as those in the nation; hence, $w_{31} = 0.003$, $w_{32} = 0.002$, and $w_{33} = 0.001$. Then simple and total regional employment effects (household employment multipliers) are, as in Eqs. (4-18) and (4-19),

$$E_1^R = (0.003)(1.169) + (0.002)(0.145) = 0.00380$$

$$E_2^R = (0.003)(0.241) + (0.002)(1.061) = 0.00285$$

and

$$\overline{E}_1^R = (0.003)(1.217) + (0.002)(0.263) + (0.001)(0.453) = 0.00463$$

$$\overline{E}_2^R = (0.003)(0.282) + (0.002)(1.164) + (0.001)(0.395) = 0.00357$$

Also, type I and type II regional employment multipliers, as in Eqs. (4-20) and (4-21), are, for this example

$$W_1^R = \frac{E_1^R}{0.003} = \frac{0.00380}{0.003} = 1.267$$

$$W_2^R = \frac{E_2^R}{0.002} = \frac{0.00285}{0.002} = 1.425$$

and

$$\overline{W}_1^R = \frac{\overline{E}_1^R}{0.003} = \frac{0.00463}{0.003} = 1.543$$

$$\overline{W}_2^R = \frac{\overline{E}_2^R}{0.002} = \frac{0.00357}{0.002} = 1.785$$

Thus, no new principles are involved in assessing multiplier effects with a single-region table instead of a national table. However, with many-region input-output models, a wider variety of multipliers is possible. We examine these in the interregional and multiregional cases in turn.

Interregional Input-Output Multipliers

The structure of an interregional input-output model was presented in section 3-3 of Chapter 3. For these models, and for multiregional input-output models also, a wider variety of multiplier measures is possible. Essentially, output, income, and employment effects can be calculated for a single region (region L), for each of the other regions, for the "rest of the economy" (aggregated over *all* regions outside of L), and for the total, many-region (national) economy. We illustrate the possibilities using (1) a set of hypothetical data for a two-region model and (2) an interregional model from data for Japan with three regions of five sectors each.

Consider the following coefficient matrices for a two-region interregional model with (the same) three sectors in each region

$$
A = \begin{bmatrix} A^{LL} & | & A^{LM} \\ ---- & + & ---- \\ A^{ML} & | & A^{MM} \end{bmatrix} = \left[\begin{array}{ccc|ccc} .150 & .250 & .050 & .021 & .094 & .017 \\ .200 & .050 & .400 & .167 & .125 & .133 \\ .300 & .250 & .050 & .050 & .050 & .000 \\ \hline .075 & .050 & .060 & .167 & .313 & .067 \\ .050 & .013 & .025 & .125 & .125 & .047 \\ .025 & .100 & .100 & .250 & .250 & .133 \end{array} \right] \qquad (4\text{-}22)
$$

and

$$
(I - A)^{-1} = \left[\begin{array}{ccc|ccc} 1.462 & .506 & .332 & .259 & .382 & .147 \\ .721 & 1.514 & .761 & .558 & .629 & .324 \\ .678 & .578 & 1.378 & .318 & .390 & .147 \\ \hline .318 & .253 & .251 & 1.428 & .649 & .190 \\ .177 & .123 & .124 & .268 & 1.315 & .114 \\ .346 & .365 & .365 & .598 & .695 & 1.300 \end{array} \right] \qquad (4\text{-}23)
$$

where the partitioning separates the two sets of within-region effects for region L and region M (upper left and lower right) and the two sets of between-region effects.

Intraregional Effects   For exogenous changes in final demands for region L goods (the first three elements in the six-element Y vector), the elements in the 3×3 submatrix in the upper left of $(I - A)^{-1}$ represent impacts on the outputs of sectors in region L. Denote this matrix as α^{LL}; here

$$
\alpha^{LL} = \begin{bmatrix} 1.462 & .506 & .332 \\ .721 & 1.514 & .761 \\ .678 & .578 & 1.378 \end{bmatrix} \qquad (4\text{-}24)
$$

Let $O_{.j}^{LL}$ denote the total output from all sectors in region L called forth by a dollar's worth of output by sector j in region L; these simple intraregional output multipliers are found as the column sums of this 3×3 matrix; here $O_{.1}^{LL} = 2.861$, $O_{.2}^{LL} = 2.598$, and $O_{.3}^{LL} = 2.471$. Arranged as a row vector, $O^{LL} = i'[\alpha^{LL}]$; here

$$
O^{LL} = \begin{bmatrix} 2.861 & 2.598 & 2.471 \end{bmatrix} \qquad (4\text{-}25)
$$

Similarly, using the column sums in the 3×3 submatrix in the lower right of $(I - A)^{-1}$, we find $O^{MM} = i'[\alpha^{MM}]$; here

$$
O^{MM} = \begin{bmatrix} 2.294 & 2.659 & 1.604 \end{bmatrix} \qquad (4\text{-}26)
$$

If we had household input coefficients in monetary terms for regions L ($a_{n+1,j}^{LL}$) and M ($a_{n+1,j}^{MM}$), we could find simple intraregional household income multipliers and type I income multipliers. Similarly, if we had intraregional physical labor input coefficients ($w_{n+1,j}^{LL}$ and $w_{n+1,j}^{MM}$), we could find simple intraregional employment multipliers and type I employment multipliers. Note that finding total intraregional output multipliers, household income multipliers, or type II income multipliers requires that we have labor input coefficients (in monetary terms) and household consumption coefficients for four different matrices. Initially, the input coefficient matrix for region L—A^{LL} in Eq. (4-22) —must be closed with respect to households. This then adds a row to A^{LM} and a column to A^{ML}. The former represents inputs of labor from region L to sector 1 and 2 production in region M (commuters). The latter represents purchases of outputs of sectors 1 and 2 in region M by consumers located in region L (imports of consumer goods). For complete consistency, in order to capture income-generating effects throughout the entire (here, two-region) system, the input coefficient matrix for region M—A^{MM} in Eq. (4-22)—should also be closed with respect to households. This then additionally requires a new row in A^{ML} and a new column in A^{LM}. These new coefficients represent inputs of labor from region M to production in L and purchases by consumers in M of goods made in L, respectively. Thus the $\bar{A}$ and $(I - \bar{A})^{-1}$ matrices, for our numerical example, would grow from 6×6 to 8×8, using overbars to represent a matrix closed with respect to households, as usual.

Given this $(I - \bar{A})^{-1}$ matrix, total intraregional output multipliers, household income multipliers, and type II income multipliers for region L would be found using the elements from the upper left submatrix—now 4×4—in $(I - \bar{A})^{-1}$. Similarly, using intraregional physical labor input coefficients for both regions, total intraregional employment multipliers and type II employment multipliers could be found.

Interregional Effects   The essence of an interregional (or multiregional) input-output model is that it includes impacts in one region that are caused by changes in another region; these are often termed the interregional spillover effects. In $(I - A)^{-1}$ in Eq. (4-23) the elements in the lower-left submatrix, which we can denote by α^{ML}, are

$$\alpha^{ML} = \begin{bmatrix} .318 & .253 & .251 \\ .177 & .123 & .124 \\ .346 & .365 & .365 \end{bmatrix} \qquad (4\text{-}27)$$

For example, $\alpha_{21}^{ML} = 0.177$; this is to be interpreted as follows: For each dollar's worth of output by sector 1 in region L, 17.7 cents' worth of the output of sector 2 in region M is used as input.

Thus, in an interregional input-output model, we can calculate simple interregional multipliers, $O_{\cdot j}^{ML}$, the total value of output from all sectors in region M used in producing a dollar's worth of output of sector j in region L. Here, then, the simple interregional output multipliers, reflecting exogenous changes in region L, are $O_{\cdot 1}^{ML} = 0.841$, $O_{\cdot 2}^{ML} = 0.741$, and $O_{\cdot 3}^{ML} = 0.740$, or, as a row vector, $O^{ML} = i'[\alpha^{ML}]$; here

$$O^{ML} = \begin{bmatrix} 0.841 & 0.741 & 0.740 \end{bmatrix} \qquad (4\text{-}28)$$

These are output impacts that are transmitted across regional boundaries—here from L to M. As the reader can perhaps imagine by now, we have the same set of possibilities for measuring various interregional income effects, interregional employment effects, and total interregional effects using the same kinds of calculations as for intraregional effects, now using α^{ML} (and $\bar{\alpha}^{ML}$ if the regions were closed with respect to households). Note that interregional effects whose origins are in new production in region M would be calculated using the elements of α^{LM} (or $\bar{\alpha}^{LM}$). Here $O^{LM} = i'[\alpha^{LM}]$

$$O^{LM} = [\,1.135 \quad 1.401 \quad 0.618\,] \tag{4-29}$$

National Effects   Assuming, once again, that there are exogenous increases in final demands for region L goods and hence in outputs of region L sectors, we can denote as national effects the sums of columns in both α^{LL} and α^{ML}. (These could logically also be termed *total* effects, but we have used *total*, as contrasted with *simple*, for effects that are calculated from a matrix that has households endogenous.) Using O_j^L for the simple output multiplier reflecting production by all sectors in all (here both) regions to provide inputs to a dollar's worth of production by sector j in region L, we find $O_1^L = 3.702$, $O_2^L = 3.339$, and $O_3^L = 3.211$. For this example, $O_{.j}^L = O_{.j}^{LL} + O_{.j}^{ML}$. Similarly, $O_1^M = 3.429$, $O_2^M = 4.060$, and $O_3^M = 2.222$. Arranged as row vectors,

$$O^L = [\,3.702 \quad 3.339 \quad 3.211\,] \tag{4-30}$$

and

$$O^M = [\,3.429 \quad 4.060 \quad 2.222\,] \tag{4-31}$$

For the two-region interregional system, let $O = [\,O^L \mathrel{\vdots} O^M\,]$. Here

$$O = [\,3.702 \quad 3.339 \quad 3.211 \quad 3.429 \quad 4.060 \quad 2.222\,] \tag{4-32}$$

A policy implication from these figures is that government spending on the output of sector 2 in region M would have the greatest impact throughout the two-region economy, as measured by total output (direct plus indirect) required from all sectors in both regions, per dollar of final demand. Similarly, if the government is interested in acquiring goods from sector 1 or sector 3, the greatest *national* (both regions) economic impact will occur if the purchases are made from firms in region L.

Again, using information on labor inputs in each region, simple and type I income and employment effects could be calculated at the national (all regions) level. Similarly, for a system in which all regions have been closed with respect to households, total national output, income, and employment effects and type II multipliers can be found.

Sectoral Effects   As a final kind of multiplier, we can find the impact *on sector i* throughout the entire country, because of a dollar's worth of output of sector j in region L. (Since this crosses regional boundaries, this is also a kind of "national" effect.) Denote this simple output multiplier as $O_{ij}^{.L}$. For our example, $O_{13}^{.L} = \alpha_{13}^{LL} + \alpha_{13}^{ML} = 0.332 + 0.251 = 0.583$, $O_{21}^{.M} = \alpha_{21}^{MM} + \alpha_{21}^{LM} = 0.268 + 0.558 = 0.826$, and so on. With region-specific labor input coefficients, we could find various simple or type I income and employment effects; with elements from $(I - \bar{A})^{-1}$, we would find total multipliers and type II effects. (These sectoral effects are most easily found when each region contains the same sectors.)

More Than Two Regions   With models of more than two regions, there are no new principles involved, although the possibilities increase. For example, with three regions (L, M, and N), one can trace interregional effects in now six different ways: (1) exogenous changes in L affecting outputs in M and/or N, (2) exogenous changes in M affecting outputs in L and/or N, and (3) exogenous changes in N affecting outputs in L and/or M. The five-sector, three-region version of the Japanese 1965 interregional system illustrated in Chapter 3 provides an example. This represents an extremely complete and detailed set of interregional input-output relationships based on actual survey data. The Leontief inverse matrix for that model is repeated here in Table 4-3. (This was Table 3-4 in Chapter 3. Recall that the regions are [1] Central, which includes Tokyo, [2] North, and [3] South. These were illustrated in Fig. 3-2 in Chapter 3.) Since this model was open with respect to households, we present the simple intra- and interregional output multipliers for this model of Japan in Table 4-4 (these are column sums of the nine submatrices in Table 4-3), along with the national (all-region) figures.

Since the North and South regions in this model are aggregates of a number of subregions (three in the North, five in the South), with large proportions of the total land area of Japan, it is not surprising that the national multipliers are quite uniform across regions. Thus, sector 2, mining, has the highest simple output multiplier, regardless of where the original stimulus in final demand occurs, and it lies within the range 1.950–2.473. Similarly, the lowest multiplier is associated with new final demand for the output of sector 5, all other sectors, and this has a range of 1.501–1.625, across originating regions, and so on. We see also that the Central region, in general, depends more heavily on the South than the North for imports of inputs to production. The South depends more heavily on the Central than the North region, as might be expected from the geography of Japan, since the South and Central regions are adjacent, while the South and North are separated by the Central region between them. Interestingly, however, the North depends approximately equally on the Central and South regions for its inputs.

Sector-specific simple output multipliers, O_{ij}^{L}, are presented in Table 4-5. Again, we find a certain amount of uniformity across regions. For example, with new demand for sector 3 output in the Central, North, and South regions, the national impact on sector 4 is 0.022, 0.022, and 0.020, respectively; new demand for sector 5 output leads to impacts of 0.375, 0.283, and 0.412 on sector 3, when originating in the Central, North, and South regions, respectively. Again, this is a reflection of the relatively large sizes of the geographical regions in this three-region division of the country. As regions get large, their economic structures look more and more alike.

Measuring Interregional Feedback Effects with Output Multipliers

In Chapter 3 we noted that one measure of the importance of interregional feedbacks in an interregional input-output model was given by the overall percentage error (OPE). This was defined to be $[(i'X_T^L - i'X_S^L)/i'X_T^L] \times 100$, where X_S^L and X_T^L represent the vectors of gross output in region L found from a single-region model and from a full interregional model, respectively, for a

TABLE 4-3 Leontief Inverse Matrix for the Five-Sector, Three-Region Japanese Interregional Input-Output System (1965)

Industry	Central Industry 1	2	3	4	5	North Industry 1	2	3	4	5	South Industry 1	2	3	4	5
Central															
1 Agriculture	1.064	.012	.015	.019	.014	.005	.006	.011	.004	.003	.003	.003	.004	.002	.002
2 Mining	.001	1.002	.001	.002	.003	.001	.001	.002	.001	.001	.000	.000	.000	.000	.000
3 Construction & Manufacturing	.639	1.016	1.380	.413	.299	.064	.067	.110	.043	.045	.082	.085	.099	.041	.051
4 Transportation	.008	.013	.016	1.107	.019	.002	.003	.005	.019	.003	.002	.002	.003	.010	.002
5 Other	.050	.088	.072	.170	1.161	.013	.017	.029	.014	.019	.013	.016	.019	.011	.025
North															
1 Agriculture	.007	.003	.001	.001	.001	1.108	.015	.024	.053	.030	.003	.002	.001	.002	.000
2 Mining	.000	.001	.000	.000	.000	.003	1.008	.003	.010	.013	.000	.000	.000	.000	.000
3 Construction & Manufacturing	.108	.087	.038	.019	.012	.488	.648	1.218	.335	.200	.059	.055	.025	.018	.009
4 Transportation	.001	.004	.001	.017	.001	.005	.015	.013	1.031	.014	.001	.001	.001	.026	.001
5 Other	.008	.042	.003	.004	.002	.028	.059	.038	.121	1.124	.004	.011	.002	.004	.002
South															
1 Agriculture	.006	.005	.005	.003	.002	.006	.006	.010	.004	.002	1.089	.016	.020	.026	.017
2 Mining	.000	.001	.001	.000	.000	.001	.001	.001	.000	.000	.002	1.006	.002	.004	.005
3 Construction & Manufacturing	.150	.173	.179	.072	.064	.075	.089	.128	.051	.038	.773	1.099	1.488	.481	.352
4 Transportation	.003	.005	.005	.031	.002	.002	.003	.004	.026	.002	.009	.016	.016	1.081	.018
5 Other	.013	.021	.017	.011	.009	.009	.012	.020	.010	.007	.049	.105	.065	.156	1.141

TABLE 4-4 Simple Intra- and Interregional Output Multipliers for the Japanese Interregional Input-Output System

Total Output in Each Region (or the Nation) to Satisfy the One-Unit Change in Final Demand

| | Region and Sector Experiencing a One-Unit Change in Final Demand | | | | | | | | | | | | | | |
| | Central | | | | | North | | | | | South | | | | |
	1	2	3	4	5	1	2	3	4	5	1	2	3	4	5
Central	1.762	2.131	1.484	1.711	1.496	.085	.094	.157	.081	.071	.100	.106	.125	.064	.080
North	.124	.137	.043	.041	.016	1.632	1.745	1.296	1.550	1.381	.067	.069	.029	.050	.012
South	.172	.205	.207	.117	.077	.093	.111	.163	.091	.049	1.922	2.242	1.591	1.748	1.533
Nation	2.058	2.473	1.734	1.869	1.589	1.810	1.950	1.616	1.722	1.501	2.089	2.417	1.745	1.862	1.625

TABLE 4-5 Sector-Specific Simple Output Multipliers for the Japanese Interregional Input-Output System

| | Sector 1 | | | Sector 2 | | | Sector 3 | | | Sector 4 | | | Sector 5 | | |
	Central	North	South	Central	North	South	Central	North	South	Central	North	South	Central	North	South
1	1.077	1.119	1.095	.022	.027	.021	.021	.045	.025	.023	.061	.030	.017	.035	.019
2	.001	.005	.002	1.004	1.010	1.006	.002	.006	.002	.002	.011	.004	.003	.014	.005
3	.897	.627	.914	1.276	.804	1.239	1.597	1.456	1.612	.504	.429	.540	.375	.283	.412
4	.012	.009	.012	.022	.021	.019	.022	.022	.020	1.155	1.076	1.117	.022	.019	.021
5	.071	.050	.066	.151	.088	.132	.092	.087	.086	.185	.145	.171	1.172	1.150	1.168

particular level of final demand, Y^L; that is, $X_S^L = (I - A^{LL})^{-1}Y^L$ and $X_T^L = \alpha^{LL}Y^L$. When the vector Y^L contains $n-1$ zeros and a 1 in the ith row, then, as we saw at the beginning of this chapter, X_S^L and X_T^L would contain just the ith columns of $(I - A^{LL})^{-1}$ and α^{LL}, respectively. Summing the elements in these columns—that is, $i'X_S^L$ and $i'X_T^L$—would give the output multiplier for sector i in region L found in the single-region and interregional models, respectively.

From the hypothetical two-region interregional data given in Eq. (4-22) we found, in Eq. (4-25),

$$i'\alpha^{LL} = O^{LL} = \begin{bmatrix} 2.861 & 2.598 & 2.471 \end{bmatrix}$$

For the elements in A^{LL} in Eq. (4-22), $(I - A^{LL})^{-1}$ was found in Chapter 3 to be

$$(I - A^{LL})^{-1} = \begin{bmatrix} 1.365 & 0.425 & 0.251 \\ 0.527 & 1.348 & 0.595 \\ 0.570 & 0.489 & 1.289 \end{bmatrix}$$

Thus the three output multipliers for region L in this single-region model are found as

$$i'(I - A^{LL})^{-1} = \begin{bmatrix} 2.462 & 2.262 & 2.135 \end{bmatrix}$$

The differences in the multipliers from the two models are

$$D^L = \begin{bmatrix} i'\alpha^{LL} - i'(I - A^{LL})^{-1} \end{bmatrix} = \begin{bmatrix} 0.399 & 0.336 & 0.336 \end{bmatrix}$$

We can express the total difference as a percent of the total "true" interregional figure. This is the analogue to the overall percentage error measure that was used in Chapter 3. We want the sum of the elements in D^L divided by the sum of the elements in $i'\alpha^{LL}$ (and multiplied by 100). For this example

$$\begin{bmatrix} D^L i / (i'\alpha^{LL})i \end{bmatrix} \times 100 = (1.071/7.930) \times 100 = 13.5$$

That is, on average the output multipliers for the sectors of region L would be underestimated by 13.5 percent when a single-region model was used instead of the full two-region interregional model.

Similarly, in Eq. (4-26) we found that

$$i'\alpha^{MM} = O^{MM} = \begin{bmatrix} 2.294 & 2.659 & 1.604 \end{bmatrix}$$

These are the three output multipliers in region M in the full two-region interregional model. Using A^{MM} from Eq. (4-22) we can find that

$$(I - A^{MM})^{-1} = \begin{bmatrix} 1.315 & 0.507 & 0.129 \\ 0.212 & 1.242 & 0.084 \\ 0.440 & 0.505 & 1.215 \end{bmatrix}$$

and therefore

$$i'(I - A^{MM})^{-1} = \begin{bmatrix} 1.967 & 2.254 & 1.428 \end{bmatrix}$$

These are the output multipliers in region M when only a single-region model is used. Therefore

$$D^M = \begin{bmatrix} i'\alpha^{MM} - i'(I - A^{MM})^{-1} \end{bmatrix} = \begin{bmatrix} 0.327 & 0.405 & 0.176 \end{bmatrix}$$

and

$$\left[D^M i / (i'\alpha^{MM})i \right] \times 100 = (0.908/6.557) \times 100 = 13.8$$

This represents the average amount (in percent) by which output multipliers for sectors in region M would be underestimated if a single-region model were used in place of the interregional model.

Over the entire two-region economy, then, the differences in multiplier values are $D^L i + D^M i = 1.071 + 0.908 = 1.979$. Similarly, over the two regions, the total of all output multipliers from the full interregional model is $(i'\alpha^{LL})i + (i'\alpha^{MM})i = 7.930 + 6.557 = 14.487$. Therefore, the average amount by which an output multiplier in a single-region model of the hypothetical two-region economy of Eq. (4-22) will underestimate the "true" multiplier from a full interregional model is 13.7 percent. This can be viewed as a measure of the error that would be associated with the use of a single-region model (for either region) for this example.

If errors of this magnitude were generally found in studies utilizing real-world input-output data, it would suggest that a single-region model would give misleading and inaccurate results, even when one is interested only in

TABLE 4-6 MEASURES OF INTERREGIONAL FEEDBACK EFFECTS IN REAL-WORLD INTERREGIONAL INPUT-OUTPUT MODELS

Author and Source	Number and Description of Regions	Number of Sectors in Each Region	Average Error in Output Multipliers when Interregional Feedbacks Were Ignored (Percent)[a]
Yamada and Ihara (1968, Tables 1-1, 5-1, and 5-2)	2 [Kinki, Tokaido (Japan)]	10	0.69
	2 [Kinki, Kanto (Japan)]	10	0.42
Riefler and Tiebout (1970, Table 4)	2 [Washington, California (U.S.)]	31 (Washington) 22 (California)	2.95
Greytak (1970, Table 1)[b]	8 (Regions of the United States)	23	14.4
Beyers (1974, Table 1)	3 (Puget Sound region, rest of Washington, rest of the United States)	22	1.62
Oosterhaven (1981, Tables 4.3, 6.5)	3 (Rijnmond region, Northern Netherlands, rest of the Netherlands)	10[c]	2.1 (Model with households exogenous) 7.0 (Model with households endogenous)
Beyers (1983, Table 1)	51 (States of the United States plus District of Columbia)	1	0.76
Eskelinen (1983, Table 3)	3 (Greater Helsinki, Northern Karelia, rest of Finland)	8	0.75

[a]Averaged over all sectors in all regions.
[b]In Greytak (1974), the two kinds of multipliers are compared from the point of their "information" content. This measure indicates a much higher error caused by ignoring interregional feedbacks.
[c]Results were chosen for 10 "large" sectors from a 23-sector model.

output effects in that single region. However, it appears that interregional feedback effects in real-world models are much smaller. Results from several studies (presented in chronological order) are summarized in Table 4-6. It should be emphasized that not all these studies were conducted expressly or even primarily to assess the magnitudes of interregional feedbacks, and that we have chosen to calculate only one measure of error (overall percentage error, as just described) that is introduced into the output multipliers by omission of such feedbacks. Some authors have questioned whether or not the initial 1.0 in the multipliers should be dropped when making these kinds of comparisons. That is, even with *no* model of sectoral interaction, one would surely estimate, at a minimum, that there would be one dollar's worth of new output from sector j in region L when final demand for output from sector j in region L increased by one dollar. Then the regional input-output model accounts for the further direct and indirect effects and the interregional input-output model adds in the interregional feedback effects. However, in Table 4-6 we have compared the entire multiplier values in both single-region and interregional models.

Multiregional Input-Output Multipliers

All of the multipliers that we found in the interregional input-output model have their counterparts in the multiregional model. This is to be expected, since the multiregional model is an attempt to capture all of the connections in the interregional model using a simpler set of data; but each of the components, for example, A^{LL} and A^{LM}, in the interregional case has its counterpart estimate, for example, $\hat{C}^{LL}A^L$ and $\hat{C}^{LM}A^M$, in the multiregional case.

Recall from Chapter 3 that the final form of the interregional model was

$$X = (I - A)^{-1}Y \tag{4-33}$$

as in Eq. (3-18) in Chapter 3, where, for the two-region case,

$$A = \begin{bmatrix} A^{LL} & A^{LM} \\ \hline A^{ML} & A^{MM} \end{bmatrix}, \qquad X = \begin{bmatrix} X^L \\ \hline X^M \end{bmatrix} \quad \text{and} \quad Y = \begin{bmatrix} Y^L \\ \hline Y^M \end{bmatrix}.$$

In the multiregional case, as in Eq. (3-30) in Chapter 3, we have

$$X = (I - CA)^{-1}CY \tag{4-34}$$

Here $A = \begin{bmatrix} A^L & 0 \\ \hline 0 & A^M \end{bmatrix}$, a block diagonal matrix whose submatrices represent

regional technical (not regional input) coefficients and $C = \begin{bmatrix} \hat{C}^{LL} & \hat{C}^{LM} \\ \hline \hat{C}^{ML} & \hat{C}^{MM} \end{bmatrix}$,

where the components of the submatrices in C represent flows between regions in the form of proportions of a commodity in a region that come from within the region and from each of the other regions.

The important point to be recalled is that in the interregional model the exogenous sectors represent final demands, wherever located, for goods made by producers in a particular region. In the multiregional model, the Y's represent demands exercised by exogenous sectors located in a given region for goods, wherever produced. For a two-region multiregional model, it is the $\hat{C}^{LL}$ and $\hat{C}^{ML}$

matrices that spatially distribute the final demand in region L between producers in L and producers in M.

For example, assume that there are two sectors in each of the two regions, L and M, and that we want to assess the impact throughout the two-region system of an increase of \$100 in final demand for good 1 by households located in region L. That is, $Y^L = \begin{bmatrix} 100 \\ 0 \end{bmatrix}$ and $Y^M = \begin{bmatrix} 0 \\ 0 \end{bmatrix}$ and thus

$$
Y = \begin{bmatrix} Y^L \\ \hline Y^M \end{bmatrix} = \begin{bmatrix} 100 \\ 0 \\ \hline 0 \\ 0 \end{bmatrix}
$$

Let

$$
\hat{C}^{LL} = \begin{bmatrix} 0.7 & 0 \\ 0 & 0.4 \end{bmatrix}, \quad \hat{C}^{LM} = \begin{bmatrix} 0.2 & 0 \\ 0 & 0.3 \end{bmatrix}, \quad \hat{C}^{ML} = \begin{bmatrix} 0.3 & 0 \\ 0 & 0.6 \end{bmatrix},
$$

and $\hat{C}^{MM} = \begin{bmatrix} 0.8 & 0 \\ 0 & 0.7 \end{bmatrix}$.

Then

$$
C = \begin{bmatrix} \hat{C}^{LL} & \hat{C}^{LM} \\ \hline \hat{C}^{ML} & \hat{C}^{MM} \end{bmatrix} = \begin{bmatrix} 0.7 & 0 & 0.2 & 0 \\ 0 & 0.4 & 0 & 0.3 \\ \hline 0.3 & 0 & 0.8 & 0 \\ 0 & 0.6 & 0 & 0.7 \end{bmatrix}
$$

and hence, the CY term that postmultiplies $(I - CA)^{-1}$ on the right-hand side of Eq. (4-34) is

$$
CY = \begin{bmatrix} 0.7 & 0 & 0.2 & 0 \\ 0 & 0.4 & 0 & 0.3 \\ \hline 0.3 & 0 & 0.8 & 0 \\ 0 & 0.6 & 0 & 0.7 \end{bmatrix} \begin{bmatrix} 100 \\ 0 \\ \hline 0 \\ 0 \end{bmatrix} = \begin{bmatrix} 70 \\ 0 \\ \hline 30 \\ 0 \end{bmatrix}
$$

That is, the impact of all of the new \$100 is not felt in region L, rather only \$70 (70 percent) is presented as new demand for good 1 made in region L, and \$30 (30 percent) turns out to be new demand for good 1 in region M.

The C matrix distributes the final demands in the multiregional model across supplying regions in accordance with the percentages embodied in the components of C. Premultiplication of CY by $(I - CA)^{-1}$ then converts these distributed final demands into necessary outputs from each sector in each region in the usual way. Thus the matrix from which the various multipliers are derived in the multiregional model is $(I - CA)^{-1}C$.

In the first numerical illustration for a multiregional model in Chapter 3, with two regions of three sectors each, we had

$$
A = \begin{bmatrix} A^L & 0 \\ \hline 0 & A^M \end{bmatrix} = \begin{bmatrix} .225 & .300 & .110 & 0 & 0 & 0 \\ .250 & .063 & .425 & 0 & 0 & 0 \\ .325 & .350 & .150 & 0 & 0 & 0 \\ \hline 0 & 0 & 0 & .188 & .406 & .083 \\ 0 & 0 & 0 & .292 & .250 & .180 \\ 0 & 0 & 0 & .300 & .300 & .133 \end{bmatrix} \tag{4-35}
$$

and

$$C = \begin{bmatrix} \hat{C}^{LL} & | & \hat{C}^{LM} \\ \hline \hat{C}^{ML} & | & \hat{C}^{MM} \end{bmatrix} = \begin{bmatrix} .721 & 0 & 0 & | & .183 & 0 & 0 \\ 0 & .812 & 0 & | & 0 & .583 & 0 \\ 0 & 0 & .735 & | & 0 & 0 & .078 \\ \hline .279 & 0 & 0 & | & .817 & 0 & 0 \\ 0 & .188 & 0 & | & 0 & .417 & 0 \\ 0 & 0 & .265 & | & 0 & 0 & .922 \end{bmatrix} \qquad (4\text{-}36)$$

and thus

$$(I - CA)^{-1}C = \begin{bmatrix} 1.127 & .447 & .300 & | & .478 & .418 & .153 \\ .628 & 1.317 & .606 & | & .552 & 1.115 & .323 \\ .512 & .526 & 1.101 & | & .335 & .470 & .247 \\ \hline .625 & .369 & .250 & | & 1.224 & .456 & .216 \\ .238 & .385 & .205 & | & .278 & .650 & .167 \\ .472 & .445 & .589 & | & .594 & .529 & 1.232 \end{bmatrix} \qquad (4\text{-}37)$$

(This was Eq. [3-31] in Chapter 3.) This matrix plays the same role for multiplier analysis in the multiregional model that $(I - A)^{-1}$ in Eq. (4-23) did for the interregional case. We examine some of these possibilities; the parallels with the interregional case should be clear, so the illustrations need not be exhaustive.

Intraregional Effects Column sums of elements in the 3×3 upper left and lower right submatrices are simple intraregional output multipliers. As before, we can denote these submatrices in the complete inverse as α^{LL} and α^{MM}, for the two-region case. These multipliers correspond to Eqs. (4-25) and (4-26), above; and, as above, $O^{LL} = i'[\alpha^{LL}]$ and $O^{MM} = i'[\alpha^{MM}]$. Here

$$O^{LL} = [2.267 \quad 2.290 \quad 2.007] \qquad (4\text{-}38)$$

and

$$O^{MM} = [2.096 \quad 1.635 \quad 1.615] \qquad (4\text{-}39)$$

For example, $O_{.2}^{LL} = 2.290$ indicates that an increase of one dollar in the demand from, say, households (exogenous) located in region L for the product of sector 2 (which may be supplied by producers in region L or region M) calls forth a total of \$2.29 worth of new output from all sectors in region L.

As before, income and employment multipliers could be found if we had additional data on labor inputs in each region in monetary and/or physical terms. Closing the multiregional model with respect to households, in order to be able to calculate total and type II multipliers, requires the addition of regional labor input coefficient rows and household consumption coefficient columns to each of the regional input matrices in A, and it requires an estimate of $c_{n+1,\,n+1}^{LL}$, $c_{n+1,\,n+1}^{LM}$, and so on—these are the proportions of household demands for labor services that are expected to be supplied from within and from outside of each region. These coefficients would be added to the lower right of each diagonal C^{LL}, C^{LM}, and so on, matrix; in general, they would be expected to be near to unity. Given $(I - \overline{CA})^{-1}\overline{C}$, using overbars to indicate a model in which households have been made endogenous, we could find these various intraregional multipliers in the usual way, from the upper left and lower right submatrices.

Interregional Effects   As in the interregional model, these effects are derived from the square matrices that are not on the main diagonal in $(I - CA)^{-1}C$ in Eq. (4-37); these are α^{ML} and α^{LM} in our previous notation, for the two-region case. Here, corresponding to Eqs. (4-28) and (4-29), above, we have the following simple interregional output multipliers, where $O^{ML} = i'[\alpha^{ML}]$, and so on

$$O^{ML} = [1.335 \quad 1.199 \quad 1.044] \tag{4-40}$$

and

$$O^{LM} = [1.365 \quad 2.003 \quad 0.723] \tag{4-41}$$

From $O_2^{ML} = 1.199$, we conclude that the sectors in region M will produce a total of \$1.20 worth of new output because of a dollar's worth of new demand for product 2 by consumers located in region L.

National Effects   Corresponding to Eqs. (4-30) and (4-31), above, we have the following simple output multipliers that reflect production in all sectors in all (here, the two) regions to support a dollar's worth of new final demand for a particular good. $O^L = O^{LL} + O^{ML}$ and $O^M = O^{MM} + O^{LM}$, as before.

$$O^L = [3.602 \quad 3.489 \quad 3.051] \tag{4-42}$$

and

$$O^M = [3.461 \quad 3.638 \quad 2.338] \tag{4-43}$$

Thus, a new dollar's worth of demand from households located in L for good 2 generates a total of \$3.49 new output throughout the entire (here, two-region) multiregional system. Arranged in a single row vector, $O = [O^L \mathrel{\vdots} O^M]$, and parallel to Eq. (4-32), we have

$$O = [3.602 \quad 3.489 \quad 3.051 \quad 3.461 \quad 3.638 \quad 2.338] \tag{4-44}$$

and similar kinds of policy implications can be drawn from these figures. For example, assume that the government could stimulate consumer demand in a particular region for a particular product (e.g., through tax credits, as for insulation and storm windows in cold regions). The greatest overall (national) effect, as measured by these simple national output multipliers, would come from consumer demand in region M for good 2.

Sectoral Effects   Finally, as with the interregional model, we can assess the impact on sector i throughout the economy of a dollar's worth of new final demand in region L for good j. As before, let $O_{ij}^{\cdot L}$ denote this particular kind of simple sector-specific output multiplier. Here, for example, $O_{13}^{\cdot L} = \alpha_{13}^{LL} + \alpha_{13}^{ML} = 0.300 + 0.250 = 0.550$, $O_{21}^{\cdot M} = \alpha_{21}^{MM} + \alpha_{21}^{LM} = 0.278 + 0.552 = 0.830$, and so on.

Final Demand for Goods Made in a Particular Region   If one is using the version of the multiregional input-output model in which impacts of new *region-specific* final demands are being assessed (as in the example of a foreign airline's new order for Boeing jetliners made in the state of Washington), where

$$X = (I - CA)^{-1} Y*$$

as in Eq. (3-32) in Chapter 3, then all of the multiplier calculations outlined above would be found from the elements in $(I - CA)^{-1}$ rather than $(I - CA)^{-1}C$. The $(I - CA)^{-1}$ matrix for this numerical example was given in Eq. (3-33) in Chapter 3. The interested reader may wish to find the various multipliers, as in Eqs. (4-38) through (4-43).

More Than Two Regions   As before, with models of more than two regions, there are no new principles involved, although the possibilities for multiplier calculations increase. For example, with three regions, there are three possible settings in which to calculate various intraregional multiplier effects and six in which to calculate interregional effects.

In section 3-4 of Chapter 3 we introduced a five-sector, three-region aggregation of the U.S. 1963 multiregional input-output model. The $(I - CA)^{-1}C$ inverse matrix for that model is repeated below, in Table 4-7. (This was Table 3-13 in Chapter 3.) The states in each regional classification were listed in Chapter 3; recall that the East includes the New England, Middle Atlantic, and South Atlantic census regions, the Central region here includes the East North Central, West North Central, East South Central, and West South Central census regions. These are obviously extremely large geographic aggregates, and the relative uniformity of the simple output multipliers across regions, as indicated in the tables to follow, reflects this. (A similar uniformity was observed in the Japanese interregional input-output model, above.) Again, if final demands are for products made in specific regions, we would use the version of the multiregional model given in Eq. (3-32), and the appropriate inverse matrix would be $(I - CA)^{-1}$ in Table 3-16 of Chapter 3.

Simple intra- and interregional output multipliers for this U.S. model are presented in Table 4-8. (These are, as usual, the column sums of the submatrices in Table 4-7.) In addition, simple national (all-region) multipliers are shown.

In the sectoral breakdown used in this model, sector 2, mining, has the largest simple output multiplier in all regions; it lies within the range 2.12–2.19. It is followed closely by sector 3, manufacturing, with a (very narrow) range of 2.03–2.07. Sector 4, services, has uniformly the smallest simple output multiplier, across all three regions; in fact, to two decimal places, it is 1.50 in all three regions.

Both the economic structure and the geographical juxtaposition of the three regions in this model are reflected in the figures in Table 4-8. For example, the East depends more heavily on the Central (adjacent) region than on the West for inputs. Similarly, the West depends more on the Central region than on the East. The Central region's total connections to the East are about twice as strong as its connections to the West, as measured by the sums of the five simple output multipliers, generated by stimuli in all sectors in the Central region, in the

TABLE 4-7 Inverse Multiplier Matrix for the U.S. Multiregional Input-Output Model (1963)

	East Industry					Central Industry					West Industry				
Industry	1	2	3	4	5	1	2	3	4	5	1	2	3	4	5
East															
1 Agriculture	.658	.005	.012	.005	.039	.062	.002	.007	.002	.016	.022	.002	.004	.001	.012
2 Mining	.004	.681	.032	.003	.005	.002	.101	.015	.002	.003	.002	.043	.010	.001	.003
3 Construction & Manufacturing	.125	.182	1.009	.085	.130	.047	.084	.292	.040	.074	.035	.061	.204	.028	.060
4 Services	.105	.144	.163	1.032	.128	.060	.074	.083	.220	.069	.039	.052	.060	.117	.054
5 Transportation and Utilities	.017	.015	.064	.008	.896	.009	.010	.039	.005	.254	.007	.008	.030	.004	.201
Central															
1 Agriculture	.383	.011	.024	.006	.050	.905	.013	.042	.011	.075	.222	.008	.021	.005	.047
2 Mining	.011	.598	.058	.007	.012	.011	1.192	.088	.009	.014	.008	.463	.048	.006	.011
3 Construction & Manufacturing	.103	.177	.448	.056	.114	.131	.229	1.134	.096	.168	.070	.134	.335	.045	.097
4 Services	.120	.147	.111	.245	.095	.222	.225	.187	1.031	.154	.091	.123	.091	.186	.083
5 Transportation and Utilities	.018	.020	.059	.008	.394	.021	.022	.096	.011	1.008	.014	.015	.050	.007	.322
West															
1 Agriculture	.039	.002	.004	.001	.009	.089	.003	.007	.002	.013	.832	.005	.026	.006	.077
2 Mining	.002	.079	.009	.001	.002	.002	.154	.014	.002	.003	.005	.941	.043	.004	.006
3 Construction & Manufacturing	.013	.025	.048	.007	.014	.019	.036	.073	.010	.019	.097	.131	.905	.071	.096
4 Services	.017	.026	.018	.034	.015	.031	.041	.025	.053	.020	.177	.172	.146	1.014	.113
5 Transportation and Utilities	.002	.003	.007	.001	.038	.003	.003	.010	.001	.063	.014	.009	.052	.006	.804

TABLE 4-8 SIMPLE INTRA- AND INTERREGIONAL OUTPUT MULTIPLIERS FOR THE U.S. MULTIREGIONAL INPUT-OUTPUT SYSTEM

Total Output in Each Region (or the Nation) to Satisfy the One-Unit Change in Final Demand	Region and Sector Experiencing a One-Unit Change in Final Demand														
	East					Central					West				
	1	2	3	4	5	1	2	3	4	5	1	2	3	4	5
East	.909	1.027	1.280	1.133	1.198	.180	.271	.364	.269	.416	.105	.166	.308	.151	.330
Central	.635	.953	.700	.322	.665	1.290	1.681	1.547	1.158	1.419	.405	.743	.545	.249	.560
West	.073	.135	.086	.044	.078	.144	.237	.129	.068	.118	1.125	1.258	1.172	1.101	1.096
Nation	1.617	2.115	2.066	1.499	1.941	1.614	2.189	2.040	1.495	1.953	1.635	2.167	2.025	1.501	1.986

TABLE 4-9 SECTOR-SPECIFIC SIMPLE OUTPUT MULTIPLIERS FOR THE U.S. MULTIREGIONAL INPUT-OUTPUT SYSTEM

	Sector 1			Sector 2			Sector 3			Sector 4			Sector 5		
	East	Central	West	East	Central	West	East	Central	West	East	Central	West	East	Central	West
1	1.080	1.056	1.076	.018	.018	.015	.040	.056	.051	.012	.015	.012	.098	.104	.136
2	.017	.015	.015	1.358	1.447	1.447	.099	.117	.101	.011	.013	.011	.019	.020	.020
3	.241	.197	.202	.384	.349	.326	1.505	1.499	1.444	.148	.146	.144	.258	.261	.253
4	.242	.313	.307	.317	.340	.347	.292	.295	.297	1.311	1.304	1.317	.238	.243	.250
5	.037	.033	.035	.038	.035	.032	.130	.145	.132	.017	.017	.017	1.328	1.325	1.327

East, and in the West (1.5 versus 0.7). This is a reflection of the broader industrial base in the East. (The multiregional input-output model available in the late 1970s and early 1980s was based on 1963 data; these regional characteristics are changing, and this would certainly be apparent in a less spatially and sectorally aggregated and more up-to-date model.)

Sector-specific simple output multipliers, O_{ij}^L, are shown in Table 4-9. Once more, there is a great deal of uniformity across regions. For example, a dollar's worth of new demand for sector 1 output by households located in the East, Central, or West region generates a national impact in terms of dollars' worth of new output in sector 2 of 0.017, 0.015, or 0.015. Similarly, a dollar's worth of new final demand for sector 4 generates 0.148, 0.146, or 0.144 dollars' worth of new output from sector 3, when the final demand originates in households in the East, Central, or West region, respectively. The figures are generally similar in other rows of Table 4-9. Again, this is primarily because of the large sizes of the three regions in this model. Clearly, if we were using the complete 51-region model, the total effects of new final demand in, say, New York for automobiles, would be widely different in Ohio, where rubber tires are made, and Nevada, where the industrial connections to automobile production are weak.

"Shortcut" Methods

Since multipliers derived from input-output models play such an important role in the analysis of real-world problems, it is not surprising that there have been attempts to estimate output multipliers, for example, from less than a full survey-based input-output table. The work of Drake (1976) and of Burford and Katz—examples of which are Burford and Katz (1977, 1981) and Katz and Burford (1982)—is representative of this line of thinking. The output multiplier is decomposed into three components, based on the power series approximation, namely that $(I - A)^{-1} = I + A + A^2 + A^3 + \cdots$ (This was Eq. [2-12] in Chapter 2.) For sector j, these three components are: (1) the initial change, which for output multipliers is unity; (2) the direct effect, which is represented by the elements in column j of A; and (3) the indirect effect, which is the remainder—in terms of the power series approximation, this means the column j elements in A^2, A^3, A^4, and so on. Letting $V_j = \sum_i a_{ij}$ (sector j's intermediate inputs), we have $O_j = 1 + V_j + R_j$, where R_j is the "remainder," as in (3). The object of short-cut methods is to estimate the components in (2) and (3) when a full A matrix is not available.

One result—developed particularly by Burford and Katz—is that an estimate of A^2 is provided by $\bar{V}A$, where $\bar{V}$ is the average of the column sums of A; $\bar{V} = (1/n)\sum_j V_j$. If this is the case, then

$$(I + A + A^2 + A^3 + A^4 + \cdots) = I + A(1 + \bar{V} + \bar{V}^2 + \bar{V}^3 + \cdots)$$

and, since $\bar{V} < 1$ (because each $V_j < 1$, except in a completely closed model), the sum in parentheses on the right-hand side is just $[1/(1 - \bar{V})]$, so $(I - A)^{-1}$ is approximated by

$$I + \left[\frac{1}{(1 - \bar{V})} \right] A$$

Thus, an estimate, $\tilde{O}_j$, of O_j, the jth column sum of $(I - A)^{-1}$, is provided by

$$\tilde{O}_j = 1 + \left[\frac{1}{(1 - \bar{V})} \right] \sum_i a_{ij} = 1 + \left[\frac{1}{(1 - \bar{V})} \right] V_j$$

There are two basic issues involved in this kind of short-cut method. One concerns the assumptions that are necessary to derive the result that $\bar{V}A$ is an acceptable approximation of A^2. A second issue is whether the methods that are used to estimate the V_j are reasonable. (Clearly, if one has a complete A matrix, then the V_j and $\bar{V}$ can easily be found, but then a "short-cut" method is unnecessary, since $[I - A]^{-1}$ can be found and its column sums examined directly.)

For more detail, the reader should consult the work of Drake and of Burford and Katz and other references in those publications. Critical comments are provided in, among others, Miernyk (1976), Phibbs and Holsman (1981), Harrigan (1982), and Jensen and Hewings (1983).

4-4 | ROW SUMS IN THE LEONTIEF INVERSE

As is explained in section A-6 of Appendix A, postmultiplication of a matrix, M, by a unity column (all 1's) generates a column vector whose elements are the row sums of M. Thus the elements in $(I - A)^{-1} \begin{bmatrix} 1 \\ 1 \\ \vdots \\ 1 \end{bmatrix} = (I - A)^{-1} i$ are the row sums

of $(I - A)^{-1}$. But since the solution to the fundamental input-output equation is $X = (I - A)^{-1}Y$, this means that the row sums of $(I - A)^{-1}$ represent the total effects on each of the sectors of the economy if there is an additional dollar's worth of final demand for each sector. (That is, when $Y = i$, $X = (I - A)^{-1}Y = (I - A)^{-1}i$.) Such "multipliers" would provide a response to the question: What is the total direct and indirect impact on a particular sector in the economy of a general expansion (by one dollar) of final demand in each of the sectors of the economy? In an n-sector economy, the total amount of final demand spending will be $\$n$.

For example, for a two-sector model, with $(I - A)^{-1} = \begin{bmatrix} \alpha_{11} & \alpha_{12} \\ \alpha_{21} & \alpha_{22} \end{bmatrix}$, using

$T = \begin{bmatrix} T_1 \\ T_2 \end{bmatrix}$ for these row sums (totals), $T = (I - A)^{-1} \begin{bmatrix} 1 \\ 1 \\ \vdots \\ 1 \end{bmatrix}$, or

$$T = (I - A)^{-1} i \qquad\qquad (4\text{-}45)$$

That is,

$$T_1 = \alpha_{11} + \alpha_{12}$$

$$T_2 = \alpha_{21} + \alpha_{22}$$

(4-46)

Output multipliers, discussed above, which are *column* sums of $(I - A)^{-1}$, translate a dollar's worth of change in final demand for a *single* sector into new output needed from *all* sectors in the economy. The "uniform demand expansion" multipliers, as they might be called, in Eq. (4-45), above, translate a dollar's worth of change in final demand for *each* sector into new output needed in an *individual* sector. In Eq. (4-46), the equation for sector 1 is really $T_1 = \alpha_{11}(\$1) + \alpha_{12}(\$1) = (\alpha_{11} + \alpha_{12})(\$1)$, and similarly for T_2. Thus, a total of \$2 worth of new final demand spending is involved (\$1 in each of two sectors). These row-sum multipliers are therefore actually composites of individual multipliers (each of the elements in a particular row of the Leontief inverse; α_{11} and α_{12} or α_{21} and α_{22} in our two-sector illustration) each multiplying a one-dollar increase in final demand (and hence, initially, a dollar's worth of necessary new output) for a different sector.

   To convert these effects to income or employment terms, we would utilize the information in H_R or W_R, as defined above. For example (using *INC* for income effects),

$$INC = \hat{H}_R (I - A)^{-1} i = \hat{H}_R T$$

(4-47)

would convert the new outputs of each sector to income earned by households because of the new output. If $H_R = [a_{31} \quad a_{32}]$, then, from Eq. (4-47)

$$INC = \begin{bmatrix} a_{31} & 0 \\ 0 & a_{32} \end{bmatrix} \begin{bmatrix} \alpha_{11} & \alpha_{12} \\ \alpha_{21} & \alpha_{22} \end{bmatrix} \begin{bmatrix} 1 \\ 1 \end{bmatrix} = \begin{bmatrix} a_{31}\alpha_{11} + a_{31}\alpha_{12} \\ a_{32}\alpha_{21} + a_{32}\alpha_{22} \end{bmatrix}$$

$$= \begin{bmatrix} a_{31}(\alpha_{11} + \alpha_{12}) \\ a_{32}(\alpha_{21} + \alpha_{22}) \end{bmatrix}$$

(4-48)

This shows that, as expected, new outputs from sector 1 are weighted by a_{31} (household input—in monetary terms—per dollar's worth of sector 1 output), and new outputs from sector 2 are weighted by a_{32}.

   It might be argued that the assumption of a uniform (one-dollar) expansion of sales to final demand in all sectors is an unrealistic way to characterize growth of an economy, because of the variation in the value of the total sales to final demand of individual sectors. If, in the current year, $Y_1 = \$100$ and $Y_2 = \$2,500$, then the "one-dollar increase" assumption is equivalent to a 1 percent increase in sector 1 sales to final demand and a 0.04 percent increase in sector 2 sales to final demand. Alternatively, then, one can form so-called "growth equalized" multipliers by assuming that final demands for all sectors increase by the same percentage of current final demands. (This notion was proposed by Gray et al. 1979.) That is, given current sales to final demand, Y, we replace the unity column in Eq. (4-45) by kY. Then the output effects on each sector, under the growth-equalized assumption, denoted by X^e, would be simply

$$X^e = (I - A)^{-1} kY$$

(4-49)

Using INC^e for this version of the row-sum multipliers,

$$INC^e = \hat{H}_R(I - A)^{-1}kY \qquad (4\text{-}50)$$

and, for the 2×2 example,

$$INC^e = \begin{bmatrix} a_{31} & 0 \\ 0 & a_{32} \end{bmatrix}\begin{bmatrix} \alpha_{11} & \alpha_{12} \\ \alpha_{21} & \alpha_{22} \end{bmatrix}\begin{bmatrix} kY_1 \\ kY_2 \end{bmatrix} = \begin{bmatrix} a_{31}(\alpha_{11}kY_1 + \alpha_{12}kY_2) \\ a_{32}(\alpha_{21}kY_1 + \alpha_{22}kY_2) \end{bmatrix}$$

$$= k\begin{bmatrix} a_{31}(\alpha_{11}Y_1 + \alpha_{12}Y_2) \\ a_{32}(\alpha_{21}Y_1 + \alpha_{22}Y_2) \end{bmatrix} \qquad (4\text{-}51)$$

Let

$$(I - A)^{-1} = \begin{bmatrix} 1.254 & .330 \\ .264 & 1.122 \end{bmatrix} \qquad (4\text{-}52)$$

as in Eq. (4-2), and $H_R = [.30 \quad .25]$, as in Eq. (4-7). Thus, as in Eq. (4-45), we have

$$T = \begin{bmatrix} 1.254 & .330 \\ .264 & 1.122 \end{bmatrix}\begin{bmatrix} 1 \\ 1 \end{bmatrix} = \begin{bmatrix} 1.584 \\ 1.386 \end{bmatrix} \qquad (4\text{-}53)$$

and, converting to new household income, as in Eq. (4-47),

$$INC = \begin{bmatrix} .30 & 0 \\ 0 & .25 \end{bmatrix}\begin{bmatrix} 1.584 \\ 1.386 \end{bmatrix} = \begin{bmatrix} 0.475 \\ 0.347 \end{bmatrix} \qquad (4\text{-}54)$$

For growth-equalized effects, recall from the same original two-sector example in Chapter 2 that $Y_1 = 350$ and $Y_2 = 1700$. Suppose we want to examine the individual sector effects of a uniform 12 percent expansion in sales by all sectors to final demand. Then, from Eq. (4-49), $k = 0.12$, $Y = \begin{bmatrix} 350 \\ 1700 \end{bmatrix}$, and

$$X^e = \begin{bmatrix} 1.254 & .330 \\ .264 & 1.122 \end{bmatrix}\begin{bmatrix} 42 \\ 204 \end{bmatrix} = \begin{bmatrix} 120 \\ 240 \end{bmatrix} \qquad (4\text{-}55)$$

Similarly, the household income effects in this case are found as in Eq. (4-50) as

$$INC^e = \begin{bmatrix} .30 & 0 \\ 0 & .25 \end{bmatrix}\begin{bmatrix} 120 \\ 240 \end{bmatrix} = \begin{bmatrix} 36 \\ 60 \end{bmatrix} \qquad (4\text{-}56)$$

Consider the total new final demand in Eq. (4-55), which is \$246, divided as \$42 for sector 1 and \$204 for sector 2. In Eq. (4-53), we assumed a \$1 increase in final demand for each of the two sectors. To make the results in Eqs. (4-53) and (4-54) more comparable with those in Eqs. (4-55) and (4-56), we can take the \$246 total new final demand from Eq. (4-55) and divide it equally between the two sectors, as was done in Eq. (4-53). Thus

$$X^e = \begin{bmatrix} 1.254 & .330 \\ .264 & 1.122 \end{bmatrix}\begin{bmatrix} 123 \\ 123 \end{bmatrix} = \begin{bmatrix} 1.584 \\ 1.386 \end{bmatrix}(123) = \begin{bmatrix} 195 \\ 170 \end{bmatrix} \qquad (4\text{-}57)$$

and, similarly,

$$INC^e = \begin{bmatrix} .30 & 0 \\ 0 & .25 \end{bmatrix} \begin{bmatrix} 195 \\ 170 \end{bmatrix} = \begin{bmatrix} 58.5 \\ 42.5 \end{bmatrix} \qquad (4\text{-}58)$$

The results in Eqs. (4-57) and (4-58) reflect an equal distribution between the two sectors of an increase in sales to final demand that is the same as total increase ($246) in the case of a uniform 12 percent increase in final demands that is reflected in Eqs. (4-55) and (4-56).

Not unexpectedly, the output and household income effects differ substantially; in particular, the proportions of the total effects in each of the two sectors vary a great deal. In the equal-percentage-increase case, output effects (in Eq. [4-55]) and household income effects (in Eq. [4-56]) are larger in sector 2 than in sector 1, precisely because in the data Y_2 was much larger than Y_1 (1700 versus 350). In the equal-dollar-increase case, in Eqs. (4-57) and (4-58), the output and household income effects are greater in sector 1 than sector 2.

The main lesson from these illustrations is simply that, as opposed to the multiplier measures discussed in the previous sections of this chapter, when we are using the Leontief inverse to assess sector-specific impacts of economywide changes, the row sums of this inverse have built into them the assumption of uniform dollar increases in sales to final demand across all sectors. If alternative expressions of economic growth are more appropriate, such as that sales to final demand expand by the same percentage in each sector, then the Leontief inverse is utilized in the usual way, namely to premultiply a vector of assumed final demand changes, kY. Equally easily, one could assume different relative increases in sales for different sectors, namely $K = [k_1, k_2, \cdots, k_n]$, meaning that we would use

$$\hat{K}Y = \begin{bmatrix} k_1 Y_1 \\ k_2 Y_2 \\ \vdots \\ k_n Y_n \end{bmatrix}$$

instead of simply kY, to be premultiplied by $(I - A)^{-1}$. In either case, the model is used in the usual way—$X = (I - A)^{-1}$ [Final Demand]—and only when uniform dollar amounts of final demand spending (or *changes* in that spending) are assumed are the row sums of the Leontief inverse of interest.

4-5 | SUMMARY

In this chapter we have introduced the reader to the rather wide variety of multipliers that are frequently calculated and used in real-world applications of the input-output framework. While the array may seem bewildering at first glance, it is, in fact, incomplete. For example, instead of using the household input coefficients, as in Eq. (4-12), to generate a household income multiplier, one can weight the elements of a column of $(I - A)^{-1}$ by the parallel concept of "government input" coefficients, representing dollar's worth of government payments by a sector per dollar's worth of that sector's output. These would be the elements needed in the added row of an A matrix that was being closed with respect to government operations, not households. In this way, we would generate government multipliers. And similarly, other multipliers associated with exogenous sectors can be calculated, for example, foreign trade multipliers.

The use of the input-output framework for impact analysis, from changing final demands, and for multiplier analysis, constitute probably the most frequent uses of the model. In subsequent chapters we will explore extensions to deal specifically with energy and environmental problems, after a discussion of alternative organizations of basic input-output data in the next chapter.

APPENDIX 4-1
INPUT-OUTPUT MULTIPLIERS EXPRESSED IN COMPACT MATRIX FORM

In this appendix we collect together, for the interested reader, the various matrix representations for each of the kinds of multipliers discussed in the text. That is, we indicate the matrix operations that will produce a vector of multipliers, one for each sector in the model.

A row vector whose elements are the *simple* output multipliers, as in Eq. (4-6) for each of the sectors in an input-output table of any size, $n \times n$, can be found by premultiplying the Leontief inverse by the unity row. Denoting the row vector of these simple output multipliers by $O = [O_1, \cdots, O_n]$, we have

$$O = i'(I - A)^{-1} \tag{4-1-1}$$

The $(n + 1)$-element row vector of *total* output multipliers, as in Eq. (4-11), for the (now) $n + 1$ sectors in the model that is closed with respect to households, would be found as $i'(I - \overline{A})^{-1}$, the $n + 1$ column sums in $(I - \overline{A})^{-1}$. Sums of the first n elements in each of the $n + 1$ columns of $(I - \overline{A})^{-1}$ represent the total output multiplier effects over the original n sectors only. They can be found as $[i' \mid 0](I - \overline{A})^{-1}$, where the $(n + 1)$-element row vector on the left contains n ones and a zero in the $(n + 1)$st position. Since interest is usually centered on the total output multipliers for the original n sectors (to be compared with the simple output multipliers for these same n sectors), we really only want the first n elements in $i'(I - \overline{A})^{-1}$. Using the notation $n; [V]$ to mean "the first n elements in the vector V," we can define $\overline{O}$ as

$$\overline{O} = n; \left[i'(I - \overline{A})^{-1} \right] \tag{4-1-2}$$

Using H_R, the n-element household input coefficient row, we can compactly represent the row vector of *simple* household income multipliers for each of the n sectors, $H = [H_1, \cdots, H_n]$, as

$$H = H_R(I - A)^{-1} \tag{4-1-3}$$

The $(n + 1)$-element row vector of *total* household income multipliers, parallel to Eq. (4-1-3), would be $H_{\overline{R}}(I - \overline{A})^{-1}$, where $H_{\overline{R}}$ is the $(n + 1)$-element row vector composed of H_R with $a_{n+1,n+1}$ added as the $(n+1)$st element. As in the case of the vector of total output multipliers, $\bar{O}$ in Eq. (4-1-2), our interest will generally be in the first n elements for the original n sectors in $H_{\bar{R}}(I - \bar{A})^{-1}$, the total household income multipliers for the original n sectors. Thus, we can define $\bar{H}$ as

$$\bar{H} = n; \left[H_{\bar{R}}(I - \bar{A})^{-1} \right] \tag{4-1-4}$$

For an n-sector economy, the n-element row vector of type I income multipliers for each sector, $Y = [Y_1, \cdots, Y_n]$, can be compactly represented using the definition of H in Eq. (4-1-3), the matrix operation of converting a vector into a diagonal matrix, and the fact that the inverse of a diagonal matrix contains the reciprocals of the diagonal elements. Namely

$$Y = H(\hat{H}_R)^{-1} = H_R(I - A)^{-1}(\hat{H}_R)^{-1} \tag{4-1-5}$$

(The reader might want to construct this expression for $n = 2$ to be convinced that a two-element row vector with elements Y_1 and Y_2 does in fact result.) Parallel to the equivalent definitions for $\bar{Y}_j$ in Eqs. (4-16) and (4-17) in the text, the n-element row vector for type II income multipliers can be defined using either $\bar{H}$ in Eq. (4-1-4) or $_{n+1}\bar{\alpha}$, which denotes the first n elements in the bottom ($[n+1]$st) row of the Leontief inverse in the model that is closed with respect to households. That is,

$$\bar{Y} = \bar{H}(\hat{H}_R)^{-1} = \left\{ n; \left[H_{\bar{R}}(I - \bar{A})^{-1} \right] \right\} (\hat{H}_R)^{-1} = (_{n+1}\bar{\alpha})(\hat{H}_R)^{-1} \tag{4-1-6}$$

(Again, the reader may wish to construct this expression exactly for a small two-sector example to be convinced that a row of elements $\bar{Y}_1$ and $\bar{Y}_2$ is generated.)

The row vector of simple household employment multipliers, $E = [E_1, \cdots, E_n]$, can be easily found, using $W_R = [w_{n+1,1}, w_{n+1,2}, \cdots, w_{n+1,n}]$, the vector of physical labor input coefficients, as

$$E = W_R(I - A)^{-1} \tag{4-1-7}$$

(Compare H in Eq. (4-1-3), above). As usual, the adjective "simple" refers to the fact that the measure is calculated from the A matrix with households exogenous. As with $\bar{H}$ in Eq. (4-1-4), above, the n-element row vector $\bar{E} = [\bar{E}_1, \cdots, \bar{E}_n]$ is found as

$$\bar{E} = n; \left[W_{\bar{R}}(I - \bar{A})^{-1} \right] \tag{4-1-8}$$

where the $(n+1)$-element row vector $W_{\bar{R}}$ is defined as $W_{\bar{R}} = [W_R \mid w_{n+1,n+1}]$.

A row vector of type I employment multipliers is found as

$$W = E(\hat{W}_R)^{-1} = W_R(I - A)^{-1}(\hat{W}_R)^{-1} \tag{4-1-9}$$

(Compare Y in Eq. (4-1-5) for the type I income multipliers. Here E replaces H and W_R replaces H_R.) For type II employment multipliers, we have

$$\bar{W} = \bar{E}(\hat{W}_R)^{-1} = \left\{ n; \left[W_{\bar{R}}(I - \bar{A})^{-1} \right] \right\} (\hat{W}_R)^{-1} \tag{4-1-10}$$

(Compare $\bar{Y}$ in Eq. (4-1-6). Again, $\bar{E}$ replaces $\bar{H}$, W_R replaces H_R, and $W_{\bar{R}}$

TABLE 4-1-1 SUMMARY OF GENERAL MULTIPLIER FORMULAS IN MATRIX FORM

Multiplier	Equation Number	Matrix Definition
Output		
Simple	(4-1-1)	$O = i'(I - A)^{-1}$
Total	(4-1-2)	$\bar{O} = n; [i'(I - A)^{-1}]$
Income		
Simple	(4-1-3)	$H = H_R(I - A)^{-1}$
Total	(4-1-4)	$\bar{H} = n; [H_R(I - \bar{A})^{-1}]$
Type I	(4-1-5)	$Y = H(\hat{H}_R)^{-1}$
Type II	(4-1-6)	$\bar{Y} = \bar{H}(\hat{H}_R)^{-1} = (_{n+1}\bar{\alpha})(\hat{H}_R)^{-1}$
Employment		
Simple	(4-1-7)	$E = W_R(I - A)^{-1}$
Total	(4-1-8)	$\bar{E} = n; [W_R(I - \bar{A})^{-1}]$
Type I	(4-1-9)	$W = E(\hat{W}_R)^{-1}$
Type II	(4-1-10)	$\bar{W} = \bar{E}(\hat{W}_R)^{-1}$

replaces $H_{\bar{R}}$.) There is no parallel in type II employment multipliers to the alternative definition of $\bar{Y} = (_{n+1}\bar{\alpha})(\hat{H}_R)^{-1}$, also in Eq. (4-1-6), for type II income multipliers.

Table 4-1-1 summarizes these matrix definitions; it is the matrix equivalent of the information in Table 4-2 in the text.

APPENDIX 4-2
THE EQUIVALENCE OF TOTAL HOUSEHOLD INCOME MULTIPLIERS AND THE ELEMENTS IN THE BOTTOM ROW OF $(I - \bar{A})^{-1}$

Consider the general representation of our 3×3 model closed with respect to households (sector $n + 1$, which here means sector 3), and its inverse, similarly partitioned.

$$(I - \bar{A}) = \begin{bmatrix} (1 - a_{11}) & -a_{12} & \vdots & -a_{13} \\ -a_{21} & (1 - a_{22}) & \vdots & -a_{23} \\ \hdashline -a_{31} & -a_{32} & \vdots & (1 - a_{33}) \end{bmatrix} = \begin{bmatrix} E & \vdots & F \\ \hdashline G & \vdots & H \end{bmatrix}$$

$$(I - \bar{A})^{-1} = \begin{bmatrix} \bar{\alpha}_{11} & \bar{\alpha}_{12} & \vdots & \bar{\alpha}_{13} \\ \bar{\alpha}_{21} & \bar{\alpha}_{22} & \vdots & \bar{\alpha}_{23} \\ \hdashline \bar{\alpha}_{31} & \bar{\alpha}_{32} & \vdots & \bar{\alpha}_{33} \end{bmatrix} = \begin{bmatrix} S & \vdots & T \\ \hdashline U & \vdots & V \end{bmatrix}$$

Since, in this case, G and U are two-element row vectors, F and T are two-element column vectors, and H and V are scalars, we have

$$\begin{bmatrix} E & \vdots & F \\ \hdashline G & \vdots & H \end{bmatrix}\begin{bmatrix} S & \vdots & T \\ \hdashline U & \vdots & V \end{bmatrix} = \begin{bmatrix} I & \vdots & \begin{matrix} 0 \\ 0 \end{matrix} \\ \hdashline 0 \quad 0 & \vdots & 1 \end{bmatrix}$$

In particular, $GS + HU = 0$. Here, this means

$$\left[\, -a_{31} \quad -a_{32} \,\right] \begin{bmatrix} \bar{\alpha}_{11} & \bar{\alpha}_{12} \\ \bar{\alpha}_{21} & \bar{\alpha}_{22} \end{bmatrix} + (1 - a_{33})\left[\, \bar{\alpha}_{31} \quad \bar{\alpha}_{32} \,\right] = \left[\, 0 \quad 0 \,\right]$$

or, carrying out the matrix multiplications,

$$-a_{31}\bar{\alpha}_{11} - a_{32}\bar{\alpha}_{21} + (1 - a_{33})\bar{\alpha}_{31} = 0$$

and

$$-a_{31}\bar{\alpha}_{12} - a_{32}\bar{\alpha}_{22} + (1 - a_{33})\bar{\alpha}_{32} = 0$$

Rearranging,

$$\bar{\alpha}_{31} = a_{31}\bar{\alpha}_{11} + a_{32}\bar{\alpha}_{21} + a_{33}\bar{\alpha}_{31}$$

and

$$\bar{\alpha}_{32} = a_{31}\bar{\alpha}_{12} + a_{32}\bar{\alpha}_{22} + a_{33}\bar{\alpha}_{32}$$

The three terms on the right-hand sides are exactly the terms in Eq. (4-13), for $j = 1$ and $j = 2$, where the $(n + 1)$st terms are those in the household row and/or column (here these are row 3 and column 3). Thus, $\bar{H}_1 = \bar{\alpha}_{31}$ and $\bar{H}_2 = \bar{\alpha}_{32}$, and this is always true, for any $\bar{H}_j$, for a model of any size with households endogenous. That is, an alternative to Eq. (4-13) for the definition of $\bar{H}_j$ is

$$\bar{H}_j = \bar{\alpha}_{n+1, j} \tag{4-2-1}$$

APPENDIX 4-3
RELATIONSHIP BETWEEN TYPE I AND TYPE II INCOME MULTIPLIERS

To examine the value of the ratio between type II and type I income multipliers, we will again utilize results on the inverse of a partitioned matrix. To begin we note, for any sector j, that both multipliers have the same denominator, $a_{n+1, j}$ and thus the ratio of the two multipliers for sector j, denoted R_j, is

$$R_j = \frac{\bar{Y}_j}{Y_j} = \frac{\bar{\alpha}_{n+1, j}}{\displaystyle\sum_{i=1}^{n} a_{n+1, i}\alpha_{ij}} \tag{4-3-1}$$

In matrix terms, eliminating $(\hat{H}_R)^{-1}$ from both row vectors (Y in Eq. [4-1-5] and $\bar{Y}$ in Eq. [4-1-6] in Appendix 4-1) by postmultiplying by $(\hat{H}_R)$, we can generate the n-element row vector of these ratios as

$$R = \left[\, R_1, R_2, \cdots, R_n \,\right] = {}_{n+1}\bar{\alpha}\left[\left\langle H_R(I - A)^{-1} \right\rangle\right]^{-1} \tag{4-3-2}$$

(The reader should be clear that this matrix operation divides each $\bar{\alpha}_{n+1, j}$ by the corresponding $\displaystyle\sum_{i=1}^{n} a_{n+1, i}\alpha_{ij}$. Recall also that the notation $\langle X \rangle$ is used instead of $\hat{X}$ when the vector being diagonalized is represented by a matrix expression containing several elements, so that the hat does not fit easily.) Notice, in Eq. (4-3-2), that the only elements that come directly from the inverse of the $(I - \bar{A})$ matrix are the $_{n+1}\bar{\alpha}$, the first n elements in the bottom row.

In section A-7 of Appendix A we have seen that, given a partitioned matrix $\begin{bmatrix} E & F \\ \hline G & H \end{bmatrix}$, where E and H are square, the elements of the inverse can be partitioned into four matrices $\begin{bmatrix} S & T \\ \hline U & V \end{bmatrix}$, where submatrices in corresponding positions in the original matrix and the inverse have the same dimensions. In particular, we saw that $U = -(H - GE^{-1}F)^{-1}GE^{-1}$.

We now want to consider the inverse to the input-output coefficients matrix in which the household sector has been made endogenous. Thus our $(I - \bar{A})$

$$= \begin{bmatrix} (I - A) & -H_C \\ \hline -H_R & (1 - h) \end{bmatrix}$$ as in Eq. (2-20) in section 2-5 of Chapter 2, and we

want to consider some of the elements in the partitioned inverse to $(I - \bar{A})$. Here $E = (I - A)$, $F = -H_C$ (an n-element column vector), $G = -H_R$ (an n-element row vector), and $H = 1 - h$ (a scalar). For the ratios of the two multipliers we need the first n elements in the bottom row of $(I - \bar{A})^{-1}$—namely, the elements in $_{n+1}\bar{\alpha}$. These correspond to the elements in U, which here is an n-element row vector.

From Eq. (4-3-2), $R = U[\langle - GE^{-1} \rangle]^{-1}$. Since $U = -(H - GE^{-1}F)^{-1}GE^{-1}$, we have

$$R = (H - GE^{-1}F)^{-1}GE^{-1}[\langle GE^{-1} \rangle]^{-1}$$

But the product of GE^{-1}—an n-element row vector—and $[\langle GE^{-1} \rangle]^{-1}$—an $n \times n$ diagonal matrix containing the reciprocals of the n elements in the row vector—is just an n-element unity row vector containing all 1's. (As an example,

$$[5 \quad 7 \quad 13] \begin{bmatrix} 1/5 & 0 & 0 \\ 0 & 1/7 & 0 \\ 0 & 0 & 1/13 \end{bmatrix} = [1 \quad 1 \quad 1].)$$

Substituting for E, F, G, and H, we find that

$$(H - GE^{-1}F)^{-1} = \left[(1 - h) - H_R(I - A)^{-1}H_C\right]^{-1}$$

But $H_R(I - A)^{-1}H_C$ is just a scalar—the dimensions in the multiplication are $(1 \times n)(n \times n)(n \times 1)$—and so the entire term in brackets is just a scalar; call it g.

$$g = \left[(1 - h) - H_R(I - A)^{-1}H_C\right] \tag{4-3-3}$$

Thus its "inverse" is just its reciprocal, $1/g$; therefore,

$$R = \left(\frac{1}{g}\right)[1, \cdots, 1] = \left[\left(\frac{1}{g}\right), \left(\frac{1}{g}\right), \cdots, \left(\frac{1}{g}\right)\right] \tag{4-3-4}$$

That is, the ratio of the type II income multiplier to the type I income multiplier is just $(1/g)$ or $1/[(1 - h) - H_R(I - A)^{-1}H_C]$. All of these elements can be found from (1) the original Leontief inverse (in which households are exogenous to the model), (2) the household input coefficient row, H_R, (3) the household consumption coefficient column H_C, and (4) the element h (which is $a_{n+1,n+1}$). Thus the type I income multiplier for any sector can be blown up to a type II income multiplier for that sector through multiplication by $(1/g)$.

For the example in section 4-2, we found that $(1/g) = 1.29$. Using the results in Eq. (4-3-3), we need $H_R = [0.3 \quad 0.25]$, $(I - A)^{-1} = \begin{bmatrix} 1.254 & 0.330 \\ 0.264 & 1.122 \end{bmatrix}$, $H_C = \begin{bmatrix} 0.05 \\ 0.40 \end{bmatrix}$, and $(1 - h) = 0.95$. Thus $H_R(I - A)^{-1}H_C = 0.174$ and $(1/g) = 1/[(1 - h) - H_R(I - A)^{-1}H_C] = 1/0.776 = 1.29$, as expected.

APPENDIX 4-4
RELATIONSHIP BETWEEN SIMPLE AND TRUNCATED TOTAL HOUSEHOLD EMPLOYMENT MULTIPLIERS

From Eq. (4-1-7) in Appendix 4-1, the vector of simple household employment multipliers is given by $E = W_R(I - A)^{-1}$ and the vector of *truncated* total household employment multipliers can be seen to be

$$\bar{E}(t) = W_R S$$

where S is the $n \times n$ matrix of inverse elements in the $n \times n$ "upper left" portion of $(I - \bar{A})^{-1}$. We consider the partitioning of $(I - \bar{A})^{-1}$ as in Appendix 4-3. From section A-7 of Appendix A,

$$S = E^{-1}(I - FU) \quad \text{where} \quad U = -(H - GE^{-1}F)^{-1}GE^{-1}$$

or

$$S = E^{-1} + E^{-1}F(H - GE^{-1}F)^{-1}GE^{-1}$$

So, for the Leontief inverse of the partitioned input-output coefficient matrix to which a household row and column have been added, as in the previous appendix, we have $E^{-1} = (I - A)^{-1}$, $F = -H_C$, $G = -H_R$, and $H = 1 - h$. In that appendix we denoted $[(1 - h) - H_R(I - A)^{-1}H_C]$ as g, so we find that

$$S = (I - A)^{-1} + (1/g)(I - A)^{-1}H_C H_R(I - A)^{-1}$$

Therefore, the differences in the elements in $E(t)$ and E are

$$D = W_R\left[S - (I - A)^{-1}\right] = \left(\frac{1}{g}\right)W_R\left[(I - A)^{-1}H_C H_R(I - A)^{-1}\right] \qquad (4\text{-}4\text{-}1)$$

For the numerical example in the text, the components of this difference vector are

$$D = (1.29)[0.003 \quad 0.002]\begin{bmatrix} 1.254 & 0.330 \\ 0.264 & 1.122 \end{bmatrix}\begin{bmatrix} 0.05 \\ 0.40 \end{bmatrix}[0.3 \quad 0.25]\begin{bmatrix} 1.254 & 0.330 \\ 0.264 & 1.122 \end{bmatrix}$$

which, through straightforward matrix multiplication, is shown to be

$$D = [0.00086 \quad 0.00074]$$

as suggested in the text.

PROBLEMS

4-1   Rank sectors in terms of their importance as measured by output multipliers in each of the economies represented by the data in problems 2-1, 2-2, and 2-4 through 2-9. (Include problems 2-10 and 2-11, if you did them—that is, if you are doing the computer problems.)

4-2   Consider one (or more) of the problems in Chapter 2. Using output multipliers, from problem 4-1, in conjunction with the new final demands in the problem in Chapter 2, derive the total value of output (across all sectors) associated with the new final demands. Compare your results with the total output obtained by summing the elements in the gross output vector which you found as the solution to the problem in Chapter 2. (In matrix notation, this is comparing $[O][\Delta Y]$ with $i'X = i'[(I-A)^{-1}\Delta Y]$; we know that they must be equal, since output multipliers are the column sums of the Leontief inverse—that is, $O = i'(I-A)^{-1}$. This is Eq. [4-1-1] in Appendix 4-1.)

4-3   Using the data in problem 2-3, find output multipliers and also both type I and type II income multipliers for the two sectors. Check that the ratio of the type II to the type I income multiplier is the same for both sectors.

4-4   Consider problem 2-8. After national elections are held, it may turn out that different government policy will be forthcoming during the first quarter of the coming year. In which of the two sectors does an increase of $100 in government purchases have the larger effect? How much larger is it than if the $100 were spent on purchases of the other sector?

4-5   Consider problem 2-9.

a   In the situation depicted in that question, if you were asked to design an advertising campaign to stimulate export sales of one of the goods produced in the country, would you concentrate your efforts on the product of sector 1 or of sector 2 or on some combination of the two? Why?

b   If labor input coefficients for the two sectors in the region were found to be $a_{31} = 0.1$ and $a_{32} = 0.18$, how might your answer to part **a** of this question be changed, if at all?

4-6   Using the elements in the full two-region interregional Leontief inverse from problem 3-2, find:

a   Simple intraregional output multipliers for sectors 1 and 2 (that is, find the elements in vectors O^{LL} and O^{MM}, as was done in Eqs. [4-25] and [4-26] in the text);

b   Simple national (total) output multipliers for sectors 1 and 2 (vectors O^{L} and O^{M}, as was done in Eqs. [4-30] and [4-31] in the text);

c   Sector-specific simple national output multipliers for sectors 1 and 2 in regions L and M. (This means finding the four multipliers in $O^{\cdot L} = [O_{11}^{\cdot L}, O_{21}^{\cdot L}, O_{12}^{\cdot L}, O_{22}^{\cdot L}]$ and in $O^{\cdot M}$, which is defined similarly.)

4-7   On the basis of the results in problem 4-6, above:

a   For which sector's output does new final demand produce the largest total intraregional output stimulus in region L? In region M?

b   For which sector in which region does an increase in final demand have the largest national (two-region) impact?

c   To increase the output of sector 1 nationally (i.e., in both regions), would it be better to institute policies that would increase household demand in region L or in region M?

d   Answer question **c** if the objective is now to increase sector 2 output nationally.

4-8   Answer problems 4-6 and 4-7, above, for the multiregional case, using the elements in $(I - CA)^{-1}C$ from problem 3-3.

4-9   The government in problem 3-4 is interested in starting an overseas advertising and promotion campaign in an attempt to increase export sales of the products of the country. There is specialization of production in the regions of the country; in particular, the products are shown in the table below:

	Region A	Region B	Region C
Manufacturing	Scissors	Cloth	Pottery
Agriculture	Oranges	Walnuts	None

For which product (or products) would increased export sales cause the greatest stimulation of the national economy?

REFERENCES

ALMON, CLOPPER, JR., MARGARET B. BUCKLER, LAWRENCE M. HOROWITZ, and THOMAS C. REIMBOLD. *1985: Interindustry Forecasts of the American Economy.* Lexington, Mass.: D.C. Heath (Lexington Books), 1974.

BEYERS, WILLIAM B. "On Geographical Properties of Growth Center Linkage Systems." *Economic Geography* 50, no. 3 (July 1974): 203–18.

———. "The Interregional Structure of the U.S. Economy." *International Regional Science Review* 8, no. 3 (December 1983): 213–31.

BURFORD, ROGER L., and JOSEPH L. KATZ. "Regional Input-Output Multipliers Without a Full I-O Table." *Annals of Regional Science* 11, no. 3 (November 1977): 21–38.

CONWAY, RICHARD S., JR. "Simulation Properties of a Regional Interindustry Econometric Model." *Papers, Regional Science Association* 43 (1979): 45–57.

———. "The Stability of Regional Input-Output Multipliers." *Environment and Planning, A* 9, no. 2 (February 1977): 197–214.

DIPASQUALE, DENISE, and KAREN R. POLENSKE. "Output, Income, and Employment Input-Output Multipliers." In *Impact Analysis: Methodology and Applications*, edited by S. Pleeter, 85–113. Leiden: Martinus Nijhoff, 1980.

DRAKE, RONALD E. "A Short-Cut to Estimates of Regional Input-Output Multipliers: Methodology and Evaluation." *International Regional Science Review* 1, no. 2 (Fall 1976): 1–17.

ESKELINEN, HEIKKI. "Core and Periphery in a Three-Region Input-Output Framework." *Annals of Regional Science* 17, no. 3 (November 1983): 41–56.

GRAY, S. LEE, et al. "Measurement of Growth Equalized Employment Multiplier Effects: An Empirical Example." *Annals of Regional Science* 13, no. 3 (November 1979): 68–75.

GREYTAK, DAVID. "Regional Impact of Interregional Trade in Input-Output Analysis." *Papers, Regional Science Association* 25 (1970): 203–17.

———. "Regional Industry Multipliers: An Analysis of Information." *Regional and Urban Economics* 4, no. 2 (October 1974): 163–72.

HARRIGAN, FRANK J. "The Estimation of Input-Output Type Output Multipliers When No Input-Output Model Exists: A Comment." *Journal of Regional Science* 22, no. 3 (August 1982): 375–81.

HIRSCH, WERNER Z. "Interindustry Relations of a Metropolitan Area." *Review of Economics and Statistics* 41, no. 4 (November 1959): 360–69.

JENSEN, RODNEY C. "Some Accounting Procedures and Their Effects on Input-Output Multipliers." *Annals of Regional Science* 12, no. 3 (November 1978): 21–38.

JENSEN, RODNEY C., and GUY WEST. "The Effect of Relative Coefficient Size on Input-Output Multipliers." *Environment and Planning, A* 12, no. 6 (June 1980):

659–70.

JENSEN, RODNEY C., and GEOFFREY J. D. HEWINGS. "Short-Cut 'Input-Output' Multipliers: A Requiem." Unpublished paper, 1983.

KATZ, JOSEPH L., and ROGER L. BURFORD. "The Estimation of Input-Output Type Output Multipliers When No Input-Output Model Exists: A Reply." *Journal of Regional Science* 22, no. 3 (August 1982): 383–87.

KUSHNIRSKY, F. I. "A Joined Input-Output and Econometric Approach to Endogenous Calculations of Final Demands and Outputs." *Journal of Policy Modeling* 4, no. 3 (November 1982): 412–23.

L'ESPERANCE, WILFORD L., ARTHUR E. KING, and RICHARD H. SINES. "Conjoining an Ohio Input-Output Model with an Econometric Model of Ohio." *Regional Science Perspectives* 7, no. 2 (1977): 54–77.

MADDEN, MOSS, and PETER W. J. BATEY. "Linked Population and Economic Models: Some Methodological Issues in Forecasting, Analysis, and Policy Optimization." *Journal of Regional Science* 23, no. 2 (April 1983) 141–64.

MIERNYK, WILLIAM H. "Comments on Recent Developments in Regional Input-Output Analysis." *International Regional Science Review* 1, no. 2 (Fall 1976): 47–55.

———. *The Elements of Input-Output Analysis*. New York: Random House, 1965.

MIERNYK, WILLIAM H. et al. *Impact of the Space Program on a Local Economy: An Input-Output Analysis*. Morgantown, W.Va.: West Virginia University Library, 1967.

MOORE, FREDERICK T. "Regional Economic Reaction Paths." *American Economic Review* 45, no. 2 (May 1955): 133–48.

MOORE, FREDERICK T., and JAMES W. PETERSEN. "Regional Analysis: An Interindustry Model of Utah." *Review of Economics and Statistics* 37, no. 4 (November 1955): 368–81.

MOSES, LEON N. "Regional Economics: Discussion." *American Economic Review* 45, no. 2 (May 1955): 150–53.

OOSTERHAVEN, JAN. *Interregional Input-Output Analysis and Dutch Regional Policy Problems*. Aldershot, Hampshire (U.K.): Gower Publishing Co., 1981.

PHIBBS, PETER J., and ANDREW J. HOLSMAN. "An Evaluation of the Burford Katz Short Cut Technique for Deriving Input-Output Multipliers." *Annals of Regional Science* 15, no. 3 (November 1981): 11–19.

RICHARDSON, HARRY W. *Input-Output and Regional Economics*. New York: John Wiley and Sons (Halsted Press), 1972.

RIEFLER, ROGER, and CHARLES M. TIEBOUT. "Interregional Input-Output: An Empirical California-Washington Model." *Journal of Regional Science* 10, no. 2 (August 1970): 135–52.

SCHAFFER, WILLIAM A. *On the Use of Input-Output Models for Regional Planning*. Leiden: Martinus Nijhoff, 1976.

STEVENS, BENJAMIN H., GEORGE I. TREYZ, and J. R. KINDAHL. "Conjoining an Input-Output Model and a Policy Analysis Model: A Case Study of the Regional Economic Effects of Expanding a Port Facility." *Environment and Planning, A* 13, no. 8 (August 1981): 1029–38.

WEST, GUY R., and RODNEY C. JENSEN. "Some Reflections on Input-Output Multipliers." *Annals of Regional Science* 14, no. 2 (July 1980): 77–89.

YAMADA, HIROYUKI, and TAKEO IHARA. "Input-Output Analysis of Interregional Repercussion." *Papers and Proceedings of the Third Far East Conference of the Regional Science Association* (1968): 3–29.

chapter 5

Organization of Basic Data for Input-Output Models

5-1 | INTRODUCTION

The most commonly used input-output tables, whether national, regional, or multiple-region tables, are generally based on historical data describing the economic area of interest. The usual source of data for such tables is a system of national (or regional) economic accounts[1] which are often routinely collected by means of a census or some other survey—hence the name survey-based tables. In Chapter 8 we examine alternatives to survey-based construction of input-output tables, which is often a prohibitively expensive and time-consuming endeavor.

In this chapter we describe the relationship between input-output tables and national (or regional) economic accounts and, in the process, show how input-output tables can be derived from such accounts. In addition, we introduce the notion of "commodity" versus "industry" accounts and discuss how input-output models must be modified to accommodate such distinctions. We also discuss the level of sectoral and spatial aggregation (numbers of industries and regions, respectively) in input-output tables and the effects of aggregating sectors and/or regions on the performance of input-output models.

5-2 | NATIONAL ECONOMIC ACCOUNTS

Overview

As far as input-output models are concerned, the most important components of a system of national economic accounts are: (1) the national income and product accounts (NIPAs) and (2) the interindustry or input-output accounts

[1]For example, the U.S. National Economic Accounts are routinely compiled by the U.S. Department of Commerce. The national input-output tables are derived from these accounts periodically. In 1968 the United Nations published a standardized system of national accounts which is consistent with the discussion presented here; this system is widely applied in the literature. (United Nations 1968.)

TABLE 5-1   BUSINESS ESTABLISHMENT PRODUCTION ACCOUNT

Debit	Credit
Purchases from	Sales to
industry 1	industry 1
industry 2	industry 2
⋮	⋮
Wages and Salaries Paid	Sales to Households
Profits	Government Purchases
Other Value Added	Other Final Demand
Total Expenses and Profits	Total Revenues

(IOAs). The former present the productive output of the national[2] economy, that is, the gross national product (GNP) both in terms of final products or final demands and in terms of income categories or value-added inputs to industries[3]. The latter present interindustry flows of goods and services which, with a number of adjustments we describe later, ultimately become the transactions matrix, Z, that was introduced in Chapter 2.

In Chapter 2 we suggested that final demand and value-added sectors of an input-output economy be viewed as somewhat exogenous to the more closely interrelated system of industrial sectors. The principal components of final demand are usually taken to be personal consumption expenditures (purchases by households), government purchases, gross private domestic capital investment, and finally, net exports of goods and services—that is, exports of goods and services less the value of imports of those same goods and services. The income categories comprising value-added inputs to industries usually include wages and salaries paid to employees, rental and proprietors' income, profits, taxes, interest, and adjustments to inventories.

Both NIPAs and IOAs are generally constructed from a set of business establishments' production accounts (BEPAs). These accounts, which comprise the basic data of the national economic accounts, are usually compiled as part of a census; hence, they are usually collected by establishment or individual business unit. Temporarily, for illustrative purposes, we will invoke four simplifying assumptions in order to facilitate our discussion of deriving the NIPAs and IOAs from the BEPAs:

1 *Imports and Exports.* We ignore the complications of imports and exports, that is, we assume all GNP is of domestic origin. For example, we assume that all automobiles purchased in the United States are domestically produced.
2 *Inventory Adjustments.* We ignore the complications of inventory adjustments, that is, we assume no changes in inventories. All automobiles produced are purchased during the current year and are not held over until the next year.
3 *Secondary Products.* We assume an industry produces one and only one distinct commodity (or service). Automobile manufacturers make only automobiles, not

[2] For the most part, the following discussion will apply to regional as well as to national accounts.
[3] Recall from Chapter 2 that the sum of all final demands equals GNP, which also equals the sum of all income types or "charges against" GNP.

additional automobile parts which may be classified as a different industry category.

4 *Capital Formation.* We ignore transactions of capital goods between industries; they are assigned to final demand (gross private domestic capital formation). New-car assembly equipment purchased by automobile manufacturers is a capital good acquisition; it is recorded as a final demand for capital by the manufacturer and not as an interindustry transaction.

Clearly these assumptions are very limiting and will have to be relaxed eventually. The first two of these simplifications will require relatively minor adjustments later, but the last two will require major changes in the way we construct input-output models. The problem of secondary production will lead to a system of "commodity-by-industry" accounts that we develop in this chapter. The accounting for capital formation is the principal concern of dynamic input-output models and is a subject of Chapter 9.

By adopting the financial accounting convention of a "T account," we can characterize a business establishment's production account (BEPA) in two

TABLE 5-2   BUSINESS ESTABLISHMENT PRODUCTION ACCOUNTS: EXAMPLE 1

Business Unit 1

Debit		Credit	
Purchases from		Sales to	
Fabricated Metal	.5	Fabricated Metal	.5
Steel	1.0	Steel	.5
Wages and Salaries	1.0	Sales to Households	2.0
Profits	1.0	Government Purchases	1.0
Other Value Added	.5	Other Final Demand	0
Total Expenses and Profits	4.0	Total Revenues	4.0

Business Unit 2

Debit		Credit	
Purchases from		Sales to	
Fabricated Metal	.5	Fabricated Metal	.5
Steel	2.0	Steel	1.5
Wages and Salaries	2.0	Sales to Households	2.0
Profits	1.0	Government Purchases	1.0
Other Value Added	.5	Other Final Demand	1.0
Total Expenses and Profits	6.0	Total Revenues	6.0

Business Unit 3

Debit		Credit	
Purchases from		Sales to	
Fabricated Metal	2.0	Fabricated Metal	3.0
Steel	4.0	Steel	4.0
Wages and Salaries	2.0	Sales to Households	0
Profits	1.0	Government Purchases	2.0
Other Value Added	1.0	Other Final Demand	1.0
Total Expenses and Profits	10.0	Total Revenues	10.0

TABLE 5-3 Input-Output Accounts: Example 1

Fabricated Metal Products

Debit		Credit	
Purchases from		Sales to	
Fabricated Metal	1.0	Fabricated Metal	1.0
Steel	3.0	Steel	2.0
Wages and Salaries	3.0	Sales to Households	4.0
Profits	2.0	Government Purchases	2.0
Other Value Added	1.0	Other Final Demand	1.0
Total Expenses and Profits	10.0	Total Revenues	10.0

Steel

Debit		Credit	
Purchases from		Sales to	
Fabricated Metal	2.0	Fabricated Metal	3.0
Steel	4.0	Steel	4.0
Wages and Salaries	2.0	Sales to Households	0
Profits	1.0	Government Purchases	2.0
Other Value Added	1.0	Other Final Demand	1.0
Total Expenses and Profits	10.0	Total Revenues	10.0

columns, with debits to the account (expenses and profits) recorded in the left-hand column and credits (sales and other revenue) recorded in the right-hand column, as shown in Table 5-1 (see page 150). (The two columns are usually separated and labeled with lines resembling a T; hence the name "T account.")

IOAs can be assembled by combining all business establishments assigned to a given industry. As our third simplifying assumption, recall that we do not permit secondary production. Hence, we assign an establishment to the industry category according to its primary product. The NIPAs can consequently be derived by combining the value-added and final-demand lines from all IOAs.

Example 1 Consider a simple economy with three business establishments, which we refer to as B_1, B_2, and B_3, respectively. The first two establishments

TABLE 5-4 National Income and Product Account: Example 1

Debit		Credit	
Wages and Salaries		Sales to Households	
Fabricated Metal	3.0	Fabricated Metal	4.0
Steel	2.0	Steel	0
Profits		Government Purchases	
Fabricated Metal	2.0	Fabricated Metal	2.0
Steel	1.0	Steel	2.0
Other Value Added		Other Final Demand	
Fabricated Metal	1.0	Fabricated Metal	1.0
Steel	1.0	Steel	1.0
Total Charges Against GNP	10.0	Total Contributions to GNP	10.0

TABLE 5-5 Input-Output Transactions: Example 1

Industry	Intermediate Transactions		Final Demand			Total Sales
	Fabricated Metal	Steel	Households	Government	Other	
Fabricated Metal	1.0	2.0	4.0	2.0	1.0	10.0
Steel	3.0	4.0	0.0	2.0	1.0	10.0
Wages and Salaries	3.0	2.0				
Profits	2.0	1.0		10.0		
Other	1.0	1.0		(GNP)		
Total Expenses and Profit	10.0	10.0				20.0 (Total Output)

both make fabricated metal products; the third produces steel. The BEPAs for the three business units are shown (page 151) in Table 5-2 (in millions of dollars).

The IOAs are then constructed by combining all business units assigned to the same industry category. In this case, B_1 and B_2 both produce fabricated metal products and B_3 produces steel; hence, we define the two IOAs as given in Table 5-3.

The NIPAs are constructed by simply combining the final-demand and value-added lines from the IOAs as given in Table 5-4.

As we found in Chapter 2, IOAs are customarily presented in the form of a matrix of interindustry transactions rather than in a series of T accounts. The debit columns of the T accounts form the columns of the transactions matrix and the credit columns (transposed) form the rows of the transactions matrix. The transactions table for the example is shown in Table 5-5.

This process that we have just described of deriving the input-output accounts from a system of BEPAs is certainly quite straightforward. The basic input-output accounts alone, however, are far from adequate for constructing a useful input-output model. In order to make the derived table a useful analytical tool, we must deal with the simplifications that were made earlier.

We now discuss a number of conventions and modifications to the basic input-output accounting framework that are designed to deal with the simplifying assumptions.

Secondary Production

In the construction of IOAs we compiled data by establishment or individual business unit; we assigned an establishment to a defined "industry" category according to the output of the establishment which comprises the primary source of revenues (primary product). Many business units, however, may produce substantial amounts of products that do not belong to the primary product industry classification; such products are termed *secondary products*. For example, as mentioned earlier, many automobile manufacturers may produce automobile parts in addition to fully assembled automobiles, or petroleum refiners may produce petrochemicals as a by-product to producing gasoline or other petroleum products.

Early input-output studies, such as the pre-1972 U.S. national tables, treated secondary products in the following manner. First, selected secondary products were "reallocated," that is, the level of secondary production *and* its constituent inputs were assigned to the sector defining that product as primary output. Such treatment was used only for industries where secondary production comprised a significant fraction of total output. All other secondary products in the economy were treated as if they had been sold by the producing sectors to the sectors for which those products were classified as primary. To accomplish this, a table of *transfers* was constructed recording these imaginary sales. This matrix of transfers was then added to the basic transactions matrix, thereby double counting the value of secondary products and consequently inflating total output. This was done in order to ensure that the secondary products were distributed correctly to consumers, at the expense of inflating the total outputs of some industries that are secondary producers.

Example 2 Reallocation (sometimes referred to as redefinition) of secondary production, as just mentioned, involves factoring out the amount of secondary product produced as well as the inputs used in that production and reassigning both to the industry for which the product is classified as primary. However, this requires that a firm allocate its inputs between the production of primary and secondary products; in effect, it is necessary to break the firm into two independent subfirms—one a producer of the primary product and the other a producer of the secondary product. Most firms do not record data in a form that permits this accounting easily, so a less desirable treatment of secondary production is often employed in input-output studies. For example, the U.S. Department of Commerce (prior to preparation of the 1972 national input-output table) reassigned the output of secondary production to the sector for which the activity was considered primary, but did not reassign the inputs. This amounted to a double counting of the inputs required for secondary production, which we see in the following example. (*Survey of Current Business* 1969, 1974; Vacarra, Shapiro, and Simon 1970.)

Consider a three-industry economy; the matrix of interindustry transactions and vector of total outputs are given in Table 5-6. Suppose that firms in both industries 1 and 3 are secondary producers of product 2, that is, industry 1 produces $100 million worth of product 2 in addition to $900 million worth of product 1, and industry 3 produces $10 million worth of product 2 as well as $1190 million worth of product 3.

TABLE 5-6 INPUT-OUTPUT TRANSACTIONS: EXAMPLE 2
(MILLIONS OF DOLLARS)

	Industry			Total Outputs
	1	2	3	
Industry 1	266	378	230	1000
Industry 2	267	110	224	1500
Industry 3	340	340	468	1200

As mentioned earlier, since the proper distribution of output is often desirable in input-output studies, the convention often employed is to treat the secondary product as if it were sold to the industry for which the product is classified as primary. In this example, if the secondary production were "transferred" to the correct primary producers, then the revised transactions matrix, $\bar{Z}$, and corresponding total outputs vector, $\bar{X}$, would be the following:

$$\bar{Z} = \begin{bmatrix} 266 & 378 & 230 \\ 367 & 110 & 234 \\ 340 & 340 & 468 \end{bmatrix} \qquad \bar{X} = \begin{bmatrix} 1000 \\ 1610 \\ 1200 \end{bmatrix}$$

Note that this is accomplished by simply adding the amount of secondary production, termed a *transfer*, to the industry for which the secondary product is classified as primary, that is, the $100 million worth of product 2 produced by industry 1 is added to the original z_{21} transaction as if it were sold by industry 2 to the secondary producer, industry 1. Similarly, the $10 million worth of product 2 produced by industry 3 is added to the original z_{23} transaction. Finally, total output of industry 2 is increased by the sum of all secondary production of product 2. However, the total outputs of industries 1 and 3 are *not* decreased, since the inputs required in secondary production were not reallocated; this inflates total output, since secondary production is counted twice.

In many input-output studies such transferring of secondary production is used except where secondary production comprises a large portion of total output of an industry, in which case secondary products and inputs are reallocated.

A more realistic classification scheme that accounts for industrial production by commodity type rather than industry category eliminates this somewhat clumsy and biased accounting of secondary production. More recent studies, such as the 1972 and 1977 U.S. National Tables, redefine all secondary production by establishing a set of "commodity-by-industry" accounts. In section 5-3 we examine the commodity-by-industry accounting framework in detail.

Producers' and Consumers' Prices

Most input-output studies value the entries in input-output accounts (and subsequently the transactions matrix) in *producers' prices*, that is, the prices at which the seller completes the transaction (sometimes called *free-on-board* or *f.o.b. prices*). The purchaser incurs the producer's price plus trade and transportation margins (and often excise taxes). The convention in most input-output studies is to assign the margins on all interindustry transactions in a column to the industry responsible for the margin. That is, all wholesale and retail trade margins on all inputs to an industry are summed and recorded as the "trade" entry in that column. Similarly, all transportation margins on inputs are summed and recorded as the input entry for "transportation." Hence, the trade and transportation sectors are not really treated as producing and consuming sectors in the economy, but only as "pass-through" sectors. This simply means that the input-output table does not actually trace flows through the trade and transportation sectors, since this would depict an economy where industries and final customers would make most of their purchases from and sales to these two industries alone. Instead, transactions are depicted as flowing directly from producer to consumer, bypassing trade and transportation. This is done to show the links between producers, consumers, and final customers.

Since trade and transportation margins for all transactions into an industry are accumulated as single values for each industry, they in effect become service inputs to that industry. Hence, the sum of all inputs measured in producers' prices plus the value of all transportation and trade margins valued as service inputs (hence, valued in de facto producers' prices) is then the value of all inputs in consumers' prices (the column sums of the transactions matrix). Margins are discussed in more detail in Elliot-Jones (1971).

Example 3   Suppose we have a four-sector input-output economy with two manufacturing sectors, A and B, and two service sectors, trade and transportation. The service sectors act as both interindustry sectors in their own right as well as a respository for all markups or margins. The interindustry transactions paid in millions of dollars *including* both trade and transportation margins—that is, in purchasers' or consumers' prices—are given by $\tilde{Z}$, final demands including margins by $\bar{Y}$, and total outputs including margins by $\bar{X}$:

$$\tilde{Z} = \begin{bmatrix} 36 & 46 & 83 & 24 \\ 76 & 78 & 94 & 35 \\ 8 & 7 & 8 & 4 \\ 3 & 1 & 5 & 1 \end{bmatrix} \qquad \bar{Y} = \begin{bmatrix} 475 \\ 263 \\ 120 \\ 150 \end{bmatrix} \qquad \bar{X} = \begin{bmatrix} 664 \\ 546 \\ 147 \\ 160 \end{bmatrix}$$

Suppose that the trade and transportation margins in millions of dollars are given by the following:

TRADE MARGINS

	A	B	Trade	Transportation	Final Demand
Industry A	9	10	11	6	50
Industry B	5	8	7	4	20
Transportation	3	1	5	1	20
Total Margins	17	19	23	11	90

TRANSPORTATION MARGINS

	A	B	Trade	Transportation	Final Demand
Industry A	7	4	9	5	75
Industry B	6	8	7	6	13
Trade	8	7	8	4	50
Total Margins	21	19	24	15	138

The sum of the margins in these two tables is the difference between the purchasers' prices and producers' prices. For example, the transaction $\tilde{z}_{11} = \$36$ million incurs a trade markup of \$9 million and a transport markup of \$7 million, leaving a so-called *direct allocation* of \$20 million. Likewise, the transaction $\tilde{z}_{43} = 5$ is transport markup on trade services, for example, transport costs associated with transactions between wholesale and retail trade. The direct allocation for this transaction is zero. Similarly, the transaction $\bar{z}_{34} = 4$ is the trade markup on transportation services, for example, the markup imposed by a principal carrier that subcontracts transport services from a secondary carrier. If we factor out (subtract) the margins from all the interindustry transactions in purchasers' prices, the result is the *direct allocations* matrix:

$$DA = \begin{bmatrix} 20 & 32 & 63 & 13 \\ 65 & 62 & 80 & 25 \\ 0 & 0 & 0 & 0 \\ 0 & 0 & 0 & 0 \end{bmatrix} \quad Y_d = \begin{bmatrix} 350 \\ 230 \\ 100 \\ 100 \end{bmatrix} \quad X_d = \begin{bmatrix} 478 \\ 462 \\ 100 \\ 100 \end{bmatrix}$$

Note that we have also factored the margins out of final demand and total output and termed these vectors Y_d and X_d, respectively. The vector of column sums of the trade margins, labeled "total margins" in the table, represents the sums of all trade margins on inputs to industries, for example, the first element of this vector, \$17 million, is the sum of all trade margins on inputs to industry A. If we add this vector to the trade row of the direct allocations matrix we are, in effect, distributing the trade margins as a service of the trade sector. Similarly, if we assign the "total transportation margins" to the transportation row of the direct allocations matrix, we account for transportation margins as a service of the transportation industry. In this way, we do not trace the flows of goods and services through the trade and transportation sectors, but instead, treat them as service inputs to producing sectors and record the flows directly from producer to consumer. The result is an interindustry transactions matrix in producers' prices:

$$Z = \begin{bmatrix} 20 & 32 & 63 & 13 \\ 65 & 62 & 80 & 25 \\ 17 & 19 & 23 & 11 \\ 21 & 19 & 24 & 15 \end{bmatrix} \quad Y = \begin{bmatrix} 350 \\ 230 \\ 190 \\ 238 \end{bmatrix} \quad X = \begin{bmatrix} 478 \\ 462 \\ 260 \\ 317 \end{bmatrix}$$

Methods of valuation in current use in the literature are discussed in more detail in Bulmer-Thomas (1982).

Accounting for Imports and Exports

Imports in an input-output framework are usually divided into two basic groups: (1) imports of commodities that are also domestically produced (competitive imports)[4] and (2) imports of commodities that are not domestically produced (noncompetitive imports). The distinction, of course, is that competitive imports can be represented in a technical coefficients matrix, while noncompetitive imports cannot. Competitive imports are usually handled by adding transactions to the domestic transactions matrix (as in the case of transfers of secondary products) as if they were domestically produced. However, the "domestic port value" (in effect, value in producers' prices) of all imports of a particular commodity is included as a negative entry in final demand. The

---

[4] Note that this treatment of competitive imports has been adopted only in more recent input-output studies such as the 1972 U.S. National Input-Output Table; earlier studies treated competitive imports in the same manner as secondary products. (Ritz 1979, 1980.)

purpose of this adjustment is to assure that the total output of an industry, computed as the row sum of the interindustry transactions to other industries and final-demand allocation, is total *domestic* production, net of imports.

Noncompetitive imports are assigned to a new industry category, but the total value of all noncompetitive imports is given a negative value in final demand so that, as in the case of competitive imports, the total output—that is, the row sum of transactions and final demand—will be total domestic production, which in this case is zero. The negative final-demand entries in both classes of imports ensure the total production and GNP of the economy are not incorrectly biased by imports.

Example 4 The following is a domestic transactions matrix, Z; final demand vector, Y; and total outputs vector, X; for a two-sector (industries A and B) input-output economy in millions of dollars:

DOMESTIC INTERINDUSTRY TRANSACTIONS (MILLIONS OF DOLLARS)

	A	B	Final Demand	Total Output
Industry A	10	20	70	100
Industry B	30	40	30	100

In addition to these domestic transactions, industry A consumes $10 million worth of B that is imported, in addition to the $30 million worth of B that is domestically produced. In addition, both industries A and B consume another product C that is only produced overseas (a noncompetitive import)—$5 million and $4 million worth for A and B, respectively. The convention usually adopted in accounting for these imports is depicted in the following modified table of transactions.

MODIFIED INTERINDUSTRY TRANSACTIONS (MILLIONS OF DOLLARS)

	A	B	C	Final Demand — Imports Adjustment	Final Demand — Other	Total Output
Industry A	10	20	0	0	70	100
Industry B	40	40	0	−10	30	100
Imports of C	5	4	0	−9	0	0

Note that the competitive import transaction of B by A is transferred—that is, added—as in the convention for transferring secondary production, to the z_{BA} transaction and also recorded as a negative final demand. The noncompetitive imports of C by both A and B are recorded as a new row in the transactions matrix and the sum of all imports of C, $9 million, is recorded as a negative final demand. Hence, the final demand, net of imports, and total outputs are unchanged from the domestic table; final demand and total outputs are customarily defined to include only domestic production.

Adjustments for Inventory Change

Inventories in an input-output model are not quite equivalent to the conventional definition of that term. In input-output models, inventory change is usually taken to mean the change in inventories of an industry's primary product, regardless of which industry or industries hold the inventories. For example, coal inventories held by electric power plants are classified as coal inventory. The traditional definition is usually restricted to the inventory actually held by the industry producing the product. This modified definition is adopted in input-output to ensure that the row total of the transactions and final demands is equal to total current output of the industry. If we ignore inventory depletion or addition, then the row totals are total consumption, not output.

5-3 | COMMODITY-BY-INDUSTRY INPUT-OUTPUT ACCOUNTS

As we mentioned in the last section, the data for most modern input-output tables are compiled through surveys (or a census) of industrial firms in the region of interest. In compiling data for a survey-based table, industries are usually grouped according to a standardized classification scheme, for example, the standard industrial classification (SIC) developed for the U.S. economy by the U.S. Department of Commerce.

Again, recall from the last section that data from an industrial survey are usually collected by establishment, that is, the economic units surveyed are generally situated at individual locations where industrial operations are performed. The information collected from a particular establishment is assigned to an industry category according to its primary product. For example, suppose a manufacturer of fabricated metal products makes both steel casings and steel rods; if the manufacturer produces more steel casings than rods, the entire value of output of the manufacturer is assigned to the industrial category—steel casings. Hence, the total output of an industry is recorded as the sum of the outputs of all establishments assigned to that industry, including both the establishment's characteristic or primary product output and its secondary product output. Such a procedure, of course, can create misleading results in economies where significant secondary production occurs, for example, in the United States[5].

An alternative way of constructing input-output tables that more accurately accounts for secondary production is to use and collect industrial data according to two distinct classification schemes. These are:

1 *Industry Accounts*, which compile data as described above and assign data to industry accounts where an industry category is a cluster of establishments as classified by the SIC code according to primary (characteristic) products, and
2 *Commodity Accounts*, which compile data in terms of the characteristic products of the SIC code, whether the product is produced as a primary or secondary good or service.

[5] Griffin (1976) reports that in some industries as much as 90 percent of output in value terms can be attributed to secondary production.

TABLE 5-7   THE MAKE MATRIX (MILLIONS OF DOLLARS)

	Commodities		Total Output (Industry)
	A	B	
Industry A	90	0	90
Industry B	10	100	110
Total Production (Commodity)	100	100	

With the above definitions, accounting for secondary production is the only difference between industry and commodity accounts—that is, if no secondary production exists, the industry and commodity accounts will be identical. In principle, however, there is no reason why the number and definition of commodities should have a one-to-one relationship with the definition and classification of industrial sectors.

As an example, consider a simple two-sector economy with industries A and B corresponding to the primary products of the establishments included in the definition of these two industries; that is, industry A's primary product is commodity A and industry B's primary product is commodity B. Industry A produces only commodity A (all establishments included in defining industry A produce only commodity A; there is no secondary product). Establishments assigned to industry B, however, while primarily producing commodity B, also produce, as a secondary product, some amount of commodity A. Suppose that industry A produces \$90 million worth of commodity A and industry B produces \$100 million worth of commodity B and \$10 million worth of commodity A.

The Make Matrix

We can display the flows just described in a matrix, the rows of which describe the commodities produced by industries in the economy and the columns of which describe the industry sources of commodity production (see Table 5-7). The on-diagonal elements of this matrix are the primary (characteristic) products of an industry (which, of course, defines the industry in the first place), while off-diagonal elements are the secondary products. This matrix of production outputs is often referred to as the *make* matrix.

The Use Matrix

The make matrix does not really provide a very complete picture of the interindustry activity in an economy, since as we recall from Chapter 2, inputs to an industry production process include not only commodities but also value-added inputs such as wages and salaries to labor, taxes, profits, and so on. In addition, the make matrix does not record the destination of commodity deliveries from an industry (either primary or secondary products)—that is, deliveries either to other industries or to final demand. In order to complete the picture of sources and disposition of industry output, we can define another matrix, often called a *use* matrix, that records the commodity inputs to an

TABLE 5-8 THE USE MATRIX* (MILLIONS OF DOLLARS)

	Industries A	Industries B	Final Demand	Total Output (Commodity)
Commodity A	10	10	80	100
Commodity B	10	7	83	100
Value Added	70	93		
Total Inputs (Industry)	90	110		

* The use matrix is defined to include only the commodity-by-industry flows; that is, the value-added row and final-demand column are not included.

industrial production process; in the literature, the use matrix is sometimes called the *absorption matrix*.

For our example (Table 5-8), let us assume that industry A uses $10 million each of commodities *A* and *B* and $70 million worth of value-added inputs in producing $90 million worth of output assigned to industry *A*. Industry *B* uses $10 million of commodity *A*, $7 million of commodity *B*, and $93 million of value-added inputs in producing $110 million worth of output assigned to industry *B*. Finally, let us assume that final demands for commodities *A* and *B* are $80 million and $83 million, respectively. All the commodity-by-industry transactions depicted in Tables 5-7 and 5-8 are collected and summarized in Table 5-9. Note that there is no industry final-demand vector included in Table 5-9. For now we will consider only final demand for commodities; we will derive industry final demand later.

Given this definition of commodity and industry accounts, we can derive the corresponding direct requirements (technical coefficients) and total requirements matrices. First let us adopt the following notation for *m* commodities and

TABLE 5-9 SUMMARY OF COMMODITY AND INDUSTRY ACCOUNTS

	Commodities A	Commodities B	Industries A	Industries B	Final Demand	Total Output
Commodities A			10	10	80	100
B			10	7 *U*	83 *E*	100 *Q*
Industries A	90	0				90
B	10	100 *V*				110 *X*
Value Added			70	93 *W*	163	
Total Inputs	100	100 *Q'*	90	110 *X'*		200

n industries in the economy:

$V = [v_{ij}]$ is the make matrix; that is, v_{ij} represents the amount of commodity j produced by industry i; V is of dimension $n \times m$.

$U = [u_{ij}]$ is the use matrix; that is, u_{ij} represents the amount of commodity i used by industry j; U is of dimension $m \times n$.

$E = [E_i]$ is the vector of commodity deliveries to final demand; E is of dimension $m \times 1$.

$Q = [Q_i]$ is the vector of commodity gross output; Q is of dimension $m \times 1$.

$W = [W_j]$ is the vector of industry value-added inputs; W is of dimension $1 \times n$.

$X = [X_j]$ is the vector of industry total outputs as defined in Chapter 2; X is of dimension $n \times 1$.

For the example (Table 5-9) we have:

$$U = \begin{bmatrix} 10 & 10 \\ 10 & 7 \end{bmatrix} \qquad E = \begin{bmatrix} 80 \\ 83 \end{bmatrix} \qquad Q = \begin{bmatrix} 100 \\ 100 \end{bmatrix}$$

$$V = \begin{bmatrix} 90 & 0 \\ 10 & 100 \end{bmatrix} \qquad\qquad\qquad X = \begin{bmatrix} 90 \\ 110 \end{bmatrix}$$

$$W = \begin{bmatrix} 70 & 93 \end{bmatrix}$$

Consider again a basic accounting identity from the general input-output model, as given in Eq. (2-1) of Chapter 2, namely

$$X_i = z_{i1} + z_{i2} + \cdots + z_{in} + Y_i$$

Recall that this identity defined total output to be the sum of all deliveries of industry i to other sectors, z_{ij}, plus deliveries to final demands.

In the commodity-by-industry framework we can state the corresponding industry output identity as

$$X_i = v_{i1} + v_{i2} + \cdots + v_{im} \tag{5-1}$$

The total output of an industry i is the sum of the values of commodities $j = 1, 2, \cdots, m$ produced by that industry, v_{ij}. Similarly, again compared to Eq. (2-1) of Chapter 2, the corresponding commodity output identity is

$$Q_i = u_{i1} + u_{i2} + \cdots + u_{in} + E_i \tag{5-2}$$

or the total production of a commodity is the sum of all the amounts of that commodity consumed by industries in the economy plus any sales of that commodity to final customers.

Consider another basic identity from the general input-output model: the sum of all interindustry inputs to a production process, plus any value-added inputs, is equal to the value of the total output of that industry, namely

$$X_j = z_{1j} + z_{2j} + \cdots + z_{nj} + W_j \tag{5-3}$$

In the commodity-by-industry framework this translates to the sum of all *commodity* inputs plus any value-added inputs is equal to the value of that industry's total output, that is,

$$X_j = u_{1j} + u_{2j} + \cdots + u_{mj} + W_j$$

Commodity-by-Industry Direct Requirements

Recall that the definition of a technical coefficient in the general input-output model was

$$a_{ij} = \frac{z_{ij}}{X_j} \qquad (5\text{-}4)$$

This defines the dollars' worth of industry i's output required to produce one dollar's worth of industry j's output. In commodity-by-industry terms this relationship is

$$b_{ij} = \frac{u_{ij}}{X_j} \qquad (5\text{-}5)$$

where b_{ij} is the dollars' worth of *commodity* i required to produce one dollar's worth of *industry* j's output. In matrix terms we recall that Eq. (5-4) can be written as

$$A = Z(\hat{X})^{-1} \qquad (5\text{-}4')$$

Similarly, Eq. (5-5) can be written

$$B = U(\hat{X})^{-1} \qquad (5\text{-}5')$$

For our example

$$B = U(\hat{X})^{-1} = \begin{bmatrix} 10 & 10 \\ 10 & 7 \end{bmatrix} \begin{bmatrix} \dfrac{1}{90} & 0 \\ 0 & \dfrac{1}{110} \end{bmatrix} = \begin{bmatrix} .111 & .091 \\ .111 & .064 \end{bmatrix}$$

Total Requirements Matrices

In Chapter 2 we defined a matrix of total requirements $(I - A)^{-1}$, the Leontief inverse; an element of this matrix, α_{ij}, defined the output of industry i required both directly and indirectly to deliver one dollar's worth of industry j's output to final demand.

In commodity-by-industry models we can derive several variations of total requirements matrices. For example, it may be convenient to collect data for a region on final demands for commodities (as opposed to industry final demands), but the desired total impacts are to be expressed in total industry output, in which case we would need an industry-by-commodity total requirements matrix. Alternatively, one might be interested in total commodity production of a region (regardless of the industry that produced the commodities), in which case we would need a commodity-by-commodity or commodity-by-industry total requirements matrix. To derive these alternative total requirements matrices, we first begin with the commodity balance equation shown earlier as Eq. (5-2).

$$Q_i = u_{i1} + u_{i2} + \cdots + u_{in} + E_i \tag{5-2}$$

In matrix terms we can rewrite Eq. (5-2) as

$$Q = Ui + E \tag{5-2'}$$

where i is a column vector of ones. In less compact form

$$\begin{bmatrix} Q_1 \\ Q_2 \\ \vdots \\ Q_m \end{bmatrix} = \begin{bmatrix} u_{11} & u_{12} & \cdots & u_{1n} \\ u_{21} & u_{22} & \cdots & u_{2n} \\ \vdots & & & \\ u_{m1} & u_{m2} & \cdots & u_{mn} \end{bmatrix} \begin{bmatrix} 1 \\ 1 \\ \vdots \\ 1 \end{bmatrix} + \begin{bmatrix} E_1 \\ E_2 \\ \vdots \\ E_m \end{bmatrix}$$

Now we recall Eq. (5-5')

$$B = U(\hat{X})^{-1}$$

which, after postmultiplying by $\hat{X}$, becomes

$$U = B\hat{X}$$

Let us substitute this expression for U into Eq. (5-2'), so that

$$Q = B\hat{X}i + E$$

Note that $\hat{X}i = X$ as shown in Appendix A. Hence,

$$Q = BX + E \tag{5-6}$$

that is, total commodity output is equal to intermediate commodity production (commodity-by-industry direct requirements multiplied by total industry output) plus commodity deliveries to final demand. This equation is analogous to the basic identity in the traditional Leontief model

$$X = AX + Y$$

or total industry output is equal to intermediate industry production (industry-by-industry direct requirements multiplied by total industry output) plus industry deliveries to final demand.

Commodity-Based Versus Industry-Based Technology The row sums of the make matrix define the vector of total outputs of industries, regardless of what combinations of commodities are produced by those industries. As in Eq. (5-1)

$$X_i = v_{i1} + v_{i2} + \cdots + v_{im}$$

In matrix, terms, this can be written as

$$X = Vi \tag{5-7}$$

Less compactly, this is

$$\begin{bmatrix} X_1 \\ X_2 \\ \vdots \\ X_n \end{bmatrix} = \begin{bmatrix} v_{11} & v_{12} & \cdots & v_{1m} \\ v_{21} & v_{22} & \cdots & v_{2m} \\ \vdots & & & \vdots \\ v_{n1} & v_{n2} & \cdots & v_{nm} \end{bmatrix} \begin{bmatrix} 1 \\ \cdot \\ \vdots \\ 1 \end{bmatrix}$$

If we divide an element of the make matrix, v_{ij}, by the total output of industry i (doing this for all elements of V is called normalizing by its *row* sums), we determine the fraction of total production of industry i that is attributable to production of commodity j; let us call this fraction

$$c_{ij} = \frac{v_{ij}}{X_i} \qquad (5\text{-}8)$$

where c_{ij} is referred to as the *industry output proportion*.[6] In matrix terms

$$C = V'(\hat{X})^{-1} \qquad (5\text{-}8')$$

Note that V' is the transpose of V; C is of dimension m commodities by n industries. If we accept the conventions used in defining the matrix C, we assume that an industry's total output is made up of commodities in fixed proportions; this is often referred to as the *commodity-based technology* assumption. For the example

$$C = V'(\hat{X})^{-1} = \begin{bmatrix} 90 & 10 \\ 0 & 100 \end{bmatrix} \begin{bmatrix} \dfrac{1}{90} & 0 \\ 0 & \dfrac{1}{110} \end{bmatrix} = \begin{bmatrix} 1 & .091 \\ 0 & .909 \end{bmatrix}$$

the first column of C indicates that industry A produces only commodity A. The second column indicates that 9.1 percent of industry B's output is commodity A and 90.9 percent is commodity B.

Let us return once again to the make matrix, V. The column sums of the make matrix we define as the vector of total production of commodities, Q, in the economy, regardless of the industry that produced them; that is,

$$Q_j = v_{1j} + v_{2j} + \cdots + v_{nj}$$

If we divide an element of the make matrix, v_{ij}, by the total production of commodity j (doing this for all elements of V is called normalizing V by its *column* sums), we determine the fraction of total production of commodity j in the economy produced by industry i. That is,

$$d_{ij} = \frac{v_{ij}}{Q_j} \qquad (5\text{-}9)$$

where d_{ij} is referred to as the *commodity output proportion*; in matrix terms

$$D = V(\hat{Q})^{-1} \qquad (5\text{-}9')$$

The matrix D is of dimension n industries by m commodities. If we accept the conventions used in constructing D, we assume that the total output of a commodity is provided by industries in fixed proportions; this is often referred to as an *industry-based-technology* assumption. For the example

$$D = V(\hat{Q})^{-1} = \begin{bmatrix} 90 & 0 \\ 10 & 100 \end{bmatrix} \begin{bmatrix} \dfrac{1}{100} & 0 \\ 0 & \dfrac{1}{100} \end{bmatrix} = \begin{bmatrix} .9 & 0 \\ .1 & 1 \end{bmatrix}$$

---

[6] Note we use c_{ij}; this should not be confused with the convention of c_{ij} to denote trade coefficients in the MRIO model of Chapter 3.

The first column of D indicates that 90 percent of commodity A consumed in the economy comes from industry A and 10 percent comes from industry B. The second column of D indicates that all of commodity B consumed in the economy is produced by industry B.

Calculation of Total Requirements: Industry-Based Technology

From this point we can calculate total requirements matrices based on an assumption of either a commodity-based technology in the input-output table, where the basic result is a commodity-by-commodity total requirements matrix, or alternatively, we can assume an industry-based technology in the input-output table, where the basic result is an industry-by-industry total requirements matrix.

The reader should recall that the purpose of the commodity-by-industry accounts is to deal with the problem of secondary production. The two alternative technology assumptions are different treatments of the same problem. Stone (1961) describes a variety of conditions under which one or the other technology assumption might be preferred. For example, he argues that subsidiary products (as opposed to by-products of an industrial process) fit the commodity-based technology assumption of fixed industry output proportions since the levels of commodity outputs of the primary and secondary commodities of an industry may change. More specifically, if an industry produces a secondary product—that is, a product considered primary (as defined earlier) to another industry—and this production is technologically similar to the primary industry's production process, the secondary product is classified as a *subsidiary* product. For example, suppose an automobile manufacturer produces a number of military tanks in a plant unrelated to that of the automobile manufacturing production (the primary activity). The tanks are subsidiary products if the production process used in manufacturing tanks by the automobile manufacturer is the same as that of producers for which manufacturing tanks is considered the primary activity. Such products seem to fit the commodity-based technology assumption of fixed industry output proportions; the commodity has the same input structure regardless of which industry produces it.

In contrast to subsidiary products, if an industry produces a secondary product that is technically related to its own main production, it is classified as a *by-product* (we discuss another treatment of by-products later). For example, if the automobile manufacturer discussed above also produces automobile parts in the course of producing fully assembled automobiles, the parts might be considered by-products. Such products seem to fit the industry-based technology assumption since their production is directly related to the production of the primary product, that is, all commodities produced by an industry are produced with the same input structure. Hence, the input structure of commodities depends upon the industry in which they are produced.

In sum, while the commodity-based assumption presumes that a commodity has the same input structure, regardless of the industry in which it is produced, industry-based technology presumes that an industry has the same input structure, regardless of its output product mix. Bulmer-Thomas (1982) discusses further additional distinctions in secondary production. For example, by-products for which no industry is considered a primary producer are often called *joint products*. If we include joint products in our input-output accounts, then there will be more commodities than industries, as in problem 5-1 at the end of this chapter.

Let us recall the matrix of commodity output proportions defined in Eq. (5-9') as

$$D = V(\hat{Q})^{-1} \tag{5-9'}$$

which, after multiplying through by $\hat{Q}$, becomes

$$V = D\hat{Q}$$

We also can recall Eq. (5-7), which simply computes total industry output as the sum of all commodities produced by each industry, that is,

$$X = Vi \tag{5-7}$$

Substituting (5-9') into (5-7), we have

$$X = D\hat{Q}i = DQ \tag{5-10}$$

Finally, if we substitute this expression for X into Eq. (5-6), the commodity balance accounting identity, we have

$$Q = BDQ + E \tag{5-10'}$$

By ordinary matrix algebra

$$Q - BDQ = E$$
$$(I - BD)Q = E$$
$$Q = (I - BD)^{-1}E \tag{5-11}$$

The matrix $(I - BD)^{-1}$ is known as the *commodity-by-commodity total require-ments matrix*; the ijth element of this matrix gives the production of commodity i required to deliver a dollar's worth of commodity j to final demand.

For our example

$$(I - BD)^{-1} = \begin{bmatrix} 1.136 & .110 \\ .129 & 1.080 \end{bmatrix}$$

In this matrix, for example, 0.129 dollars' worth of commodity 2 is required to deliver a dollar's worth of commodity 1 to final demand.

If we recall once again the commodity output proportions matrix, D, we can redefine final demand for commodities, E, in terms of industry output as opposed to commodity output. That is, an element of $D = [d_{ij}]$ gives the proportion of total production of commodity j produced by industry i, so that

$$Y_i = d_{ij}E_j$$

or in matrix terms

$$Y = DE \tag{5-12}$$

In our example

$$Y = DE = \begin{bmatrix} .9 & 0 \\ .1 & 1 \end{bmatrix} \begin{bmatrix} 80 \\ 83 \end{bmatrix} = \begin{bmatrix} 72 \\ 91 \end{bmatrix}$$

If we multiply through by D^{-1}, then

$$E = D^{-1}Y \tag{5-12'}$$

which translates industry final demand, Y, into commodity final demand, E. By substituting the expression for E into Eq. (5-11), the definition of commodity-by-commodity total requirements, we obtain the *commodity-by-industry total requirements matrix*, namely the bracketed quantity in

$$Q = \left[(I - BD)^{-1} D^{-1} \right] Y \tag{5-13}$$

For our example,

$$(I - BD)^{-1} D^{-1} = \begin{bmatrix} 1.250 & .110 \\ .023 & 1.080 \end{bmatrix}$$

In this matrix, for example, 0.023 dollars' worth of commodity 2 is required to deliver a dollar's worth of industry 1's output to final demand.

Recall Eq. (5-10), $X = DQ$, and Eq. (5-11), $Q = (I - BD)^{-1}E$. By combining these two equations we obtain

$$X = \left[D(I - BD)^{-1} \right] E \tag{5-14}$$

Hence, the bracketed quantity is the *industry-by-commodity total requirements matrix*; for the example

$$D(I - BD)^{-1} = \begin{bmatrix} 1.022 & .099 \\ .243 & 1.092 \end{bmatrix}$$

In this matrix, for example, 0.243 dollars' worth of industry 2's product is required to deliver a dollar's worth of commodity 1 to final demand.

Finally, if we use Eq. (5-12) to write industry final demands in terms of commodity final demands, we can write (by ordinary matrix algebra)

$$X = D(I - BD)^{-1}E$$
$$D^{-1}X = (I - BD)^{-1}E$$
$$(I - BD)D^{-1}X = E$$
$$(D^{-1} - B)X = E$$
$$D(D^{-1} - B)X = DE$$
$$(I - DB)X = DE$$
$$X = (I - DB)^{-1}DE$$
$$X = \left[(I - DB)^{-1} \right] Y \tag{5-15}$$

where the bracketed quantity is the *industry-by-industry total requirements matrix*; for the example

$$(I - DB)^{-1} = \begin{bmatrix} 1.125 & .099 \\ .148 & 1.092 \end{bmatrix}$$

In this matrix, for example, 0.148 dollars' worth of industry 2's output is required to deliver a dollar's worth of industry 1's output to final demand.

Calculation of Total Requirements: Commodity-Based Technology Instead of employing D as a basis for technology in the input-output economy—that is, assuming that industries have the same input structure regardless of the output product mix—we can alternatively employ C, thereby assuming that commodity input structure is independent of the producing industry.

Let us recall, once again, the accounting identity given in Eq. (5-2'), namely

$$Q = Ui + E \tag{5-2'}$$

which we showed is equivalent to

$$Q = BX + E \tag{5-6}$$

We can recall the definition of *industry output proportions*, C, in Eq. (5-8')

$$C = V'(\hat{X})^{-1}$$

After multiplying through by $\hat{X}$, this becomes

$$V' = C\hat{X}$$

Equivalently,

$$\hat{X} = C^{-1}V'$$

Multiplying through by i yields

$$X = \hat{X}i = C^{-1}V'i \tag{5-16}$$

However, the term $V'i$ is simply summing the rows of V' (or equivalently summing down the columns of V), that is, computing the total commodity outputs Q. More succinctly,

$$Q = V'i$$

so that Eq. (5-16) can be written as

$$X = C^{-1}Q \tag{5-17}$$

The matrix C^{-1} simply translates total commodity output, Q, into total industry output, X.

Finally, if we substitute Eq. (5-17) into the modified commodity balance accounting identity (Eq. [5-6]), we have

$$Q = BC^{-1}Q + E \tag{5-18}$$

Again, by ordinary matrix algebra

$$Q - BC^{-1}Q = E$$
$$(I - BC^{-1})Q = E$$
$$Q = (I - BC^{-1})^{-1}E \tag{5-19}$$

which is simply another definition of the *total commodity-by-commodity requirements matrix*. This time, however, the total requirements matrix is derived in terms of C, industry output proportions, rather than in terms of D, commodity output proportions for an industry, as in the industry-based technology total requirements matrices. For this example

$$(I - BC^{-1})^{-1} = \begin{bmatrix} 1.139 & .113 \\ .136 & 1.086 \end{bmatrix}$$

In this matrix, for example, 0.136 dollars' worth of commodity 2's output is required to deliver a dollar's worth of commodity 1 to final demand. Note that this commodity-by-commodity table is different from the corresponding table using the industry-based technology assumption, $(I - BD)^{-1}$.

Recall that the industry output proportions matrix, C, can be used, just as we used D earlier in Eq. (5-12), to redefine final demand for commodities, E, in terms of industry output as opposed to commodity output:

$$E_k = c_{kj} Y_j \tag{5-20}$$

Or in matrix terms

$$E = CY \tag{5-20'}$$

Hence, we can rewrite Eq. (5-19) as

$$Q = \left[(I - BC^{-1})^{-1} C \right] Y$$

where the bracketed quantity is the *commodity-by-industry total requirements matrix*; for the example

$$(I - BC^{-1})^{-1} C = \begin{bmatrix} 1.139 & .207 \\ .136 & 1.0 \end{bmatrix}$$

In this matrix, for example, 0.136 dollars' worth of commodity 2 is required to deliver a dollar's worth of industry 1's output to final demand. Again, compare with the corresponding table using the industry-based technology assumption.

If we multiply Eq. (5-17) through by C, we can substitute the resulting expression, $Q = CX$, into Eq. (5-19) to obtain

$$CX = (I - BC^{-1})^{-1} E$$

or by ordinary matrix algebra

$$(I - BC^{-1})CX = E$$

$$(C - B)X = E$$

$$C^{-1}(C - B)X = C^{-1}E$$

$$(I - C^{-1}B)X = C^{-1}E$$

$$X = \left[(I - C^{-1}B)^{-1} C^{-1} \right] E \tag{5-21}$$

where the bracketed quantity is the *industry-by-commodity total requirements matrix*;

TABLE 5-10 SUMMARY OF COMMODITY-BY-INDUSTRY TOTAL REQUIRE-MENTS MATRICES

	Industry-Based Technology	Commodity-Based Technology
Commodity-by-Commodity	$(I - BD)^{-1}$	$(I - BC^{-1})^{-1}$
Commodity-by-Industry*	$(I - BD)^{-1}D^{-1}$ or $D^{-1}(I - DB)^{-1}$	$(I - BC^{-1})^{-1}C$ or $C(I - C^{-1}B)^{-1}$
Industry-by-Commodity*	$D(I - BD)^{-1}$ or $(I - DB)^{-1}D$	$C^{-1}(I - BC^{-1})^{-1}$ or $(I - C^{-1}B)^{-1}C^{-1}$
Industry-by-Industry	$(I - DB)^{-1}$	$(I - C^{-1}B)^{-1}$

*It should be clear by now that for two square matrices α and β, $\alpha(I - \beta\alpha)^{-1} = (I - \alpha\beta)^{-1}\alpha$ and $\alpha^{-1}(I - \alpha\beta)^{-1} = (I - \beta\alpha)^{-1}\alpha^{-1}$.

for the example

$$(I - C^{-1}B)^{-1}C^{-1} = \begin{bmatrix} 1.125 & 0 \\ .148 & 1.183 \end{bmatrix}$$

In this matrix, for example, 0.148 dollars' worth of industry 2's output is required to deliver a dollar's worth of commodity 1 output to final demand. Again, compare this table with the corresponding table using the industry-based technology assumption.

Finally, if we multiply Eq. (5-20′) through by C^{-1}, we can once again rewrite Eq. (5-21) as

$$X = (I - C^{-1}B)^{-1}C^{-1}E$$

$$X = \left[(I - C^{-1}B)^{-1} \right] Y$$

where the bracketed quantity is the *industry-by-industry total requirements matrix*; for the example

$$(I - C^{-1}B)^{-1} = \begin{bmatrix} 1.125 & .102 \\ .148 & 1.089 \end{bmatrix}$$

In this matrix, for example, 0.148 dollars' worth of industry 2's output is required to deliver a dollar's worth industry 1's output to final demand. All the total requirements matrices are summarized in Table 5-10.

Direct Definition of Technology Assumptions

Recall the commodity-based technology assumption accounting identity given as Equation (5-18):

$$Q = BC^{-1}Q + E \tag{5-18}$$

Let us define the commodity-by-commodity direct requirements matrix under this assumption as A_C where

$$A_C = BC^{-1} \tag{5-22}$$

so that Equation (5-18) can be written as

$$Q = A_C Q + E \tag{5-23}$$

If we substitute the definition of B and C^{-1} given earlier in Eqs. (5-5′) and (5-8′), respectively, Eq. (5-22) becomes:

$$A_C = BC^{-1}$$
$$= \left[U(\hat{X})^{-1} \right] \left[V'(\hat{X})^{-1} \right]^{-1}$$
$$= \left[U(\hat{X})^{-1} \right] \left[(\hat{X})(V')^{-1} \right]$$
$$= U(V')^{-1} \tag{5-24}$$

Hence, we can define the commodity-by-commodity direct requirements matrix for the commodity-based technology assumption directly in terms of the original make and use matrices. Use of B and C^{-1}, as defined earlier, serves only to specify the underlying technology assumptions.

Recall that the make matrix, V, depicts the levels of commodity production of each industry in the economy. If V is a diagonal matrix then there is no secondary production in the economy at all. Hence the on-diagonal elements of V depict primary production in the economy while off-diagonal elements depict secondary production. As discussed in Appendix A, let us define the matrix made up of only the on-diagonal elements of V as $\hat{V}$ and the corresponding matrix of only off-diagonal elements of V as $\check{V}$. (If V is a nonsquare matrix, $\hat{V}$ will still contain elements v_{ii} only.) Hence,

$$V = \hat{V} + \check{V} \tag{5-25}$$

Note that in traditional input-output tables, since secondary production is not recognized and no distinction is made between industries and commodities, $U = Z$, $\hat{V} = \hat{X}$, and $\check{V} = 0$. Hence, the basic definition of the direct requirements matrix becomes

$$A = Z(\hat{X})^{-1} = U(\hat{V})^{-1} \tag{5-26}$$

Note also that, since $\hat{V}$ is a diagonal matrix, in this case, $\hat{V} = (\hat{V}')$ and Eqs. (5-24) and (5-26) are equivalent.

The industry-based technology assumption can also be defined directly in terms of U and V. Recall the industry-based technology assumption accounting identity given earlier as Eq. (5-10′):

$$Q = BDQ + E \tag{5-10′}$$

Let us define the commodity-by-commodity direct requirements matrix under the industry-based technology assumption as A_I where

$$A_I = BD \tag{5-27}$$

so that Eq. (5-10′) can be written as

$$Q = A_I Q + E \tag{5-28}$$

Substituting the definition of B and D given earlier as Eqs. (5-5′) and (5-9′), respectively, Eq. (5-27) becomes

$$A_I = BD$$

$$= \left[U(\hat{X})^{-1} \right] \left[V(\hat{Q})^{-1} \right]$$

$$= U\langle Vi \rangle^{-1} V\langle V'i \rangle^{-1} \tag{5-29}$$

While this is clearly a good deal more cumbersome than A_C, it is also directly defined in terms of U and V. Similar but more complicated expressions can be derived for the direct definition of technical coefficients in terms of U and V for industry-based matrices.

The By-product Technology Assumption

Some researchers have criticized the industry technology assumption on several counts (ten Raa et al. 1984), the most important of which has to do with its sensitivity to base-year prices. Ten Raa et al. show that the underlying base-year prices become a fundamental determinant of the description of the technology under the industry-based technology assumption, for example, much more so than with other technology assumptions. As an alternative to the industry-based technology, if we are interested principally in the input structure of an industry's primary production process, we can define what is called the *by-product technology* assumption. This assumption defines all secondary products as by-products and excludes them from the calculation of the commodity-by-commodity direct requirements matrix. That is, the direct requirements are defined as net of any secondary production. Hence, industry j, in order to deliver primary production v_{jj}, would require net inputs (exclusive of inputs required for secondary production) of

$$a_{ij} = \frac{u_{ij} - \check{v}_{ji}}{v_{jj}} \tag{5-30}$$

As before, if there is no secondary production, then $u_{ij} = z_{ij}$, $\check{v}_{ji} = 0$, and $v_{jj} = X_j$ so that $a_{ij} = z_{ij}/X_j$.

In matrix terms, defining the commodity-by-commodity direct requirements matrix under the by-product technology assumption as A_B, we can write

$$A_B = \left[U - (\check{V}') \right] (\hat{V})^{-1} \tag{5-31}$$

For our example

$$\check{V} = \begin{bmatrix} 0 & 0 \\ 10 & 0 \end{bmatrix} \quad \text{and} \quad \hat{V} = \begin{bmatrix} 90 & 0 \\ 0 & 100 \end{bmatrix}$$

so

$$(I - A_B)^{-1} = \begin{bmatrix} 1.125 & 0 \\ .134 & 1.075 \end{bmatrix}$$

where

$$A_B = \begin{bmatrix} .111 & 0 \\ .111 & .070 \end{bmatrix}$$

For the example, we can compare this with the corresponding commodity-by-commodity direct requirements matrices under the industry-based and commodity-based technology assumptions, defining $A_I = BD = U\langle Vi \rangle^{-1} V \langle V'i \rangle^{-1}$ and $A_C = BC^{-1} = U(V')^{-1}$:

$$A_I = \begin{bmatrix} .109 & .091 \\ .106 & .064 \end{bmatrix} \qquad A_C = \begin{bmatrix} .111 & .089 \\ .111 & .059 \end{bmatrix}$$

The reader should trace the implications of the underlying assumptions through the calculations of each of these cases.

Mixed Technology Assumptions

In practice, it is not necessary to rely completely on industry-based (or the alternative by-product) or commodity-based technology assumptions alone. These assumptions can be mixed so that some commodities/industries rely on the former while others rely on the latter. This can be accomplished in a variety of ways (see United Nations, 1968); in Appendix 5-1 we illustrate several techniques. Basically, these mixed procedures involve dividing the make matrix, V, into two separate matrices (which when added together form V); the commodity-based assumption is invoked for one matrix while the industry-based technology is invoked for the other. (We can also replace the industry-based technology assumption with the by-product technology assumption in these mixed technology formulations.) Commodity-by-industry accounts have also been extended to interregional input-output models by Hoffman and Kent (1970).

5-4 | AGGREGATION OF INPUT-OUTPUT TABLES

The number of industrial sectors defined in an output-output table (often referred to as the level of *sectoral* aggregation) is usually decided in the context of the problem being considered, for example, whether or not it is important to distinguish between fully assembled automobiles and automobile parts produced separately by Ford Motor Company; a more aggregated sector labeled "automobiles and parts" may be sufficient. Other considerations such as computational expense or availability of data may also weigh heavily in this decision. Similarly, in multiple-region models—that is, interregional or multiregional models as defined in Chapter 3—the number of regions considered in the model (the level of *spatial* aggregation) must also be selected in the problem being considered, for example, if we are interested in the impacts of increased coal development on regions in the United States, how should states be grouped into regions (assuming the basic data are state-specific) to construct an applicable model? Moreover, what information, if any, is lost in performing this aggregation?

Since the early 1950s there has been considerable attention in the literature given to establishing criteria for and measuring the effects of aggregation of sectors in input-output models. Representative examples include Ara (1950), Balderston and Whitin (1954), Hatanka (1952), McManus (1956), Malinvaud

(1956), Morimoto (1970), and Theil (1957). The question is likely to be even more important at the regional level, where good data are often unavailable or difficult and prohibitively expensive to obtain (see Doeksen and Little 1960, Williamson 1970, and Hewings 1972). More recently the spatial aggregation question has also been considered for interregional and multiregional input-output models (Miller and Blair 1981 or Blair and Miller 1983.)

In this section we examine the effects of aggregation on input-output models. In particular, we investigate several measures of the bias or error introduced by aggregation.

The Aggregation Matrix

Before examining the effects of aggregation, let us develop a systematic way of accomplishing aggregation of sectors in an input-output table. First, let us define a matrix S, the aggregation matrix, to be a $k \times n$ matrix of ones and zeros, where k is the number of sectors in the to-be-created aggregated version of the input-output table and n is the number of sectors in the existing unaggregated version of the table. The locations of ones in row i of S indicate which sectors of the unaggregated table will be grouped together as sector i in the aggregated table.

For example, let $n = 4$ and $k = 3$; suppose that sectors 2 and 3 of the disaggregated table are to be combined. Then the aggregation matrix that accomplishes this is

$$S = \begin{bmatrix} 1 & 0 & 0 & 0 \\ 0 & 1 & 1 & 0 \\ 0 & 0 & 0 & 1 \end{bmatrix}$$

Let Z denote the unaggregated 4×4 transactions matrix and Z^* be the corresponding aggregated 3×3 transactions matrix. Similarly, Y and Y^* are the unaggregated and aggregated vectors of final demand, respectively. Recall that our aim is to aggregate sectors 2 and 3 of the unaggregated model; for Y this can easily be accomplished by premultiplying by S:

$$Y^* = SY = \begin{bmatrix} 1 & 0 & 0 & 0 \\ 0 & 1 & 1 & 0 \\ 0 & 0 & 0 & 1 \end{bmatrix} \begin{bmatrix} Y_1 \\ Y_2 \\ Y_3 \\ Y_4 \end{bmatrix} = \begin{bmatrix} Y_1 \\ Y_2 + Y_3 \\ Y_4 \end{bmatrix} \tag{5-32}$$

For Z, this can be accomplished by

$$Z^* = SZS' = \begin{bmatrix} 1 & 0 & 0 & 0 \\ 0 & 1 & 1 & 0 \\ 0 & 0 & 0 & 1 \end{bmatrix} \begin{bmatrix} z_{11} & z_{12} & z_{13} & z_{14} \\ z_{21} & z_{22} & z_{23} & z_{24} \\ z_{31} & z_{32} & z_{33} & z_{34} \\ z_{41} & z_{42} & z_{43} & z_{44} \end{bmatrix} \begin{bmatrix} 1 & 0 & 0 \\ 0 & 1 & 0 \\ 0 & 1 & 0 \\ 0 & 0 & 1 \end{bmatrix} \tag{5-33}$$

$$Z^* = \begin{bmatrix} z_{11} & z_{12} + z_{13} & z_{14} \\ z_{21} + z_{31} & z_{22} + z_{23} + z_{32} + z_{33} & z_{24} + z_{34} \\ z_{41} & z_{42} + z_{43} & z_{44} \end{bmatrix}$$

The new corresponding vector of total outputs X^* can be computed as

$$X^* = Z^*i + Y^* \tag{5-34}$$

where, as before, i is a column vector of ones.

We can also use the aggregation matrix to reorder sectors. For example, the matrix S given above is the one that introduces the least sector labeling rearrangement into the aggregated matrix; that is, the original first sector remains sector 1 and the original "last" sector, 4, becomes the "last" sector, 3, in the aggregated model. Alternatively, $S = \begin{bmatrix} 0 & 1 & 1 & 0 \\ 1 & 0 & 0 & 0 \\ 0 & 0 & 0 & 1 \end{bmatrix}$ groups original sectors 2 and 3 together and labels them sector 1 in the aggregated matrix, labels original sector 1 as sector 2 in the aggregated matrix, and the original sector 4 as sector 3 in the aggregated matrix.

If we are given a new set of final demands, $\tilde{Y}$, for which we wish to compute the corresponding total output needed to support that final demand, we can compute the Leontief inverse matrices for both unaggregated and aggregated versions of the model

$$A = Z\hat{X}^{-1} \quad \text{and} \quad A^* = Z^*(\hat{X}^*)^{-1}$$

$$(I - A)^{-1} \quad \text{and} \quad (I - A^*)^{-1}$$

As in the case of the initial set of final demands, the aggregated vector of new final demands is

$$\tilde{Y}^* = S\tilde{Y}$$

Hence, impact analysis yields

$$\tilde{X} = (I - A)^{-1}\tilde{Y} \quad \text{and} \quad \tilde{X}^* = (I - A^*)^{-1}\tilde{Y}^*$$

Note that, except under very special circumstances which we describe later, $\tilde{X}^* \neq S\tilde{X}$; the difference between $\tilde{X}^*$ and $S\tilde{X}$ is one indication of the bias introduced by aggregating the input-output table from four to three sectors.

Example 5: Sectoral Aggregation We begin with a four-sector input-output model defined by the following:

$$Z = \begin{bmatrix} 26.5 & 75.0 & 46.0 & 53.0 \\ 34.0 & 5.0 & 68.0 & 68.0 \\ 41.5 & 38.0 & 52.0 & 83.0 \\ 33.5 & 6.0 & 53.0 & 67.0 \end{bmatrix} \quad Y = \begin{bmatrix} 659.5 \\ 1835.0 \\ 2515.5 \\ 1560.5 \end{bmatrix} \quad X = \begin{bmatrix} 860 \\ 2010 \\ 2730 \\ 1720 \end{bmatrix}$$

Let us consider two alternative sectoral aggregations of this model, given respectively by the aggregation matrices S_1 and S_2:

$$S_1 = \begin{bmatrix} 1 & 0 & 0 & 0 \\ 0 & 1 & 0 & 0 \\ 0 & 0 & 1 & 1 \end{bmatrix} \quad S_2 = \begin{bmatrix} 0 & 1 & 0 & 0 \\ 0 & 0 & 1 & 0 \\ 1 & 0 & 0 & 1 \end{bmatrix}$$

S_1 combines sectors 3 and 4 of the four-sector model into sector 3 of a three-sector model, leaving sectors 1 and 2 unaggregated. S_2 combines sectors 1 and 4 of the four-sector model into sector 3 of a three-sector model and assigns sectors 2 and 3 of the four-sector model to sectors 1 and 2, respectively, in a three-sector model.

From Eqs. (5-32), (5-33), and (5-34) we can compute the corresponding aggregated values of Y, Z, and X for the two alternative aggregation schemes. For the S_1 aggregation scheme, we have

$$Y_1^* = S_1 Y = \begin{bmatrix} 659.5 \\ 1835.0 \\ 4076.0 \end{bmatrix}$$

$$Z_1^* = S_1 Z S_1' = \begin{bmatrix} 26.5 & 75.0 & 99.0 \\ 34.0 & 5.0 & 136.0 \\ 75.0 & 44.0 & 255.0 \end{bmatrix}$$

$$X_1^* = Z_1^* i + Y_1^* = \begin{bmatrix} 860 \\ 2010 \\ 4450 \end{bmatrix}$$

Similarly, for the S_2 aggregation scheme, we have

$$Y_2^* = S_2 Y = \begin{bmatrix} 1835.0 \\ 2515.5 \\ 2220.0 \end{bmatrix}$$

$$Z_2^* = S_2 Z S_2' = \begin{bmatrix} 5.0 & 68.0 & 102.0 \\ 38.0 & 52.0 & 124.5 \\ 81.0 & 99.0 & 180.0 \end{bmatrix}$$

$$X_2^* = Z_2^* i + Y_2^* = \begin{bmatrix} 2010 \\ 2730 \\ 2580 \end{bmatrix}$$

Let us now compute the technical coefficients matrix and Leontief inverse for each of the aggregation schemes. For S_1, we have

$$A_1^* = Z_1^* \left(\hat{X}_1^* \right)^{-1} = \begin{bmatrix} 0.031 & 0.037 & 0.022 \\ 0.040 & 0.003 & 0.031 \\ 0.087 & 0.022 & 0.057 \end{bmatrix};$$

$$\left(I - A_1^* \right)^{-1} = \begin{bmatrix} 1.036 & 0.039 & 0.026 \\ 0.044 & 1.005 & 0.034 \\ 0.097 & 0.027 & 1.064 \end{bmatrix}$$

and for S_2, we have

$$A_2^* = Z_2^* \left(\hat{X}_2^* \right)^{-1} = \begin{bmatrix} 0.002 & 0.025 & 0.040 \\ 0.019 & 0.019 & 0.048 \\ 0.040 & 0.036 & 0.070 \end{bmatrix};$$

$$\left(I - A_2^* \right)^{-1} = \begin{bmatrix} 1.005 & 0.027 & 0.044 \\ 0.022 & 1.022 & 0.054 \\ 0.044 & 0.041 & 1.079 \end{bmatrix}$$

Suppose we are given a new final demand, $\tilde{Y}$, which is presented to the economy as

$$\tilde{Y} = \begin{bmatrix} 10 \\ 10 \\ 10 \\ 10 \end{bmatrix}$$

For the two alternative aggregations, the corresponding final-demand vectors are

$$\tilde{Y}_1^* = S_1\tilde{Y} = \begin{bmatrix} 10 \\ 10 \\ 20 \end{bmatrix}; \qquad \tilde{Y}_2^* = S_2\tilde{Y} = \begin{bmatrix} 10 \\ 10 \\ 20 \end{bmatrix}$$

The corresponding total output vectors are

$$\tilde{X}_1^* = \left(I - A_1^*\right)^{-1}\tilde{Y}_1^* = \begin{bmatrix} 11.26 \\ 11.16 \\ 22.52 \end{bmatrix}; \qquad \tilde{X}_2^* = \left(I - A_2^*\right)^{-1}\tilde{Y}_2^* = \begin{bmatrix} 11.20 \\ 11.51 \\ 22.43 \end{bmatrix}$$

If we use the unaggregated model in impact analysis, the total output vector is

$$\tilde{X} = \left(I - A\right)^{-1}\tilde{Y} = \begin{bmatrix} 11.30 \\ 11.20 \\ 11.51 \\ 11.13 \end{bmatrix}$$

where $A = Z(\hat{X})^{-1}$ from the original unaggregated matrix of transactions, Z, and vector of total outputs, X. If we aggregate the vector $\tilde{X}$ by the two aggregation schemes, we obtain

$$S_1\tilde{X} = \begin{bmatrix} 11.30 \\ 11.20 \\ 22.64 \end{bmatrix} \quad \text{and} \quad S_2\tilde{X} = \begin{bmatrix} 11.20 \\ 11.51 \\ 22.43 \end{bmatrix}$$

Note that while $\tilde{X}_1^*$ and $S_1\tilde{X}$ are quite different, $\tilde{X}_2^*$ and $S_2\tilde{X}$ are identical. That is, no error is introduced in the second aggregation scheme, S_2. We will see more formally later why this is true, but for the time being, we look at the original unaggregated matrix of technical coefficients, A:

$$A = Z(\hat{X})^{-1} = \begin{bmatrix} 0.031 & 0.037 & 0.017 & 0.031 \\ 0.040 & 0.003 & 0.025 & 0.040 \\ 0.048 & 0.019 & 0.019 & 0.048 \\ 0.039 & 0.003 & 0.019 & 0.039 \end{bmatrix}$$

Note that the first and last columns of A are identical, that is, the two industries have identical production characteristics. In the S_2 aggregation scheme, these two industries are aggregated into one; this was not the case in the S_1 aggregation scheme.

Measures of Aggregation Bias

Total aggregation bias has been defined—for example, in Morimoto (1970)—as the difference between the vector of total outputs in the aggregated system and the vector obtained by aggregating the total outputs in the original unaggregated system. As in the last example, for some new vector of final demands, Y, the total output vector in the unaggregated model is $X = (I - A)^{-1}Y$. The total output vector in the aggregated model is $X^* = (I - A^*)^{-1}Y^*$, and the total aggregation bias is defined as

$$T = X^* - SX \tag{5-35}$$

That is, $T = (I - A^*)^{-1}Y^* - S(I - A)^{-1}Y$, or

$$T = \left[(I - A^*)^{-1}S - S(I - A)^{-1} \right]Y$$

Using the power series results,

$$\begin{aligned}
T &= \left[(I + A^* + A^{*2} + \cdots)S - S(I + A + A^2 + \cdots) \right]Y \\
&= \left[(A^*S - SA) + (A^{*2}S - SA^2) + \cdots \right]Y
\end{aligned} \tag{5-36}$$

The first term in this series has been defined as the "first-order" aggregation bias (Theil 1957); that is,

$$F = (A^*S - SA)Y \tag{5-37}$$

We present two basic theorems regarding aggregation bias and, in particular, when it will vanish. One has to do with the nature of the A and A^* matrices, that is, with the structural characteristics of the economy; the other has to do with the nature of the final-demand vectors, Y and Y^*, being studied. The former is

Theorem I   The total aggregation bias vanishes (i.e., $T = 0$) for any Y if and only if $A^*S = SA$.

This follows from the expression for T in Eq. (5-36) since, if $A^*S = SA$, $A^{*2}S - SA^2 = A^*A^*S - SAA = A^*(SA) - (A^*S)A = 0$, and similarly, for higher-order terms in the series. This theorem suggests that if two (or more) sectors have identical interindustry structures (i.e., equal columns in the A matrix, as we found in the example), then aggregation of these sectors will result in zero total aggregation bias.

For example, consider a three-sector economy in which sectors 1 and 3 have the same interindustry input structure:

$$A = \begin{bmatrix} a_{11} & a_{12} & a_{11} \\ a_{21} & a_{22} & a_{21} \\ a_{31} & a_{32} & a_{31} \end{bmatrix} \qquad X = \begin{bmatrix} X_1 \\ X_2 \\ X_3 \end{bmatrix}$$

The corresponding transactions matrix is found by

$$Z = A\hat{X} = \begin{bmatrix} a_{11} & a_{12} & a_{11} \\ a_{21} & a_{22} & a_{21} \\ a_{31} & a_{32} & a_{31} \end{bmatrix} \begin{bmatrix} X_1 & 0 & 0 \\ 0 & X_2 & 0 \\ 0 & 0 & X_3 \end{bmatrix} = \begin{bmatrix} a_{11}X_1 & a_{12}X_2 & a_{11}X_3 \\ a_{21}X_1 & a_{22}X_2 & a_{21}X_3 \\ a_{31}X_1 & a_{32}X_2 & a_{31}X_3 \end{bmatrix}$$

The proper aggregation matrix for combining sectors 1 and 3 is

$$S = \begin{bmatrix} 1 & 0 & 1 \\ 0 & 1 & 0 \end{bmatrix}$$

Hence, the aggregated transactions matrix and total outputs vector are

$$Z^* = SZS' = \begin{bmatrix} 1 & 0 & 1 \\ 0 & 1 & 0 \end{bmatrix} \begin{bmatrix} a_{11}X_1 & a_{12}X_2 & a_{11}X_3 \\ a_{21}X_1 & a_{22}X_2 & a_{21}X_3 \\ a_{31}X_1 & a_{32}X_2 & a_{31}X_3 \end{bmatrix} \begin{bmatrix} 1 & 0 \\ 0 & 1 \\ 1 & 0 \end{bmatrix}$$

$$Z^* = \begin{bmatrix} a_{11}X_1 + a_{31}X_1 + a_{11}X_3 + a_{31}X_3 & a_{12}X_2 + a_{32}X_2 \\ a_{21}X_1 + a_{21}X_3 & a_{22}X_2 \end{bmatrix}$$

$$X^* = SX = \begin{bmatrix} 1 & 0 & 1 \\ 0 & 1 & 0 \end{bmatrix} \begin{bmatrix} X_1 \\ X_2 \\ X_3 \end{bmatrix} = \begin{bmatrix} X_1 + X_3 \\ X_2 \end{bmatrix}$$

Hence, the aggregated technical coefficients matrix is found by

$$A^* = Z^*(\hat{X}^*)^{-1} = \begin{bmatrix} \dfrac{(a_{11} + a_{31})(X_1 + X_3)}{X_1 + X_3} & \dfrac{(a_{12} + a_{32})X_2}{X_2} \\ \dfrac{a_{21}(X_1 + X_3)}{X_1 + X_3} & \dfrac{a_{22}X_2}{X_2} \end{bmatrix}$$

$$A^* = \begin{bmatrix} a_{11} + a_{31} & a_{12} + a_{32} \\ a_{21} & a_{22} \end{bmatrix}$$

Theorem I asserts that there will be no aggregation bias when two columns are identical, that is, when $A^*S = SA$. For our general example this can be shown by

$$A^*S = \begin{bmatrix} a_{11} + a_{31} & a_{12} + a_{32} \\ a_{21} & a_{22} \end{bmatrix} \begin{bmatrix} 1 & 0 & 1 \\ 0 & 1 & 0 \end{bmatrix} = \begin{bmatrix} a_{11} + a_{31} & a_{12} + a_{32} & a_{11} + a_{31} \\ a_{21} & a_{22} & a_{21} \end{bmatrix}$$

and

$$SA = \begin{bmatrix} 1 & 0 & 1 \\ 0 & 1 & 0 \end{bmatrix} \begin{bmatrix} a_{11} & a_{12} & a_{11} \\ a_{21} & a_{22} & a_{21} \\ a_{31} & a_{32} & a_{31} \end{bmatrix} = \begin{bmatrix} a_{11} + a_{31} & a_{12} + a_{32} & a_{11} + a_{31} \\ a_{21} & a_{22} & a_{21} \end{bmatrix}$$

which are clearly the same.

The second theorem on aggregation bias is

Theorem II If some sectors are not aggregated and the new final demands occur only in unaggregated sectors, the first-order aggregation bias will vanish.

For a general three-sector economy, the unaggregated and aggregated technical coefficients matrices, A and A^*, respectively, are:

$$A = \begin{bmatrix} \dfrac{z_{11}}{X_1} & \dfrac{z_{12}}{X_2} & \dfrac{z_{13}}{X_3} \\[2mm] \dfrac{z_{21}}{X_1} & \dfrac{z_{22}}{X_2} & \dfrac{z_{23}}{X_3} \\[2mm] \dfrac{z_{31}}{X_1} & \dfrac{z_{32}}{X_2} & \dfrac{z_{33}}{X_3} \end{bmatrix} \qquad A^* = \begin{bmatrix} \dfrac{z_{11}}{X_1} & \dfrac{z_{12}+z_{13}}{X_2+X_3} \\[2mm] \dfrac{z_{21}+z_{31}}{X_1} & \dfrac{z_{22}+z_{23}+z_{32}+z_{33}}{X_2+X_3} \end{bmatrix}$$

The unaggregated sector is sector 1 (in both the aggregated and unaggregated models). Consider final-demand vectors for which only the unaggregated elements are nonzero:

$$Y = \begin{bmatrix} Y_1 \\ 0 \\ 0 \end{bmatrix} \qquad Y^* = SY = \begin{bmatrix} Y_1 \\ 0 \end{bmatrix}$$

This theorem asserts that the first-order aggregation bias, $F = (A^*S - SA)Y$ is zero for final demands such as those given as Y and Y^* above. For the example:

$$SA = \begin{bmatrix} 1 & 0 & 0 \\ 0 & 1 & 1 \end{bmatrix} \begin{bmatrix} \dfrac{z_{11}}{X_1} & \dfrac{z_{12}}{X_2} & \dfrac{z_{13}}{X_3} \\[2mm] \dfrac{z_{21}}{X_1} & \dfrac{z_{22}}{X_2} & \dfrac{z_{23}}{X_3} \\[2mm] \dfrac{z_{31}}{X_1} & \dfrac{z_{32}}{X_2} & \dfrac{z_{33}}{X_3} \end{bmatrix} = \begin{bmatrix} \dfrac{z_{11}}{X_1} & \dfrac{z_{12}}{X_2} & \dfrac{z_{13}}{X_3} \\[2mm] \dfrac{z_{21}+z_{31}}{X_1} & \dfrac{z_{22}+z_{32}}{X_2} & \dfrac{z_{23}+z_{33}}{X_3} \end{bmatrix}$$

and

$$A^*S = \begin{bmatrix} \dfrac{z_{11}}{X_1} & \dfrac{z_{12}+z_{13}}{X_2+X_3} & \dfrac{z_{12}+z_{13}}{X_2+X_3} \\[2mm] \dfrac{z_{21}+z_{31}}{X_1} & \dfrac{z_{22}+z_{23}+z_{32}+z_{33}}{X_2+X_3} & \dfrac{z_{22}+z_{23}+z_{32}+z_{33}}{X_2+X_3} \end{bmatrix}$$

Hence, the first-order bias, given Y as defined earlier, is

$$F = (A^*S - SA)Y =$$

$$\begin{bmatrix} 0 & \left(\dfrac{z_{12}+z_{13}}{X_2+X_3} - \dfrac{z_{12}}{X_2}\right) & \left(\dfrac{z_{12}+z_{13}}{X_2+X_3} - \dfrac{z_{13}}{X_3}\right) \\[3mm] 0 & \left(\dfrac{z_{22}+z_{23}+z_{32}+z_{33}}{X_2+X_3} - \dfrac{z_{22}+z_{32}}{X_2}\right) & \left(\dfrac{z_{22}+z_{23}+z_{32}+z_{33}}{X_2+X_3} - \dfrac{z_{23}+z_{33}}{X_3}\right) \end{bmatrix}$$

$$\times \begin{bmatrix} Y_1 \\ 0 \\ 0 \end{bmatrix} = \begin{bmatrix} 0 \\ 0 \end{bmatrix}$$

Thus, if one is studying the effect of new final demand only for sector 1's output in an n-sector model, any and all combinations of sectors 2 through n into fewer sectors will generate no first-order aggregation bias.

Although these theorems are stated in terms of sectoral aggregation, they also have implications for spatial aggregation in interregional models. In general, the conditions of Theorem I are almost certain not to be met as one combines regions in an interregional input-output model, but the conditions of Theorem II will be met in many cases. Aggregation bias in interregional and multiregional input-output models is discussed in detail in Miller and Blair (1981) and Blair and Miller (1983). Additional theorems on sectoral aggregation bias based on statistical properties are discussed in Gibbons et al. (1982).

We now consider two examples of *spatial* aggregation for the three-region Japanese interregional and the U.S. multiregional input-output models introduced in Chapter 3.

Example 6: Spatial Aggregation of IRIO Models   Spatial aggregation of interregional input-output models is in many respects identical to sectoral aggregation. In Chapter 3 we presented a three-region, five-sector version of the Japanese IRIO models. Let us consider the case of aggregating this model to two regions, the first being region 1 (Central), unaggregated, of the three-region model. The second aggregated model region is to be composed by combining regions 2 (North) and 3 (South) of the three-region model. Hence, using the notation of Chapter 3 for IRIO transactions and denoting the regions of the aggregated model by a (Central) and b (North plus South), the new transactions matrix is found by (for $i, j = 1, \cdots, 5$ in all cases)

$$z_{ij}^{aa} = z_{ij}^{11}$$

$$z_{ij}^{ab} = z_{ij}^{12} + z_{ij}^{13}$$

$$z_{ij}^{ba} = z_{ij}^{21} + z_{ij}^{31}$$

$$z_{ij}^{bb} = z_{ij}^{22} + z_{ij}^{23} + z_{ij}^{32} + z_{ij}^{33}$$

Similarly, final demands are found by

$$Y_i^a = Y_i^1$$

$$Y_i^b = Y_i^2 + Y_i^3$$

Note that we can easily accomplish this spatial aggregation by constructing an aggregation matrix, S, as we did in the case of sectoral aggregation:

$$S = \begin{bmatrix}
1 & 0 & 0 & 0 & 0 & 0 & 0 & 0 & 0 & 0 & 0 & 0 & 0 & 0 & 0 \\
0 & 1 & 0 & 0 & 0 & 0 & 0 & 0 & 0 & 0 & 0 & 0 & 0 & 0 & 0 \\
0 & 0 & 1 & 0 & 0 & 0 & 0 & 0 & 0 & 0 & 0 & 0 & 0 & 0 & 0 \\
0 & 0 & 0 & 1 & 0 & 0 & 0 & 0 & 0 & 0 & 0 & 0 & 0 & 0 & 0 \\
0 & 0 & 0 & 0 & 1 & 0 & 0 & 0 & 0 & 0 & 0 & 0 & 0 & 0 & 0 \\
0 & 0 & 0 & 0 & 0 & 1 & 0 & 0 & 0 & 0 & 1 & 0 & 0 & 0 & 0 \\
0 & 0 & 0 & 0 & 0 & 0 & 1 & 0 & 0 & 0 & 0 & 1 & 0 & 0 & 0 \\
0 & 0 & 0 & 0 & 0 & 0 & 0 & 1 & 0 & 0 & 0 & 0 & 1 & 0 & 0 \\
0 & 0 & 0 & 0 & 0 & 0 & 0 & 0 & 1 & 0 & 0 & 0 & 0 & 1 & 0 \\
0 & 0 & 0 & 0 & 0 & 0 & 0 & 0 & 0 & 1 & 0 & 0 & 0 & 0 & 1
\end{bmatrix}$$

We can use S to create

$$Y^* = SY$$

$$Z^* = SZS'$$

where Y^* is the 10×1 aggregated vector of final demands (the unaggregated vector, Y, is 15×1); Z^* is the aggregated 10×10 interindustry transactions matrix (the unaggregated transactions matrix, Z, is 15×15).

We can subsequently compute the new aggregated total outputs vector as

$$X^* = Z^*i + Y^* = \begin{bmatrix} 151 \\ 113 \\ 211 \\ 122 \\ 175 \\ 157 \\ 116 \\ 423 \\ 136 \\ 213 \end{bmatrix}$$

The new aggregated matrix of IRIO input coefficients, A^*, is

$$A^* = Z^*(\hat{X}^*)^{-1}$$

$$= \begin{bmatrix}
.053 & .000 & .009 & .011 & .009 & .001 & .000 & .002 & .000 & .001 \\
.000 & .001 & .001 & .001 & .002 & .000 & .000 & .000 & .000 & .000 \\
.428 & .723 & .250 & .240 & .180 & .015 & .005 & .046 & .000 & .014 \\
.000 & .001 & .010 & .090 & .012 & .000 & .000 & .001 & .009 & .001 \\
.012 & .029 & .042 & .117 & .125 & .000 & .000 & .008 & .001 & .013 \\
.006 & .000 & .002 & .000 & .000 & .080 & .000 & .014 & .020 & .012 \\
.000 & .000 & .000 & .000 & .000 & .001 & .004 & .002 & .003 & .005 \\
.104 & .063 & .102 & .000 & .015 & .463 & .692 & .297 & .258 & .185 \\
.000 & .003 & .002 & .039 & .000 & .000 & .005 & .010 & .083 & .011 \\
.004 & .039 & .006 & .001 & .003 & .013 & .052 & .037 & .109 & .110
\end{bmatrix}$$

The corresponding Leontief inverse, $(I - A^*)^{-1}$, is

$$\begin{bmatrix}
1.063 & .012 & .015 & .019 & .014 & .004 & .004 & .005 & .002 & .002 \\
.001 & 1.002 & .001 & .002 & .003 & .000 & .001 & .001 & .000 & .000 \\
.639 & 1.016 & 1.380 & .413 & .299 & .075 & .081 & .101 & .041 & .050 \\
.008 & .013 & .016 & 1.107 & .019 & .002 & .002 & .003 & .012 & .002 \\
.050 & .088 & .071 & .170 & 1.161 & .012 & .016 & .021 & .011 & .023 \\
.013 & .008 & .007 & .004 & .002 & 1.099 & .018 & .023 & .033 & .021 \\
.001 & .001 & .001 & .000 & .000 & .003 & 1.007 & .003 & .005 & .007 \\
.267 & .267 & .217 & .092 & .076 & .754 & 1.050 & 1.480 & .477 & .335 \\
.005 & .009 & .006 & .049 & .003 & .009 & .018 & .017 & 1.098 & .018 \\
.021 & .064 & .020 & .015 & .010 & .049 & .105 & .065 & .155 & 1.140
\end{bmatrix}$$

Let us now compute the aggregation bias introduced by grouping regions 2 and 3. Consider the following vector of final demands for the unaggregated (three-region, five-sector) model:

$$\tilde{Y} = (100 \quad 100 \quad \cdots \quad 100)'$$

The corresponding aggregated (two-region, five-sector) version is

$$\tilde{Y}^* = (100 \quad 100 \quad 100 \quad 100 \quad 100 \quad 200 \quad 200 \quad 200 \quad 200 \quad 200)'$$

We can compute $\tilde{X}^* = (I - A^*)^{-1}\tilde{Y}^*$ and $\tilde{X} = (I - A)^{-1}\tilde{Y}$ where A is the original unaggregated technical coefficients matrix. In order to compare $\tilde{X}^*$ and $\tilde{X}$, we must aggregate $\tilde{X}$, which can be accomplished with the sectoral aggregation matrix, S, given earlier, that is, $S\tilde{X}$. Table 5-11 gives the vectors $\tilde{X}^*$, $S\tilde{X}$, and the differences between the corresponding elements. The sum of absolute differences $|S\tilde{X} - \tilde{X}^*|$ for the unaggregated region a (Central) as a percentage of the total outputs in that region, that is, $S\tilde{X}i$, is

$$100\left(\frac{|S\tilde{X} - \tilde{X}^*|i}{S\tilde{X}i} \right) = 100\left(\frac{3.768}{954.792} \right) = .395\%$$

and the corresponding value for region b (North and South) is

$$100\left(\frac{73.319}{1851.735} \right) = 3.96\%$$

This indicates, as expected, that more error is introduced into the prediction of outputs in the aggregated region than in the unaggregated region. The overall error (for both regions) is

$$100\left(\frac{77.087}{2806.527} \right) = 2.747\%$$

Notice that the aggregation bias is quite small in all three calculations, that is, region a, region b, and overall, particularly in the unaggregated region. Miller and Blair (1981) show that spatial aggregation of IRIO models generally seems to introduce only modest bias. This suggests, for example, that if one is interested in the impacts in one region in an interconnected interregional system of a change in final demands for some of the sectors in that region (e.g., effects on the California economy of new federal spending in California, which is one of the interconnected 48 continental states), then a "two-region" model of California and the rest of the United States may be sufficient.

Example 7: Spatial Aggregation of MRIO Models   In Chapter 3 we presented a three-region, five-sector multiregional input-output model of the United States (Tables 3-11 through 3-13). Suppose we wish to aggregate regions 2 (Central) and 3 (West) of the basic three-region model, leaving region 1 (East) unaggregated. We designate the regions in the aggregated model by superscripts a (East) and b (Central plus West) so that the new *intraregional* flow matrices are

TABLE 5-11 Spatial Aggregation of IRIO Models: Example 6

		Aggregated Gross Outputs from the Three-Region Model $S\tilde{X}$	Outputs from the Aggregated Two-Region Model $\tilde{X}*$	Aggregation Error $S\tilde{X} - \tilde{X}*$	Aggregation Error as a Percent of Gross Outputs of the Three-Region Model $100\left(\dfrac{\|S\tilde{X} - \tilde{X}*\|}{S\tilde{X}}\right)$
	Sector				
	1	116.801	115.749	1.052	.901
	2	101.649	101.394	.255	.251
Region a	3	443.529	444.330	− .801	− .181
	4	121.260	120.363	.896	.739
	5	171.553	170.789	.764	.446
Total (Absolute)		954.792	952.625	3.768	
	Sector				
	1	246.876	242.116	4.760	1.928
	2	206.519	205.343	1.176	.570
Region b	3	853.242	911.145	− 57.904	− 6.786
	4	235.381	238.800	− 3.418	− 1.452
	5	309.717	315.778	6.061	− 1.957
Total (Absolute)		1851.735	1913.182	73.319	
Total (Absolute)		2806.527	2865.807	77.087	

found by (for $i, j = 1, \cdots, 5$ in all cases)

$$z^a_{ij} = z^1_{ij}$$

$$z^b_{ij} = z^2_{ij} + z^3_{ij}$$

Similarly, total regional outputs are

$$X^a_i = X^1_i$$

$$X^b_i = X^2_i + X^3_i$$

Hence the input coefficients for the aggregated model are found by

$$a^a_{ij} = \frac{z^a_{ij}}{X^a_j}$$

$$a^b_{ij} = \frac{z^b_{ij}}{X^b_j}$$

The resulting block diagonal aggregated technical coefficients matrix, which we denote A^*, is

$$A^* = \begin{bmatrix} .082 & .003 & .012 & .005 & .061 & .000 & .000 & .000 & .000 & .000 \\ .000 & .196 & .043 & .000 & .000 & .000 & .000 & .000 & .000 & .000 \\ .156 & .211 & .302 & .076 & .110 & .000 & .000 & .000 & .000 & .000 \\ .096 & .133 & .131 & .220 & .101 & .000 & .000 & .000 & .000 & .000 \\ .012 & .001 & .061 & .002 & .234 & .000 & .000 & .000 & .000 & .000 \\ \hline .000 & .000 & .000 & .000 & .000 & .046 & .002 & .030 & .007 & .075 \\ .000 & .000 & .000 & .000 & .000 & .000 & .302 & .057 & .001 & .000 \\ .000 & .000 & .000 & .000 & .000 & .103 & .143 & .281 & .075 & .115 \\ .000 & .000 & .000 & .000 & .000 & .207 & .151 & .127 & .216 & .101 \\ .000 & .000 & .000 & .000 & .000 & .010 & .001 & .075 & .002 & .230 \end{bmatrix}$$

Note that, as is to be expected, the elements in the upper left 5×5 submatrix are the same as those in the upper-left 5×5 submatrix in Table 3-11 in Chapter 3. This is because the East (region 1) remains spatially distinct.

The *interregional* commodity flow matrices for the original unaggregated model are $z_i = z_i^{LM}$ for $L, M = 1, 2, 3$ regions and $i = 1, \cdots, 5$ sectors, a total of five 3×3 matrices. Aggregation from three to two regions for the commodity flows can be accomplished by constructing a spatial aggregation matrix R, as in the case of sectoral aggregation; for this example

$$R = \begin{bmatrix} 1 & 0 & 0 \\ 0 & 1 & 1 \end{bmatrix}$$

We define R to be distinct from the sectoral aggregation matrix, S, defined earlier. The aggregated (2×2) interregional flow matrices, Z_i^*, are found by

$$Z_i^* = R Z_i R' \qquad \text{for } i = 1, \cdots, 5 \text{ industries}$$

We can then construct the aggregated trade coefficients

$$c_i^{ab} = \frac{z_i^{ab}}{T_i^b}$$

where, as defined in Chapter 3, T_i is the vector of column sums of Z_i^*. The trade coefficients matrix for the aggregated MRIO model, C^*, is

$$C^* = \begin{bmatrix} \hat{C}^{aa} & \hat{C}^{ab} \\ \hline \hat{C}^{ba} & \hat{C}^{bb} \end{bmatrix}$$

$$C^* = \begin{bmatrix} .621 & .000 & .000 & .000 & .000 & .047 & .000 & .000 & .000 & .000 \\ .000 & .586 & .000 & .000 & .000 & .000 & .053 & .000 & .000 & .000 \\ .000 & .000 & .738 & .000 & .000 & .000 & .000 & .144 & .000 & .000 \\ .000 & .000 & .000 & .824 & .000 & .000 & .000 & .000 & .121 & .000 \\ .000 & .000 & .000 & .000 & .721 & .000 & .000 & .000 & .000 & .157 \\ \hline .379 & .000 & .000 & .000 & .000 & .953 & .000 & .000 & .000 & .000 \\ .000 & .414 & .000 & .000 & .000 & .000 & .947 & .000 & .000 & .000 \\ .000 & .000 & .262 & .000 & .000 & .000 & .000 & .856 & .000 & .000 \\ .000 & .000 & .000 & .176 & .000 & .000 & .000 & .000 & .879 & .000 \\ .000 & .000 & .000 & .000 & .279 & .000 & .000 & .000 & .000 & .843 \end{bmatrix}$$

Again, the elements in the upper-left submatrix of C^* are the same as those in a similar position in Table 3-12 in Chapter 3, reflecting the fact that the East (region 1) remains unaggregated. The corresponding matrix of MRIO multipliers, $(I - C^*A^*)^{-1}C^*$, is

$$
\begin{bmatrix}
.658 & .004 & .012 & .005 & .039 & .053 & .002 & .006 & .002 & .015 \\
.004 & .680 & .032 & .003 & .004 & .002 & .088 & .014 & .002 & .003 \\
.124 & .180 & 1.007 & .084 & .129 & .045 & .078 & .271 & .037 & .071 \\
.103 & .142 & .161 & 1.031 & .127 & .055 & .068 & .077 & .193 & .065 \\
.017 & .015 & .063 & .008 & .895 & .008 & .010 & .036 & .005 & .243 \\
.425 & .013 & .028 & .007 & .061 & 1.008 & .015 & .048 & .012 & .095 \\
.013 & .678 & .066 & .008 & .014 & .013 & 1.358 & .100 & .010 & .017 \\
.118 & .202 & .493 & .064 & .128 & .153 & .264 & 1.213 & .109 & .189 \\
.138 & .176 & .131 & .281 & .111 & .257 & .274 & .218 & 1.115 & .180 \\
.021 & .022 & .066 & .009 & .433 & .025 & .025 & .105 & .013 & 1.083
\end{bmatrix}
$$

We now compute the aggregation bias introduced by this spatial consolidation. Consider the following 15-element vector of hypothesized final demands for the unaggregated (three-region, five-sector) model

$$\tilde{Y} = \begin{bmatrix} 100 & 100 & \cdots & 100 \end{bmatrix}'$$

The corresponding aggregated (two-region, five-sector) version is

$$\tilde{Y}^* = \begin{bmatrix} 100 & 100 & 100 & 100 & 100 & 200 & 200 & 200 & 200 & 200 \end{bmatrix}'$$

We can compute $\tilde{X}^* = (I - C^*A^*)^{-1}C^*\tilde{Y}^*$ and $\tilde{X} = (I - CA)^{-1}C\tilde{Y}$ where A and C are from the original unaggregated model. In order to compare $\tilde{X}^*$ and $\tilde{X}$, we must aggregate $\tilde{X}$, which we can accomplish with the following sectoral aggregation matrix, S:

$$
S\tilde{X} =
\begin{bmatrix}
1 & 0 & 0 & 0 & 0 & 0 & 0 & 0 & 0 & 0 & 0 & 0 & 0 & 0 & 0 \\
0 & 1 & 0 & 0 & 0 & 0 & 0 & 0 & 0 & 0 & 0 & 0 & 0 & 0 & 0 \\
0 & 0 & 1 & 0 & 0 & 0 & 0 & 0 & 0 & 0 & 0 & 0 & 0 & 0 & 0 \\
0 & 0 & 0 & 1 & 0 & 0 & 0 & 0 & 0 & 0 & 0 & 0 & 0 & 0 & 0 \\
0 & 0 & 0 & 0 & 1 & 0 & 0 & 0 & 0 & 0 & 0 & 0 & 0 & 0 & 0 \\
0 & 0 & 0 & 0 & 0 & 1 & 0 & 0 & 0 & 0 & 1 & 0 & 0 & 0 & 0 \\
0 & 0 & 0 & 0 & 0 & 0 & 1 & 0 & 0 & 0 & 0 & 1 & 0 & 0 & 0 \\
0 & 0 & 0 & 0 & 0 & 0 & 0 & 1 & 0 & 0 & 0 & 0 & 1 & 0 & 0 \\
0 & 0 & 0 & 0 & 0 & 0 & 0 & 0 & 1 & 0 & 0 & 0 & 0 & 1 & 0 \\
0 & 0 & 0 & 0 & 0 & 0 & 0 & 0 & 0 & 1 & 0 & 0 & 0 & 0 & 1
\end{bmatrix}
\begin{bmatrix}
117 \\ 127 \\ 254 \\ 240 \\ 155 \\ 139 \\ 192 \\ 293 \\ 277 \\ 175 \\ 126 \\ 145 \\ 191 \\ 219 \\ 135
\end{bmatrix}
$$

Table 5-12 gives the vectors $\tilde{X}^*$, $S\tilde{X}$, and the differences between corresponding elements. The sum of absolute differences $S\tilde{X} - \tilde{X}^*$ for the unaggre-

188   Organization of Basic Data for Input-Output Models

TABLE 5-12   SPATIAL AGGREGATION OF MRIO MODELS: EXAMPLE 7

		Aggregated Gross Outputs from the Three-Region Model $S\tilde{X}$	Outputs from the Aggregated Two-Region Model $\tilde{X}*$	Aggregation Error $S\tilde{X} - \tilde{X}*$	Aggregation Error as a Percent of Gross Outputs of the Three-Region Model $100\left(\dfrac{\lvert S\tilde{X} - \tilde{X}*\rvert}{S\tilde{X}}\right)$
	Sector				
	1	134.718	135.265	.547	.405
	2	109.863	110.036	.173	.157
Region a	3	352.078	358.354	6.276	1.751
	4	133.305	134.171	.866	.645
	5	215.715	216.205	.490	.226
Total (Absolute)		954.679	954.031	8.352	
	Sector				
	1	311.061	318.149	7.088	2.228
	2	229.036	229.359	.324	.141
Region b	3	658.678	633.958	−24.720	−3.899
	4	262.909	257.744	−5.164	−2.004
	5	392.772	388.443	−4.329	−1.115
Total (Absolute)		1854.456	1827.653	41.625	
Total (Absolute)		2800.135	2781.684	49.977	

gated region a (East) as a percentage of the total outputs in that region, that is, $S\tilde{X}i$, is

$$100\left(\frac{\lvert S\tilde{X} - \tilde{X}*\rvert i}{S\tilde{X}i}\right) = 100\left(\frac{8.352}{945.679}\right) = .883\%$$

and the corresponding value for region b (Central plus West) is

$$100\left(\frac{41.625}{1854.456}\right) = 2.245\%$$

This indicates, as expected, that more error is introduced into the prediction of outputs in the aggregated region than in the unaggregated region. The overall error (for both regions) is

$$100\left(\frac{49.977}{2800.135}\right) = 1.785\%$$

As we found with the IRIO model, it appears that spatial aggregation in MRIO models produces only modest aggregation bias, at least judging from the results of the example (see Blair and Miller 1983 for a more detailed discussion). Hence, for questions pertaining to one or more specific regions, it appears that an MRIO model in which those regions are distinct, while the rest of the economy is aggregated into the "remaining" region, is likely to be entirely adequate.

5-5 | SUMMARY

In this chapter we have discussed the development of input-output models from basic data given from, for example, a system of national economic accounts. In particular, we examined a number of conventions routinely adopted in deriving input-output models. These conventions included the use of producers' prices in valuation of transactions in the economy and the method of handling trade and transportation margins on such transactions. We also examined the common methods used for dealing with imports and exports in input-output models and in accounting for changes in inventories. The techniques for dealing with secondary production in an economy led us to specification of commodity-by-industry input-output models. We examined alternative assumptions for the treatment of secondary production in such models and the implications of each. Finally, we investigated the problem of aggregation in input-output models, including both sectoral (combining sectors) and spatial (combining regions in a multiple-region model) aggregation. We examined several theorems relating to the bias introduced by aggregating input-output models and conditions under which this bias is minimized.

APPENDIX 5-1
MIXED TECHNOLOGY ASSUMPTIONS IN COMMODITY-BY-INDUSTRY INPUT-OUTPUT MODELS

Introduction

In section 5-3 a number of alternative formulations for commodity-by-industry input-output models were examined based on two alternative assumptions concerning the underlying technology of the input-output economy, namely so-called commodity-based or industry-based technology. It was also suggested that under some circumstances it might be appropriate or desirable to represent some commodities/industries using the former assumption while representing others using the latter assumption. In this appendix we derive two alternative methods for mixing commodity-based and industry-based technology assumptions.

Method I

We divide the make matrix, V, into two parts, V_1 and V_2, where V_1 includes the distribution of outputs of commodities for which we wish to invoke the commodity-based technology assumption and V_2 includes the corresponding distribution of outputs for which we wish to invoke the industry-based technology assumption. Moreover, we select V_1 and V_2 such that

$$V = V_1 + V_2$$

Note that even individual elements of V could be divided between V_1 and V_2. With such a decomposition of the make matrix, we can actually invoke both technology assumptions and write:

$$X_1 = V_1 i = C_1^{-1} Q_1 \tag{5-1-1}$$

$$X_2 = V_2 i = D_2 Q \tag{5-1-2}$$

where X_1 and X_2 are the industry output vectors for V_1 and V_2, respectively (so that $X = X_1 + X_2$); Q_1 is the commodity outputs vector for V_1; and Q is the total commodity outputs vector (note that this is not Q_2, the reason for which will become apparent); C_1^{-1} is the inverse of the matrix of *industry output proportions*, as defined earlier, for V_1 (recall that the use of C is equivalent to assuming a commodity-based technology); and D_2 is the matrix of *commodity output proportions* (the use of which is equivalent to assuming an industry-based technology). This mixed technology formulation was proposed by Gigantes (1970).

Note that we can also write the companion equation to (5-1-2), that is,

$$Q_2 = V_2' i \tag{5-1-3}$$

which we can recall is the vector of column sums of the make matrix, V_2, that is, total commodity outputs for V_2. Equivalently,

$$Q_2 = [D_2 \hat{Q}]' i$$

which can be found by substituting $V_2 = D_2 \hat{Q}$ into Eq. (5-1-3); this follows directly from Eq. (5-1-2) since if we postmultiply both sides of $V_2 = D_2 \hat{Q}$ by i we obtain

$$V_2 i = D_2 \hat{Q} i = D_2 Q$$

which is Eq. (5-1-2). Finally, we can write

$$Q_2 = \langle D_2' i \rangle Q \tag{5-1-4}$$

where $\langle D_2' i \rangle$ is a diagonal matrix formed from the vector $D_2 i$. We illustrate this for the two-by-two case:

$$[D_2 \hat{Q}]' i = \left\{ \begin{bmatrix} d_{11} & d_{12} \\ d_{21} & d_{22} \end{bmatrix} \begin{bmatrix} q_1 & 0 \\ 0 & q_2 \end{bmatrix} \right\}' \begin{bmatrix} 1 \\ 1 \end{bmatrix} = \begin{bmatrix} d_{11}q_1 & d_{21}q_1 \\ d_{12}q_2 & d_{22}q_2 \end{bmatrix} \begin{bmatrix} 1 \\ 1 \end{bmatrix} = \begin{bmatrix} d_{11}q_1 + d_{21}q_1 \\ d_{12}q_2 + d_{22}q_2 \end{bmatrix}$$

$$\langle D_2' i \rangle Q = \left\langle \begin{bmatrix} d_{11} & d_{21} \\ d_{12} & d_{22} \end{bmatrix} \begin{bmatrix} 1 \\ 1 \end{bmatrix} \right\rangle \begin{bmatrix} q_1 \\ q_2 \end{bmatrix} = \begin{bmatrix} d_{11} + d_{21} & 0 \\ 0 & d_{12} + d_{22} \end{bmatrix} \begin{bmatrix} q_1 \\ q_2 \end{bmatrix}$$

$$= \begin{bmatrix} d_{11}q_1 + d_{21}q_1 \\ d_{12}q_2 + d_{22}q_2 \end{bmatrix}$$

This simply allows us to write Q_1 as a function of Q. Since $Q_1 = Q - Q_2$, we can use Eq. (5-1-4) to write

$$Q_1 = Q - \langle D_2' i \rangle Q = [I - \langle D_2' i \rangle] Q \tag{5-1-5}$$

which expresses Q_1 as a function of Q. Finally, we can substitute Eq. (5-1-5) into Eq. (5-1-1) to obtain

$$X_1 = C_1^{-1}Q_1 = C_1^{-1}\big[I - \langle D_2'i \rangle\big]Q \tag{5-1-6}$$

Also recall

$$X_2 = D_2 Q$$

Since $X = X_1 + X_2$,

$$X = C_1^{-1}\big[I - \langle D_2'i \rangle\big]Q + D_2 Q$$
$$X = \big\{C_1^{-1}\big[I - \langle D_2'i \rangle\big] + D_2\big\}Q \tag{5-1-7}$$

which is analogous to Eq. (5-10) for industry-based technology alone or to Eq. (5-17) for commodity-based technology alone. Let us refer to the bracketed quantity as R, parallel to D for industry-based technology and C^{-1} for commodity-based technology. Hence, the corresponding total requirements matrix is

$$X = \big[(I - RB)^{-1}R\big]E \quad \text{or} \quad X = \big[(I - BR)^{-1}R^{-1}\big]E \tag{5-1-8}$$

which is analogous to Eq. (5-21) earlier.

Thus, we can extend Table 5-10 to include the "mixed-technology" assumption; this is done in table 5-1-1.

Example 5-1-1 Consider a three-commodity, three-industry economy described by the following commodity and industry accounts:

$$U = \begin{bmatrix} 10 & 10 & 0 \\ 10 & 7 & 10 \\ 10 & 10 & 5 \end{bmatrix} \qquad E = \begin{bmatrix} 80 \\ 73 \\ 15 \end{bmatrix} \qquad Q = \begin{bmatrix} 100 \\ 100 \\ 40 \end{bmatrix}$$

$$V = \begin{bmatrix} 90 & 0 & 0 \\ 10 & 100 & 10 \\ 0 & 0 & 30 \end{bmatrix} \qquad \qquad X = \begin{bmatrix} 90 \\ 120 \\ 30 \end{bmatrix}$$

$$W = \begin{bmatrix} 60 & 93 & 15 \end{bmatrix}$$

TABLE 5-1-1 Summary of Commodity-by-Industry Total Requirements Matrices

	Industry-Based Technology	Commodity-Based Technology	Mixed Technology
Commodity-by-Commodity	$(I - BD)^{-1}$	$(I - BC^{-1})^{-1}$	$(I - BR)^{-1}$
Commodity-by-Industry*	$(I - BD)^{-1}D^{-1}$ or $D^{-1}(I - DB)^{-1}$	$(I - BC^{-1})^{-1}C$ or $C(I - C^{-1}B)^{-1}$	$(I - BR)^{-1}R^{-1}$ or $R^{-1}(I - RB)^{-1}$
Industry-by-Commodity*	$D(I - BD)^{-1}$ or $(I - DB)^{-1}D$	$C^{-1}(I - BC^{-1})^{-1}$ or $(I - C^{-1}B)^{-1}C^{-1}$	$R(I - BR)^{-1}$ or $(I - RB)^{-1}R$
Industry-by-Industry	$(I - DB)^{-1}$	$(I - C^{-1}B)^{-1}$	$(I - RB)^{-1}$

*It should be clear by now that for two square matrices α and β, $\alpha(I - \beta\alpha)^{-1} = (I - \alpha\beta)^{-1}\alpha$ and $\alpha^{-1}(I - \alpha\beta)^{-1} = (I - \beta\alpha)^{-1}\alpha^{-1}$.

Note that if we denote the industries as I, II, and III and the commodities as a, b, and c, we can see from the make matrix, V, that industries I and III produce only commodities a and c, respectively (the first and third rows of V have only one nonzero entry each). Industry II, however, while primarily producing commodity b, also produces commodities a and c as secondary products. Suppose we divide V into two parts as described earlier such that $V = V_1 + V_2$:

$$V_1 = \begin{bmatrix} 90 & 0 & 0 \\ 0 & 100 & 0 \\ 0 & 0 & 30 \end{bmatrix} \qquad V_2 = \begin{bmatrix} 0 & 0 & 0 \\ 10 & 0 & 10 \\ 0 & 0 & 0 \end{bmatrix}$$

Suppose that we wish, arbitrarily, to assume commodity-based technology for V_1 and industry-based technology for V_2. Since $X_1 = V_1 i$ and $X_2 = V_2 i$,

$$C_1 = V_1'(\hat{X}_1)^{-1} = \begin{bmatrix} 1 & 0 & 0 \\ 0 & 1 & 0 \\ 0 & 0 & 1 \end{bmatrix}; \qquad C_1^{-1} = \begin{bmatrix} 1 & 0 & 0 \\ 0 & 1 & 0 \\ 0 & 0 & 1 \end{bmatrix}$$

$$D_2 = V_2(\hat{Q})^{-1} = \begin{bmatrix} 0 & 0 & 0 \\ .1 & 0 & .25 \\ 0 & 0 & 0 \end{bmatrix}$$

Note that, as discussed earlier, the computation of D_2 uses Q, not Q_2. Hence, R found by Eq. (5-1-7) is

$$R = C_1^{-1}\left[I - \langle D_2' i \rangle \right] + D_2 = \begin{bmatrix} 9/10 & 0 & 0 \\ 1/10 & 1 & 1/4 \\ 0 & 0 & 3/4 \end{bmatrix}$$

We can use R in computing the industry-by-commodity total requirements matrix $(I - RB)^{-1}R$ so that

$$X = (I - RB)^{-1}RE = \begin{bmatrix} 1.027 & .096 & .055 \\ .328 & 1.149 & .657 \\ .121 & .091 & .909 \end{bmatrix} \begin{bmatrix} 80 \\ 73 \\ 15 \end{bmatrix} = \begin{bmatrix} 90 \\ 120 \\ 30 \end{bmatrix}$$

where

$$B = U(\hat{X})^{-1} = \begin{bmatrix} .111 & .083 & 0 \\ .111 & .058 & .333 \\ .111 & .083 & .167 \end{bmatrix}$$

Method II

Consider a second mixed-technology assumption in which we divide V again into two parts, but this time we reverse the roles of V_1 and V_2. That is, we assume V_1 captures industries/commodities for which we invoke the industry-based technology assumption; V_2 captures industries/commodities for which we invoke the commodity-based technology assumption. The reason for this will become apparent in the following. Hence, as before, $V = V_1 + V_2$, but we define

D_1 and C_2 such that

$$X_1 = V_1 i = D_1 Q_1 \tag{5-1-9}$$

$$Q_2 = V_2' i = C_2 X \tag{5-1-10}$$

These two expressions should be compared with the alternative assumptions we used for the previous mixed-technology assumption given in Eqs. (5-1-1) and (5-1-2). Total industry outputs of V_2 are found by taking the row sums

$$X_2 = V_2 i \tag{5-1-11}$$

If we solve Eq. (5-1-10) for V_2 we obtain

$$V_2' = C_2 \hat{X}$$

or, equivalently,

$$V_2 = \hat{X} C_2' \tag{5-1-12}$$

Consider the two-by-two case:

$$V_2 = \hat{X} C_2' = \begin{bmatrix} X_1 & 0 \\ 0 & X_2 \end{bmatrix} \begin{bmatrix} c_{11} & c_{21} \\ c_{12} & c_{22} \end{bmatrix} = \begin{bmatrix} c_{11}X_1 & c_{21}X_1 \\ c_{12}X_2 & c_{22}X_2 \end{bmatrix}$$

$$V_2' = C_2 \hat{X} = \begin{bmatrix} c_{11} & c_{12} \\ c_{21} & c_{22} \end{bmatrix} \begin{bmatrix} X_1 & 0 \\ 0 & X_2 \end{bmatrix} = \begin{bmatrix} c_{11}X_1 & c_{12}X_2 \\ c_{21}X_1 & c_{22}X_2 \end{bmatrix}$$

We can now substitute Eq. (5-1-12) into (5-1-11) to obtain

$$X_2 = \left(\hat{X} C_2' \right) i = \langle C_2' i \rangle X \tag{5-1-13}$$

This is illustrated for the two-by-two case as follows

$$\left(\hat{X} C_2' \right) i = \begin{bmatrix} X_1 & 0 \\ 0 & X_2 \end{bmatrix} \begin{bmatrix} c_{11} & c_{21} \\ c_{12} & c_{22} \end{bmatrix} \begin{bmatrix} 1 \\ 1 \end{bmatrix}$$

$$= \begin{bmatrix} c_{11}X_1 + c_{21}X_1 \\ c_{12}X_2 + c_{22}X_2 \end{bmatrix} = \begin{bmatrix} (c_{11} + c_{21})X_1 \\ (c_{12} + c_{22})X_2 \end{bmatrix}$$

$$\langle C_2' i \rangle X = \left\langle \begin{bmatrix} c_{11} & c_{21} \\ c_{12} & c_{22} \end{bmatrix} \begin{bmatrix} 1 \\ 1 \end{bmatrix} \right\rangle \begin{bmatrix} X_1 \\ X_2 \end{bmatrix}$$

$$= \begin{bmatrix} c_{11} + c_{21} & 0 \\ 0 & c_{12} + c_{22} \end{bmatrix} \begin{bmatrix} X_1 \\ X_2 \end{bmatrix} = \begin{bmatrix} (c_{11} + c_{21})X_1 \\ (c_{12} + c_{22})X_2 \end{bmatrix}$$

Hence, since $X = X_1 + X_2$, we can use Eqs. (5-1-9) and (5-1-13) to write

$$X = X_1 + X_2 = D_1 Q_1 + \langle C_2' i \rangle X \tag{5-1-14}$$

Also, since $Q_1 = Q - Q_2$, we can use Eq. (5-1-10) to write

$$Q_1 = Q - Q_2 = Q - C_2 X \tag{5-1-15}$$

Substituting Eq. (5-1-15) into (5-1-14) we obtain

$$X = D_1 (Q - C_2 X) + \langle C_2' i \rangle X \tag{5-1-16}$$

By ordinary matrix algebra

$$X = D_1 Q - D_1 C_2 X + \langle C_2' i \rangle X$$

$$D_1 Q = \left(I + D_1 C_2 - \langle C_2' i \rangle \right) X$$

$$X = \left[\left(I + D_1 C_2 - \langle C_2' i \rangle \right)^{-1} D_1 \right] Q \qquad (5\text{-}1\text{-}17)$$

As before, the quantity in brackets, which we denote as T, is parallel to D for industry-based technology alone, C^{-1} for commodity-based technology alone, and R for the first mixed-technology assumption. Hence, the corresponding total industry-by-commodity total requirements matrix is the bracketed quantity in

$$X = \left[(I - TB)^{-1} T \right] E \qquad (5\text{-}1\text{-}18)$$

Consider the technology assumptions given in Eqs. (5-10), (5-17), (5-1-7), and (5-1-17) and their corresponding industry-by-commodity total requirements expressions:

$$X = DQ; \qquad X = D(I - BD)^{-1} E \qquad (5\text{-}10)$$

$$X = C^{-1} Q; \qquad X = (I - C^{-1} B)^{-1} C^{-1} E \qquad (5\text{-}17)$$

$$X = \underbrace{\left[C_1^{-1} (I - \langle D_2' i \rangle) + D_2 \right]}_{R} Q; \qquad X = R(I - BR)^{-1} E \qquad (5\text{-}1\text{-}7)$$

$$X = \underbrace{\left[\left(I + D_1 C_2 - \langle C_2' i \rangle \right)^{-1} D_1 \right]}_{T} Q; \qquad X = T(I - BT)^{-1} E \qquad (5\text{-}1\text{-}17)$$

First note that if there are no distinctions between commodities and industries, then $C = D = I$ (and, hence, $R = T = I$) and all four total requirements expressions reduce to

$$X = (I - B)^{-1} E \qquad (5\text{-}1\text{-}19)$$

Further, if commodities and industries are indistinguishable, then $U = Z$ and $Y = E$ so that

$$B = U(\hat{X})^{-1} = Z(\hat{X})^{-1} = A$$

Hence, the total requirements expression in Eq. (5-1-19) further reduces to the traditional Leontief model

$$X = (I - A)^{-1} Y$$

Note also that both Eqs. (5-17) and (5-1-7) require computation of C^{-1} (or C_1^{-1} in [5-1-7]), which generally requires that C be a square matrix, that is, that the number of commodities equals the number of industries in the economy. A number of approaches to computing inverses of nonsquare matrices (often termed generalized or pseudo-inverses) have been developed (see, for example, Rao and Mitra 1971), but these techniques are beyond the scope of this text. The expression in Eqs. (5-10) and (5-1-17) does not require computation of C^{-1}. Moreover, in Eq. (5-1-17) the product $D_1 C_2$ will result in a square matrix even if D_1 and C_2 are nonsquare.

Example 5-1-2 Consider a two-industry, three-commodity economy described by the following commodity and industry accounts in millions of dollars:

$$U = \begin{bmatrix} 10 & 10 \\ 5 & 4 \\ 5 & 3 \end{bmatrix} \quad E = \begin{bmatrix} 60 \\ 91 \\ 12 \end{bmatrix} \quad Q = \begin{bmatrix} 80 \\ 100 \\ 20 \end{bmatrix}$$

$$V = \begin{bmatrix} 70 & 0 & 20 \\ 10 & 100 & 0 \end{bmatrix} \qquad\qquad X = \begin{bmatrix} 90 \\ 110 \end{bmatrix}$$

$$W = \begin{bmatrix} 70 & 93 \end{bmatrix}$$

If we denote the industries as I and II and the commodities as a, b, and c, then we can see from the make matrix, V, that industry I is primarily a producer of commodity a ($70 million) but it also produces, as a secondary product, $20 million worth of commodity c. Industry II primarily produces commodity b ($100 million) and also produces $10 million worth of commodity a.

Let us consider this example under each of the technology assumptions, that is, the commodity-based and industry-based technologies considered separately and the two mixed-technology assumptions given in Eqs. (5-1-7) and (5-1-17). From Eqs. (5-5'), (5-8'), and (5-9') we can compute

$$B = U(\hat{X})^{-1} = \begin{bmatrix} .111 & .091 \\ .056 & .036 \\ .056 & .027 \end{bmatrix}$$

$$C = V'(\hat{X})^{-1} = \begin{bmatrix} .778 & .091 \\ 0 & .909 \\ .222 & 0 \end{bmatrix}$$

$$D = V(\hat{Q})^{-1} = \begin{bmatrix} .875 & 0 & 1 \\ .125 & 1 & 0 \end{bmatrix}$$

Note, as just discussed, that we cannot generally invoke the commodity-based technology assumption, since in this case this would involve the computation of C^{-1} which, for this example, is impossible because C is nonsquare. We can, however, quite easily invoke the industry-based technology assumption. The industry-by-commodity total requirements matrix (from Table 5-1-1) is

$$D(I - BD)^{-1} = \begin{bmatrix} 1.059 & .114 & 1.191 \\ .209 & 1.060 & .087 \end{bmatrix}$$

The first mixed technology assumption (Eq. [5-1-7]) also involves the computation of C_1^{-1} which, for this example, is impossible as we found in considering the commodity-based technology alone. The second mixed technology assumption, however, does not require computation of C_1^{-1} and will work quite nicely for nonsquare U's and V's. That is, recalling Eq. (5-1-17), we obtain

$$T = \left[I + D_1 C_2 - \langle C_2' i \rangle \right]^{-1} D_1$$

$$T = \begin{bmatrix} 1 & -.1 & 1 \\ 0 & 1.1 & 0 \end{bmatrix}$$

for

$$V_1 = \begin{bmatrix} 70 & 0 & 10 \\ 0 & 100 & 0 \end{bmatrix} \qquad V_2 = \begin{bmatrix} 0 & 0 & 10 \\ 10 & 0 & 0 \end{bmatrix}$$

and hence, rearranging Eqs. (5-1-9) and (5-1-10),

$$D_1 = V_1 (\hat{Q}_1)^{-1} = \begin{bmatrix} 1 & 0 & 1 \\ 0 & 1 & 0 \end{bmatrix} \qquad \text{for} \qquad Q_1 = \begin{bmatrix} 70 \\ 100 \\ 10 \end{bmatrix}$$

$$C_2 = V_2' (\hat{X})^{-1} = \begin{bmatrix} 0 & .091 \\ 0 & 0 \\ .111 & 0 \end{bmatrix}$$

Note that T has little intuitive meaning, particularly since it can contain negative elements (as it does in this example). Armstrong (1975) discusses the significance of negative elements in this matrix. Almon (1970) presents a method for dealing with negative elements.

The industry-by-commodity total requirements matrix is found by recalling Eq. (5-1-17) to obtain

$$T(I - BT)^{-1} = \begin{bmatrix} 1.203 & .038 & 1.203 \\ .077 & 1.148 & .077 \end{bmatrix}$$

The By-Product Technology in Mixed Technology Models

As discussed in Chapter 5, ten Raa et al. (1984) argue that the industry-based technology assumption can lead to direct requirements matrices that are overly sensitive to base year prices. As an alternative, the industry-based technology assumption can be replaced by the by-product technology assumption. In a similar fashion, the mixed technology assumptions can be modified by replacing the terms involving the industry-based technology assumption with corresponding terms involving the by-product assumption, for example, terms involving V_1 in Method II just discussed.

Summary

The use of commodity-by-industry accounts in constructing input-output tables is very important if the issue of secondary production in the economy is significant (as in the United States). In 1977 the U.S. Department of Commerce issued the first commodity-by-industry version of the U.S. national input-output tables for 1972. The 1977 U.S. tables (issued in 1984) also followed this format. Moreover, as we consider the incorporation of nonmarket commodities in subsequent chapters—for example, environmental commodities—the use of commodity-by-industry accounts is especially important.

PROBLEMS

5-1 In a system of commodity-by-industry accounts, suppose we have defined three commodities and two industries. The make matrix, V, and the use matrix, U, are given below.

$$U = \begin{bmatrix} 3 & 5 \\ 2 & 7 \\ 2 & 3 \end{bmatrix} \qquad V = \begin{bmatrix} 15 & 5 & 10 \\ 5 & 25 & 0 \end{bmatrix}$$

  a Compute the vector of commodity final demands, the vector of industry value added inputs, the vector of total commodity outputs, and the vector of total industry outputs.

  b Assuming an "industry-based" technology, compute the industry-by-commodity total requirements matrix.

5-2 Consider the following system of commodity and industry accounts for a region

	Commodities		Industries		Final Demand	Total Output
			1	2	7	10
			3	4	3	10
	10	2				12
	0	8				8
Value Added			8	2	10	
Total Inputs	10	10	12	8		20

  a Compute the commodity-by-industry matrix of direct requirements.

  b Compute the industry-by-commodity total requirements matrices under both assumptions of industry-based and commodity-based technology.

  c If a new naval facility is being constructed in the region, represented by commodity final demands $\Delta E' = [6 \quad 5]$, what would be the total production of each industry in the region required to support this facility? Do this for both technology assumptions.

5-3 Consider again the system of accounts given in problem 5-1. Which of the two "mixed technology" assumptions that were covered in Chapter 5 (Appendix 5-1) can we invoke in computing the industry-by-commodity total requirements matrix for this system of accounts? Compute the matrix. Why can we not invoke the other assumption? Can we invoke either the commodity-based or industry-based technology assumptions?

5-4 Use both mixed technology assumptions in deriving industry-by-commodity total requirements matrices for the system of accounts given in problem 5-2.

5-5* Consider the transactions data given in problem 2-11. One way of assessing the effects of aggregation is as follows. Using a final-demand vector of all 1's, determine the effect on total outputs throughout the entire economy (i.e., summed over all the sectors) of the following set of increasingly aggregated models. (Remember to aggregate the final-demand vector appropriately each time you aggregate the sectors.)

- Run 1 (8 × 8)   No sectoral aggregation
- Run 2 (7 × 7)   Combine sector 6 with sector 2
- Run 3 (6 × 6)   Also combine sector 5 with sector 1
- Run 4 (5 × 5)   Also combine sector 8 with sector 3
- Run 5 (4 × 4)   Also combine sector 7 with previously combined 6 and 2
- Run 6 (3 × 3)   Also combine sector 4 with previously combined 5 and 1

5-6*   Consider the seven-sector input-output table of technical coefficients for the U.S. economy (1972) given in Appendix B. Given a vector final demands of $\Delta Y' = [100\ 100\ 100\ 100\ 100\ 100\ 100]$, compute the first-order and total aggregation bias associated with combining agriculture with mining, construction with manufacturing, and transportation-utilities with services and other sectors to yield a new three-sector model.

5-7*   Using the seven-sector make and use tables for the 1972 U.S. economy given in Appendix B (Table B-23), compute the industry-by-commodity total requirements matrices under both assumptions of commodity-based and industry-based technology. What is the mean absolute difference between the two matrices?

| REFERENCES

ALMON, CLOPPER. "Investment in Input-Output Models and the Treatment of Secondary Products." In *Input-Output Techniques*, Vol. 2, *Applications of Input-Output Analysis*, edited by Anne P. Carter and Andrew Bródy, 103–16. Proceedings of the Fourth International Conference on Input-Output Techniques, Geneva, January 1968. Amsterdam: North-Holland, 1970.

ARA, K. "The Aggregation Problem in Input-Output Analysis." *Econometrica* 27, no. 2 (April 1959): 257–62.

ARMSTRONG, A. G. "Technology Assumptions in the Construction of U. K. Input-Output Tables." In *Estimating and Projecting Input-Output Coefficients*, edited by R. I. G. Allen and W. F. Gossling, 68–93. London: Input-Output Publishing Co., 1975.

BALDERSTON, J. B., and T. M. WHITIN. "Aggregation in the Input-Output Model." In *Economic Activity Analysis*, edited by O. Morgenstern, 79–128. New York: John Wiley & Sons, 1954.

BLAIR, PETER D., and RONALD E. MILLER. "Spatial Aggregation of Multiregional Input-Output Models." *Environment and Planning A* 15, no. 2 (February 1983): 187–206.

BULMER-THOMAS, V. *Input-Output Analysis in Developing Countries*. New York: John Wiley and Sons, 1982.

DOEKSEN, G. A., and C. H. LITTLE. "Effects of the Size of the Input-Output Model on the Results of an Impact Analysis." *Agricultural Economics Research* 20, no. 4 (October 1968): 134–38.

ELLIOT-JONES, M. F. *Input-Output Analysis: A Nontechnical Description*. New York: The Conference Board, Conference Board Report No. 533, 1971.

GIBBONS, JOEL C., ALAN WOLSKY, and GEORGE TOLLEY. "Approximate Aggregation and Error in Input-Output Models." *Resources and Energy* 4, no. 3 (September 1982): 203–30.

GIGANTES, T. "The Representation of Technology in Input-Output Systems." In *Input-Output Techniques*, Vol. 1, *Contributions to Input-Output Analysis*, edited by Anne P. Carter and Andrew Bródy, 270–90. Proceedings of the Fourth International Conference on Input-Output Techniques, Geneva, January 1968. Amsterdam: North-Holland, 1970.

GRIFFIN, JAMES. "Energy Input-Output Modeling." Electric Power Research Institute, Palo Alto, California (November 1976).

HATANAKA, M. "Note on Consolidation Within a Leontief System." *Econometrica* 20, no. 2 (April 1952): 301–3.

HEWINGS, GEOFFREY J. D. "Aggregation for Regional Impact Analysis." *Growth and Change* 2, no. 1 (January 1972): 15–19.

HOFFMAN, R. B., and J. N. KENT. "Design of Commodity-by-Industry Interregional Input-Output Models." In *Advances in Input-Output Analysis*, edited by Karen R. Polenske and Jiri V. Skolka, 251–62. Proceedings of the Sixth International Conference on Input-Output Techniques, Vienna, April 22–26, 1974. Cambridge, Massachusetts: Ballinger, 1976.

MALINVAUD, E. "Aggregation Problems in Input-Output Models." In *The Structural Interdependence of the Economy*, edited by T. Barna, 189–202. New York: John Wiley and Sons, 1956.

McMANUS, M. "General Consistent Aggregation in Leontief Models." *Yorkshire Bulletin of Economic and Social Research* 8 (June 1956): 28–48.

MILLER, RONALD E., and PETER BLAIR. "Spatial Aggregation in Interregional Input-Output Models." *Papers, Regional Science Association* 48 (1981): 150–64.

MORIMOTO, Y. "On Aggregation Problems in Input-Output Analysis." *Review of Economic Studies* 37, no. 109 (January 1970): 119–26.

RAO, C. RADHAKRISHNA, and SUJIT KUMAR MITRA. *Generalized Inverse of Matrices and its Applications.* New York: John Wiley and Sons, 1971.

RITZ, PHILIP. "Definitions and Conventions of the 1972 Input-Output Study." Washington, D.C.: U.S. Government Printing Office, 1980.

———. "The Input-Output Structure of the U.S. Economy: 1972." *Survey of Current Business* 59, no. 2 (February 1979): 34–72.

STONE, RICHARD. *Input-Output and National Accounts.* Paris: Organization for European Economic Cooperation, 1961.

Survey of Current Business. "The Input-Output Structure of the U.S. Economy: 1967" 54, no. 2 (February 1974): 24–56.

———. "The Input-Output Structure of the U.S. Economy: 1963" 49, no. 11 (November 1969): 16–47.

TEN RAA, THIJS, DEBESH CHAKRABORTY, and J. ANTHONY SMALL. "An Alternative Treatment of Secondary Products in Input-Output Analysis." *Review of Economics and Statistics* 66, no. 1 (February 1984): 88–97.

THEIL, HENRI. "Linear Aggregation in Input-Output Analysis." *Econometrica* 25, no. 1 (January 1957): 111–22.

UNITED NATIONS, DEPARTMENT OF ECONOMIC AND SOCIAL AFFAIRS. *A System of National Accounts.* Series F, No. 2, revision 3. New York: United Nations, 1968.

VACARRA, BEATRICE, ARLENE SHAPIRO, and NANCY SIMON. "The Input-Output Structure of the U.S. Economy: 1947." U.S. Department of Commerce, Office of Business Economics (March 1970). Mimeograph.

WILLIAMSON, ROBERT B. "Simple Input-Output Models for Area Analysis." *Land Economics* 46, no. 3 (August 1970): 333–38.

chapter 6 | Energy Input-Output Analysis

6-1 | INTRODUCTION

Input-output provides a useful framework for tracing energy use and other activities such as environmental pollution associated with interindustry activity. In recent years much attention has been focused on extending the Leontief input-output framework to account for such activities. Ayres and Kneese (1969), Bullard and Herendeen (1975b), Griffin (1976), Cumberland (1966), and many others have reported these developments. In this chapter we examine how input-output has been extended to account for interindustry energy flows; we explore several approaches in the current literature, detailing the limitations and usefulness of each approach. In Chapter 7 we deal with other extensions such as accounting for pollution elimination and generation, employment, and recycling of materials. The mathematical structure of these extensions almost mirrors the classical Leontief model we have discussed in earlier chapters. However, when we attempt to ensure consistency between, for example, levels of energy consumption and economic activity, we must add to the basic analytical framework.

Energy input-output typically determines the total energy required to deliver a product to final demand, both directly as the energy consumed by an industry's production process and indirectly as the energy embodied in that industry's inputs. In engineering parlance, this is a *process analysis*: A target product is identified either as a good or service, then a list is compiled of the goods and services directly required to deliver the product. These inputs to the target production process include fuels (direct energy) and nonenergy goods and services. The nonenergy inputs are then analyzed to determine the inputs to their production processes, which again include some fuels and nonenergy goods and services. The process traces inputs back to primary resources; the first round of energy inputs is the *direct energy requirement*; subsequent rounds of energy inputs comprise the *indirect energy requirement*. The sum of these two is the *total energy requirement.* For example, the energy used in assembling automobiles would be a direct energy requirement, while the energy embodied in (used in providing) the materials employed at the assembly plant (tires, engines, etc.) would comprise an indirect energy requirement.

In the input-output framework, computing the total energy requirement, sometimes called the *energy intensity*, of industries is analogous to computing the total dollar requirement or Leontief inverse of the traditional input-output model. In energy input-output analysis, we are most often concerned with energy measured in physical units—for example, British thermal units (Btus), barrels of oil, or tons of coal, rather than in dollars or value terms. As may be expected, one way to obtain these quantities in physical units is to first compute the total dollar requirement by conventional input-output analysis, then convert these values to Btus or some other appropriate physical units by means of prices relating dollar outputs to energy outputs. We eventually see, however, that such a procedure introduces inconsistencies in the resultant accounting of energy consumption, necessitating adjustments in the procedure to insure reasonable results.

For example, in computing the energy intensity of a product (as defined above) we will distinguish between *primary* energy sectors (e.g., crude oil or coal mining) and *secondary* energy sectors (e.g., refined petroleum or electricity). The latter receive primary energy as an input and convert it into secondary energy forms. Hence, if we compute both the total amount of primary energy required to produce an industry's output and the total amount of secondary energy required to produce that same output, they must be equal, net of any energy lost in converting energy from primary to secondary energy forms, for example, electric power production from coal. Different technologies, of course, have different energy conversion efficiencies. Hence, our energy input-output formulation should include the condition that the total primary energy intensity of a product should equal the total secondary energy intensity of the product plus the amount of energy lost in energy conversion. We refer to this condition as an *energy conservation condition.* This condition will be a fundamental determinant in assessing whether or not a particular energy input-output model formulation (several of which will be discussed in what follows) accurately depicts the energy flows in the economy.

6-2 | ENERGY INPUT-OUTPUT ANALYSIS

A Basic Formulation

We begin with the most contemporary framework of energy input-output where we construct a transactions table in so-called "hybrid-units"—that is, we trace energy flows in the economy in Btus (or some other convenient energy units) and nonenergy flows in dollars. We will see later in Appendix 6-1 that such a formulation is generally superior to alternative formulations widely applied in the literature, albeit in some cases less easy to implement practically because of availability of data.

In energy input-output we seek an analogous set of matrices to Z, A, and $(I - A)^{-1}$, that is, an energy transactions or flows matrix (this time measured in physical inputs of *energy*, e.g., Btus), a direct *energy* requirements matrix, and finally a total *energy* requirements matrix. With only a minor change in the way we represent interindustry transactions in the basic input-output framework of Chapter 2, we can construct these energy input-output matrices.

First we begin by constructing a matrix of energy flows in physical units. That is, given an n-sector input-output economy, let us assume that m of the n sectors are energy sectors. Hence, the matrix of energy flows, E, would be of dimension m by n; if we also assume that energy consumed by final demand (in physical units) is given by E_y and total energy consumption in the economy is given by F (E_y and F are both m-element column vectors), the energy flows accounting identity analogous to $Zi + Y = X$ is given by:

$$Ei + E_y = F \tag{6-1}$$

The sum of energy (of each type depicted by the rows of E) consumed by interindustry sectors plus that consumed by final demand is the total amount of energy consumed (and produced) by the economy.

Next, we can construct an interindustry transactions matrix in hybrid units as defined earlier by taking the original interindustry transactions matrix, Z, and replacing the energy rows by the corresponding rows in the energy flows matrix, E. We define a new transactions matrix, Z^*, for which the energy rows are measured in energy units and the nonenergy rows are measured in dollars, as usual.[1] We must, of course, define corresponding total output, X^*, and final demand, Y^*, vectors for which the energy and nonenergy sector quantities are similarly measured in energy units and dollars, respectively. In terms of our earlier notation these quantities are defined as the following:

$$Z_i^* = \begin{cases} Z_j & \text{for nonenergy rows} \\ E_k & \text{for energy rows} \end{cases} \tag{6-2}$$

$$Y_i^* = \begin{cases} Y_j & \text{for nonenergy rows} \\ e_{ky} & \text{for energy rows} \end{cases} \tag{6-3}$$

$$X_i^* = \begin{cases} X_j & \text{for nonenergy rows} \\ F_k & \text{for energy rows} \end{cases} \tag{6-4}$$

$$F_i^* = \begin{cases} 0 & \text{for nonenergy rows} \\ F_k & \text{for energy rows} \end{cases} \tag{6-5}$$

The corresponding matrices, $A^* = Z^*(\hat{X}^*)^{-1}$ and $(I - A^*)^{-1}$, follow directly from these definitions. However, some of the characteristics of these matrices differ from the traditional Leontief model. For example, the column sums of A^* are not necessarily less than unity as in the traditional model. Note also the units of the direct requirements matrix, A^*, and the total requirements

---

[1] This "hybrid" formulation was suggested by Bullard and Herendeen (1975a); it is discussed in Blair (1979), Dossani and Preziosi (1980), Griffin (1976) and others.

matrix, $(I - A^*)^{-1}$. Consider, for example, the two-sector case where the first sector is an energy sector and the second is a nonenergy sector. The units of such a model formulated in hybrid units can be depicted by

$$Z^* = \begin{bmatrix} \text{Btus} & \text{Btus} \\ \$ & \$ \end{bmatrix}; \quad Y^* = \begin{bmatrix} \text{Btus} \\ \$ \end{bmatrix}; \quad X^* = \begin{bmatrix} \text{Btus} \\ \$ \end{bmatrix}; \quad F^* = \begin{bmatrix} \text{Btus} \\ 0 \end{bmatrix}$$

Hence, we obtain

$$A^* = Z^*(\hat{X}^*)^{-1} = \begin{bmatrix} \dfrac{\text{Btu}}{\text{Btu}} & \dfrac{\text{Btu}}{\$} \\ \dfrac{\$}{\text{Btu}} & \dfrac{\$}{\$} \end{bmatrix}$$

The matrix $(I - A^*)^{-1}$ will have the same units as A^* except, of course, that they are in terms of the requirement (Btus or dollars) per unit (Btu or dollar) of final demand (i.e., total requirement) instead of per unit of total output (direct requirement).

To obtain the matrices we referred to earlier as the *direct energy requirements matrix* and *total energy requirements matrix* we need only extract the energy rows from A^* and $(I - A^*)^{-1}$, respectively. To isolate the energy rows we can first construct the matrix product $F^*(\hat{X}^*)^{-1}$; the elements of F^*, F_i^*, were defined in Eq. (6-5). Since the nonzero elements of F^* are identical to the corresponding values in X^* (recall also the definition of X_i^* in Eq. [6-4]), the result of this product is a vector of ones and zeros, the ones denoting the locations of energy sectors. We postmultiply this vector by $(I - A^*)^{-1}$ to retrieve *only* the total energy coefficients, that is, the energy rows of $(I - A^*)^{-1}$. Equivalently, we can premultiply A^* by this matrix to retrieve only the direct energy coefficients from A^*, that is, the energy rows of A^*. Let us define the direct and total energy coefficients matrices to be δ and α, respectively:

$$\delta = F^*(\hat{X}^*)^{-1}A^* \tag{6-6}$$

$$\alpha = F^*(\hat{X}^*)^{-1}(I - A^*)^{-1} \tag{6-7}$$

Example 1 We consider a two-sector example that will illustrate the essential properties of this "hybrid-units" formulation of the energy input-output problem. In the following table, energy flows in Btus corresponding to the dollar transactions from the energy sector to the other sectors (including final demand and total output) are given in the parentheses.

TABLE 6-1 ENERGY AND DOLLAR FLOWS: EXAMPLE 1 (MILLIONS OF DOLLARS AND 10^{15} BTUS)

	Widgets	Energy	Final Demand	Total Output
Widgets	10	20	70	100
Energy	30 (60)	40 (80)	50 (100)	120 (240)

From the conventions just described for the hybrid-units formulation we can derive:

$$Z^* = \begin{bmatrix} 10 & 20 \\ 60 & 80 \end{bmatrix} \qquad X^* = \begin{bmatrix} 100 \\ 240 \end{bmatrix}$$

$$A^* = Z^*(\hat{X}^*)^{-1} = \begin{bmatrix} .100 & .083 \\ .600 & .333 \end{bmatrix}$$

$$(I - A^*)^{-1} = \begin{bmatrix} 1.212 & 1.515 \\ 1.091 & 1.636 \end{bmatrix}$$

From Eqs. (6-6) and (6-7) we compute the direct and total energy requirements matrices:

$$\delta = F^*(\hat{X}^*)^{-1} A^* = \begin{bmatrix} 0 & 240 \end{bmatrix} \begin{bmatrix} 100 & 0 \\ 0 & 240 \end{bmatrix} \begin{bmatrix} .100 & .083 \\ .600 & .353 \end{bmatrix} = \begin{bmatrix} .600 & .333 \end{bmatrix}$$

$$\alpha = F^*(\hat{X}^*)^{-1}(I - A^*)^{-1} = \begin{bmatrix} 0 & 240 \end{bmatrix} \begin{bmatrix} 100 & 0 \\ 0 & 240 \end{bmatrix} \begin{bmatrix} 1.212 & 1.515 \\ 1.091 & 1.636 \end{bmatrix}$$
$$= \begin{bmatrix} 1.091 & 1.636 \end{bmatrix}$$

Note that in using the energy input-output model in impact analysis—that is, analogous to $X = (I - A)^{-1}Y$ in the traditional Leontief model—the final demand presented to the total requirements matrix *must* be in hybrid units, that is, $F = \alpha Y^*$. We can verify for this example, since $Y^* = \begin{bmatrix} 70 \\ 100 \end{bmatrix}$, that $F = \alpha Y^* = \begin{bmatrix} 1.091 & 1.636 \end{bmatrix} \begin{bmatrix} 70 \\ 100 \end{bmatrix} = 240$.

Generalization to Several Energy Types

In the initial energy input-output formulation, we defined the vector F to be of length m (the number of energy sectors) denoting the total energy output (in Btus) of energy sectors. In developing the hybrid-units notation further, we defined the vector F^* in Eq. (6-5) to be of length n (the total number of industry sectors, including energy sectors) where the elements representing energy sectors (m of the n elements) denote total energy output (in Btus) of those sectors; the remaining elements were defined to be zero. We can easily extend this notion to facilitate accounting for several energy types by creating a matrix $\hat{F}^*$ of dimension $m \times n$ where the elements of F^* are placed along the principal diagonal; all other elements are zero.[2] We illustrate the use of $\hat{F}^*$ in Example 2.

Example 2   Consider a four-sector economy, in which three sectors are energy sectors, namely crude oil, refined petroleum, and electric power. The fourth sector, autos, is the only nonenergy sector. Note that the only primary energy sector in this economy is crude oil. The dollar transactions for the

---

[2]We define the principal diagonal of a nonsquare matrix A to be the a_{ii} elements.

TABLE 6-2 Interindustry Economic Transactions: Example 2 (millions of dollars)

	Crude Oil	Refined Petroleum	Electric Power	Autos	Final Demand	Total Output
Crude Oil	0	5	5	0	0	10
Refined Petroleum	2.5	2.5	0	2.5	12.5	20
Electric Power	2.5	1.25	1.25	2.5	12.5	20
Autos	0	0	0	0	20	20

economy are given in Table 6-2; the energy flows in the economy (measured in 10^{15} Btus) are as given in Table 6-3.

The hybrid-units energy input-output formulation is the following:

$$Z^* = \begin{bmatrix} 0 & 20 & 20 & 0 \\ 1 & 3 & 0 & 1 \\ 2.5 & 1.25 & 1.25 & 2.5 \\ 0 & 0 & 0 & 0 \end{bmatrix}; \quad Y^* = \begin{bmatrix} 0 \\ 15 \\ 12.5 \\ 20 \end{bmatrix}$$

$$A^* = \begin{bmatrix} 0 & 1 & 1 & 0 \\ 0.025 & 0.15 & 0 & 0.05 \\ 0.0625 & 0.0625 & 0.0625 & 0.0125 \\ 0 & 0 & 0 & 0 \end{bmatrix}; \quad X^* = \begin{bmatrix} 40 \\ 20 \\ 20 \\ 20 \end{bmatrix}$$

$$(I - A^*)^{-1} = \begin{bmatrix} 1.109 & 1.391 & 1.183 & 0.217 \\ 0.033 & 1.217 & 0.035 & 0.065 \\ 0.076 & 0.174 & 1.148 & 0.152 \\ 0.000 & 0.000 & 0.000 & 1.000 \end{bmatrix}$$

In deriving the matrix of total energy coefficients for each energy type, α, which should be of dimension 3×4, we first compute the matrix $\hat{F}^*$, as defined earlier, describing the total energy consumption of each type:

$$\hat{F}^* = \begin{bmatrix} X_1^* & 0 & 0 & 0 \\ 0 & X_2^* & 0 & 0 \\ 0 & 0 & X_3^* & 0 \end{bmatrix} = \begin{bmatrix} 40 & 0 & 0 & 0 \\ 0 & 20 & 0 & 0 \\ 0 & 0 & 20 & 0 \end{bmatrix}$$

Recall that $\hat{F}^*$ is created by taking the values of total energy production for each of the energy sectors (40, 20, and 20, respectively, for crude oil, refined petroleum, and electricity) and defining them as the f_{ii}^* elements of $\hat{F}^*$.

TABLE 6-3 Energy Flows: Example 2 (quadrillions of Btus)

	Crude Oil	Refined Petroleum	Electric Power	Autos	Final Demand	Total Output
Crude Oil	0	20	20	0	0	40
Refined Petroleum	1	3	0	1	15	20
Electric Power	2.5	1.25	1.25	2.5	12.5	20

Given $\hat{F}^*$ and X^*, we can obtain

$$\hat{F}^*(\hat{X}^*)^{-1} = \begin{bmatrix} 40 & 0 & 0 & 0 \\ 0 & 20 & 0 & 0 \\ 0 & 0 & 20 & 0 \end{bmatrix} \begin{bmatrix} \dfrac{1}{40} & 0 & 0 & 0 \\ 0 & \dfrac{1}{20} & 0 & 0 \\ 0 & 0 & \dfrac{1}{20} & 0 \\ 0 & 0 & 0 & \dfrac{1}{20} \end{bmatrix}$$

$$= \begin{bmatrix} 1 & 0 & 0 & 0 \\ 0 & 1 & 0 & 0 \\ 0 & 0 & 1 & 0 \end{bmatrix}$$

and

$$\alpha = \hat{F}^*(\hat{X}^*)^{-1}(I - A^*)^{-1} = \begin{bmatrix} 1 & 0 & 0 & 0 \\ 0 & 1 & 0 & 0 \\ 0 & 0 & 1 & 0 \end{bmatrix} \begin{bmatrix} 1.109 & 1.391 & 1.183 & 0.217 \\ 0.033 & 1.217 & 0.035 & 0.065 \\ 0.076 & 0.174 & 1.148 & 0.152 \\ 0 & 0 & 0 & 1.000 \end{bmatrix}$$

which simply retrieves the first three (energy) rows of $(I - A^*)^{-1}$:

$$\alpha = \begin{bmatrix} 1.109 & 1.391 & 1.183 & .217 \\ .033 & 1.217 & .035 & .065 \\ .076 & .174 & 1.148 & .152 \end{bmatrix}$$

Energy Conservation Conditions

Earlier, we noted that a fundamental requirement of a suitable energy input-output model is that it satisfy a set of energy conservation conditions. Let us now more formally define these conditions for an energy input-output model and see if they are fulfilled in our formulation. The energy conservation conditions can be stated (Herendeen, 1974) as

$$\alpha_{kj}X_j = \left(\sum_{i=1}^{n} \alpha_{ki}z_{ij} \right) + f_{kj}^* \qquad (6\text{-}8)$$

where, as before, α_{kj} is the amount of energy required to produce a dollar's worth of sector j's output; X_j is the total dollar output of sector j; and z_{ij} is the dollar value of sector i's product consumed by sector j. For this discussion, we restrict f_{kj}^* to be the total energy output of only primary energy sectors.[3] That is, the energy embodied in any sector output X_j equals the amount of energy embodied in all that sector's inputs z_{ij} $(i = 1, \cdots, n)$ plus the primary energy input, f_{kj}^*, which is nonzero only for primary energy sectors. Translated into

---

[3] In defining energy conservation, the energy inputs depicted in Equation (6-8) as f_{kj}^* are the only inputs exogenous to the economy, i.e., primary inputs; all other inputs are embodied in consuming sector j's inputs $i = 1, \ldots, n$.

matrix terms:

$$\alpha \hat{X} = \alpha Z + \hat{F}^* \tag{6-9}$$

For the three-sector $(i, j = 1, 2, 3)$, two-energy-sector $(k = 1, 2)$ case this can be illustrated by:

$$
\begin{bmatrix} \alpha_{11} & \alpha_{12} & \alpha_{13} \\ \alpha_{21} & \alpha_{22} & \alpha_{23} \end{bmatrix}
\begin{bmatrix} X_1 & 0 & 0 \\ 0 & X_2 & 0 \\ 0 & 0 & X_3 \end{bmatrix}
$$

$$
= \begin{bmatrix} \alpha_{11} & \alpha_{12} & \alpha_{13} \\ \alpha_{21} & \alpha_{22} & \alpha_{23} \end{bmatrix}
\begin{bmatrix} z_{11} & z_{12} & z_{13} \\ z_{21} & z_{22} & z_{23} \\ z_{31} & z_{32} & z_{33} \end{bmatrix}
+ \begin{bmatrix} f_{11}^* & 0 & 0 \\ 0 & 0 & 0 \end{bmatrix}
$$

Note that in this example there is only one nonzero element in $\hat{F}^*$, that is, only one *primary* energy sector. Expanding this equation we obtain

$$
\begin{bmatrix} \alpha_{11}X_1 & \alpha_{12}X_2 & \alpha_{13}X_3 \\ \alpha_{21}X_1 & \alpha_{22}X_2 & \alpha_{23}X_3 \end{bmatrix} =
$$

$$
\begin{bmatrix} \alpha_{11}z_{11} + \alpha_{12}z_{21} + \alpha_{13}z_{31} & \alpha_{11}z_{12} + \alpha_{12}z_{22} + \alpha_{13}z_{32} & \alpha_{11}z_{13} + \alpha_{12}z_{23} + \alpha_{13}z_{33} \\ \alpha_{21}z_{11} + \alpha_{22}z_{21} + \alpha_{23}z_{31} & \alpha_{21}z_{12} + \alpha_{22}z_{22} + \alpha_{23}z_{32} & \alpha_{21}z_{13} + \alpha_{22}z_{23} + \alpha_{23}z_{33} \end{bmatrix}
$$

$$
+ \begin{bmatrix} f_{11}^* & 0 & 0 \\ 0 & 0 & 0 \end{bmatrix}
$$

Each term of this matrix is defined generally by Eq. (6-8), for example, the upper-left term is

$$\alpha_{11}X_1 = (\alpha_{11}z_{11} + \alpha_{12}z_{21} + \alpha_{13}z_{31}) + f_{11}^*$$

which is identical to Eq. (6-8) for $k = 1$, $j = 1$, and $i = 1, 2$, and 3.

Since $Z = A\hat{X}$, we can write directly from Eq. (6-9)

$$\alpha \hat{X} = \alpha A \hat{X} + \hat{F}^*$$

$$\alpha \hat{X} - \alpha A \hat{X} = \hat{F}^*$$

$$\alpha (I - A)\hat{X} = \hat{F}^*$$

$$\alpha (I - A) = \hat{F}^*(\hat{X})^{-1}$$

$$\alpha = \hat{F}^*(\hat{X})^{-1}(I - A)^{-1} \tag{6-10}$$

In the hybrid-units formulation, both X and A in Eq. (6-10) are replaced by corresponding values of X^* and A^*. This formulation completely coincides with our energy conservation given in Eqs. (6-8) and (6-9).

Example 2 (Revisited) Recall the total energy requirements matrix from Example 2:

$$
\alpha = \begin{bmatrix} 1.109 & 1.391 & 1.183 & .217 \\ .033 & 1.217 & .035 & .065 \\ .076 & .174 & 1.148 & .152 \end{bmatrix}
$$

Recall that the first energy sector, oil, was the primary energy sector while the remaining energy sectors, refined petroleum and electricity, are secondary energy sectors. Consider the last column of α, that is, the automobile sector (the only nonenergy sector in this example). The term $\alpha_{14} = 0.217$ is the total primary energy intensity of producing automobiles in the economy. That is, it takes 0.217×10^9 Btus of crude oil to produce (including both direct and indirect energy requirements) one dollar's worth of output in the automobile sector. Similarly, $\alpha_{24} = 0.065$ and $\alpha_{34} = 0.152$ are the secondary energy intensities of automobile production, namely, it takes 0.065 and 0.152 billion Btus of refined petroleum and electricity, respectively, to produce a dollar's worth of automobiles. However, since both refined petroleum and electricity ultimately come from crude oil in this economy (since oil is the only primary energy sector), the energy-conservation condition requires that the sum of secondary energy intensities for automobile production equals the primary energy intensity (minus any losses, which we ignore for the time being). That is, for this example,

$$\alpha_{24} + \alpha_{34} = \alpha_{14} = 0.217$$

This condition, of course, should hold for all sectors in the economy except for the primary energy sectors, which extract their energy from outside the economy (primary resources).

In other words, if we sum the secondary energy rows (rows 2 and 3 in our example)—the total secondary energy intensity—the result should be the same as the primary energy intensity (row 1 in the example). If there were more primary energy sectors, the total primary energy intensity would be the sum of the primary energy rows. For column 1 (crude oil), however, total secondary energy intensity is $\alpha_{21} + \alpha_{31} = 0.109$ while $\alpha_{11} = 1.109$. The difference can be interpreted as the amount of crude oil received from outside the economy per unit of output of crude oil, namely *all* of it, since it is a primary resource.

6-3 | FURTHER METHODOLOGICAL CONSIDERATIONS

We now examine a number of additional methodological considerations in the application of energy input-output analysis.

Adjusting for Energy Conversion Efficiencies

In the version of the energy input-output model discussed thus far that deals with secondary energy production, we ignored the effect of energy conversion efficiencies. We assumed that the energy produced by secondary sources must equal the sum of the amounts of primary sources consumed in producing that secondary energy. It is a quite straightforward extension to modify our hybrid-units model to account for conversion efficiencies.

This adjustment must first recognize that for secondary energy sources $F_k^* \neq X_k^*$, where the value of F_k^* refers to the total energy *input* of type k to the production process, and X_k^* refers to the total energy *output*. The ratio of F_k^* to X_k^* is the conversion efficiency.

Example 3 Let us consider a three-sector economy with one primary energy sector (coal) and one secondary energy sector (electricity) as depicted in Table 6-4.

TABLE 6-4 REVISED TRANSACTIONS: EXAMPLE 3

	Coal	Electric	Autos	Final Demand	Total Output
Coal (10^{15} Btus)	0	300	0	0	300
Electric (10^{15} Btus)	20	20	20	60	120
Automobiles ($\$10^6$)	0	0	0	100	100

$$(I - A^*)^{-1} = \begin{bmatrix} 1.25 & 3.75 & .75 \\ .1 & 1.5 & .3 \\ 0 & 0 & 1 \end{bmatrix}$$

In this example the coal sector delivers all of its output to electricity, and that output is 300×10^{15} Btus, that is, $F_1^* = 300$, but the total output of electricity is $X_2^* = 120$; hence the implied conversion of efficiency of producing electricity from coal is $X_2^*/F_1^* = 0.4$. Therefore we write

$$\hat{F}^*(\hat{X}^*)^{-1} = \begin{bmatrix} 0 & 0 & 0 \\ 0 & \dfrac{300}{120} & 0 \end{bmatrix}$$

and subsequently

$$\alpha = \hat{F}^*(\hat{X}^*)^{-1}(I - A^*)^{-1} = \begin{bmatrix} 1.25 & 3.75 & .75 \\ .25 & 3.75 & .75 \end{bmatrix}$$

Each element in α reflects the energy conversion efficiency implied in $\hat{F}^*(\hat{X}^*)^{-1}$. For example, the total amount of coal required to deliver the amounts of electricity given in the second row of $(I - A^*)^{-1}$ is 2.5 times the amount given in that row, since the energy conversion efficiency is 0.4. Hence, the second row in α is 2.5 times the second row in $(I - A^*)^{-1}$.

Accounting for Imports

As described in Chapter 5, many input-output studies include, as part of the total outputs, transferred or competitive imports, that is, imported goods competing with domestically produced goods. To correctly compute the *domestic* total energy intensity via our total energy requirements matrix, the matrix must somehow be adjusted to reflect only domestic output. Reducing total outputs, X^*, by transferred imports, X_I^*, we write

$$D = E(\hat{X}^* - \hat{X}_I^*)^{-1} \quad \text{and} \quad A^* = Z^*(\hat{X}^* - \hat{X}_I^*)^{-1} \qquad (6\text{-}11)$$

Recall that:

$$\alpha = \hat{F}^*(\hat{X}^*)^{-1}(I - A^*)^{-1} \qquad (6\text{-}12)$$

Using the adjusted total outputs vector,

$$\alpha = \hat{F}^*\left(\hat{X}^* - \hat{X}_I^*\right)^{-1}\left[I - Z^*\left(\hat{X}^* - \hat{X}_I^*\right)^{-1}\right]^{-1}$$

$$\alpha\left[I - Z^*\left(\hat{X}^* - \hat{X}_I^*\right)^{-1}\right] = \hat{F}^*\left(\hat{X}^* - \hat{X}_I^*\right)^{-1}$$

$$\alpha\left[\left(\hat{X}^* - \hat{X}_I^*\right) - Z^*\left(\hat{X}^* - \hat{X}_I^*\right)^{-1}\left(\hat{X}^* - \hat{X}_I^*\right)\right]$$

$$= \hat{F}^*\left(\hat{X}^* - \hat{X}_I^*\right)^{-1}\left(\hat{X}^* - \hat{X}_I^*\right)$$

$$\alpha\left[\hat{X}^* - \hat{X}_I^* - Z^*\right] = \hat{F}^* \tag{6-13}$$

$$\alpha = \hat{F}^*\left[\hat{X}^* - \hat{X}_I^* - Z^*\right]^{-1} \tag{6-14}$$

For the case where $X_I^* = 0$, then

$$\alpha = \hat{F}^*\left(\hat{X}^* - Z^*\right)^{-1} \tag{6-15}$$

This is, of course, equivalent to our previous definition of α:

$$\alpha = \hat{F}^*\left(\hat{X}^*\right)^{-1}\left(I - A^*\right)^{-1}$$

$$\alpha\left(I - A^*\right) = \hat{F}^*\left(\hat{X}^*\right)^{-1}$$

$$\alpha - \alpha Z^*\left(\hat{X}^*\right)^{-1} = \hat{F}^*\left(\hat{X}^*\right)^{-1}$$

$$\alpha\hat{X}^* - \alpha Z^* = \hat{F}^*$$

$$\alpha = \hat{F}^*\left(\hat{X}^* - Z^*\right)^{-1} \tag{6-16}$$

In studies where the domestic production of energy is the central focus, the adjustment just described would be important. Herendeen (1974) deals with this adjustment in detail.

Commodity-by-Industry Energy Models

In Chapter 5 we introduced the following commodity-by-industry accounting identity:

$$X = Vi \tag{6-17}$$

This was Eq. (5-7) in Chapter 5, the industry output identity.

$$Q = Ui + E \tag{6-18}$$

This was Eq. (5-2′) in Chapter 5, the commodity output identity. Recall that V is the make matrix of commodity outputs by industries, Q is the vector of total commodity outputs, E is the vector of final demands for commodities, and U is the use matrix of commodity inputs.

In Chapter 5 we could invoke either of two assumptions for deriving a total requirements matrix, that is, either an industry-based or commodity-based definition of technologies in the input-output economy. For this discussion we assume the former, but similar results could easily be derived for the latter. Again from Chapter 5, with an industry-based technology, we have

$$U = B\hat{X} \tag{6-19}$$

which follows directly from Eq. (5-5′) in Chapter 5, and

$$V = D\hat{Q} \tag{6-20}$$

which follows directly from Eq. (5-9′) in Chapter 5. Substituting Eq. (6-19) into (6-18) we obtain

$$Q = B\hat{X}i + E = BX + E$$

and substituting Eq. (6-17) for X we obtain

$$Q = BVi + E$$

Finally, substituting Eq. (6-20) for V we obtain

$$Q = BD\hat{Q}i + E = BDQ + E \tag{6-21}$$

or

$$Q = (I - BD)^{-1}E \tag{6-22}$$

Recall that $(I - BD)^{-1}$ is the commodity-by-commodity total requirements matrix.

Let us now return to the energy-balance equation stated earlier for the traditional Leontief model:

$$\alpha\hat{X} = \alpha Z + \hat{F}^* \tag{6-23}$$

The corresponding equation for the commodity-by-commodity model is

$$\alpha\hat{Q} = \alpha(BD\hat{Q}) + \hat{F}^* \tag{6-24}$$

where α, as before, is the matrix of total energy intensities; however, this time we define them as commodity energy intensities rather than industry energy intensities (F^* must also be defined in terms of commodities). Rewriting Eq. (6-24) by ordinary matrix algebra, we have

$$\alpha = \hat{F}^*(\hat{Q})^{-1}(I - BD)^{-1} \tag{6-25}$$

As before, where we computed $\hat{F}^*(\hat{X}^*)^{-1}$ to identify the energy rows of $(I - A^*)^{-1}$, $\hat{F}^*(\hat{Q})^{-1}$ accomplishes the same for $(I - BD)^{-1}$ if Q is measured in "hybrid units," as before—Btus for energy sectors and dollars for nonenergy sectors.

As discussed in Chapter 5, in some industries a significant fraction of total output (in value terms) can be attributed to secondary production. In such situations the use of commodity-by-industry accounts is important. Moreover, the secondary production of energy by nonenergy sectors—for example, industrial cogeneration of electricity—can be easily accommodated in this framework.

6-4 | APPLICATIONS

We now consider a number of applications of the energy input-output formulation to several contemporary problems. The intent is not to examine these applications in detail, but only to illustrate the kinds of questions that have been considered in the energy input-output framework.

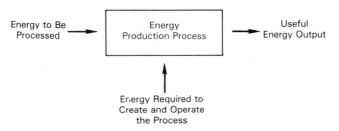

FIGURE 6-1 Net energy analysis.

Net Energy Analysis

Fraley et al. (1980) define net energy analysis as a comparison of the energy produced by a process (or a series of processes) to the energy required to create and sustain that process (Fig. 6-1). The amount of energy to be processed for a given energy production system is the direct energy requirement, as we defined it for the energy input-output model. Similarly, the sum of the direct energy required to create and operate the process and the energy embodied in the industry's inputs is interpreted as the total energy requirement.

Example 4 Consider a highly aggregated hybrid-units input-output model of the U.S. economy for 1963 depicted in Table 6-5. Note that there are five energy sectors: (1) coal, (2) crude oil and gas, (3) refined petroleum, (4) electricity, and (5) natural gas utilities. The primary energy in the economy consists of crude oil and gas, coal, and the electricity produced from nuclear and hydroelectric plants. The nuclear and hydroelectric amounts are relatively small, so that for convenience, this energy is often represented in terms of its fossil fuel equivalent by dividing it by the efficiency of converting fossil fuels to electricity. We can write an expression for the total *primary energy intensity*[4] of an industry as $\bar{\alpha} = [\bar{\alpha}_j]$ where

$$\bar{\alpha}_j = \alpha_{1j} + \alpha_{2j} + \frac{\beta}{\eta}\alpha_{4j} \tag{6-26}$$

where β is the fraction of electricity produced directly from hydroelectric and nuclear sources; η is the conversion efficiency of producing electricity from fossil fuels. Recall that α_{kj} is the total energy intensity of energy type k per dollar's worth of final demand of industry j.

The A^* and $(I - A^*)^{-1}$ matrices for the U.S. transactions shown in Table 6-5 are given in Table 6-6. The total primary energy intensities, $\bar{\alpha}$, as found in Eq. (6-26), are given in Table 6-7. Recall from before that the energy rows of $(I - A^*)^{-1}$ are the total energy coefficients, α. For purposes of our illustration we assume that $\beta = .1$ and $\eta = .33$. In Appendix 6-2 we present the energy

[4] This concept is developed in detail in Bullard and Herendeen (1975a) and in many other articles by these authors.

TABLE 6-5 INPUT-OUTPUT TRANSACTIONS FOR THE U.S. ECONOMY IN HYBRID UNITS (1963)*

Industry Sector	1	2	3	4	5	6	7	8	9	10	Final Demand	Total Output
1. Coal Mining	96	0	0	7750	14	551	71	4702	0	0	2740	15922
2. Crude Oil and Natural Gas	0	1113	23326	0	17737	148	0	0	0	0	499	42825
3. Refined Petroleum	32	43	1624	906	14	741	847	4030	3691	2037	14037	28003
4. Electric Utilities	16	43	56	445	0	381	71	1343	75	509	1181	4120
5. Gas Utilities	0	86	896	3148	977	868	212	1343	151	1528	4948	14156
6. Chemical Products	48	171	616	41	0	4025	2540	10075	75	1018	2572	21182
7. Agriculture	0	0	0	0	0	763	19898	36270	75	3055	10498	70559
8. Mining & Manufacturing	350	1328	868	943	283	3008	6562	255235	4897	49902	348295	671671
9. Transport & Communication	32	171	1344	610	42	635	1552	16120	6102	17313	31412	75334
10. Rest of the Economy	366	4197	2968	3650	849	1271	11007	82616	13108	99294	289873	509200

*Transactions are in millions of dollars for nonenergy sectors and in Quads (10^{15} Btu) for energy sectors.

TABLE 6-6 Technical Coefficients and Leontief Inverse: Example 4*

A*	1	2	3	4	5	6	7	8	9	10
1. Coal Mining	.006	.000	.000	1.881	.001	.026	.001	.007	.000	.000
2. Crude Oil	.000	.026	.833	.000	1.253	.007	.000	.000	.000	.000
3. Refined Petroleum	.002	.000	.058	.220	.001	.035	.012	.006	.049	.004
4. Electric Utilities	.001	.001	.002	.108	.000	.018	.001	.002	.001	.001
5. Gas Utilities	.000	.002	.032	.764	.069	.041	.003	.002	.002	.003
6. Chemical Products	.003	.004	.022	.010	.000	.190	.036	.015	.001	.002
7. Agriculture	.000	.000	.000	.000	.000	.036	.282	.054	.001	.006
8. Mining & Manufacturing	.022	.031	.031	.229	.020	.142	.093	.380	.065	.098
9. Transportation & Communication	.002	.004	.048	.148	.003	.030	.022	.024	.081	.034
10. Rest of the Economy	.023	.098	.106	.886	.060	.060	.156	.123	.174	.195

$(I - A^*)^{-1}$	1	2	3	4	5	6	7	8	9	10
1. Coal Mining	1.010	.003	.012	2.153	.007	.087	.013	.022	.006	.007
2. Crude Oil	.005	1.036	.976	1.489	1.397	.168	.043	.033	.062	.020
3. Refined Petroleum	.003	.003	1.071	.304	.007	.062	.028	.021	.061	.012
4. Electric Utilities	.002	.001	.005	1.132	.002	.027	.005	.005	.002	.003
5. Gas Utilities	.002	.005	.046	.955	1.081	.082	.015	.011	.008	.008
6. Chemical Products	.005	.007	.039	.064	.011	1.250	.071	.039	.007	.009
7. Agriculture	.004	.008	.018	.094	.015	.095	1.421	.133	.017	.029
8. Mining & Manufacturing	.046	.079	.176	.966	.159	.391	.298	1.704	.174	.222
9. Transportation & Communication	.006	.012	.079	.310	.025	.075	.060	.064	1.108	.056
10. Rest of the Economy	.042	.146	.322	1.842	.289	.351	.361	.320	.289	1.302

*A^* and $(I - A^*)^{-1}$ are given in hybrid units; note that, as discussed earlier, the column sums of A^* are not necessarily less than unity.

intensities developed by Hannon et al. (1984) for the U.S. economy for the years 1963, 1967, and 1972.

Suppose that we are considering two alternative designs of a power plant, both of which are rated at 1000 megawatts of electric power and will operate approximately 7000 hours per year for 30 years. This means that each power plant will produce 21×10^{10} kilowatt-hours (kwh) of electrical energy (or 0.7×10^{15} Btus) over its lifetime. The lists of materials required for construction,

TABLE 6-7 Total Primary Energy Intensities

Sector	Primary Energy Intensity
1. Coal Mining	1.016
2. Crude Oil	1.039
3. Refined Petroleum	.980
4. Electric Utilities	3.985
5. Gas Utilities	1.405
6. Chemical Products	.263
7. Agriculture	.058
8. Mining and Manufacturing	.057
9. Transportation and Communication	.069
10. Rest of the Economy	.028

TABLE 6-8 POWER PLANT INPUTS: EXAMPLE 4

Sector	Power Plant I	Power Plant II
1	0	0
2	0	0
3	0	0
4	100	200
5	100	0
6	100	100
7	0	0
8	1000	1000
9	500	1000
10	1000	500

operation, and maintenance (excluding fuel) for the two plants are given in Table 6-8. We will interpret these expenditures as new final demands presented to the U.S. economy.

Let us refer to the vectors of expenditures for the two power plants as Y^{I} and Y^{II}, respectively. The total primary energy intensities for Y^{I} and Y^{II} are found in 10^{12} Btus by

$$\bar{\alpha}Y^{I} = 683$$

$$\bar{\alpha}Y^{II} = 962$$

As a measure of energy efficiency of technologies, the so-called energy ratio (ER) is defined to be the ratio of total energy output of the power plant over its lifetime to the total primary energy intensity. For our example, the energy ratios of Y^{I} and Y^{II} are 1.05 and 0.7, respectively; from a net energy standpoint, power plant design I is more efficient than design II. If the total production is the same for both power plants, then the primary energy intensity gives the same ranking as the ER.

Energy Cost of Goods and Services

We can use the energy input-output model to convert the total energy cost of final demand expenditures, for example, the total fuel (direct) and indirect energy consumed in using a family automobile. Bullard and Herendeen (1975a) show that only about 30 percent of the total energy consumption attributable to automobile usage is gasoline; the rest includes the "energy cost of energy" (e.g., refinery losses), the manufacture of the auto, parts, maintenance, road construction, and so on. We can, of course, use this calculation to compare the energy efficiency of alternative modes of transportation, for example, automobile versus urban mass transit. This problem has been examined in detail by Hannon and Puleo (1974).

Similarly, we might wish to examine the energy intensity of family expenditures as a function of income (see Herendeen 1974). The U.S. Bureau of Labor Statistics routinely compiles personal consumption expenditure data that can be used in energy input-output analysis. Perhaps the most interesting result of this work is that *direct* energy consumption (e.g., gasoline) appears to level off with increasing income. The result, when personal consumption expenditures are translated to indirect energy consumption via the energy input-output model, is that *total* energy consumption attributable to family expenditure does not level off with increasing income. Hence, Herendeen argues, estimates of impacts of energy shortfalls on consumers based on direct energy consumption alone could be quite misleading.

This concept of examining the energy impacts of changes in final demand can, of course, also be used to investigate changes in final demand other than that part which comprises personal consumption. Bezdek and Hannon (1974), for example, examined the impacts of various federal "public works" programs, and Blair (1979) examined the regional impact of constructing new electric-power-generating facilities.

Impacts of New Energy Technologies

Just (1974) has used the input-output model to examine the impact of new energy technologies such as coal gasification or combined gas-and-steam-cycle electric power generation on the U.S. economy. His approach was to estimate the column of technical coefficients, A_N, that would describe the new technology. If A_j is the technology that might be replaced by A_N, then the new column A_j^{new}, reflecting incorporation of the new technology, would be

$$A_j^{new} = gA_N + (1 - g)A_j$$

where g is the fraction of the total production of sector j for which replacement is expected.

An Energy Tax

Bullard (1974) examined the impact of a tax on energy use (per Btu). He assumed that all of the tax would be passed on directly to the consumer. The results indicate that the tax would be distributed in such a way as to substantially increase the prices of energy-intensive products. The impacts of such a tax have been estimated for the U.S. economy based on the 367-sector input-output model developed by Herendeen (1974).

Other Applications

The energy input-output model has been used to examine a wide variety of other problems in addition to those just outlined. These include a detailed characterization of the U.S. import-export balance (Bullard and Herendeen 1975b), analysis of the costs versus benefits of alternative energy conservation programs (Henry 1977), energy consumption analysis (Bullard and Herendeen 1975a), regional energy trade balance relationships (Bourque 1981), and others listed in the references (for example, Almon et al. 1974, Bullard, Penner, and Pilati 1978, Polenske 1976, and Proops 1977, 1984).

TABLE 6-9 SUMMARY OF ENERGY INPUT-OUTPUT RELATIONSHIPS: INITIAL FORMULATION

	Economic (n × n)	Energy (m × n)
Transactions	Z	Z^*, E
		$Z^* i + Y^* = X^*$
	$Zi + Y = X$	$Ei + E_y = F$
Direct Requirements	$A = Z(\hat{X})^{-1}$	$A^* = Z^*(X^*)^{-1}; \delta = (\hat{F}^*)(\hat{X}^*)^{-1} A^*$
		$A^* X^* + Y^* = X^*$
	$AX + Y = X$	$\delta X^* + E_y = F$
Total Requirements	$(I - A)^{-1}$	$(I - A^*)^{-1}; \alpha = (\hat{F}^*)(\hat{X}^*)^{-1}(I - A^*)^{-1}$
		$X^* = (I - A^*)^{-1} Y^*$
	$X = (I - A)^{-1} Y$	$F = \alpha Y^*$

6-5 | SUMMARY

In this chapter we have presented an energy input-output model by constructing matrices of direct and total energy coefficients in so-called "hybrid units." Alternative approaches discussed in Appendix 6-1, which were widely used in the late 1960s and early 1970s, produced energy coefficients dependent upon the level of final demand that was presented to the energy input-output model. The hybrid-units approach does not suffer from this limitation. We show that the hybrid-units approach yields energy coefficients that conform to a fundamental definition of energy conservation conditions; the alternative formulations are shown in Appendix 6-1 to conform only to these conditions when interindustry prices of energy are uniform across all consuming sectors. Table 6-9 summarizes the energy input-output relationships developed in this chapter. An analogous table is presented in Appendix 6-1 (Table 6-1-3) showing the relationship between the original Leontief model and the hybrid-units and alternative energy input-output formulations.

APPENDIX 6-1
EARLIER FORMULATION OF ENERGY INPUT-OUTPUT MODELS

Introduction

In this appendix we present an alternative formulation of the energy input-output model. While still widely applied in the literature, this approach suffers from limitations that in some cases should preclude its use (this formulation was initially adopted by Strout 1967 and Bullard and Herendeen 1975b). In other cases, as we will show, however, the model can be acceptable or even equivalent to the formulation presented in section 6-2.

Recall the $m \times n$ matrix of energy flows, E, which we defined at the beginning of Chapter 6 and for which we defined the basic accounting relationship

$$Ei + E_y = F \tag{6-1-1}$$

We can define an alternative set of *direct energy coefficients*, $D = [d_{kj}]$ where $d_{kj} = e_{kj}/X_j$, that is, the amount of energy type k (in Btus) $(k = 1, \cdots, m)$ required directly to produce a dollar's worth of each producing sector's output $(j = 1, \cdots, n)$ as:

$$D = E(\hat{X})^{-1} \tag{6-1-2}$$

This is directly analogous to the direct input coefficients, $a_{ij} = z_{ij}/X_j$ and $A = Z(\hat{X})^{-1}$. Note, however, the D will in general not be square.

Alternatively, we define a matrix Q of *implied inverse energy prices* (Herendeen 1974 coined this term) with elements:

$$q_{kj} = \frac{e_{kj}}{z_{kj}} \qquad (k = 1, \cdots, m; \; j = 1, \cdots, n) \tag{6-1-3}$$

defined only for $z_{kj} \neq 0$. The units of q_{kj} are then Btus of energy of type k delivered to sector j per dollar transacted from k to j. Thus, the term *inverse price*, for these are Btus per dollar rather than dollars per Btu (the implied price rarely corresponds to the price actually paid for energy, but its significance will become clear shortly). For now, it generates the matrix of direct energy coefficients by:

$$d_{kj} = q_{kj} a_{kj} \tag{6-1-4}$$

This is actually equivalent to our previous definition of D, since

$$d_{kj} = q_{kj} a_{kj} = \left(\frac{e_{kj}}{z_{kj}} \right) \left(\frac{z_{kj}}{X_j} \right) = \frac{e_{kj}}{X_j} \tag{6-1-5}$$

It follows directly from Eqs. (6-1-1) and (6-1-2) that

$$E = D\hat{X} \tag{6-1-6}$$

and

$$D\hat{X}i + E_y + F \tag{6-1-7}$$

but since $\hat{X}i = X$,

$$DX + E_y = F \tag{6-1-8}$$

which is analogous to $AX + Y = X$ of the traditional Leontief model.

In the basic input-output model, we easily calculate the accounting relationships $AX + Y = X = (I - A)^{-1}Y$, where the Leontief inverse elements represent total *dollar* requirements. We appropriately ask, as we did with the hybrid-units energy input-output formulation, whether we can derive the corresponding total *energy* requirements matrix from the relationship in Eq. (6-1-8).

First, we note that the two terms in Eq. (6-1-8), namely DX and E_y, refer respectively to energy consumption by intermediate producers and energy consumption by final demand. To express total *interindustry* energy consumption for a given final demand we simply write

$$DX = D(I - A)^{-1}Y \qquad (6\text{-}1\text{-}9)$$

where $D(I - A)^{-1}$ is the matrix of total interindustry energy coefficients.

In order to account for the energy consumed directly by final demand, the second term in Eq. (6-1-8), we return to the notion of implied inverse energy prices, this time for the energy that is delivered to final demand (as we did for interindustry transactions when the q's were defined in Eq. [6-1-3]). Now we have $Q_y = [q_{ky}]$ where

$$q_{ky} = \frac{e_{ky}}{Y_k} \qquad (6\text{-}1\text{-}10)$$

Here Y_k is the final demand in dollars for the output of energy sector k, and q_{ky} is the corresponding implied inverse price in units of Btus per dollar of final demand (for $Y_k \neq 0$; for $Y_k = 0$ we will define $q_{ky} = 0$). This allows us to transform final demand into the corresponding energy requirements as we did in Eq. (6-1-4) for interindustry requirements translated into energy requirements, by rewriting Eq. (6-1-10) as

$$e_{ky} = q_{ky}Y_k \qquad (6\text{-}1\text{-}11)$$

In matrix terms, Eq. (6-1-11) is written as:

$$E_y = \tilde{Q}Y \qquad (6\text{-}1\text{-}12)$$

where $\tilde{Q} = [\tilde{q}_{ky}]$ is an $m \times n$ matrix whose elements are defined as

$$\tilde{q}_{ky} = \begin{cases} q_{ky}, & k = j \text{ (when energy sector index } k \text{ and} \\ & \text{industry sector index } j \text{ describe} \\ & \text{the same industrial sector)} \\ 0, & \text{otherwise.} \end{cases} \qquad (6\text{-}1\text{-}13)$$

There will, of course, be at most m nonzero elements in $\tilde{Q}$ since there are only m elements in Q_y.

By constructing $\tilde{Q}$ of dimension $m \times n$, we can combine it with the interindustry energy coefficients to produce a matrix of total (interindustry and final-demand) energy coefficients. Altogether, Eqs. (6-1-8), (6-1-9), and (6-1-12) can be combined to obtain

$$F = DX + E_y \qquad (6\text{-}1\text{-}8)$$

$$F = D(I - A)^{-1}Y + \tilde{Q}Y \qquad (6\text{-}1\text{-}14)$$

$$F = [D(I - A)^{-1} + \tilde{Q}]Y \qquad (6\text{-}1\text{-}15)$$

The bracketed quantity, which we denote by ε, is the matrix of *total energy coefficients* analogous to α in the hybrid-units formulation which gives the total amount of energy (Btus) required, both directly and indirectly, to support a given level of final demand, Y.

Example 6-1-1 Consider a simple three-sector input-output economy where two of the sectors are energy sectors, for example, coal and electricity. Assume that the following transactions (in millions of dollars) are observed for a given year:

TABLE 6-1-1 DOLLAR TRANSACTIONS (Z): EXAMPLE 6-1-1 (MILLIONS OF DOLLARS)

	Coal	Electricity	Autos	Final Demand	Total Output
Coal	0	40	0	0	40
Electricity	10	10	10	30	60
Autos	0	0	0	100	100

Suppose that the corresponding energy flows of this economy, expressed in quadrillions of Btus, are given by

TABLE 6-1-2 ENERGY FLOWS (E): EXAMPLE 6-1-1 (QUADRILLIONS OF BTUS)

	Coal	Electricity	Autos	Energy Consumed by Final Demand	Total Energy Production
Coal	0	120	0	0	120
Electricity	20	20	20	60	120

Note that in our example, the coal sector delivers all its product to electricity, another energy sector. Hence, as discussed earlier, the coal sector is known as a primary energy sector and electricity is a secondary energy sector; this distinction will become more important later.

For the example, D, the matrix of direct energy coefficients, is given, as in Eq. (6-1-2), by

$$D = E(\hat{X})^{-1} = \begin{bmatrix} 0 & 120 & 0 \\ 20 & 20 & 20 \end{bmatrix} \begin{bmatrix} \dfrac{1}{40} & 0 & 0 \\ 0 & \dfrac{1}{60} & 0 \\ 0 & 0 & \dfrac{1}{100} \end{bmatrix} = \begin{bmatrix} 0 & 2 & 0 \\ .5 & .333 & .2 \end{bmatrix}$$

(6-1-16)

The matrix of implied inverse energy prices, Q, whose elements are defined in Eq. (6-1-3), is given by

$$Q = \begin{bmatrix} 0 & \dfrac{120}{40} & 0 \\ \dfrac{20}{10} & \dfrac{20}{10} & \dfrac{20}{10} \end{bmatrix} = \begin{bmatrix} 0 & 3 & 0 \\ 2 & 2 & 2 \end{bmatrix}$$

(6-1-17)

Note that the implied inverse prices of coal and electricity are uniform across all consuming sectors, that is, the same for each energy type across all consuming sectors. This is also true for energy delivered to final demand. That is, the implied prices for energy delivered to final demand, q_{ky}, as defined in Eq. (6-1-10), are given by $q_{1y} = 0$ (by definition since $Y_1 = 0$) and $q_{2y} = e_{2y}/Y_2 = 60/30 = 2$. Notice that the price of electricity delivered to final demand is the same as that for interindustry sectors. By Eq. (6-1-13), the matrix $\tilde{Q}$ becomes

$$\tilde{Q} = \begin{bmatrix} q_{1y} & 0 & 0 \\ 0 & q_{2y} & 0 \end{bmatrix} = \begin{bmatrix} 0 & 0 & 0 \\ 0 & 2 & 0 \end{bmatrix} \tag{6-1-18}$$

from which we can easily verify Eq. (6-1-12) (for our example)

$$E_y = \tilde{Q}Y = \begin{bmatrix} 0 & 0 & 0 \\ 0 & 2 & 0 \end{bmatrix} \begin{bmatrix} 0 \\ 30 \\ 100 \end{bmatrix} = \begin{bmatrix} 0 \\ 60 \end{bmatrix} \tag{6-1-19}$$

From Table 6-1-1 we can easily compute A and $(I - A)^{-1}$

$$A = Z(\hat{X})^{-1} = \begin{bmatrix} 0 & .667 & 0 \\ .25 & .167 & .1 \\ 0 & 0 & 0 \end{bmatrix}; \quad (I - A)^{-1} = \begin{bmatrix} 1.25 & 1.00 & .10 \\ .38 & 1.50 & .15 \\ .00 & .00 & 1.00 \end{bmatrix} \tag{6-1-20}$$

Knowing D, $(I - A)^{-1}$, and $\tilde{Q}$, the total energy requirements ε can be computed, as in Eq. (6-1-15), by

$$\varepsilon = D(I - A)^{-1} + \tilde{Q} = \begin{bmatrix} .75 & 3 & .3 \\ .75 & 3 & .3 \end{bmatrix} \tag{6-1-21}$$

It should not seem unusual, at least for this example, that the rows of ε are identical. Indeed, this is a peculiarity of this example which follows from an examination of the original energy flows in Table 6-1-2. Note that coal (the primary energy sector) delivers all of its energy, 120×10^{15} Btus, to electricity (the secondary energy sector)—that is, coal is a "pass-through" sector for energy that is ultimately distributed as electricity. This implies that, since electricity receives all of its energy from coal, the total amount of electricity consumed by the economy cannot exceed the amount of primary energy (coal) required to produce that electricity.[5] Moreover, for a given final demand, the amount of electrical energy must equal the amount of coal energy necessary to produce it. For example as shown in ε, supplying one dollar's worth of automobiles to final demand required 0.3×10^{15} Btus of coal and also of electricity (the elements in the third column of ε). Hence, this energy conservation condition requires that the rows of ε be equal and that the elements of F be identical. We can easily verify that for the original vector of final demands,

$$F = \varepsilon Y = \begin{bmatrix} .75 & 3 & .3 \\ .75 & 3 & .3 \end{bmatrix} \begin{bmatrix} 0 \\ 60 \\ 100 \end{bmatrix} = \begin{bmatrix} 120 \\ 120 \end{bmatrix} \tag{6-1-22}$$

[5]As discussed at the beginning of this chapter, after adjusting for an appropriate energy conversion efficiency of generating electric power from coal, these two amounts must be equal; for now we measure the energy conversion efficiency as 100 percent.

TABLE 6-1-3 Summary of Input-Output Relationships

	Economic	Hybrid-Units Energy Model	Alternate Energy Model
Transactions	Z	Z^*	E
	$Zi + Y = X$	$Z^*i + Y^* = X^*$	$Ei + E_y = F$
Direct Requirements	$A = Z(\hat{X})^{-1}$	$\delta = (\hat{F}^*)(\hat{X}^*)^{-1}A^*$	$D = E(\hat{X})^{-1}$
	$AX + Y = X$	$A^*X^* + Y^* = X^*$	$DX + E_y = F$
		$\delta X^* + E_y = F$	
Total Requirements	$(I - A)^{-1}$	$\alpha = (\hat{F}^*)(\hat{X}^*)^{-1}(I - A^*)^{-1}$	$\varepsilon = D(I - A)^{-1} + \tilde{Q}$
	$X = (I - A)^{-1}Y$	$X^* - (I - A^*)^{-1}Y^*$	$F - \varepsilon Y$
		$F = \alpha Y^*$	

as in Eq. (6-1-15). (Of course, it will always be true that if the rows of ε are equal, then εY, for any Y, will generate a column vector of equal elements.) Note that this will generally not be true for more than one primary energy sector.

We will see soon that this formulation, which is widely applied in the literature, has several serious shortcomings; any attempt at resolving them will have only limited success. The fundamental difficulty is a violation of consistency among energy transactions (the energy conservation condition discussed in Chapter 6) except under very specific conditions (namely, uniform interindustry prices). Before examining these shortcomings, we summarize the input-output relationships derived thus far; we have developed a set of three tables analogous to the original transactions, technical coefficients, and total requirements matrices of the traditional Leontief model. In these new relationships, however, we define energy flows in Btus rather than dollars. Table 6-1-3 summarizes these alternative energy input-output relationships along with the hybrid-units energy input-output relationships.

We now modify the E matrix in Example 6-1-1 to reflect a different distribution of output of electricity without changing the corresponding dollars transacted in Z. This simply changes the implied prices of electricity for different consumers; that is, the price at which electricity is sold is no longer the same for all consumers.

Example 6-1-1 (Revisited) Redefine E and E_y for Example 6-1-1 as follows:

TABLE 6-1-4 Revised Energy Flows (E) for Example 6-1-1 (quadrillions of Btus)

	Coal	Electricity	Autos	Final Demand	Total Energy Consumption
Coal	0	120	0	0	120
Electricity	20	20	30	50	120

Note that we do not change the total energy consumption in Table 6-1-1, only the energy flows; the corresponding implied prices for interindustry and final-demand sales, respectively, are given by

$$Q = \begin{bmatrix} 0 & 3 & 0 \\ 2 & 2 & 3 \end{bmatrix}; \qquad Q_y = \begin{bmatrix} 0 \\ 1.67 \end{bmatrix} \qquad \textbf{(6-1-23)}$$

Hence, the $\tilde{Q}$ matrix, as defined in Eq. (6-1-13), becomes

$$\tilde{Q} = \begin{bmatrix} 0 & 0 & 0 \\ 0 & 1.67 & 0 \end{bmatrix} \qquad (6\text{-}1\text{-}24)$$

and finally, ε becomes

$$\varepsilon = D(I - A)^{-1} + \tilde{Q} = E(\hat{X})^{-1}(I - A)^{-1} + \tilde{Q}$$

$$= \begin{bmatrix} 0 & 120 & 0 \\ 20 & 20 & 30 \end{bmatrix} \begin{bmatrix} \dfrac{1}{40} & 0 & 0 \\ 0 & \dfrac{1}{60} & 0 \\ 0 & 0 & \dfrac{1}{100} \end{bmatrix} \qquad (6\text{-}1\text{-}25)$$

$$\times \begin{bmatrix} 1.25 & 1.0 & 0.1 \\ 0.38 & 1.5 & 0.15 \\ 0 & 0 & 1.0 \end{bmatrix} + \begin{bmatrix} 0 & 0 & 0 \\ 0 & 1.67 & 0 \end{bmatrix} = \begin{bmatrix} .75 & 3 & .3 \\ .75 & 2.667 & .4 \end{bmatrix}$$

Looking at the elements in the third column, this new total energy requirements matrix implies that one dollar's worth of automobiles requires 0.4×10^{15} Btus of electricity to produce that output, but only 0.3×10^{15} Btus of coal. This violates the energy conservation condition for this example, discussed earlier, since the electricity-producing sector received all its primary energy from coal—that is, for this example the two total energy requirements matrix rows should be the same.

It should be readily apparent that application of this alternative energy input-output formulation simply yields the output of the traditional Leontief model multiplied by a set of conversion factors—the implied energy prices. We show more generally later that this formulation is only satisfactory when these energy prices are the same across *all* consuming sectors (including final demand) for each energy type. Griffin (1976) shows that this condition does not hold at all in the U.S. economy. However, in some developing countries, such an assumption may be reasonable. This might encourage adoption of this formulation, since final demands can be posed entirely in value terms instead of hybrid units, as required in the formulation developed in Chapter 6.

Extensions of Example 1   Recall the two-sector economy given in Example 1 of the text of this chapter where we constructed the following hybrid-units energy input-output relationships:

$$Z^* = \begin{bmatrix} 10 & 20 \\ 60 & 80 \end{bmatrix}; \qquad X^* = \begin{bmatrix} 100 \\ 240 \end{bmatrix}$$

$$A^* = Z^*(\hat{X}^*)^{-1} = \begin{bmatrix} .100 & .083 \\ .600 & .333 \end{bmatrix}; \qquad (I - A^*)^{-1} = \begin{bmatrix} 1.212 & 1.515 \\ 1.091 & 1.636 \end{bmatrix}$$

$$\delta = F^*(\hat{X}^*)^{-1}A^* = \begin{bmatrix} .600 & .333 \end{bmatrix}$$

$$\alpha = F^*(\hat{X}^*)^{-1}(I - A^*)^{-1} = \begin{bmatrix} 1.091 & 1.636 \end{bmatrix}$$

The analogous information for the alternative-energy input-output formulation is

$$Z = \begin{bmatrix} 10 & 20 \\ 30 & 40 \end{bmatrix}; \qquad X = \begin{bmatrix} 100 \\ 200 \end{bmatrix};$$

$$A = Z(\hat{X})^{-1} = \begin{bmatrix} .100 & .167 \\ .300 & .333 \end{bmatrix}; \qquad (I-A)^{-1} = \begin{bmatrix} 1.212 & .303 \\ .546 & 1.636 \end{bmatrix};$$

$$D = E(\hat{X})^{-1} = [.600 \quad .667]$$

$$\varepsilon = E(\hat{X})^{-1}(I-A)^{-1} + \tilde{Q} = [60 \quad 80] \begin{bmatrix} \dfrac{1}{100} & 0 \\ 0 & \dfrac{1}{120} \end{bmatrix}$$

$$\times \begin{bmatrix} 1.212 & .303 \\ .546 & 1.636 \end{bmatrix} + [0 \quad 2] = [1.091 \quad 3.273]$$

Note that ε is identical to α, where the elements corresponding to energy sectors are multiplied by the relevant price; ε used in conjunction with Y (not Y^*) necessitates this price adjustment. In other words, $(Y^*)' = [70 \quad 50]$ with an energy price of 2 (10^{15} Btus/10^6)

$$\varepsilon Y = [1.091 \quad 3.272] \begin{bmatrix} 70 \\ 50 \end{bmatrix} = 240$$

$$\alpha Y^* = [1.091 \quad 1.636] \begin{bmatrix} 70 \\ 100 \end{bmatrix} = 240$$

The first expression, εY, generates the total energy requirement (240×10^{15} Btus) needed to support final demand Y. The second expression, αY^*, yields the same result but in terms of supporting the equivalent final demand, Y^*, measured in hybrid units.

The result should not be surprising, since under conditions of uniform interindustry energy prices, the computation of ε is simply a price adjustment[6] of α. Note, however, that result will in general be true *only* under conditions of uniform prices, which we will illustrate in the following. Recall that in the case of using the alternative formulation in Example 6-1-1, when this condition was not met, the model gave inappropriate results. Let us test to see if the hybrid units model fares better when we relax the condition of uniform energy prices.

[6] Generally, let us define a two-element vector $R = [1 \quad 2]$ where the first element is the value that converts the nonenergy units of the original model to the nonenergy units of the hybrid-units model. Clearly these units are the same, so the value of this element is always unity. The second element is the interindustry inverse energy price.

Given this vector R, we can easily write $Y^* = \hat{R}Y$. Here $\begin{bmatrix} 70 \\ 100 \end{bmatrix} = \begin{bmatrix} 1 & 0 \\ 0 & 2 \end{bmatrix}\begin{bmatrix} 70 \\ 50 \end{bmatrix}$. Also, $X^* = \hat{R}X$ or $X = (\hat{R})^{-1}X^*$. Here $\begin{bmatrix} 100 \\ 240 \end{bmatrix} = \begin{bmatrix} 1 & 0 \\ 0 & 2 \end{bmatrix}\begin{bmatrix} 100 \\ 120 \end{bmatrix}$.

The result: For the case of uniform interindustry energy prices, there is no need to account for energy in Btus, since this is equivalent to deriving outputs in dollars and converting to Btus by simply multiplying by the energy price. However, as we found before, if prices are not uniform for all consumers (both interindustry *and* final-demand consumers), such procedures are inappropriate.

Consider, again, the two-sector model of Example 6-1-1 with new energy flows and corresponding energy prices:

TABLE 6-1-5 ENERGY AND DOLLAR FLOWS FOR EXAMPLE 6-1-1 (REVISED) (MILLIONS OF DOLLARS AND 10^{15} BTUS)

	Widgets	Energy	Final Demand	Total Output
Widgets	10	20	70	100
Energy	30 (60)	40 (100)	50 (80)	120 (240)

The dollar quantities $(Z, Y, X, A,$ and $[I - A]^{-1})$ do not change from the earlier case. However, the hybrid-units quantities change since the energy transactions have changed. The energy prices have, of course, changed and are not uniform for all consumers. Energy prices are given in the following table:

TABLE 6-1-6 IMPLIED ENERGY PRICES FOR EXAMPLE 6-1-1 (REVISED) (10^{15} BTUS $/$10^6$)

	Widgets	Energy	Final Demand	Total Output
Energy	2	2.5	1.6	2

From the conventions of the alternative formulation (Method I) and of the hybrid-units formulation (Method II) we can derive the following:

Method I: Alternate Formulation	Method II: Hybrid-Units Model

$$Z = \begin{bmatrix} 10 & 20 \\ 30 & 40 \end{bmatrix} \quad X = \begin{bmatrix} 100 \\ 120 \end{bmatrix} \qquad Z^* = \begin{bmatrix} 10 & 20 \\ 60 & 100 \end{bmatrix} \quad X^* = \begin{bmatrix} 100 \\ 240 \end{bmatrix}$$

$$A = Z(\hat{X})^{-1} = \begin{bmatrix} .100 & .167 \\ .300 & .333 \end{bmatrix} \qquad A^* = Z^*(\hat{X}^*)^{-1} = \begin{bmatrix} .100 & .083 \\ .600 & .417 \end{bmatrix}$$

$$(I - A)^{-1} = \begin{bmatrix} 1.212 & .303 \\ .546 & 1.636 \end{bmatrix} \qquad (I - A^*)^{-1} = \begin{bmatrix} 1.228 & .175 \\ 1.263 & 1.895 \end{bmatrix}$$

We can now calculate the total energy coefficients by the two methods.

METHOD I.

$$D = E(\hat{X})^{-1} = \begin{bmatrix} 60 & 100 \end{bmatrix} \begin{bmatrix} \dfrac{1}{100} & 0 \\ 0 & \dfrac{1}{120} \end{bmatrix} = \begin{bmatrix} .6 & .833 \end{bmatrix}$$

$$\varepsilon = D(I - A)^{-1} + \tilde{Q} = \begin{bmatrix} .6 & .833 \end{bmatrix} \begin{bmatrix} 1.212 & .303 \\ .546 & 1.636 \end{bmatrix} + \begin{bmatrix} 0 & \dfrac{8}{5} \end{bmatrix} = \begin{bmatrix} 1.182 & 3.145 \end{bmatrix}$$

From this we can verify that, since $Y = \begin{bmatrix} 70 \\ 50 \end{bmatrix}$,

$$\varepsilon Y = \begin{bmatrix} 1.182 & 3.145 \end{bmatrix} \begin{bmatrix} 70 \\ 50 \end{bmatrix} = 240$$

METHOD II.

$$F^*(\hat{X}^*)^{-1} = \begin{bmatrix} 0 & 240 \end{bmatrix} \begin{bmatrix} \dfrac{1}{100} & 0 \\ 0 & \dfrac{1}{240} \end{bmatrix} = \begin{bmatrix} 0 & 1 \end{bmatrix}$$

$$\alpha = F^*(\hat{X}^*)^{-1}(I - A^*)^{-1} = \begin{bmatrix} 0 & 1 \end{bmatrix} \begin{bmatrix} 1.228 & .175 \\ 1.263 & 1.895 \end{bmatrix} = \begin{bmatrix} 1.263 & 1.895 \end{bmatrix}$$

From this we can verify that, since $Y^* = \begin{bmatrix} 70 \\ 80 \end{bmatrix}$,

$$\alpha Y^* = \begin{bmatrix} 1.263 & 1.895 \end{bmatrix} \begin{bmatrix} 70 \\ 80 \end{bmatrix} = 240$$

Both methods thus yield the same total energy requirements for the basic data. However, this is not generally true. Consider two cases of *new* final-demand vectors for which we wish to compute the total energy requirement by both Methods I and II.

Case 1 Consider the following final-demand vectors, Y and Y^*, which describe the same final demand since the energy price to final demand is 8/5, that is, $Y_2^* = Y_2(8/5) = (331.1)(8/5) = 533$.

$$Y = \begin{bmatrix} 100 \\ 333.1 \end{bmatrix} \qquad Y^* = \begin{bmatrix} 100 \\ 533 \end{bmatrix}$$

Computing the total energy requirement by the two methods:

Method I: $\varepsilon Y = \begin{bmatrix} 1.182 & 3.145 \end{bmatrix} \begin{bmatrix} 100 \\ 333.1 \end{bmatrix} = 1166$

Method II: $\alpha Y^* = \begin{bmatrix} 1.263 & 1.895 \end{bmatrix} \begin{bmatrix} 100 \\ 533 \end{bmatrix} = 1136$

Case 2 Consider another equivalent pair of final demands:

$$Y = \begin{bmatrix} 1000 \\ 10 \end{bmatrix} \qquad Y^* = \begin{bmatrix} 1000 \\ 16 \end{bmatrix}$$

Computing the total energy requirement by the two methods:

Method I: $\varepsilon Y = \begin{bmatrix} 1.182 & 3.145 \end{bmatrix} \begin{bmatrix} 1000 \\ 10 \end{bmatrix} = 1031.90$

Method II: $\alpha Y = \begin{bmatrix} 1.263 & 1.895 \end{bmatrix} \begin{bmatrix} 1000 \\ 16 \end{bmatrix} = 1293.32$

Limitations of Alternative Formulation

In the following we will show that Method II correctly computes the total energy requirement, so that in Cases 1 and 2 (above), Method I overestimates and underestimates, respectively, the total energy requirement.

Let us return, briefly, to the alternative formulation of total energy coefficients defined in Eq. (6-1-15):

$$F = \left[D(I - A)^{-1} + \tilde{Q} \right] Y \qquad (6\text{-}1\text{-}15)$$

We denote an arbitrary final demand as Y^{new} and the corresponding total energy requirement as F^{new}. Similarly, we denote the total output vector used in defining the total energy coefficients X^{old}, that is, D was computed as

$$D = E(\hat{X}^{old})^{-1} \qquad (6\text{-}1\text{-}26)$$

Combining Eqs. (6-1-15) and (6-1-26) we obtain

$$F^{new} = E(\hat{X}^{old})^{-1}(I - A)^{-1}Y^{new} + \tilde{Q}Y^{new} = E(\hat{X}^{old})^{-1}X^{new} + \tilde{Q}Y^{new} \qquad (6\text{-}1\text{-}27)$$

If $X^{old} = X^{new}$, then the product $(\hat{X}^{old})^{-1}X^{new}$ will be a column vector of ones and, by definition, $E_y = \tilde{Q}Y^{new}$, and

$$F^{new} = Ei + E_y \qquad (6\text{-}1\text{-}28)$$

which is Eq. (6-1) from which the total energy coefficients were originally derived. If $X^{old} \neq X^{new}$, however, which is the case for most applications, the model does not reduce to Eq. (6-1) and does not appropriately reflect the energy flows generated by a new final demand. Hence, we can conclude that while Method II (the hybrid-units formulation) correctly computes the total energy requirement for any arbitrary vector of final demands consistent with our energy conservation condition, Method I yields correct results only for the base case of final demands from which the model was originally derived. The only defense for using Method I in practice, therefore, is when impact analysis involves new final demands that are not substantially different from the basic data or when there are uniform interindustry energy prices.[7]

APPENDIX 6-2
ENERGY INTENSITIES FOR THE UNITED STATES: 1963, 1967, AND 1972

The computation of energy intensities for the U.S. economy has been completed by Hannon et al. (1984) for the years 1963, 1967, and 1972. The methods adopted for reconciling differences among accounting frameworks and aggregation for those years are discussed at length in that paper. Among other complications, recall that, beginning with the 1972 U.S. national input-output

---

[7]Herendeen (1974) suggested a modification procedure for enforcing consistency.

table, the U.S. Department of Commerce adopted the commodity-by-industry accounting framework. Hannon et al.'s approach was to generate make and use matrices from the original input-output data for 1963 and 1967, that is, the data prior to the application of the conventions used at that time for dealing with secondary production (discussed in Chapter 5); hence, the energy intensities reported here and in Hannon et al. (1984) are for specific commodities per unit of output. The data are presented in hybrid units, as defined in Chapter 6, so that energy intensities are expressed for energy commodities per Btu and for nonenergy commodities per dollar of final demand.

The method for computing total primary intensity, again as defined in Chapter 6, was to begin with total energy intensity defined as

$$\alpha = \hat{F}^*(\hat{Q})^{-1}(I - BD)^{-1}$$

TABLE 6-2-1   U.S. COMMODITY ENERGY INTENSITIES: 1963

Sector	Coal Mining	Crude Oil & Gas	Refined Petroleum	Electric Utilities	Gas Utilities	Total Primary
1 Agriculture, Forestry, & Fishing	8808	37089	24836	2709	10149	49306
2 Metal Mining	52851	65506	33537	9565	31838	127275
3 Crude Oil & Gas (see 25)	—	—	—	—	—	—
4 Other Mining (excluding coal; see 24)	34209	126628	34921	10874	92429	173859
5 Construction	15200	31153	17458	2829	13785	49632
6 Food, Feed, & Tobacco Products	12595	31716	17561	2854	13554	47596
7 Textile Products & Apparel	18568	38123	17024	5126	16549	61392
8 Wood Products & Furniture	18237	29143	13528	3758	14086	50988
9 Paper, Printing, & Publishing	28306	45371	19365	4718	23816	78668
10 Chemicals & Chemical Products	40680	119697	44191	10343	49590	171268
11 Petroleum & Coal Products (excluding refined petroleum; see 26)	23126	346083	317634	5546	47057	391904
12 Rubber, Plastics, & Leather	19871	39219	16581	4640	17493	63544
13 Stone, Clay, & Glass Products	29775	82070	18815	6439	62175	119861
14 Primary & Fabricated Metals	51219	50703	18643	7941	31064	109084
15 Machinery, Except Electrical	26351	27951	11871	3981	15673	58033
16 Electrical Equipment & Supplies	22240	30852	12300	4951	17354	57484
17 Transport Equipment & Ordnance	30204	31107	12934	4552	17486	65519
18 Other Manufacturing	19115	33288	14586	4253	16086	56455
19 Transportation & Trade	4946	24692	18177	1908	7338	32086
20 Utilities (excluding electricity and gas; see 27, 28)	15001	51412	31387	4018	20738	71486
21 Other Services	4273	12997	7148	1624	5826	18885
22 Government Enterprises	5724	18147	9986	2388	8216	26198
23 Scrap & Secondhand Goods	—	—	—	—	—	—
24 Coal Mining	1.00648	.00619	.00327	.00193	.00278	1.01409
25 Crude Petroleum & Natural Gas	.00282	1.05387	.00327	.00113	.00627	1.05784
26 Refined Petroleum	.01319	1.07253	1.08301	.00490	.05896	1.14968
27 Electric Utilities	1.97097	1.15398	.28196	1.11615	.90221	3.81815
28 Gas Utilities	.00591	1.10054	.00981	.00177	1.11095	1.16836

Source: Hannon et al. (1984); nonenergy intensities expressed per 1972 dollar.

Tables 6-2-1, 6-2-2, and 6-2-3 are derived by aggregation of the data given in Hannon et al. (1984) for coal, crude petroleum and natural gas, refined petroleum, electric utilities, and natural gas utilities. Total primary intensity is computed in a manner similar to that discussed in Example 4 of Chapter 6. Hannon et al. define primary intensity as

$$\alpha_p = s\alpha$$

where s is a $1 \times n$ vector of scaling factors that adjust the total energy intensity to reflect only primary energy production. Such adjustments include electricity produced from hydroelectric and nuclear sources (as discussed in Example 4), natural gas sold directly to industry (without passing through gas utilities), and

TABLE 6-2-2   U.S. Commodity Energy Intensities: 1967

Sector	Coal Mining	Crude Oil & Gas	Refined Petroleum	Electric Utilities	Gas Utilities	Total Primary
1 Agriculture, Forestry, & Fishing	8426	45640	27330	2725	13937	58004
2 Metal Mining	32107	69525	18735	13315	49986	113514
3 Crude Oil & Gas (see 25)	—	—	—	—	—	—
4 Other Mining (excluding coal; see 24)	31376	126329	22939	12505	105065	172894
5 Construction	13169	34072	20386	2798	14516	50884
6 Food, Feed, & Tobacco Products	11393	34171	17170	3062	15974	49279
7 Textile Products & Apparel	16700	37468	13789	5233	18763	59128
8 Wood Products & Furniture	15361	28063	11278	3770	15536	47200
9 Paper, Printing, & Publishing	22995	45770	17805	5108	25945	74533
10 Chemicals & Chemical Products	30552	107081	20746	8748	54742	147305
11 Petroleum & Coal Products (excluding refined petroleum; see 26)	26839	328041	297181	5068	52556	377216
12 Rubber, Plastics, & Leather	17383	38814	13394	4659	19966	60883
13 Stone, Clay, & Glass Products	29814	77620	16548	6467	61367	115995
14 Primary & Fabricated Metals	47083	48039	13928	8505	33790	102937
15 Machinery, Except Electrical	22468	25718	8889	4158	16806	52138
16 Electrical Equipment & Supplies	17401	26152	8749	4625	16480	47745
17 Transport Equipment & Ordnance	23275	27147	9281	4543	17478	54660
18 Other Manufacturing	15242	29705	10386	4155	16768	48975
19 Transportation & Trade	5303	24447	18046	2231	7622	32497
20 Utilities (excluding electricity & gas; see 27, 28)	17367	34451	12670	4378	21781	56421
21 Other Services	4951	14000	7772	1910	6424	20881
22 Government Enterprises	6437	22846	13874	2618	9483	32147
23 Scrap & Secondhand Goods	—	—	—	—	—	—
24 Coal Mining	1.00477	.00549	.00254	.00177	.00277	1.01159
25 Crude Petroleum & Natural Gas	.00335	1.05154	.00244	.00129	.00947	1.05638
26 Refined Petroleum	.01277	1.04170	1.06995	.00509	.06318	1.11921
27 Electric Utilities	1.92536	1.11907	.30630	1.10956	.86218	3.75424
28 Gas Utilities	.00601	1.07305	.00491	.00200	1.10395	1.15154

Source: Hannon et al. (1984); nonenergy intensities expressed per 1972 dollar.

TABLE 6-2-3 U.S. COMMODITY ENERGY INTENSITIES: 1972

Sector	Coal Mining	Crude Oil & Gas	Refined Petroleum	Electric Utilities	Gas Utilities	Total Primary
1 Agriculture, Forestry, & Fishing	8054	58815	35623	4203	20120	72916
2 Metal Mining	29888	70728	27786	15237	43550	114126
3 Crude Oil & Gas (see 25)	—	—	—	—	—	—
4 Other Mining (excluding coal; see 24)	25034	134265	50646	12180	88868	175646
5 Construction	11878	42274	27088	3585	16325	59045
6 Food, Feed, & Tobacco Products	9355	38627	19107	3997	19185	52808
7 Textile Products & Apparel	13482	47494	20581	6420	23718	67598
8 Wood Products & Furniture	13739	37345	17150	4969	19796	56387
9 Paper, Printing, & Publishing	17487	59077	27641	6456	31273	84177
10 Chemicals & Chemical Products	17543	94747	29085	6936	46369	121320
11 Petroleum & Coal Products (excluding refined petroleum; see 26)	16327	376042	346698	6292	51708	421347
12 Rubber, Plastics, & Leather	14299	51599	20984	6079	26189	72524
13 Stone, Clay, & Glass Products	24545	90584	25681	7936	66218	125900
14 Primary & Fabricated Metals	41229	55691	20066	9775	36029	106291
15 Machinery, Except Electrical	19293	30544	11809	5075	18945	54806
16 Electrical Equipment & Supplies	14593	30415	12103	5449	18179	50151
17 Transport Equipment & Ordnance	20046	32835	13233	5367	19604	58153
18 Other Manufacturing	13101	34448	14519	4916	18722	52581
19 Transportation & Trade	4852	26111	19999	2942	7345	34416
20 Utilities (excluding electricity and gas; see 27, 28)	6872	36023	23935	2823	12498	46886
21 Other Services	3863	13485	7274	2141	6487	19484
22 Government Enterprises	4670	27246	16110	2502	11360	35153
23 Scrap & Secondhand Goods	—	—	—	—	—	—
24 Coal Mining	1.01007	.01039	.00645	.00275	.00410	1.02272
25 Crude Petroleum & Natural Gas	.00278	1.05556	.00558	.00159	.00649	1.06006
26 Refined Petroleum	.01093	1.06221	1.07908	.00632	.06065	1.14875
27 Electric Utilities	1.57502	1.44651	.62877	1.13073	.89369	3.77136
28 Gas Utilities	.00457	1.06630	.00864	.00266	1.10223	1.14965

Source: Hannon et al. (1984); nonenergy intensities expressed per 1972 dollar.

TABLE 6-2-4 TOTAL PRIMARY ENERGY INTENSITY ADJUSTMENT FACTORS

	1963	1967	1972
Coal Mining	1	1	1
Crude Oil & Natural Gas	1	1	1
Refined Petroleum	.0536	.0540	.0628
Electric Utilities	.5463	.5748	.5732
Natural Gas Utilities	.0543	.0644	.0696

Source: Hannon et al. (1984).

TABLE 6-2-5 88-SECTOR TO 28-SECTOR AGGREGATION CODE

28-Sector Aggregation	88-Sector Aggregation
1 Agriculture, Forestry, & Fishing	6-9
2 Metal Mining	10, 11
3 Crude Oil & Gas	(See sector 25)
4 Other Mining	12, 13 (excluding coal; see sector 24)
5 Construction	14, 15
6 Food, Feed, & Tobacco Products	17, 18
7 Textile Products & Apparel	19-22
8 Wood Products & Furniture	23-26
9 Paper, Printing, & Publishing	27-29
10 Chemicals & Chemical Products	30-33
11 Petroleum & Coal Products	34, 35 (excluding refined petroleum; see sector 26)
12 Rubber, Plastics, & Leather	36-38
13 Stone, Clay, & Glass Products	39, 40
14 Primary & Fabricated Metals	41-46
15 Machinery, Except Electrical	47-56
16 Electrical Equipment & Supplies	57-62
17 Transport Equipment & Ordnance	63-65, 16
18 Other Manufacturing	66-68
19 Transportation & Trade	69-75, 79
20 Utilities	78 (excluding electricity and gas; see sectors 27 and 28)
21 Other Services	76, 77, 80-86
22 Government Enterprises	87, 88
23 Scrap & Secondhand Goods	(Excluded; no energy intensity)
24 Coal Mining	1
25 Crude Oil Petroleum & Natural Gas	2
26 Refined Petroleum	3
27 Electric Utilities	4
28 Gas Utilities	5

others discussed in Hannon et al. (1984). Table 6-2-4 gives the values of s used for the calculation of total primary energy intensity in Tables 6-2-1, 6-2-2, and 6-2-3. Table 6-2-5 provides the aggregation scheme from 88 sectors to a 28-sector version with five distinct energy sectors and the remaining 23 sectors the same as those used in Appendix B (except for adjustments as noted in Table 6-2-5).

PROBLEMS

6-1 Consider the following three-sector input-output economy; two sectors are energy sectors (oil is the primary energy sector and refined petroleum is the secondary energy sector):

INTERINDUSTRY TRANSACTIONS (MILLIONS OF DOLLARS)

	Oil	Refined Petroleum	Manufacturing	Final Demand	Total Output
Oil	0	20	0	0	20
Refined Petroleum	2	2	2	24	30
Manufacturing	0	0	0	20	20

The energy sector transactions are also measured in quadrillions of Btus in the following table:

ENERGY SECTOR TRANSACTIONS (10^{15} Btus)

	Oil	Refined Petroleum	Manufacturing	Final Demand	Total Energy Output
Oil	0	20	0	0	20
Refined Petroleum	1	1	1	17	20

Given this information, do the following:

a Compute (1) the matrix of implied inverse energy prices, (2) the direct energy requirements matrix, and (3) the total energy requirements matrix (including an accounting for energy consumed by final demand) using Method I. Is there anything peculiar about the total energy requirements matrix?

b Reformulate this problem as a hybrid-units input-output model; that is, recompute the technical coefficients and Leontief inverse using value terms for nonenergy sectors and energy units (Btus) for energy sectors. Does this model obey the conditions of energy conservation?

6-2 Consider the following input-output transactions table in value terms (millions of dollars) for two industries—*A* and *B*:

	A	B	Total Output
A	2	4	100
B	6	8	100

Suppose we have a direct energy requirements matrix for this economy that is given by:

$$D = \begin{bmatrix} .2 & .3 \\ .1 & .4 \end{bmatrix} \quad \begin{array}{l} 10^{15} \text{ Btus of oil per million dollars of output} \\ 10^{15} \text{ Btus of coal per million dollars of output} \end{array}$$

a Compute the total energy requirements matrix (neglecting energy consumption by final demand).

b Suppose that the final demands for industries *A* and *B* are projected to be $200 million and $100 million respectively for the next year. What is the *net* increase in energy (both oil and gas) required to support this new final demand (neglect energy consumed directly by final demand, since you do not have the information to do this calculation anyway)? What fraction of this net increase is a direct energy requirement and what fraction is indirect (total minus direct)?

c Suppose an energy conservation measure in industry *B* caused the direct energy requirement of that industry for coal to be reduced from 0.4 to 0.3 (10^{15} Btus of coal per dollar of output of industry *B*). How does this change the direct and total energy requirements needed to support the new final demand given in **b**?

6-3 Consider the following input-output table (10^6)

	Transactions			Total Output
	Autos	Oil	Electricity	
Autos	2	6	1	10
Oil	4	4	5	20
Electricity	3	2	1	10

Assume that the implied inverse energy price matrix for this economy is given by the following (in Btus/dollar).

	Autos	Oil	Electricity
Oil	3	1	5
Electricity	5	1	7

a Compute the current energy flows matrix, that is, the distribution of each energy type among the industries in the economy.

b Compute the direct energy coefficients matrix.

c If a final demand of $(2, 14, 18)'$ is presented to this economy, what would be the total amount of energy (of each type) required to support this final demand (assume no energy is consumed directly by final demand).

6-4 Recall that the conditions for energy conservation in an input-output model can be expressed as the following:

$$\alpha \hat{X} = \alpha Z + \hat{F}*$$

where α is the matrix of total energy coefficients, Z is the matrix of interindustry transactions, X is the vector of total outputs, and $F*$ is the matrix of primary energy outputs.

a Show that the hybrid-units formulation of the energy input-output model—that is, $X = X*$ and $Z = Z*$—satisfies these conditions in general.

b Given the following total energy coefficients matrices, explain which of them satisfy the conditions of energy conservation and why. Use the convention that crude oil is a primary energy sector and refined petroleum and electricity are secondary energy sectors.

	Crude	Refined Petroleum	Electricity	Autos
Crude Oil	0	.6	.5	.3
Refined Petroleum	0	.4	.5	.2
Electricity	0	.2	0	.1

	Crude	Refined Petroleum	Electricity	Autos
Crude Oil	0	.6	.5	.3
Refined Petroleum	0	.4	.2	.1
Electricity	0	.2	0	.1

6-5 An energy input-output model is defined by the following (in 10^6 units):

$$Z = \begin{matrix} & \begin{matrix} \text{I} & \text{II} & \text{III} \end{matrix} \\ \begin{matrix} \text{I} \\ \text{II} \\ \text{III} \end{matrix} & \begin{bmatrix} 0 & 10 & 0 \\ 5 & 5 & 5 \\ 0 & 0 & 0 \end{bmatrix} \end{matrix} \qquad Y = \begin{bmatrix} 0 \\ 25 \\ 20 \end{bmatrix} \qquad X = \begin{bmatrix} 10 \\ 40 \\ 20 \end{bmatrix}$$

Industries I and II are energy industries whose patterns of allocation of output are described in energy terms (10^{15} Btus) by

$$E = \begin{bmatrix} 0 & 40 & 0 \\ 5 & 5 & 15 \end{bmatrix} \qquad E_y = \begin{bmatrix} 0 \\ 15 \end{bmatrix}$$

a   Compute F (the vector of total outputs in *energy units*).
b   Compute ε, the total energy requirements matrix (via Method I). Now compute α, the hybrid-units total energy requirements matrix.

| REFERENCES

ALMON, CLOPPER, JR., MARGARET B. BUCKLER, LAWRENCE M. HOROWITZ, and THOMAS C. REIMBOLD. *1985: Interindustry Forecasts of the American Economy.* Lexington, Massachusetts: D. C. Heath (Lexington Books), 1974.

AYRES, ROBERT, and ALAN KNEESE. "Production, Consumption, and Externalities." *American Economic Review* 59, no. 3 (June 1969): 282–97.

BEZDEK, ROGER, and BRUCE HANNON. "Energy, Manpower and the Highway Trust Fund." *Science* 185, no. 4152 (August 1974): 669–75.

BLAIR, PETER. *Multiobjective Regional Energy Planning.* Boston: Martinus Nijhoff, 1979.

BOURQUE, PHILIP. "Embodied Energy Trade Balances Among Regions." *International Regional Science Review* 6, no. 2 (Winter 1981): 121–36.

BULLARD, CLARK. "Sector Outputs and Intraindustry Transactions: Definition of System Boundaries." Center for Advanced Computation, Document No. 40, University of Illinois, 1974.

BULLARD, CLARK, PETER PENNER, and DAVID PILATI. "Net Energy Analysis: A Handbook for Combining Process and Input-Output Analysis." *Resources and Energy* 1, no. 3 (November 1978): 267–313.

BULLARD, CLARK, and ROBERT HERENDEEN. "Energy Impact of Consumption Decisions." *Proceedings of the IEEE* 63, no. 3 (March 1975a): 484–93.

———. "The Energy Costs of Goods and Services." *Energy Policy* 1, no. 4 (December 1975b): 268–77.

CUMBERLAND, JOHN H. "A Regional Interindustry Model for Analysis of Development Objectives." *Papers of the Regional Science Association*, 17 (1966): 65–94.

DOSSANI, NAZIR, and A. PREZIOSI. "Employment-Energy-Economic Interactions." *Final Report to the U.S. Department of Energy.* Consad Research Corporation, 1980.

FRALEY, DAVID W., C. L. MCDONALD, and N. E. CARTER. "A Review of Issues and Applications of Net Energy Analysis." PNL-SA-6619, Battelle Memorial Institute (May 1980).

GRIFFIN, JAMES. "Energy Input-Output Modeling." Electric Power Research Institute, November 1976, Palo Alto, Calif.

HANNON, BRUCE, and F. PULEO. "Transferring from Urban Cars to Buses: The Energy and Employment Impacts." Center for Advanced Computation, Document 98, University of Illinois at Urbana-Champaign, 1974.

HANNON, BRUCE, THOMAS BLAZCEK, DOUGLAS KENNEDY, and ROBERT ILLYES. "A Comparison of Energy Intensities: 1963, 1967 and 1972." *Resources and Energy* 5, no. 1 (March 1984): 83–102.

HENRY, E. W. "An Input-Output Approach to Cost-Benefit Analysis of Energy Conservation Methods." *Economic and Social Review* 9, no. 1, (October 1977): 1–26.

HERENDEEN, ROBERT. "Affluence and Energy Demand." *Mechanical Engineering* 96, no. 10 (October 1974): 18–22.

JUST, JAMES. "Impacts of New Energy Technology Using Generalized Input-Output Analysis." In *Energy*, edited by M. Macrakis, 113–27. Cambridge, Mass.: MIT Press, 1974.

POLENSKE, KAREN R. "Multiregional Interactions Between Energy and Transportation." In *Advances in Input-Output Analysis*, edited by Karen R. Polenske and Jiri V.

Skolka, 433–60. Proceedings of the Sixth International Conference on Input-Output Techniques, Vienna, April 22–26, 1974. Cambridge, Mass.: Ballinger, 1976.

PROOPS, JOHN L. "Input-Output Analysis and Energy Intensities: A Comparison of Some Methodologies." *Applied Mathematical Modelling* 1, no. 4 (March 1977): 181–88.

———. "Modeling the Energy-Output Ratio." *Energy Economics* 6, no. 1 (January 1984): 47–51.

STROUT, ALAN. "Technological Change and U.S. Energy Consumption." Ph.D. diss., University of Chicago, 1967.

7

Environmental Input-Output Analysis

7-1 | INTRODUCTION

The input-output framework has been extended by many researchers to account for environmental pollution generation and abatement associated with interindustry activity. These extensions have been appearing since the late 1960s; in this chapter we will examine several of the most prominent environmental input-output formulations and discuss the limitations of each.

Much like the discussion in Chapter 6—that is, modification of the traditional Leontief model to deal with energy flows—in the environmental extensions we must include some additional conditions in order to enforce consistency among interindustry production, pollution generation, and pollution abatement activities.

The principal problem to be resolved in environmental models is the appropriate unit of measurement of environmental (or ecological) quantities—for example, in monetary or physical units. In the alternatives we consider here, we will see formulations using each approach.

We will examine briefly three basic categories of environmental input-output models:

1 *Generalized Input-Output Models*. These are formed by augmenting the technical coefficients matrix with additional rows and columns to reflect pollution generation and abatement activities.

2 *Economic-Ecologic Models*. These models result from extending the interindustry framework to include "ecosystem" sectors, where flows will be recorded between economic and ecosystem sectors along the lines of an interregional input-output model.

3 *Commodity-by-Industry Models*. Such models express environmental factors as "commodities" in a commodity-by-industry input-output table, as described in Chapter 5.

7-2 | GENERALIZED INPUT-OUTPUT ANALYSIS

Accounting for Pollution Impacts

A very straightforward approach to accounting for pollution generation associated with interindustry activity is to first assume a matrix of pollution output or direct impact coefficients, $v = [v_{kj}]$, each element of which is the amount of pollutant type k, for example, sulfur dioxide or hydrocarbons, generated per dollar's worth of industry j's output. Hence, the level of pollution associated with a given vector of total outputs can be expressed as

$$v^* = vX \qquad (7\text{-}1)$$

where v^* is the vector of pollution levels. Hence, by adding the traditional Leontief model, $X = (I - A)^{-1}Y$, we can compute v^* as a function of final demand, that is, the total pollution of each type generated by the economy directly and indirectly in supporting that final demand:

$$v^* = \left[v(I - A)^{-1}\right]Y \qquad (7\text{-}2)$$

We can view the bracketed quantity as a matrix of total impact coefficients; that is, an element of this matrix is the total pollution impact generated per dollar's worth of final demand presented to the economy.

Even though we are concerned primarily with environmental extensions to input-output analysis in this chapter, we could easily replace the pollution coefficients matrix with a corresponding matrix for any factor associated with interindustry activity that we assume varies linearly with output, for example, employment or energy consumption (as we did in Chapter 6 in the case of energy in the alternate formulation). The use of employment coefficients is essentially equivalent to the notion of employment multipliers introduced in Chapter 4.

Example 1 Consider the two-sector input-output table of transactions shown in Table 7-1. The corresponding technical coefficients and Leontief

TABLE 7-1 INPUT-OUTPUT TRANSACTIONS (MILLIONS OF DOLLARS)

	Industry A	Industry B	Final Demand	Total Output
Industry A	3	2	5	10
Industry B	1	7	2	10

TABLE 7-2 DIRECT IMPACT COEFFICIENTS

	Industry		
Coefficient	A	B	Direct Impact per Million Dollars of Output
Energy	$u = \begin{bmatrix} .2 & .3 \\ .1 & .4 \end{bmatrix}$		Oil Consumption (10^9 Btus)
			Coal Consumption (10^9 Btus)
Pollution	$v = \begin{bmatrix} .5 & 1.1 \\ .7 & .7 \end{bmatrix}$		SO_2 generation (10^2 lbs)
			HC generation (10^2 lbs)
Employment	$w = [.1 \quad .2]$		Employment (10^3 man-years)

inverse matrices are

$$A = \begin{bmatrix} .3 & .2 \\ .1 & .7 \end{bmatrix} \qquad (I-A)^{-1} = \begin{bmatrix} 1.58 & 1.05 \\ 0.53 & 3.68 \end{bmatrix}$$

We now define three direct-impact coefficient matrices relating energy requirements, pollution generation, and employment to total output[1] (see Table 7-2).

For convenience, we can easily *concatenate* these matrices (that is, stack these matrices u, v, and w on top of one another), to yield a single direct-impact coefficient matrix D.

$$D = \begin{bmatrix} u \\ \hline v \\ \hline w \end{bmatrix} = \begin{bmatrix} .2 & .3 \\ .1 & .4 \\ \hline .5 & 1.1 \\ .7 & .7 \\ \hline .1 & .2 \end{bmatrix}$$

We can similarly define a vector of total impacts, X^*, by concatenating the following:

$$X^* = \begin{bmatrix} u^* \\ \hline v^* \\ \hline w^* \end{bmatrix} \qquad (7\text{-}3)$$

where $u^* = uX$; $v^* = vX$, and $w^* = wX$. Hence, we can write

$$X^* = DX \qquad (7\text{-}4)$$

For convenience, we may wish to record X^* along with the corresponding final demands associated with the generation of a particular X^*. We can accomplish this easily by defining a new vector of total impacts, concatenating the vector of final demands with X^*; let us define this expanded vector of total impacts as $\tilde{X}$, so that

$$\tilde{X} = \begin{bmatrix} X^* \\ \hline Y \end{bmatrix} \qquad (7\text{-}5)$$

We can similarly expand the matrix of direct-impact coefficients by concatenating D with $(I - A)$; let us define this new expanded direct-impact coefficients

---

[1] Recall from Chapter 6 that developing such coefficients for energy, in particular, is in effect using the methodology of Appendix 6-1, which must be applied carefully in order to avoid inconsistent results.

matrix to be G:

$$G = \left[\frac{D}{I - A} \right] \tag{7-6}$$

In our example, for $10 million worth of total production of each industry, A and B, a total of 5 million Btus each of oil and coal is required to support that production. Similarly, 16,000 and 14,000 pounds, respectively, of SO_2 and hydrocarbons are generated by this production; 3000 man-years of employment are also associated with the level of industrial production. Hence, we can write

$$\tilde{X} = GX \tag{7-7}$$

which, for our example, is

$$GX = \begin{bmatrix} .2 & .3 \\ .1 & .4 \\ \hline .5 & 1.1 \\ .7 & .7 \\ \hline .1 & .2 \\ \hline .7 & -.2 \\ -.1 & .3 \end{bmatrix} \begin{bmatrix} 10 \\ 10 \end{bmatrix} = \begin{bmatrix} 5 \\ 5 \\ \hline 16 \\ 14 \\ \hline 3 \\ \hline 5 \\ 2 \end{bmatrix} = \left[\frac{X^*}{Y} \right] \tag{7-8}$$

This formulation is particularly well suited to using input-output with mathematical programming models as in Thoss (1976) and Blair (1979).

As an alternative to the preceding formulation, we may wish to express total impacts as a function of final demands. For example, we may wish to use the coefficients in impact analysis in much the same way we traditionally use the Leontief inverse. That is, we may find the total impacts in terms of energy, pollution generation, and employment associated with some given level of final demand. This formulation has been applied by Just (1974) and Folk and Hannon (1974) to examine the impacts of new energy technologies.

In this case we can write our earlier expression for total impacts, Eq. (7-4), equivalently as:

$$X^* = \left[D(I - A)^{-1} \right] Y \tag{7-9}$$

where, as before for pollution coefficients alone, the bracketed quantity is the matrix of total-impact coefficients. Let us denote the bracketed quantity by D^* so that, for our example, we can find the levels of energy needs, pollution generation, and employment associated with the basic data.

$$X^* = D^*Y = \begin{bmatrix} .2 & .3 \\ .1 & .4 \\ \hline .5 & 1.1 \\ .7 & .7 \\ \hline .1 & .2 \end{bmatrix} \begin{bmatrix} 1.58 & 1.05 \\ .53 & 3.68 \end{bmatrix} \begin{bmatrix} 5 \\ 2 \end{bmatrix} = \begin{bmatrix} 5 \\ 5 \\ \hline 16 \\ 14 \\ \hline 3 \end{bmatrix} \tag{7-10}$$

Note that here we compute X^* as a function of Y; in Eq. (7-4) we computed X^* as a function of X. Finally, for convenience, we may wish to include X itself in our vector of total impacts. This can be accomplished easily by concatenating X with the vector of total impacts in the same manner we concatenated X^* with Y in constructing $\tilde{X}$ in Eq. (7-5); we define a new expanded vector of total impacts to be $\overline{X}$:

$$\overline{X} = \left[\frac{X^*}{X}\right] = \begin{bmatrix} 5 \\ 5 \\ \hline 16 \\ 14 \\ \hline 3 \\ \hline 10 \\ 10 \end{bmatrix} \tag{7-11}$$

We can similarly expand the total-impacts coefficients matrix by concatenating the Leontief inverse with the total-impact coefficients; let us call the new expanded total-impacts coefficients matrix H, so that

$$H = \left[\frac{D^*}{(I-A)^{-1}}\right] \tag{7-12}$$

Hence,

$$\overline{X} = \left[\frac{X^*}{X}\right] = HY = \begin{bmatrix} .48 & 1.31 \\ .37 & 1.58 \\ 1.37 & 4.57 \\ 1.48 & 3.31 \\ .26 & .84 \\ \hline 1.58 & 1.05 \\ .53 & 3.68 \end{bmatrix} \begin{bmatrix} 5 \\ 2 \end{bmatrix} = \begin{bmatrix} 5 \\ 5 \\ 16 \\ 14 \\ 3 \\ \hline 10 \\ 10 \end{bmatrix} \tag{7-13}$$

Note that $\tilde{X}$ and $\overline{X}$ are equivalent descriptions of the same situation, since X and Y uniquely define one another in a Leontief model. That is, for every given Y, there is one and only one X, and vice versa. Note also that we can generate a matrix of impacts generated by each industry separately by diagonalizing Y to yield $H\hat{Y}$. For the last example,

$$H\hat{Y} = \begin{bmatrix} 2.40 & 2.62 \\ 1.85 & 3.16 \\ 6.85 & 9.14 \\ 7.40 & 6.62 \\ 1.30 & 1.68 \\ \hline 7.90 & 2.10 \\ 2.65 & 7.36 \end{bmatrix}$$

Hence, for example, of the 5×10^9 Btus of oil consumed by the economy in the course of satisfying final demand $Y' = [5 \quad 2]$, 2.4×10^9 Btus are attributed to industry 1; 2.62×10^9 Btus are attributed to industry 2. (These values do not sum to those in Eq. (7-13) due to rounding.) This is analogous to retrieving the matrix of transactions, Z, from $Z = A\hat{X}$.

Ecological Commodities

In the preceding discussion and in Chapter 6, we defined a set of direct and indirect impacts as factors—such as energy consumption, pollution generation, and employment—that are associated with interindustry activity. In evaluating many environmental issues, we may wish to distinguish between such factors viewed as inputs to an industry production process, for example, energy and employment, and those factors viewed as outputs generated by a production process, for example, pollution.

We might view all these factors as flows into and out of the ecosystem in which the interindustry economic system exists, that is, as ecological input and output commodities. Further, we might restrict our consideration of ecological commodities to nonmarket materials, since we can adequately deal with the marketable commodities through the Leontief model itself (sometimes with modifications, as we found in Chapters 5 and 6).

Let us define a set of ecological commodity inputs—for example, water, land, or air—the magnitudes of which we will capture in a matrix $M = [m_{kj}]$, an element of which reflects the amount of ecological input of type k used in the production of economic sector j's total output. Similarly, we define a set of ecological commodity outputs—for example, pounds of sulfur dioxide air pollution. The corresponding matrix of ecological commodity output flows is $N = [n_{jk}]$, an element of which specifies the amount of ecological commodity output k associated with the output of sector j.

Johnson and Bennett (1981) classify ecological commodities according to the sources from which they are extracted and the sinks to which they are eventually discharged. For example, consider the table of economic and ecologic commodity flows in Table 7-3.

We can define ecological commodity input and output coefficients in the same way we define technical coefficients in the Leontief model. Recall that

$$A = Z(\hat{X})^{-1}$$

defines the technical coefficients; similarly

$$R = M(\hat{X})^{-1} \tag{7-14}$$

defines the ecological commodity input coefficients, that is, that elements of $R = [r_{kj}]$ specify the amount commodity k required per dollar's worth of output of industry j. Also,

$$Q = N'(\hat{X})^{-1} \tag{7-15}$$

defines the ecological commodity output coefficients, that is, $Q = [q_{kj}]$ specifies the amount of commodity k generated per dollar's worth of output of industry j. Note that N' is the transpose of the matrix of ecological commodity output flows. For the data given in Table 7-3, we find

$$A = Z(\hat{X})^{-1} = \begin{bmatrix} 1 & 3 & 5 \\ 0 & 2 & 10 \\ 0 & 2 & 6 \end{bmatrix} \begin{bmatrix} \dfrac{1}{12} & 0 & 0 \\ 0 & \dfrac{1}{12} & 0 \\ 0 & 0 & \dfrac{1}{24} \end{bmatrix} = \begin{bmatrix} .083 & .25 & .208 \\ 0 & .167 & .417 \\ 0 & .167 & .250 \end{bmatrix}$$

$$\tag{7-16}$$

TABLE 7-3 Economic-Ecologic Commodity Flows

| | | Interindustry Transactions | | | | | Ecological Commodity Outputs | |
| | | Consuming Sectors | | | Final Demand | Total Output | SO$_2$ | HC |
		Agriculture	Mining	Manufacturing				
Producing Sectors	Agriculture	1	3	5	3	12	0	1
	Mining	0	2	10	0	12	0	2
	Manufacturing	0	2	6	16	24	4	3
Ecological Commodity Inputs	Water	5	4	8				
	Land	10	10	1				

$$R = M(\hat{X})^{-1} = \begin{bmatrix} 5 & 4 & 8 \\ 10 & 10 & 1 \end{bmatrix} \begin{bmatrix} \dfrac{1}{12} & 0 & 0 \\ 0 & \dfrac{1}{12} & 0 \\ 0 & 0 & \dfrac{1}{24} \end{bmatrix} = \begin{bmatrix} .417 & .333 & .333 \\ .833 & .833 & .042 \end{bmatrix}$$

$$(7\text{-}17)$$

$$Q = N'(\hat{X})^{-1} = \begin{bmatrix} 0 & 0 & 4 \\ 1 & 2 & 3 \end{bmatrix} \begin{bmatrix} \dfrac{1}{12} & 0 & 0 \\ 0 & \dfrac{1}{12} & 0 \\ 0 & 0 & \dfrac{1}{24} \end{bmatrix} = \begin{bmatrix} 0 & 0 & .167 \\ .083 & .167 & .125 \end{bmatrix}$$

$$(7\text{-}18)$$

Using R and Q as computed in Eqs. (7-17) and (7-18), total impact coefficients—that is, in this case, ecological commodity input and output coefficients as a function of final demands—can be written as $R^* = R(I - A)^{-1}$ and $Q^* = Q(I - A)^{-1}$, respectively. For the example,

$$R^* = R(I - A)^{-1} = \begin{bmatrix} .417 & .333 & .333 \\ .833 & .833 & .042 \end{bmatrix} \begin{bmatrix} 1.091 & .436 & .545 \\ 0 & 1.350 & .750 \\ 0 & .300 & 1.500 \end{bmatrix}$$

$$= \begin{bmatrix} .455 & .732 & .977 \\ .909 & 1.501 & 1.142 \end{bmatrix} \quad (7\text{-}19)$$

$$Q^* = Q(I - A)^{-1} = \begin{bmatrix} 0 & 0 & .167 \\ .083 & .167 & .125 \end{bmatrix} \begin{bmatrix} 1.091 & .436 & .545 \\ 0 & 1.350 & .750 \\ 0 & .300 & 1.500 \end{bmatrix}$$

$$= \begin{bmatrix} 0 & .050 & .250 \\ .011 & .299 & .358 \end{bmatrix} \quad (7\text{-}20)$$

The elements in $R^* = [r_{ij}^*]$ reflect the amount of ecologic input i required directly and indirectly to deliver a dollar's worth of industry j's output to final demand. Hence $r_{11}^* = 0.455$ indicates that 0.455 units of water are required to deliver a dollar's worth of agricultural products to final demand. Similarly, the elements in $Q^* = [q_{ij}^*]$ reflect the amount of ecologic output i associated with delivering a dollar's worth of industry j's output to final demand directly and indirectly. For example, $q_{23}^* = 0.358$ means that associated with delivering one dollar's worth of manufacturing goods to final demand is production of 0.358 units of hydrocarbon pollutants.

7-3 | AN AUGMENTED LEONTIEF MODEL

Another straightforward approach to accounting for pollution generation and abatement in a traditional Leontief model is simply to augment the technical coefficients matrix with a set of pollution generation and/or abatement coefficients. In the case of pollution generation, the coefficients reflect the amount of a particular pollutant generated per dollar's worth of industry output. Similarly, the pollution abatement coefficients reflect inputs to pollution-elimination activities. This procedure was first proposed in Leontief (1970).

Pollution Generation

Consider the two-sector input-output model presented in Chapter 2:

TABLE 7-4 POLLUTION-GENERATION EXAMPLE: DOLLAR TRANSACTIONS

		Purchasing Sector		Final Demand	Total Output
		1	2		
Selling	1	150	500	350	1000
Sector	2	200	100	1700	2000

Suppose that sector 1, in producing the $1000 output indicated in Table 7-4, generates 50 units of "pollution" or "waste"—for example, emits 50 pounds of solid pollutant into the air.[2] Sector 2, while producing its $2000 output, may have been observed to have generated 80 pounds of the same solid pollutant. Dividing each of these by the total output of the sector responsible for their production would give a kind of pollution-generation or waste-generation coefficient—pounds of pollutant generated per dollar's worth of output (as in Q in the last section). Since these pollutants are outputs or by-products of a given production process, they could be interpreted as "negative inputs," in which case we might define them in the A matrix in the columns of the producing sectors, 1 or 2, with a minus sign. This is unnecessary, however, if we interpret pollutant generation in terms of the services required to dispose of pollution, for example, waste-disposal services. Hence we measure waste-disposal services in units of pollution disposed of or generated.

Letting p denote pollution generation, $z_{p1} = 50$ pounds says that sector 1 *generated* 50 pounds of pollutant; similarly, $z_{p2} = 80$ indicates that sector 2 *generated* 80 pounds of pollutant. Thus, the pollution-generation coefficients are $z_{p1}/X_1 = a_{p1} = 50/100 = 0.05$, and $z_{p2}/X_2 = 80/2000 = 0.04$; both are in units of pounds per dollar of output.

If the technological relationships implied by these coefficients are assumed to remain as stable as the others in input-output analysis, then the total amount of solid pollutant emitted into the air, X_p, for any given values of X_1 and X_2,

---

[2] Of course, there may (and generally will) be several kinds of pollution generation associated with any production process. The basic ideas, however, are adequately illustrated with the example of a single pollutant. Extension to several pollution types is covered in Ayres and Kneese (1969), Gutmanis (1975) and Leontief and Ford (1972).

would be given by

$$X_p = a_{p1}X_1 + a_{p2}X_2 \tag{7-21}$$

or, in this example, $X_p = (.05)X_1 + (.04)X_2$.

This relationship, defining the total pollution output, can be added directly to the general two-sector model. From before we have

$$(1 - a_{11})X_1 - a_{12}X_2 = Y_1$$
$$- a_{21}X_1 + (1 - a_{22})X_2 = Y_2 \tag{7-22}$$

Adding Eq. (7-21), a third linear equation involving a third variable, X_p, which does not appear in the previous two equations, is accomplished easily.

$$(1 - a_{11})X_1 - a_{12}X_2 + 0X_p = Y_1$$
$$- a_{21}X_1 + (1 - a_{22})X_2 + 0X_p = Y_2 \tag{7-23}$$
$$- a_{p1}X_1 - a_{p2}X_2 + X_p = 0$$

or, in more compact matrix terms

$$\begin{bmatrix} (I-A) & \vdots & \begin{matrix} 0 \\ 0 \end{matrix} \\ \hline - a_{p1} \quad - a_{p2} & \vdots & 1 \end{bmatrix} \begin{bmatrix} X_1 \\ X_2 \\ \hline X_p \end{bmatrix} = \begin{bmatrix} Y_1 \\ Y_2 \\ \hline 0 \end{bmatrix} \tag{7-24}$$

The original $(I - A)$ matrix is essentially bordered by a row of (the negatives of) pollution-generation coefficients and a column of zeros, and the X and Y vectors are appropriately expanded. Denote this expanded coefficient matrix as $(I - A_p)$. Note that this is, in practice, similar to closing the basic Leontief model with respect to households, as we did in Chapter 2.

Fundamentally, this simply enables the amount of pollution generated, X_p, to be calculated along with X_1 and X_2 for any given Y_1 and Y_2. This could also be done in two steps, using the smaller two-equation input-output model, (7-22), and then using the resulting gross outputs, X_1 and X_2 to evaluate X_p via Eq. (7-21)—as in section 7-2, with the matrix of direct-impact coefficients.

With the expanded inverse, and the data from the example in section 2-3 (in particular, from Numerical Example: Hypothetical Figures—Approach I), and the hypothesized values for a_{p1} and a_{p2}, we have

$$\begin{bmatrix} X_1 \\ X_2 \\ \hline X_p \end{bmatrix} = \begin{bmatrix} .85 & -.25 & \vdots & 0 \\ -.20 & .95 & \vdots & 0 \\ \hline -.05 & -.04 & \vdots & 1 \end{bmatrix}^{-1} \begin{bmatrix} 600 \\ 1500 \\ \hline 0 \end{bmatrix}$$

The reader should find the required inverse, using the standard determinant-adjoint definition (and selecting column 3 for evaluating the determinant, because of the presence of zeros). He will find that the elements of the original $(I - A)^{-1}$ matrix still appear in the upper-left area of the expanded inverse, $(I - A_p)^{-1}$; this same result follows from observations on the inverse of a partitioned matrix, in section A-7 of Appendix A. This new inverse is

$$
(I - A_p)^{-1} = \left(\frac{1}{.758}\right)
\begin{bmatrix}
.05 & .25 & 0 \\
.20 & .85 & 0 \\
\hline
.055 & .046 & .758
\end{bmatrix}
$$

or

$$
(I - A_p)^{-1} =
\begin{bmatrix}
1.254 & .330 & 0 \\
.264 & 1.122 & 0 \\
\hline
.073 & .061 & 1
\end{bmatrix}
\tag{7-25}
$$

and hence

$$
\begin{bmatrix} X_1 \\ X_2 \\ \hline X_p \end{bmatrix} =
\begin{bmatrix}
1.254 & .330 & 0 \\
.264 & 1.122 & 0 \\
\hline
.073 & .061 & 1
\end{bmatrix}
\begin{bmatrix} 600 \\ 1500 \\ \hline 0 \end{bmatrix}
$$

Thus the pollution generated during production to meet final demands of $Y_1 = 600$ and $Y_2 = 1500$ is $X_p = (.073)(600) + (.061)(1500) = 43.98 + 92.10 = 136.08$ pounds.

Clearly, having $X_1 = 1247$ and $X_2 = 1842$ from our earlier calculations, and having the pollution-generation coefficients ($a_{p1} = .05$, $a_{p2} = .04$), the pollution generated by this production could have been found straightforwardly as $X_p = (.05)(1247) + (.04)(1842) = 62.35 + 73.68 = 136.03$. The small differences in the two approaches are due to rounding errors that occur in working with decimals in finding the inverse of $(I - A_p)$; in either case, we would estimate that 136 pounds of waste would be generated.

Since finding $(I - A_p)^{-1}$ involves additional calculations, we would expect the approach using this inverse to have some advantages, and it does. It allows us to impute the total amount of pollution generated back to the final users, whose demands, Y_1 and Y_2, were responsible for production in the first place. The first two elements in the bottom row of $(I - A_p)^{-1}$ do just that; each dollar of final demand for the output of sector 1 causes the generation of 0.073 pounds of pollutant, and each dollar of final demand for the output sector 2 causes 0.061 pounds. Thus, of the 136 pounds produced, Y_1 is the cause of 44 pounds and Y_2 is the cause of 92 pounds. Note that from the point of view of producers, sector 1's gross output, X_1, generates 62 pounds; sector 2's gross output, X_2, accounts for the remaining 74 pounds. The division of responsibility differs, depending on whether one is viewing the production (supply) side or the final consumption (demand) side. That is, a $100 reduction of sector 1's gross output means 5 pounds less of solid waste; a $100 reduction of final demand for sector 1's output means 7.33 pounds less.

For some kinds of environmental policy questions it is useful to be able to assign responsibility not to producers themselves but to the ultimate consumers. The "pollution multipliers" in the bottom row of $(I - A_p)^{-1}$ give an indication of the effects on pollution generation that might be expected to accompany, for example, a government tax policy aimed at decreasing final demands by consumers by, say, a selective sales tax.[3]

---

[3]Chatterji (1975) extends the augmented Leontief model to include the concepts of a balanced regional model discussed earlier in Chapter 3.

Pollution Elimination

In a similar fashion, pollution abatement or waste disposal could be introduced into a Leontief framework as one or more columns representing sectors whose function it is to reduce or eliminate various pollutants. Consider only one such sector in a model which includes a pollution-generation row, as above. The coefficients in this column (except for the last one) would represent inputs to the technological process that removes (or disposes of) the pollutant. If the process itself generates additional pollution, this would appear in the form of a coefficient in the pollution-generation row. Let X_p now represent pollution *eliminated*. If all pollution is to be eliminated, the appropriate set of equations, similar to Eq. (7-23), would be

$$(1 - a_{11})X_1 - a_{12}X_2 - a_{1p}X_p = Y_1$$

$$- a_{21}X_1 + (1 - a_{22})X_2 - a_{2p}X_p = Y_2 \qquad (7\text{-}26)$$

$$- a_{p1}X_1 - a_{p2}X_2 + (1 - a_{pp})X_p = 0$$

The coefficients a_{1p} and a_{2p} represent inputs from the other sectors to pollution abatement, and the third equation simply defines the total amount of pollution generated and eliminated:

$$X_p = a_{p1}X_1 + a_{p2}X_2 + a_{pp}X_p \qquad (7\text{-}27)$$

If it is not technologically or economically feasible for *all* waste to be eliminated, let X_p be the amount *eliminated*, only, and let Y_p be the amount not eliminated (and hence, in some way, "tolerated" by society, if not exactly "demanded"). The total pollution *generated* is $a_{p1}X_1 + a_{p2}X_2 + a_{pp}X_p$, analogous to the intermediate output in the traditional Leontief model. We must subtract the amount of pollution tolerated (add a negative value, Y_p) to yield total pollution eliminated, X_p. Then the third equation in (7-26) would simply be

$$- a_{p1}X_1 - a_{p2}X_2 + (1 - a_{pp})X_p = - Y_p$$

Hence, the relationships in (7-26) would be

$$(1 - a_{11})X_1 - a_{12}X_2 - a_{1p}X_p = Y_1$$

$$- a_{21}X_1 + (1 - a_{22})X_2 - a_{2p}X_p = Y_2 \qquad (7\text{-}26')$$

$$- a_{p1}X_1 - a_{p2}X_2 + (1 - a_{pp})X_p = - Y_p$$

and the total amount of pollution generated would be

$$X_p + Y_p = a_{p1}X_1 + a_{p2}X_2 + a_{pp}X_p \qquad (7\text{-}28)$$

Example 2 Consider the following example of a pollution-activity-augmented Leontief model. The transactions, including pollution levels, are given in Table 7-5.

The row sums of the interindustry transactions matrix yield intermediate industry output for the economic sectors and total pollution *generated* for the pollution-generation sector. In the final-demand column are industry final demands for the economic sectors and the amount of pollution tolerated by

TABLE 7-5 INPUT-OUTPUT TRANSACTIONS: POLLUTION-EXPANDED MODEL EXAMPLE

	Manufacturing	Services	Pollution Abatement	Intermediate Output	Final Demand	Total Output
Manufacturing	15.0	25.0	.6	40.6	59.4	100.0
Services	20.0	5.0	1.2	26.2	73.8	100.0
Pollution						
Generation	5.0	4.0	0	9.0	−3.0	6.0

society, which is entered as a negative value since the term X_p is a measure of the total amount of pollution *eliminated*; that is, the total amount eliminated, $X_p = 6$ units, should equal the total amount produced, z_{p1} (5) plus z_{p2} (4) or 9 units, less the amount tolerated, which is recorded in the table, as discussed earlier, by the value $-Y_p = -3$. Viewing tolerated pollution as a negative final demand allows us to retain the Leontief identity of intermediate outputs *plus* final demands equals total outputs for pollution sectors as well as economic sectors. Note also that for purposes of this example we presume that the pollution-abatement sector does not generate pollution in the process of eliminating pollution from other sectors and the final demand.

The A_p matrix for this example is

$$A_p = Z_p(\hat{X})^{-1} = \begin{bmatrix} 15 & 25 & .6 \\ 20 & 5 & 1.2 \\ 5 & 4 & 0 \end{bmatrix} \begin{bmatrix} \dfrac{1}{100} & 0 & 0 \\ 0 & \dfrac{1}{100} & 0 \\ 0 & 0 & \dfrac{1}{6} \end{bmatrix} = \begin{bmatrix} .15 & .25 & .1 \\ .20 & .05 & .2 \\ .05 & .04 & 0 \end{bmatrix}$$

The last row, the pollution-generation row, indicates that the economic sectors, manufacturing and services, generate 0.05 and 0.04 units of pollution, respectively, per dollar's worth of output. Hence

$$(I - A_p) = \begin{bmatrix} .85 & -.25 & -.1 \\ -.2 & .95 & -.2 \\ -.05 & -.04 & 1.00 \end{bmatrix}$$

and

$$X_p = (I - A_p)^{-1} Y_p = \begin{bmatrix} 1.630 & 1.806 & .195 \\ .283 & 1.138 & .256 \\ .075 & .063 & 1.020 \end{bmatrix} \begin{bmatrix} 59.4 \\ 73.8 \\ -3.0 \end{bmatrix} = \begin{bmatrix} 100.0 \\ 100.0 \\ 6.0 \end{bmatrix}$$

Existence of Nonnegative Solutions

In Chapter 2 we presented a set of conditions ensuring the nonnegativity of total outputs computed in a Leontief model for a set of given (positive vector of) final demands, the Hawkins-Simon conditions. These conditions will turn out to be much more important in the context of environmental input-output models for assuring the existence of nonnegative solutions than they were in the traditional Leontief framework. The corresponding conditions for the Leontief model augmented with pollution-generation and/or pollution-abatement sectors can be derived directly from original Hawkins-Simon conditions.

Let us recall the simple extended model given in Eq. (7-26′), which includes both generation and elimination of pollution; in matrix terms we can rewrite (7-26′) as:

$$
\begin{bmatrix}
1 - a_{11} & -a_{12} & \vdots & -a_{1p} \\
-a_{21} & 1 - a_{22} & \vdots & -a_{2p} \\
\cdots & \cdots & \vdots & \cdots \\
-a_{p1} & -a_{p2} & \vdots & 1 - a_{pp}
\end{bmatrix}
\begin{bmatrix}
X_1 \\
X_2 \\
\cdots \\
X_p
\end{bmatrix}
=
\begin{bmatrix}
Y_1 \\
Y_2 \\
\cdots \\
-Y_p
\end{bmatrix}
\qquad (7\text{-}29)
$$

We can rewrite this relationship in terms of its submatrix components as

$$
\begin{bmatrix}
1 - a_{11} & -a_{12} \\
-a_{21} & 1 - a_{22}
\end{bmatrix}
\begin{bmatrix}
X_1 \\
X_2
\end{bmatrix}
+
\begin{bmatrix}
-a_{1p} \\
-a_{2p}
\end{bmatrix}
[X_p]
=
\begin{bmatrix}
Y_1 \\
Y_2
\end{bmatrix}
\qquad (7\text{-}29a)
$$

$$
\begin{bmatrix} -a_{p1} & -a_{p2} \end{bmatrix}
\begin{bmatrix} X_1 \\ X_2 \end{bmatrix}
+
\begin{bmatrix} 1 - a_{pp} \end{bmatrix}
\begin{bmatrix} X_p \end{bmatrix}
=
-\begin{bmatrix} Y_p \end{bmatrix}
\qquad (7\text{-}29b)
$$

Note that in Eq. (7-29a) we can recognize the 2×2 submatrix $\begin{bmatrix} 1 - a_{11} & -a_{12} \\ -a_{21} & 1 - a_{22} \end{bmatrix}$ as simply $(I - A)$, that is, the Leontief matrix of economic sectors unexpanded by the pollution-elimination and -generation sectors. We can assume that $(I - A)$ alone satisfies the Hawkins-Simon conditions. Rearranging terms in Eq. (7-29a):

$$
\begin{bmatrix} X_1 \\ X_2 \end{bmatrix}
= (I - A)^{-1} \left\{
\begin{bmatrix} Y_1 \\ Y_2 \end{bmatrix}
+
\begin{bmatrix} a_{1p} \\ a_{2p} \end{bmatrix}
[X_p]
\right\}
\qquad (7\text{-}29a')
$$

We want to show the conditions for ensuring that all elements of the vector $X = \begin{bmatrix} X_1 \\ X_2 \end{bmatrix}$ are positive. Since we assume that $(I - A)$ by itself satisfies the Hawkins-Simon conditions, all the elements of $(I - A)^{-1}$ are positive. Moreover, $Y = \begin{bmatrix} Y_1 \\ Y_2 \end{bmatrix}$ is a vector of positive final demands presented to the economy and, since a_{1p} and a_{2p} represent inputs from other sectors to the pollution-abatement sector, they are also nonnegative. Hence all elements of the vector X will be nonnegative when X_p is nonnegative. The conditions for nonnegativity of X_p are found by first rearranging Eq. (7-29b) to obtain

$$
X_p = (1 - a_{pp})^{-1} \left\{
\begin{bmatrix} a_{p1} & a_{p2} \end{bmatrix}
\begin{bmatrix} X_1 \\ X_2 \end{bmatrix}
- [Y_p]
\right\}
\qquad (7\text{-}29b')
$$

As discussed earlier, the term a_{pp} is simply the technical coefficient describing pollution generation associated with pollution-abatement activities; it is therefore nonnegative. Hence the terms $(1 - a_{pp})$ and, consequently, $\dfrac{1}{(1 - a_{pp})}$ are nonnegative if $a_{pp} < 1$, that is, if the amount of pollution generated by the pollution-abatement sector is less than the amount it eliminates. Finally, therefore, X_p will be nonnegative if the expression $[a_{p1} \quad a_{p2}]\begin{bmatrix} X_1 \\ X_2 \end{bmatrix} - Y_p$ is nonnegative, that is, when

$$[a_{p1} \quad a_{p2}]\begin{bmatrix} X_1 \\ X_2 \end{bmatrix} > Y_p \tag{7-30}$$

As defined earlier, Y_p represents the amount of pollution not eliminated, or tolerated; the coefficients a_{p1} and a_{p2} give the pollution generated per unit of output X_1 and X_2, respectively. Hence, Eq. (7-30) simply implies that X_p will be positive; consequently, the Hawkins-Simon conditions are satisfied for the extended model (7-29) when the amount of pollution generated in the economy is greater than the amount desired. More generally, this indicates that in polluted areas where pollution generally exceeds the tolerated or desired levels, the augmented model satisfies the Hawkins-Simon conditions. If this is not the case, this augmented model is not necessary.

Example 2 (Revisited) Applying Eqs. (7-29a′) and (7-29b′) to the expanded Leontief model given in Example 2, we obtain

$$\begin{bmatrix} X_1 \\ X_2 \end{bmatrix} = \begin{bmatrix} 1.250 & .330 \\ .264 & 1.122 \end{bmatrix} \left\{ \begin{bmatrix} Y_1 \\ Y_2 \end{bmatrix} + \begin{bmatrix} .1 \\ .2 \end{bmatrix}[X_p] \right\}$$

$$[X_p] = [1.0]\left\{ [.05 \quad .04]\begin{bmatrix} X_1 \\ X_2 \end{bmatrix} - [Y_p] \right\}$$

Clearly $(I - A)$, alone, satisfies the Hawkins-Simon conditions (as defined in Chapter 2):

(a) $|I - A| = .15 > 0$

(b) $1 - a_{11} = .15 > 0; \qquad 1 - a_{22} = .05 > 0$

Therefore, all the elements of $(I - A)^{-1}$ are nonnegative, as shown above. Recall that in this example $a_{pp} = 0$ and therefore $(1 - a_{pp}) = 1$, which satisfies the Hawkins-Simon conditions. Since $(1 - a_{pp}) > 0$, this ensures that the pollution-abatement sector eliminates more pollution than it generates. Finally, since $(1 - a_{pp})$ is nonnegative, X_p will be nonnegative if Eq. (7-30) is satisfied. For the example, this condition is

$$[a_{p1} \quad a_{p2}]\begin{bmatrix} X_1 \\ X_2 \end{bmatrix} = [.05 \quad .04]\begin{bmatrix} X_1 \\ X_2 \end{bmatrix} > Y_p$$

We demonstrate the implications of this condition as follows. First, recall that the expanded Leontief inverse was found to be

$$(I - A_p)^{-1} = \begin{bmatrix} 1.630 & 1.806 & .195 \\ .283 & 1.138 & .256 \\ .075 & .063 & 1.020 \end{bmatrix}$$

Consider two cases, I and II, defined by the following Y vectors:

$$Y_p^{\mathrm{I}} = \begin{bmatrix} 1 \\ 1 \\ -.1 \end{bmatrix} \qquad Y_p^{\mathrm{II}} = \begin{bmatrix} 1 \\ 1 \\ -.5 \end{bmatrix}$$

Case I depicts unit final demands for economic sectors and a level of "tolerated" pollution output of 0.1, shown as negative final demand. Case II depicts the same unit economic sector final demands with an *increased* level of tolerable pollution generation, 0.5 units. The corresponding values of X_p^{I} and X_p^{II} are

$$X_p^{\mathrm{I}} = \left(I - A_p \right)^{-1} Y_p^{\mathrm{I}} = \begin{bmatrix} 1.591 \\ 1.395 \\ .035 \end{bmatrix}$$

and

$$X_p^{\mathrm{II}} = \left(I - A_p \right)^{-1} Y_p^{\mathrm{II}} = \begin{bmatrix} 1.513 \\ 1.293 \\ -.373 \end{bmatrix}$$

In Case II, $X_p = -0.373$, the total amount of pollution eliminated, is negative. This is difficult to interpret; that is, it violates the Hawkins-Simon conditions. More specifically, recalling the condition defined in Eq. (7-30), for Case I,

$$\begin{bmatrix} a_{p1} & a_{p2} \end{bmatrix} \begin{bmatrix} X_1 \\ X_2 \end{bmatrix} = \begin{bmatrix} .05 & .04 \end{bmatrix} \begin{bmatrix} 1.591 \\ 1.395 \end{bmatrix} = .135 > \begin{bmatrix} Y_p \end{bmatrix} = .1$$

For Case II

$$\begin{bmatrix} a_{p1} & a_{p2} \end{bmatrix} \begin{bmatrix} X_1 \\ X_2 \end{bmatrix} = \begin{bmatrix} .05 & .04 \end{bmatrix} \begin{bmatrix} 1.513 \\ 1.293 \end{bmatrix} = .127 < \begin{bmatrix} Y_p \end{bmatrix} = .5$$

In Case I the total amount of pollution generated is 0.135 units, which is greater than the amount tolerated by society, that is, $Y_p = 0.1$ units. In Case II, however, the total pollution generated is 0.127 units, less than the amount tolerated ($Y_p = 0.5$ units), so the Hawkins-Simon conditions are not fulfilled, that is, X_p can be negative. In this case the augmented model is unnecessary. The -0.373 thus represents the fact that the amount of pollution generated in Case II is 0.373 units *less* than the amount tolerated.

The discussion we have presented here has been restricted to a single pollutant. The general framework can be easily extended to several pollutants (see Ayres 1978). Additional comments and enhancements to the augmented Leontief model are given in Flick (1974), Steenge (1978), Lee (1982), Chen (1973), and Rhee and Miranowski (1984).

Finally, possibilities of recycling (certainly only feasible for certain kinds of generated pollutants) can be incorporated into the model through changes in the coefficients in the pollution-generation row. For example, sector 2 might generate only one half as much pollutant per dollar's worth of output, due to its ability to use some of the waste as an input to production (for example a_{p2} might be 0.02

instead of 0.04). In addition, entirely new recycling sectors could be introduced. Their output would be the end product of recycling (scrap metal, for example); their inputs would be purchases from other productive sectors and from the waste-generation sector.

7-4 | ECONOMIC-ECOLOGIC MODELS

In section 7-2 we introduced the notion of ecological commodities, which we defined as nonmarketable quantities that are either inputs used or outputs discharged from a production process. Given this definition, we can quite easily extend the notion of commodity-by-industry accounts to accommodate environmental activities in terms of these ecological commodities. Moreover, as an alternative to simply appending environmental intensity rows to the technical coefficients, as we did in the last section when dealing with pollution and its elimination, we can account more specifically for environmental (or ecosystem) flows by creating an "ecosystem submatrix" that is linked to interindustry economic flows matrix in the same manner that regions are interconnected in an interregional input-output model. Such a model is often called a fully integrated model.

Fully Integrated Models

Both Daly (1968) and Isard et al. (1968) have developed similar procedures along these lines for incorporating environmental activities into an input-output framework. Both approaches employ flow matrices within and between both economic activities and environmental processes (see Table 7-6). As shown in Table 7-6, transactions can be grouped into four basic submatrices; the diagonal submatrices depict flows within the economy and the ecosystem, and the off-diagonal submatrices depict flows between the economy and the ecosystem and vice versa.

Daly's version employs a highly aggregated industry-by-industry characterization of the economic submatrix (upper-left submatrix of Table 7-6) and a classification of ecosystem processes, including life processes such as plants and animals and nonlife processes such as chemical reactions in the atmosphere. Isard refines this basic paradigm by recognizing that secondary production of ecologic outputs—for example, pollution generation, is incompatible with the assumption of one-product industries inherent in traditional Leontief models.

TABLE 7-6 BASIC STRUCTURE OF ECONOMIC-ECOLOGIC MODELS

	Industries	Ecologic Processes
Industries	Flows between economic sectors	Flows from industry to the ecosystem
Ecologic Processes	Flows from the ecosystem to industry	Flows within the ecosystem

Instead, Isard adopts the commodity-by-industry accounting scheme along the lines described earlier in Chapter 5, which permits an accounting of multiple commodities, economic and ecologic, produced by a single industry. The technical coefficients in Isard's model are estimated directly from technical data, but since this model was never fully implemented, the adequacy of available data for such estimation is very difficult to judge. Richardson (1972), Victor (1972), and Isard et al. (1971) discuss the strengths and weaknesses of this approach in more detail. The availability of data for the ecosystem submatrix appears to be the most troublesome point.

Limited Models

Victor (1972) limits the scope of Isard's fully integrated economic-ecologic model to account only for flows of ecological commodities from the environment into the economy and of the waste products from the economy into the environment. Thus, by limiting the scope of the analysis, the data are generally available and the model can be implemented with little difficulty. The basic accounting framework is shown schematically in Table 7-7. It is a conventional commodity-by-industry table augmented with additional rows of ecological inputs (P and T) and columns of ecological outputs (R and S).

The submatrices are defined as follows:

Economic Subsystem

$U = [u_{ij}]$ is the economic "use" matrix; u_{ij} represents the amount of economic commodity i used by industry j. For n industries and m commodities, U is $m \times n$.

$V = [v_{ij}]$ is the economic "make" matrix; v_{ij} represents the amount of economic commodity i produced by industry j; V is $n \times m$.

$E = [E_i]$ is the vector of economic commodity final demands; E_i is the final demand for commodity i; E is $m \times 1$.

$Q = [Q_i]$ is the vector of economic commodity gross outputs; Q_i is the total production of commodity i; Q is $m \times 1$.

TABLE 7-7   LIMITED COMMODITY-BY-INUDSTRY ECONOMIC-ECOLOGIC MODEL

	Economic Subsystem				Ecosystem
	Commodities	Industries	Final Demand	Total Output	Ecologic Commodities
Commodities		U	E	Q	R
Industries	V			X	S
Value Added		W	GNP		
Total Output	Q'	X'			
Ecologic Commodities	P	T			

$W = [W_j]$ is the vector of industry value-added inputs; w_j represents the total of value-added inputs to industry j; W is $1 \times n$.

$X = [X_j]$ is the vector of industry total outputs; X_j represents the total output of industry j; X is $n \times 1$.

Note that all of these submatrices of the economic subsystem are defined in the discussion of commodity-by-industry accounts in Chapter 5.

Ecologic Subsystem

$R = [r_{ik}]$ is the matrix of economic commodity by ecologic commodity outputs; r_{ik} is the amount of ecologic commodity k discharged as a result of production of economic commodity i; for l ecologic commodities, R is $m \times l$.

$S = [s_{jk}]$ is the matrix of industry by ecologic commodity outputs; s_{jk} is the amount of ecologic commodity k discharged by industry j; s is $n \times l$.

$P = [p_{ki}]$ is the matrix of ecologic commodity by economic commodity inputs; p_{ki} is the amount of ecologic commodity k used in the production of economic commodity i; P is $l \times m$.

$T = [t_{kj}]$ is the matrix of ecologic commodity by industry inputs; t_{kj} is the amount of ecologic commodity k used by industry j; T is $l \times n$.

As before, with the conventional commodity-by-industry accounts, we can recall Eqs. (5-5′) and (5-8′) from Chapter 5.

$$B = U(\hat{X})^{-1} \tag{5-5′}$$

$B = [b_{ij}]$ is the matrix of economic commodity-by-industry direct requirements; b_{ij} is the amount of economic commodity i required per dollar's worth of output of industry j; B is $m \times n$.

$$C = V'(\hat{X})^{-1} \tag{5-8′}$$

$C = [c_{ij}]$ is the matrix of industry output proportions; c_{ij} is the fraction of industry j's output that is distributed as commodity i; C is $m \times n$.

With the accounting system expanded to include ecologic commodities, we can also define

$$F = S'(\hat{X})^{-1} \tag{7-31}$$

$F = [f_{kj}]$ is the matrix of ecologic commodity output coefficients; the term $f_{kj} = s_{kj}/X_j$ is the amount of ecologic commodity k discharged per dollar's worth of output of industry j; F is $l \times n$.

$$G = T(\hat{X})^{-1} \tag{7-32}$$

$G = [g_{kj}]$ is the matrix of ecologic commodity input coefficients; the term $g_{kj} = t_{kj}/X_j$ is the amount of ecologic commodity k used in the production of a dollar's worth of industry j's output; G is $l \times n$.

Example 3 To illustrate Victor's approach, first we review the system of commodity-by-industry accounts given earlier in the example in section 5-3. To this system we append the ecologic commodity accounts, that is, the production of ecologic commodities by industry (S) and by economic commodity (R) as well as the use of ecologic commodities in producing industry output (T) and commodities (P) (see Table 7-8).

For purposes of illustration, we restrict the model to an industry-based technology, as described in Chapter 5. Recall that this simply means we assume that an industry consumes economic (and ecologic) commodities in fixed proportions. In this case we need to compute the matrix of commodity input proportions, D, and the matrix of commodity-by-industry direct requirements, B:

$$B = U(\hat{X})^{-1} = \begin{bmatrix} .111 & .091 \\ .111 & .064 \end{bmatrix} \qquad D = V(\hat{Q})^{-1} = \begin{bmatrix} .9 & 0 \\ .1 & 1 \end{bmatrix}$$

Hence, as before, the industry-by-commodity total requirements matrix is

$$D(I - BD)^{-1} = \begin{bmatrix} 1.022 & .099 \\ .243 & 1.092 \end{bmatrix}$$

The ecologic commodity output and input coefficient matrices F and G, respectively, are

$$F = S(\hat{X})^{-1} = \begin{bmatrix} .022 & .091 \\ 0 & 0 \end{bmatrix} \qquad G = T(\hat{X})^{-1} = \begin{bmatrix} 0 & 0 \\ .111 & .182 \end{bmatrix}$$

If we are interested in the total ecologic commodity production (*output*) by industries in the economy, we can simply sum down the columns of the

TABLE 7-8 ECONOMIC-ECOLOGIC MODELS: EXAMPLE 3

		Commodities A	B	Industries A	B	Final Demand	Total Output	Ecologic Commodities SO$_2$	Water
Commodities	A			10	10	80	100	3	0
					U	E	Q		R
	B			10	7	83	100	9	0
Industries	A	90	0				90	2	0
			V				X		S
	B	10	100				110	10	0
Value Added				70	93	W GNP 163			
Total Inputs		Q' 100	100	X' 90	110		200	12	S̄ 0
SO$_2$		0	20	0	0		0		
			P		T		T̄		
Water		0	10	10	20		30		

industry-by-ecologic commodity flows matrix S. Industry A produces 2 units of SO_2 and industry B produces 10 units of SO_2, so production of SO_2 by the entire economy is 12 units. We denote the vector of total ecologic commodity production (outputs) by $\bar{S}$; hence in matrix terms

$$\bar{S} = i'S = [1 \quad 1]\begin{bmatrix} 2 & 0 \\ 10 & 0 \end{bmatrix} = [12 \quad 0]$$

and, moreover, $S = F\hat{X}$, so $\bar{S} = i'F\hat{X}$. For an arbitrary vector of final demands for economic commodities, E, the total ecologic commodity output associated with that vector of final demands, is then found by

$$X = D(I - BD)^{-1}E \tag{7-33}$$

$$\bar{S} = i'F\hat{X} = i'F\left(\left\langle D(I - BD)^{-1}E\right\rangle\right) \tag{7-34}$$

Similarly, we can find the vector of total ecologic commodity *inputs* for all industries of the economy as the vector of row sums of T. That is, industry A consumes 10 units of water in its production process and industry B consumes 20 units of water; total water consumption is 30 units. We denote the vector of total ecologic commodity consumption (inputs) by $\bar{T}$; hence, in matrix terms

$$\bar{T} = Ti = \begin{bmatrix} 0 & 0 \\ 10 & 20 \end{bmatrix}\begin{bmatrix} 1 \\ 1 \end{bmatrix} = \begin{bmatrix} 0 \\ 30 \end{bmatrix}$$

Since $T = G\hat{X}$ then $\bar{T} = G\hat{X}i$; but since $\hat{X}i = X$, $\bar{T} = GX$. Hence, the total ecologic commodity requirement for a given vector of economic commodity final demands, E, is found by

$$X = D(I - BD)^{-1}E$$

$$\bar{T} = GX$$

or, compactly, $\bar{T} = [GD(I - BD)^{-1}]E$. The bracketed quantity is the ecologic input *intensity* (ecologic commodity inputs by economic commodity total requirements matrix).

Note that by using the alternative commodity-by-industry total requirements matrices we derived in Chapter 5 we could easily compute, for example, ecologic inputs and outputs as a function of final demands for industries rather than for commodities, as we have shown here. Hannon et al. (1983) have shown circumstances under which the commodity-based and industry-based technology assumptions give equivalent results in specifying ecosystem models.

7-5 | POLLUTION DISPERSION

In the environmental extensions to input-output that we have dealt with so far, we have measured pollution in terms of total emissions or discharges of various pollutants. The ultimate effect of pollutant emissions on a region depends not only on the total amount of pollutant generated, but also on the manner in which that pollutant is discharged into the environment. For example, sulfur dioxide produced in electric power plants is emitted and dispersed from tall smokestacks. The concentrations of that pollutant at various points in the region surrounding the plant depend upon a variety of technical, climatic, and geo-

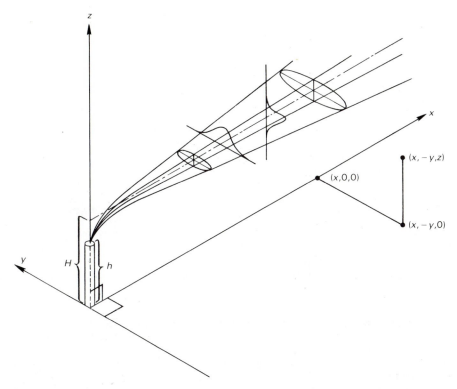

FIGURE 7-1 Illustration of the Gaussian plume structure for concentrations downwind from a single point source.

graphic factors such as the stack height, wind direction and speed, and local topography.

Gaussian Dispersion Models

A number of researchers—for example, Berlinsky et al. (1973) and Coupé (1977)—have coupled models of pollution dispersion to input-output models. Most of these approaches assume that air pollution from point sources (as opposed to mobile sources, such as automobiles) is dispersed as a "Gaussian plume," as shown in Fig. 7-1.[4] Note that the pollutant is assumed to disperse symmetrically about the centerline (the x-axis) of the plume in both the y and z directions (horizontal and vertical, respectively).

The cross section of the plume is an ellipse which, at least in the figure, indicates that the rate of dispersion is greater in the horizontal direction than in the vertical direction. Pasquill (1962), Gifford (1961), Seinfeld (1975), and others derive a formula describing this dispersion, which gives the pollutant concentration at a "receptor point" (x, y, z) measured downwind from that pollution source. The x-axis measures distance downwind, the y-axis measures

---

[4]Alternatives to Gaussian dispersion models are described in Seinfeld (1975) and Turner (1961).

horizontal distance from the x-axis, and the z-axis measures vertical distance from the x-axis. The formula for computing pollutant concentrations at ground level ($z = 0$) is

$$C(x, y, 0) = \frac{Q}{2\pi u \sigma_y \sigma_z} \exp\left\{ -\frac{1}{2}\left[\left(\frac{y}{\sigma_y}\right)^2 + \left(\frac{H}{\sigma_z}\right)^2 \right] \right\} \qquad (7\text{-}35)$$

where

$C(x, y, 0)$ = the pollutant concentration in $\mu g/m^3$ (micrograms per cubic meter);
H = height of the pollution source (stack height) in meters;
Q = the pollution emission rate in $\mu g/\text{minute}$;
σ_y, σ_z = the standard deviation of the horizontal and vertical dispersion distributions, respectively (usually a function of x);
u = the wind speed (meters/minute).

The parameters σ_y and σ_z are functions of the local meteorology and, in particular, the stability of the atmosphere or the air turbulence characteristics. Derivation of specific values of σ_y and σ_z are beyond the scope of this book, but the subject is dealt with in detail in Seinfeld (1975) and elsewhere in the literature.

Coupling Pollution Dispersion and Input-Output Models

In coupling dispersion models with input-output models, Hordijk (1980) and others distinguish among pollution emissions (at the source), primary concentrations (at specified receptor points), and "cumulated" levels of pollution (accumulated over time at the receptor points). The emission rate is usually assumed to vary linearly with economic output of the industry. Hence, we can determine the location of a pollution source or a number of locations over which total emissions of this type of pollutant in the region are averaged and subsequently dispersed from these locations. We can then select a number of receptor points for which we wish to record pollutant concentrations. This could be a collection of several strategic points or an entire map of all points in the region. We then add the values of pollutant concentration resulting from each pollution source to yield total concentration of that pollutant at that receptor point.

Example 4   Consider the region defined in Fig. 7-2. Note that there are two pollution sources and four receptor points where we wish to measure pollutant concentrations. The following input-output model describes interindustry activity in the region (millions of dollars):

$$Z = \begin{bmatrix} 1 & 2 \\ 3 & 4 \end{bmatrix} \qquad X = \begin{bmatrix} 10 \\ 10 \end{bmatrix}$$

where Z is the matrix of interindustry transactions and X is the vector of total outputs.

The local government has decided to stimulate industrial activity through fiscal measures which, in terms of the input-output model, translate to increased final-demand activity. Suppose the stimulus amounts to $Y = (Y_1, Y_2)'$, where Y_1 and Y_2 are \$4 million and \$3 million, respectively. The amount Y_1 is the

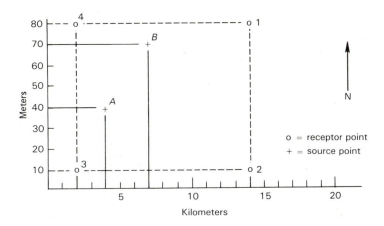

FIGURE 7-2 Location of air pollution sources and receptor points.

increased final demand presented to industry A, and Y_2 is the increased final demand presented to industry B.

Assume that the economic activity is related to pollution emission by average values of 30.77 grams per second per million dollars' worth of output from industry A and 27.59 grams per second per million dollars' worth of output from industry B. Further, we assume that $u = 15$ meters/second prevailing from the West, $H = 250$ meters, and $\sigma_y = \sigma_z = ax^b$ where $a = 0.24$ and $b = 0.88$ are empirically derived constants. We are interested in pollutant concentrations at the receptor points (at ground level, that is, where $z = 0$) so we can apply Eq. (7-35). With the increased interindustry activity, pollutant concentrations increase proportionally with the level of increased total output. We can compute the region's new level of total production as the sum of current production, X, and the production prompted by the new final demand, that is,

$$X^{new} = X + (I - A)^{-1} Y = \begin{bmatrix} 10 \\ 10 \end{bmatrix} + \begin{bmatrix} 1.250 & .416 \\ .625 & 1.875 \end{bmatrix}\begin{bmatrix} 4 \\ 3 \end{bmatrix} = \begin{bmatrix} 16.25 \\ 18.125 \end{bmatrix}$$

Since the prevailing wind is from the West, and the pollution sources are east of receptor points 3 and 4, the ambient pollutant concentrations at these points are both zero. The concentrations at receptor points 1 and 2, however, must be computed by the dispersion formula:

Receptor Point 1: $C = 4.31 \times 10^{-5} \ \mu g/m^3$

Receptor Point 2: $C = 4.16 \times 10^{-5} \ \mu g/m^3$

A map of pollutant concentrations for all points in the region is given in Fig. 7-3.

7-6 | SUMMARY

In this chapter we examined several approaches to accounting for pollution generation and elimination in input-output models. The models ranged from using a matrix of pollution-generation coefficients in conjunction with the

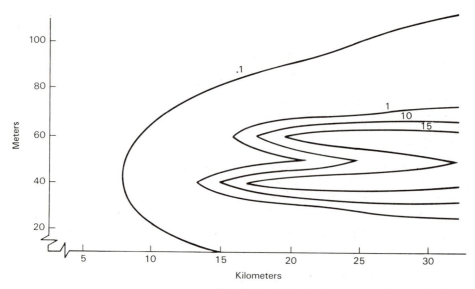

Note: Contour lines are in micrograms per cubic meter of pollutant.

FIGURE 7-3 Map of pollutant concentrations: Example 4.

Leontief inverse to an economic-ecologic model that couples a Leontief model of economic flows with an ecosystem model of environmental commodity flows. Finally we discussed coupling an environmental input-output model to a model of pollution dispersion over a geographic region.

Many input-output models applied to environmental problems appeared in the 1970s, including the Strategic Environmental Assessment System (SEAS) (House 1977), Miernyk and Sears (1974), Cumberland and Stram (1976), Leontief and Ford (1972), Converse (1971), Page (1973), Stone (1972), and Lowe (1979). More recently applications to pollution control technology assessment have appeared in Ketkar (1983) and Rose (1983), which built upon the earlier work of Miernyk (1973), Cumberland (1966), and Giarratani (1974).

PROBLEMS

7-1   Assume that we have the following direct coefficient matrices for energy, air pollution, and employment (u, v, and w, respectively) for two industries, 1 and 2:

$$u = \begin{bmatrix} .1 & .2 \\ .2 & .4 \end{bmatrix} \quad \begin{array}{l} \text{oil} \left(10^{15} \text{ Btus per } 10^6 \text{ dollars' output}\right) \\ \text{coal} \left(10^{15} \text{ Btus per } 10^6 \text{ dollars' output}\right) \end{array}$$

$$v = \begin{bmatrix} .2 & .5 \\ .2 & .3 \end{bmatrix} \quad \begin{array}{l} \text{SO}_2 \left(\text{tons per } 10^6 \text{ dollars' output}\right) \\ \text{NO}_x \left(\text{tons per } 10^6 \text{ dollars' output}\right) \end{array}$$

$$w = \begin{bmatrix} .2 & .5 \end{bmatrix} \quad \text{employment} \left(\text{man-years per } 10^6 \text{ dollars' output}\right)$$

Notice that industry 2 is both a high-polluting and high-employment industry. Suppose that the local government has an opportunity to spend a total of $10 million on a regional development project. Two projects are candidates: (1) Project 1 would spend appropriated dollars in the ratio of 60% to industry 1 and 40% to industry 2; the minimum size of this project is $4 million; (2) Project 2 would spend appropriated dollars in the ratio of 30% to industry 1 and 70% to industry 2; the minimum size of this project is $2 million. The government can adopt either project or a combination of the two projects (as long as the minimum size of each project is at least maintained and the total budget is not overrun). In other words, we might describe the options available to the government as:

$$\begin{bmatrix} \beta_a \\ \beta_b \end{bmatrix} = \alpha_1 \begin{bmatrix} .6 \\ .4 \end{bmatrix} + \alpha_2 \begin{bmatrix} .3 \\ .7 \end{bmatrix}$$

$$10 \geq \beta_a + \beta_b$$

where α_1 and α_2 are budgets allocated to projects 1 and 2, respectively. β_a and β_b are the total final demands presented to the regional economy by the combination of projects for industries A and B, respectively.

Suppose that four alternative compositions of these projects are being considered

(1) $\begin{aligned} \alpha_1 &= 4 \\ \alpha_2 &= 2 \end{aligned}$ (2) $\begin{aligned} \alpha_1 &= 5 \\ \alpha_2 &= 5 \end{aligned}$ (3) $\begin{aligned} \alpha_1 &= 10 \\ \alpha_2 &= 0 \end{aligned}$ (4) $\begin{aligned} \alpha_1 &= 0 \\ \alpha_2 &= 10 \end{aligned}$

and that the following table of constraints describes the local regulation on energy consumption and environmental pollution in the region:

	Maximum Allowable Collectively by All Industries
Oil Consumption (10^{15} Btus)	3.0
Coal Consumption (10^{15} Btus)	no limit
SO_2 Emissions (tons)	14.5
NO_x Emissions (tons)	10

Finally, suppose that the regional economy is currently described by the following input-output transactions table (in millions of dollars):

	A	B	X
A	1	3	10
B	5	1	10

a   Which of the proposed combinations of projects (1), (2), (3), and (4) permit the region to operate within the above constraints on energy consumption and air-pollution emission and within the established budget constraint?

b   Which of these "legal" projects that you identified in a should be adopted to maximize the employment in the region?

7-2   Assume that a regional economy has two primary industries: A and B. In producing these two products it was observed last year that 3 pounds of SO_2 and 1 pound of NO_x were emitted per dollar's worth of output of industry A, and 5 pounds of SO_2 and 2 pounds of NO_x were emitted per dollar's worth of output of industry B. It was also observed that industries A and B consumed 1×10^6 tons and 6×10^6 tons of coal respectively during that year. Industry A also consumed 2×10^7 barrels of oil. Total employment in the region was 100,000 (40% of which were employed by industry A and the rest by industry B).

The regional planning agency has constructed the following input-output table of interindustry activity in the region (in $\$10^6$).

	A	B	Total Output
A	2	6	20
B	6	12	30

Assume that with growth in the region during the next year the new final-demand vector will be $(15, 25)'$.

Using what you know about constructing a generalized input-output model, determine the following:

a   the total consumption of each energy type (coal and oil) during the next year.

b   the total pollution emission (of each type) during the next year.

c   the level of total employment during the next year.

7-3   A regional planning agency initiates a regional development plan. Four projects are being considered that would represent government purchases of regionally produced products, that is, final demands presented to the regional economy (see table).

Regional Industry	Project Expenditures (10^6 dollars)			
	Project 1	Project 2	Project 3	Project 4
A	2	4	2	2
B	2	0	0	2
C	2	2	4	3

You are given additional information. The matrix of technical coefficients is:

$$A = \begin{bmatrix} .04 & .23 & .38 \\ .33 & .52 & .47 \\ 0 & 0 & .1 \end{bmatrix}$$

The relationships between the following quantities and total output are also known:

	Industry		
	1	2	3
Pollution Emission (grams / $ output)	4.2	7.0	9.1
Energy Consumption (bbls oil / $ output)	7.6	2.6	.5
Employment (workers / $ output)	7.3	3.3	6.3

a   Which of the four projects contributes most to gross regional product?

b   Which of the projects causes regional consumption of energy to increase the most?

c   Which of the projects contributes most to regional employment?

7-4   Imagine that the data presented in Problem 2-9 depict an economy in deep economic trouble. Suppose that the federal government has at its disposal policy tools that can be implemented to stimulate demand for goods from one sector or the other. Also suppose that the plants in sector 1 discharge 0.3 lbs. of airborne particulate substances for every dollar of output (0.3 lbs/$ output), while sector 2 pollutes at 0.5 lbs/$ output. Finally, let labor input coefficients be 0.005 and 0.07 for sectors 1 and 2, respectively. Would a conflict of interest arise between unions and environmentalists in determining the sector toward which the government should direct its policy effort? (You need not *close* the matrix with respect to either households or pollution generation to answer this question.) Can you think of a technological reason why or why not a dispute might arise?

REFERENCES

Ayres, Robert, and Allen Kneese. "Production, Consumption, and Externalities." *American Economic Review* 59, no. 3 (June 1969): 282–97.

Ayres, Robert. *Resources, Environment and Economics: Applications of the Materials/Energy Balance Principle*. New York: Wiley Interscience, 1978.

Berlinsky, E., Anne Carter, and Michael First. "National Production, Emissions Control and Local Air Pollution in the Integration Iron and Steel Industry: An Input-Output Model." Third International Clean Air Congress, Düsseldorf, West Germany, 1973.

Blair, Peter. *Multiobjective Regional Energy Planning*. Boston: Martinus Nijhoff, 1979.

Chatterji, Manas. "A Balanced Regional Input-Output Model for Identifying Responsibility for Pollution Created by Industries which Serve National Markets." *International Regional Science Review* 1, no. 1 (Spring 1975): 87–94.

Chen, Kan. "Input-Output Economic Analysis of Environmental Impacts." *IEEE Transactions on Systems, Man and Cybernetics* SMC-3, no. 6 (November 1973): 539–47.

Converse, A. O. "On the Extension of Input-Output Analysis to Account for Environmental Externalities." *American Economic Review* 61, no. 1 (March 1971): 197–98.

Coupé, B. E. M. G. *Regional Economic Structure and Environmental Pollution*. Leiden, Netherlands: Martinus Nijhoff, 1977.

Cumberland, John H. "A Regional Interindustry Model for Analysis of Development Objectives." *Papers of the Regional Science Association* 17 (1966): 64–94.

Cumberland, John H., and Bruce Stram. "Empirical Application of Input-Output Models to Environmental Problems." In *Advances in Input-Output Analysis*, edited by Karen R. Polenske and Jiri V. Skolka, 365–82. Proceedings of the Sixth International Conference on Input-Output Techniques, Vienna, April 22–26, 1974. Cambridge, Massachusetts: Ballinger, 1976.

Daly, Herman. "On Economics as a Life Science." *Journal of Political Economy* 76, no. 3 (May/June 1968): 392–406.

Flick, Warren A. "Environmental Repercussions and the Economic Structure: An Input-Output Approach (A Comment)." *Review of Economics and Statistics* 56, no. 1 (February 1974): 107–9.

Folk, Hugh, and Bruce Hannon. "An Energy, Pollution, and Employment Policy Model." In *Energy*, edited by Michael Macrakis, 159–73. Cambridge, Massachusetts: MIT Press, 1974.

Giarratani, Frank. "Air Pollution Abatement: Output and Relative Price Effects, A Regional Input-Output Simulation." *Environment and Planning, A* 6, no. 3 (May–June 1974): 307–12.

Gifford, F. A. "Uses of Routine Meteorological Observations for Estimating Atmospheric Dispersion." *Nuclear Safety* 2, no. 4 (1961): 47–51.

Gutmanis, Ivars. "Input-Output Models in Economic and Environmental Policy Analyses." *Proceedings of the IEEE* 63, no. 3 (March 1975): 431–37.

HANNON, BRUCE, ROBERT COSTANZA, and ROBERT HERENDEEN. "Measures of Energy Cost and Value in Ecosystems." University of Illinois at Urbana-Champaign. September, 1983.

HORDIJK, L. "Economic Structure and the Environment." In *Production and Energy Consumption in the Netherlands 1973/1985*. Institute for Environmental Studies, Free University, Amsterdam, Netherlands, 1980.

HOUSE, PETER. *Trading Off Environment, Economics and Energy*. Lexington, Massachusetts: Lexington Books, 1977.

ISARD, WALTER, et al. *Ecologic-Economic Analysis for Regional Planning*. New York: The Free Press, 1971.

———. "On the Linkage of Socio-Economic and Ecological Systems." *Papers of the Regional Science Association* 21 (1968): 79–99.

JOHNSON, M., and JAMES BENNETT. "Regional Environmental and Economic Impact Evaluation." *Regional Science and Urban Economics* 11, no. 2 (May 1981): 215–30.

JUST, JAMES. "Impacts of New Energy Technology Using Generalized Input-Output Analysis." In *Energy*, edited by Michael Macrakis, 113–28. Cambridge, Mass.: MIT Press, 1974.

KETKAR, KUSUM W. "Pollution Control and Inputs to Production." *Journal of Environmental Economics and Management* 10, no. 1 (March 1983): 50–59.

LEE, KWANG-SOO. "A Generalized Input-Output Model of an Economy with Environmental Protection." *Review of Economics and Statistics* 64, no. 3 (August 1982): 466–73.

LEONTIEF, WASSILY. "Environmental Repercussions and the Economic Structure: An Input-Output Approach." *Review of Economics and Statistics* 52, no. 3 (August 1970): 262–71.

LEONTIEF, WASSILY, and DANIEL FORD. "Air Pollution and Economic Structure: Empirical Results of Input-Output Computations." In *Input-Output Techniques*, edited by Andrew Bródy and Anne P. Carter, 9–30. Proceedings of the Fifth International Conference on Input-Output Techniques, Geneva, 1971. New York: American Elsevier, 1972.

LOWE, PETER R. "Pricing Problems in an Input-Output Approach to Environmental Protection." *Review of Economics and Statistics* 61, no. 1 (February 1979): 110–17.

MIERNYK, WILLIAM H. "A Regional Input-Output Pollution Abatement Model." *IEEE Transactions on Systems, Man and Cybernetics* SMC-3, no. 6 (November 1973): 575–77.

MIERNYK, WILLIAM H., and JOHN T. SEARS. *Air Pollution Abatement and Regional Economic Development*. Lexington, Massachusetts: Lexington Books, 1974.

PAGE, TALBOT. "Pollution Affecting Producers in an Input-Output Context." *IEEE Transactions on Systems, Man and Cybernetics* SMC-3, no. 6 (November 1973): 555–61.

PASQUILL, F. *Atmospheric Diffusion*. London: Van Nostrand, 1962.

RHEE, JEONG J., and JOHN A. MIRANOWSKI. "Determination of Income, Production and Employment under Pollution Control: An Input-Output Approach." *Review of Economics and Statistics* 66, no. 1 (February 1984): 146–50.

RICHARDSON, HARRY. *Input-Output and Regional Economics*. New York: John Wiley and Sons (Halsted Press), 1972.

ROSE, ADAM. "Modeling the Macroeconomic Impact of Air Pollution Abatement." *Journal of Regional Science* 23, no. 4 (November 1983): 441–59.

SEINFELD, JOHN. *Air Pollution*. New York: McGraw-Hill, Inc., 1975.

STEENGE, ALBERT E. "Environmental Repercussions and the Economic Structure: Further Comments." *Review of Economics and Statistics* 60, no. 3 (August 1978): 482–86.

STONE, RICHARD. "The Evaluation of Pollution: Balancing Gains and Losses." *Minerva* 10, no. 3 (July 1972): 412–25.

THOSS, RAINER. "A Generalized Input-Output Model for Residuals Management." In *Advances in Input-Output Analysis*, edited by Karen R. Polenske and Jiri V. Skolka, 411–32. Proceedings of the Sixth International Conference on Input-Output Techniques, Vienna, April 22–26, 1974. Cambridge, Massachusetts: Ballinger, 1976.

TURNER, DAVID. *Workbook of Atmospheric Diffusion Estimates*. U.S. Public Health Service, Publication No. 999-AP-26, 1961.

VICTOR, PETER A. *Pollution: Economy and Environment*. London: George Allen and Unwin, Ltd., 1972.

8

Nonsurvey and Partial-Survey Methods

8-1 | INTRODUCTION

The heart of any input-output analysis is the table of input-output coefficients which describes the relationships between inputs and outputs for a particular economy. To produce a table based on a survey of establishments in the economy is an expensive and time-consuming task, not only at the national level, but also for regions (states, counties, metropolitan areas, etc.). In this chapter we examine some of the more widely used approaches that attempt to adapt older tables to reflect more recent economic conditions or to borrow information in a table for one economy to use for a different economy. In a very general way, these may be thought of as modifications of tables over time or across space, respectively. We consider these two types of problems in turn, and we see that there is one kind of adjustment technique that is often used in either the temporal or the spatial situation.

8-2 | THE QUESTION OF STABILITY OF INPUT-OUTPUT DATA

One of the most serious concerns of those who use input-output models in applied work is that the table of technical coefficients available to them for the economy that they are studying may reflect data from a much earlier year. For example, the U.S. input-output table based upon 1977 transactions between and among sectors was not generally available to researchers until 1984. And this is not exclusively a problem that is associated with a large and complex economy, such as the United States; the 1972 input-output table for the state of Washington was not completed until 1977. These time lags reflect the fact that when establishments in different industries are surveyed for information regarding their purchases of inputs and their sales of output, it takes a great deal of time (and, usually, money) to obtain the data, organize the information, and reconcile inconsistencies—for example, reported purchases of sector i goods by sector j establishments may differ from reported sales by sector i to sector j establishments. (We will return to this reconciliation problem in section 8-6 below.) This is a general and continuing problem with survey-based tables.

It is clear that techniques of production will and do change over time, for a variety of reasons. Among others:

1 There is technological change itself, whereby new techniques of production are introduced in a sector (e.g., replacement of some human labor with robots in automobile production).

2 If there is a large increase in demand for the products of a particular sector, output will increase (subject, of course, to capacity constraints), and the producer may experience economies of scale. For example, if the scale of operation of a firm was very small at the time it was sampled, relatively large inputs per dollar of its output might be recorded. Later, after the level of production is increased, economies of scale might be reflected in lower amounts of at least some inputs per dollar of output. (In terms of the usual production function geometry, as in Fig. 2-1(a), such scale economies mean that each isoquant represents a higher level of output than under the original conditions of production.)

3 New products are invented (e.g., plastics) which means both that (a) there may be an entirely new sector—row and column—in a sufficiently disaggregated table or at least the product mix will change in an existing sector if the new product is classified there, and (b) it may be used to replace an older product as an input to production in other sectors (e.g., plastic bottles rather than glass for soft drinks).

4 Relative prices change, and this may cause substitution among inputs in a production process (e.g., a switch from oil to natural gas as an energy source as the price of oil jumped sharply during the mid-1970s).

5 The more aggregated the input-output table, the greater the number of distinct products that are encompassed under one sectoral classification. To recall an extreme example from Chapter 3, if the food and kindred products sector produces mostly tomato soup in one year, there will be a need for tin cans in which to package the output. If, in a later year, the output of the food and kindred products sector is primarily chocolate bars, paper will be required for wrapping the product, not tin. Thus the relative proportions of products that are mixed together in a sector will influence the aggregate production recipe (column of input coefficients) for that sector.

6 Changes from domestically produced to imported inputs—or from imported to domestically produced—will alter the economic interrelationships between sectors in the domestic economy. This is particularly noticeable in interregional and multiregional input-output models.

For reasons such as these, an economy's technical coefficients matrix will change over time. The real question, however, is an empirical one—how quickly and how dramatically does the matrix change, and, more importantly, how much difference does this make in actual applications of the input-output model?

National Coefficients

Following the pioneering work of Leontief (1953, pp. 17–52), Carter (1970) analyzed in some detail the changes in the U.S. economy as they were reflected in the 1939, 1947, and 1958 U.S. input-output data. With, say, a 50-sector classification, each year's table of technical coefficients would contain some 2500 a_{ij} coefficients, or there would be 2500 elements in each of the Leontief inverse matrices. It is not immediately obvious how best to compare three sets of 2500 coefficients. In general, then, summary measures of comparison become useful. We briefly explore two kinds of comparisons, below; one of these uses a_{ij} coefficients directly, and one employs the Leontief inverse.

Comparisons of Direct-Input Coefficients If one constructs two-dimensional plots, in which the horizontal axis is used to measure the size of particular coefficients in the earlier year (t_0) and the vertical axis measures the size of coefficients in the later year (t_1), where the scales along the two axes are the same, then a particular a_{ij} coefficient will have as its horizontal/vertical coordinates the value of that coefficient at time t_0 and at time t_1, that is, $a_{ij}(t_0)$ and $a_{ij}(t_1)$. For an n-sector economy, there will be n^2 points in such a figure.

If all coefficients remained unchanged over the period from t_0 to t_1, then all the points would fall along a 45-degree line, as indicated in Fig. 8-1. On the other hand, if there has been a tendency for coefficients to increase over time, then the points will tend to fall above the 45-degree line (that is, a given a_{ij} at time t_0 will have a larger value at time t_1). Similarly, if coefficients have decreased over time, then the points will tend to fall below the 45-degree line (e.g., $a_{ij}[t_0] = 0.4$ and $a_{ij}[t_1] = 0.3$). Carter examined figures of this sort for given sets of sectors as inputs (that is, the a_{ij}'s for specific i's) and found, for example, that input coefficients for the "general inputs" sectors (energy, transportation, trade, communications, and other services) tended to increase over time, while those for materials inputs did not. Industry-specific analyses showed, for example, that coefficients measuring iron and steel inputs to productive sectors (a_{ij}, where $i =$ iron and steel) clustered generally below the 45-degree line, when $t_0 = 1947$ and $t_1 = 1958$; similarly, those for aluminum inputs (a_{ij}, where $i =$ aluminum) tended to cluster above the 45-degree line, for the same time period. This reflects the fact of decreased use of iron and steel and increased use of aluminum as inputs to productive processes over the 1947–1958 period.

Comparisons of Leontief Inverse Matrices One way to quantify in an aggregate way the effects of input-output coefficient change over time is to

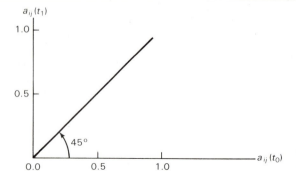

FIGURE 8-1 The case of temporal stability, $A(t_0) = A(t_1)$

compare the total output vector that would be needed for a given set of final demands, using the Leontief inverses from various technical coefficients matrices. For example, Carter used actual U.S. final demand in 1961, $Y(1961)$, in conjunction with $[I - A(1939)]^{-1}$, $[I - A(1947)]^{-1}$, and $[I - A(1958)]^{-1}$ to calculate $X(1961/1939)$, $X(1961/1947)$, and $X(1961/1958)$—where, for example, $X(1961/1939) = [I - A(1939)]^{-1}Y(1961)$. That is, $X(1961/1939)$ represents the gross output that would be needed in each sector of the economy to satisfy 1961 final demands if the structure of production were that of the United States in 1939. In all cases, these were technical coefficients matrices that did not include households. Representative results (Carter 1970, Table 4.1, pp. 35–36.) were as follows for total intermediate output—total output, $X(1961/19xx)$, less final demand, $Y(1961)$—to satisfy known 1961 final demands (in millions of 1947 dollars and for xx = 39, 47, or 58):

- Using 1939 Coefficients — 324,288
- Using 1947 Coefficients — 336,296
- Using 1958 Coefficients — 336,941
- Actual 1961 Output   — 334,160

The implications of results of this sort are that, over time, intermediate input requirements are relatively stable. Carter suggests that the small increase in total intermediate input represents a slight increase in specialization within sectors and a relative decrease in the use of labor and capital in later years. Overall, while there were noteworthy changes in specific sectors, it appeared from this study that in most sectors structural change was very gradual. This, of course, supports the contention that input-output coefficients tables may remain useful for a number of years, even though the year in which they were constructed may appear to make them out of date.

Other Summary Measures   Column sums of A matrices (with, say, households exogenous) show how a given sector depends on other sectors for inputs. If $\sum_i a_{ij}(t_0) = 0.32$ and $\sum_i a_{ij}(t_1) = 0.54$, we would conclude that sector j became more dependent upon other sectors in the economy in the period from t_0 to t_1; that is, that sector j depended less on labor, capital, imports, and so on as inputs. Similarly, row sums of an A matrix show how dependent all n sectors of the economy are on a particular input. If $\sum_j a_{ij} = 4.72$ and $n = 10$, this means that in producing a total of ten dollars' worth of output (one dollar of output in each of the ten sectors), the amount of input i needed, across all sectors, would be $4.72. Thus if $\sum_j a_{ij}(t_0) < \sum_j a_{ij}(t_1)$, we would conclude that sector i has become relatively more important as a supplier of inputs to industries in the economy over the period from t_0 to t_1. (This is the case, for example, for aluminum in the United States between 1947 and 1958.) These represent kinds of sectoral "linkage" in an economy, as do column sums (output multipliers) and row sums of the Leontief inverse matrices. These linkage notions will be taken up in Chapter 9. The point here is simply to note that they provide alternative kinds of summary measures by which to compare coefficients over time.

   Data for the U.S. Economy   Appendix B contains consistently aggregated
input-output information on the U.S. economy for 1947, 1958, 1963, 1967, 1972,
and 1977. Both technical coefficients and their associated Leontief inverses are
shown for each of these years. The interested reader may wish to make
comparisons along the lines indicated in this section. Note, however, that if the
highly aggregated tables are used, many of the most interesting kinds of changes
may well be hidden by the extremely broad sectoral classification scheme.

Constant versus Current Prices

   In studies, such as Carter's, that attempt to identify structural (technological) change, it is appropriate to express the input-output relationships in constant
dollars. Suppose that $z_{ij}(t_0) = \$40$, $X_j(t_0) = \$1000$, $z_{ij}(t_1) = \$160$, and $X_j(t_1)$
$= \$2000$. Recall that a transaction in value terms, z_{ij}, is a physical flow from i
to j, f_{ij}, multiplied by the price of input i, p_i. Then, in terms of current (at time
t_0 and at time t_1) values, $a_{ij}(t_0) = 0.04$ and $a_{ij}(t_1) = 0.08$. This doubling of the
input coefficient from sector i to sector j might be interpreted as a reflection of
technological change—a doubling of the importance of good i in industry j's
production process. However, if the price of input i had increased over the
period, then the difference between $a_{ij}(t_0)$ and $a_{ij}(t_1)$ would be at least partly
due to this price change and to the extent that this was the case would not reflect
any changed technological relationships at all. To cite an extreme case, if the
price of good i had doubled and if the same physical flow was used in time t_1,
then the $z_{ij}(t_1) = f_{ij}(t_1)p_i(t_1) = \$160$ reflects entirely a change in the price of i.
If this were reduced to the price level at t_0—namely, if $p_i(t_1)$ were divided by 2
—then in constant (t_0-level) not current (t_1-level) dollars $z_{ij}(t_1)$ is just \$80; thus,
expressed in constant dollars, $a_{ij}(t_1) = \$80/\$2000 = 0.04$, and we would conclude that there has been no structural change at all in the way input i is used in
production by sector j. This is why constant-dollar comparisons are generally
used in studies that attempt to identify structural change in an economy.
   However, in addressing the question of coefficient stability over time
(which is, ultimately, the question of whether or not "old" tables can be used
reasonably in "new" times), current values are appropriate. There are two
reasons for this. In the first place, when input prices increase, the price of the
output produced from them will tend to increase also. Recall that the denominator of an a_{ij} is X_j, which is a physical output, F_j, multiplied by the price of j,
p_j. In the example above, if good i were the only input to sector j whose price
had increased, it is not likely that the price of j would have doubled also, but it
might well have increased slightly in the period from t_0 to t_1. However, if prices
of all (or most) inputs to j had increased over the period, then the price of j is
almost certain to have gone up also, so there will be some compensating
movement in the numerators and the denominators of the a_{ij}'s. Thus, coefficients using current prices are likely to exhibit more stability, since price changes
will be reflected in both numerators and denominators. This has been noted in
several studies—for example, Tilanus and Rey (1964) at a national level and
Conway (1980) at a regional level.
   Secondly, due to the necessity of dealing with aggregated classifications,
sectors contain a wide variety of individual products. Suppose that products a

and b are classified as belonginging to sector i (for example, heating oil and natural gas in the energy sector). If the price of one of these products, say a, rises relative to the other, then in establishments in sector j where substitution between a and b is possible, there will tend to be replacement of the higher-priced input, a, by the lower-priced one, b. This substitution, in turn, will tend to stabilize the value of the transaction z_{ij}, when that value is measured in current dollars, even though the physical composition of the transaction may be quite different at t_1 from what it was at t_0. (For example, if the price of oil rises relative to that of natural gas, a transaction from the energy sector to sector j may contain relatively more natural gas than oil in t_1 as compared with t_0.)

Regional Coefficients

In Chapter 3 we saw that a regional technical coefficient, a_{ij}^R, can be broken down to the sum of the regional input coefficient, a_{ij}^{RR}, and the coefficient representing the amount of good i produced in other regions per dollar's worth of output of sector j in region R, $a_{ij}^{\tilde{R}R}$ (where $\tilde{R}$ indicates regions other than R). That is, $a_{ij}^{RR} = a_{ij}^R - a_{ij}^{\tilde{R}R}$. (For studies that concentrate on a specific region, where it is not necessary to use a superscript to designate the particular region, the simpler notation $r_{ij} = a_{ij} - m_{ij}$ is sometimes used for regional input coefficients, technical coefficients, and import coefficients.) Both the technical coefficients and the import coefficients, which represent trade patterns, are likely to be subject to variations over time. This has led to the speculation that regional coefficients are likely to be more unstable than technical coefficients, since they are made up of two unstable components—technical coefficients and import coefficients. For example, suppose $a_{ij}(t_0) = 0.1$, $a_{ij}(t_1) = 0.2$, $m_{ij}(t_0) = 0.05$, and $m_{ij}(t_1) = 0.1$. Then $r_{ij}(t_0) = 0.05$, $r_{ij}(t_1) = 0.1$, and the percentage increases in a_{ij}, m_{ij}, and r_{ij} are all 100. On the other hand, if $m_{ij}(t_1) = 0.08$, then $r_{ij}(t_0) = 0.05$, $r_{ij}(t_1) = 0.12$, and the percentage increases are 100, 60, and 140, for a_{ij}, m_{ij}, and r_{ij}, respectively. Thus, in this case, the regional input coefficient *is* more unstable than either the technical coefficient or the import coefficient, even though the latter two moved in the same direction over the period from t_0 to t_1.

Three survey-based input-output tables for the state of Washington, for 1963, 1967, and 1972, have been used in a number of studies of coefficient change at the regional level. The tables are available in Bourque and Weeks (1969), Beyers et al. (1970), and Bourque and Conway (1977), respectively. Results of an examination of the regional input coefficients for the 1963 and 1967 Washington survey-based tables, in current dollars, are not conclusive (Beyers 1972, Table 4, p. 372). Of the 888 coefficients for which a_{ij} experienced a change over the 1963–1967 period, in 21.3 percent of the cases there was no change in m_{ij}, and hence the change in r_{ij} was the same as in a_{ij}. In 16.2 percent of the cases, a_{ij} and m_{ij} moved in the same direction and there was no change in r_{ij}; hence in these cases the presence of both a_{ij} and m_{ij} in the definition of r_{ij} was "compensating." (For example, if $a_{ij}[t_0] = 0.2$, $a_{ij}[t_1] = 0.18$, $m_{ij}[t_0] = 0.05$, $m_{ij}[t_1] = 0.03$, then $r_{ij}[t_0] = 0.15$ and $r_{ij}[t_1] = 0.15$, even though both a_{ij} and m_{ij} have fallen over the period.) In 10.4 percent of the cases, a_{ij} and m_{ij} moved in opposite directions and hence led to a more unstable

r_{ij}. However, in the remaining 52.1 percent of the cases, the effects were ambiguous—either a_{ij}, m_{ij}, and r_{ij} all moved in the same direction or a_{ij} and m_{ij} moved in the opposite direction (both of these kinds of movements may or may not lead to more instability in r_{ij} than in either a_{ij} or m_{ij}). For example, if $a_{ij}(t_0) = 0.2$, $a_{ij}(t_1) = 0.19$, $m_{ij}(t_0) = 0.05$, $m_{ij}(t_1) = 0.01$, then $r_{ij}(t_0) = 0.15$ and $r_{ij}(t_1) = 0.18$. While both a_{ij} and m_{ij} have decreased over time, r_{ij} has increased, and the percentage change in r_{ij} (in absolute terms) is larger than the percentage change in a_{ij}—a 20 percent increase versus a 5 percent decrease, respectively.

Examination of the Leontief inverses for the regional input coefficients and regional technical coefficients for the two years showed "the regional [input coefficients] matrix appears somewhat less stable than the [regional] technical requirements matrix." (Beyers 1972, p. 372.) However, the amount of change was relatively unimportant for overall impact analysis. For example, in an analysis of the Leontief-Carter type, total 1967 output calculated by using the 1963 coefficients matrix and the 1967 final demand was found to be only 2.3 percent larger than total actual 1967 output; intermediate output (gross output less sales to final demand) was 10.5 percent larger. However, the usual caveat applies; namely, some individual sectoral outputs were badly estimated using the 1963 matrix (the worst being overestimated by 77 percent).

Further analyses of the Washington survey-based data arrive at similar conclusions. Conway (1977) investigated the variation over the period in several types of multipliers derived from the Leontief inverse of the regional inputs matrix for the state. Again, current-value data were used. For example, in the case of output multipliers (column sums of these inverses), the simple average multipliers for the three years were: 1963, 1.33; 1967, 1.29; and 1972, 1.33. Of course, individual sectors did exhibit more variation (up to about 18 percent, for the 1963–1972 period). Continuing the Leontief-Carter type of analysis (Conway 1980), it was found that

1 Total predicted 1972 output using the 1967 input-output table and 1972 final demand was 1.2 percent lower than total actual 1972 output and
2 Total predicted 1972 output using the 1963 input-output table and 1972 final demand was only 0.8 percent higher than total actual 1972 output.

These results partly reflect the fact that the 1967 Washington economy included a relatively high level of imports, due to extremely rapid expansion of the economy between 1963 and 1967, with the consequence that many regional sectors were operating at or near full capacity and it was necessary to turn to sources of supply outside of the region. They also confirm that, for overall predictions, an "old" regional table may work quite well. As usual, however, individual sectoral outputs can be badly forecast.[1]

---

[1]Conway also stresses the fact that forecasting the final-demand components (the Y vector for the forecast period) is a critical problem in that errors in these elements can add significant prediction error to that caused by unstable coefficients. "To reduce forecasting errors efforts must initially be directed at improving the quality of final demand projections, especially those of gross exports." (Conway 1980, 170) The importance and difficulty of final demand forecasting was noted at the beginning of Chapter 4.

Emerson (1976) examined survey-based tables for Kansas for 1965 and 1970, including full import and export matrices. The results are, like those for Washington, not terribly conclusive. Although there were some changes in the import coefficients, and consequently in the Kansas regional input coefficients, the problem was judged to be "not acute but...of sufficient importance to warrant concern" (Emerson 1976, p. 275). Also, Baster (1980) supplied some evidence on relative stability of trade coefficients in a study for the Strathclyde region in Scotland. At the level of the individual firm or establishment, 79 percent of the coefficients showing imports from the rest of Scotland were constant over the 1974–1976 period, and an additional 13.5 percent of the coefficients varied by no more than 10 percent over the period. At the sectoral level (that is, aggregating establishments), over 90 percent of the import coefficients were stable. This study also noted that most instability was exhibited by products that have a high value-to-weight ratio, where transport costs are therefore relatively unimportant (for example, engineering goods as opposed to agricultural products).

Summary

There is no question but that coefficients change over time, at both a national and at a regional level. It is also apparent that for aggregate kinds of measures, such as total sectoral output associated with a specific vector of final demand, the error introduced by using an "old" table may not be large. On the other hand, there may be other, even simpler methods for forecasting total output that are not much worse. Conway (1975) estimates total Washington 1967 output, $i'X^W(1967)$, using known total final demands for 1963 and 1967; $i'Y^W(1963)$ and $i'Y^W(1967)$; and total 1963 output, $i'X^W(1963)$. His estimate is simply

$$i'X^W(1967) = \left[i'X^W(1963)\right]\left[\frac{i'Y^W(1967)}{i'Y^W(1963)}\right].$$

This is sometimes referred to as a "final demand blowup" approach; in the Washington case it led to an overestimate of 3.1 percent (Conway 1975, p. 67), as opposed to the input-output generated error of 2.3 percent noted above (Beyers 1972, p. 368). That is, there may be much simpler ways to be not much worse off, at this very aggregate level. Thus one of the particular advantages of the input-output model is precisely that it generates results at the sectoral level, and here, as we have seen, out-of-date tables *can* produce considerable error. For this reason, there is continuing concern with the issue of updating or projecting input-output data.

8-3 | TEMPORAL STABILITY: UPDATING AND PROJECTING COEFFICIENTS. TRENDS, MARGINAL COEFFICIENTS, AND BEST PRACTICE METHODS.

Trends and Extrapolation

Analysis of the trends in input-output coefficients might appear to be a tempting approach to the problem of estimating probable changes in input-output coefficients over time. Given two or more coefficient matrices defined for an economy over the same set of sectors, linear (or nonlinear) trends could be established for each particular coefficient, and then extrapolations could be made to the year in question (with negative coefficients set equal to zero). For example, if a particular a_{ij} at time t_0 equals 0.2 and if the coefficient for the same i and j is 0.15 five years later, at time $t_0 + 5$, then a linear trend extrapolation would suggest that at $t_0 + 10$, a_{ij} would be equal to 0.10.

In a study that used ten Dutch input-output tables, Tilanus (1966) found that in fact such extrapolations generated worse results than simply using the most recent coefficients table. Barker (Allen and Gossling 1975, Ch. 2) considered the same approach for U.K. tables. Given technical coefficients matrices for 1954 and 1960, estimates were made of 1963 intermediate demand, using actual 1963 final demand and the Leontief inverses associated with the 1954 and 1960 coefficients matrices. Estimates were also made using a matrix for 1963 that was derived by trend projection, coefficient by coefficient, from the 1954 and 1960 data. Finally, a naive final-demand blowup method was used, sector by sector, with 1960 as the base year. The average absolute percentage errors, over all sectors, were 17.3, 13.7, 15.9, and 18.9, respectively, for the 1954, 1960, trend extrapolation, and naive approaches. (Calculated from Barker, Table 2.1, pp. 30–31.) Note in particular that trend extrapolation was worse than simply using the most recent (here 1960) matrix.

Marginal Input Coefficients

Suppose that one is forecasting into the future from the current year, t, to some future year, $t + s$. Given a forecast of $Y(t + s)$, one could then estimate $X(t + s)$ as

$$X(t + s) = [I - A(t)]^{-1}Y(t + s) \tag{8-1}$$

Suppose that, in addition to the current-year data, there is a set of input-output data for a previous year, $t - r$. Then one could generate a set of *marginal* input coefficients, a_{ij}^*, defined as

$$a_{ij}^* = \frac{z_{ij}(t) - z_{ij}(t - r)}{X_j(t) - X_j(t - r)} = \frac{\Delta z_{ij}}{\Delta X_j}$$

That is, these coefficients relate the *change* (from year $t - r$ to year t) in the amount of input i purchased by industry j to the *change* (over the same period) in the total amount of j produced. To the extent that the average and marginal coefficients, a_{ij} and a_{ij}^*, differ, the latter may reflect scale effects. The argument can be made that the marginal coefficient better reflects the inputs from i to j that would be used when the output of sector j changes, due to new (forecast) final demands.

For example, let $z_{ij}(t - r) = \$500$, $z_{ij}(t) = \$560$, $X_j(t - r) = \$5000$, and $X_j(t) = \$6000$, so that $a_{ij}(t) = \$560/\$6000 = 0.0933$ and $a_{ij}^*(t) = \$60/\$1000 = 0.06$. Putting ourselves back to year $t - r$, $a_{ij}(t - r) = \$500/\$5000 = 0.1$. If at time $t - r$ we had "forecast" $X_j(t)$ to be $\$6000$, our estimate of $z_{ij}(t)$, based on the usual average input coefficient, would have been $a_{ij}(t - r)X_j(t) = (0.1)(\$6000) = \$600$. However, if we had had a marginal coefficient at $t - r$,

$a_{ij}^*(t - r)$, we could have made a forecast of $z_{ij}(t)$ as $z_{ij}(t) = z_{ij}(t - r) + \Delta z_{ij} = z_{ij}(t - r) + a_{ij}^*(t - r)\Delta X_j = \$500 + a_{ij}^*(t - r)(\$1000)$. In particular, if our estimate of $a_{ij}^*(t - r)$ had been 0.06, our estimate of $z_{ij}(t)$ would have been perfect, at \$560. This is the basic idea behind the use of marginal coefficients for forecasting. The alternative to estimating directly the level of new output, at time $t + s$, as in Eq. (8-1), is to forecast the change in output, using marginal coefficients, and add it to the current level; that is,

$$X(t + s) = X(t) + \Delta X = [I - A(t)]^{-1}Y(t) + [I - A^*(t)]^{-1}\Delta Y \quad (8\text{-}2)$$

where $\Delta Y = Y(t + s) - Y(t)$ and $A^*(t)$ is the matrix of marginal input coefficients. Since the elements in $X(t + s)$ are found using a combination of current average coefficients, $A(t)$, and marginal coefficients, $A^*(t)$, this is in effect a way of introducing changing coefficients over time into the analysis.

Although the idea of using marginal coefficients to reflect changes in input-output structure has a certain logical appeal, experiments by Tilanus (1967) on a series of Dutch national input-output tables for 13 consecutive years (1948 through 1960) were not encouraging. For $r = 5$ (that is, calculating marginal coefficients over the previous five-year period) and $s = 1, 2, 3, 4\frac{1}{2}$, and $6\frac{1}{2}$ (years of projection), using marginal coefficients in this way gave results that were not as good as when the most recent table of average coefficients was used; that is, the approach in Eq. (8-1) turned out to be better than that in Eq. (8-2).

"Best Practice" Firms

An alternative approach for projecting the technology in an input-output table in the future is the "best practice" firm idea of Professor William Miernyk (for example, in Miernyk 1965). In constructing a table for short-term forecasting into the future—say, three to six years—Miernyk suggests that one not gather current information from *all* firms in each sector, or even from some random sample of firms. Rather, one should obtain data only from the "best practice" firms in a sector—those that are technologically most advanced at present. Such firms can be defined as those for which the ratios of employment or wage payments to total gross output are relatively low ("low labor intensity") or those with relatively high ratios of profits to total gross output. Firms could be identified as best practice ones if they satisfied any one or only if they satisfied several of these (or similar) criteria simultaneously.

The logic is that these firms, which are somewhat unusual now (in the sense of being better than average for their sector), represent the technology that will be generally in use in the future—the best of today will be the average of the future. There are many obvious objections to this idea—why should "best" today be "average" in five years for *all* sectors? Is this approach valid for three years, or five years, or seven years in the future? And so on. But in its favor is the fact that it is a workable, feasible way of constructing technical coefficients matrices that are more likely to represent the future structure of production than would a table that was constructed to represent the average structure in each sector today.

8-4 | TEMPORAL STABILITY: UPDATING AND PROJECTING COEFFICIENTS. THE RAS APPROACH

The RAS Technique

Early work at updating input-output information, done under Stone's direction, is reported in Stone (1961); Stone and Brown (1962); Cambridge University, Department of Applied Economics (1963); and Bacharach (1970). Because many of these techniques do not require all the information that is usually forthcoming from a survey of the sort that underlies survey-based input-output tables, they are often referred to as partial-survey methods, or nonsurvey methods, if all of the data needed can be found in generally available published sources. We concentrate here on the "RAS" procedure; the origin of the name will become clear in what follows.

To begin, assume that we have an input-output direct input coefficients table for an n-sector economy for a given year in the past (which, in what follows, we will designate year "0") and that we would like to update those coefficients to a more recent year (for example, last year, which we will designate year "1"). Using obvious notation, we have $A(0)$ and want $A(1)$, the n^2 coefficients for the n sectors in the economy for the more recent year.

If one were to conduct a survey of establishments in each of the sectors in the economy, it would be to determine: (1) the dollar value of purchases by sector j from each sector i (alternatively, the sales from sector i to each sector j), z_{ij}, and (2) the total output of each sector j, X_j. Thus, the technical coefficients, $a_{ij} = z_{ij}/X_j$, would be found from these $n^2 + n = n(n+1)$ pieces of information. (Ultimately, our interest is primarily in the n^2 coefficients, a_{ij}. However, if we obtain transactions data, z_{ij}—and not a_{ij} directly—from a survey, then we also need the relevant X_j in order to derive the $n \times n$ direct input coefficients matrix, A.)

The RAS technique attempts to estimate the n^2 coefficients, a_{ij}, from $3n$ pieces of information for the year of interest (year 1). These are: (1) total gross outputs, X_j, (which are also needed with survey-based transactions information); (2) total interindustry (or "intermediate") sales, by sector; for any given sector, i, this is $\sum_{j=1}^{n} z_{ij}$, which is the same as total output of sector i less sector i's sales to final demand (since $X_i = \sum_{j=1}^{n} z_{ij} + Y_i$) and (3) total interindustry purchases, by sector; for sector j, this is $\sum_{i=1}^{n} z_{ij}$, which is the same as $X_j - \overline{W}_j$ (that is, total output of sector j less total purchases by j from the payments sector—labor inputs to sector j, imported inputs to sector j, taxes paid for government services, interest paid on capital loans, rental payments for land, etc.)

It has become conventional in the RAS literature to use U_i to represent $\sum_{j=1}^{n} z_{ij}$—that is, total interindustry sales by sector i—and V_j to represent $\sum_{i=1}^{n} z_{ij}$

—total interindustry input purchases by sector j. Define $U = \begin{bmatrix} U_1 \\ \vdots \\ U_n \end{bmatrix}$ and $V =$

$[V_1, \cdots, V_n]$ as n-element column and row vectors, respectively, of interindustry sales and purchases, by sector. Since these need to be known for year 1, they will be designated $U(1)$ and $V(1)$. (In using U and V, we are following established convention in the literature on nonsurvey techniques. It has also become established in the literature to use U and V for the "use" and "make" matrices, respectively, when discussing the commodity-by-industry input-output accounting framework, as we did in Chapter 5. It will always be clear in the context of the discussion which definition of U and V is relevant.)

Thus, the problem that the RAS procedure addresses is: Given an $n \times n$ matrix $A(0)$ and given three n-element vectors for the more recent year (year 1), $X(1)$, $U(1)$, and $V(1)$, estimate $A(1)$. We denote the estimate that is generated by this procedure as $\tilde{A}(1)$. If we are dealing with, say, a 25-sector economy, we are trying to estimate 625 coefficients (the elements of $A[1]$) from 75 pieces of information. These are: (1) the row sums of the unknown transactions matrix, $Z(1)$, namely $U(1)$; (2) the column sums of the same matrix, namely $V(1)$; and (3) the $X(1)$, which are essential primarily to convert an estimate of a $z_{ij}(1)$ into an estimate of a technical coefficient $a_{ij}(1)$, since $a_{ij}(1) = z_{ij}(1)/X_j(1)$.

We develop the procedure for the general 3×3 case, and then present a 3×3 numerical example. The potential usefulness of the technique is in real-world applications, where n, the number of sectors, is much larger than three and hence the difference between n^2 and $3n$ is large. For an 80-sector table, $n^2 = 6400$, whereas $3n = 240$. For the general 3×3 case, we assume given, from the "base" year (year 0),

$$A(0) = \begin{bmatrix} a_{11}(0) & a_{12}(0) & a_{13}(0) \\ a_{21}(0) & a_{22}(0) & a_{23}(0) \\ a_{31}(0) & a_{32}(0) & a_{33}(0) \end{bmatrix} \tag{8-3}$$

and from the "target" year (year 1),

$$X(1) = \begin{bmatrix} X_1(1) \\ X_2(1) \\ X_3(1) \end{bmatrix}, \qquad U(1) = \begin{bmatrix} U_1(1) \\ U_2(1) \\ U_3(1) \end{bmatrix}, \qquad V(1) = [V(1)\, V(2)\, V(3)]$$

$$\tag{8-4}$$

Initially, suppose we hypothesize that $A(0) = A(1)$, namely that the technical coefficients have remained stable over time. To test the credibility of this hypothesis, we must investigate whether or not it is consistent with our year 1 information on intermediate sales and purchases. Since these are row and column sums of the transactions matrix, it will be necessary to convert coefficients, a_{ij}, into transactions, z_{ij}, via the relationship $z_{ij} = a_{ij}X_j$. In matrix terms, since $A = Z(\hat{X})^{-1}$, we have $Z = A\hat{X}$. Therefore, the matrix of interindustry transactions that is implied by our assumption that $A(1) = A(0)$ is given by $A(0)\hat{X}(1)$. Here this is

$$A(0)\hat{X}(1) = \begin{bmatrix} a_{11}(0) & a_{12}(0) & a_{13}(0) \\ a_{21}(0) & a_{22}(0) & a_{23}(0) \\ a_{31}(0) & a_{32}(0) & a_{33}(0) \end{bmatrix} \begin{bmatrix} X_1 & 0 & 0 \\ 0 & X_2 & 0 \\ 0 & 0 & X_3 \end{bmatrix}$$

$$= \begin{bmatrix} a_{11}(0)X_1(1) & a_{12}(0)X_2(1) & a_{13}(0)X_3(1) \\ a_{21}(0)X_1(1) & a_{22}(0)X_2(1) & a_{23}(0)X_3(1) \\ a_{31}(0)X_1(1) & a_{32}(0)X_2(1) & a_{33}(0)X_3(1) \end{bmatrix}$$

(8-5)

The issue is whether (or how well) the row sums and the column sums of the matrix in Eq. (8-5) correspond to our information about the target year economy, namely $U(1)$ and $V(1)$. Recall that postmultiplication of a matrix, M, by i (a column vector of 1's) generates a column vector whose elements are the row sums of M. Hence we want to compare $[A(0)\hat{X}(1)]i$ with $U(1)$. Let U^1 denote $[A(0)\hat{X}(1)]i$; that is, U^1 is the estimate of interindustry sales, by sector, under the assumption of no technical change.[2]

If $U^1 = U(1)$, our estimate of $Z(1)$ has the correct row sums. It then remains to be determined whether the column sums of $[A(0)\hat{X}(1)]$ correspond to the known interindustry purchases, by sector, namely $V(1)$. Recall that premultiplication of a matrix, M, by i', a row of 1's, generates a row vector whose elements are the column sums of M. Therefore, if $i'[A(0)\hat{X}(1)] = V(1)$, then our work is finished, since the old technical coefficient matrix, $A(0)$, in conjunction with the new gross outputs, $X(1)$, generates the proper target year interindustry sales and purchases. Since the $U(1)$ and $V(1)$ are row and column sums of the (unknown) $Z(1)$ matrix, they are sometimes referred to as "marginals" or "row and column margins" of $Z(1)$.

Much more likely is the situation in which the no-change hypothesis fails in the sense that $U^1 \neq U(1)$ and/or $V^1 \neq V(1)$. Specifically, suppose that the row sums of the matrix in Eq. (8-5) are unsatisfactory; that is

$$a_{11}(0)X_1(1) + a_{12}(0)X_2(1) + a_{13}(0)X_3(1) = U_1^1 \neq U_1(1)$$

$$a_{21}(0)X_1(1) + a_{22}(0)X_2(1) + a_{23}(0)X_3(1) = U_2^1 \neq U_2(1) \qquad (8\text{-}6)$$

$$a_{31}(0)X_1(1) + a_{32}(0)X_2(1) + a_{33}(0)X_3(1) = U_3^1 \neq U_3(1)$$

If a particular $U_i^1 > U_i(1)$, this means that the elements in row i—a_{i1} (0), $a_{i2}(0)$, $a_{i3}(0)$, in our example—are larger than they should be, since the $X_1(1)$, $X_2(1)$, and $X_3(1)$ contain "updated" (target year) information. (Similarly, if $U_k^1 < U_k(1)$, the elements of row k in $A(0)$ are smaller than they should be.)

Denote the ratio $U_i(1)/U_i^1$ by r_i^1; when $U_i(1) < U_i^1$, this ratio will be less than 1. Let $i = 1$ for illustration. If each element in row 1 of $A(0)$ is multiplied by this r_1^1, each of those elements will be reduced. In particular, this operation

---

[2] We use the superscript notation, here U^1, because, as we will see below, this represents the *first* of several estimates of the true $U(1)$. The next (better) estimate will be denoted U^2, the third will be U^3, and so on. This may appear cumbersome, but we want to distinguish, for example, U^1, our first *estimates* of interindustry sales, from $U(1)$, our exogenously determined target year *data*.

will generate a new set of technical coefficients in that row which, when multiplied by the $X(1)$'s, will sum to $U_1(1)$ exactly, which is what we want.[3] Letting $r_1^1 a_{11}(0) = a_{11}^1$, $r_1^1 a_{12}(0) = a_{12}^1$, and $r_1^1 a_{13}(0) = a_{13}^1$, we see that row 1 of $A(0)$ has been altered to produce a new set of coefficients $(a_{11}^1, a_{12}^1, a_{13}^1)$ which constitute our *first* estimate (hence the superscript 1) of a better set of values, in the sense that they satisfy the target year information in $U_1(1)$ exactly.

Similarly, if $U_2^1 < U_2(1)$, we form $r_2^1 = U_2(1)/U_2^1$, which will now be greater than unity. Multiplying the elements in row 2 of $A(0)$ by r_2^1 has the effect of *increasing* each of them sufficiently so that, when thus altered, the second row sum will equal the known value $U_2(1)$.[4] Letting $r_2^1 a_{21}(0) = a_{21}^1$, $r_2^1 a_{22}(0) = a_{22}^1$, and $r_2^1 a_{23}(0) = a_{23}^1$, we find a modified second row of $A(0)$, where in this example all elements in this row have been increased. These are our first estimates of a better set of values for row 2 of $A(0)$. Similarly, for row 3, since $U_3^1 \neq U_3(1)$ in Eq. (8-6), we use $r_3^1 = U_3(1)/U_3^1$ to multiply each coefficient in the third row of $A(0)$—reducing them if $U_3(1) < U_3^1$ and expanding if $U_3(1) > U_3^1$—so as to reflect correctly the known target year row sum (interindustry sales from sector 3) of $U_3(1)$.

Algebraically, we want to multiply row 1 of $A(0)$ by r_1^1, row 2 of $A(0)$ by r_2^1, and row 3 of $A(0)$ by r_3^1. Recall that premultiplication of a matrix, M, by a diagonal matrix, $D = [d_i]$, has the effect of multiplying row i of M by the element d_i. Thus our first estimate of a target-year A matrix, which we denote A^1, is given by

$$A^1 = \begin{bmatrix} r_1^1 & 0 & 0 \\ 0 & r_2^1 & 0 \\ 0 & 0 & r_3^1 \end{bmatrix} A(0) \tag{8-7}$$

It is to be emphasized that the superscripts—here 1—in the description of the RAS technique will refer to the "step" in the procedure. Thus A^1 is our first estimate, which means our estimate after the first step of the procedure; A^2 will refer to our second estimate (and not to "A squared"), and so on. This may appear cumbersome at first, but it turns out to be useful notation, as we will see

---

[3] From Eq. (8-6) we have

$$a_{11}(0)X_1(1) + a_{12}(0)X_2(1) + a_{13}(0)X_3(1) = U_1^1$$

where $U_1^1 > U_1(1)$. Letting $r_1^1 = U_1(1)/U_1^1$, and multiplying through by r_1^1, we have

$$r_1^1 a_{11}(0)X_1(1) + r_1^1 a_{12}(0)X_2(1) + r_1^1 a_{13}(0)X_3(1) = r_1^1 U_1^1 = \left[\frac{U_1(1)}{U_1^1}\right] U_1^1 = U_1(1)$$

[4] Again, from Eq. (8-6),

$$a_{21}(0)X_1(1) + a_{22}(0)X_2(1) + a_{23}(0)X_3(1) = U_2^1$$

where $U_2^1 < U_2(1)$. Then, with $r_2^1 = U_2(1)/U_2^1$, we have

$$r_2^1 a_{21}(0)X_1(1) + r_2^1 a_{22}(0)X_2(1) + r_2^1 a_{23}(0)X_3(1) = r_2^1 U_2^1 = \left[\frac{U_2(1)}{U_2^1}\right] U_2^1 = U_2(1)$$

below. Letting

$$R^1 = \begin{bmatrix} r_1^1 & 0 & 0 \\ 0 & r_2^1 & 0 \\ 0 & 0 & r_3^1 \end{bmatrix}$$

the result in Eq. (8-7) can be expressed as

$$A^1 = R^1 A(0) \tag{8-8}$$

For this example, $U(1) = \begin{bmatrix} U_1(1) \\ U_2(1) \\ U_3(1) \end{bmatrix}$ and $U^1 = \begin{bmatrix} U_1^1 \\ U_2^1 \\ U_3^1 \end{bmatrix}$. Then, employing the

"hat" notation once again to convert a vector into a diagonal matrix and recalling that the inverse of a diagonal matrix is a diagonal matrix whose elements are the reciprocals of the elements in the original matrix, note that

$$R^1 = [\hat{U}(1)](\hat{U}^1)^{-1} \tag{8-9}$$

With this set of adjustments to the rows of $A(0)$, we know that now

$$[R^1 A(0)\hat{X}(1)]i = [A^1\hat{X}(1)]i = Z^1 i = U(1) \tag{8-10}$$

precisely, since it was to ensure this equality that the modification of $A(0)$ to A^1 was made.

The next issue, then, is whether or not the *column* sum information for the target year, $V(1)$, is captured in the improved matrix, A^1. That is, the task is now to compare each V_j^1 and $V_j(1)$. The column sums in the transactions matrix associated with A^1 and $X(1)$ are

$$a_{11}^1 X_1(1) + a_{21}^1 X_1(1) + a_{31}^1 X_1(1) = \left(a_{11}^1 + a_{21}^1 + a_{31}^1\right) X_1(1) = V_1^1$$

$$a_{12}^1 X_2(1) + a_{22}^1 X_2(1) + a_{32}^1 X_2(1) = \left(a_{12}^1 + a_{22}^1 + a_{32}^1\right) X_2(1) = V_2^1 \tag{8-11}$$

$$a_{13}^1 X_3(1) + a_{23}^1 X_3(1) + a_{33}^1 X_3(1) = \left(a_{13}^1 + a_{23}^1 + a_{33}^1\right) X_3(1) = V_3^1$$

More compactly, $V(1) = i'[A^1\hat{X}(1)]$. If $V_1^1 = V_1(1)$, $V_2^1 = V_2(1)$, and $V_3^1 = V_3(1)$, then A^1 is $\tilde{A}(1)$, our estimate of $A(1)$, since it generates row *and* column sums that correspond to the observed $U(1)$ and $V(1)$. Letting $V^1 = [V_1^1, V_2^1, V_3^1]$, this is the case in which $V^1 = V(1)$.

In most cases, however, $V^1 \neq V(1)$ and so it is then necessary to modify the elements in A^1 column by column. If, for example, $V_1^1 > V_1(1)$—the first column sum in Eq. (8-11), using A^1, is larger than we want it to be—we form the ratio $V_1(1)/V_1^1$, denote it by s_1^1, and multiply through the first equation in (8-11).[5] (The superscript 1, on s, indicates that this is our *first* modification of coefficients in order to meet *column* sum information.) The modified coefficients in column 1 are then $s_1^1 a_{11}^1$, $s_1^1 a_{21}^1$, and $s_1^1 a_{31}^1$; we denote these by a_{11}^2, a_{21}^2, and a_{31}^2. The

---

[5] This gives $s_1^1(a_{11}^1 + a_{21}^1 + a_{31}^1)X_1(1) = s_1^1 V_1^1 = [V_1(1)/V_1^1]V_1^1 = V_1(1)$ which is what we want.

superscript 2 on the a_{i1} coefficients denotes the fact that this is our second modification of elements from the original $A(0)$ matrix.

Similarly, we form $s_2^1 = V_2(1)/V_2^1$ and $s_3^1 = V_3(1)/V_3^1$. If a particular $V_j(1) > V_j^1$, then the associated $s_j^1 > 1$ and the elements in the jth column of A^1 are all increased, when multiplied by s_j^1. On the other hand, if $V_k(1) < V_k^1$, then $s_k^1 < 1$, and each of the elements in the kth column of A^1 is reduced when it is multiplied by s_k^1. When a particular $V_m(1) = V_m^1$, then the corresponding $s_m^1 = 1$, and so the elements in column m of A^1 will be multiplied by 1, that is, they will not be changed.

Algebraically, we now want to multiply column 1 of A^1 by s_1^1, column 2 by s_2^1, and column 3 by s_3^1. Since postmultiplication of a matrix, M, by a diagonal matrix, $D = [d_j]$, has the effect of multiplying column j of M by the element d_j, we form our *second* estimate of our matrix for the target year, A^2, as

$$A^2 = A^1 \begin{bmatrix} s_1^1 & 0 & 0 \\ 0 & s_2^1 & 0 \\ 0 & 0 & s_3^1 \end{bmatrix} \tag{8-12}$$

Letting $S^1 = \begin{bmatrix} s_1^1 & 0 & 0 \\ 0 & s_2^1 & 0 \\ 0 & 0 & s_3^1 \end{bmatrix}$, this is

$$A^2 = A^1 S^1 \tag{8-13}$$

Given $V(1)$ and V^1, we see that

$$S^1 = [\hat{V}(1)](\hat{V}^1)^{-1} \tag{8-14}$$

(Compare R^1 in Eq. [8-9].) With this set of adjustments, we know that the column sums are correct; that is, $Z^2 = A^2[\hat{X}(1)]$, and

$$i'[A^2 \hat{X}(1)] = i'Z^2 = V(1) \tag{8-15}$$

precisely, since it was to ensure this equality that the modification of A^1 to A^2 was made.

Note, from Eqs. (8-8) and (8-13), that

$$A^2 = R^1 A(0) S^1 \tag{8-16}$$

Ignoring superscripts and the (0), denoting base-year information, we have "RAS" on the right-hand side of Eq. (8-16). This is the origin of the name of the technique; we will comment on this further below. The point here is that the R is seen to refer to a diagonal matrix of elements modifying rows, the A to the coefficient matrix being modified, and the S to a diagonal matrix of column modifiers.

Note also that while A^2 in Eq. (8-13) now contains elements that, in conjunction with $X(1)$, satisfy the $V(1)$ marginals (as in Eq. [8-15]), it will generally be the case that in modifying A^1 to produce A^2 we will have disturbed the row sum property of A^1, given in Eq. (8-10). (Except in the case where

$S^1 = I$, meaning that A^1 also satisfies all of the column marginals exactly, in which case A^1 is our desired new matrix, $\tilde{A}[1]$.) Therefore, we must now test A^2 for row sum conformability, in the same way that we did $A(0)$, originally. Thus, we now find $[A^2\hat{X}(1)]i$; that is

$$
\begin{bmatrix} a_{11}^2 & a_{12}^2 & a_{13}^2 \\ a_{21}^2 & a_{22}^2 & a_{23}^2 \\ a_{31}^2 & a_{32}^2 & a_{33}^2 \end{bmatrix}\begin{bmatrix} X_1(1) & 0 & 0 \\ 0 & X_2(1) & 0 \\ 0 & 0 & X_3(1) \end{bmatrix}\begin{bmatrix} 1 \\ 1 \\ 1 \end{bmatrix} = \begin{bmatrix} U_1^2 \\ U_2^2 \\ U_3^2 \end{bmatrix} \qquad \text{(8-17)}
$$

and let $U^2 = \begin{bmatrix} U_1^2 \\ U_2^2 \\ U_3^2 \end{bmatrix}$. The superscript on U reminds us that this is our *second* set of row sum estimates. If, as is likely, $U^2 \neq U(1)$, we repeat the steps used in forming the diagonal row-modifying matrix. That is, let $r_1^2 = U_1(1)/U_1^2$, $r_2^2 = U_2(1)/U_2^2$, and $r_3^2 = U_3(1)/U_3^2$, and define

$$
R^2 = \begin{bmatrix} r_1^2 & 0 & 0 \\ 0 & r_2^2 & 0 \\ 0 & 0 & r_3^2 \end{bmatrix} = [\hat{U}(1)](\hat{U}^2)^{-1} \qquad \text{(8-18)}
$$

(Compare R^1 in Eq. [8-9]; note that the numerators in the r_i ratios are always the same, namely $U_i(1)$—the number that we know we want. The denominators change, since they represent the "latest" estimates—here U_i^2 instead of U_i^1, which we had initially.)

The entire procedure now follows the pattern that we have already established. If $R^2 = I$, then A^2 contains elements that satisfy both column and row marginals, and we use it as $\tilde{A}(1)$, our estimate of $A(1)$. If not—that is, if $U^2 \neq U(1)$—then we generate a further estimate of $A(0)$ as

$$
A^3 = R^2A^2 \qquad \text{(8-19)}
$$

The construction of R^2 assures us that the row marginals are now met.

The issue now is whether or not the column sum properties of A^3 satisfy the known target-year information in $V(1)$. Thus V_1^2, V_2^2, and V_3^2 are generated, as in Eq. (8-11), with a_{ij}^3 here replacing a_{ij}^1 in Eq. (8-11). Let $V^2 = \begin{bmatrix} V_1^2 \\ V_2^2 \\ V_3^2 \end{bmatrix}$; if $V^2 = V(1)$, then we have in A^3 a matrix that satisfies both row and column marginals, and we use it for $\tilde{A}(1)$. If $V^2 \neq V(1)$, we form

$$
S^2 = [\hat{V}(1)](\hat{V}^2)^{-1} \qquad \text{(8-20)}
$$

exactly as in Eq. (8-14), but using the elements in V^2 rather than those in V^1. Then our next estimate of $A(0)$ is given by

$$
A^4 = A^3S^2 \qquad \text{(8-21)}
$$

Note, from Eqs. (8-16) and (8-19), that

$$A^3 = [R^2 R^1] A(0) [S^1]$$ (8-22)

and from Eq. (8-21)

$$A^4 = [R^2 R^1] A(0) [S^1 S^2]$$ (8-23)

Note that R^1, R^2, S^1, and S^2 are all (in this example) 3×3 diagonal matrices. By $[R^2 R^1]$ we mean the 3×3 matrix that is the product of these two matrices. In fact, as the reader can easily verify,

$$[R^2 R^1] = \begin{bmatrix} r_1^2 r_1^1 & 0 & 0 \\ 0 & r_2^2 r_2^1 & 0 \\ 0 & 0 & r_3^2 r_3^1 \end{bmatrix}$$

And similarly for $[S^1 S^2]$. By repetition of these procedures, we would find

$$A^5 = [R^3 R^2 R^1] A(0) [S^1 S^2]$$
$$A^6 = [R^3 R^2 R^1] A(0) [S^1 S^2 S^3]$$ (8-24)
$$\vdots$$
$$A^{2n} = [R^n \cdots R^1] A(0) [S^1 \cdots S^n]$$

Letting $R = [R^n \cdots R^1]$ and $S = [S^1 \cdots S^n]$—both of which in this illustration are 3×3 diagonal matrices—then the right-hand side of Eq. (8-24) is "RAS." As mentioned earlier, this is the origin of the name of the procedure.

One may reasonably ask: How many alterations using row and column balancing factors will be needed until the adjusted matrix satisfies the row and column marginal totals for year 1? And, for that matter, do we know that, eventually, they *will* be satisfied, or may the sequence of row and column adjustments make things continually worse instead of better? In general, it has been found that the RAS procedure in fact does converge. That is, after row adjustment R^{k+1} we are closer to $U(1)$ than we were after the previous adjustment, R^k, and after column adjustment S^{k+1} we are closer to $V(1)$ than we were previously, after S^k.[6] The number of adjustments needed depends at least in part on how close one wants the row and column margins of the adjusted matrix to be to the known target-year values of $U(1)$ and $V(1)$. One usual kind of criterion is to continue the matrix adjustments until all elements in both $|U(1) - U^k|$ and $|V(1) - V^k|$ are less than or equal to ε, where ε is some small positive number, say 0.01. This means that each U_i^k is within 0.01 of the desired $U_i(1)$, and also that each V_j^k is within 0.01 of its associated $V_j(1)$.

For cases in which one is interested in assessing impacts on an economy of some *future* event, a *projection* of an existing technical coefficients matrix is called

[6] These technical matters, dealing with properties of the RAS technique, including convergence, are beyond the scope of this book. The interested reader will find discussions in Bacharach (1970) and Cambridge University, Department of Applied Economics (1963). An excellent overview of RAS and similar matrix adjustment techniques is to be found in several of the chapters in Allen and Gossling (1975), which also contains a good list of references.

for. One approach is again to use the RAS procedure, where now the values in the U, V, and X vectors must be forecast into the future year T; that is, we need to estimate $U(T)$, $V(T)$, and $X(T)$, to be used along with the current or most recent base matrix, $A(0)$.

Example of the RAS Procedure

The following 3×3 example illustrates the RAS procedure. Let the base year coefficients matrix be, as in Eq. (8-3),

$$A(0) = \begin{bmatrix} .120 & .100 & .049 \\ .210 & .247 & .265 \\ .026 & .249 & .145 \end{bmatrix} \tag{8-25}$$

The information that would be necessary for a full survey-based coefficients table for the target year, $A(1)$, would be interindustry flows, $Z(1)$, and total outputs, $X(1)$. Suppose that, in fact, we have

$$Z(1) = \begin{bmatrix} 98 & 72 & 75 \\ 65 & 8 & 63 \\ 88 & 27 & 44 \end{bmatrix} \tag{8-26}$$

and

$$X(1) = \begin{bmatrix} 421 \\ 284 \\ 283 \end{bmatrix} \tag{8-27}$$

Thus,

$$U(1) = \begin{bmatrix} 245 \\ 136 \\ 159 \end{bmatrix} \tag{8-28}$$

and

$$V(1) = \begin{bmatrix} 251 & 107 & 182 \end{bmatrix} \tag{8-29}$$

and $A(1)$ can be found as $A(1) = [Z(1)][\hat{X}(1)]^{-1}$;

$$A(1) = \begin{bmatrix} .2328 & .2535 & .2650 \\ .1544 & .0282 & .2226 \\ .2090 & .0951 & .1555 \end{bmatrix} \tag{8-30}$$

The point of partial-survey techniques is to develop reasonable estimates of the elements in $A(1)$ in the absence of information on the full set of transactions in $Z(1)$. To use the RAS approach, we need only the marginal information in $U(1)$ and $V(1)$, along with $X(1)$—as in (8-27), (8-28), and (8-29)—and the original or base year coefficients table, $A(0)$, as in Eq. (8-25).

Beginning with the conjecture that, perhaps, $A(1) = A(0)$—that is, that the coefficients have not changed—we want to see if the row and column sums of $A(0)\hat{X}(1)$, as in Eq. (8-5), satisfy the information in $U(1)$ and $V(1)$. Here

$$A(0)X(1) = \begin{bmatrix} 50.520 & 28.400 & 13.867 \\ 88.410 & 70.148 & 74.995 \\ 10.946 & 70.716 & 41.035 \end{bmatrix}$$

and

$$U^1 = [A(0)\hat{X}(1)]\, i = \begin{bmatrix} 92.787 \\ 233.553 \\ 122.697 \end{bmatrix}$$

Thus, $r_1^1 = U_1(1)/U_1^1 = 245/92.787 = 2.6405$. Similarly, $r_2^1 = 0.5823$ and $r_3^1 = 1.2959$. Forming R^1 as in Eq. (8-9), we have

$$R^1 = [\hat{U}(1)](\hat{U}^1)^{-1} = \begin{bmatrix} 2.6405 & 0 & 0 \\ 0 & 0.5823 & 0 \\ 0 & 0 & 1.2959 \end{bmatrix}$$

and our first adjusted matrix, A^1, as in Eq. (8-8), is

$$A^1 = R^1 A(0) = \begin{bmatrix} .3169 & .2640 & .1294 \\ .1223 & .1438 & .1543 \\ .0337 & .3227 & .1879 \end{bmatrix} \tag{8-31}$$

The elements in R^1 assure us that the row sums of $A^1\hat{X}(1)$ will equal $U(1)$, as in Eq. (8-10). Thus, checking the column sums of $A^1\hat{X}(1)$ against the requirements in $V(1)$, we have

$$V^1 = i'[A^1 X(1)] = [199.06 \quad 207.48 \quad 133.46]$$

and

$$V(1) = [251 \quad 107 \quad 182]$$

Then, as in Eq. (8-14),

$$S^1 = [\hat{V}(1)](\hat{V}^1)^{-1} = \begin{bmatrix} 1.2609 & 0 & 0 \\ 0 & 0.5157 & 0 \\ 0 & 0 & 1.3637 \end{bmatrix}$$

and, as in Eq. (8-13),

$$A^2 = A^1 S^1 = \begin{bmatrix} .3995 & .1362 & .1764 \\ .1542 & .0742 & .2104 \\ .0425 & .1664 & .2562 \end{bmatrix}$$

In this example, we set $\varepsilon = 0.005$, meaning that the alternating row and column adjustments would continue through the kth adjustment, when $|U(1) - U^k| \le 0.005$ and $|V(1) - V^k| \le 0.005$. For this example, $k = 12$, which means that six full modifications were needed—six row adjustments and six column adjustments. The final matrix, A^{12}, is shown in Eq. (8-32), below.

$$\tilde{A}(1) = A^{12} = \begin{bmatrix} .3924 & .1219 & .1596 \\ .1509 & .0661 & .1897 \\ .0529 & .1887 & .2938 \end{bmatrix} \tag{8-32}$$

Rather than print all the preceding matrices, A^1 through A^{11}, Table 8-1 presents the successive values of two representative coefficients, a_{11} and a_{23}, beginning with the original $A(0)$ matrix and continuing through each iteration of the RAS procedure. In Table 8-2 we record the three elements in $[U(1) - U^k]$

TABLE 8-1 Values of a_{11} and a_{23} at Each Step in the RAS Adjustment Procedure

k	a_{11}	a_{23}
0	.120	.265
1	.3169	.1543
2	.3995	.2104
3	.3812	.1966
4	.3957	.1913
5	.3902	.1912
6	.3931	.1900
7	.3920	.1900
8	.3926	.1898
9	.3923	.1898
10	.3925	.1897
11	.3924	.1897
12	.3924	.1897

(transposed, to make it a row vector, for ease of presentation) and the three elements in $[V(1) - V^k]$, for $k = 0$ through 13. The $k = 0$ line shows the row and column differences using $A(0)\hat{X}(1)$—that is, assuming $A(0) = A(1)$. As expected, at $k = 1$ the row marginals, in $U(1)$, are satisfied exactly—all zero elements in $[U(1) - U^1]'$—but the column marginals, in $V(1)$, are not. Thus step 2 adjusts for these column constraints—generating zeros in $[V(1) - V^2]$—but throwing the row sums out of balance with $U(1)$. Therefore, for the odd values of k—that is, the first, third, fifth, $\cdots$, etc. iteration—the U differences are all zero; for the even values of k, the V differences are all zero. At $k = 13$ (that is, *after $k = 12$*), all differences are less than 0.005 in absolute value (for the first time), and hence the RAS adjustment is terminated, since our stopping criterion was $\varepsilon = 0.005$. Finally, in Table 8-3 we present the elements of each of the diagonal matrices, R^1 through R^7 and S^1 through S^7, as in A^{2n} in Eq. (8-24).

It is of interest to compare our nonsurvey-generated target-year matrix, $\tilde{A}(1)$ in Eq. (8-32), with $A(1)$ in Eq. (8-30), which we would have available to us if the entire set of interindustry transactions in $Z(1)$ were known. For ease of

TABLE 8-2 Differences from Row and Column Margins at Each Step in the RAS Adjustment Procedure

k	$[U(1) - U^k]'$			$[V(1) - V^k]$		
0	152.2130	-97.5530	36.3030	101.1240	-62.2640	52.1030
1	0	0	0	51.9376	-100.4759	48.5383
2	-11.8055	-9.5328	21.3383	0	0	0
3	0	0	0	9.2120	-4.1679	-5.0441
4	-3.4458	$-.0723$	3.5181	0	0	0
5	0	0	0	1.8586	$-.6862$	-1.1724
6	$-.7098$	$-.0024$	.7122	0	0	0
7	0	0	0	.3798	$-.1394$	$-.2404$
8	$-.1452$	$-.0007$	.1459	0	0	0
9	0	0	0	.0778	$-.0286$	$-.0492$
10	$-.0297$	$-.0002$	.0299	0	0	0
11	0	0	0	.0159	$-.0059$	$-.0101$
12	$-.0061$	0	.0061	0	0	0
13	0	0	0	.0033	$-.0012$	$-.0021$

TABLE 8-3 Elements in the Diagonal Matrices R^k and S^k, for $k = 1, \cdots, 7$

k	R			S		
1	2.6405	.5823	1.2959	1.2609	.5157	1.3637
2	.9540	.9345	1.1550	1.0381	.9625	.9730
3	.9861	.9995	1.0226	1.0075	.9936	.9936
4	.9971	1.0000	1.0045	1.0015	.9987	.9987
5	.9994	1.0000	1.0009	1.0003	.9997	.9997
6	.9999	1.0000	1.0002	1.0001	.9999	.9999
7	1.0000	1.0000	1.0000	1.0000	1.0000	1.0000

comparison, we present $\tilde{A}(1)$ and $A(1)$ below.

$$\tilde{A}(1) = \begin{bmatrix} .3924 & .1219 & .1596 \\ .1509 & .0661 & .1897 \\ .0529 & .1887 & .2938 \end{bmatrix} \qquad A(1) = \begin{bmatrix} .2328 & .2535 & .2650 \\ .1544 & .0282 & .2226 \\ .2090 & .0951 & .1555 \end{bmatrix}$$

Define an error matrix, E, as $E = \tilde{A}(1) - A(1)$. Here

$$E = \begin{bmatrix} .1596 & -.1316 & -.1054 \\ -.0035 & .0379 & -.0329 \\ -.1561 & .0936 & .1383 \end{bmatrix}$$

An alternative way to express the errors in each of the coefficients is to convert the elements in E to percentage terms. Define $P = [\,p_{ij}\,]$ where $p_{ij} = [|e_{ij}|/a_{ij}(1)] \times 100$. That is, P contains the absolute values of the errors as a percentage of the corresponding true coefficients in $A(1)$. For this example,

$$P = \begin{bmatrix} 68.6 & 51.9 & 39.8 \\ 2.3 & 134.4 & 14.8 \\ 74.7 & 98.4 & 88.9 \end{bmatrix}$$

Viewed in this way, it is clear that some of the nonsurvey-estimated coefficients are very different from their survey counterparts. For example, the error in a_{22} is over 100 percent; indeed, six of the nine nonsurvey coefficients are in error by more than 50 percent.

We illustrate several measures that are used to compare two matrices—that is, to measure the "difference" between two matrices. The *mean absolute deviation* (MAD) simply averages the elements in E, ignoring sign. Formally,

$$\text{MAD} = \left(\frac{1}{n^2} \right) \sum_{i=1}^{n} \sum_{j=1}^{n} |e_{ij}|$$

where $n = 3$ in this example; here, MAD $= (1/9)(0.8589) = 0.0954$. This represents the average amount (whether positive or negative) by which an estimated coefficient differs from the true coefficient. The *mean absolute percentage error* (MAPE) performs the same averaging on the elements in P. Formally,

$$\text{MAPE} = \left(\frac{1}{n^2} \right) \sum_{i=1}^{n} \sum_{j=1}^{n} p_{ij}$$

For this example, MAPE $= (1/9)(575.38) = 63.76$, which means that, on average, each coefficient will be either 63.8 percent larger or smaller than its true value; that is, it will be "in error" by 63.8 percent. (If the *direction* of error is thought to be important, then we could generate the elements in the P matrix, retaining the signs. However, in that case, it is not very meaningful to find an average over all elements, since positive and negative errors would tend to offset each other.) By these measures (and others, which we need not explore here), the matrix produced by the RAS procedure does not appear to be a particularly good reflection of $A(1)$, the survey-based matrix. At least this is the implication of these measures that examine the element-by-element accuracy of $\tilde{A}(1)$ as compared with $A(1)$.

Another point of view is that while this individual cell accuracy (sometimes called *partitive* accuracy) may be important for some kinds of problems, the ultimate test of a set of coefficients is how well they perform in practice (also sometimes known as *holistic* accuracy).[7] That is, we should be more concerned with the relative accuracy in the Leontief inverse matrices associated with $\tilde{A}(1)$ and $A(1)$. Here

$$[I - A(1)]^{-1} = \begin{bmatrix} 1.5651 & .4684 & .6146 \\ .3463 & 1.1599 & .4144 \\ .4264 & .2465 & 1.3829 \end{bmatrix} \tag{8-33}$$

and

$$[I - \tilde{A}(1)]^{-1} = \begin{bmatrix} 1.7703 & .3298 & .4888 \\ .3310 & 1.1940 & .3955 \\ .2210 & .3438 & 1.5583 \end{bmatrix} \tag{8-34}$$

Comparing column sums of these two matrices—that is, the true output multipliers, $O(1)$, from Eq. (8-33), and the nonsurvey-generated output multipliers, $\tilde{O}(1)$, from Eq. (8-34)—we find

$$O(1) = \begin{bmatrix} 2.3378 & 1.8748 & 2.4119 \end{bmatrix}$$

and

$$\tilde{O}(1) = \begin{bmatrix} 2.3223 & 1.8676 & 2.4426 \end{bmatrix}$$

These appear to be remarkably close. In particular, expressing the differences, $\tilde{O}(1) - O(1)$, as percentages of the true values in $O(1)$, we have

$$\text{Percentage errors in output multipliers} = \begin{bmatrix} -0.66 & -0.38 & 1.27 \end{bmatrix}$$

That is, the worst of the three estimates is in error by only 1.27 percent.

Alternatively, we can compare the performance of $\tilde{A}(1)$ and $A(1)$ in assessing the impact on total outputs associated with an arbitrarily chosen ΔY vector. Let $\Delta Y = \begin{bmatrix} 800 \\ 700 \\ 300 \end{bmatrix}$; then, using the Leontief inverses in Eqs. (8-33) and

---

[7]These terms are from Jensen. See, for example, Jensen (1980).

(8-34), we find

$$\Delta X(1) = \begin{bmatrix} 1764.20 \\ 1213.29 \\ 928.54 \end{bmatrix}$$

and

$$\Delta \tilde{X}(1) = \begin{bmatrix} 1793.74 \\ 1219.25 \\ 884.95 \end{bmatrix}$$

Again, expressing the differences, $\Delta \tilde{X}_i(1) - \Delta X_i(1)$, as a percentage of $\Delta X_i(1)$, we have

$$\text{Percentage errors in output impacts} = \begin{bmatrix} 1.67 \\ 0.49 \\ -4.69 \end{bmatrix}$$

Thus, the effect on the gross output of sector 3 is underestimated by almost 5 percent; the other two outputs are much more accurately estimated.

Conclusions that can be drawn from this example are: (1) the RAS procedure may generate a technical coefficients matrix that does not look very much like an associated full-survey matrix, but (2) an A matrix estimated by RAS may perform relatively well, when converted to its associated Leontief inverse, in terms of such measures as its output multipliers or the sectoral gross outputs that it produces in conjunction with a given ΔY vector.

Economic Content of the RAS Procedure

In the preceding sections, we have illustrated the mathematics of the RAS procedure for adjusting, sequentially, rows and columns of a given coefficient matrix, $A(0)$, in order to generate an estimate of a more recent matrix, $A(1)$, where only $X(1)$, $U(1)$, and $V(1)$ are assumed known for the target year, 1. When the adjustment process is terminated (because the row and column margins are then within the prespecified level of error, ε, from the elements in the observed $U(1)$ and $V(1)$, we have

$$A(1) = RA(0)S \qquad (8\text{-}35)$$

As we have seen, R is a diagonal matrix that is the product of a series of diagonal matrices; $R = [R^n \cdots R^1]$. Similarly, $S = [S^1 \cdots S^n]$ is also a diagonal matrix. The element r_i of R multiplies each element in row i of $A(0)$—for $i = 1, \cdots, n$. The element s_j of S multiplies each element in column j of $A(0)$—for $j = 1, \cdots, n$.

In this "updating" procedure, one might well ask why this kind of uniform proportional change should be expected for the elements in any given row or column of $A(0)$. In the early development of the RAS procedure, Stone (1961) described the uniform changes along any row and down any column as reflecting what he termed the economic phenomena of *substitution effects* and *fabrication effects*, respectively. The former—substitution effects—refers to the emergence of substitutes as production inputs; that is, the substitution of one input for another

—for example, the use (throughout industrial processes) of plastic products in place of metal ones. The implication is that all a_{ij} in the plastics row would increase (for example, be multiplied by 1.4) and all a_{ij} in the metals row would decrease (for example, be multiplied by 0.82). The term *fabrication effect* refers to the altered proportion of value-added items in a sector's total purchases. For example, over time, the product of a particular sector may come to depend more on high-technology capital equipment and/or skilled labor. Thus, a dollar's worth of the product embodies proportionately less of interindustrial inputs and proportionately more of value-added inputs. Thus the a_{ij} in the column representing the industry in question would decrease (for example, be multiplied by 0.79).

To the extent that technological change in the style of production may be reflected in such substitution and fabrication effects, the RAS procedure has a logical economic basis. However, many researchers discount this oversimplified view of the way in which such change is distributed throughout an economy. Instead, they view RAS as a purely mathematical procedure. It can be shown that the RAS technique in fact emerges as the solution to a constrained optimization problem in which, subject to the row and column marginals given in $U(1)$ and $V(1)$, we want to generate a new coefficient matrix, $A(1)$, that "differs" as little as possible from our previous observation, $A(0)$. The underlying logic is simply that, in the absence of *any* new information, we would assume that $A(0)$ is still the best representation of interindustrial relationships. However, *given* some updated information—in $X(1)$, $U(1)$, and $V(1)$—a modified matrix, $A(1)$, will usually be called for. The notion of the "difference" between two matrices is a rather subtle one. Any number of measures of this difference are possible and have been proposed in certain situations. The measure that is minimized by the RAS procedure is

$$D[A(0):A(1)] = \sum_i \sum_j \left\{ a_{ij}(1)\ln\left[\frac{a_{ij}(1)}{a_{ij}(0)}\right] \right\}$$

This turns out to have an interpretation as the "information" measure of distance between $A(0)$ and $A(1)$. In a sense, it generates the $A(1)$ which, given $A(0)$ and the information in $X(1)$, $U(1)$, and $V(1)$, generates the least "surprise." (For the reader who is familiar with constrained optimization problems and Lagrange multiplier techniques, this connection is explored in Appendix 8-1 to this chapter.)

There are two properties of the RAS procedure that bear noting. Signs are preserved in the sense that no original $a_{ij}(0) > 0$ will ever be changed to a negative-valued coefficient. As the fundamental definitions of R and S make clear, all the r_i and s_j modifiers of $A(0)$ are nonnegative. Thus, no matter how much a particular $a_{ij}(0)$ is modified, it will remain nonnegative. Secondly, any $a_{ij}(0)$ that equals zero will remain zero throughout the RAS procedure, since all that happens to it is that it is multiplied by nonnegative numbers. Suppose that sector i represents potatoes and sector j is automobiles. If $a_{ij}(0) = 0$, this represents the (believable) fact that potatoes were not purchased as direct inputs to automobile manufacturing in year 0. The RAS technique assures us that in the updated matrix, $A(1)$, $a_{ij}(1)$ will still be zero. This feature is a mixed blessing. In some cases, such as potatoes and automobiles, it is probably good that a zero-valued coefficient is preserved; potatoes were not used as a direct input to automobiles in year 0 and most probably were not in year 1, either. On the other hand, if sector k is plastics and sector j is automobiles, it may be (if year 0 was long enough ago) that $a_{kj}(0) = 0$, but we know that for our more recent year 1, $a_{kj}(1) \neq 0$. Nevertheless, the RAS procedure by itself will predict $a_{kj}(1) = 0$.

There are a number of other potentially attractive measures of the difference between the elements in the estimated matrix and those in the base-year matrix. Each leads to a different constrained optimization problem and to a different method of generating the estimates from the known data. However, most of these have some disadvantage in comparison to the RAS procedure; for example, they may fail to preserve nonnegativity or they may require solution of large and complex nonlinear programming problems. For a summary of RAS along with some of these alternatives, see Lecomber (Allen and Gossling 1975, Ch. 1) and the Appendix in Hewings and Janson (1980).

Additional Exogenous Information in an RAS Calculation

The RAS technique, as discussed above, assumes only target-year—that is, year 1—information on X, U, and V. It is of course entirely conceivable that one may have particular information about specific transactions or specific coefficients. (If a particular $z_{ij}[1]$ is exogenously known, then since $X_j[1]$ is also known, this is equivalent to knowing $a_{ij}[1]$ exogenously, since $a_{ij}[1] = z_{ij}[1]/X_j[1]$.) The information may come from a survey of a "key" industry in the economy, from an independent forecast of a particular sector's sales to one or more local sectors, and so on.

Suppose that a single $z_{ij}(1)$ is known. Then one can subtract $z_{ij}(1)$ from both $U_i(1)$ and $V_j(1)$, inserting instead a zero in the i, jth cell of $Z(0)$ and hence of $A(0)$. Continuing with our general 3×3 example, suppose $z_{31}(1)$ is known. Since gross output of sector 1 in the target year $X_1(1)$ is also known, this means that $a_{31}(1)$, an element of the matrix $A(1)$, which we want to estimate, is known as well.

We can define $\bar{A}(0)$ to be the original $A(0)$ matrix, as in Eq. (8-1), except that $a_{31}(0)$ has been replaced with a zero. Define a 3×3 matrix K as

$$K = \begin{bmatrix} 0 & 0 & 0 \\ 0 & 0 & 0 \\ a_{31}(1) & 0 & 0 \end{bmatrix}$$

That is, K is the null matrix, with k_{31} replaced by the known target-year coefficient, $a_{31}(1)$. With the amount $z_{31}(1)$ subtracted from $U_3(1)$ and $V_1(1)$, we denote the resulting vectors $\bar{U}(1)$ and $\bar{V}(1)$. These become the relevant marginals, and the RAS procedure is utilized, as usual, but with $\bar{A}(0)$ as the base-year matrix, to be modified according to the (altered) row and column sum information for the target year, $\bar{U}(1)$ and $\bar{V}(1)$. The RAS technique will leave the new zero element, $a_{31}(0)$, unchanged. Thus, when the approximating technique is completed we will have

$$\tilde{A}(1) = K + R\bar{A}(0)S \qquad (8\text{-}36)$$

Clearly, in an economy represented by a larger number of sectors, we may choose to derive estimates of several $z_{ij}(1)$ and hence of several of the target-year coefficients, $a_{ij}(1)$. In fact, if there is a certain "key" sector that is known to play a particularly important role in the economy, an entire column (interindustry inputs to the key sector) and/or an entire row (interindustry sales by the key sector) may be known or independently determined. And indeed there may be more than one key sector. In all of these cases, there is no difference in the approach outlined. Of course, the matrix K will contain more nonzero (known) elements, and the adjustments to $U(1)$ and $V(1)$—to generate $\bar{U}(1)$ and $\bar{V}(1)$—will be more extensive.

Modified Example: One Coefficient Known in Advance

We now present examples in which one of the coefficients in our previous three-sector illustration is set equal to its actual target-year value, $a_{ij}(1)$. Initially, we select a_{31}, and proceed as discussed above. From Eq. (8-30) $a_{31}(1) = 0.2090$, and therefore

$$K = \begin{bmatrix} 0 & 0 & 0 \\ 0 & 0 & 0 \\ .2090 & 0 & 0 \end{bmatrix}$$

and

$$\bar{A}(0) = \begin{bmatrix} .120 & .100 & .049 \\ .210 & .247 & .265 \\ 0 & .249 & .145 \end{bmatrix}$$

(This is $A(0)$ in Eq. (8-25) with a_{31} replaced by 0).

We employ the RAS procedure on $\bar{A}(0)$. We find $\bar{U}(1) = \begin{bmatrix} 245 \\ 136 \\ 71.011 \end{bmatrix}$, which

represents the original $U(1)$, with $U_3(1) = 159$ replaced by $159 - (0.2090)(421) = 159 - 87.989 = 71.011$. That is, the fixed interindustry flow in the target year, from sector 3 to sector 1, is $z_{31}(1) = a_{31}(1)X_1(1) = (0.2090)(421) = 87.989$; this therefore must be netted out of both $U_3(1)$ and $V_1(1)$. Thus, also, $\bar{V}(1) = [163.011 \quad 107 \quad 182]$. As in Eq. (8-36) we find, in this case,

$$\tilde{A}(1) = \begin{bmatrix} .2909 & .1892 & .3527 \\ .0963 & .0884 & .3608 \\ .2090 & .0992 & .2197 \end{bmatrix} \qquad (8\text{-}37)$$

Recall, from Eq. (8-30), that

$$A(1) = \begin{bmatrix} .2328 & .2535 & .2650 \\ .1544 & .0282 & .2226 \\ .2090 & .0951 & .1555 \end{bmatrix}$$

If we calculate the error matrix, $E = \tilde{A}(1) - A(1)$, we find

$$E = \begin{bmatrix} .0581 & -.0643 & .0877 \\ -.0581 & .0602 & .1382 \\ 0 & .0041 & .0642 \end{bmatrix}$$

Using, for illustration, the mean absolute deviation (MAD) measure, we find that here MAD $= (1/9)(0.5349) = 0.0594$. Recall that in the original example, without any prior information on coefficient values, we had a MAD of 0.0954. By this measure, then, the RAS estimate in Eq. (8-37), which includes exogenous information on the value of a_{31} in the target year, is more accurate than was $\tilde{A}(1)$ in Eq. (8-32), above.

Although it may appear logical that the estimate in $\tilde{A}(1)$ will be better whenever we can incorporate prior information about one or more coefficients in the target year, this is not always the case. We illustrate this possibly surprising result by selecting a_{21} instead of a_{31} as the coefficient about which we have prior knowledge. Thus, now

$$K = \begin{bmatrix} 0 & 0 & 0 \\ .1544 & 0 & 0 \\ 0 & 0 & 0 \end{bmatrix}$$

and hence

$$\bar{A}(0) = \begin{bmatrix} .120 & .100 & .049 \\ 0 & .247 & .265 \\ .026 & .249 & .145 \end{bmatrix}$$

Using the RAS procedure, this time with $\bar{U}(1)$ and $\bar{V}(1)$ reflecting changes in $U_2(1)$ and $V_1(1)$, we find

$$\tilde{A}(1) = \begin{bmatrix} .3898 & .1599 & .1621 \\ .1544 & .0838 & .1860 \\ .0520 & .2449 & .2950 \end{bmatrix} \tag{8-38}$$

and

$$E = \begin{bmatrix} .1570 & -.0936 & -.1029 \\ 0 & .0556 & -.0366 \\ -.1570 & .1498 & .1395 \end{bmatrix}$$

Again, using MAD as a measure of closeness of $A(1)$ and $\tilde{A}(1)$, we now find MAD $= (1/9)(0.8920) = 0.0991$. Our original example had MAD $= 0.0954$; hence, at least by this measure of the difference between two matrices, the prior information about one coefficient has resulted in an estimate of $A(1)$ that is worse than the one that was generated with no prior information at all. Thus it is clear that prior information on the true value of a particular cell will not guarantee that the final nonsurvey-generated matrix will be more accurate. (This phenomenon was also noted in Miernyk 1977.)

Table 8-4 presents the MAD measure associated with each of the $\tilde{A}(1)$ matrices that can be generated using prior information on one of the cells in

TABLE 8-4 Mean Absolute Deviation
(MAD), $\tilde{A}(1)$ versus $A(1)$, When
One $a_{ij}(1)$ Is Known in Advance

Element Known in Advance	MAD
None	.0954
a_{11}	.0588
a_{12}	.0824
a_{13}	.0962
a_{21}	.0991
a_{22}	.0882
a_{23}	.0988
a_{31}	.0594
a_{32}	.0925
a_{33}	.0783

$A(1)$. In this small example it happens that there is improvement (as measured by MAD) over the no-prior-information case if a_{11}, a_{12}, a_{22}, a_{31}, a_{32}, or a_{33} is fixed in advance at its target-year value. On the other hand, if the target-year values of a_{13}, a_{21}, or a_{23} are known in advance, the $\tilde{A}(1)$ matrix that results from utilization of the RAS procedure on (in each case) the remaining eight elements in the coefficient matrix is further from $A(1)$, by the MAD measure, than was the $\tilde{A}(1)$ matrix in Eq. (8-32), where no prior information about any target year coefficient was available in advance.

The fact that completely accurate prior information about one of the target-year coefficients can lead to a less-accurate total matrix does not, at first glance, seem very logical. Essentially, the explanation for this odd result is that when one (or more) coefficients are eliminated from the $A(0)$ matrix and replaced by zero, there are fewer nonzero cells available to be altered to meet the remaining row and column marginal requirements. That is, the necessary modifications must be absorbed by a smaller number of elements, with the result that there is an increase in the "burden" of change that is put on each of these elements. The outcome can be a vastly changed smaller number of cells with a resulting overall accuracy measure, such as MAD, that is worse than in the case of no prior information at all.

Summary

This section has described the RAS procedure for updating input-output coefficient tables. It has only discussed the most rudimentary aspects of this partial-survey technique, however. Since RAS was first proposed, there have been many applications at both the national and regional levels. These have also led to developments and modification of the procedure itself. The interested reader is referred to Allen and Gossling (1975) for an overview of some of this work. Also, an examination of the tables of contents or annual indexes of journals in this field—for example, the *Journal of Regional Science*, *Environment and Planning*, *A*, and the *International Regional Science Review*—will disclose a large number of articles with "RAS," "partial-survey techniques," or "nonsurvey techniques" in the title.

8-5 | SPATIAL STABILITY: REGIONALIZING AND EXCHANGING COEFFICIENTS

As noted in Chapter 3, some of the earliest attempts at estimating interindustry relationships at a regional level employed national input coefficients along with estimates of regional supply percentages showing, for each supplying sector, the proportion of total regional requirements of that good that could be expected to originate within the region. Recall that one procedure for obtaining this estimate for sector i was to find the ratio of total regional output, less exports, of sector i, to the total output, less exports, plus imports, of sector i. As in Chapter 3, for a particular region R,

$$p_i^R = \frac{X_i^R - E_i^R}{X_i^R - E_i^R + M_i^R}$$

Thus, when none of good i was imported, $p_i^R = 1$ and the assumption is that all of the region's needs can be supplied internally. The regional input coefficient matrix is then estimated as

$$A^{RR} = \hat{P}A$$

where P is the n-element vector of regional supply proportions and A is the national technical coefficients matrix. As we saw in Chapter 3, this represents a uniform alteration of each of the coefficients in row i of A by p_i^R.

One of the empirical problems with this approach is that data on exports and imports by sector are often not readily available. For that reason, a number of alternatives has been used for estimating the regional proportion of total needs, by sector. As in the case of updating and projecting input-output coefficients, we can distinguish partial-survey and purely nonsurvey techniques for regionalization. By purely nonsurvey techniques we mean those methods that estimate regional input coefficients through adjustment of national technical coefficients entirely on the basis of published information on regional employment, income, or output, by industry. Examples of such approaches are provided by Schaffer and Chu (1969), Hewings (1969, 1971), Round (1972), Morrison and Smith (1974), Eskelinen and Suorsa (1980), Cartwright et al. (1981), and Alward and Palmer (1981). In an early but very complete study, Schaffer and Chu used five such nonsurvey techniques to estimate 1963 regional coefficients, interindustry flows, and exports, and imports (given regional total outputs and final demands by industry) for the state of Washington from the 1958 U.S. input-output tables. The nonsurvey techniques included several versions of location quotients, namely the simple location quotient (SLQ), the purchases-only location quotient (PLQ), the cross-industry quotient (CIQ), and also a supply-demand pool technique (SDP). We will examine these in turn. (Round 1983 provides a thorough overview of various partial survey and nonsurvey approaches.)

As we saw in Section 8-2, above, a regional input coefficient, a_{ij}^{RR}, is defined as the difference between a regional technical coefficient, a_{ij}^{R}, and a regional import coefficient, $a_{ij}^{\bar{R}R}$. (Also as above, when it is clear what particular region is intended, the simpler notation $r_{ij} = a_{ij} - m_{ij}$ is used.) If we have available a complete set of intra- and interregional data (as is needed in constructing an interregional input-output model, for example), then we observe the a_{ij}^{RR}'s (and $a_{ij}^{\tilde{R}R}$'s) directly. However, if we are trying to estimate a_{ij}^{RR} from national data, it is often more useful to pose the estimation problem in the following way: (1) estimate a regional technical coefficient, a_{ij}^{R}, from the corresponding national coefficient, a_{ij}^{N}, and (2) estimate the regional input coefficient, a_{ij}^{RR}, as some proportion of the regional technical coefficient; that is, $a_{ij}^{RR} = p_{ij}^{R} a_{ij}^{R}$ (where $0 \le p_{ij}^{R} \le 1$). Instead of estimating a_{ij}^{R} and a_{ij}^{RR}, we estimate a_{ij}^{R} and p_{ij}^{R}. The two steps in this procedure for estimating a_{ij}^{RR} from a_{ij}^{N} would therefore be: (1) find $\alpha_{ij}^{R} \ge 0$ such that

$$a_{ij}^{R} = \left(\alpha_{ij}^{R} \right) \left(a_{ij}^{N} \right) \qquad (8\text{-}39)$$

and (2) find β_{ij}^{R} ($0 \le \beta_{ij}^{R} \le 1$) such that

$$a_{ij}^{RR} = \left(\beta_{ij}^{R} \right) \left(a_{ij}^{R} \right) \qquad (8\text{-}40)$$

Of course, if we indeed can find α_{ij}^{R} and β_{ij}^{R} for every i and j, this is equivalent to finding

$$a_{ij}^{RR} = \left(\gamma_{ij}^{R} \right) \left(a_{ij}^{N} \right)$$

where $\gamma_{ij}^{R} = (\alpha_{ij}^{R})(\beta_{ij}^{R})$

The basic point is that in general we do not have enough regional information to find the α_{ij}^{R}'s and β_{ij}^{R}'s.[8] For example, in the simple procedure described at the beginning of this section, we see that (1) a_{ij}^{R} was assumed equal to a_{ij}^{N}; in terms of Eq. (8-39), $\alpha_{ij}^{R} = 1$ for all i and j (region R and national production recipes are identical) and (2) each regional purchaser, j, of input i was assumed to buy the same proportion of those inputs from within the region; in terms of Eq. (8-40), $\beta_{ij}^{R} = p_{i}^{R}$ for all i. We will now see where several of the nonsurvey techniques for regionalization of national coefficients fit in the general scheme given by Eqs. (8-39) and (8-40).

Location Quotients and Related Techniques

Simple Location Quotients   Let X_{i}^{R} and X^{R} denote gross output of sector i and total output, respectively, in region R and, similarly, X_{i}^{N} and X^{N} denote these totals at the national level. Then the simple location quotient for sector i in region R is defined as

$$LQ_{i}^{R} = \left[\frac{X_{i}^{R}/X^{R}}{X_{i}^{N}/X^{N}} \right] \qquad (8\text{-}41)$$

---

[8]Some writers—for example, Round (1978a), have termed the β_{ij}^{R}'s "trading coefficients." This should not be confused with the use of the term "trade coefficients" for the a_{ij}^{LM} ($L \ne M$) in the interregional input-output model or for the c_{i}^{LM} ($L \ne M$) in the multiregional input-output model, as in Chapter 3.

In cases where output data are not consistently available (for example, at the regional level), other measures of relative size are often used—employment, personal income earned, value added, and so on, by sector.

The interpretation of this measure is as follows. The numerator in Eq. (8-41) represents the proportion of region R's total output contributed by sector i. The denominator in Eq. (8-41) represents the proportion of total national output that is contributed by sector i, nationally. If $LQ_i^R = (0.034)/(0.017) = 2$, we understand that sector i output represents 3.4 percent of all region R's gross output while, at the national level, sector i's output represents only 1.7 percent of the total national output. In a case like this—in fact, whenever $LQ_i^R > 1$—it is said that sector i is more localized, or concentrated, in region R than in the nation as a whole. Conversely, if $LQ_i^R = (0.015)/(0.045) = 0.33$, we understand that while sector i's output is 4.5 percent of the total national gross output, it represents only 1.5 percent of the gross output in region R. In this situation, sector i is less localized, or less concentrated, in region R than in the nation as a whole.

In estimating regional from national coefficients, the simple location quotient has been viewed as a measure of the ability of regional industry i to supply the demands placed upon it by other industries in the region and by regional final demand. If industry i is less concentrated in the region than in the nation ($LQ_i^R < 1$), it is viewed as less capable of satisfying regional demand for its output, and its regional direct input coefficients, a_{ij}^{RR} ($j = 1, \cdots, n$) are estimated from the national coefficients, a_{ij}^N, by multiplying them by LQ_i^R. However, if industry i is more highly concentrated in the region than in the nation ($LQ_i^R > 1$), then it is assumed that the national coefficients, a_{ij}^N ($j = 1, \cdots, n$) will apply to the region, and the regional "surplus" produced by i will be exported to the rest of the nation. Thus, for row i of an estimated regional table,

$$a_{ij}^{RR} = \begin{cases} a_{ij}^N (LQ_i^R) & \text{if } LQ_i^R < 1 \\ a_{ij}^N & \text{if } LQ_i^R \geq 1 \end{cases} \tag{8-42}$$

In terms of the general scheme in Eqs. (8-39) and (8-40), we see that this procedure is equivalent to (1) assuming $\alpha_{ij}^R = 1$ for all i and j and (2) letting $\beta_{ij}^R = LQ_i^R$ when $LQ_i^R < 1$ and $\beta_{ij}^R = 1$ when $LQ_i^R \geq 1$. There is therefore a kind of asymmetry in this approach. When a sector is import oriented ($LQ_i^R < 1$), the modification of the national coefficient varies with the strength of the import orientation—$a_{ij}^{RR} = (LQ_i^R)a_{ij}^N$. When a sector is export oriented ($LQ_i^R > 1$), the strength of this orientation is not reflected in the modification—$a_{ij}^{RR} = (1)a_{ij}^N$.

The SLQ technique requires only comparably defined data on regional and national output, or employment, or value added, and so on, by industry. However, a complication arises from the fact that the estimates of regional industry output that are obtained using SLQ coefficients may exceed actual output for some industries. Thus, coefficients developed by this method have often been "balanced" to ensure that they do not overestimate regional output by sector. The notion of a balancing method is simply that if estimated regional coefficients generate a regional output for sector i that is too large, then the estimates of a_{ij}^{RR} (for all j) should be uniformly reduced.

For example, calculate estimated sector i output on the basis of *actual* regional industry outputs (if they are available) and the *SLQ*-estimated regional input coefficients (and regional final-demand purchase coefficients). For sector i, this is

$$\tilde{X}_i = \sum_j a_{ij}^{RR} X_j + \sum_f c_{if}^{RR} y_f \tag{8-43}$$

where

$\tilde{X}_i$ = estimated regional output of sector i,

y_f = total regional final demand of final-demand sector f, and

c_{if}^{RR} = estimated regional final-demand purchase coefficient of regional final-demand sector f from industry i.

The c_{if}^{RR} elements reflect purchases of regionally produced output i by regional final-demand sector f. Typically, the regional final-demand sectors will be personal consumption expenditures, investment, state and local government, as well as both foreign and rest-of-the-country exports (a part of which will be federal government purchases, except for those purchases made by federal installations located in the region). Estimates of c_{if}^{RR} are found in much the same manner as were the a_{ij}^{RR}; that is, using national data and the region-specific location quotients. In particular,

$$c_{if}^{RR} = \begin{cases} c_{if}^N \left(LQ_i^R \right) & \text{if } LQ_i^R < 1 \\ c_{if}^N & \text{if } LQ_i^R \geq 1 \end{cases} \tag{8-44}$$

where

$c_{if}^N = \dfrac{Y_{if}}{Y_f}$, and

Y_{if} = national sales of industry i to final-demand sector f, and

Y_f = total national purchases of final-demand sector f.

Thus, when $LQ_i^R \geq 1$, it is assumed that purchases of good i by final-demand sector f are the same proportion of total sector f purchases in the region as in the nation. For example, if purchases of electricity (sector i) by consumers (final-demand sector f) constitute 3 percent of total consumer expenditures nationally, and if $LQ_i^R \geq 1$, then it is assumed that 3 percent of the total expenditures by consumers in region R will be on electricity produced in region R; $c_{if}^{RR} = 0.03$. When $LQ_i^R < 1$, then the national proportion is modified downward. If $LQ_i^R = 0.67$, then it would be assumed that only 2 percent of the total expenditures by consumers in region R will be on electricity produced in region R: $c_{if}^{RR} = 0.02$.

The next step in the balancing procedure is to calculate the ratio of estimated to actual regional output; denote this by Z_i. Then

$$Z_i = \frac{\tilde{X}_i}{X_i} \tag{8-45}$$

Each row of estimated regional input coefficients for which Z_i is greater than one is adjusted downward. That is, an adjusted ("balanced") set of regional input coefficients are estimated as

$$\bar{a}_{ij}^{RR} = \begin{cases} a_{ij}^{RR}(1/Z_i) & \text{if } Z_i > 1 \\ a_{ij}^{RR} & \text{if } Z_i \leq 1 \end{cases} \tag{8-46}$$

There are several variants of the simple location quotient approach, all of which are used in the same general way in adjusting national to regional coefficients. Since the SLQ approach in Eq. (8-42), above, will never increase a national coefficient (they are either left unchanged or made smaller), this procedure is also called *reducing* the national coefficients table, and hence these are sometimes referred to as *reduction* techniques.

Purchases-Only Location Quotients   The purchases-only location quotient (PLQ) for sector i in region R relates regional to national ability to supply sector i inputs, but only to those sectors that use i as an input. That is,

$$PLQ_i^R = \left[\frac{X_i^R / X^{*R}}{X_i^N / X^{*N}} \right] \tag{8-47}$$

where X_i^R and X_i^N are regional and national output of good i, as before, and where X^{*R} and X^{*N} are total regional and national output of only those sectors that use i as an input. The idea here is simply that if input i is not used by sector k, then the size of sector k's output is not really relevant in determining whether or not the region can supply all of its needs for input i. (Whether or not region R can supply all of its needs for potatoes [sector i] is not affected by the automobile production [sector k] in region R, since potatoes are not a direct input to automobile manufacturing.) PLQ_i^R is used in the same way as LQ_i^R to uniformly adjust the elements in row i of a national coefficients table.

Cross-Industry Quotients   Another variant is the cross-industry quotient (CIQ). This allows for differing modifiers within a given row of the national matrix; that is, it allows for differing cell-by-cell adjustments within $A(N)$ rather than uniform adjustments along each row. What is now of interest is the relative importance of both selling sector i and buying sector j in the region and in the nation. That is,

$$CIQ_{ij}^R = \left[\frac{X_i^R / X_i^N}{X_j^R / X_j^N} \right] \tag{8-48}$$

Then

$$a_{ij}^{RR} = \begin{cases} a_{ij}^N(CIQ_{ij}^R) & \text{if } CIQ_{ij}^R < 1 \\ a_{ij}^N & \text{if } CIQ_{ij}^R \geq 1 \end{cases} \tag{8-49}$$

The idea is that if the output of regional sector i relative to the national output of i is larger than the output of regional sector j relative to the national output of sector j (that is, $CIQ_{ij}^R > 1$), then all of j's needs of input i can be supplied from within the region. Similarly, if sector i at the regional level is relatively smaller than sector j at the regional level ($CIQ_{ij}^R < 1$), then it is assumed that some of j's needs for i inputs will have to be imported. Note that, algebraically, $CIQ_{ij}^R = LQ_i^R/LQ_j^R$.

Supply-Demand Pool Approaches The supply-demand pool technique estimates regional from national coefficients in much the same way as the procedure described above was used to balance the regional coefficients estimated by the simple location quotient technique. National technical coefficients are taken as the first approximation to regional coefficients. Regional output by sector is then found, as above, by multiplying each of these coefficients by the appropriate actual regional output of that sector (and similarly for final-demand sectors, but using the *national* final-demand input proportions, c_{if}^N) and summing. That is,

$$\tilde{X}_i^R = \sum_j a_{ij}^N X_j^R + \sum_f c_{if}^N Y_f \tag{8-50}$$

Then the regional commodity balance, b_i, is calculated for industry i as $b_i = X_i^R - \tilde{X}_i^R$. If this balance is positive (or zero), using national coefficients as estimates of regional coefficients does not generate an overestimate of regional production and $a_{ij}^{RR} = a_{ij}^N$ and $c_{if}^{RR} = c_{if}^N$. However, if the balance is negative, national coefficients are "too large" in the sense that they generate unrealistically high regional outputs, by sector, so $a_{ij}^{RR} = a_{ij}^N(X_i^R/\tilde{X}_i^R)$ and $c_{if}^{RR} = c_{if}^N(X_i^R/\tilde{X}_i^R)$. That is, the national coefficients are reduced by the amount necessary to make the regional balance for that sector exactly zero.

$$a_{ij}^{RR} = \begin{cases} a_{ij}^N(X_i^R/\tilde{X}_i^R) & \text{if } b_i < 0 \\ a_{ij}^N & \text{if } b_i \geq 0 \end{cases} \tag{8-51}$$

In terms of the general approaches in Eqs. (8-39) and (8-40), we see that the supply-demand pool technique assumes that $\alpha_{ij}^R = 1$, as do all of the quotient techniques mentioned above. Further, $\beta_{ij}^R = X_i^R/\tilde{X}_i^R$ when $X_i^R - \tilde{X}_i^R < 0$ and $\beta_{ij}^R = 1$ when $X_i^R - \tilde{X}_i^R \geq 0$.

Fabrication Effects Round (1972, 1978) has suggested an adjustment of a national coefficient, a_{ij}^N, to estimate a regional technical coefficient, a_{ij}^R. Define the regional fabrication effect for sector j in region R, ρ_j^R,

$$\rho_j^R = \frac{[1 - (W_j^R/X_j^R)]}{[1 - (W_j^N/X_j^N)]} \tag{8-52}$$

In the numerator, W_j^R is value-added payments by sector j in region R and X_j^R is, as usual, gross output of sector j in R. Thus (W_j^R/X_j^R) is the proportion of the total output of sector j in region R accounted for by value-added elements; hence $[1 - (W_j^R/X_j^R)]$ is the proportion of total output due to inputs from the processing sectors (including imports). Roughly, then, the expression in brackets represents the relative dependence of sector j in region R on inputs from itself and all other sectors. For example, if $W_j^R = \$400$ and $X_j^R = \$1000$, then

$[1 - (W_j^R/X_j^R)] = 0.6$; 60 percent of the value of sector j's total output is derived from inputs from the producing sectors. The denominator in Eq. (8-52) is this same measure of industrial dependence for sector j nationally. Suppose $W_j^N = \$3000$ and $X_j^N = \$10,000$, so that the denominator in Eq. (8-52) is 0.7; at the aggregate national level sector j is relatively more dependent on industrial inputs and relatively less dependent on value-added inputs. For this example, $\rho_j^R = 0.6/0.7 = 0.857$.

Round suggests that ρ_j^R be used as α_{ij}^R in Eq. (8-39); that is, that the estimate of a_{ij}^R (for $i = 1, \cdots, n$) be found as

$$a_{ij}^R = \left(\rho_j^R\right)\left(a_{ij}^N\right)$$

That is, the entire jth column of $A(N)$ is multiplied by ρ_j^R to generate an estimate of the jth column of $A(R)$. The idea is that since sectoral outputs are relatively less important to industry j's production at the regional than at the national level, national input coefficients for sector j should be scaled down. Similarly, if $\rho_k^R > 1$, then all of the elements in the kth column of $A(N)$ would be scaled upward, to generate the estimates of a_{ik}^R ($i = 1, \cdots, n$).

Note that this "fabrication" adjustment is similar in spirit to the column adjustments (the s's) in the RAS updating procedure, which multiply all elements in the kth column of the coefficient matrix by s_k. (This was, in fact, to adjust for what Stone termed the "fabrication effect"—the possibility that there is a change in the proportion of value-added inputs in a sector's output over time.)

Regional Purchase Coefficients   Work at the Regional Science Research Institute (as discussed, for example, in Stevens and Trainer 1976, 1980 and in Stevens et al. 1983) has concentrated on estimation of what are essentially the regional supply proportions, p_i^R, that were mentioned at the beginning of this section (and earlier in Chapter 3). These have been termed *regional purchase coefficients* (*RPC*'s) in the RSRI work. In contrast to Round's fabrication effect that operates uniformly on columns of $A(N)$, the regional purchase coefficient approach alters $A(N)$ uniformly across rows. In terms of Eq. (8-39), $\alpha_{ij}^R = 1$ and, in Eq. (8-40), $\beta_{ij}^R = p_i^R$ ($= RPC_i^R$).

The regional purchase coefficient for a sector is defined as the proportion of regional demand for that sector's output that is fulfilled from regional production. Formally, for region R and good i,

$$RPC_i^R = z_i^{RR}/\left(z_i^{RR} + z_i^{\tilde{R}R}\right)$$

where, as in Chapter 3, z_i^{RR} accounts for shipments of good i from producers in R to all buyers in R and $z_i^{\tilde{R}R}$ represents imports of i from outside R to buyers in R.[9] Rewriting, by dividing numerator and denominator by z_i^{RR},

$$RPC_i^R = 1/\left[1 + 1/\left(z_i^{RR}/z_i^{\tilde{R}R}\right)\right]$$

---

[9] In the context of the multiregional input-output model (Chapter 3), these coefficients are the c_i^{RR}'s—for example, as in Eq. (3-27). However, in the MRIO model, they are used to modify a *regional* matrix, $A(R)$, that is not assumed simply to be the same as $A(N)$, the national table. In terms of Eqs. (8-39) and (8-40), in the MRIO model $\alpha_{ij}^R \neq 1$, at least for some i, j and R, and $\beta_{ij}^R = c_i^{RR}$ for all i.

Effort has been concentrated on estimating the magnitude of the *relative shipments* term, $z_i^{RR}/z_i^{\bar{R}R}$. Assuming that *relative* terms designate ratios of region R values to national values, relative shipments are estimated as a function of relative delivered costs (made up of relative unit production costs and relative unit shipment costs). These, in turn, depend on relative wages, relative output levels, and average shipping distances from producers within and outside region R. A relationship between RPC_i^R and proxies for these relative terms has been proposed and fitted by regression techniques to data that are available in U.S. published sources such as *County Business Patterns*, *Census of Transportation*, and *Census of Manufactures*, as well as a national input-output technical coefficients table. Comparisons of a survey-based table for the state of Washington with a table generated using regional purchase coefficients were viewed as "not disappointing" (Stevens et al. 1983, p. 280), and efforts at refining the approach are continuing.

Summary   It has been shown in empirical studies—for example, in Morrison and Smith (1974) and in Sawyer and Miller (1983)—that in general the simple location quotient method is the best of the various location quotient techniques and is also generally better than the supply-demand pool approaches. Thus, although there have been other variations or refinements on both location quotient and supply-demand pool techniques, we do not review them here. (The interested reader should turn, for example, to Schaffer 1976 or Isserman 1980.) In fact, it is generally recognized that these nonsurvey approaches (as might be expected) provide less-accurate estimates than do partial-survey techniques. In particular, the RAS procedure, while originally devised for updating input-output information, has been employed, with some success, for regionalization. We turn to it next.

The RAS Procedure in a Regional Setting

The RAS technique generates a coefficient matrix for a particular year, $A(1)$, given observations on total outputs, total interindustry sales, and total interindustry purchases for that year—$X(1)$, $U(1)$, and $V(1)$, and using as a starting point an earlier coefficient matrix, $A(0)$. While it is inherently a mathematical technique, we have seen that the economic notions of uniform substitution and fabrication effects are compatible with the procedure. Since coefficient tables for regional input-output models are essential for regional analysis, one way to have a wider variety of tables available for various regions of a nation is to apply the same RAS principles, where we utilize a *national* input-output table, $A(N)$, and marginal information about *regional* economic activity—$X(R)$, $U(R)$, and $V(R)$. Or, for that matter, instead of $A(N)$, one may have an input-output table for some *other* region in the country, R', and then use the known $A(R')$ as the matrix to be adjusted to satisfy the observed marginal information for the region of interest, R. Thus, instead of using the RAS procedure to adjust coefficient matrices across time (the updating problem), it has also been used to adjust coefficient matrices across space (the regionalization problem). To the extent that a national table, $A(N)$, reflects an average of input-output relationships in various regions of the nation, the minimization of "information distance" or "surprise" that is inherent in the RAS technique may also be appropriate at the regional level. Or if there is an input-output coefficient table for a region, R', that is thought to be economically similar to the region in question, R, then this same "minimal surprise" characteristic of the RAS procedure is possibly an attractive one.

Many studies have included the RAS approach, often along with one or more of the purely nonsurvey techniques mentioned above, in examining the feasibility of regionalization of a national input-output table. An early example is provided by Czamanski and Malizia (1969); other examples are to be found in Morrison and Smith (1974) and Sawyer and Miller (1983). On the problem of updating a regional table via RAS-like techniques, see, among others, McMenamin and Haring (1974) (and also the Giarratani 1975 comment on this work)[10] and Malizia and Bond (1974). There has been a great deal of work by Jensen and his colleagues in Australia deriving input-output tables for various regions of that country, using a national table and an RAS approach modified when additional region-specific data are available. They have named this the GRIT technique—for *g*eneration of *r*egional *i*nput-output *t*ables. (See, for example, Jensen et al. 1979.) As was also noted at the end of section 8-4 in a national context, there are many, many more examples of the use of the RAS technique, with or without modifications, at the regional level. Indeed, because of the relative scarcity of regional data, RAS procedures are probably more intensively utilized for regionalization of a national (or other-region) table or for updating a regional table than for updating national tables.

Exchanging Coefficients Matrices

An alternative to adapting a national table to reflect the economic characteristics of a particular region might be to adapt an existing table for some other region or, indeed, simply to use a table for one region as representing another region as well. For example, a coefficients table for a particular wheat-growing county in North Dakota could reflect very well the economic interrelations in another wheat-growing county in North Dakota, or probably also in South Dakota or Nebraska. However, whether or not the survey-based table for Philadelphia would be directly transferable to Boston or (less likely) San Francisco—or how much and what kind of modification would be necessary before it was useful for a different city—are more complicated questions. In this regard, one can only make very broad and general statements; for example, if in the opinion of experts two regions are very similar economically, then it is possible that a coefficients table for one of them will prove to be useful for the other also. Or it may be useful with appropriate modification; the problem is always how to decide what needs to be modified and how to go about doing it.

[10]A particular feature of the McMenamin-Haring approach is that it employs the RAS technique on an entire transactions table, including the sales to final-demand sectors and the purchases from value-added sectors. That is, $U(R)$ and $V(R)$ are not needed; only $X(R)$ is used. This relaxes the data requirements but imposes the biproportionality assumption on not only the interindustry transactions but also on final-demand and value-added data. This is the basic point raised by Giarratani (1975).

As an example of coefficient exchange at the regional level, Hewings (1977) used a survey-based table for Washington State for 1963 (Bourque and Weeks 1969) to estimate Kansas interindustry structure in 1965; he also used a survey-based Kansas table for 1965 (Emerson 1969) to estimate Washington's structure in 1963. After appropriate classification of the two tables into a comparable set of sectors, it was clear from inspection that there were many individual coefficients that were vastly different in the two tables. In a simple coefficient change, estimating Washington sectoral output with Kansas technology, as $X^W = (I - A^{KK})^{-1} Y^W$ and similarly, estimating Kansas sectoral output with Washington technology, $X^K = (I - A^{WW})^{-1} Y^K$, it was found that aggregate errors (for total output, summed over all sectors) were 4.8 percent (overestimate) for Washington and -12.6 percent (underestimate) for Kansas. However, as usual, individual sector estimates were often very far off; the worst in Washington was overestimated by 336 percent and the worst in Kansas was overestimated by 114 percent. Thus, straightforward coefficient exchange was not particularly satisfactory.

However, using the RAS procedure in conjunction with Kansas survey-based information on total intermediate outputs, total intermediate inputs, and total output, by sector, produced far superior results. That is, the Washington table (instead of a national table) was "balanced" by the RAS technique to conform to the observed Kansas marginal information. With the modification, total estimated Kansas output was underestimated by only 0.008 percent, and the largest error for an individual sector's output was only 0.195 percent.

To emphasize the relative importance of the marginal information in the RAS procedure, Hewings also "balanced" an artificial coefficient matrix made up of random numbers (but with column sums less than one, to conform to expected Hawkins-Simon conditions for an input coefficients matrix). That is, the "base" matrix was a totally artificial one, which did not correspond to any national or regional table. Using a randomly generated new final-demand vector, Hewings compared "true" gross outputs (using the actual Kansas table) with the RAS-adjusted Washington table and the RAS-adjusted random table. In these two cases, the total Kansas output, summed over all sectors, was overestimated by only 0.028 percent and underestimated by 0.192 percent, respectively. The worst errors in individual sector outputs were 3.7 percent (Washington table) and 5.6 percent (random table). The main lesson from this experiment appears to be that region-specific sectoral total intermediate output and input information, along with sectoral gross outputs, are of dominant importance in an RAS adjustment procedure. (For a comment on the Hewings study and a reply, see Thumann 1978 and Hewings and Janson 1980.)

Estimating Interregional Flows

We have examined some of the techniques that have been proposed and used to estimate regional input coefficients from existing regional or national tables. If two or more regions are to be connected in the model, then some kind of interregional coefficients are also needed. In Chapter 3 we saw what data are necessary in both the interregional and multiregional cases, and examples were provided from the Japanese interregional and the U.S. multiregional models.

Because of the extremely detailed data that are necessary for a full interregional model and because the U.S. multiregional model was itself an extremely ambitious and time-consuming project, there are not many existing tables of interregional coefficients available to be used as "base" tables to be updated, projected, or exchanged. Rather, a number of proposals have been explored for estimating these flows between sectors and regions. The techniques are sometimes relatively advanced, and a thorough survey is beyond the scope of this book. We indicate only some of the broad ideas that have been used.

Some methods are simplifications or variants of the quotient techniques that were discussed above. Essentially, they use some measure of a region's import or export orientation with respect to each good; and if region R is found to be an exporter of good i, then it is assumed that all the requirements for i in region R will be met by local production and hence there will be no imports of i to region R. One important feature in the two-region interregional case is that one region's exports of a particular good are the other region's imports. From Eq. (8-40), $a_{ij}^{RR} = (\beta_{ij}^R)(a_{ij}^R)$ and so, in a two-region interregional model (with regions R and S), $a_{ij}^{SR} = (1 - \beta_{ij}^R)(a_{ij}^R)$. Moreover, the logic behind location quotient kinds of procedures is that if $\beta_{ij}^R < 1$ then $\beta_{ij}^S = 1$. (That is, if sector j in region R cannot have its needs for good i supplied wholly from within that region, then some i will be imported from region S. But region S will only be an exporter of good i if it produces more than enough to completely satisfy demands for i by sector j in the region.)

A simple quotient-like procedure was used in Nevin, Roe, and Round (1966) for a two-region model in the United Kingdom and by Vanwynsberghe (1976) for a three-region Belgian model. Examination of a wide variety of nonsurvey techniques in an interregional setting is contained in a series of papers by Round (1972, 1978a, 1978b, 1979), to which the interested reader is referred. An alternative approach used in several Swedish regional studies is outlined in Andersson (1975) and modifications are suggested in Bigsten (1981).

Versions of gravity model formulations have also been proposed and explored for the purpose of estimating commodity flows between regions. The basic idea is that the flow of good i from region R to region S can be looked upon as a function of (1) some measure of the total output of i in R, X_i^R, (2) some measure of the total purchases of i in S, P_i^S, and (3) the distance between the two regions, D^{RS}. One straightforward function, taking inspiration from Newton's observations on gravity (and hence the name for this class of models), would involve the product of the two "masses" (X_i^R and P_i^S) divided by the square of the distance. A bit more generally,

$$z_i^{RS} = \frac{\left(c_i^R X_i^R\right)\left(d_i^S P_i^S\right)}{\left(D^{RS}\right)^{e_i}} = \left(k_i^{RS}\right)\frac{X_i^R P_i^S}{\left(D^{RS}\right)^{e_i}}$$

where c_i^R, d_i^S (alternatively, k_i^{RS}) and e_i are parameters to be estimated. (In the strictest Newtonian form, $e_i = 2$.) Extensions would attempt to estimate the specific flow from i in R to j in S; that is, z_{ij}^{RS}. This might be attempted as

$$z_{ij}^{RS} = \frac{\left(c_i^R X_i^R\right)\left(d_j^S X_j^S\right)}{\left(D^{RS}\right)^{e_i}} = \left(k_{ij}^{RS}\right)\frac{X_i^R X_j^S}{\left(D^{RS}\right)^{e_i}}$$

Alternatively, the "mass" terms have also been represented as $(X_i^R)^{c_i^R}$ rather than $(c_i^R X_i^R)$, and so forth.

The gravity approach was suggested in Leontief and Strout (1963) and explored in Theil (1967). Polenske (1970a) tested the gravity approach, using Japanese interregional flow data. She also compared the gravity formulation with the approach used in the MRIO model (section 3-4) and one other alternative. The gravity and MRIO estimates were about equally good and far better than those obtained by the alternative method (Polenske 1970b). Estimates based on gravity models have also appeared in Uribe, de Leeuw, and Theil (1966) and Gordon (1976) among others. The gravity approach was embedded in a general entropy-maximizing framework in a number of papers by Wilson. An overview is provided by Wilson (1970, especially Chapter 3). Connections with information theory have been suggested, and this has been thoroughly explored by Batten (1982, 1983) and applied in Snickars (1979). Batten's empirical studies combine iterative (RAS-like) methods with a maximum entropy formulation and, if required, additional variations ("minimum information gain" procedures). (See Batten 1983, especially Chapter 5 and Appendix E.)

8-6 | THE RECONCILIATION ISSUE

In section 8-1, above, we noted that problems can arise in constructing survey-based interindustry transactions tables when the row total for a sector differs from the column total for that same sector. Since one approach to the resolution of this reconciliation problem uses an RAS approach, this discussion was postponed until we had introduced the RAS technique in its more usual updating or regionalization role.

Some input-output tables (especially at the regional level) have been constructed exclusively on the basis of information on purchases by sectors in the economy. Establishments in each sector (usually a *sample* of those establishments) are asked to identify the magnitudes of their inputs, by sector and by region—or at least whether the input came from inside the region in question or was imported from outside that region. This is sometimes known as the "purchases only" or "columns only" approach, since the transactions table (and hence the direct-input coefficients matrix) is compiled column by column. It depends on information from establishments regarding the distribution of their costs. (This was used in constructing the 496-sector Philadelphia table for 1959; see Isard and Langford 1971.) Similarly, a "sales only" or "rows only" procedure depends entirely upon information on the magnitudes of sales from a particular sector to all other regional sectors, and to final-demand purchasers. This relies on information from establishments regarding the distribution of their products. (For a study that used this approach, see Hansen and Tiebout 1963.)

Frequently, one will have some (but not complete) information on purchases and some (but also not complete) information on sales. (For example, from a questionnaire in which firms are asked for data on both sales and purchases.) Thus for many cells there may be two estimates of the z_{ij} transaction. If one has independent estimates of regional total gross outputs, X_j, from published sources, this of course means that there will be two estimates of the regional direct-input coefficient. The issue then is one of reconciling the two estimates. (Examples of empirical studies using both row and column information include Bourque et al. 1967, Beyers et al. 1970, Bourque and Conway 1977, Miernyk et al. 1967, and Miernyk et al. 1970.)

Often, the reconciliation is made entirely on the basis of the judgment of the researchers, reflecting their knowledge of the regional economy and comparisons with national coefficients; Bourque et al. (1967) provides one such example. Building on the general discussion in Miernyk et al. (1970), in which an attempt was made to estimate the relative accuracy (reliability) of various pieces of information, Jensen and McGaurr (1976) propose a two-stage procedure. Let the two transactions estimates for the i, jth cell be r_{ij} and c_{ij}, from the "rows-only" and "columns-only" information. On the basis of knowledge of sampling procedures and other features of the data and of probable sources of error, a pair of what have been termed *reliability weights* (Jensen and McGaurr 1976) are chosen for the two estimates. Let k_{ij} denote this weight for the rows-only estimate ($k_{ij} \geq 0$), then ($1 - k_{ij}$) will be the weight for the columns-only estimate. Then, a first approximation to the reconciled transactions estimate for the i, jth cell is found as the simple weighted sum $z_{ij}(1) = k_{ij}r_{ij} + (1 - k_{ij})c_{ij}$. The 1 represents the fact that this is a first estimate. For example, if one were certain that a rows-only estimate, r_{ij}, were completely accurate, its k_{ij} would be 1.0; if, in the judgment of the researchers, the row and column estimates for a particular cell were equally likely to be correct, k_{ij} would be 0.5 for that cell, and so on.

In addition to the total output vector, X, suppose that independent estimates have been made of the magnitudes of final-demand purchases from each sector, Y_i, so that the final-demand column vector is known, and also assume that there are estimates of all value-added payments by each sector (including imports), $\overline{W}_j$, so that the value-added row vector, $\overline{W}$, is also known. Then the total value of interindustry transactions is given by $T = i'(X - Y) = \sum_i (X_i - Y_i)$, or, equivalently, by $T = (X - \overline{W})i = \sum_j (X_j - \overline{W}_j)$. It is then necessary to check the total of the estimated transactions, $Z(1) = \sum_i \sum_j z_{ij}(1)$, against this (independently estimated) total figure, T. If, as is very likely, these are not equal, each $z_{ij}(1)$ is scaled upward or downward through multiplication by $T/Z(1)$. This produces a second set of estimates of reconciled transactions, $z_{ij}(2) = z_{ij}(1)[T/Z(1)]$. These estimates are consistent in the aggregate, in that $\sum_i \sum_j z_{ij}(2) = T$. This concludes stage one.

While the transactions $z_{ij}(2)$ have now been adjusted so that they sum to the proper aggregate flow, they must also be consistent with the *individual* row and column sums. Since X_i and Y_i have been independently estimated, then total intermediate output for each sector, U_i, is found as $U_i = X_i - Y_i$. Similarly, given estimates of $\overline{W}_j$ also, then total intermediate input for each sector, V_j, is found as $V_j = X_j - \overline{W}_j$. The issue then is whether or not $\sum_j z_{ij}(2) = U_i$, for each sector $(i = 1, \cdots, n)$ and also whether or not $\sum_i z_{ij}(2) = V_j$, for each sector $(j = 1, \cdots, n)$. In general, not all of these constraining equations will be met, and so the estimates in $z_{ij}(2)$ must be further adjusted to conform to the marginal information for each row and each column. This is exactly the kind of problem for which the RAS technique is suited, and it is the procedure that is suggested by Jensen and McGaurr. This is stage two of the adjustment. The result will be a third and final set of transactions estimates, $z_{ij}(3)$. Given the estimates of X_j, the direct input coefficients can then be estimated.[11]

This approach has been discussed because it represents one formalized way of attempting to incorporate subjective judgments (via the reliability weights) and also a certain amount of objective structure (via the RAS adjustments) in the reconciliation procedure. An alternative approach has been suggested by Gerking, in the context of his stochastic view of input-output models (Gerking 1976a, b). He proposes that coefficients can be estimated and that the reconciliation problem can be addressed using regression techniques (Gerking 1976c, 1979b). This has generated a good deal of critical comment—and response—in the literature. (For example, Brown and Giarratani 1979, Miernyk 1976, 1979, Gerking 1979a, c.) It appears that the reconciliation issue is far from settled; the range of possibilities from wholly subjective to entirely mathematical is very wide indeed.

8-7 | SUMMARY

In this chapter we have introduced the reader to several alternative approaches to estimating tables of input-output coefficients when a full matrix of interindustry transactions is not available. No nonsurvey or partial-survey technique can be expected to generate a table that is a perfect copy of what could be obtained if a complete survey were undertaken. On the other hand, errors and compromises of many sorts enter into the production of even the best survey-based table, so it can be argued that even a survey-based table is not a completely accurate snapshot of an economy. The updating problem and the regionalization problem have given rise to a number of different adjustment techniques—for example, best practice methods in the former case and location quotient techniques in the latter. It has been shown empirically that, of the various quotient techniques, the simple location quotient is generally as good or better than more complicated versions. We have also seen that variations on the RAS approach are appropriate in either the temporal or the spatial setting.

[11]If independent estimates of Y_i and $\overline{W}_j$ are not available, then one can employ the same procedure as outlined above on an expanded transactions table; this would include estimates from firms on not only their interindustry transactions but also on sales to final-demand sectors and purchases from value-added sectors. In this case the first reconciliation would scale all transactions so that their total was just $\sum_i X_i$ $(= i'X)$, and the second reconciliation would compare row and column sums against each X_i and X_j. This is, in fact, the procedure used by Jensen and McGaurr (1976, 1977) in their discussion and in their empirical work.

APPENDIX 8-1
RAS as a Solution to the Constrained Minimum Information Distance Problem

The problem is to choose the elements of $A(1)$ so as to minimize the information measure of distance between $A(0)$ and $A(1)$, namely

$$D[A(0):A(1)] = \sum_{i=1}^{n} \sum_{j=1}^{n} a_{ij}(1)\ln\left[\frac{a_{ij}(1)}{a_{ij}(0)}\right] \qquad (8\text{-}1\text{-}1)$$

subject to

$$\sum_{j=1}^{n} a_{ij}(1)X_j(1) = U_i(1) \qquad (i=1,\cdots,n) \qquad (8\text{-}1\text{-}2)$$

$$\sum_{i=1}^{n} a_{ij}(1)X_j(1) = V_j(1) \qquad (j=1,\cdots,n) \qquad (8\text{-}1\text{-}3)$$

Notice that the expression in Eq. (8-1-1) is only defined for $a_{ij}(0) \neq 0$. Forming the associated Lagrangian expression,

$$\begin{aligned}
L = \sum_{i=1}^{n} \sum_{j=1}^{n} a_{ij}(1)\ln\left[\frac{a_{ij}(1)}{a_{ij}(0)}\right] - \sum_{i=1}^{n} \lambda_i\left[\sum_{j=1}^{n} a_{ij}(1)X_j(1) - U_i(1)\right] \\
- \sum_{j=1}^{n} \mu_j\left[\sum_{i=1}^{n} a_{ij}(1)X_j(1) - V_j(1)\right]
\end{aligned} \qquad (8\text{-}1\text{-}4)$$

we find that the appropriate first-partial derivatives are

$$\partial L/\partial a_{ij}(1) = 1 + \ln a_{ij}(1) - \ln a_{ij}(0) - \lambda_i X_j(1) - \mu_j X_j(1) \qquad (8\text{-}1\text{-}5)$$

Setting $\partial L/\partial a_{ij}(1) = 0$ yields

$$\ln a_{ij}(1) = \ln a_{ij}(0) - 1 + \lambda_i X_j(1) + \mu_j X_j(1)$$

and, taking antilogarithms,

$$a_{ij}(1) = a_{ij}(0)e^{[-1+\lambda_i X_j(1)+\mu_j X_j(1)]}$$

or, rearranging,

$$a_{ij}(1) = e^{[\lambda_i X_j(1)-1/2]}a_{ij}(0)e^{[\mu_j X_j(1)-1/2]} \qquad (8\text{-}1\text{-}6)$$

Let $r_i = e^{[\lambda_i X_j(1)-1/2]}$ which is a function of λ_i only (that is, a row constraint) and $s_j = e^{[\mu_j X_j(1)-1/2]}$ which is a function of μ_j only (that is, a column constraint). Then the right-hand side of Eq. (8-1-6) can be shown as

$$a_{ij}(1) = r_i a_{ij}(0)s_j \qquad (8\text{-}1\text{-}7)$$

Thus the new coefficient, $a_{ij}(1)$, is derived as the old coefficient, $a_{ij}(0)$, modified by a row-constraint term, r_i, and a column-constraint term, s_j.

The constraints of the problem, Eqs. (8-1-2) and (8-1-3), are reproduced in the remaining first-order conditions, as usual, when we set $\partial L/\partial\lambda_i = 0$ ($i = 1,\cdots,n$) and $\partial L/\partial\mu_j = 0$ ($j=1,\cdots,n$). Inserting Eq. (8-1-7) into these two constraints, we find

$$r_i = U_i(1) \bigg/ \sum_{j=1}^{n} a_{ij}(0) s_j X_j(1)$$

and

$$s_j = V_j(1) \bigg/ \sum_{j=1}^{n} r_i a_{ij}(0) X_j(1)$$

The values of r_i and s_j are found through iterative solution of these two equations. This is what the RAS procedure accomplishes. (The interested reader may wish to consult Macgill 1977 or Bacharach 1970 for details.)

For an entire matrix, $A(1) = [a_{ij}(1)]$, there is a diagonal matrix

$$R = \begin{bmatrix} r_1 & 0 & \cdots & 0 \\ 0 & r_2 & & \cdot \\ \cdot & & & \cdot \\ \cdot & & & \cdot \\ 0 & & \cdots & r_n \end{bmatrix}$$

and a diagonal matrix

$$S = \begin{bmatrix} s_1 & 0 & \cdots & 0 \\ 0 & s_2 & & \cdot \\ \cdot & & & \cdot \\ \cdot & & & \cdot \\ 0 & & \cdots & s_n \end{bmatrix}.$$

(Recall that premultiplication by a diagonal matrix modifies each element in a particular row uniformly, and postmultiplication by a diagonal matrix modifies each element in a given column uniformly.) Then

$$A(1) = RA(0)S \tag{8-1-8}$$

as in Eq. (8-35) in the text.

Examining second-partial derivatives, we find

$$\frac{\partial^2 L}{\partial a_{ij}(1)^2} = \frac{1}{a_{ij}(0)} \tag{8-1-9}$$

This is strictly positive for all $a_{ij}(0) \neq 0$, which is the set of $a_{ij}(0)$ elements over which the information distance measure in Eq. (8-1-1) is defined. Thus $D[A(0): A(1)]$ is minimized by the choice of $a_{ij}(1)$ shown in Eq. (8-1-6) or Eq. (8-1-7).

| PROBLEMS

8-1   (Two-sector version; with apologies to *Gulliver's Travels*) The economy of the Land of Lilliput is described by the following input-output table:

	Interindustry Transactions		Total Outputs
	A	B	X
A	1	6	20
B	4	2	15

The economy of the neighboring Land of Brobdingnag is described by another input-output table:

	A	B	X
A	7	4	35
B	1	5	15

The economy of the distant land of the Houyhnhnms is described by yet another input-output table:

A	B	X
20	30.67	100
2.86	38.33	115

a Compute the vectors of value-added, intermediate inputs, final-demand, and intermediate outputs for each economy.

b A Lilliputian economist is interested in examining the structure of the Brobdingnagian economy. Likewise, a Brobdingnagian economist is interested in examining the structure of the Lilliputian economy.

However, each economist only has available to him the value-added, final-demand, and total-output vectors for the foreign economy. Each economist knows the RAS modification procedure and uses it with the technical coefficients matrix of his own economy serving as the base A matrix. Which of the two economists calculates a better estimate of the foreign economy's technical coefficients matrix in terms of mean absolute deviation (all elements of A)? (Set a tolerance limit for RAS convergence of 0.1).

c An economist in the distant land of the Houyhnhnms learned of the two other economies from a world traveler. He becomes interested in the economic structures of these foreign lands but is only able to obtain the final-demand, value-added, and total-output vectors for each economy from the world traveler. The economist uses RAS with his own country's A matrix as a base to estimate the interindustry structure of the two distant lands. Which economy does he estimate more accurately in terms of a mean absolute deviation? Do you notice anything peculiar about the comparative structures of the Lilliputian, Brobdingnagian, and Houyhnhnm economies?

d The Land of Lilliput plans to build a new power plant which will require the following value of output (in millions of dollars) from each of the economy's industries (directly, so it can be thought of as a final demand presented to the Lilliputian economy):

A	100
B	150

How accurate, measured as an average mean absolute deviation, is the Houyhnhnms' estimate of the total industrial activity (output) in the Lilliputian economy required to construct this power plant?

8-2 Suppose the economies given in problem 8-1 are really three-sector economies where the economy of the Land of Lilliput is described by the following input-output table:

	Interindustry Transactions			Total Outputs
	A	B	C	X
A	1	6	6	20
B	4	2	1	15
C	4	1	1	12

The economy of the neighboring land of Brobdingnag is described by another input-output table:

	A	B	C	X
A	7	4	8	35
B	1	5	1	15
C	6	2	7	30

The economy of the distant land of Houyhnhnms is described by yet another input-output table:

	A	B	C	X
A	5.5	33	33	110
B	22	11	5.5	82.5
C	22	5.5	5.5	66

Solve parts **a**, **b**, and **c** of problem 8-1 for these new economies.

8-3 Consider the following input-output table for region 1:

	A	B	X
A	1	2	10
B	3	4	10

We are interested in determining the impact of a particular final demand in another region (region 2). Suppose we have the following data concerning region 2.

	Value Added	Final Demand	Total Outputs
A	10	11	15
B	13	12	20

Suppose that the cost of computing an RAS estimate of region 2's input-output table using region 1's A matrix as a base table is given by nc_1, where n is the number of RAS iterations. One iteration is defined by one row *and* one column adjustment, that is, $A' = RAS$ (a row adjustment alone as the last iteration would also be counted as an iteration).

We ultimately wish to compute the impact of a new final demand in region 2. This impact (the total outputs required to support the new final demand) can be computed exactly or by using the round-by-round approximation of the inverse. We know that: (1) The cost of computing the inverse exactly on a computer is c_2 and the cost of using this inverse in impact analysis is c_1 (let us assume that $c_2 = 10c_1$, that is, the cost of computing the inverse is ten times the cost of using it in impact analysis.) (2) The cost of a round-by-round approximation of impact analysis is mc_1, where m is the order of the round-by-round approximation, that is, $Y + AY + A^2Y + \cdots + A^mY$.

a Assuming that a fourth-order round-by-round approximation is sufficiently accurate ($m = 4$), which method of impact analysis should we use to minimize cost—(1) or (2)?

b What is the total cost of performing impact analysis, including the cost of the RAS approximation (tolerance of 0.01) and of the impact analysis scheme you chose in **a**?

c If the budget for the entire impact-analysis calculation is $7c_1$, what level of tolerance can you afford?: 0.01, 0.001, 0.0001, 0.00001, or 0.000001?

| REFERENCES

ALLEN, R. I. G., and W. F. GOSSLING, eds. *Estimating and Projecting Input-Output Coefficients*. London: Input-Output Publishing Co., 1975.

ALWARD, G. S., and C. J. PALMER. "IMPLAN: An Input-Output Analysis System for Forest Service Planning." Fort Collins, Colorado: U.S. Forest Service, 1981.

ANDERSSON, ÅKE E. "A Closed Nonlinear Growth Model for International and Interregional Trade and Location." *Regional Science and Urban Economics* 5, no. 4 (December 1975): 427–44.

BACHARACH, MICHAEL. *Biproportional Matrices and Input-Output Change*. Cambridge, U.K.: Cambridge University Press, 1970.

BASTER, J. "Stability of Trade Patterns in Regional Input-Output Tables." *Urban Studies* 17, no. 1 (February 1980): 71–75.

BATTEN, DAVID F. *Spatial Analysis of Interacting Economies*. Boston: Kluwer-Nijhoff Publishing, 1983.

———. "The Interregional Linkages Between National and Regional Input-Output Models." *International Regional Science Review* 7, no. 1 (May 1982): 53–67.

BEYERS, WILLIAM B. "On the Stability of Regional Interindustry Models: The Washington Data for 1963 and 1967." *Journal of Regional Science* 12, no. 3 (December 1972): 363–74.

BEYERS, WILLIAM B. et al. *Input-Output Tables for the Washington Economy, 1967*. Seattle: University of Washington, Graduate School of Business Administration, December 1970.

BIGSTEN, ARNE. "A Note on the Estimation of Interregional Input-Output Cofficients." *Regional Science and Urban Economics* 11, no. 1 (February 1981): 149–53.

BOURQUE, PHILIP J., and E. WEEKS. *Detailed Input-Output Tables for Washington State, 1963*. Pullman: Washington State University, Washington Agricultural Experiment Station, Circular 508, September 1969.

BOURQUE, PHILIP J., and RICHARD S. CONWAY, JR. *The 1972 Washington Input-Output Study*. Seattle: University of Washington, Graduate School of Business Administration, 1977.

BOURQUE, PHILIP J. et al. *The Washington Economy: An Input-Output Study*. Seattle: University of Washington, Graduate School of Business Administration, 1967.

BROWN, DOUGLAS M., and FRANK GIARRATANI. "Input-Output as a Simple Econometric Model: A Comment." *Review of Economics and Statistics* 61, no. 4 (November 1979): 621–23.

CAMBRIDGE UNIVERSITY, DEPARTMENT OF APPLIED ECONOMICS. *Input-Output Relationships, 1954–1966*. Vol. 3, *A Programme for Growth*. London: Chapman and Hall, 1963.

CARTER, ANNE P. *Structural Change in the American Economy*. Cambridge: Harvard University Press, 1970.

CARTWRIGHT, J., R. BEEMILLER, and R. GUSTELEY. "RIMS II: Regional Input-Output Modelling System. Estimation, Evaluation and Application of a Disaggregated Regional Impact Model." Washington, D.C.: U.S. Department of Commerce, Bureau of Economic Analysis, April 1981.

CONWAY, RICHARD S., JR. "A Note on the Stability of Regional Interindustry Models." *Journal of Regional Science* 15, no. 1 (April 1975): 67–72.

———. "Changes in Regional Input-Output Coefficients and Regional Forecasting." *Regional Science and Urban Economics* 10, no. 1 (March 1980): 158–71.

———. "The Stability of Regional Input-Output Multipliers." *Environment and Planning*, A 9, no. 2 (February 1977): 197–214.

CZAMANSKI, STANISLAW, and EMIL E. MALIZIA. "Applicability and Limitations in the Use of National Input-Output Tables for Regional Studies." *Papers, Regional Science Association* 23 (1969): 65–77.

EMERSON, M. JARVIN. "Interregional Trade Effects in Static and Dynamic Input-Output Models." In *Advances in Input-Output Analysis*, edited by Karen R. Polenske and Jiri V. Skolka, 263–77. Proceedings of the Sixth International Conference on Input-Output Techniques, Vienna, April 22–26, 1974. Cambridge, Massachusetts: Ballinger, 1976.

———. "The Interindustry Structure of the Kansas Economy." Topeka, Kansas: Kansas Office of Economic Analysis and Planning Division, Kansas Department of Economic Development, 1969.

ESKELINEN, H., and M. SUORSA. "A Note on Estimating Interindustry Flows." *Journal of Regional Science* 20, no. 2 (May 1980): 261–66.

GERKING, SHELBY D. *Estimation of Stochastic Input-Output Models*. Leiden: Martinus Nijhoff, 1976a.

———. "Input-Output as a Simple Econometric Model." *Review of Economics and Statistics* 58, no. 3 (August 1976b): 274–82.

———. "Input-Output as a Simple Econometric Model: Reply." *Review of Economics and Statistics* 61, no. 4 (November 1979a): 623–26.

———. "Reconciling Reconciliation Procedures in Regional Input-Output Analysis." *International Regional Science Review* 4, no. 1 (Fall 1979b): 23–36.

———. "Reconciling 'Rows Only' and 'Columns Only' Coefficients in an Input-Output Model." *International Regional Science Review* 1, no. 2 (Fall 1976c): 30–46.

———. "Reply to 'Reconciling Reconciliation Procedures in Regional Input-Output Analysis.'" *International Regional Science Review* 4, no. 1 (Fall 1979c): 38–40.

GIARRATANI, FRANK. "A Note on the McMenamin-Haring Input-Output Projection Technique." *Journal of Regional Science* 15, no. 3 (December 1975): 371–73.

GORDON, IAN R. "Gravity Demand Functions, Accessibility and Regional Trade." *Regional Studies* 10, no. 1 (1976): 25–37.

HANSEN, W. LEE, and CHARLES M. TIEBOUT. "An Intersectoral Flows Analysis of the California Economy." *Review of Economics and Statistics* 45, no. 4 (November 1963): 409–18.

HEWINGS, GEOFFREY J. D. "Evaluating the Possibilities for Exchanging Regional Input-Output Coefficients." *Environment and Planning*, A 9, no. 8 (August 1977): 927–44.

———. "Regional Input-Output Models in the U.K.: Some Problems and Prospects for the Use of Nonsurvey Techniques." *Regional Studies* 5, no. 1 (1971): 11–22.

———. "Regional Input-Output Models Using National Data: the Structure of the West Midlands Economy." *Annals of Regional Science* 3, no. 1 (June 1969): 179–190.

HEWINGS, GEOFFREY J. D., and BRUCE N. JANSON. "Exchanging Regional Input-Output Coefficients: A Reply and Further Comments." *Environment and Planning*, A 12, no. 7 (July 1980): 843–54.

ISARD, WALTER, and THOMAS LANGFORD. *Regional Input-Output Study: Recollections, Reflections, and Diverse Notes on the Philadelphia Experience*. Cambridge, Mass.: The MIT Press, 1971.

ISSERMAN, ANDREW. "Estimating Export Activity in a Regional Economy: A Theoretical and Empirical Analysis of Alternative Methods." *International Regional Science Review* 5, no. 2 (Winter 1980): 155–84.

JENSEN, RODNEY C. "The Concept of Accuracy in Regional Input-Output Models." *International Regional Science Review* 5, no. 2 (Winter 1980): 139–54.

JENSEN, RODNEY C., and D. MCGAURR. "Reconciliation of Purchases and Sales Estimates in an Input-Output Table." *Urban Studies* 13, no. 1 (February 1976): 59–65.

———. "Reconciliation Techniques in Input-Output Analysis: Some Comparisons and Implications." *Urban Studies* 14, no. 3 (October 1977): 327–38.

JENSEN, RODNEY C., T. D. MANDEVILLE, and N. D. KARUNARATNE. *Regional Economic Planning: Generation of Regional Input-Output Analysis.* London: Croom Helm, 1979.

LEONTIEF, WASSILY, and ALAN STROUT. "Multiregional Input-Output Analysis." In *Structural Interdependence and Economic Development*, edited by Tibor Barna, 119–49. London: Macmillan, 1963. Reprinted in Wassily Leontief, *Input-Output Economics.* New York: Oxford University Press, 1966, pp. 223–57.

LEONTIEF, WASSILY et al. *Studies in the Structure of the American Economy.* New York: Oxford University Press, 1953.

MACGILL, S. M. "Theoretical Properties of Biproportional Matrix Adjustments." *Environment and Planning, A* 9, no. 6 (June 1977): 687–701.

MALIZIA, EMIL, and DANIEL L. BOND. "Empirical Tests of the RAS Method of Interindustry Coefficient Adjustment." *Journal of Regional Science* 14, no. 3 (December 1974): 355–65.

MCMENAMIN, DAVID G., and JOSEPH E. HARING. "An Appraisal of Nonsurvey Techniques for Estimating Regional Input-Output Models." *Journal of Regional Science* 14, no. 2 (August 1974): 191–205.

MIERNYK, WILLIAM H. "Comment on 'Reconciling Reconciliation Procedures in Regional Input-Output Analysis.'" *International Regional Science Review* 4, no. 1 (Fall 1979): 36–38.

———. "Comments on Recent Developments in Regional Input-Output Analysis." *International Regional Science Review* 1, no. 2, (Fall 1976): 47–55.

———. *The Elements of Input-Output Analysis.* New York: Random House, 1965.

———. "The Projection of Technical Coefficients for Medium-Term Forecasting." In *Medium-Term Dynamic Forecasting*, edited by W. F. Gossling, 29–41. (The 1975 London Input-Output Conference) London: Input-Output Publishing Co., 1977.

MIERNYK, WILLIAM H., et al. *Impact of the Space Program on a Local Economy: An Input-Output Analysis.* Morgantown, W.Va.: West Virginia University Library, 1967.

———. *Simulating Regional Economic Development.* Lexington, Mass.: D.C. Heath and Co., 1970.

MORRISON, WILLIAM I and P. SMITH. "Nonsurvey Input-Output Techniques at the Small Area Level: An Evaluation." *Journal of Regional Science* 14, no. 1 (April 1974): 1–14.

NEVIN, E. T., A. R. ROE, and JEFFERY I. ROUND. *The Structure of the Welsh Economy.* Cardiff: University of Wales Press, 1966.

POLENSKE, KAREN R. "An Empirical Test of Interregional Input-Output Models: Estimation of 1963 Japanese Production." *American Economic Review* 60, no. 2 (May 1970a): 76–82.

———. "Empirical Implementation of a Multiregional Input-Output Gravity Trade Model." In *Input-Output Techniques*, Vol. 1, *Contributions to Input-Output Analysis*, edited by Anne P. Carter and Andrew Bródy, 143–63. Proceedings of the Fourth International Conference on Input-Output Techniques, Geneva, January 1968. Amsterdam: North-Holland, 1970b.

ROUND, JEFFERY I. "An Interregional Input-Output Approach to the Evaluation of Nonsurvey Methods." *Journal of Regional Science* 18, no. 2 (August 1978a): 179–94.

———. "Compensating Feedback Effects in Interregional Input-Output Models." *Journal of Regional Science* 19, no. 2 (May 1979): 145–55.

ROUND, JEFFERY I. "Nonsurvey Techniques: A Critical Review of the Theory and the Evidence." *International Regional Science Review* 8, no. 3 (December 1983): 189–212.
———. "On Estimating Trade Flows in Interregional Input-Output Models." *Regional Science and Urban Economics* 8, no. 3 (September 1978b): 289–302.
———. "Regional Input-Output Models in the U.K.: A Reappraisal of Some Techniques." *Regional Studies* 6, no. 1 (March 1972): 1–9.
SAWYER, CHARLES, and RONALD E. MILLER. "Experiments in Regionalization of a National Input-Output Table." *Environment and Planning*, A 15, no. 11 (November 1983): 1501–20.
SCHAFFER, WILLIAM. *On the Use of Input-Output Models Regional Planning.* Leiden: Martinus Nijhoff, 1976.
SCHAFFER, WILLIAM, and KONG CHU. "Nonsurvey Techniques for Constructing Regional Interindustry Models." *Papers, Regional Science Association* 23 (1969): 83–101.
SNICKARS, FOLKE. "Construction of Interregional Input-Output Tables by Efficient Information Adding." In *Exploratory and Explanatory Statistical Analysis of Spatial Data*, edited by C. P. A. Bartels and Ronald H. Ketellapper, 73–112. Boston: Martinus Nijhoff, 1979.
STEVENS, BENJAMIN H., and GLYNNIS A. TRAINER. "Error Generation in Regional Input-Output Analysis and Its Implications for Nonsurvey Models." In *Economic Impact Analysis: Methodology and Applications*, edited by Saul Pleeter, 68–84. Boston: Martinus Nijhoff, 1980.
———. "The Generation of Error in Regional Input-Output Impact Models." Working paper No. A1–76, Regional Science Research Institute, Amherst, Massachusetts, 1976.
STEVENS, BENJAMIN H., GEORGE I. TREYZ, DAVID J. EHRLICH, and JAMES R. BOWER. "A New Technique for the Construction of Non-Survey Regional Input-Output Models and Comparison with Two Survey-Based Models." *International Regional Science Review* 8, no. 3 (December 1983): 271–86.
STONE, RICHARD. *Input-Output and National Accounts.* Paris: Organization for European Economic Cooperation, 1961.
STONE, RICHARD, and A. BROWN. *A Computable Model of Economic Growth.* Vol. 1, *A Programme for Growth.* London: Chapman and Hall, 1962.
THEIL, HENRI. *Economics and Information Theory.* New York: American Elsevier, 1967.
THUMANN, R. G. "A Comment on 'Evaluating the Possibilities for Exchanging Regional Input-Output Coefficients.'" *Environment and Planning*, A 10, no. 3 (March 1978): 321–25.
TILANUS, C. B. *Input-Output Experiments: The Netherlands, 1948–1961.* Rotterdam: Rotterdam University Press, 1966.
———. "Marginal vs. Average Input Coefficients in Input-Output Forecasting." *Quarterly Journal of Economics* 81, no. 1 (February 1967): 140–45.
TILANUS, C. B., and G. REY. "Input-Output Volume and Value Predictions for the Netherlands, 1948–1958." *International Economic Review* 5, no. 1 (January 1964): 34–45.
URIBE, PEDRO, C. G. DE LEEUW, and HENRI THEIL. "The Information Approach to the Prediction of Interregional Trade Flows." *Review of Economic Studies* 33, no. 3 (July 1966): 209–20.
VANWYNSBERGHE, D. "An Operational Nonsurvey Technique for Estimating a Coherent Set of Interregional Input-Output Tables." In *Advances in Input-Output Analysis*, edited by Karen R. Polenske and Jiri V. Skolka, 279–94. Proceedings of the Sixth International Conference on Input-Output Techniques, Vienna, April 22–26, 1974. Cambridge, Massachusetts: Ballinger, 1976.
WILSON, ALAN. *Entropy in Urban and Regional Modelling.* London: Pion, 1970.

chapter 9

Selected Topics

In this chapter we present several additional topics and extensions of the input-output framework. Section 9-1 deals with supply-side input-output models, in which factor supplies instead of final demands are viewed as the exogenous driving force in the model. One area in which the coefficients matrices of supply-side models are used is in industrial linkage analysis, which is the topic of Section 9-2. Another variation on the standard model of Chapter 2 is one in which some final demands and some gross outputs are exogenously determined (instead of all final demands and no outputs being exogenous); this is the subject matter of section 9-3. Some of the approaches that have been used to measure the impact of a new firm or a new sector on an economy are examined in section 9-4, which draws on the material in section 9-3. The basics of incorporating dynamic considerations into an input-output framework are discussed in section 9-5. In section 9-6 we examine the notion and role of prices in the input-output model.

9-1 | SUPPLY-SIDE INPUT-OUTPUT MODELS

To recapitulate the fundamental relationships in the standard input-output model, we have the following observed data: a matrix of transactions between sectors, Z, and a vector of sales to final demand, Y. From these, total gross outputs, X, are found as $X = Zi + Y$. The technical, or direct-input, coefficients are found as $a_{ij} = z_{ij}/X_j$; the matrix of these coefficients, A, is $A = Z(\hat{X})^{-1}$. That is, each element in the jth column of Z is divided by the gross output for that sector, X_j. In the 2×2 case,

$$Z = \begin{bmatrix} z_{11} & z_{12} \\ z_{21} & z_{22} \end{bmatrix}, \qquad X = \begin{bmatrix} X_1 \\ X_2 \end{bmatrix}, \qquad \text{and}$$

$$A = \begin{bmatrix} a_{11} & a_{12} \\ a_{21} & a_{22} \end{bmatrix} = \begin{bmatrix} \dfrac{z_{11}}{X_1} & \dfrac{z_{12}}{X_2} \\ \dfrac{z_{21}}{X_1} & \dfrac{z_{22}}{X_2} \end{bmatrix} = \begin{bmatrix} z_{11} & z_{12} \\ z_{21} & z_{22} \end{bmatrix} \begin{bmatrix} \dfrac{1}{X_1} & 0 \\ 0 & \dfrac{1}{X_2} \end{bmatrix} = Z(\hat{X})^{-1}$$

The direct-input coefficients matrix is, of course, the core of the model. Since total output is equal to interindustry sales plus sales to final demand, we have $X = AX + Y$, from which $X = (I - A)^{-1}Y$ is easily derived. Then, given an A matrix for an economy, the necessary new output, X^{new}, needed to satisfy some exogenously determined new final demand, Y^{new}, is found as $X^{new} = (I - A)^{-1}Y^{new}$. In this sense, the standard input-output model is said to be a demand-side model or a demand-driven model. Once a set of demands on outputs is established, the model assumes that all the necessary inputs to satisfy the needs for production to meet that demand will be supplied.

In the standard input-output model, the Leontief inverse relates sectoral gross outputs to the amount of final product—that is, to a unit of product leaving the interindustry system at the end of the process. Several writers—for example, Ghosh (1958), and Augustinovics (1970)—have suggested that an alternative point of view can be taken with the basic input-output data. This alternative interpretation relates sectoral gross production to the primary inputs —that is, to a unit of value entering the interindustry system at the beginning of the process. This approach is made operational by essentially "rotating" or transposing our vertical (column) view of the model to a horizontal (row) one. Instead of dividing each *column* of Z by the gross output of the sector associated with that column, divide each *row* of Z by the gross output of the sector associated with that row. We use $\vec{A}$ to denote the direct-output coefficients matrix that results. (Some writers also use $A\downarrow$ for the traditional demand-side coefficients, which we have denoted simply by A. This serves to make explicit the two points of view—$A\downarrow$ resulting from division of all elements in *column j* of Z by X_j, and $\vec{A}$ resulting from division of all elements in *row i* of Z by X_i.) For our two-sector example

$$\vec{A} = \begin{bmatrix} \vec{a}_{11} & \vec{a}_{12} \\ \vec{a}_{21} & \vec{a}_{22} \end{bmatrix} = \begin{bmatrix} \dfrac{z_{11}}{X_1} & \dfrac{z_{12}}{X_1} \\ \dfrac{z_{21}}{X_2} & \dfrac{z_{22}}{X_2} \end{bmatrix} = \begin{bmatrix} \dfrac{1}{X_1} & 0 \\ 0 & \dfrac{1}{X_2} \end{bmatrix} \begin{bmatrix} z_{11} & z_{12} \\ z_{21} & z_{22} \end{bmatrix}$$

$$= (\hat{X})^{-1}Z$$

The motivation for this set of coefficients is as follows. From the basic flow table for a two-sector economy, as in Table 2-2 in Chapter 2, we found that gross outputs could be calculated not only as row sums (interindustry sales plus sales to final demand) but also as column sums, provided that all elements in the payments sector were included. We now use W_j for the sum of all of the elements in the payments column for sector j (for example, labor inputs to sector j, imports used by sector j, and all other value-added items—government services [paid for in taxes], capital [paid for in interest], land [rental payments], entrepreneurship [profits], etc.)[1] Thus, for the two-sector example

$$X_1 = z_{11} + z_{21} + W_1 \quad \text{and} \quad X_2 = z_{12} + z_{22} + W_2 \quad (9\text{-}1)$$

or

$$[X_1 \quad X_2] = i'Z + [W_1 \quad W_2] \quad (9\text{-}2)$$

(We now present total gross outputs as a row vector, suggesting that these elements are found as the sum down the columns of Z, then adding W_1 to the first column sum and W_2 to the second column sum.) In matrix form

$$X' = i'Z + W \quad (9\text{-}3)$$

The parallel in the demand-side model was $X = Zi + Y$. Note that X has been transposed; the vector of payments sector elements, W, is simply defined as a row vector.

Now, using $z_{ij}/X_i = \vec{a}_{ij}$,

$$Z = \hat{X}\vec{A} \quad (9\text{-}4)$$

For example,

$$\begin{bmatrix} X_1 & 0 \\ 0 & X_2 \end{bmatrix}\begin{bmatrix} \vec{a}_{11} & \vec{a}_{12} \\ \vec{a}_{21} & \vec{a}_{22} \end{bmatrix} = \begin{bmatrix} \vec{a}_{11}X_1 & \vec{a}_{12}X_1 \\ \vec{a}_{21}X_2 & \vec{a}_{22}X_2 \end{bmatrix} = \begin{bmatrix} z_{11} & z_{12} \\ z_{21} & z_{22} \end{bmatrix}$$

Thus from Eqs. (9-3) and (9-4) we have

$$X' = i'\hat{X}\vec{A} + W$$

Since $i'\hat{X} = [X_1 \quad X_2] = X'$, this becomes

$$X'(I - \vec{A}) = W$$

and so

$$X' = W(I - \vec{A})^{-1} \quad (9\text{-}5)$$

Given exogenously determined values for, say, changes in W, ΔW, we find the associated values of $\Delta X'$ as

$$\Delta X' = \Delta W(I - \vec{A})^{-1} \quad (9\text{-}6)$$

The basic assumption of the supply-side approach is that output distribution patterns are stable in an economic system, meaning that if output of sector i is, say, doubled, then one might expect that the sales from i to each of the sectors that purchase from i will also be doubled. That is, instead of fixed input coefficients, fixed output coefficients are assumed in the supply-side model.

[1] Following general convention (e.g., Giarratani 1978), we will use W_i here in the sense that $\overline{W}_i$ was used in Chapter 2, to denote the total outlays to the payments sector by sector i. Recall from Chapter 2 that W_i denoted the total of value-added payments, while $\overline{W}_i$ was value-added plus imports bought by sector i; $\overline{W}_i = W_i + M_i$. When the exports component of final demand is net exports, then imports are zero and $\overline{W}_i = W_i$. Despite the fact that this terminology is a little inexact, we will now use W_i to represent total payments-sector outlays by sector i, whether or not $M_i = 0$.

We consider the relationships in Eq. (9-5) in more detail. Denote the elements of $(I - \vec{A})^{-1}$ by q_{ij}. This is sometimes termed the *output inverse*, in contrast to the usual Leontief inverse, $(I - A)^{-1}$, which is also known as the *input inverse*. Then, for the n-sector case, we have

$$[X_1, \cdots, X_n] = [W_1, \cdots, W_n] \begin{bmatrix} q_{11} & \cdots & q_{1n} \\ \vdots & & \vdots \\ q_{n1} & \cdots & q_{nn} \end{bmatrix} \qquad (9\text{-}7)$$

For sector j,

$$X_j = W_1 q_{1j} + W_2 q_{2j} + \cdots + W_i q_{ij} + \cdots + W_n q_{nj} \qquad (9\text{-}8)$$

Recall the typical equation in the solution to the demand-driven model, from Eqs. (2-8) in Chapter 2:

$$X_i = \alpha_{i1} Y_1 + \alpha_{i2} Y_2 + \cdots + \alpha_{ij} Y_j + \cdots + \alpha_{in} Y_n$$

where the α_{ij} are elements in $(I - A)^{-1}$, the Leontief inverse. The effect on output of sector i, ΔX_i, of a \$1.00 change in final demand for sector j goods ($\Delta Y_j = 1$), is given by α_{ij}. (Again, for readers who are familiar with differential calculus, $\partial X_i / \partial Y_j = \alpha_{ij}$.) Column sums of $(I - A)^{-1} = [\alpha_{ij}]$ were seen (Chapter 4) to be output multipliers; $\sum_{i=1}^{n} \alpha_{ij}$ denotes the total new output throughout all n sectors of the economy that is associated with a \$1.00 increase in final demand for sector j. Row sums of $(I - A)^{-1}$ can also be interpreted; $\sum_{i=1}^{n} \alpha_{ij}$ shows the total new sector i sales to all sectors that would be needed if there were a \$1.00 increase in the final demands for the outputs of *each* of the n sectors in the economy.

Looking again at the typical equation in the solution to the supply-driven model, in Eq. (9-8), we see that the effect on sector j output, ΔX_j, of a \$1.00 change in the availability of primary inputs to sector i ($\Delta W_i = 1$) is given by q_{ij}. (In calculus terms, $\partial X_j / \partial W_i = q_{ij}$; note that the order of the subscripts in this partial derivative is the opposite of that for α_{ij} from the usual Leontief inverse.) For example, if $q_{ij} = 0.67$, this can be interpreted to mean that if there is \$1.00 less labor available to sector i as an input to production (due, say, to a strike), then the amount of reduction in sector j output will be \$0.67. The reduction comes about because, in the input-output framework, a decrease in the available labor to sector i means a decrease in sector i output and hence in the outputs of all sectors that depend on sector i 's product as an input to their own production processes. This represents the same kind of effect, originating in an exogenous supply change, as is captured in the usual input-output system, which responds to exogenous demand changes. (Appendix 9-1 to this chapter traces through the repercussions in round-by-round fashion, for the interested reader.)

Consider row and column sums in the output inverse, $(I - \vec{A})^{-1} = [q_{ij}]$.

1   Row sums. $\sum_{j=1}^{n} q_{ij} = q_{i1} + q_{i2} + \cdots + q_{ij} + \cdots + q_{in}$ ($= \partial X_1 / \partial W_i + \partial X_2 / \partial W_i + \cdots + \partial X_j / \partial W_i + \cdots + \partial X_n / \partial W_i$); this represents the effect on total output throughout all sectors of the economy associated with a \$1.00 change in primary inputs for sector i. This is the supply-side model's analog to an output (or demand) multiplier, which was a *column* sum in $(I - A)^{-1}$. These supply model *row* sums can be termed input (or supply) multipliers.

2 Column sums. $\sum_{i=1}^{n} q_{ij} = q_{1j} + q_{2j} + \cdots + q_{ij} + \cdots + q_{nj}$ $(= \partial X_j / \partial W_1$

$+ \partial X_j / \partial W_2 + \cdots + \partial X_j / \partial W_i + \cdots + \partial X_j / \partial W_n)$; this is the total effect on sector j output if there were a \$1.00 change in the supply of primary factors for *each* of the n sectors in the economy. These *column* sums are the supply-side model's parallel to the *row* sums of $(I - A)^{-1}$ in the demand model.

Appendix 9-2 examines the mathematical connections between A and $\vec{A}$ (and their corresponding Leontief inverses) in detail for the interested reader.

Example (Hypothetical Data)

From the example in earlier chapters, let

$$Z = \begin{bmatrix} 150 & 500 \\ 200 & 100 \end{bmatrix} \quad \text{and} \quad Y = \begin{bmatrix} 350 \\ 1200 \end{bmatrix}, \text{ so that } X = \begin{bmatrix} 1000 \\ 2000 \end{bmatrix},$$

$$A = Z(\hat{X})^{-1} = \begin{bmatrix} .15 & .25 \\ .20 & .05 \end{bmatrix} \tag{9-9}$$

and

$$(I - A)^{-1} = \begin{bmatrix} 1.254 & .330 \\ .264 & 1.122 \end{bmatrix} \tag{9-10}$$

We are now interested in

$$\vec{A} = \begin{bmatrix} 150/1000 & 500/1000 \\ 200/2000 & 100/2000 \end{bmatrix} = \begin{bmatrix} .15 & .50 \\ .10 & .05 \end{bmatrix} \tag{9-11}$$

and hence

$$(I - \vec{A})^{-1} = \begin{bmatrix} 1.254 & .660 \\ .132 & 1.122 \end{bmatrix} \tag{9-12}$$

Thus, for example, if there were \$100 less labor available for sector 1 production and \$300 less for sector 2 production, we would find, as in Eq. (9-6),

$$[\Delta X_1 \quad \Delta X_2] = [-100 \quad -300] \begin{bmatrix} 1.254 & .660 \\ .132 & 1.122 \end{bmatrix} = [-165 \quad -402.6]$$

These figures, $\Delta X_1 = -165$ and $\Delta X_2 = -402.6$, can be interpreted as the amounts by which the outputs of sectors 1 and 2 would be reduced, given the decreases in labor inputs to the two sectors.

If $\Delta W_1 = 1$ and $\Delta W_2 = 0$, we would find, again using Eq. (9-6), $[\Delta X_1 \quad \Delta X_2] = [1.254 \quad 0.660]$. These figures represent the total additional outputs possible in sectors 1 and 2, respectively, due to the availability of one more unit of value-added input to sector 1. If $\Delta W_1 = -1$ and $\Delta W_2 = 0$, these numbers will be negative, representing reduced output in the two sectors. Thus, the sum of the elements in row 1 of $(I - \vec{A})^{-1}$, 1.914, represents the total potential impact throughout the economy of a \$1.00 change in the availability of value-added inputs to sector 1. As was noted above, this is the parallel to the concept of the output multiplier for sector 1 in the ordinary, demand-driven input-output model. It is, in the context of this supply-side model, an input multiplier for sector 1. Similarly, if $\Delta W_1 = 0$ and $\Delta W_2 = 1$, the total effects in the two-sector economy are [0.132 1.122], and hence the input multiplier for sector 2 is $0.132 + 1.122 = 1.254$. Thus, in the context of a supply-side model, one might want to decide where an additional dollar's worth of provision of primary resources (labor, etc.) would be most beneficial to the total economy, in terms of potential for supporting expanded output. Conversely, these input multipliers can indicate the potential contracting effects of shortages in primary inputs to a particular sector. From this point of view, a reduction by $1.00 in the availability of a scarce resource could lead to a reduction in economywide output of $1.914 or $1.254, depending on whether the reduction in availability was in sector 1 or sector 2.

Example (U.S. Data)

Giarratani (1978) calculated output coefficients, $\vec{a}_{ij}$, and the associated output inverse matrix of elements q_{ij}, using the 78-sector 1967 U.S. data. Supply multipliers ranged from a high of 4.01 for iron and ferroalloy-ores mining to 1.09 for medical and educational services and nonprofit organizations. With ranking of sectors such as this, it is possible to determine where primary factor constraints would have the greatest potential for limiting aggregate economic output. (For example, a contemplated labor strike in one or more sectors.)

Looking down the jth column of $(I - \vec{A})^{-1}$ allows one to identify supply linkages that have potential for significantly limiting the output of sector j. Among others, Giarratani considered sector 31, petroleum refining and related industries (the only secondary energy sector in the 78-sector 1967 U.S. table). Examination of column 31 in the output inverse identifies the following among the largest coefficients: for sector 8, crude petroleum and natural gas, $q_{8,31} = 0.8605$; for sector 27, chemicals and chemical products, $q_{27,31} = 0.0513$; and for sector 12, maintenance and repair construction, $q_{12,31} = 0.0504$. The interpretation here is that interruptions in primary inputs to these sectors have the potential for disruptions in refined petroleum output.

The output multipliers in Chapter 4 are concerned with the sensitivity of aggregate gross outputs throughout the economy to changes in the strength of (exogenous) final demands for outputs. Here, the input multipliers in a supply-side model provide one way of measuring the sensitivity of aggregate gross outputs to changes in the availability of (exogenous) scarce resource inputs. (The interested reader might want to consider the potential usefulness of the supply-side model in the regional, interregional, or multiregional setting and in particular whether the assumptions behind this model are any more or less plausible than they are at the national level.)

9-2 | INTERINDUSTRIAL LINKAGE ANALYSIS

In the framework of an input-output model, production by a particular sector has two kinds of economic effects on other sectors in the economy. If sector j increases its output, this means there will be increased *demands* from sector j (as a purchaser) on the sectors whose products are used as inputs to production in j. This is the direction of causation in the usual demand-side model. The term *backward linkage* is used to indicate this kind of interconnection of a particular sector to those sectors from which it purchases inputs. On the other hand, increased output in sector j also means additional amounts of product j that are available to be used as inputs to other sectors for their own production. That is, there will be increased *supplies* from sector j (as a seller) for the sectors which use good j in their production. This is the direction of causation in the supply-side model. The term *forward linkage* is used to indicate this kind of interconnection of a particular sector to those sectors to which it sells its output.

Measures have been proposed to quantify such backward and forward linkages for the sectors in an economy. Examination of these measures for similar sectors in different countries provides one method of making international comparisons of the structure of production. On the other hand, comparison of the strengths of backward and forward linkages for the sectors in a single economy provide one mechanism for identifying "key" or "leading" sectors in that economy and for grouping sectors into spatial clusters. If the backward linkage of sector i is larger than that of sector j, one might conclude that a dollar's worth of expansion of sector i output would be more beneficial to the economy than would an equal expansion in sector j's output, in terms of the productive activity throughout the economy that would be generated by it. Similarly, if the forward linkage of sector r is larger than that of sector s, it could be said that a dollar's worth of expansion of the output of sector r is more essential to the economy than a similar expansion in the output of sector s, from the point of view of the overall productive activity that it would support.

Several authors have proposed differing definitions of these linkage measures (for example, Rasmussen 1956, Hirschman 1958, Chenery and Watanabe 1958, Yotopoulos and Nugent 1973, Laumas 1975, and Jones 1976), and there has been, and continues to be, a good deal of discussion on the "proper" definition (for example, see the several additional articles and Yotopoulos and Nugent's reply in the May 1976 issue of the *Quarterly Journal of Economics*, or the exchange in Diamond 1976, Schultz and Schumacher 1976 and Laumas 1976). Questions on the exact role of linkage measures and the identification of key sectors in development planning have been raised in McGilvray (1977) and Hewings (1982) among others. Our purpose here is simply to introduce the reader to some of the most prevalent of these measures and, in particular, to indicate how they are derived from information in either the demand-side or the supply-side input-output model.

Backward Linkage

In its simplest form, a measure of the strength of the backward linkage of sector j—the amount by which sector j production depends on inputs—is given by the sum of the elements in the jth column of the direct-input coefficients matrix, A, namely $\sum_{i=1}^{n} a_{ij}$. Since the coefficients in A are measures of direct effects only, this is usually known as the *direct* backward linkage. Thus

$$B(d)_j = \sum_{i=1}^{n} a_{ij} \tag{9-13}$$

Let $B(d)$ represent the n-element row vector of these direct backward-linkage measures for each of the sectors in the economy. Recalling that premultiplication of a matrix by a unity row generates a vector of column sums of that matrix, we have

$$B(d) = i'A \tag{9-14}$$

As we have seen, the elements of the Leontief inverse incorporate both direct and indirect connections between sectors. Therefore, a possibly more useful and comprehensive measure of the backward linkage of sector j would be given by the sum of the elements in the jth column of the direct and indirect coefficients matrix, $(I - A)^{-1}$, whose elements we have denoted as α_{ij}. Thus, the *total* backward linkage for sector j is

$$B(d + i)_j = \sum_{i=1}^{n} \alpha_{ij} \tag{9-15}$$

These are, of course, the *output multipliers* for each sector, as defined in Chapter 4. The corresponding row vector of direct and indirect backward-linkage measures for each sector is

$$B(d + i) = i'(I - A)^{-1} \tag{9-16}$$

Forward Linkage

As might be expected from the discussion of supply-side input-output models in section 9-1, the most frequently used measures of forward linkage utilize elements from the direct output coefficients matrix, $\vec{A}$, or from the output inverse, $(I - \vec{A})^{-1}$. Parallel to the direct backward-linkage measure, the direct forward linkage of sector i is defined as the sum of the ith row of elements in $\vec{A}$; that is

$$F(d)_i = \sum_{j=1}^{n} \vec{a}_{ij} \tag{9-17}$$

and the n-element column vector of direct forward linkages for each of the sectors in the economy is

$$F(d) = \vec{A}i \tag{9-18}$$

Similarly, a measure of the direct and indirect forward linkage of sector i is given by the sum of the elements in the ith row of $(I - \vec{A})^{-1}$, whose elements we denote as q_{ij}; namely, the total forward linkage is

$$F(d + i)_i = \sum_{j=1}^{n} q_{ij} \tag{9-19}$$

and

$$F(d + i) = (I - \vec{A})^{-1}i \tag{9-20}$$

These are what were termed the *input multipliers* in our earlier discussion of supply-side input-output models.

Example

Using the example in Eqs. (9-9) through (9-12), above, we can find

$$B(d) = [\ .35 \quad .30\ ]$$

$$B(d + i) = [\ 1.518 \quad 1.452\ ]$$

$$F(d) = \begin{bmatrix} .65 \\ .15 \end{bmatrix}$$

$$F(d + i) = \begin{bmatrix} 1.914 \\ 1.254 \end{bmatrix}$$

In this small example, it turns out that sector 1 is the more important of the two by any of these four measures. In more complex economies with a large number of sectors, the ranking may vary, depending upon which measure is employed. From our discussion of output multipliers in Chapter 4 and of input multipliers earlier in this chapter, it seems clear that these two (direct plus indirect) measures—$B(d + i)$ and $F(d + i)$—are potentially the most useful.

When linkages are being measured in order to make comparisons of the structure of production between countries, the underlying coefficients matrices, whether A or $\vec{A}$, should be derived from total interindustry transactions data—that is, a particular z_{ij} should include good i used by sector j, whether good i comes from domestic producers or is imported. This is simply because interest is concentrated on how things are made in various economies, not on where the inputs come from. On the other hand, if linkages are being used to define "key" sectors in a particular economy, then the A or $\vec{A}$ matrices should be derived from a flow matrix that includes only domestically supplied inputs, since it is the impact on the domestic economy that is of interest. The distinction is the same as that between what at the regional level we denoted A^L and A^{LL}—for example, in Chapter 3. In studying the economies of less developed countries, it has been suggested (Bulmer-Thomas 1982, p. 196) that linkage analysis is the most common use that is made of input-output data. The interested reader might wish to think about the definitions of these linkage measures in regional, interregional, and multiregional input-output models, and what kinds of region- and sector-specific information they might contain.

9-3 | MIXED EXOGENOUS/ENDOGENOUS VARIABLES

In the usual form of the standard demand-side input-output model, $(I - A)X = Y$ and $X = (I - A)^{-1}Y$, the final-demand elements, Y, are considered exogenous. Changes in the Y_i's come about as a result of forces that are outside the model (e.g., changes in consumer tastes, government purchases), and it is the effects of these changes on sectoral gross outputs, the X_i's, that are quantified through the input-output model.

In certain situations a mixed type of input-output model may be employed, in which final demands for some sectors and gross outputs for the remaining sectors are specified exogenously. For example, due to a strike of a major supplier, output from a particular sector might be fixed at the amounts currently on hand in warehouses, awaiting transportation and delivery to buyers. Or, in a planned economy, a target might be to increase agricultural production (output) by 12 percent by the end of the next planning period.

Exogenous Specifications of $Y_1, \cdots, Y_{n-1}$ and X_n

As an example, in a three-sector model, assume that Y_1, Y_2, and X_3 are treated as exogenous. (Since the numbering of sectors is arbitrary, we can always assume that sector n is the one whose output, not final demand, is fixed.) The basic input-output relationships are still embodied in the following three equations:

$$(1 - a_{11})X_1 - a_{12}X_2 - a_{13}X_3 = Y_1$$
$$- a_{21}X_1 + (1 - a_{22})X_2 - a_{23}X_3 = Y_2$$
$$- a_{31}X_1 - a_{32}X_2 + (1 - a_{33})X_3 = Y_3$$

Now, however, we rearrange all three equations in order to have the exogenous variables (Y_1, Y_2, and X_3) on the right-hand side and the endogenous variables (X_1, X_2, and Y_3) on the left. We emphasize exogenous variables by using an overbar; this gives

$$(1 - a_{11})X_1 - a_{12}X_2 + 0Y_3 = \overline{Y}_1 + 0\overline{Y}_2 + a_{13}\overline{X}_3$$
$$- a_{21}X_1 + (1 - a_{22})X_2 + 0Y_3 = 0\overline{Y}_1 + \overline{Y}_2 + a_{23}\overline{X}_3$$
$$- a_{31}X_1 - a_{32}X_2 - Y_3 = 0\overline{Y}_1 + 0\overline{Y}_2 - (1 - a_{33})\overline{X}_3$$

Or, in matrix form,

$$\begin{bmatrix} (1 - a_{11}) & -a_{12} & 0 \\ -a_{21} & (1 - a_{22}) & 0 \\ -a_{31} & -a_{32} & -1 \end{bmatrix} \begin{bmatrix} X_1 \\ X_2 \\ Y_3 \end{bmatrix} = \begin{bmatrix} \overline{Y}_1 + a_{13}\overline{X}_3 \\ \overline{Y}_2 + a_{23}\overline{X}_3 \\ -(1 - a_{33})\overline{X}_3 \end{bmatrix} \quad \textbf{(9-21)}$$

Note that the matrix of coefficients on the left-hand side of Eq. (9-21), which we will denote M, no longer has the $(I - A)$ character of the basic input-output model (Chapter 2). In fact, using the results on the inverse of a partitioned matrix, from section A-7 of Appendix A, it can be shown that the inverse of this matrix will be of the form

$$M^{-1} = \begin{bmatrix} \alpha_{11} & \alpha_{12} & 0 \\ \alpha_{21} & \alpha_{22} & 0 \\ \hline \beta_1 & \beta_2 & -1 \end{bmatrix} \quad \textbf{(9-22)}$$

where the α_{ij} are elements of $\begin{bmatrix} (1 - a_{11}) & -a_{12} \\ -a_{21} & (1 - a_{22}) \end{bmatrix}^{-1}$, the Leontief inverse for the model with sectors 1 and 2 only. Thus

$$\begin{bmatrix} X_1 \\ X_2 \\ Y_3 \end{bmatrix} = \begin{bmatrix} \alpha_{11} & \alpha_{12} & 0 \\ \alpha_{21} & \alpha_{22} & 0 \\ \beta_1 & \beta_2 & -1 \end{bmatrix} \begin{bmatrix} \overline{Y}_1 + a_{13}\overline{X}_3 \\ \overline{Y}_2 + a_{23}\overline{X}_3 \\ -(1 - a_{33})\overline{X}_3 \end{bmatrix} \quad \textbf{(9-23)}$$

It will later be useful to view Eq. (9-21) as

$$
\begin{bmatrix}
(1-a_{11}) & -a_{12} & 0 \\
-a_{21} & (1-a_{22}) & 0 \\
-a_{31} & -a_{32} & -1
\end{bmatrix}
\begin{bmatrix}
X_1 \\
X_2 \\
Y_3
\end{bmatrix}
=
\begin{bmatrix}
1 & 0 & a_{13} \\
0 & 1 & a_{23} \\
0 & 0 & -(1-a_{33})
\end{bmatrix}
\begin{bmatrix}
\bar{Y}_1 \\
\bar{Y}_2 \\
\bar{X}_3
\end{bmatrix}
\qquad (9\text{-}24)
$$

Let $N = \begin{bmatrix} 1 & 0 & a_{13} \\ 0 & 1 & a_{23} \\ 0 & 0 & -(1-a_{33}) \end{bmatrix}$. The solution will then be of the form

$$
\begin{bmatrix}
X_1 \\
X_2 \\
Y_3
\end{bmatrix}
= M^{-1}N
\begin{bmatrix}
\bar{Y}_1 \\
\bar{Y}_2 \\
\bar{X}_3
\end{bmatrix}
=
\begin{bmatrix}
\alpha_{11} & \alpha_{12} & 0 \\
\alpha_{21} & \alpha_{22} & 0 \\
\beta_1 & \beta_2 & -1
\end{bmatrix}
\begin{bmatrix}
1 & 0 & a_{13} \\
0 & 1 & a_{23} \\
0 & 0 & -(1-a_{33})
\end{bmatrix}
\begin{bmatrix}
\bar{Y}_1 \\
\bar{Y}_2 \\
\bar{X}_3
\end{bmatrix}
$$

$$(9\text{-}25)$$

In this form, the matrix $M^{-1}N$ is seen to relate the exogenously determined values of Y_1, Y_2, and X_3 to the endogenous variables, X_1, X_2, and Y_3.

Suppose that sector j decides to increase output, for whatever reason (for example, to fill back orders, or because of *anticipated* new demand, etc.). The framework described here would be useful for assessing the impact of only this new activity in sector j on all other sectors of the economy. Let sector 3 be the one whose output is increased. Then, using Eq. (9-21), we have $\bar{Y}_1 = 0$, $\bar{Y}_2 = 0$, and $\bar{X}_3$ is known. In this case, the right-hand side of Eq. (9-21) is just $\begin{bmatrix} a_{13}\bar{X}_3 \\ a_{23}\bar{X}_3 \\ -(1-a_{33})\bar{X}_3 \end{bmatrix}$. From Eq. (9-23)

$$
\begin{bmatrix}
X_1 \\
X_2 \\
Y_3
\end{bmatrix}
=
\left[
\begin{array}{cc|c}
\alpha_{11} & \alpha_{12} & 0 \\
\alpha_{21} & \alpha_{22} & 0 \\
\hline
\beta_1 & \beta_2 & -1
\end{array}
\right]
\begin{bmatrix}
a_{13}\bar{X}_3 \\
a_{23}\bar{X}_3 \\
-(1-a_{33})\bar{X}_3
\end{bmatrix}
\qquad (9\text{-}26)
$$

In particular, because of the structure of the inverse matrix in Eq. (9-26), the gross outputs of sectors 1 and 2 can be found from

$$
\begin{bmatrix}
X_1 \\
X_2
\end{bmatrix}
=
\begin{bmatrix}
\alpha_{11} & \alpha_{12} \\
\alpha_{21} & \alpha_{22}
\end{bmatrix}
\begin{bmatrix}
a_{13}\bar{X}_3 \\
a_{23}\bar{X}_3
\end{bmatrix}
\qquad (9\text{-}27)
$$

The vector $\begin{bmatrix} a_{13}\bar{X}_3 \\ a_{23}\bar{X}_3 \end{bmatrix}$ translates output of sector 3 into new demands on sectors 1 and 2, and the inverse of the coefficients matrix for the two-sector model converts these inputs into total necessary gross outputs from those two sectors.

An Alternative Approach When $Y_1, \cdots, Y_{n-1}$ and X_n Are Exogenously Specified[2]

The basic interpretation of the elements of the Leontief inverse matrix, α_{ij}, is that they translate a change in final demand for a particular sector, j, into a change in gross output of sector i; $\alpha_{ij} = \Delta X_i/\Delta Y_j$ or $\Delta X_i = \alpha_{ij}\Delta Y_j$. This was clear from Eqs. (2-8) in Chapter 2 and is at the core of the notion of multipliers in Chapter 4. It would be slightly cumbersome but completely accurate to call α_{ij} a final-demand-to-output multiplier. Consider α_{jj}, the on-diagonal element in the jth column of the Leontief inverse. Using the same interpretation, $\alpha_{jj} = \Delta X_j/\Delta Y_j$ or $\Delta X_j = \alpha_{jj}\Delta Y_j$. Suppose that we define α_{ij}^* as the ratio of α_{ij} to α_{jj}; that is, $\alpha_{ij}^* = \alpha_{ij}/\alpha_{jj} = [\Delta X_i/\Delta Y_j]/[\Delta X_j/\Delta Y_j] = \Delta X_i/\Delta X_j$ or $\Delta X_i = \alpha_{ij}^*\Delta X_j$. Thus, α_{ij}^* could be termed an output-to-output multiplier.

Consider the matrix of these multipliers, $(I - A^*)^{-1} = [\alpha_{ij}^*]$, found by dividing each element in a column of $(I - A)^{-1}$ by the on-diagonal element for that column. Then each of the elements in column j of $(I - A^*)^{-1}$ indicates by how much the output of that sector (the row label) would change if the output of sector j changed by one dollar. Suppose, then, that sector j increases its output to some amount, $\overline{X}_j$. Then postmultiplication of $(I - A^*)^{-1}$ by a vector, $\overline{X}$, with $\overline{X}_j$ as its jth element and zeros elsewhere, will generate a vector of total outputs necessary from each sector in the economy because of the exogenously determined output of sector j. That is,

$$X = (I - A^*)^{-1}\overline{X} \qquad (9\text{-}28)$$

This kind of calculation should give the same results as those found using the approach in Eq. (9-27), above. This equivalence is demonstrated in the following examples.

Examples

Suppose that we have a three-sector model in which Y_1, Y_2, and X_3 are treated as exogenous; that is, we want to specify the level of output (not final demand) for sector 3. Let $A = \begin{bmatrix} .15 & .25 & .30 \\ .20 & .05 & .18 \\ .20 & .20 & .10 \end{bmatrix}$; in the format of Eq. (9-21),

$$\begin{bmatrix} .85 & -.25 & 0 \\ -.20 & .95 & 0 \\ -.20 & -.20 & -1 \end{bmatrix} \begin{bmatrix} X_1 \\ X_2 \\ Y_3 \end{bmatrix} = \begin{bmatrix} \overline{Y}_1 + (.3)\overline{X}_3 \\ \overline{Y}_2 + (.18)\overline{X}_3 \\ -(.9)\overline{X}_3 \end{bmatrix}$$

Let $\overline{Y}_1 = 100{,}000$, $\overline{Y}_2 = 200{,}000$, and $\overline{X}_3 = 150{,}000$; we find the inverse of the coefficients matrix on the left, M^{-1}, to be

$$M^{-1} = \begin{bmatrix} 1.254 & .330 & 0 \\ .264 & 1.122 & 0 \\ -.304 & -.290 & -1 \end{bmatrix}$$

[2] We thank Professor Andrew M. Isserman for calling this approach to our attention. It is mentioned in Ritz and Spaulding (1975, p. 14).

Then, as in Eq. (9-23),

$$\begin{bmatrix} X_1 \\ X_2 \\ Y_3 \end{bmatrix} = \begin{bmatrix} 1.254 & .330 & 0 \\ .264 & 1.122 & 0 \\ -.304 & -.290 & -1 \end{bmatrix} \begin{bmatrix} 145,000 \\ 227,000 \\ -135,000 \end{bmatrix} = \begin{bmatrix} 256,740 \\ 292,974 \\ 25,090 \end{bmatrix}$$

Notice that the 2×2 upper-left submatrix in this inverse is indeed just the inverse of $\begin{bmatrix} .85 & -.25 \\ -.20 & .95 \end{bmatrix}$, as was suggested in Eq. (9-22).

If only $\bar{X}_3 = 150,000$ is exogenously specified, then $\bar{Y}_1 = 0$ and $\bar{Y}_2 = 0$. The approach of Eq. (9-23) leads to

$$\begin{bmatrix} X_1 \\ X_2 \\ Y_3 \end{bmatrix} = \begin{bmatrix} 1.254 & .330 & 0 \\ .264 & 1.122 & 0 \\ -.304 & -.290 & -1 \end{bmatrix} \begin{bmatrix} 45,000 \\ 27,000 \\ -135,000 \end{bmatrix}$$

from which $X_1 = 65,340$, $X_2 = 42,174$, and $Y_3 = 113,490$. If only the gross outputs of sectors 1 and 2 are of interest, then the approach in Eq. (9-27) is completely adequate. That is,

$$\begin{bmatrix} X_1 \\ X_2 \end{bmatrix} = \begin{bmatrix} 1.254 & .330 \\ .264 & 1.122 \end{bmatrix} \begin{bmatrix} 45,000 \\ 27,000 \end{bmatrix}$$

which will clearly give the same results for X_1 and X_2.

Continuing with the same numerical example and using the alternative approach, we create $(I - A^*)^{-1}$ for that three-sector illustration. Here, $(I - A)^{-1}$

$$= \begin{bmatrix} 1.429 & .497 & .576 \\ .377 & 1.230 & .372 \\ .401 & .384 & 1.322 \end{bmatrix}, \text{ and so}$$

$$(I - A^*)^{-1} = \begin{bmatrix} 1.0000 & .4041 & .4537 \\ .2638 & 1.0000 & .2814 \\ .2806 & .3122 & 1.0000 \end{bmatrix}$$

Consider again the case in which sector 3 output is increased to $150,000. Here, then,

$$\bar{X} = \begin{bmatrix} 0 \\ 0 \\ 150,000 \end{bmatrix}$$

and, as in Eq. (9-28),

$$X = (I - A^*)^{-1}\bar{X} = \begin{bmatrix} 65,355 \\ 42,210 \\ 150,000 \end{bmatrix}$$

Except for rounding error, created in forming $(I - A^*)^{-1}$, these values for X_1 and X_2 are the same as our earlier results, and of course $X_3 = 150,000$, which is part of the stipulation of the problem and is assured by the fact that $a_{33}^* = 1$. (The manner of constructing $[I - A^*]^{-1}$ assures that all $a_{jj}^* = 1$.)

In Appendix 9-3 we demonstrate for the interested reader that these two approaches for the case when X_n is exogenously specified must always give the same results for the outputs of X_1 through X_{n-1}. (Again, results on the inverse of a partitioned matrix turn out to be useful.) If one already has the Leontief inverse for the *n*-sector model, then $(I - A^*)^{-1}$ is easily calculated, and it provides information on the potential impacts of a change in output of *any* of the sectors. In cases where the Leontief inverse for the system has yet to be calculated, it may be easier to use the approach in Eq. (9-27), since the coefficients matrix is smaller (by one row and column).

Note that the vector $\overline{X}$ may only contain one nonzero element. That is, the approach in Eq. (9-28) is not valid in a situation in which more than one sector's output is specified exogenously. For example, if one tried *also* to set X_1 at $100,000, making

$$\overline{X} = \begin{bmatrix} 100,000 \\ 0 \\ 150,000 \end{bmatrix}$$

we see that

$$X = (I - A^*)^{-1}\overline{X} = \begin{bmatrix} 165,355 \\ 68,590 \\ 178,060 \end{bmatrix}$$

which satisfies neither $X_1 = 100,000$ nor $X_3 = 150,000$.

Consider the same three-sector model, but now let the exogenous values be $\overline{Y}_1 = 100,000$, $\overline{Y}_2 = 200,000$ (both as before), but $\overline{X}_3 = 100,000$ (instead of 150,000). Using Eq. (9-25) instead of (9-23), with M^{-1} as before and $N = \begin{bmatrix} 1 & 0 & .3 \\ 0 & 1 & .18 \\ 0 & 0 & -.9 \end{bmatrix}$, we have

$$\begin{bmatrix} X_1 \\ X_2 \\ Y_3 \end{bmatrix} = \begin{bmatrix} 1.254 & .330 & 0 \\ .264 & 1.122 & 0 \\ -.304 & -.290 & -1 \end{bmatrix} \begin{bmatrix} 1 & 0 & .3 \\ 0 & 1 & .18 \\ 0 & 0 & -.9 \end{bmatrix} \begin{bmatrix} 100,000 \\ 200,000 \\ 100,000 \end{bmatrix}$$

$$= \begin{bmatrix} 1.254 & .330 & .436 \\ .264 & 1.122 & .281 \\ -.304 & -.290 & .757 \end{bmatrix} \begin{bmatrix} 100,000 \\ 200,000 \\ 100,000 \end{bmatrix} = \begin{bmatrix} 234,960 \\ 278,916 \\ -12,740 \end{bmatrix}$$

This simply means that the exogenously specified values of Y_1, Y_2, and X_3 in this example cannot possibly be satisfied unless Y_3 is negative. If all variables are read as "changes in," then to increase *final demand* for sectors 1 and 2 by 100,000 and 200,000, while increasing *output* of sector 3 by only 100,000, can only be accomplished by decreasing final demand for sector 3 by 12,740. This is not unusual in planned economies; increased *production* targets ($\Delta X_i > 0$) may be attainable only through decreases in allocations to consumption ($\Delta Y_i < 0$). Similarly, in the case of a shortage (due to a strike, for example), increases in consumption in other sectors may require a decrease in consumption of the product that is in short supply. Whether or not negative values for Y_3 make sense depends entirely on the context of the problem. If all X's and Y's are *not* changes in, it still is possible to attach meaning to a negative Y_j. For example, if the exports component of final demand is defined as *net* exports, then a negative value here for Y_j simply means net *imports* of j-type goods.

Given the a_{ij} values, Eq. (9-23) makes clear that the values of X_1 and X_2 do not depend on Y_3, but that Y_3 does depend on the solution values for X_1 and X_2. With exogenously given $\bar{Y}_1$, $\bar{Y}_2$, and $\bar{X}_3$, the first two equations in (9-23) can be solved for X_1 and X_2. This is a straightforward 2×2 input-output system

$$\begin{bmatrix} X_1 \\ X_2 \end{bmatrix} = \begin{bmatrix} \alpha_{11} & \alpha_{12} \\ \alpha_{21} & \alpha_{22} \end{bmatrix} \begin{bmatrix} \bar{Y}_1 + a_{13}\bar{X}_3 \\ \bar{Y}_2 + a_{23}\bar{X}_3 \end{bmatrix} \qquad \textbf{(9-29)}$$

in which a positive right-hand side vector will lead to positive X_1 and X_2. (This was the structure of Eq. [9-27], when $\bar{Y}_1 = 0$ and $\bar{Y}_2 = 0$.) Then, from the third equation in (9-21), we obtain

$$Y_3 = (1 - a_{33})\bar{X}_3 - a_{31}X_1 - a_{32}X_2$$

This, too, is a standard input-output equation for sector 3 in a three-sector model. However, with an exogenously given value for X_3 and with the values for X_1 and X_2 found from solving the two-sector model, the value of Y_3 can be positive, zero, or negative; that is, it is found simply as a *residual* in the system. It is influenced by the values of other variables, but does not influence them.

From the form of the solution that is given in Eq. (9-25), using the example values of $\bar{Y}_1 = 100,000$ and $\bar{Y}_2 = 200,000$, we can find the critical value of $\bar{X}_3$ that makes $Y_3 = 0$. (For $\bar{X}_3$ above this value, Y_3 will be positive; for $\bar{X}_3$ below this value, Y_3 will be negative.) Replacing 100,000 by $\bar{X}_3^c$ and setting $Y_3 = 0$, we have

$$\begin{bmatrix} X_1 \\ X_2 \\ 0 \end{bmatrix} = \begin{bmatrix} 1.254 & .330 & .436 \\ .264 & 1.122 & .281 \\ -.304 & -.290 & .757 \end{bmatrix} \begin{bmatrix} 100,000 \\ 200,000 \\ \bar{X}_3^c \end{bmatrix}$$

From the third equation, we see

$$0 = (-.304)(100,000) + (-.290)(200,000) + (.757)\bar{X}_3^c$$

from which $\bar{X}_3^c = 116,777$.

From these examples we see that $M^{-1}N$ is the matrix that relates the exogenously given values of X and Y, $\bar{X}$ and $\bar{Y}$, to those X's and Y's that are endogenous variables. Thus, the elements in this matrix have the same kind of "multiplier" interpretation as we explored in Chapter 4 for the usual input-output system, in which $X = (I - A)^{-1}Y$. In this example,

$$M^{-1}N = \begin{bmatrix} 1.254 & .330 & .436 \\ .264 & 1.122 & .281 \\ -.304 & -.290 & .757 \end{bmatrix}$$

For example, with $\bar{Y}_1 = 1$, $\bar{Y}_2 = \bar{X}_3 = 0$, we find $\bar{X}_1 = 1.254$, $\bar{X}_2 = 0.264$, and $\bar{Y}_3 = -0.304$. If only final demand for sector 1 increases, then output in sectors 1 and 2 must increase while final demand for sector 3 goods must decrease. The elements in the second column have a similar interpretation. From the third column, we find that when the only change is $\bar{X}_3 = 1$, then $X_1 = 0.436$ and $X_2 = 0.281$, as would be expected (the outputs of both sectors 1 and 2 are inputs to sector 3 production). We also find that $Y_3 = 0.757$; this represents the new amount of final demand that can be sustained by the new dollar's worth of sector 3 output, after account has been taken of interindustry needs.

Exogenous Specification of $Y_1, \cdots, Y_k, X_{k+1}, \cdots, X_n$

The reader can easily work out the matrix representation of, say, a four-sector model with Y_1, Y_2, X_3, and X_4 exogenous. For the general n-sector case, assume that sectors have been labeled so that the first k sectors are those for which final demands $(Y_1, \cdots, Y_k)$ are the exogenous elements and the last $(n - k)$ sectors are those for which gross outputs $(X_{k+1}, \cdots, X_n)$ are the exogenous elements. Then the parallel to Eq. (9-24) is

$$\begin{bmatrix} P & 0 \\ R & -1 \end{bmatrix} \begin{bmatrix} X \\ Y \end{bmatrix} = \begin{bmatrix} I & Q \\ 0 & S \end{bmatrix} \begin{bmatrix} \bar{Y} \\ \bar{X} \end{bmatrix} \tag{9-30}$$

where the submatrices are as follows:

P = the $k \times k$ matrix containing the elements from the first k rows and the first k columns in $(I - A)$,

R = the $(n - k) \times k$ matrix containing elements from the last $(n - k)$ rows and the first k columns of $(I - A)$,

X = the k-element column vector containing elements X_1 through X_k, whose values are to be found,

Y = the $(n - k)$-element column vector with elements Y_{k+1} through Y_n, whose values are to be found,

Q = the $k \times (n - k)$ matrix of elements from the first k rows and the last $(n - k)$ columns of $-(I - A)$,

S = the $(n - k) \times (n - k)$ matrix of elements from the last $(n - k)$ rows and columns of $-(I - A)$,

$\bar{Y}$ = the k-element column vector of elements Y_1 through Y_k, whose values are exogenously determined, and

$\bar{X}$ = the $(n - k)$-element column vector of elements X_{k+1} through X_n, whose values are exogenously determined,

and where the I and 0 matrices are of appropriate dimension in each case. The solution procedure is the same for any square set of linear equations. Using the same notation as earlier, in the case when only X_n was exogenously determined, we have

$$M \begin{bmatrix} X \\ Y \end{bmatrix} = N \begin{bmatrix} \bar{Y} \\ \bar{X} \end{bmatrix}$$

and

$$\begin{bmatrix} X \\ Y \end{bmatrix} = M^{-1} N \begin{bmatrix} \bar{Y} \\ \bar{X} \end{bmatrix} \tag{9-31}$$

The parallel result for the earlier case is in Eq. (9-25).

Again, if one's interest is only in the effects on gross outputs of the k endogenous sectors that are caused by specifying the outputs of the last $(n - k)$ sectors exogenously, then $\bar{Y} = 0$ in Eq. (9-30), and the same kind of partitioned inverse argument can be used to show that

$$X = P^{-1}Q\bar{X}$$

where $Q = \begin{bmatrix} a_{1, k+1} & \cdots & a_{1n} \\ \vdots & & \vdots \\ a_{k, k+1} & \cdots & a_{kn} \end{bmatrix}$. For example, the first element in $Q\bar{X}$ will be $a_{1, k+1}X_{k+1} + a_{1, k+2}X_{k+2} + \cdots + a_{1n}X_n$; this represents the inputs that are needed from endogenous sector 1 to allow production of the fixed amounts of output in sectors $k + 1$ through n. (In an early application of input-output analysis at the regional level, Tiebout 1969 specified [projected] the outputs of 13 out of 57 local sectors exogenously and found the consequent outputs of the remaining 44 sectors in the regional economy in just this way.) We will see in the next section that a mix of X's and Y's in the endogenous and exogenous categories can also be useful in assessing the impact of a new industry on an economy.

9-4 | NEW INDUSTRY IMPACTS IN THE INPUT-OUTPUT MODEL

The input-output model provides a framework within which to assess the economic impact associated with the introduction of a new industry into an economy—for example, a basic manufacturing activity in a less-developed country, an export-oriented industry in a region, and so on. A quantitative approach to this kind of problem is extremely important. Individuals with responsibility for planning economic development (for a nation or a region) need to be able to make quantitative estimates of the total amount of economic benefit that can be expected from policies that are designed to attract certain kinds of industry to an area. Then the costs associated with attracting the activity—for example, reduced business taxes as an incentive, possible environmental degradation—can be weighed against the benefits of the new economic activity associated with the new industry. For convenience, in this section we will consider that the in-movement of the new industry is to a region, whether studied in isolation or as part of an interregional or multiregional system. It will be clear that the same principles apply if the "region" is in fact an entire country. In the input-output literature, one finds discussions of essentially two ways of introducing a new production activity into an economic area—through a new final-demand vector only and through the addition of new elements into the technical coefficients table for the economy. We will examine these in turn.

New Industry: The Final-Demand Approach

For illustration, we again consider a two-sector regional economy, for which we have a 2×2 input coefficient matrix, $A = \begin{bmatrix} a_{11} & a_{12} \\ a_{21} & a_{22} \end{bmatrix}$. If a firm in a different industry, which we will denote sector 3, were to locate in the region, one way of attempting to quantify the impact of this in-movement on the region is as follows. (This is essentially the approach used by Isard and Kuenne 1953 and by Miller 1957 in relatively early applications of the input-output framework at the regional level.) From an input-output coefficient table for another region of the country, or from a national table, or from surveys, assume that it is possible to estimate what the inputs will be from sectors 1 and 2 per dollar's worth of output of the new sector 3; that is, a_{13} and a_{23}.

In order to quantify the impact of the in-movement of sector 3 to the economy, we must have some measure of the *magnitude* of new economic activity associated with sector 3. In input-output terms, this means that either sector 3's level of production (gross output), X_3, or of sales to final demand, Y_3, must be specified. For this example, assume that the measure of new activity by sector 3 is in terms of gross output; denote this proposed level of sector 3 production by $\overline{X}_3$. This is often the case. A new firm plans to build, say, a \$2.5 million plant with a planned annual output of \$850,000, for example. Then the new demand on sectors 1 and 2 that arises because of production by the new sector 3 is $a_{13}\overline{X}_3$ and $a_{23}\overline{X}_3$, respectively. That is, we can view these new demands as an *exogenous* change imposed on the original two sectors; $\Delta Y = \begin{bmatrix} a_{13}\overline{X}_3 \\ a_{23}\overline{X}_3 \end{bmatrix}$, and so the impacts, in terms of the outputs from these two sectors, will be given by $\Delta X = (I - A)^{-1}\Delta Y$. Using α_{ij}'s to denote elements of the Leontief inverse, as usual, we have

$$X = \begin{bmatrix} \alpha_{11} & \alpha_{12} \\ \alpha_{21} & \alpha_{22} \end{bmatrix} \begin{bmatrix} a_{13}\overline{X}_3 \\ a_{23}\overline{X}_3 \end{bmatrix} = \begin{bmatrix} \alpha_{11}a_{13}\overline{X}_3 + \alpha_{12}a_{23}\overline{X}_3 \\ \alpha_{21}a_{13}\overline{X}_3 + \alpha_{22}a_{23}\overline{X}_3 \end{bmatrix} \tag{9-32}$$

Given that there are also the usual kinds of final demands, $\overline{Y}_1$ and $\overline{Y}_2$, for the products of the two sectors, total gross outputs in sectors 1 and 2 will be

$$\begin{bmatrix} X_1 \\ X_2 \end{bmatrix} = \begin{bmatrix} \alpha_{11} & \alpha_{12} \\ \alpha_{21} & \alpha_{22} \end{bmatrix} \begin{bmatrix} \overline{Y}_1 + a_{13}\overline{X}_3 \\ \overline{Y}_2 + a_{23}\overline{X}_3 \end{bmatrix}$$

$$= \begin{bmatrix} \alpha_{11}(\overline{Y}_1 + a_{13}\overline{X}_3) + \alpha_{12}(\overline{Y}_2 + a_{23}\overline{X}_3) \\ \alpha_{21}(\overline{Y}_1 + a_{13}\overline{X}_3) + \alpha_{22}(\overline{Y}_2 + a_{23}\overline{X}_3) \end{bmatrix} \tag{9-33}$$

This is exactly the structure of the model in Eq. (9-29), and for the same reason. We are specifying $\overline{Y}_1$ and $\overline{Y}_2$ and, in addition, the value of X_3. When $\overline{X}_3 = 0$, that is, without the new sector in the region, this is a standard input-output exercise. When $\overline{Y}_1 = 0$ and $\overline{Y}_2 = 0$, then in Eq. (9-33) we find the impact of the new industry alone—as in Eq. (9-32), above.

For example, using the same illustration, let $A = \begin{bmatrix} .15 & .25 \\ .20 & .05 \end{bmatrix}$. Then $(I - A)^{-1} = \begin{bmatrix} 1.254 & .330 \\ .264 & 1.122 \end{bmatrix}$. Assume that our estimates of the direct input coefficients for the new sector 3 are $a_{13} = 0.30$ and $a_{23} = 0.18$, and that the plant in the new sector 3 that is moving into the region expects to produce at a level of \$100,000 per year. So $\overline{X}_3 = 100,000$, $\Delta Y = \begin{bmatrix} 30,000 \\ 18,000 \end{bmatrix}$, and, as in Eq. (9-32),

$$\Delta X = \begin{bmatrix} 1.254 & .330 \\ .264 & 1.122 \end{bmatrix} \begin{bmatrix} 30,000 \\ 18,000 \end{bmatrix} = \begin{bmatrix} 43,560 \\ 28,116 \end{bmatrix} \tag{9-34}$$

Sector 1, in satisfying the new demand for \$30,000 worth of its product, will ultimately have to increase its output by \$43,560. Similarly, the new demands on sector 2 from sector 3 are \$18,000, but in the end sector 2 will need to produce a total of \$28,116 more output. These figures represent one way of measuring the impact on an economy that comes about from the in-movement of new industrial activity.

With a_{13} and a_{23} assumed known, but $a_{31} = a_{32} = a_{33} = 0$, the basic equations in this approach are

$$(1 - a_{11}) X_1 - a_{12}X_2 - a_{13}X_3 = Y_1$$

$$- a_{21}X_1 + (1 - a_{22})X_2 - a_{23}X_3 = Y_2$$

$$0X_1 + 0X_2 + X_3 = Y_3$$

The first two equations reflect the fact that sector 1 and 2 outputs are used as inputs to (the new) sector 3. The third equation shows that all of sector 3's output can be used to satisfy final demand, since it is not used as an input to production in the region. (For example, a sector may move to a region to be closer to the sources of inputs, while continuing to produce a product for export.)

In matrix terms, with

$$\bar{A} = \begin{bmatrix} a_{11} & a_{12} & a_{13} \\ a_{21} & a_{22} & a_{23} \\ 0 & 0 & 0 \end{bmatrix} \quad \text{and} \quad (I - \bar{A}) = \begin{bmatrix} (1 - a_{11}) & -a_{12} & -a_{13} \\ -a_{21} & (1 - a_{22}) & -a_{23} \\ 0 & 0 & 1 \end{bmatrix}$$

we have partially included the new sector in the A matrix. To assess the impact of new sector 3 production, $\bar{X}_3$, we let $Y_1 = 0$, and $Y_2 = 0$. Also, $Y_3 = X_3 = \bar{X}_3$, from the third equation above. Thus

$$X = (I - \bar{A})^{-1} \begin{bmatrix} 0 \\ 0 \\ \bar{X}_3 \end{bmatrix}$$

Because of the zeros in the Y vector, $\underline{X}_1, = \bar{\alpha}_{13}\bar{X}_3$, $X_2 = \bar{\alpha}_{23}\bar{X}_3$ and $X_3 = \bar{\alpha}_{33}\bar{X}_3$, using $\bar{\alpha}_{ij}$'s for the elements of $(I - \bar{A})^{-1}$. That is, only the third column of the inverse is of interest. Using results on the inverse of a partitioned matrix (once again from section A-7 of Appendix A) it is easily shown that

$$\begin{bmatrix} \bar{\alpha}_{13} \\ \bar{\alpha}_{23} \end{bmatrix} = \begin{bmatrix} \alpha_{11} & \alpha_{12} \\ \alpha_{21} & \alpha_{22} \end{bmatrix} \begin{bmatrix} a_{13} \\ a_{23} \end{bmatrix} \quad \text{and} \quad \bar{\alpha}_{33} = 1$$

In particular, then,

$$\begin{bmatrix} X_1 \\ X_2 \end{bmatrix} = \begin{bmatrix} \alpha_{11} & \alpha_{12} \\ \alpha_{21} & \alpha_{22} \end{bmatrix} \begin{bmatrix} a_{13} \\ a_{23} \end{bmatrix} \bar{X}_3$$

exactly as in Eq. (9-32), above. Note also that, as expected, $X_3 = (1)\bar{X}_3$.

New Industry: Complete Inclusion in the Technical Coefficients Matrix

The estimate of the impact of the new industry that was given above is clearly conservative; the complete impact of a new sector of an economy would reflect the fact that not only would the new industry buy inputs from existing sectors, but it would probably also sell its own product as an input to other producing sectors in the economy. That is, ultimately the entire technical structure of the economy may change. In the first place, there will be a new column and row of direct-input coefficients associated with purchases by and sales of the new sector. In addition, there may be changes in the elements of the original A matrix, reflecting, for example, substitution of the newly available input for one previously used.

To completely "close" the previous 2×2 coefficient matrix with respect to the new industry, we need a_{13} and a_{23} (which we have already assumed can be estimated), and we also need a_{31} and a_{32}, estimates of how much each of the old industries (1 and 2) will buy from the new sector (3) per dollar's worth of their outputs, plus a_{33}, the intrasectoral input coefficient for the new industry. For in-movement of a new industry into a region with n original sectors, the previous approach required that we estimate n new coefficients (a column for the new sector, except for the last element). For the present approach we need an additional $(n + 1)$ coefficients (a row for the new sector, including intraindustry use per dollar's worth of output); that is, we need $(2n + 1)$ new coefficients in all.

Again, assuming that X_3, the level of gross output of the new sector, is known, our three-equation model, relating the endogenous variables X_1, X_2, and Y_3 to the values $\overline{Y}_1$, $\overline{Y}_2$, and $\overline{X}_3$, is still

$$(1 - a_{11})X_1 - a_{12}X_2 - a_{13}\overline{X}_3 = \overline{Y}_1$$
$$- a_{21}X_1 + (1 - a_{22})X_2 - a_{23}\overline{X}_3 = \overline{Y}_2 \qquad (9\text{-}35)$$
$$- a_{31}X_1 - a_{32}X_2 + (1 - a_{33})\overline{X}_3 = Y_3$$

Rearranging, to put exogenous variables on the right-hand side,

$$(1 - a_{11})X_1 - a_{12}X_2 + 0Y_3 = \overline{Y}_1 + a_{13}\overline{X}_3$$
$$- a_{21}X_1 + (1 - a_{22})X_2 + 0Y_3 = \overline{Y}_2 + a_{23}\overline{X}_3 \qquad (9\text{-}36)$$
$$- a_{31}X_1 - a_{32}X_2 - Y_3 = -(1 - a_{33})\overline{X}_3$$

The matrix representation for (9-36) is

$$\begin{bmatrix} (1 - a_{11}) & -a_{12} & 0 \\ -a_{21} & (1 - a_{22}) & 0 \\ -a_{31} & -a_{32} & 1 \end{bmatrix} \begin{bmatrix} X_1 \\ X_2 \\ Y_3 \end{bmatrix} = \begin{bmatrix} \overline{Y}_1 + a_{13}\overline{X}_3 \\ \overline{Y}_2 + a_{23}\overline{X}_3 \\ -(1 - a_{33})\overline{X}_3 \end{bmatrix} \qquad (9\text{-}37)$$

This is exactly the structure of the model in Eq. (9-21), in the previous section, and so solution possibilities are the same as we saw in the examples of that section. In particular, there is no guarantee that the Y_3 associated with given values of Y_1, Y_2, and X_3 will be positive.

Instead of specification of the level of gross output of the new sector, one could quantify the magnitude of the new operation by exogenously fixing the level of sales to final demand—that is, by specifying Y_3 at $\overline{Y}_3$, instead of X_3 at $\overline{X}_3$. But then, from Eq. (9-35), with X_3 now a variable to be determined, not specified at $\overline{X}_3$, we see that this is a standard kind of input-output problem. Whether $\overline{Y}_1 = 0$ or not, and whether $\overline{Y}_2 = 0$ or not, given some $\overline{Y}_3 > 0$, we find the associated values of the necessary gross outputs, X_1, X_2, and X_3, through the use of the Leontief inverse to the 3×3 $(I - A)$ matrix in Eq. (9-35). Thus, when the level of new sector activity is specified in terms of sales to final demand rather than gross output, no new principles are involved in assessing the impact on the economy into which the industry moves.

For example, for our illustrative problem, the 3×3 technical coefficients matrix is

$$\overline{A} = \begin{bmatrix} .15 & .25 & .30 \\ .20 & .05 & .18 \\ .20 & .20 & .10 \end{bmatrix}$$

(using an overbar to distinguish this from the original 2×2 A matrix). Thus the matrix of coefficients in the equations in (9-35) is

$$(I - \overline{A}) = \begin{bmatrix} .85 & -.25 & -.30 \\ -.20 & .95 & -.18 \\ -.20 & -.20 & .90 \end{bmatrix} \qquad (9\text{-}38)$$

and the corresponding inverse is

$$(I - \overline{A})^{-1} = \begin{bmatrix} 1.429 & .497 & .576 \\ .377 & 1.230 & .372 \\ .401 & .384 & 1.322 \end{bmatrix} \qquad (9\text{-}39)$$

Given $\overline{Y}_1 = 100{,}000$, $\overline{Y}_2 = 200{,}000$, and, say, $\overline{Y}_3 = 50{,}000$, we find that

$$\begin{bmatrix} X_1 \\ X_2 \\ X_3 \end{bmatrix} = \begin{bmatrix} 1.429 & .497 & .576 \\ .377 & 1.230 & .372 \\ .401 & .384 & 1.322 \end{bmatrix} \begin{bmatrix} 100{,}000 \\ 200{,}000 \\ 50{,}000 \end{bmatrix} = \begin{bmatrix} 271{,}100 \\ 302{,}300 \\ 183{,}000 \end{bmatrix} \qquad (9\text{-}40)$$

in standard input-output fashion.

A New Firm in an Existing Industry

If the firm that moves into a region belongs to a sector that is already established in the region, so that the effect is to augment the production capacity of a particular existing industry, *not* introduce it into the local economy for the first time, the assessment of its impact is fairly straightforward. In particular, an input-output table for the economy in question will already include interindustry and intraindustry relationships for the sector in which the new firm is classified.

Assume that we have a three-sector economy and that the new firm is classified as a member of sector 3. Thus a 3×3 A matrix and its Leontief inverse are known. If the level of activity in the new firm is specified as a certain total amount of production, then we have a positive X_3^*, and the relationships among sectors are exactly those shown in Eq. (9-35), above, where now we use X_3^* in place of $\overline{X}_3$ to distinguish the two cases ($\overline{X}_3$ when the industry was new to the region, X_3^* when the new firm only represents an increase in capacity of the existing sector). The new demands on the three original sectors are found as

$$\begin{bmatrix} a_{13}X_3^* \\ a_{23}X_3^* \\ a_{33}X_3^* \end{bmatrix} \qquad (9\text{-}41)$$

and impacts on all three sectors are found in the standard input-output way, using the 3×3 Leontief inverse. With $\Delta X = \begin{bmatrix} \Delta X_1 \\ \Delta X_2 \\ \Delta X_3 \end{bmatrix}$,

$$\Delta X = (I - A)^{-1} \begin{bmatrix} a_{13}X_3^* \\ a_{23}X_3^* \\ a_{33}X_3^* \end{bmatrix} \qquad (9\text{-}42)$$

If the level of new capacity in sector 3 is specified through an additional amount of sales to final demand, that is, as ΔY_3, then the impact is found in the usual input-output way. The new final-demand vector is just

$$\begin{bmatrix} 0 \\ 0 \\ \Delta Y_3 \end{bmatrix}$$

and

$$\Delta X = (I - A)^{-1} \begin{bmatrix} 0 \\ 0 \\ \Delta Y_3 \end{bmatrix} \qquad (9\text{-}43)$$

Using α_{ij}'s for the elements of this 3×3 Leontief inverse, this is just

$$\Delta X_1 = \alpha_{13}\Delta Y_3$$

$$\Delta X_2 = \alpha_{23}\Delta Y_3 \qquad \text{or} \qquad \Delta X = \begin{bmatrix} \alpha_{13} \\ \alpha_{23} \\ \alpha_{33} \end{bmatrix}(\Delta Y_3) \qquad (9\text{-}44)$$

$$\Delta X_3 = \alpha_{33}\Delta Y_3$$

For example, assume that the Leontief inverse for the three-sector economy is as shown in Eq. (9-39). If a new firm in sector 3 moves into the economy and its projected level of annual production is \$120,000 (that is, $X_3^* = 120,000$), then, using the elements in the third column of the technical coefficients matrix, we find the new final demands in Eq. (9-41) as

$$\begin{bmatrix} (.30)(120,000) \\ (.18)(120,000) \\ (.10)(120,000) \end{bmatrix} = \begin{bmatrix} 36,000 \\ 21,600 \\ 12,000 \end{bmatrix}$$

and, as in Eq. (9-42)

$$\Delta X = \begin{bmatrix} 1.429 & .497 & .576 \\ .377 & 1.230 & .372 \\ .401 & .384 & 1.322 \end{bmatrix} \begin{bmatrix} 36,000 \\ 21,600 \\ 12,000 \end{bmatrix} = \begin{bmatrix} 69,127 \\ 44,604 \\ 38,594 \end{bmatrix}$$

Notice that the *total* new output from sector 3 is $158,594. This figure includes the $120,000 from the new firm and $38,594 of additional output from the old (existing) firms in sector 3. On the other hand, if increased capacity in sector 3 is specified as, say, $70,000 more sales to final demand for sector 3 goods, then, as in Eq. (9-43),

$$\Delta X = \begin{bmatrix} 1.429 & .497 & .576 \\ .377 & 1.230 & .372 \\ .401 & .384 & 1.322 \end{bmatrix} \begin{bmatrix} 0 \\ 0 \\ 70,000 \end{bmatrix} = \begin{bmatrix} 40,320 \\ 26,880 \\ 92,540 \end{bmatrix}$$

which is just $\begin{bmatrix} .576 \\ .372 \\ 1.322 \end{bmatrix}$ (70,000), as in Eq. (9-44).

Other Structural Changes

As was already mentioned, when a new industry moves into an economic area, or when the capacity of an existing sector is increased, it is of course entirely possible that current transaction patterns for existing sectors in the region will change. For example, sector j, which formerly bought input i from a firm located outside the region, may now purchase some (or all) of input i from the new local establishment. Or, indeed, sector j may replace formerly used input k, bought from a producer in the region, with input i, bought from the new establishment in the region. Such changes in transactions, the elements of the Z matrix, will generate changes in direct-input coefficients in columns and rows other than those for the new sector (or for the sector whose capacity has been increased.)

It should be clear that out-movement of a firm or an entire sector from a local economy can be treated in much the same way. Usually output, income, and employment multipliers provide an adequate approach to quantifying such decreases in economic activity—particularly if, say, one plant closes but other plants in the same sector remain. If all economic activity in a sector is stopped—for example, all shoe manufacturing leaves Massachusetts and moves to the South—then the column and row for that sector disappear from the Massachusetts A matrix, and local producers in other sectors that use the product as an input will either have to import the good that has disappeared from the local economy or else they will substitute alternative locally produced inputs. Similarly, local firms that previously supplied inputs to the now-absent sector will find their sales patterns altered. Again, changes will occur in other columns and/or rows of the A matrix. However, it is extremely difficult to predict exactly where these changes will be and exactly what their magnitude will be.

9-5 | DYNAMIC CONSIDERATIONS IN INPUT-OUTPUT ANALYSIS

General Relationships

Thus far, we have considered analysis using the A matrix of technical coefficients, which was derived from measurement of *flows* of goods between sectors, purchased for current production needs during a particular period of time. Each of the flows, z_{ij}, is viewed as serving as an input for current output, X_j, and these relations are reflected in the technical coefficients, $a_{ij} = z_{ij}/X_j$. Actually, however, some input goods contribute to the production process but are not immediately used up during that production—machines, buildings, and so on. In other words, a sector has a certain capital *stock* that is also necessary for production. If one could measure the value of the output of sector i that is held by sector j as stock, v_{ij}, then one could estimate a "capital coefficient," by dividing this holding of stock by the output of sector j, over some period. Along with fixed investment items such as buildings and machinery, goods bought as inventory by sector j, to use as inputs to later production, may also be included in the v_{ij} term. Let $b_{ij} = v_{ij}/X_j$; this coefficient is interpreted as the amount of sector i's product (in dollars) held as capital stock for production of one dollar's worth of output by sector j. For example, if sector i is the construction industry and sector j is automobiles, b_{ij} might represent the dollars' worth of factory space per dollar's worth of automobiles produced. Clearly, for *current* production, the machinery, buildings, and so forth must already be in place. But if an economy is growing, then *anticipated* production (next year) is different from current production (this year), and the amount of supporting capital may change. One simple assumption (often used) is that the amount of new production from sector i for capital stocks in sector j in time period $t + 1$ (say next year) will be given by $b_{ij}(X_j^{t+1} - X_j^t)$, where the superscripts denote time periods (here years); that is, the amount of sector i production necessary to satisfy the added demand in sector j for goods from sector i as capital stocks for next year's production is given by the observed capital coefficient, b_{ij}, times the change in sector j output between this year and next year, $(X_j^{t+1} - X_j^t)$. This use of the capital coefficients assumes that production is at or near effective capacity in sector j, since the anticipated increase in production (if $[X_j^{t+1} - X_j^t]$ is positive) requires new capital goods.[3]

The typical equation for the output of sector i in period t would become

$$X_i^t = \sum_{j=1}^{n} a_{ij}X_j^t + \sum_{j=1}^{n} b_{ij}\left(X_j^{t+1} - X_j^t\right) + Y_i^t \qquad (9\text{-}45)$$

or

$$X_i^t - \sum_{j=1}^{n} a_{ij}X_j^t + \sum_{j=1}^{n} b_{ij}X_j^t - \sum_{j=1}^{n} b_{ij}X_j^{t+1} = Y_i^t \qquad (9\text{-}46)$$

---

[3]The $X_j^{t+1} - X_j^t$ term could also be negative or zero. Thus, if $b_{ij} = 0.02$ and $X_j^{t+1} - X_j^t = \$100$, there will be a need for \$2 more output from sector i for sector j; if $X_j^{t+1} - X_j^t = -\$300$, the model would forecast a decrease of \$6 in purchases from i by j. In general, we are usually concerned with the sectoral consequences of economic *growth*, so that the usual setting in which the dynamic model is used is when $X_j^{t+1} - X_j^t$ is strictly positive.

The matrix form, given an $n \times n$ capital coefficients matrix B, made up of elements b_{ij}, would be

$$(I - A + B)X^t - BX^{t+1} = Y^t \qquad (9\text{-}47)$$

or, rearranging,

$$BX^{t+1} = (I - A + B)X^t - Y^t$$

for $t = 0, 1, \cdots, T$. For example, if the time superscripts denote years, this represents a set of relationships between gross outputs and final demands starting now (year $t = 0$) and extending T years into the future.

These are so-called linear *difference equations*, since the values of the variables—the X_j's—are related, via the coefficients in A and B and the final demands, for different periods of time. Solution methods for sets of difference equations, and analysis of the values of the variables over time, are topics that go beyond the level of this text. The intention here is primarily to acquaint the reader with the notion of capital coefficients and with one of the ways in which the existence of stocks of capital goods for production could be incorporated into input-output analysis.[4] Clearly, the assumptions inherent in this model—for example, the stability of capital coefficients over time—deserve just as careful scrutiny as those in the static model. Moreover, data and measurement problems for estimating capital coefficients are even more severe than those for technical coefficients. (Richardson 1972, pp. 183–93, discusses the many problems involved in implementing a dynamic model at the regional level.) Several operational models have been developed, however, such as Miernyk et al. (1970), which examines alternative economic development strategies for the state of West Virginia, and Miernyk and Sears (1974), where the impacts of pollution-control technologies on regional economies are analyzed, using a dynamic input-output model.

In developing capital coefficients, we may also wish to distinguish between "replacement capital"—for example, investment for replacing depreciated equipment—which is a function of current production, X^t, and "expansion capital"—for example, investment in new equipment for expanded production capacity—which is a function of industry growth. These represent the difference between current and past production, $X^{t+1} - X^t$. In this case we might write the analog to Eq. (9-47) as

$$(I - A - D + B)X^t - BX^{t+1} = Y^t \qquad (9\text{-}48)$$

where D is the newly added matrix of replacement capital coefficients and B is now the matrix of expansion capital coefficients.

---

[4] For the reader who is somewhat familiar with differential calculus, there is a *continuous* version of this model. As the time interval between periods becomes very small, the difference $X_j^{t+1} - X_j^t$ approaches the derivative dX_j/dt. The continuous analog to Eq. (9-45) is thus $X_i = \sum_{j=1}^{n} a_{ij}X_j + \sum_{j=1}^{n} b_{ij}(dX_j/dt) + Y_i$, and, denoting the time derivative of the vector X by $\dot{X}$, we would have $B\dot{X} = (I - A)X - Y$. These are linear *differential equations* for which solution procedures and stability analysis are also possible but beyond the level of this text.

A Three-Period Example

Consider Eq. (9-47) again; denote $(I - A + B)$ by G and let $T = 3$. Then the difference equation relationships are

$$
\begin{array}{l}
GX^0 - BX^1 = Y^0 \\
GX^1 - BX^2 = Y^1 \\
GX^2 - BX^3 = Y^2 \\
GX^3 - BX^4 = Y^3
\end{array}
\quad \text{or} \quad
\begin{bmatrix}
G & -B & 0 & 0 & 0 \\
0 & G & -B & 0 & 0 \\
0 & 0 & G & -B & 0 \\
0 & 0 & 0 & G & -B
\end{bmatrix}
\begin{bmatrix}
X^0 \\ X^1 \\ X^2 \\ X^3 \\ X^4
\end{bmatrix}
=
\begin{bmatrix}
Y^0 \\ Y^1 \\ Y^2 \\ Y^3
\end{bmatrix}
$$

$$(9\text{-}49)$$

Notice that there are four matrix equations involving five unknown vectors, X^0 through X^4. If there are n sectors in the economy, we have $4n$ linear equations in $5n$ variables. An issue that arises in many dynamic models, including the input-output system, is which values to specify as fixed in the dynamic process. Generally, there are *initial* values, at the beginning ($t = 0$), when one starts with a given amount of, say, output in the economy, or else there are *terminal* values, specifying desired characteristics of the system at the end of the period over which the model is being used ($t = T$ or $T + 1$). We investigate several possibilities in the case where $T = 3$.

Terminal Conditions In (9-49), when $T = 3$, this means $X^{T+1} = X^4$. In some versions of the dynamic input-output model (for example, Leontief 1970), it is simply assumed that we cannot see beyond year T, the last year that is of interest, and so $X^{T+1} = 0$. In that case, the equations in (9-49) are represented in compact matrix form as

$$
\begin{bmatrix}
G & -B & 0 & 0 \\
0 & G & -B & 0 \\
0 & 0 & G & -B \\
0 & 0 & 0 & G
\end{bmatrix}
\begin{bmatrix}
X^0 \\ X^1 \\ X^2 \\ X^3
\end{bmatrix}
=
\begin{bmatrix}
Y^0 \\ Y^1 \\ Y^2 \\ Y^3
\end{bmatrix}
\qquad (9\text{-}50)
$$

Since $X^4 = 0$, it disappears from the X vector in (9-49), and the last column of the coefficient matrix in (9-49) is also unnecessary.

Given a set of final demands in the current year and in the next three years—Y^0, Y^1, Y^2, and Y^3—we could find the associated gross outputs in each of those years—X^0, X^1, X^2, and X^3—using the inverse of the matrix on the left in Eq. (9-50), provided that it exists. (We will come back to this point soon.) Notice that for an n-sector economy, this will be a square matrix of order $4n$. In general, for a time horizon of T years, this matrix will be of order $(T + 1)n$; that is, it can become a fairly large matrix for "reasonable" problems. For a ten-year planning problem in a 100-sector economy this matrix will be 1100×1100. However, the particular structure of these equations when $X^{T+1} = 0$, as in Eq. (9-50), allows for an alternative and simple *recursive* solution procedure.

Given Y^3, find X^3 from

$$
X^3 = G^{-1}Y^3 \qquad (9\text{-}51)
$$

Using this value for X^3, find X^2 from the third equation in (9-49) as

$$X^2 = G^{-1}(Y^2 + BX^3) = G^{-1}(Y^2 + BG^{-1}Y^3) \qquad (9\text{-}52)$$

Similarly, knowing X^3 and X^2,

$$\begin{aligned}X^1 &= G^{-1}(Y^1 + BX^2) = G^{-1}\left[Y^1 + BG^{-1}(Y^2 + BX^3)\right]\\ &= G^{-1}\left[Y^1 + BG^{-1}Y^2 + BG^{-1}BG^{-1}Y^3\right]\end{aligned} \qquad (9\text{-}53)$$

and finally

$$X^0 = G^{-1}(Y^0 + BX^1) = G^{-1}\left[Y^0 + (BG^{-1})Y^1 + (BG^{-1})^2Y^2 + (BG^{-1})^3Y^3\right] \qquad (9\text{-}54)$$

Notice that this approach moves backward in time, starting at the end (X^3) and finishing at the beginning (X^0).[5] This sequential solution procedure depends on the nonsingularity of G; that is, we must be able to find $(I - A + B)^{-1}$. In practice, G is not likely to be singular. Also, there is a result in matrix algebra which states that a matrix with the structure of the coefficient matrix on the left-hand side of Eq. (9-50) will be nonsingular if and only if G is nonsingular, and that G^{-1} will appear along the main diagonal of this large inverse.[6] Therefore the sequential approach in Eqs. (9-51) through (9-54) is possible if and only if the inverse in Eq. (9-50) exists.

Instead of assuming that $X^{T+1} = 0$ in Eq. (9-49), we could have some target value of X for the first postterminal year; that is, we could specify that

---

[5]An interesting special case emerges from Eq. (9-54). Suppose that we are interested in a τ-year planning period with production to meet a constant level of final demand, Y^*, each year. Then extension of the result in Eq. (9-54) leads to

$$X^0 = G^{-1}\left[I + (BG^{-1}) + (BG^{-1})^2 + \cdots + (BG^{-1})^\tau\right]Y^*$$

If, as τ gets large, the power series in brackets converges—as we saw in Chapter 2 in the case for $(I + A + A^2 + \cdots + A^m)$—then

$$X^0 = G^{-1}\left[I - (BG^{-1})\right]^{-1}Y^*$$

From the matrix result that $B^{-1}A^{-1} = (AB)^{-1}$, this is

$$X^0 = \left\{\left[I - (BG^{-1})\right]G\right\}^{-1}Y^* = (G - B)^{-1}Y^*$$

and since $G = (I - A + B)$, this means that

$$X^0 = (I - A)^{-1}Y^*$$

Finally, as $\tau \to \infty$, $X^0 = X^1 = \cdots = X = X^*$, so

$$X^* = (I - A)^{-1}Y^*$$

This reflects the logical limiting case. When final demand is constant and the time horizon infinite, the output level is constant and there is no need for capital growth.

[6]That this is true for the $T = 1$ case, where the relevant matrix is $\begin{bmatrix} G & -B \\ 0 & G \end{bmatrix}$, is easily shown using results on the inverse of a partitioned matrix (Appendix A, section A-7). The extension to larger systems is fairly straightforward. It also is clear, from the $T = 1$ case, that the matrices in the upper-left and lower-right positions in the inverse are both G^{-1}.

$X^4 = \bar{X}^4$. Then the matrix structure in Eq. (9-50) would be altered only in that Y^3 on the right-hand side would be replaced by $Y^3 + B\bar{X}^4$. The solution could still be found using the inverse of the matrix on the left of Eq. (9-50), or the recursive solution, as in Eqs. (9-51) through (9-54), could proceed as before.

Alternatively, one can specify that $X^{T+1} = HX^T$, where H is a diagonal matrix whose elements are exogenously set growth rates for each of the sectors in the first postterminal year. In that case, the last equation in (9-49) would be $GX^3 - BHX^3 = Y^3$ and the matrix structure would be

$$
\begin{bmatrix}
G & -B & 0 & 0 \\
0 & G & -B & 0 \\
0 & 0 & G & -B \\
0 & 0 & 0 & (G-BH)
\end{bmatrix}
\begin{bmatrix}
X^0 \\
X^1 \\
X^2 \\
X^3
\end{bmatrix}
=
\begin{bmatrix}
Y^0 \\
Y^1 \\
Y^2 \\
Y^3
\end{bmatrix}
\tag{9-55}
$$

and solution procedures would be as above.

Initial Conditions As in the case with general systems of difference equations, it is often assumed that the initial ($t = 0$) values of *all* elements in the system are known and that the usefulness of the model comes from its description of the values to be taken by the variables that are of interest in subsequent years. From that point of view, we would assume that both Y^0 *and* X^0 have given initial values. This reduces the system in Eq. (9-49) to $4n$ linear equations in $4n$ variables. Then, given exogenous values for Y^1, Y^2, and Y^3, we could proceed sequentially from X^1 to X^4. As opposed to the sequence in Eqs. (9-51) through (9-54), this one moves forward in time, not backward. From Eq. (9-49),

$$
\begin{aligned}
X^1 &= B^{-1}(GX^0 - Y^0) \\
X^2 &= B^{-1}(GX^1 - Y^1) \\
X^3 &= B^{-1}(GX^2 - Y^2) \\
X^4 &= B^{-1}(GX^3 - Y^3)
\end{aligned}
\tag{9-56}
$$

Notice that this sequential solution procedure depends on the nonsingularity of B, so that B^{-1} can be found.

The results found sequentially in (9-56) can also be found in matrix form if the system in (9-49) is written as

$$
\begin{bmatrix}
-B & 0 & 0 & 0 \\
G & -B & 0 & 0 \\
0 & G & -B & 0 \\
0 & 0 & G & -B
\end{bmatrix}
\begin{bmatrix}
X^1 \\
X^2 \\
X^3 \\
X^4
\end{bmatrix}
=
\begin{bmatrix}
Y^0 - GX^0 \\
Y^1 \\
Y^2 \\
Y^3
\end{bmatrix}
\tag{9-57}
$$

This reflects the fact that X^0 is now exogenously determined; it disappears from the top of the X vector on the left and hence the first column in the coefficient matrix in Eq. (9-49) also is removed. Then X^1 through X^4 can be found by premultiplying both sides of Eq. (9-57) by the inverse of the coefficient matrix on the left, provided that inverse exists. As before, the matrix on the left-hand side of Eq. (9-57) will be nonsingular if and only if the matrix on its main diagonal, here B, is nonsingular.

In fact, singularity of the B matrix is a problem in dynamic input-output models. It is easy to see why it might be that $|B| = 0$. In a model with a fairly large number of sectors (a relatively disaggregated model), it is very likely that there will be sectors that do not supply capital goods to any sectors—that is, sectors whose row in the B matrix will contain all zeros. (For example, if there were a sector labeled "Agriculture, potatoes"). When one or more rows of a matrix is all zeros, the determinant of the matrix is zero and so the matrix has no inverse (Appendix A, section A-5).[7] In the examples to follow, we will see that even when B is nonsingular, it may be somewhat "ill-conditioned" and contain unusually large elements in its inverse. This, in turn, introduces complications for the problem with initial conditions specified.

Numerical Example 1

We illustrate the general workings of the dynamic input-output model using hypothetical figures for a two-sector economy. Let $A = \begin{bmatrix} .1 & .2 \\ .3 & .4 \end{bmatrix}$ and $B = \begin{bmatrix} .05 & .001 \\ .001 & .05 \end{bmatrix}$; then $G = \begin{bmatrix} .95 & -.199 \\ -.299 & .65 \end{bmatrix}$. For simplicity, let $T = 2$.

Terminal Conditions Suppose that $Y^0 = \begin{bmatrix} 100 \\ 100 \end{bmatrix}$, $Y^1 = \begin{bmatrix} 120 \\ 150 \end{bmatrix}$, and $Y^2 = \begin{bmatrix} 140 \\ 200 \end{bmatrix}$. If we assume that $X^3 = 0$, then, as in Eqs. (9-51) through (9-54)—but with $T = 2$ rather than $T = 3$, as in that set of illustrations—we can find the backward sequence X^2, X^1, X^0. Here $G^{-1} = \begin{bmatrix} 1.1649 & 0.3566 \\ 0.5358 & 1.7025 \end{bmatrix}$, so

$$X^2 = G^{-1}Y^2 = \begin{bmatrix} 234.41 \\ 415.51 \end{bmatrix} \tag{9-58}$$

Then

$$X^1 = G^{-1}(Y^1 + BX^2) = \begin{bmatrix} 214.91 \\ 361.94 \end{bmatrix} \tag{9-59}$$

and

$$X^0 = G^{-1}(Y^0 + BX^1) = \begin{bmatrix} 171.62 \\ 260.96 \end{bmatrix} \tag{9-60}$$

Alternatively, using the full matrix form, as in Eq. (9-50), where

$$\begin{bmatrix} G & -B & 0 \\ 0 & G & -B \\ 0 & 0 & G \end{bmatrix}^{-1}$$

$$= \begin{bmatrix} 1.1649 & .3566 & .0784 & .0532 & .0061 & .0061 \\ .5358 & 1.7025 & .0791 & .1560 & .0090 & .0149 \\ 0 & 0 & 1.1649 & .3566 & .0784 & .0532 \\ 0 & 0 & .5358 & 1.7025 & .0791 & .1560 \\ 0 & 0 & 0 & 0 & 1.1649 & .3566 \\ 0 & 0 & 0 & 0 & .5358 & 1.7025 \end{bmatrix} \tag{9-61}$$

[7] There is a large literature on the singularity problem in the dynamic Leontief model, but the subject is beyond the scope of this book. The interested reader might want to refer to Leontief (1970), Kendrick (1972), Livesey (1976), Luenberger and Arbel (1977), Schinnar (1978), or Leontief and Duchin (1984).

we could find, simultaneously, these same values for X^0, X^1, and X^2. (Note that G^{-1} does indeed appear repeated along the main diagonal of the large inverse.)

If, instead of $X^3 = 0$, we specify $X^3 = \begin{bmatrix} 250 \\ 450 \end{bmatrix}$ (target values for sectoral outputs in the first postterminal year), then $BX^3 = \begin{bmatrix} 12.95 \\ 22.75 \end{bmatrix}$, so that only the equation for X^2 changes slightly from the sequence in Eqs. (9-58) through (9-60), and

$$X^2 = G^{-1}(Y^2 + BX^3) = \begin{bmatrix} 257.60 \\ 461.18 \end{bmatrix}$$

$$X^1 = G^{-1}(Y^1 + BX^2) = \begin{bmatrix} 217.13 \\ 366.52 \end{bmatrix}$$

$$X^0 = G^{-1}(Y^0 + BX^1) = \begin{bmatrix} 171.83 \\ 261.41 \end{bmatrix}$$

In comparison with the X^0, X^1, and X^2 found above when $X^3 = 0$, notice that the initial-year outputs are affected very little by this change in postterminal year conditions. However, X^1 is changed more than X^0 and X^2 more than X^1. In matrix form,

$$\begin{bmatrix} G & -B & 0 \\ 0 & G & -B \\ 0 & 0 & G \end{bmatrix} \begin{bmatrix} X^0 \\ X^1 \\ X^2 \end{bmatrix} = \begin{bmatrix} Y^0 \\ Y^1 \\ Y^2 + BX^3 \end{bmatrix}$$

and, using Eq. (9-61), the same values of the gross outputs from both sectors in each period can be found simultaneously.

Using the $X^3 = 0$ example again, let $Y^0 = Y^1 = Y^2 = \begin{bmatrix} 100 \\ 100 \end{bmatrix}$. Then, from the inverse in Eq. (9-61), or from the backward recursive procedure, as above, we can find

$$X = \begin{bmatrix} X^0 \\ X^1 \\ X^2 \end{bmatrix} = \begin{bmatrix} 166.53 \\ 249.73 \\ 165.31 \\ 247.34 \\ 152.15 \\ 223.83 \end{bmatrix} \qquad \textbf{(9-62)}$$

Recall (from footnote 4) that with constant final demands, Y^*, as the time period lengthens, the results in each X^t approach $(I - A)^{-1}Y^*$. Here $A = \begin{bmatrix} .1 & .2 \\ .3 & .4 \end{bmatrix}$, so

$$(I - A)^{-1} \begin{bmatrix} 100 \\ 100 \end{bmatrix} = \begin{bmatrix} 166.70 \\ 250.00 \end{bmatrix}$$

which is closely approximated by X^0 in Eq. (9-62), the outputs in the earliest year. As the time period lengthens (that is, as T gets larger), subsequent values of X^t will also approach $\begin{bmatrix} 166.70 \\ 250.00 \end{bmatrix}$. (The reader with access to a computer may wish to experiment by letting $T = 3$, $T = 4$, and so on, using the same A and B and constant final demand of 100 for both sectors.)

Initial Conditions   Taking an alternative point of view, suppose

$$Y^0 = \begin{bmatrix} 100 \\ 100 \end{bmatrix}, Y^1 = \begin{bmatrix} 120 \\ 150 \end{bmatrix}, \text{and } Y^2 = \begin{bmatrix} 140 \\ 200 \end{bmatrix},$$

as before, but let $X^0 = \begin{bmatrix} 180 \\ 270 \end{bmatrix}$. Originally, with these final demands and X^0 determined endogenously, we found $X^0 = \begin{bmatrix} 171.61 \\ 260.96 \end{bmatrix}$, as in Eq. (9-60). We now select an X^0 that is larger. Here, using the forward recursive procedure of Eq. (9-56), with $B^{-1} = \begin{bmatrix} 20.008 & -0.4 \\ -0.4 & 20.008 \end{bmatrix}$, we find

$$X^1 = B^{-1}(GX^0 - Y^0) = \begin{bmatrix} 336.87 \\ 426.87 \end{bmatrix}$$

and

$$X^2 = B^{-1}(GX^1 - Y^1) = \begin{bmatrix} 2291.66 \\ 488.91 \end{bmatrix}$$

Essentially the same values are found, using the inverse of $\begin{bmatrix} -B & 0 \\ G & -B \end{bmatrix}$, as in Eq. (9-57). Here this inverse is

$$\begin{bmatrix} -20.008 & 0.4 & 0 & 0 \\ 0.4 & -20.008 & 0 & 0 \\ -384.395 & 92.522 & -20.008 & 0.4 \\ 132.538 & -264.347 & 0.4 & -20.008 \end{bmatrix}$$

(Again, note that $-B^{-1}$ is repeated along the main diagonal of this inverse.) This example illustrates that the dynamic input-output model, at least in the simplified form presented here, is very sensitive to the specification of initial conditions. We return to this point in Numerical Example 2, below.

If we use the same structure as in Eqs. (9-56) and (9-57), but with $X^0 = \begin{bmatrix} 171.62 \\ 260.96 \end{bmatrix}$, which is the actual initial output found in Eq. (9-60) when X^0 is endogenous, we will generate exactly the values of X^1 and X^2 that were found initially in Eqs. (9-59) and (9-58). Similarly, if we use $X^0 = \begin{bmatrix} 166.53 \\ 249.73 \end{bmatrix}$, from Eq. (9-62), in conjunction with $Y^0 = Y^1 = Y^2 = \begin{bmatrix} 100 \\ 100 \end{bmatrix}$, we generate exactly the sequence of outputs already found for that example—X^1 and X^2 in Eq. (9-62). For either of these earlier examples, if we take the forward sequential approach but with an initial X^0 that is less than that found with X^0 endogenous (and using the same final demands), we will generate one or more negative gross outputs in years after $t = 0$. Since the values for X^0 in Eqs. (9-60) and (9-62) represent what is necessary to satisfy the specified sequences of final demands with an economy whose structure is reflected in the given A and B matrices, then any initial output that is less than that X^0 will produce a sequence of additions to capital stock that eventually become inadequate for future production. (Recall that, unlike the static input-output case, in the dynamic model it is assumed that all sectors are producing at full capacity.)

Numerical Example 2

In order to illustrate a particularly sensitive feature of the dynamic input-output model in its forward sequential form (starting from *initial* conditions), we select an alternative capital coefficients matrix. In this new case, sector 1 is far more important as a supplier of capital goods than is sector 2; here B

$$= \begin{bmatrix} .05 & .06 \\ .0004 & .0007 \end{bmatrix}.$$ Using the same A matrix as in the preceding example, we

find $G = \begin{bmatrix} .95 & -.14 \\ -.2996 & .6007 \end{bmatrix}$. Note that while B is quite different from the

preceding example, the current G matrix is close to that in Example 1. This, of course, is because $G = (I - A + B)$, and A is unchanged in the two examples.

Terminal Conditions   We use the same sequence of final demands—namely

$$Y^0 = \begin{bmatrix} 100 \\ 100 \end{bmatrix}, \; Y^1 = \begin{bmatrix} 120 \\ 150 \end{bmatrix}, \text{ and } Y^2 = \begin{bmatrix} 140 \\ 200 \end{bmatrix}.$$

Again, letting $X^3 = 0$, we can find X^2, X^1, and X^0 sequentially, exactly as in Eqs. (9-58) through (9-60). Here $G^{-1} = \begin{bmatrix} 1.1361 & .2648 \\ .5667 & 1.7968 \end{bmatrix}$ (which is not a great deal different from G^{-1} in the previous example) and

$$X^2 = \begin{bmatrix} 212.01 \\ 438.70 \end{bmatrix}$$

$$X^1 = \begin{bmatrix} 218.10 \\ 359.15 \end{bmatrix}$$

$$X^0 = \begin{bmatrix} 177.05 \\ 255.35 \end{bmatrix}$$

While these results are different from those in the previous example, as is to be expected, the individual differences are never terribly large (not more than about $25).

Initial Conditions   Using the same Y^0, Y^1, and Y^2 along with X^0

$$= \begin{bmatrix} 180 \\ 270 \end{bmatrix},$$ from the previous example, illustrates the sensitivity problem. Here, because B has a row of elements that are smaller than any of the elements in the previous capital coefficients matrix, its inverse can be expected to contain at least some larger elements. And indeed it does; here $B^{-1} = \begin{bmatrix} 63.636 & -5454.545 \\ -36.364 & 4545.455 \end{bmatrix}$.

Unlike G^{-1} in the two examples, we see that this B^{-1} is very different from its counterpart in the previous example. Thus

$$X^1 = B^{-1}(GX^0 - Y^0) = B^{-1} \begin{bmatrix} 33.20 \\ 8.26 \end{bmatrix} = \begin{bmatrix} -42942 \\ 36338 \end{bmatrix}$$

and, much worse (the results have been rounded)

$$X^2 = B^{-1}(GX^1 - Y^1) = B^{-1}\begin{bmatrix} -45882 \\ 34694 \end{bmatrix} = \begin{bmatrix} -192{,}000{,}000 \\ 159{,}000{,}000 \end{bmatrix}$$

This illustrates that as the elements in one or more rows of B become small, B^{-1} contains very large numbers. Here $|B| = 0.000011$; if one were working with four-decimal accuracy, one would conclude that B was singular.

Consider the determination of X^1. Rewriting, $BX^1 = GX^0 - Y^0$, and with A and B (and hence G) given, along with Y^0, the choice of X^0 then specifies the right-hand side vector for this set of n linear equations in n unknowns. (In our examples, $n = 2$). Denote a specific right-hand side vector as R^0. In the easily visualized two-variable case, we could explore the solution-space geometry of the pair of equations. Here

$$B = \begin{bmatrix} b_{11} & b_{12} \\ b_{21} & b_{22} \end{bmatrix}, \qquad X^1 = \begin{bmatrix} X_1^1 \\ X_2^1 \end{bmatrix}, \qquad \text{and } R^0 = \begin{bmatrix} r_1^0 \\ r_2^0 \end{bmatrix}$$

so

$$b_{11}X_1^1 + b_{12}X_2^1 = r_1^0$$

$$b_{21}X_1^1 + b_{22}X_2^1 = r_2^0$$

We leave it to the interested reader to make sketches in solution space. However, it is easy to show that both lines will have positive intercepts on the vertical axis (when $R^0 > 0$, which by definition it must be) and that both will have negative slopes. Then the conditions for the intersection of the two lines to be in the positive quadrant or on its boundaries (that is, $X^1 \geq 0$) can be shown to be as follows. The values of X_1^0 and X_2^0 must be chosen so that r_1^0/r_2^0 lies within the bounds set by b_{11}/b_{21} and b_{12}/b_{22}. The generalization to more sectors and to nonnegativity of outputs further in the future—X^2, X^3, and so on—is beyond this text. The point of the illustration is simply to highlight the kinds of problems that can arise in the dynamic model when one wants to calculate forward from initial conditions, using B^{-1}.

Note that in the first numerical example, $b_{11}/b_{21} = 50$ and $b_{12}/b_{22} = 0.02$. In that example, in fact, $(GX^0 - Y^0) = R^0 = \begin{bmatrix} 18.77 \\ 21.71 \end{bmatrix}$, so that $r_1^0/r_2^0 = 0.86$, which is indeed within the bounds. In the second example, $b_{11}/b_{21} = 125$ and $b_{12}/b_{22} = 85.7$. For our initial choice of $X^0 = \begin{bmatrix} 180 \\ 270 \end{bmatrix}$, $r_1^0/r_2^0 = 33.2/8.26 = 4.02$, which is outside the admissible range. A choice of $X^0 = \begin{bmatrix} 180 \\ 256.8 \end{bmatrix}$, however, would lead to $X^1 \geq 0$, since $r_1^0/r_2^0 = 105.6$, while an initial $X^0 = \begin{bmatrix} 180 \\ 256.7 \end{bmatrix}$ generates $r_1^0/r_2^0 = 129.1$, which means that X^1 will not be nonnegative. By any reasonable definition, this would appear to be extreme sensitivity to initial values.

Turnpike Growth and Dynamic Models

In Chapter 2 we introduced the notion of a completely closed input-output model as

$$(I - A)X = 0$$

or

$$AX = X$$

Recall that such an input-output model is in fact a homogeneous system of linear equations which has a nontrivial solution, that is, one other than $X = 0$, if and only if $|I - A| = 0$.

The corresponding closed dynamic model is the following

$$AX^t + B(X^{t+1} - X^t) = X^t \qquad (9\text{-}63)$$

If we assume for simplicity that we can find an X^{t+1} and X^t such that all industries grow at the same rate in the economy, say, at rate λ, then

$$X^{t+1} = \lambda X^t \qquad (9\text{-}64)$$

This rate, λ, is often referred to as a *turnpike growth rate* (all industries are growing or declining on the same path—the "turnpike"), and it is interpreted as a general indicator of the "health" of the economy, that is, $\lambda > 1$ indicates that the economy is expanding, $0 < \lambda < 1$ indicates that the economy is contracting, and $\lambda < 0$ indicates that the economy is unstable, that is, experiencing periods of both decline and growth over time. Since λ is really only a theoretical number, how can it be computed? Substituting Eq. (9-64) into Eq. (9-63), we obtain by ordinary matrix algebra

$$AX^t + B(\lambda X^t - X^t) = X^t$$

$$B\lambda X^t = (I - A + B)X^t$$

$$B^{-1}(I - A + B)X^t = \lambda X^t$$

or

$$QX^t = \lambda X^t \qquad (9\text{-}65)$$

where $Q = B^{-1}(I - A + B)$. Note that Eq. (9-65) has a very interesting feature, namely a *scalar*, λ, multiplied by X^t, yields precisely the same value as a *matrix*, Q, postmultiplied by X^t.

Such a problem is actually well known is applied mathematics as an *eigenvalue* problem where λ is the *eigenvalue* (sometimes called a characteristic value or latent root), and X^t corresponding to λ, that is, such that Eq. (9-65) holds, is the *eigenvector* (sometimes called characteristic vector or latent vector). This problem is closely related to the solution of systems of homogeneous linear equations discussed in section A-9 of Appendix A. Note that we can rewrite Eq. (9-65) as

$$(Q - \lambda I)X = 0 \qquad (9\text{-}66)$$

for which there is a nontrivial solution if and only if

$$|Q - \lambda I| = 0 \qquad (9\text{-}67)$$

We consider the 2×2 case, with

$$Q = \begin{bmatrix} q_{11} & q_{12} \\ q_{21} & q_{22} \end{bmatrix}$$

so that

$$|Q - \lambda I| = \left| \begin{bmatrix} q_{11} - \lambda & q_{12} \\ q_{21} & q_{22} - \lambda \end{bmatrix} \right| = (q_{11} - \lambda)(q_{22} - \lambda) - q_{12}q_{22} = 0 = \lambda^2 + b\lambda + c$$

where $b = -(q_{11} + q_{22})$ and $c = q_{11}q_{22} - q_{12}q_{21}$. We find the solution to $QX = \lambda X$ by solving

$$|Q - \lambda I| = 0$$

or

$$\lambda^2 + b\lambda + c = 0$$

Note that this is a polynomial (sometimes called the characteristic polynomial) which, when set equal to zero, is called the characteristic equation; in this case it has two solutions, given by

$$\lambda = \frac{-(q_{11} + q_{22}) \pm \left[(q_{11} + q_{22})^2 - 4(q_{11}q_{22} - q_{12}q_{21})\right]^{1/2}}{2}$$

Denote these solutions as λ_1 and λ_2. The turnpike growth rate is defined to be the largest eigenvalue found (see Carter 1974), which we define as λ_{max}.

Example Suppose $Q = B^{-1}(I - A + B) = \begin{bmatrix} 1.0 & .5 \\ 2.0 & 1.0 \end{bmatrix}$

$$|Q - \lambda I| = (1 - \lambda)(1 - \lambda) - 1 = 0$$
$$\lambda^2 - 2\lambda = 0$$
$$\lambda(\lambda - 2) = 0$$

so $\lambda_1 = 0$ and $\lambda_2 = 2$. The turnpike growth rate is $\lambda_{max} = \lambda_2 = 2$. As mentioned earlier, if $\lambda_{max} < 0$ then the economy is unstable, that is, oscillating. The interpretation of negative λ's can be specified more precisely by relating it to the solution of a system of ordinary differential equations, but this is beyond the scope of this text. Carter (1974) and Leontief and Duchin (1984) examine the notion of turnpike growth as an indicator economic stability resulting from changes in technology in the United States.

9-6 | THE PRICE MODEL

Structural relationships between sectors in an economy would perhaps be measured most accurately in physical units. At least this would eliminate the influence of prices. For example, a steel manufacturer may use 375 kilowatt-hours of electricity in making 1000 tons of steel. Whether the price of a kilowatt-hour of electricity is $2.00 or $2.50, the production needs of electricity for 1000 tons of steel will most likely not be changed. But under the $2.00 price, the cost of

TABLE 9-1 Physical-Value Flows, s_{ij}

Sectors	1	2	Sectors ...	n	Final Demand F_i	Total (Gross) Output Q_i
1	s_{11}	s_{12}	...	s_{1n}	F_1	Q_1
2	s_{21}	s_{22}	...	s_{2n}	F_2	Q_2
$\vdots$	$\vdots$	$\vdots$			$\vdots$	$\vdots$
n	s_{n1}	s_{n2}	...	s_{nn}	F_n	Q_n
$n+1$	$s_{n+1,1}$	$s_{n+1,2}$	...	$s_{n+1,n}$	F_{n+1}	Q_{n+1}

electricity inputs into 1000 tons of steel will be \$750.00, whereas at \$2.50 per kilowatt-hour, the cost will be \$937.50. Thus, the z_{ij} (in value terms) representing electricity used by steel will change with the price of electricity, even though the basic structural relationship is unchanged.

Suppose, then, that sales between and among sectors in *physical* units, denoted s_{ij}, have been found, as in Table 9-1. Let F_i denote final demand for sector i output in physical units and Q_i represent total production (gross output), in physical units, for sector i. For simplicity, let the exogenous payments sector—the $(n+1)$st sector—be labor inputs (this implies, in the notation of Chapter 2, that $L_j = W_j = \overline{W}_j$), and hence final demand will be consumer (household) demand. The physical units for this sector will be man-days (or person-days). Reading across any row, say the ith, we find the basic accounting relationship when we are measuring in physical units.

$$Q_i = s_{i1} + s_{i2} + \cdots + s_{in} + F_i = \sum_{j=1}^{n} s_{ij} + F_i \qquad (9\text{-}68)$$

Letting $S = [s_{ij}]$, $Q = [Q_i]$, and $F = [F_i]$, we have

$$Q = Si + F \qquad (9\text{-}69)$$

Now, suppose that we know the prices *per unit* of physical output for each of the productive sectors, and for labor, P_{n+1}. To convert to a set of value-based data, we note that

$$X_i = P_i Q_i \qquad (9\text{-}70)$$

$$z_{ij} = P_i s_{ij} \qquad (9\text{-}71)$$

$$Y_i = P_i F_i \qquad (9\text{-}72)$$

Hence, multiplying Eq. (9-68) through by P_i, we find

$$X_i = P_i Q_i = \sum_{j=1}^{n} z_{ij} + Y_i \qquad (9\text{-}73)$$

In matrix form, the parallel to Eq. (9-69) is (also as we have seen in earlier chapters)

$$X = Zi + Y \qquad (9\text{-}74)$$

TABLE 9-2 DOLLAR-VALUE FLOWS, z_{ij}

Sectors	1	2	Sectors ...	n	Final Demand Y_i	Total (Gross) Output X_i
1	z_{11}	z_{12}	...	z_{1n}	Y_1	X_1
2	z_{21}	z_{22}	...	z_{2n}	Y_2	X_2
$\vdots$	$\vdots$	$\vdots$		$\vdots$	$\vdots$	$\vdots$
n	z_{n1}	z_{n2}	...	z_{nn}	Y_n	X_n
n+1	$z_{n+1,1}$	$z_{n+1,2}$	...	$z_{n+1,n}$	Y_{n+1}	X_{n+1}

Therefore, the dollar-value flows, parallel to the physical-value data in Table 9-1, can be found through multiplication of all elements in row i of Table 9-1 by P_i. These flows are represented in Table 9-2, which is exactly like the tables of data that were first introduced in Chapter 2. This is the form in which virtually all data in real-world applications are collected. One notable exception is the *ex ante* approach, which uses engineering production data to construct input-output tables; see Fisher (Allen and Gossling 1975, Ch. 6).

While column sums in Table 9-1 are not meaningful, because the elements in each row are measured in different units, the elements in a column of Table 9-2 represent dollar values of inputs bought by the producing sector in that column. As we saw in Chapter 2, when *all* inputs are accounted for in the processing *and* payments sectors, then the jth column sum, total outlays, is equal to the jth row sum, total output. Let W_j represent the total value of payments to the exogenous sector; this represents a price, P_{n+1}, times a physical-units amount of value added (for us, labor), $s_{n+1,j}$. Thus, summing down the jth column in Table 9-2,

$$X_j = \sum_{i=1}^{n} z_{ij} + W_j \tag{9-75}$$

or, using Eqs. (9-70) and (9-71)

$$P_j Q_j = \sum_{i=1}^{n} P_i s_{ij} + P_{n+1} s_{n+1,j} \tag{9-76}$$

We can define a technical coefficient, in physical terms, as

$$c_{ij} = \frac{s_{ij}}{Q_j} \tag{9-77}$$

For the example of electricity input into steel, this would be $375/1000 = 0.375$ (kilowatt-hours of electricity per ton of steel). Recall, from Chapter 2, that our technical coefficients in value terms are found as

$$a_{ij} = \frac{z_{ij}}{X_j}$$

Thus, using Eqs. (9-70), (9-71), and (9-77),

$$a_{ij} = \frac{P_i s_{ij}}{P_j Q_j} = c_{ij} \left(\frac{P_i}{P_j} \right) \tag{9-78}$$

The assumption of fixed-input coefficients in the basic input-output model can be applied to either value-based technical coefficients, the a_{ij}'s, or physical technical coefficients, the c_{ij}'s. Assuming fixed c_{ij}'s (in effect, a fixed "engineering" production function) is much less restrictive than assuming fixed a_{ij}'s, that is, a fixed "economic" production function. By assuming the latter, we see that both a physical technical coefficient, c_{ij}, *and* a price ratio P_i/P_j, are assumed fixed. In most input-output studies, data are not generally available to develop physical technical coefficients, so fixed a_{ij}'s are assumed.

Dividing Eq. (9-76) by Q_j, we have

$$P_j = \sum_{i=1}^{n} \frac{P_i s_{ij}}{Q_j} + \frac{P_{n+1} s_{n+1,j}}{Q_j} \tag{9-79}$$

Let $d_j = P_{n+1} s_{n+1,j}/Q_j = P_{n+1} c_{n+1,j}$. That is, d_j represents the dollar value of exogenous inputs per physical unit of output—for example, cost of labor per ton of steel. Using this and Eq. (9-77), we can rewrite Eq. (9-79) as

$$P_j = \sum_{i=1}^{n} P_i c_{ij} + d_j \tag{9-80}$$

For $n = 2$, the relationships in Eq. (9-80) are

$$
\begin{aligned}
P_1 &= P_1 c_{11} + P_2 c_{21} + d_1 \\
P_2 &= P_1 c_{12} + P_2 c_{22} + d_2
\end{aligned}
\tag{9-81}
$$

and

$$
\begin{aligned}
(1 - c_{11})P_1 - c_{21}P_2 &= d_1 \\
- c_{12}P_1 + (1 - c_{22})P_2 &= d_2
\end{aligned}
\tag{9-82}
$$

Letting $P = \begin{bmatrix} P_1 \\ P_2 \end{bmatrix}$, $C = \begin{bmatrix} c_{11} & c_{12} \\ c_{21} & c_{22} \end{bmatrix}$, and $D = \begin{bmatrix} d_1 \\ d_2 \end{bmatrix}$, this is

$$(I - C')P = D \tag{9-83}$$

That is, given the physical coefficients from some base period and assuming some exogenously determined value added per unit of physical output figures, D, for the target year, the effect on prices in the target year is found as

$$P = (I - C')^{-1} D \tag{9-84}$$

This is the Leontief price model.

Example

Consider a two-sector economy (electricity and manufacturing) and, for simplicity, let the $(n + 1)$st sector (here, sector 3) represent labor inputs (row 3) and consumer demand (column 3). Suppose that the base-period physical flows, s_{ij} as in Table 9-1, are as shown in Table 9-3.

Assume that base-period prices per unit of physical output are

$$P_1 = \$2.00 \qquad P_2 = \$5.00 \qquad P_3 = \$10.00$$

TABLE 9-3 HYPOTHETICAL EXAMPLE — PHYSICAL FLOWS

	1	2	F_i	Q_i
1	75	250	175	500
2	40	20	340	400
3 (Labor)	65	140	110	315

These may be, for example, $2.00 per 1000 kilowatt-hours of electricity, $5.00 per ton of manufactures, $10.00 per person-day of labor. Then the value-based flows, z_{ij}, as in Table 9-2, are as shown in Table 9-4. (These are, in fact, the numbers in the two-sector value-based example that has been used several times earlier in this book.)

Thus, as in Eq. (9-77), we can find the physical technical coefficients

$$\bar{C} = \begin{bmatrix} .15 & .625 & .556 \\ .08 & .05 & 1.079 \\ .13 & .35 & .349 \end{bmatrix} \tag{9-85}$$

We use $\bar{C}$ for the technical coefficients matrix that includes households. C will represent the 2×2 matrix in the upper-left corner; that is, the matrix of technical coefficients connecting the two producing sectors in the economy. Note that, unlike their value-based counterparts in an A matrix, there is no reason for a c_{ij} to be less than one, and there is no reason for column sums of $\bar{C}$ or C to be less than one.

The relationships in Eq. (9-81) are

$$\begin{aligned} 2 &= (2)(.15) + (5)(.08) + (10)(.13) = .30 + .40 + 1.30 \\ 5 &= (2)(.625) + (5)(.05) + (10)(.35) = 1.25 + .25 + 3.50 \end{aligned} \tag{9-86}$$

If we use the base-period value added per unit of output figures, $d_1 = 1.30$ and $d_2 = 3.50$, along with $(I - C')^{-1}$ for the C matrix in Eq. (9-85), in the price model of Eq. (9-84) we should generate the base-year prices, $P_1 = 2$ and $P_2 = 5$. Here

$$(I - C')^{-1} = \begin{bmatrix} 1.254 & .107 \\ .825 & 1.122 \end{bmatrix} \tag{9-87}$$

and Eq. (9-84) gives

$$\begin{bmatrix} P_1 \\ P_2 \end{bmatrix} = \begin{bmatrix} 1.254 & .107 \\ .825 & 1.122 \end{bmatrix} \begin{bmatrix} 1.3 \\ 3.5 \end{bmatrix} = \begin{bmatrix} 2.00 \\ 5.00 \end{bmatrix} \tag{9-88}$$

as expected.

TABLE 9-4 HYPOTHETICAL EXAMPLE — VALUE-BASED FLOWS

	1	2	Y_i	X_i
1	150	500	350	1000
2	200	100	1700	2000
3 (Labor)	650	1400	1100	3150

The problem is that one does not generally have the physical coefficients, c_{ij}. How, then, do the value-based coefficients, a_{ij}, contribute to a Leontief price model? The important observation is that per-unit prices for each sector in the value-based model are all one dollar, since the a_{ij} coefficients are derived on a "per-dollar's-worth-of-output" basis. So the price of a unit of output (which is defined as a dollar's worth of output) is one dollar. In this sense, they are "normalized" prices. Suppose that one has coefficients of value added per unit (dollar's worth) of output, say k_1 and k_2. (When value added consists entirely of labor, as we have assumed for this example, these are simply the so-called labor-input coefficients from earlier chapters.) Let $K = \begin{bmatrix} k_1 \\ k_2 \end{bmatrix}$ and $\bar{P} = \begin{bmatrix} \bar{P}_1 \\ \bar{P}_2 \end{bmatrix}$ represent these coefficients and the normalized prices, respectively. Then the value-based counterpart to Eq. (9-84) is

$$\bar{P} = (I - A')^{-1} K \qquad (9\text{-}89)$$

From Table 9-2, we find

$$\bar{A} = \begin{bmatrix} .15 & .25 & .11 \\ .20 & .05 & .54 \\ .65 & .70 & .35 \end{bmatrix} \qquad (9\text{-}90)$$

and, using A for the 2×2 submatrix of sector 1 and sector 2 coefficients,

$$(I - A')^{-1} = \begin{bmatrix} 1.254 & .264 \\ .330 & 1.122 \end{bmatrix} \qquad (9\text{-}91)$$

From the base-year data, we have $k_1 = 0.65$ and $k_2 = 0.70$ (from the bottom row of $\bar{A}$ in Eq. [9-90]). These are the dollar values of labor inputs per dollar's worth of output from sectors 1 and 2 (labor-input coefficients). Thus, in Eq. (9-89),

$$\bar{P} = \begin{bmatrix} 1.254 & .264 \\ .330 & 1.122 \end{bmatrix} \begin{bmatrix} .65 \\ .70 \end{bmatrix} = \begin{bmatrix} 1.00 \\ 1.00 \end{bmatrix} \qquad (9\text{-}92)$$

as expected.

The way in which the Leontief price model is often used is to assess the impact on prices throughout the economy of an increase in value-added costs in one or more sectors. Again, suppose that these costs consist entirely of wage payments. Assume that wages in sector 1 increase by 30 percent, while those in sector 2 are unchanged. Thus $\Delta K = \begin{bmatrix} .195 \\ 0 \end{bmatrix}$ where $(0.195) = (0.30)(0.65)$; that is, $\Delta k_1 = (0.30)k_1$. Using Eq. (9-89),

$$\Delta\bar{P} = (I - A')^{-1}\Delta K = \begin{bmatrix} 1.254 & .264 \\ .330 & 1.122 \end{bmatrix} \begin{bmatrix} .195 \\ 0 \end{bmatrix} = \begin{bmatrix} .245 \\ .064 \end{bmatrix} \qquad (9\text{-}93)$$

This says that the economywide effect of the 30 percent wage increase in sector 1 is that the price of sector 1 output goes up by 24.5 percent and that of sector 2 by 6.4 percent. This can be confirmed by forming a vector of new value-added costs

$$K^{new} = \begin{bmatrix} .845 \\ .700 \end{bmatrix}$$

where $(0.845) = (0.65)(0.195)$; that is, $k_1^{new} = k_1 + \Delta k_1$. Then

$$\bar{P}^{new} = (I - A')^{-1} K^{new} = \begin{bmatrix} 1.254 & .264 \\ .330 & 1.122 \end{bmatrix} \begin{bmatrix} .845 \\ .700 \end{bmatrix} = \begin{bmatrix} 1.245 \\ 1.064 \end{bmatrix} \quad (9\text{-}94)$$

Relative to the original normalized prices of $\bar{P}_1 = 1.00$ and $\bar{P}_2 = 1.00$, we see indeed that sector 1's price has gone up to 1.245, which represents a 24.5 percent increase, and sector 2's price has gone up to 1.064, which is a 6.4 percent increase. (Note that if labor costs are only a part of the value-added component for sector 1, then a 30 percent increase in wages in sector j will generate a less than 30 percent increase in k_j—for example, if wages comprise 40 percent of sector j's value-added payments, a 30 percent wage increase translates into a 12 percent increase in k_j.)

An example of the use of this version of the input-output model is provided by Melvin (1979), where the price effects of changes in corporate income taxes are estimated for both the United States and Canada, using an 82-sector U.S. table for 1965 and a 110-sector Canadian table for 1966.

A number of researchers have developed variations of the basic Leontief price model, for example, Gupta (1967), Lee et al. (1977), Moses (1974), Pai (1979), Polenske (1978), and Young (1978). These variations fall into three basic categories: (1) models that deal with disaggregated value-added components, (2) models based on changes in commodity output prices (a selected industry is made exogenous instead of the value-added sector), and (3) so-called "price-output" models that use both the price model to determine relative price changes and the output model to determine total output impacts. Pai (1979) also extends the multiregional price model, that is, $P = [I - (CA)']^{-1}D$, to deal with environmental pollution. Finally, some researchers (e.g., Hudson and Jorgenson 1974) have considered econometric approaches to determining technical coefficients as a function of relative changes in prices of inputs. This area of research addresses the most fundamental limitation of Leontief models, that is, the fixed-input-requirements assumption.

9-7 | SUMMARY

In this chapter we have introduced the reader to several extensions of or variations on the basic input-output model of earlier chapters. The supply-side version provides a framework for analyzing impacts on individual sectors throughout an economy that result from curtailment of exogenous inputs—the primary factors used in production. The assumption of constant output coefficients, which is inherent in this model, deserves just as careful scrutiny as is given the constant-input-coefficient assumption in the standard input-output model.

Measurements of industrial linkages, or interconnectedness of sectors in the economy, utilize both the conventional (demand-side) input-output framework and also the supply-side model, depending upon whether one's interest is primarily on the backward linkages (related to a sector's purchases) or forward linkages (related to a sector's sales). These linkage measures are useful in helping to identify logical clusters of industries in which the connections of each industry in the cluster (in terms of flows of goods and services) to other industries in the cluster are stronger than to industries outside the cluster. If, in addition to these strong intracluster connections, the industries are near to one another spatially, they form what is termed an *industrial complex*. Thus, when linkage analyses are carried out at a small enough regional level, they can help to identify industrial complexes.[8]

While the conventional input-output model takes final demands as the exogenous driving force and calculates sectoral gross outputs necessary to satisfy those demands, there are circumstances under which one might want, instead, to specify at least some of the gross outputs exogenously—as with production targets in planned economies—and let the amounts of some of the goods available for final demands be determined endogenously. This sometimes is the case when we try to measure the impact of a new industry on an economy.

The extension of the input-output framework into dynamic modeling introduces the distinction between interindustry transactions of inputs for current production and for accumulation of stocks to increase the future productive capacity of the economy. In this model, both input coefficients and capital coefficients are assumed constant, although at least in principle it may be possible to update or project both kinds of coefficients over time. The dynamic extension of the input-output model can also be applied at the regional level—for example, to investigate the growth potential of a regional economy.

Finally, the distinction between transactions in physical terms and in value terms allows development of a price-sensitive version of the input-output model. This provides a framework within which to trace through economywide repercussions of changes in prices of exogenous inputs, such as wage increases.

APPENDIX 9-1
THE ROUND-BY-ROUND APPROACH IN THE SUPPLY-SIDE
INPUT-OUTPUT MODEL

In Chapter 2 we saw that the solution provided by the Leontief inverse to the demand-side model could also be understood as the result of a series of round-by-round effects originating with an initial new final-demand vector. A similar approach is also possible for the supply-side input-output model. For the two-sector case, suppose that there is a decrease in the availability (or supply of) W_1 and W_2, the exogenous inputs for sectors 1 and 2; let these be ΔW_1 and ΔW_2. Since we are considering decreases, both ΔW_1 and ΔW_2 will be negative. Building up the total effects in terms of changes in outputs, ΔX_1 and ΔX_2, we have:

  1 An *initial* estimate of how much X_1 will decrease would be given by ΔW_1. Clearly, if $\Delta W_1 = -\$5.00$, we would expect the total decrease in output

---

[8]Alternative approaches for identification of industrial complexes, incorporating input-output data, have been discussed widely in the literature; to cover the topic thoroughly is beyond the scope of this book. Representative references—which contain some conflicting opinions—include Czamanski (1972, Ch. 5; 1977), Czamanski and Czamanski (1977), Harrigan (1982), Latham (1976, 1977), and Roepke et al. (1974).

from sector 1 to exceed five dollars, since five dollars' worth of exogenous inputs to sector 1 would surely lead to production of more than five dollars' worth of sector 1 output; otherwise, sector 1 would not be a profitable segment of the economy. And similarly, the minimum output decrease to be expected from sector 2 is ΔW_2. Thus, initially, we would estimate $\Delta X_1 = \Delta W_1$ and $\Delta X_2 = \Delta W_2$. (Since we are considering decreases, where both ΔW_1 and ΔW_2 are negative, ΔX_1 and ΔX_2 will be negative throughout what follows.)

  2 From the supply-side point of view, the process does not stop here, since, using the supply-driven coefficients, $\vec{a}_{ij}$, we know that the ΔW_1 and ΔW_2 mean reduced inputs to sector 1 production of $\vec{a}_{11}\Delta W_1$, because of ΔW_1, and $\vec{a}_{21}\Delta W_2$, because of ΔW_2. (Recall that $\vec{a}_{11} = z_{11}/X_1$, so $\Delta z_{11} = \vec{a}_{11}\Delta X_1$, and here our first-round estimate of ΔX_1 is ΔW_1, so $\Delta z_{11} = \vec{a}_{11}\Delta W_1$.) Similarly, $\vec{a}_{21} = z_{21}/X_2$ and so, since our initial estimate of ΔX_2 is ΔW_2, $\Delta z_{21} = \vec{a}_{21}\Delta W_2$.

  On the basis of the reduced availability of these inputs to sector 1, our estimates of expected next-round reduced production from sector 1 will be

$$\vec{a}_{11}\Delta W_1 + \vec{a}_{21}\Delta W_2 \qquad (9\text{-}1\text{-}1)$$

For example, if $\vec{a}_{21} = 0.3$ and $\Delta W_2 = \$100$, then there will be $30 less sector 2 output shipped as an input to sector 1 for sector 1 production; therefore, in this supply-side model, the minimum amount of reduction in sector 1 production that comcs about because of the reduced availability of this input from sector 2 is $30. Similarly, our next-round estimate of the production decrease in sector 2 because of reduced interindustry and intraindustry inputs is

$$\vec{a}_{12}\Delta W_1 + \vec{a}_{22}\Delta W_2 \qquad (9\text{-}1\text{-}2)$$

  3 Now, in exactly the same way as further rounds were investigated in section 2-3 of Chapter 2, we would next find that the reduced outputs in (9-1-1) and (9-1-2), above, generated yet further reductions from sectors 1 and 2, of

$$\vec{a}_{11}(\vec{a}_{11}\Delta W_1 + \vec{a}_{21}\Delta W_2) + \vec{a}_{21}(\vec{a}_{12}\Delta W_1 + \vec{a}_{22}\Delta W_2)$$

for sector 1, and

$$\vec{a}_{12}(\vec{a}_{11}\Delta W_1 + \vec{a}_{21}\Delta W_2) + \vec{a}_{22}(\vec{a}_{12}\Delta W_1 + \vec{a}_{22}\Delta W_2)$$

for sector 2. That is, the amounts in (9-1-1) and (9-1-2), estimated in step 2, replace ΔW_1 and ΔW_2, estimated in step 1, to be multiplied by $\vec{a}_{11}$ and $\vec{a}_{21}$, for our estimate of additional reductions in sector 1 production, or by $\vec{a}_{12}$ and $\vec{a}_{22}$, for our estimate of new reductions in sector 2 production.

  4 Further "rounds" are derived in exactly the same fashion as in the demand-driven model in Chapter 2.

Using matrix notation, one can see that our first estimates of the new outputs, in step 1 above, are

$$\begin{bmatrix} \Delta X_1 & \Delta X_2 \end{bmatrix} = \begin{bmatrix} \Delta W_1 & \Delta W_2 \end{bmatrix}$$

In step 2, these have added to them

$$\begin{bmatrix} \Delta W_1 & \Delta W_2 \end{bmatrix} \begin{bmatrix} \vec{a}_{11} & \vec{a}_{12} \\ \vec{a}_{21} & \vec{a}_{22} \end{bmatrix}$$

In step 3, we add

$$\begin{bmatrix} \Delta W_1 & \Delta W_2 \end{bmatrix} \begin{bmatrix} \vec{a}_{11} & \vec{a}_{12} \\ \vec{a}_{21} & \vec{a}_{22} \end{bmatrix}^2$$

$$= \begin{bmatrix} \Delta W_1 & \Delta W_2 \end{bmatrix} \begin{bmatrix} (\vec{a}_{11}^2 + \vec{a}_{12}\vec{a}_{21}) & (\vec{a}_{11}\vec{a}_{12} + \vec{a}_{12}\vec{a}_{22}) \\ (\vec{a}_{21}\vec{a}_{11} + \vec{a}_{22}\vec{a}_{21}) & (\vec{a}_{21}\vec{a}_{12} + \vec{a}_{22}^2) \end{bmatrix}$$

and so forth. Through logic that is exactly similar to that in Chapter 2, we would find eventually that

$$\Delta X' = \Delta W (I + \vec{A} + \vec{A}^2 + \vec{A}^3 + \cdots + \vec{A}^n)$$

and, for exactly the same kinds of reasons as those that underlie the power-series approximation to the usual Leontief inverse matrix, it turns out that here

$$(I + \vec{A} + \vec{A}^2 + \vec{A}^3 + \cdots + \vec{A}^n) = (I - \vec{A})^{-1}$$

for "large enough" n. Thus the relationship in Eq. (9-6) in the text, which is an algebraic result, conforms to our more intuitive result here.

APPENDIX 9-2
RELATIONSHIPS BETWEEN A AND $\vec{A}$ AND BETWEEN THE OUTPUT AND INPUT INVERSES

We define $A = Z(\hat{X})^{-1}$ and $\vec{A} = (\hat{X})^{-1}Z$. From the latter, $Z = (\hat{X})\vec{A}$; putting this into the former, we see that

$$A = (\hat{X})\vec{A}(\hat{X})^{-1} \tag{9-2-1}$$

When two matrices, P and Q, are connected by the relation $P = MQM^{-1}$, they are said to be *similar*; this is denoted $P \sim Q$. Thus, from Eq. (9-2-1), we see that A and $\vec{A}$ are similar matrices.

Consider $(I - A)$. From Eq. (9-2-1), $(I - A) = I - (\hat{X})\vec{A}(\hat{X})^{-1}$. Since $(\hat{X})I(\hat{X})^{-1} = I$,

$$(I - A) = (\hat{X})(I - \vec{A})(\hat{X})^{-1}$$

That is, $(I - A) \sim (I - \vec{A})$. Using a basic result on the inverse of a product—namely, that $(PQR)^{-1} = R^{-1}Q^{-1}P^{-1}$—we find that since $(I - A)^{-1} = [(\hat{X})(I - \vec{A})(\hat{X})^{-1}]^{-1}$,

$$(I - A)^{-1} = (\hat{X})(I - \vec{A})^{-1}(\hat{X})^{-1} \tag{9-2-2}$$

Thus $(I - A)^{-1} \sim (I - \vec{A})^{-1}$. The interested reader may wish to check the results in Eqs. (9-2-1) and (9-2-2) using the data in the small example in section 9-1—specifically, in Eqs. (9-9) through (9-12).

Because of Eqs. (9-2-1) and (9-2-2), any measures that are defined for A—such as output multipliers and backward linkages (section 9-2)—can be found from $\vec{A}$, provided that X is also known. Conversely, input multipliers and forward linkages—defined on $\vec{A}$—can be found using A and X.

APPENDIX 9-3
EQUIVALENCE OF ALTERNATIVE MODELS WITH X_n
EXOGENOUSLY SPECIFIED

We consider a three-sector case, to parallel the illustrations in section 9-3. The extension to an n-sector model involves no new principles. The outputs of sectors 1 and 2 necessitated by an exogenously determined X_3 were shown in Eq. (9-27).

$$\begin{bmatrix} X_1 \\ X_2 \end{bmatrix} = \begin{bmatrix} \alpha_{11} & \alpha_{12} \\ \alpha_{21} & \alpha_{22} \end{bmatrix} \begin{bmatrix} a_{13}\overline{X}_3 \\ a_{23}\overline{X}_3 \end{bmatrix} = \begin{bmatrix} \alpha_{11} & \alpha_{12} \\ \alpha_{21} & \alpha_{22} \end{bmatrix} \begin{bmatrix} a_{13} \\ a_{23} \end{bmatrix} \overline{X}_3 \qquad (9\text{-}3\text{-}1)$$

The alternative approach utilizes elements from the complete 3×3 Leontief inverse in forming $(I-A^*)^{-1} = [\alpha_{ij}^*]$, where $\alpha_{ij}^* = \alpha_{ij}/\alpha_{jj}$. In the three-sector illustration

$$(I-A^*)^{-1} = \begin{bmatrix} \dfrac{\alpha_{11}}{\alpha_{11}} & \dfrac{\alpha_{12}}{\alpha_{22}} & \dfrac{\alpha_{13}}{\alpha_{33}} \\[2mm] \dfrac{\alpha_{21}}{\alpha_{11}} & \dfrac{\alpha_{22}}{\alpha_{22}} & \dfrac{\alpha_{23}}{\alpha_{33}} \\[2mm] \dfrac{\alpha_{31}}{\alpha_{11}} & \dfrac{\alpha_{32}}{\alpha_{22}} & \dfrac{\alpha_{33}}{\alpha_{33}} \end{bmatrix}$$

with

$$\overline{X} = \begin{bmatrix} 0 \\ 0 \\ \overline{X}_3 \end{bmatrix}$$

we have

$$X = (I-A^*)^{-1}\overline{X}$$

and, in particular,

$$\begin{bmatrix} X_1 \\ X_2 \end{bmatrix} = \begin{bmatrix} \alpha_{13}^* \\ \alpha_{23}^* \end{bmatrix} \overline{X}_3 = \begin{bmatrix} \dfrac{\alpha_{13}}{\alpha_{33}} \\[2mm] \dfrac{\alpha_{23}}{\alpha_{33}} \end{bmatrix} \overline{X}_3 \qquad (9\text{-}3\text{-}2)$$

Our interest is therefore in examining the two alternative expressions for X_1 and X_2 in Eqs. (9-3-1) and (9-3-2).

Consider the three-sector $(I-A)$ matrix partitioned as

$$\begin{bmatrix} 1-a_{11} & -a_{12} & -a_{13} \\ -a_{21} & 1-a_{22} & -a_{23} \\ \hline -a_{31} & -a_{32} & 1-a_{33} \end{bmatrix} = \begin{bmatrix} E & F \\ \hline G & H \end{bmatrix}$$

and its inverse, similarly partitioned as $(I - A)^{-1} = \left[\begin{array}{c|c} S & T \\ \hline U & V \end{array}\right]$. In particular, T $= \left[\begin{array}{c} \alpha_{13} \\ \alpha_{23} \end{array}\right]$ and $V = \alpha_{33}$. Thus, the results in Eq. (9-3-2) can be expressed as

$$\left[\begin{array}{c} X_1 \\ X_2 \end{array}\right] = (TV^{-1})\bar{X}_3 \tag{9-3-3}$$

From section A-7 of Appendix A, on the inverse of a partitioned matrix, we know that $T = -E^{-1}FV$ and thus

$$TV^{-1} = -E^{-1}F \tag{9-3-4}$$

Since $E^{-1} = \left[\begin{array}{cc} \alpha_{11} & \alpha_{12} \\ \alpha_{21} & \alpha_{22} \end{array}\right]$ and $F = \left[\begin{array}{c} -a_{13} \\ -a_{23} \end{array}\right]$, we see that the expression in Eq. (9-3-1) is

$$\left[\begin{array}{c} X_1 \\ X_2 \end{array}\right] = (-E^{-1}F)\bar{X}_3 \tag{9-3-5}$$

From Eq. (9-3-4), the expressions for X_1 and X_2 in Eqs. (9-3-1) and (9-3-2) are identical.

Since the results on partitioned inverses are general and valid for nonsingular square matrices of any size, the argument above holds for an n-sector economy in which $Y_1, \cdots, Y_{n-1}$ and X_n are specified exogenously. And since the numbering of sectors is arbitrary, we can always designate as sector n the one whose gross output is fixed.

❘ PROBLEMS

9-1 Create a supply-driven model for the U.S. economy for one or more years from the data that are presented in Appendix B. Determine the sensitivity of the national economy to an interruption in a scarce-factor input—for example, a strike—in one of the sectors.

9-2 Using the A and $(I - A)^{-1}$ matrices for the United States that are presented in Appendix B, find both the direct and the direct and indirect forward and backward linkages for the sectors in the U.S. economy and examine how these linkages may have changed over time.

9-3 The centrally planned economy of Czaria is involved in its planning for the next fiscal year. The matrix of technical coefficients for Czaria is given below:

	1	2	3	4
1. Agriculture	0.168	0.155	0.213	0.212
2. Mining	0.194	0.193	0.168	0.115
3. Military Manufacturing	0.105	0.025	0.126	0.124
4. Civilian Manufacturing	0.178	0.101	0.219	0.186

Projected total outputs in millions of dollars for agriculture, mining, and civilian manufacturing in Czaria next year are 4558, 5665, and 5079, respectively. Final demand (government purchases and exports) of military manufactured products is $2050 million. Compute the GNP and total gross production for the economy next year.

9-4 Consider the impact on the economy of problem 2-1 of the establishment of a new sector, finance and insurance (sector 3).

a Suppose you know that the total output of this new sector will be $900 during the current year (its first year of operation), and that its needs for agricultural and manufactured goods are represented by $a_{13} = 0.001$ and $a_{23} = 0.07$. In the absence of any further information, what would you estimate to be the impact of this new sector on the economy?

b You later learn (1) that the agriculture and manufacturing sectors bought $20 and $40 in finance and insurance services last year from foreign firms (i.e., that they imported these inputs), and (2) that sector 3 will use $15 of its own product for each $100 worth of its output. Assuming that they will now buy from the domestic sector, how might you now assess the impact of the new sector on this economy?

9-5 Consider the following closed dynamic input-output model:

$$AX + B(X' - X) = X$$

where: X' = future outputs, X = current outputs, and where $A = \begin{bmatrix} .5 & .1 \\ .1 & .5 \end{bmatrix}$ and $B = \begin{bmatrix} 0 & .1 \\ .1 & 0 \end{bmatrix}$. Assume that $X' = cX$, where c is some scalar (the turnpike growth rate); compute c.

9-6 Using the dynamic input-output model developed in section 9-5, where $Q = B^{-1}(I - A + B)$, suppose $Q = \begin{bmatrix} 1 & .1 \\ 10 & 1 \end{bmatrix}$. Find the turnpike growth rate.

9-7 Given the closed dynamic input-output model $AX + B(X' - X) = X$, where $A = \begin{bmatrix} .1 & .2 \\ .3 & .4 \end{bmatrix}$ and $B = \begin{bmatrix} .1 & 0 \\ 0 & .1 \end{bmatrix}$,

a Compute the turnpike growth rate for this example.

b If both the capital coefficients for the first industry (the first column of $B0$ are changed to 0.1, then what is the new turnpike growth rate and what has happened to the apparent "health" of the economy?

| REFERENCES

ALLEN, R. I. G., and W. F. GOSSLING, eds. *Estimating and Projecting Input-Output Coefficients.* London: Input-Output Publishing Co., 1975.

AUGUSTINOVICS, MARIA. "Methods of International and Intertemporal Comparison of Structure." In *Contributions to Input-Output Analysis*, edited by A. P. Carter and A. Bródy, 249–269, Amsterdam: North-Holland, 1970.

BULMER-THOMAS, V. *Input-Output Analysis in Developing Countries.* New York: John Wiley and Sons, 1982.

CARTER, ANNE. "Energy, Environment and Economic Growth." *Bell Journal of Economics* 5, no. 2 (Autumn 1974): 578–94.

CHENERY, HOLLIS B., and T. WATANABE. "International Comparisons of the Structure of Production." *Econometrica* 26, no. 4 (October 1958): 487–521.

CZAMANSKI, DANIEL, and STAN CZAMANSKI. "Industrial Complexes: Their Typology, Structure and Relation to Economic Development." *Papers, Regional Science Association* 35 (1977): 93–111.

CZAMANSKI, STAN. "Needless Complexity in the Identification of Industrial Complexes: A Comment." *Journal of Regional Science* 17, no. 3 (December 1977): 455–57.

———. *Regional Science Techniques in Practice: The Case of Nova Scotia.* Lexington, Mass.: Lexington Books (D. C. Heath and Co.), 1972.

DIAMOND, J. "Key Sectors in Some Underdeveloped Countries: A Comment." *Kyklos* 29, no. 4 (1976): 762–64.

GHOSH, A. "Input-Output Approach to an Allocative System." *Economica* 25, no. 1 (February 1958): 58–64.

GIARRATANI, FRANK. "Application of an Industry Supply Model to Energy Issues." In *Regional Impacts of Rising Energy Prices*, edited by William Miernyk, Frank Giarratani and Charles Socher, 89–102, Cambridge, Mass.: Ballinger Publishing Co., 1978.

GUPTA, T. R. "A Note on the Determination of Wage Increases with Price Rises Using Input-Output Analysis." Cambridge, Mass.: Harvard Economics Research Project, 1967.

HARRIGAN, F. J. "The Relationship Between Industrial and Geographical Linkages: A Case Study of the United Kingdom." *Journal of Regional Science* 22, no. 1 (February 1982): 19–31.

HEWINGS, GEOFFREY J. D. "The Empirical Identification of Key Sectors in an Economy: A Regional Perspective." *The Developing Economies* 20, no. 2 (June 1982): 173–95.

HIRSCHMAN, ALBERT O. *The Strategy of Economic Development*. New Haven: Yale University Press, 1958.

HUDSON, E., and D. JORGENSON. "U.S. Energy Policy and Economic Growth, 1975–2000." *Bell Journal of Economics* 5, no. 2 (Autumn 1974): 461–514.

ISARD, WALTER, and ROBERT E. KUENNE. "The Impact of Steel upon the Greater New York–Philadelphia Industrial Region." *Review of Economics and Statistics* 35, no. 4 (November 1953): 289–301.

JONES, LEROY P. "The Measurement of Hirschmanian Linkages." *Quarterly Journal of Economics* 90, no. 2 (May 1976): 323–33.

KENDRICK, DAVID. "On the Leontief Dynamic Inverse." *Quarterly Journal of Economics* 86, no. 4 (November 1972): 693–96.

LATHAM, WILLIAM R., III. "Needless Complexity in the Identification of Industrial Complexes." *Journal of Regional Science* 16, no. 1 (April 1976): 45–55.

———. "Needless Complexity in the Identification of Industrial Complexes: A Reply." *Journal of Regional Science* 17, no. 3 (December 1977): 459–61.

LAUMAS, PREM S. "Key Sectors in Some Underdeveloped Countries." *Kyklos* 28, no. 1 (1975): 62–79.

———. "Key Sectors in Some Underdeveloped Countries: A Reply." *Kyklos* 29, no. 4 (1976): 767–69.

LEE, GENE K., LEROY L. BLAKESLEY, and WALTER R. BUTCHER. "Effects of Exogenous Price Changes on a Regional Economy: An Input-Output Analysis." *International Regional Science Review* 2, no. 1 (Fall 1977): 15–27.

LEONTIEF, WASSILY. "The Dynamic Inverse." In *Contributions to Input-Output Analysis* 1, edited by A. Carter and A. Bródy, 17–46, Amsterdam: North-Holland, 1970.

LEONTIEF, WASSILY, and FAYE DUCHIN et al. "The Impacts of Automation on Employment, 1963–2000." Final report to the National Science Foundation, PRA-8012844. April, 1984.

LIVESEY, D. A. "A Minimal Realization of the Leontief Dynamic Input-Output Model." In *Advances in Input-Output Analysis*, edited by Karen R. Polenske and Jiri V. Skolka, 527–41. Proceedings of the Sixth International Conference on Input-Output Techniques, Vienna, April 22–26, 1974. Cambridge, Massachusetts: Ballinger, 1976.

LUENBERGER, D. G., and A. ARBEL. "Singular Dynamic Leontief Systems." *Econometrica* 45, no. 4 (May 1977): 991–95.

McGILVRAY, JAMES W. "Linkages, Key Sectors and Development Strategy." In *Structure, System and Economic Policy*, edited by Wassily Leontief, 49–56. Proceedings of Section

F of the British Association for the Advancement of Science, University of Lancaster, 1–8 September 1976. Cambridge: Cambridge University Press, 1977.

MELVIN, JAMES R. "Short-Run Price Effects of the Corporate Income Tax and Implications for International Trade." *American Economic Review* 69, no. 5 (December 1979): 765–74.

MIERNYK, WILLIAM H., et al. *Simulating Regional Economic Development: An Interindustry Model of the West Virginia Economy.* Lexington, Mass.: Lexington Books, D. C. Heath and Co., 1970.

MIERNYK, WILLIAM H., and JOHN T. SEARS. *Air Pollution Abatement and Regional Economic Development.* Lexington, Mass.: Lexington Books, D. C. Heath and Co., 1974.

MILLER, RONALD E. "The Impact of the Aluminum Industry on the Pacific Northwest: A Regional Input-Output Analysis." *Review of Economics and Statistics* 39, no. 2 (May 1957): 200–209.

MOSES, LEON N. "Output and Prices in Interindustry Models." *Papers of the Regional Science Association* 32 (1974): 7–18.

PAI, GREGORY G. Y. *Environmental Pollution Control Policy: An Assessment of Regional Economic Impacts.* Ph.D. diss., Massachusetts Institute of Technology, 1979.

POLENSKE, KAREN R. "Energy Analysis and the Determination of Multiregional Prices." *Papers of the Regional Science Association* 43 (1978): 83–97.

RASMUSSEN, P. N. *Studies in Intersectoral Relations.* Amsterdam: North-Holland, 1956.

RICHARDSON, HARRY W. *Input-Output and Regional Economics.* New York: John Wiley and Sons (Halsted Press), 1972.

RITZ, PHILIP M. and ELIZABETH SPAULDING. "Basic I-O Terminology." U. S. Department of Commerce, Bureau of Economic Analysis, Interindustry Economics Division, February 25, 1975.

ROEPKE, HOWARD, DAVID ADAMS, and ROBERT WISEMAN. "A New Approach to the Identification of Industrial Complexes Using Input-Output Data." *Journal of Regional Science* 14, no. 1 (April 1974): 15–29.

SCHINNAR, ARIE P. "The Leontief Generalized Dynamic Inverse." *Quarterly Journal of Economics* 92, no. 4 (November 1978): 641–52.

SCHULTZ, SIEGFRIED, and DIETER SCHUMACHER. "Key Sectors in Some Underdeveloped Countries: A Comment." *Kyklos* 29, no. 4 (1976): 765–66.

TIEBOUT, CHARLES M. "An Empirical Regional Input-Output Projection Model: The State of Washington 1980." *Review of Economics and Statistics* 51, no. 3 (August 1969): 334–40.

YOTOPOULOS, PAN A., and JEFFREY B. NUGENT. "A Balanced-Growth Version of the Linkage Hypothesis: A Test." *Quarterly Journal of Economics* 90, no. 2 (May 1973): 157–71.

YOUNG, JEFFREY. "The Multiregional Input-Output Price Model Applied to Transportation." Master's thesis, Massachusetts Institute of Technology, 1978.

appendix

A

Mathematical
Background:
Matrix Algebra
and Solutions
to Systems
of Linear Equations

A-1 | INTRODUCTION

The mathematical structure of the input-output model is a system of linear equations. Being able to represent these relations in matrix form turns out to be a great advantage, both conceptually and computationally. From the conceptual point of view, we will be able to determine a great deal about the solution to an input-output problem from the matrix representation. Also, in many actual applications, the input-output model that is used may contain 50, or 100, or more, linear equations containing the same number of unknowns. From the computational point of view, modern computers can deal with such large matrix systems very efficiently because, even though they are large, they are algebraically relatively simple.

A matrix is a collection of elements arranged in a grid, that is, in a pattern of rows and columns. In all cases that are of interest to the discussion in this book, the elements will be the numbers whose values are either known or unknown and to be determined. Matrices are defined in this "rectangular" way so that they can be used to represent systems of linear relations among variables, as we will see.

Consider one equation and one unknown; for example, $3x = 12$. In concluding that $x = 4$, we have divided both sides of the equation by 3 or, equivalently, multiplied both sides by $1/3$. One linear equation is all that is needed to find the value of the one unknown[1]. If we had a second linear equation involving x, one of two possibilities would arise. Either the equation would

---

[1]The equation is linear because x appears raised to the first power, not squared or cubed, and not in any trigonometric or exponential expression, like $\cos x$ or e^x. The general case would be represented as $ax = b$. The straightforward geometric representation of a linear equation will be clear below, when we consider two unknowns, x_1 and x_2.

contain the same information—for example, $12x = 48$—in which case either equation is redundant, since one is all that is needed to determine that $x = 4$, or else the second equation would contain contradictory information about the variable—for example, $12x = 60$—in which case there is no value of x that satisfies both $3x = 12$ and $12x = 60$; the equations are inconsistent and there is no solution. Observations such as these, which are very apparent for these simple cases of linear equations with one variable, can be extended to more equations and more variables. The definitions and operations of matrix algebra facilitate this greatly, and this is essentially the motivation for investigating this subject in some detail.

With two unknowns, x_1 and x_2, we expect that not one but two linear equations will be needed in order to determine unique values for the variables.[2] The geometry of linear equations makes this clear. Using one axis—say, the horizontal one—along which to measure x_1, and another—vertical—axis for measurement of x_2, we can easily represent an equation such as $x_1 + 2x_2 = 10$ in two-dimensional space.[3] If we also have a second linear relation between the variables—$2x_1 - 2x_2 = 8$, say—we can find, using simple algebra, that $x_1 = 6$ and $x_2 = 2$. For example, from the former equation, $x_1 = 10 - 2x_2$; this substituted into the latter equation gives $-6x_2 = -12$, from which the results follow. Thus we conclude that the pair of equations

$$\text{(a)} \qquad x_1 + 2x_2 = 10$$
$$\text{(A-1)}$$
$$\text{(b)} \qquad 2x_1 - 2x_2 = 8$$

has a unique solution, $x_1 = 6$ and $x_2 = 2$. However, had the second equation been (1) $2x_2 + 4x_2 = 20$ or (2) $2x_1 + 4x_2 = 30$, the simple algebraic approach used above would not lead to unique value for x_1 and x_2. In the case of (1), we conclude from the same algebraic substitution that $20 = 20$, which does not define x_2 for us as in the pair of equations in (A-1); in the case of (2) we first of all obtain the contradiction $20 = 30$ and, secondly, do not have any value for x_2.

The nature of the problem is made clear by two-dimensional geometry. Sketching the pair of equations in (A-1), we see that the straight lines representing the two equations intersect in a single point, the coordinates of which represent the solution to the system (pair) of equations. Figure A-1 is said to be a geometric representation in solution space.[4] The equations are *linear* since the

---

[2] It is preferable to use x_1 and x_2, rather than, for example, x and y to denote the two unknown variables, since this notation generalizes so easily to the case of three variables (x_1, x_2, x_3) —or, ultimately, n variables ($x_1, x_2, \cdots, x_n$).

[3] One axis (or direction, or dimension) is needed for each of the variables, hence the space is two-dimensional for the present case.

[4] This is simply a space which has an axis for each variable and in which the solution to the equation system will appear as one point—or several, as we will see below—in that space. The correspondence is between algebraic solutions to equations and geometric points in space. It is assumed that the reader has sketched linear equations in this kind of picture before. A simple approach for each equation is to set one variable (say, x_1) equal to zero and then find the resulting value of the other (x_2), which will be the intercept on the x_2-axis; then repeat, setting x_2 equal to zero and find the resulting value of x_1. In the case of the first equation in (A-1), this procedure gives $x_2 = 5$ and $x_1 = 10$ for the two intercepts.

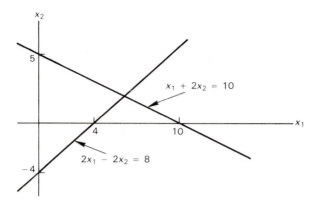

FIGURE A-1 Equations (A-1).

values of x_1 and x_2 satisfying either one of them fall along a straight line in solution space.

The second set of equations

$$\text{(a)} \quad x_1 + 2x_2 = 10$$
$$\text{(b)} \quad 2x_1 + 4x_2 = 20 \tag{A-2}$$

is represented in solution space by only one line, since Eq. (A-2b) gives us the same information about x_1 and x_2 as does Eq. (A-2a). Dividing both sides of Eq. (A-2b) by 2 gives exactly Eq. (A-2a). Thus *any* pair of values of x_1 and x_2 that fall along this single line—for example, $x_1 = 10$, $x_2 = 0$, or $x_1 = 0$, $x_2 = 5$, or $x_1 = 8$, $x_2 = 1$, and so on—will be a solution to Eqs. (A-2). There are infinitely many such solutions, as in Fig. A-2. The third set

$$\text{(a)} \quad x_1 + 2x_2 = 10$$
$$\text{(b)} \quad 2x_1 + 4x_2 = 30 \tag{A-3}$$

has a solution-space picture which is a pair of parallel lines. Thus there are *no* values of x_1 and x_2 that satisfy both equations (i.e., that simultaneously lie on both lines). As a system of linear relationships, the two equations in (A-3) are inconsistent (Fig. A-3).

These kinds of situations—namely, equations that have a unique solution, an infinite number of solutions, and no solution—can of course occur in larger

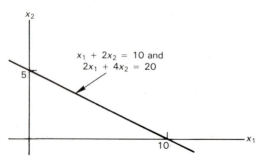

FIGURE A-2 Equations (A-2).

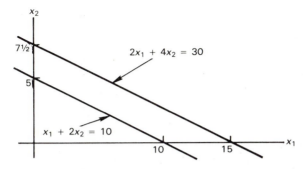

FIGURE A-3 Equations (A-3).

systems as well: three linear equations in three unknowns, four linear equations in four unknowns, and so on. Since the geometry for more than three unknowns (three dimensions) is not easily visualized, it will be well to have an algebraic approach to sets of linear equations. Matrix notation and matrix operations supply such a representation. Full advantage of this approach can only be taken after we become familiar in some detail with these notations and operations (such as addition, multiplication, etc.), that is, with the algebra of matrices.

A-2 | MATRICES—FUNDAMENTAL DEFINITIONS

Since matrices contain elements arranged in a rectangular grid, we can denote the *general* case as one with m rows and n columns. If $m = 2$ and $n = 3$, a particular matrix might be

$$\begin{bmatrix} 2 & 1 & 3 \\ 4 & 6 & 12 \end{bmatrix} \tag{A-4}$$

where brackets are used to denote the collection, which here is two rows of three elements each (or, equivalently, three columns of two elements each). Matrices are *always* rectangular. This includes the possibility of a square matrix ($m = n$), a matrix of only one row ($m = 1$) or only one column ($n = 1$) or both ($m = n = 1$). Examples of each are, respectively:

$$\begin{bmatrix} 2 & 1 \\ 4 & 6 \end{bmatrix}, \quad \begin{bmatrix} 1 & 3 & 7 \end{bmatrix}, \quad \begin{bmatrix} 2 \\ 5 \\ 8 \\ 9 \end{bmatrix}, \quad \text{and} \quad \begin{bmatrix} 6 \end{bmatrix}$$

The number of rows and the number of columns are termed the *dimensions* of a matrix; the matrix in (A-4) is 2×3 (read "2 by 3"; the number of rows is always indicated first), those immediately above are 2×2, 1×3, 4×1, and 1×1, respectively. The latter three are sometimes given special names: an n-element (here $n = 3$) row *vector*, an m-element (here $m = 4$) column *vector* and a *scalar* (a matrix consisting of one row and one column, that is, one element, only).

Matrices are required to have a rectangular shape precisely because of the use to which they are put in the representation and analysis of systems of linear equations. Since an element in a matrix has both a row and a column location, it is logical to denote a particular element in a matrix by the specific row and column in which it sits. If we denote the matrix in (A-4) as A, and its individual elements as a_{ij}, then by a_{23} we will understand the element in row 2, column 3, that is, the number 12. Thus for

$$A = \begin{bmatrix} 2 & 1 & 3 \\ 4 & 6 & 12 \end{bmatrix}$$

$a_{23} = 12$; in addition, $a_{13} = 3$, $a_{21} = 4$, and so on. This is simply a straightforward way of addressing the elements in a rectangular arrangement. In general, uppercase letters are used to denote matrices, and corresponding lowercase letters (with double subscripts for particular location) are used for individual elements of that matrix. The dimensions of a matrix are often shown directly under the uppercase designation—for example, $\underset{(2 \times 3)}{A}$.

The four principal *operations* of ordinary algebra—addition, subtraction, multiplication, and division—have their counterparts in matrix algebra. In defining these, it will be necessary to recall and perhaps reexamine some *definitions* from ordinary algebra as well.

A-3 | MATRIX OPERATIONS—ADDITION AND SUBTRACTION

Addition

Let $A = \begin{bmatrix} 2 & 1 & 3 \\ 4 & 6 & 12 \end{bmatrix}$ and $B = \begin{bmatrix} 1 & 0 & 7 \\ 3 & 6 & 9 \end{bmatrix}$. Then their sum is $S = A + B$

$= \begin{bmatrix} 3 & 1 & 10 \\ 7 & 12 & 21 \end{bmatrix}$. The process of addition is simply that of adding elements *in corresponding positions*. Consequently, only matrices of the same dimension can be added. The addition operation is not much different from the same operation in ordinary algebra. One need only remember that to add matrices, one needs to have elements in corresponding positions, so that it is only possible to add matrices of exactly the same dimension. Note that in the process, the matrix that is the sum will also be of the same dimension. Since the operation is element-by-element addition, $S = A + B = B + A$; that is, the order in which the addition is carried out does not matter. It is also clear that the sum of more than two matrices, all of the same dimension, will be a matrix whose elements are, in turn, the sums of those in corresponding positions in the matrices being added. Let

$C = \begin{bmatrix} 0 & 0 & 6 \\ 0 & 5 & 1 \end{bmatrix}$; then, using the A and B given above, $A + B + C$

$= \begin{bmatrix} 3 & 1 & 16 \\ 7 & 17 & 22 \end{bmatrix}$.

Equality

Implicit in the above is the idea of matrix equality, namely the fact that two matrices are defined to be equal when their elements, in corresponding positions, are equal. Thus $S = \begin{bmatrix} s_{11} & s_{12} & s_{13} \\ s_{21} & s_{22} & s_{23} \end{bmatrix} = \begin{bmatrix} 3 & 1 & 10 \\ 7 & 12 & 21 \end{bmatrix}$ means, clearly, that $s_{12} = 1$, $s_{23} = 21$, and so on. Matrix equality is element-by-element equality; thus, again, only matrices of the same dimension can possibly be equal. Given $E = \begin{bmatrix} 1 & 0 & 7 \\ 3 & 6 & 9 \end{bmatrix}$, we may write that $B = E$.

Subtraction

As with addition, the operation of subtraction, for matrices, is exactly parallel to that in ordinary algebra. Only matrices of the same dimension can be subtracted, and the algebra is element-by-element subtraction. Taking A and B from above, the difference, $D = A - B = \begin{bmatrix} 2 & 1 & 3 \\ 4 & 6 & 12 \end{bmatrix} - \begin{bmatrix} 1 & 0 & 7 \\ 3 & 6 & 9 \end{bmatrix}$ $= \begin{bmatrix} 1 & 1 & -4 \\ 1 & 0 & 3 \end{bmatrix}$. Similarly, $A - B - C = \begin{bmatrix} 1 & 1 & -10 \\ 1 & -5 & 2 \end{bmatrix}$. (As with ordinary algebra, order *does* make a difference in subtraction; just as $a - b$ is not usually the same as $b - a$—except when a and b are equal—so $A - B \neq B - A$, except in this same case, namely when matrices A and B are equal.)

Null Matrix

The *identity element for addition* is, in ordinary algebra, the number that does not affect an expression when added to it; this is, clearly, zero (for example $21 + 0 = 21$). In matrix algebra, a matrix of all zero elements plays the same role. Such a matrix, provided it has the proper dimensions, will contribute nothing when added to some other matrix. In matrix algebra, a matrix of all zeros, termed the *null* or *zero matrix*, is generally represented by 0. Thus, let $\underset{(2 \times 3)}{0} = \begin{bmatrix} 0 & 0 & 0 \\ 0 & 0 & 0 \end{bmatrix}$; then $A + 0 = A = \begin{bmatrix} 2 & 1 & 3 \\ 4 & 6 & 12 \end{bmatrix}$. Note that subtracting any particular $m \times n$ matrix from itself will produce an $m \times n$ null matrix—m rows of n zeros each.[5]

A-4 | MATRIX OPERATIONS—MULTIPLICATION

Multiplication

To multiply a matrix by a single number, each element of the matrix is simply multiplied by that number. Thus, using the same A as above, $2A$ $= \begin{bmatrix} 4 & 2 & 6 \\ 8 & 12 & 24 \end{bmatrix}$. As with addition and subtraction, this seems to follow logically from ordinary algebra. Multiplication of one matrix by another, however, is a different matter; this is the first instance in which the definition of a matrix algebraic operation differs markedly from that in ordinary algebra. The reason for the definition is precisely because of the way in which matrix notation is used

---

[5] Note, also, that the null matrix might equally well be termed the identity element for subtraction, since $A - 0 = A$; that is, a matrix of all zeros (just as with the single element zero in ordinary algebra) will not affect a matrix from which it is subtracted.

to represent systems of linear equations. If $A = \begin{bmatrix} 2 & 1 & 3 \\ 4 & 6 & 12 \end{bmatrix}$ and F

$= \begin{bmatrix} 2 & 1 & 3 \\ 4 & 0 & 7 \\ 1 & 1 & 6 \end{bmatrix}$, then the product, AF, is $\begin{bmatrix} 11 & 5 & 31 \\ 44 & 16 & 126 \end{bmatrix}$. This is obtained as

follows: The element in the ith row and jth column of the product matrix is the result of multiplying each element in row i of A by the corresponding element in column j of F and then summing these products. For example, the element in row 1, column 2 of the product, namely 5, is derived from the operation $(2)(1) + (1)(0) + (3)(1)$.

Representing A and F more generally:

$$A = \begin{bmatrix} a_{11} & a_{12} & a_{13} \\ a_{21} & a_{22} & a_{23} \end{bmatrix} \qquad F = \begin{bmatrix} f_{11} & f_{12} & f_{13} \\ f_{21} & f_{22} & f_{23} \\ f_{31} & f_{32} & f_{33} \end{bmatrix}$$

Denote their product by the matrix P (that is, $AF = P$), with elements p_{ij}. Then $p_{12} = a_{11} f_{12} + a_{12} f_{22} + a_{13} f_{32}$, the sum of products of elements from row 1 of A and column 2 of F. Similarly, $p_{23} = a_{21} f_{13} + a_{22} f_{23} + a_{23} f_{33}$ (across row 2 in A, down column 3 in F). Because of this definition of multiplication of two matrices, it is clear that the rows in the matrix on the left must have the same number of elements as there are in the columns of the matrix on the right. This is known as the *conformability requirement* for matrix multiplication; the second dimension of the matrix on the left (here A) must equal the first dimension of the matrix on the right (here F). The reader should also be convinced that the product will be a matrix whose dimensions are the first dimension (number of rows) of the matrix on the left and the second dimension (number of columns) of the matrix on the right. That is, in general, $\underset{(m \times n)}{G} \underset{(n \times p)}{H} = \underset{(m \times p)}{K}$. In the previous example, $\underset{(2 \times 3)}{A} \underset{(3 \times 3)}{F} = \underset{(2 \times 3)}{P}$.

Since this operation is by no means parallel with its counterpart in ordinary algebra, we illustrate with a further example, which will also serve to show clearly that order of multiplication will usually make a difference in matrix algebra. Let

$$\underset{(2 \times 3)}{L} = \begin{bmatrix} 1 & 2 & 5 \\ 6 & 0 & 1 \end{bmatrix}, \qquad \underset{(3 \times 1)}{M} = \begin{bmatrix} 3 \\ 6 \\ 9 \end{bmatrix}, \qquad \underset{(3 \times 2)}{N} = \begin{bmatrix} 1 & 10 \\ -1 & 1 \\ 0 & -3 \end{bmatrix}$$

The following products can be formed (that is, the matrices are conformable for multiplication in the order indicated):

$$\underset{(2 \times 3) \, (3 \times 1)}{L \quad M} = \begin{bmatrix} 3 + 12 + 45 \\ 18 + 0 + 9 \end{bmatrix} = \begin{bmatrix} 60 \\ 27 \end{bmatrix}$$

$$\underset{(2 \times 3) \, (3 \times 2)}{L \quad N} = \begin{bmatrix} 1 - 2 + 0 & 10 + 2 - 15 \\ 6 - 0 + 0 & 60 + 0 - 3 \end{bmatrix} = \begin{bmatrix} -1 & -3 \\ 6 & 57 \end{bmatrix}$$

$$\underset{(3 \times 2) \, (2 \times 3)}{N \quad L} = \begin{bmatrix} 1 + 60 & 2 + 0 & 5 + 10 \\ -1 + 6 & -2 + 0 & -5 + 1 \\ 0 - 18 & 0 + 0 & 0 - 3 \end{bmatrix} = \begin{bmatrix} 61 & 2 & 15 \\ 5 & -2 & -4 \\ -18 & 0 & -3 \end{bmatrix}$$

Note that the following products are not defined: $\underset{(3\times 1)}{M}\ \underset{(3\times 2)}{N}$, $\underset{(3\times 2)}{N}\ \underset{(3\times 1)}{M}$, $\underset{(3\times 1)}{M}\ \underset{(2\times 3)}{L}$. All three fail the conformability test that the number of columns in the matrix on the left be equal to the number of rows in the matrix on the right. Note also that although it is possible to calculate both LN and NL, the results are vastly different (differently sized matrices with differing elements). Since order of multiplication makes a difference, there is terminology to distinguish the two products of L and N. In the case of LN, L is said to premultiply N or, equivalently, N is said to postmultiply L. This makes clear the relative positions of the two matrices in the product.

Representation of Linear Equation Systems

Consider again the pair of linear equations given in (A-1); they were

$$x_1 + 2x_2 = 10$$

$$2x_1 - 2x_2 = 8$$

Define the following matrices:

$$\underset{(2\times 2)}{A} = \begin{bmatrix} 1 & 2 \\ 2 & -2 \end{bmatrix}, \qquad \underset{(2\times 1)}{X} = \begin{bmatrix} x_1 \\ x_2 \end{bmatrix}, \qquad \underset{(2\times 1)}{B} = \begin{bmatrix} 10 \\ 8 \end{bmatrix}$$

The matrix A contains the coefficients multiplying the unknowns; X is a column vector of unknown variables, listed in order; and B is a column vector of the right-hand sides of the equations. Then, precisely because of (1) the way in which matrix multiplication is defined and (2) the definition of matrix equality, the pair of linear equations can be represented as

$$AX = B \qquad\qquad (A-5)$$

That is, $\begin{bmatrix} 1 & 2 \\ 2 & -2 \end{bmatrix} \begin{bmatrix} x_1 \\ x_2 \end{bmatrix} = \begin{bmatrix} 10 \\ 8 \end{bmatrix}$. By the rules for matrix multiplication, this is $\begin{bmatrix} x_1 + 2x_2 \\ 2x_1 - 2x_2 \end{bmatrix} = \begin{bmatrix} 10 \\ 8 \end{bmatrix}$. This, in turn, by matrix equality, is $x_1 + 2x_2 = 10$ and $2x_1 - 2x_2 = 8$, exactly the original pair of equations. Note the similarity with the form of one equation in one unknown—$3x = 12$, mentioned earlier; or, more generally, $ax = b$. In the single-variable case, the solution was obtained by dividing both sides by a or, equivalently, multiplying by $(1/a)$, the reciprocal of a. (Recall that the reciprocal of a number is also denoted by the exponent -1; that is, $3^{-1} = 1/3$, $a^{-1} = 1/a$.) The form of the equations in (A-5) suggests that, parallel to the one-variable case, a "solution" might be found by dividing both sides of $AX = B$ by A or, alternatively, by multiplying both sides by the "reciprocal" of A. To pursue this line of reasoning we need to explore the matrix operation that parallels division in ordinary algebra; we will find it useful to view division in its alternate form, multiplication by a reciprocal.

A-5 | MATRIX OPERATIONS—DIVISION

Identity Matrix

In ordinary algebra, the *identity element for multiplication* is the element that does not affect another element when multiplying it; this is, clearly, unity—for example, $(21)(1) = 21$. In matrix algebra, the so-called identity matrix plays the same role. By considering the way in which matrix multiplication was defined, it will be clear that a matrix that has the property of not altering a matrix which it multiplies will be square, with 1's along the main diagonal—strung out from upper left to lower right—and 0's elsewhere. A *diagonal* matrix is a square matrix all of whose nonzero elements are on the main diagonal—that is, in positions a_{ii} $(i = 1, \cdots, n)$ only—with zeros elsewhere—in positions $a_{ij}(i, j = 1, \cdots, n; \ i \neq j)$. Thus the identity matrix is a special case of a diagonal matrix in which all $a_{ii} = 1$.

For example, for $A = \begin{bmatrix} 2 & 1 & 3 \\ 4 & 6 & 12 \end{bmatrix}$—the matrix in (A-4)—$\begin{bmatrix} 2 & 1 & 3 \\ 4 & 6 & 12 \end{bmatrix}$ $\begin{bmatrix} 1 & 0 & 0 \\ 0 & 1 & 0 \\ 0 & 0 & 1 \end{bmatrix} = \begin{bmatrix} 2 & 1 & 3 \\ 4 & 6 & 12 \end{bmatrix}$. Thus, a 3×3 identity matrix can be found so that, when used to postmultiply A, we are left with A. An identity matrix is generally denoted by I. As with the null matrix, the proper dimensions will always be clear—it will be square and have the proper number of rows and columns to be conformable in the multiplication statement. Thus, $AI = A$. Moreover, $\begin{bmatrix} 1 & 0 \\ 0 & 1 \end{bmatrix} \begin{bmatrix} 2 & 1 & 3 \\ 4 & 6 & 12 \end{bmatrix} = \begin{bmatrix} 2 & 1 & 3 \\ 4 & 6 & 12 \end{bmatrix}$; here I is a 2×2 matrix; again $IA = A$.

Division

The concept of an identity matrix is essential for development of the fourth algebraic operation, division. We will consider matrix division to be multiplication by a reciprocal matrix. In ordinary algebra, the reciprocal is the number which, when multiplied by the number of which it is a reciprocal, generates the identity element for multiplication. That is $(3)(1/3) = 1$ or, more generally, $(a)(1/a) = 1$. In alternative notation, $(3)(3^{-1}) = 1$; $(a)(a^{-1}) = 1$.

The reciprocal, or *inverse*, of a matrix is defined similarly. The major exception is that inverses, for the purposes for which we will find them useful in input-output analysis, will be defined only for square matrices. Consider again the A matrix in (A-5), namely $A = \begin{bmatrix} 1 & 2 \\ 2 & -2 \end{bmatrix}$. Using notation similar to that for reciprocals of ordinary numbers, its inverse, A^{-1}, must be a matrix of elements that satisfy the following (definitional) equation: $AA^{-1} = I$. Since, in the present case, A is a 2×2 matrix, we know that the product, I, will have two rows (same as the number of rows in A). We also know that I is square, hence it must have two columns as well; but this means that A^{-1} also has two columns. Finally, to satisfy the conformability requirement for multiplication, the number of rows in A^{-1} must be the same as the number of columns in A, which is two. Hence, A^{-1}

is a 2×2 matrix.[6] Unfortunately, as the reader can soon establish, A^{-1} does not simply contain the reciprocals of all the elements in A:

$$\begin{bmatrix} 1 & 2 \\ 2 & -2 \end{bmatrix}\begin{bmatrix} 1 & 1/2 \\ 1/2 & -1/2 \end{bmatrix} = \begin{bmatrix} 2 & -1/2 \\ 1 & 2 \end{bmatrix} \neq \begin{bmatrix} 1 & 0 \\ 0 & 1 \end{bmatrix}.$$

Here, for $A = \begin{bmatrix} 1 & 2 \\ 2 & -2 \end{bmatrix}$, $A^{-1} = \begin{bmatrix} 1/3 & 1/3 \\ 1/3 & -1/6 \end{bmatrix}$, as the reader can easily check by finding the product AA^{-1}. In fact, since (for our purposes) inverses are to be found for square matrices only, it turns out that the identity matrix is generated whether A is premultiplied or postmultiplied by A^{-1}, that is $AA^{-1} = A^{-1}A = I$.[7]

Before turning to the somewhat involved procedure for finding the elements of an inverse matrix, note how we might now approach the equation system represented in (A-5) as $AX = B$. If (as in the particular case above) we knew A^{-1}, then (1) *premultiplying* both sides of the equation by this inverse gives $A^{-1}AX = A^{-1}B$, (2) by definition $A^{-1}A = I$, hence the equation reads $IX = A^{-1}B$, (3) since I contributes nothing in the multiplication statement, we really have $X = A^{-1}B$. Since A^{-1} and B contain known numbers, we can perform the

multiplication, giving $X = \begin{bmatrix} 1/3 & 1/3 \\ 1/3 & -1/6 \end{bmatrix} \begin{bmatrix} 10 \\ 8 \end{bmatrix} = \begin{bmatrix} 10/3 + 8/3 \\ 10/3 - 8/6 \end{bmatrix} = \begin{bmatrix} 6 \\ 2 \end{bmatrix}$. Fi-

nally, since $X = \begin{bmatrix} x_1 \\ x_2 \end{bmatrix}$, and by the definition of matrix equality, we conclude (as we already knew from earlier exploration of this example) that $x_1 = 6$, $x_2 = 2$. What we have gained is not necessarily an easier way to deal with the case of two linear equations with two unknowns, but rather a format for solution of a system of n linear equations in n unknowns, irrespective of the size of n. Moveover, as we will soon see, we also have a framework which will help us identify and distinguish between the two cases illustrated by Eqs. (A-2) and (A-3) above, namely the situations where the equations contain too little information for a unique solution (for example, two equations defining only one line in solution space) or conflicting information and thus no solution (for example, two equations defining two parallel lines in solution space).

In developing the definition of an inverse that will be most useful for purposes of analyzing linear equation systems, we will need to make use of several matrix concepts: determinants, minors, and cofactors.

Determinants A determinant is a number that is associated with any square matrix. For the general 2×2 case, that is, $A = \begin{bmatrix} a_{11} & a_{12} \\ a_{21} & a_{22} \end{bmatrix}$, the determi-

[6] This is easily seen to be generally true. For any $n \times n$ matrix the inverse matrix (if it exists, which is a question soon to be investigated) will also be of size $n \times n$.

[7] For a given square A matrix, let B be the postmultiplying inverse and C be the premultiplying inverse; $AB = I$, $CA = I$. Since A and I are square, B and C must have the same (square) dimensions. Multiplying both sides of the first statement by C gives $CAB = CI$. But, from the second statement, $CA = I$; thus CAB can be written IB. Thus $IB = CI$, and since I does not affect the multiplications, $B = C$; the two inverses for A must be the same. In more advanced matrix algebra discussions, the concept of pseudo-inverses, right and left inverses, and generalized inverses for nonsquare matrices are introduced. However, they are not necessary for an understanding of the input-output equation system.

nant, denoted $|A|$, is defined as $a_{11}a_{22} - a_{12}a_{21}$. For example, for $A = \begin{bmatrix} 1 & 2 \\ 2 & -2 \end{bmatrix}$, $|A| = (-2) - (4) = -6$. In words, the determinant for a 2×2 matrix is the product of the elements on the main diagonal less the product of the elements on the other diagonal. Unfortunately, this simplicity does not extend to finding

determinants of larger matrices. For a 3×3 matrix, $A = \begin{bmatrix} a_{11} & a_{12} & a_{13} \\ a_{21} & a_{22} & a_{23} \\ a_{31} & a_{32} & a_{33} \end{bmatrix}$,

$|A| = (a_{11}a_{22}a_{33} + a_{12}a_{23}a_{31} + a_{13}a_{32}a_{21}) - (a_{13}a_{22}a_{31} + a_{23}a_{32}a_{11} + a_{33}a_{12}a_{21})$.
This looks worse than it is; rewrite A and repeat columns 1 and 2 as columns 4 and 5.

$$\begin{bmatrix} a_{11} & a_{12} & a_{13} & a_{11} & a_{12} \\ a_{21} & a_{22} & a_{23} & a_{21} & a_{22} \\ a_{31} & a_{32} & a_{33} & a_{31} & a_{32} \end{bmatrix}$$

Then $|A|$ is the sum of the products of elements along the three solid arrows less the sum of the products of elements along the three broken arrows. For example, from previously, if $F = \begin{bmatrix} 2 & 1 & 3 \\ 4 & 0 & 7 \\ 1 & 1 & 6 \end{bmatrix}$, then $|F| = 0 + 7 + 12 - (0 + 14 + 24) =$
-19. For square matrices of larger dimension, a more general rule for evaluation of the determinant is necessary; there is no simple "diagonals" rule. To understand this more general rule we need some further terminology.

Minor   The minor of an element a_{ij} in a square matrix A, sometimes denoted $|a_{ij}|$, is the determinant of the square matrix that remains when row i and column j are removed from A. In the general 3×3 matrix A, above,
$|a_{12}| = \begin{vmatrix} a_{21} & a_{23} \\ a_{31} & a_{33} \end{vmatrix} = a_{21}a_{33} - a_{23}a_{31}$. For example, referring again to F, $|f_{12}|$
$= \begin{vmatrix} 4 & 7 \\ 1 & 6 \end{vmatrix} = 24 - 7 = 17$. The definition of a minor is needed to understand what a cofactor is.

Cofactor   The cofactor of an element a_{ij} in a square matrix A, sometimes denoted A_{ij}, is the minor of a_{ij} multiplied by $(-1)^{i+j}$—that is, $A_{ij} = (-1)^{i+j}|a_{ij}|$. Again, $A_{12} = (-1)^3 \begin{vmatrix} a_{21} & a_{23} \\ a_{31} & a_{33} \end{vmatrix} = -a_{21}a_{33} + a_{23}a_{31}$; $F_{12} =$
$(-1)^3(17) = -17$. Thus the cofactor and the minor of an element differ at most by sign (hence the cofactor is sometimes called the *signed minor*). They will differ only when the sum of a_{ij}'s row and column location is odd, since (-1) raised to an odd power is -1, but (-1) raised to an even power is just $+1$, the identity element for ordinary multiplication.

We are now prepared for a more general definition of the determinant of any $n \times n$ square matrix A. It is because of this definition that we need to know what a cofactor is. (The rules, above, for 2×2 and 3×3 matrices, are in fact the result of applications of this rule in the two smallest cases.) The determinant can be found as the sum of the products of each of the elements in *any* particular row, i, times their corresponding cofactors, or each of the elements in *any* column, j, times their corresponding cofactors. That is,

$$|A| = \sum_{j=1}^{n} a_{ij} A_{ij} \quad (\text{across any row } i)$$

or

$$|A| = \sum_{i=1}^{n} a_{ij} A_{ij} \quad (\text{down any column } j)$$

For example, expanding the general 3×3 matrix A, above, along row 3, gives

$$|A| = a_{31} A_{31} + a_{32} A_{32} + a_{33} A_{33}$$

$$= a_{31} \begin{vmatrix} a_{12} & a_{13} \\ a_{22} & a_{23} \end{vmatrix} + a_{32}(-1) \begin{vmatrix} a_{11} & a_{13} \\ a_{21} & a_{23} \end{vmatrix} + a_{33} \begin{vmatrix} a_{11} & a_{12} \\ a_{21} & a_{22} \end{vmatrix}$$

$$= a_{31}(a_{12}a_{23} - a_{13}a_{22}) - a_{32}(a_{11}a_{23} - a_{13}a_{21}) + a_{33}(a_{11}a_{22} - a_{12}a_{21})$$

This is the same set of terms (although in a different order) as was given by the "diagonal" rule, above. Using the matrix F, and again expanding along row 3,

$$|F| = 1 \begin{vmatrix} 1 & 3 \\ 0 & 7 \end{vmatrix} + 1(-1) \begin{vmatrix} 2 & 3 \\ 4 & 7 \end{vmatrix} + 6 \begin{vmatrix} 2 & 1 \\ 4 & 0 \end{vmatrix}$$

$$= 1(7 - 0) - 1(14 - 12) + 6(0 - 4) = -19,$$

again, as before.

Expanding A down column 2:

$$|A| = a_{12} A_{12} + a_{22} A_{22} + a_{32} A_{32}$$

$$= a_{12}(-1) \begin{vmatrix} a_{21} & a_{23} \\ a_{31} & a_{33} \end{vmatrix} + a_{22} \begin{vmatrix} a_{11} & a_{13} \\ a_{31} & a_{33} \end{vmatrix} + a_{32}(-1) \begin{vmatrix} a_{11} & a_{13} \\ a_{21} & a_{23} \end{vmatrix}$$

$$= -a_{12}(a_{21}a_{33} - a_{23}a_{31}) + a_{22}(a_{11}a_{33} - a_{13}a_{31}) - a_{32}(a_{11}a_{23} - a_{13}a_{21})$$

which is simply a rearrangement of the same terms as before. Finding $|F|$ down row 2:

$$|F| = -1 \begin{vmatrix} 4 & 7 \\ 1 & 6 \end{vmatrix} + 0 \begin{vmatrix} 2 & 3 \\ 1 & 6 \end{vmatrix} - 1 \begin{vmatrix} 2 & 3 \\ 4 & 7 \end{vmatrix}$$

$$= -1(24 - 7) + 0(12 - 3) - 1(14 - 12) = -19.$$

These rules for evaluation of determinants suggest that if one selects a row or column with many 0's and 1's, the arithmetic involved will be simplified.

Several useful properties of determinants can be deduced from the general definition of expansion along a row or column. In particular, because of the role that the determinant, $|A|$, will be found to play in the general definition of the inverse, A^{-1}, we are interested in situations in which $|A| = 0$.

1 If a square matrix A contains one or more rows or columns whose elements are all zeros, $|A| = 0$. This follows immediately, since one can select a row or column of zeros along which to expand; each a_{ij} in the sum $\sum a_{ij} A_{ij}$ will be zero and hence the sum will be zero.

2 If two or more rows or columns in a square matrix A are equal, $|A| = 0$.[8]

3 If two or more rows or columns in a square matrix A are proportional, $|A| = 0$.[9]

4 If we apply the determinant rule by selecting elements a_{ij} from one row and cofactors from some other row, A_{kj}, the result will be zero. That is, $\sum_{j=1}^{n} a_{ij}A_{kj} = 0$

$(i \neq k)$. This is also true for the column expansion; $\sum_{i=1}^{n} a_{ij}A_{il} = 0$ $(j \neq l)$. These are known as expansions by *alien* cofactors, since the cofactors used do not belong to the same row or column as the individual elements a_{ij}. This property is useful in developing a general definition for an inverse.

Transposition   One further matrix operation is needed. The transpose of an $m \times n$ matrix A, denoted A' or A^T, is the matrix formed by interchanging rows with columns. For example, if $A = \begin{bmatrix} a_{11} & a_{12} & a_{13} \\ a_{21} & a_{22} & a_{23} \end{bmatrix}$, $A' = \begin{bmatrix} a_{11} & a_{21} \\ a_{12} & a_{22} \\ a_{13} & a_{23} \end{bmatrix}$; row 1 of A becomes column 1 of A', and so on. (The transpose of a transpose is the original matrix; $[A']' = A$.) The transposition operation is part of the definition of an adjoint matrix which is needed, in turn, in the definition of an inverse.

Adjoint Matrix   The adjoint of a square matrix A, denoted adj A, is a matrix whose element in row i, column j is the *cofactor* of the element in row i, column j of the *transpose* of A. (Deriving adjoint matrices is, in general, a tedious procedure; our chief interest in them comes from the role that the adjoint plays in the general definition of an inverse.)

For $A = \begin{bmatrix} a_{11} & a_{12} & a_{13} \\ a_{21} & a_{22} & a_{23} \\ a_{31} & a_{32} & a_{33} \end{bmatrix}$, adj $A = \begin{bmatrix} A_{11} & A_{21} & A_{31} \\ A_{12} & A_{22} & A_{32} \\ A_{13} & A_{23} & A_{33} \end{bmatrix}$. The element in

row 1, column 2 of the adjoint is the cofactor of the element in row 2, column 1 of A (that is, the element in row 1, column 2 of the transpose of A), namely A_{21}. And $A_{21} = (-1)^3 \begin{vmatrix} a_{12} & a_{13} \\ a_{32} & a_{33} \end{vmatrix} = -(a_{12}a_{33} - a_{13}a_{32})$. Thus, each element in the adjoint of an $n \times n$ matrix requires evaluation of the determinant of an $(n-1) \times (n-1)$ matrix. The reader may wish to check to be convinced that, for F

$= \begin{bmatrix} 2 & 1 & 3 \\ 4 & 0 & 7 \\ 1 & 1 & 6 \end{bmatrix}$, adj $F = \begin{bmatrix} -7 & -3 & 7 \\ -17 & 9 & -2 \\ 4 & -1 & -4 \end{bmatrix}$.

Now, finally, we are in a position to investigate the nature of the inverse matrix. Consider the general 3×3 case. Suppose that we were to postmultiply A

---

[8] This follows from another property, namely that the interchange of any two rows or columns in a square matrix A changes the sign of $|A|$. (Proof of this property can be found in more advanced discussions of determinants.) If two rows (or columns) are equal, then interchanging them will not alter the determinant at all. Yet the sign of the determinant must be changed. Zero is the only number that is the same regardless of sign.

[9] This follows from property (2), immediately above, and also from the fact that multiplication of any row or column in a square matrix A by a constant, k, produces a matrix whose determinant is $k|A|$.

by its adjoint:

$$A(\text{adj } A) = \begin{bmatrix} a_{11} & a_{12} & a_{13} \\ a_{21} & a_{22} & a_{23} \\ a_{31} & a_{32} & a_{33} \end{bmatrix} \begin{bmatrix} A_{11} & A_{21} & A_{31} \\ A_{12} & A_{22} & A_{32} \\ A_{13} & A_{23} & A_{33} \end{bmatrix}$$

$$= \begin{bmatrix} \sum\limits_{j=1}^{3} a_{1j}A_{1j} & \sum\limits_{j=1}^{3} a_{1j}A_{2j} & \sum\limits_{j=1}^{3} a_{1j}A_{3j} \\ \sum\limits_{j=1}^{3} a_{2j}A_{1j} & \sum\limits_{j=1}^{3} a_{2j}A_{2j} & \sum\limits_{j=1}^{3} a_{2j}A_{3j} \\ \sum\limits_{j=1}^{3} a_{3j}A_{1j} & \sum\limits_{j=1}^{3} a_{3j}A_{2j} & \sum\limits_{j=1}^{3} a_{3j}A_{3j} \end{bmatrix}$$

The subscripts are of great importance. The sum of the upper-left corner of the product matrix (row 1, column 1) is just the determinant of A, evaluated along row 1 by the general rule for determinants. Similarly, the elements in row 2, column 2, and row 3, column 3 (i.e., along the main diagonal) in the product matrix also equal $|A|$. On the other hand, consider the sum in row 1, column 2 of the product matrix. This involves elements from row 1 of A and cofactors from row 2; it is an expansion by alien cofactors and hence equals zero. All other off-diagonal elements represent such alien cofactor expansions and hence are also zero. Thus, in this 3×3 case,

$$A(\text{adj } A) = \begin{bmatrix} |A| & 0 & 0 \\ 0 & |A| & 0 \\ 0 & 0 & |A| \end{bmatrix}$$

and, since $|A|$ is a scalar, from the definition of the identity matrix, I, and of multiplication by a scalar, this can be written

$$A(\text{adj } A) = |A| \begin{bmatrix} 1 & 0 & 0 \\ 0 & 1 & 0 \\ 0 & 0 & 1 \end{bmatrix} = |A|I.$$

Then, dividing both sides by the scalar $|A|$:

$$\left(\frac{1}{|A|} \right) [A(\text{adj } A)] = I \quad \text{or} \quad A\left[\left(\frac{1}{|A|} \right) (\text{adj } A) \right] = I$$

This tells us that the quantity in square brackets, postmultiplying A, must be A^{-1}, precisely by the definition of what an inverse does, namely that $AA^{-1} = I$. So

$$A^{-1} = \left(\frac{1}{|A|} \right) (\text{adj } A)$$

That is, the inverse consists of a scalar part, $\left(\dfrac{1}{|A|} \right)$, and a matrix part, the adjoint. Since division by zero is not defined, we see that when $|A| = 0$, the inverse will not be defined. When a matrix has a determinant of zero, the matrix is termed singular, it has no inverse; a nonsingular matrix has a nonzero determinant and this means that it has an inverse.

The Inverse in Linear Equation Systems

To return to the matrix representation of systems of linear equations, $AX = B$, we recognize that only if A is nonsingular so that $|A| \neq 0$ and therefore A^{-1} exists, can we perform the matrix algebra $A^{-1}AX = A^{-1}B$, which generates the unique solution for X. If $|A| = 0$, there is no inverse and we cannot "divide through" by A.

Returning now to the pairs of equations in (A-1), (A-2), and (A-3), recall that we have already written equations (A-1) in $AX = B$ form by defining

$$A = \begin{bmatrix} 1 & 2 \\ 2 & -2 \end{bmatrix}, \qquad X = \begin{bmatrix} x_1 \\ x_2 \end{bmatrix}, \qquad \text{and} \qquad B = \begin{bmatrix} 10 \\ 8 \end{bmatrix}.$$

We can also see that $|A| = -6$ and hence A^{-1} can be found; it was already used, above, in finding $X = \begin{bmatrix} 6 \\ 2 \end{bmatrix}$.

For Eqs. (A-2), the A, X, and B matrices are

$$A = \begin{bmatrix} 1 & 2 \\ 2 & 4 \end{bmatrix}, \qquad X = \begin{bmatrix} x_1 \\ x_2 \end{bmatrix}, \qquad \text{and} \qquad B = \begin{bmatrix} 10 \\ 20 \end{bmatrix}$$

and for (A-3) they are

$$A = \begin{bmatrix} 1 & 2 \\ 2 & 4 \end{bmatrix}, \qquad X = \begin{bmatrix} x_1 \\ x_2 \end{bmatrix}, \qquad \text{and} \qquad B = \begin{bmatrix} 10 \\ 30 \end{bmatrix}.$$

Equations (A-2) and (A-3) have the same coefficient matrix, A, and $|A| = 4 - 4 = 0$. Recall that the solution-space picture for (A-2) was one line, hence an infinite number of solutions exist; the picture for (A-3) was a pair of parallel lines. This suggests: (1) that a singular coefficient matrix characterizes a set of linear equations which does not have a unique solution and (2) that to distinguish the underdetermined case (multiple solutions) from the inconsistent case (no solutions) must require consideration of the B vector, along with the A matrix, since in matrix notation the only difference between equation sets (A-2) and (A-3) lies in the right-hand side vector, B.

We can summarize our results thus far; they have been explored with examples for the 2×2 case but are, in fact, valid for an $n \times n$ system of linear equations of any size. In matrix representation, A is the $n \times n$ coefficient matrix of parameters (coefficients) attached to the unknown x's, X is an $n \times 1$ column vector of those unknown variables, and B is an $n \times 1$ column vector of right-hand side values. The equation system is thus $AX = B$, due to the definitions of matrix multiplication and matrix equality. If A^{-1} exists (which means, if A is nonsingular, i.e., has a nonzero determinant), then the unique solution to the equations is given by $X = A^{-1}B$. (This involves matrix multiplication, the definition of the inverse and identity matrices, and matrix equality.) If A^{-1} does not exist (A is singular, i.e., has a zero determinant), then apparently either there is no solution or there are many.

The sharp distinction between the 2×2 multiple solution and no-solution cases is not maintained in larger systems ($3 \times 3, \cdots, n \times n$). That this will be so can be visualized for the case of three linear equations in three unknowns. Each equation will define a plane (in three-dimensional solution space) instead of a line as in the 2×2 case. For a unique solution ($|A| \neq 0$), all three planes must intersect in a single point—that is, two planes must intersect in a line and the third plane must cut through that line. When $|A| = 0$, all three equations may define the same plane (this corresponds to Eqs. [A-2]), or the three planes may be distinct and parallel (corresponding to Eqs. [A-3]). In addition, however, two planes may be parallel and the third plane intersect them, the three planes may intersect in a common line, or each pair of planes may intersect in a line, and the three lines may be parallel. These represent situations in which a unique solution is not possible but which do not correspond to the underdetermined and overdetermined 2×2 cases.

A complete analysis of the various possibilities which only emerge in systems of size 3×3 or larger is beyond the scope of our interest in this book. However, the fundamental distinction between the 2×2 cases of multiple solutions and an inconsistent system can be made most clearly via the vector notion of linear dependence and independence and the definition of the rank of a matrix. This is useful for analysis of larger systems, and the accompanying and new geometric view of linear equation systems which it is based upon is of interest in its own right. We will introduce these concepts in section A-8. In the next two sections we examine some special properties of diagonal matrices and the potential importance of the notion of partitioning. These can be particularly useful in dealing with input-output equation systems.

A-6 | DIAGONAL MATRICES AND UNITY VECTORS

Diagonal Matrices

At some points in the text, it will be useful to employ additional matrix notation for diagonal matrices, which is particularly pertinent to input-output models. Consider an n-element column vector X; in Eqs. (2-6) and (2-7) in Chapter 2 this represents gross outputs. The "hat" symbol placed over an n-element vector indicates that the elements of the vector have been "strung out" along the main diagonal of an $n \times n$ diagonal matrix. When the expression for the vector being diagonalized contains several elements, so that the hat does not easily extend over the entire width of the expression, the alternative notation $\langle X \rangle$ is used—for example, if the vector is denoted $M^{-1}AMB$. That is

$$\hat{X} = \langle X \rangle = \begin{bmatrix} X_1 & 0 & \cdots & 0 \\ 0 & X_2 & & \\ \vdots & & & \\ 0 & 0 & \cdots & X_n \end{bmatrix} \tag{A-6}$$

When a diagonal matrix *post*multiplies another matrix, the jth element in the diagonal matrix multiplies all of the elements in the jth *column* of the matrix on the left. For example, for $A = \begin{bmatrix} a_{11} & a_{12} \\ a_{21} & a_{22} \end{bmatrix}$ and $X = \begin{bmatrix} X_1 \\ X_2 \end{bmatrix}$,

$$A\hat{X} = \begin{bmatrix} a_{11} & a_{12} \\ a_{21} & a_{22} \end{bmatrix} \begin{bmatrix} X_1 & 0 \\ 0 & X_2 \end{bmatrix} = \begin{bmatrix} a_{11}X_1 & a_{12}X_2 \\ a_{21}X_1 & a_{22}X_2 \end{bmatrix} \tag{A-7}$$

Similarly, *pre*multiplication by a diagonal matrix results in multiplication of each element in the ith *row* of the matrix on the right by the ith element of the diagonal matrix. Using the same A and X as above,

$$\hat{X}A = \begin{bmatrix} X_1 & 0 \\ 0 & X_2 \end{bmatrix} \begin{bmatrix} a_{11} & a_{12} \\ a_{21} & a_{22} \end{bmatrix} = \begin{bmatrix} X_1 a_{11} & X_1 a_{12} \\ X_2 a_{21} & X_2 a_{22} \end{bmatrix} \tag{A-8}$$

Another useful fact about diagonal matrices is that the inverse of a diagonal matrix is another diagonal matrix, each of whose elements is just the reciprocal of the original element. (The reader can easily show this in the 2×2 or 3×3 case, using the most basic rule for finding an inverse, from section A-5, above.) Thus, for example, for the same two-element column vector X,

$$(\hat{X})^{-1} = \begin{bmatrix} X_1 & 0 \\ 0 & X_2 \end{bmatrix}^{-1} = \begin{bmatrix} \dfrac{1}{X_1} & 0 \\ 0 & \dfrac{1}{X_2} \end{bmatrix} \tag{A-9}$$

The usefulness of this notation is illustrated if we consider Table 2-1 in Chapter 2, which contains interindustry flows, z_{ij}, between the n sectors in an economy, Define Z to be the $n \times n$ matrix of these flows:

$$Z = \begin{bmatrix} z_{11} & \cdots & z_{1n} \\ \vdots & & \\ z_{n1} & \cdots & z_{nn} \end{bmatrix}$$

Then, because of the particular characteristics of the inverse of a diagonal matrix and of postmultiplication by a diagonal matrix, the matrix A, containing the technical coefficients $a_{ij} = z_{ij}/X_j$, as defined in Eq. (2-3) in Chapter 2, can be represented as

$$A = Z(\hat{X})^{-1} \tag{A-10}$$

Again, to illustrate, for the 2×2 case,

$$A = \begin{bmatrix} z_{11} & z_{12} \\ z_{21} & z_{22} \end{bmatrix} \begin{bmatrix} \dfrac{1}{X_1} & 0 \\ 0 & \dfrac{1}{X_2} \end{bmatrix} = \begin{bmatrix} \dfrac{z_{11}}{X_1} & \dfrac{z_{12}}{X_2} \\ \dfrac{z_{21}}{X_1} & \dfrac{z_{22}}{X_2} \end{bmatrix} = \begin{bmatrix} a_{11} & a_{12} \\ a_{21} & a_{22} \end{bmatrix}$$

When the hat appears over a square $n \times n$ matrix, M, it denotes the $n \times n$ diagonal matrix that is formed by setting all off-diagonal elements in M equal to zero. For $M = \begin{bmatrix} m_{11} & m_{12} & m_{13} \\ m_{21} & m_{22} & m_{23} \\ m_{31} & m_{32} & m_{33} \end{bmatrix}$, $\hat{M} = \begin{bmatrix} m_{11} & 0 & 0 \\ 0 & m_{22} & 0 \\ 0 & 0 & m_{33} \end{bmatrix}$. In addition, an inverted hat over an $n \times n$ square matrix designates the $n \times n$ matrix that results when all main diagonal elements in M are set equal to zero. Thus $\check{M}$

$$= \begin{bmatrix} 0 & m_{12} & m_{13} \\ m_{21} & 0 & m_{23} \\ m_{31} & m_{32} & 0 \end{bmatrix}$$. It follows that $M = \hat{M} + \check{M}$. This notation can be useful

in discussing commodity-by-industry input-output models, as in Chapter 5. This notation can be used with nonsquare matrices also. If M has dimensions $m \times n$ ($m \neq n$), then $\hat{M}$ denotes the $m \times n$ matrix with elements m_{ii} from M and zeros elsewhere. For example, if $M = \begin{bmatrix} m_{11} & m_{12} & m_{13} \\ m_{21} & m_{22} & m_{23} \end{bmatrix}$, $\hat{M} = \begin{bmatrix} m_{11} & 0 & 0 \\ 0 & m_{22} & 0 \end{bmatrix}$ and,

analogously, $\check{M} = \begin{bmatrix} 0 & m_{12} & m_{13} \\ m_{21} & 0 & m_{23} \end{bmatrix}$.

Unity Rows and Columns

Closely related to the (diagonal) identity matrix, I, is the *unity* column, denoted by i, or its transpose, the unity row, i'. This is a column or row containing all 1's. (An *identity* column or row is a vector all of whose elements are 0's except for one, which is 1. That is, identity columns or rows are columns or rows from an identity matrix. Somewhat confusingly, these are also called unit—not unity—columns and rows.) The two-element unity column is $i = \begin{bmatrix} 1 \\ 1 \end{bmatrix}$. *Post*multiplication of a matrix A by the unity column generates a *column vector* whose elements are the sums of the elements in each *row* of A; *pre*multiplication of A by i' creates a *row vector* each of whose elements is a *column* sum from A. To continue with illustrations from the 2×2 case:

$$Ai = \begin{bmatrix} a_{11} & a_{12} \\ a_{21} & a_{22} \end{bmatrix} \begin{bmatrix} 1 \\ 1 \end{bmatrix} = \begin{bmatrix} (a_{11} + a_{12}) \\ (a_{21} + a_{22}) \end{bmatrix}$$

$$i'A = \begin{bmatrix} 1 & 1 \end{bmatrix} \begin{bmatrix} a_{11} & a_{12} \\ a_{21} & a_{22} \end{bmatrix} = [(a_{11} + a_{21}) \ (a_{12} + a_{22})]$$

In some chapters of this book, for example when some simple input-output multiplier concepts are presented, and in later chapters, when dealing with so-called nonsurvey methods for generating input-output coefficient matrices, we will find that row sums and/or column sums of matrices will be important. The unity row and column will be notationally useful at those points.

A-7 | PARTITIONED MATRICES

Multiplication of Partitioned Matrices

Suppose that the product AB is to be found, where A is of dimension $m \times n$, and B is of dimension $n \times p$. Suppose, further, that both are large matrices (that is, that m, n, and p are large numbers). Each element in the product will contain the sum of n products of pairs of elements. It is possible to divide up, or partition, A and B so that the multiplication can be carried out with smaller submatrices (that is, with smaller numbers of pairs of elements). We redefine A as composed of four submatrices, as follows, with dimensions as shown.

$$A = \begin{matrix} q \\ (m-q) \end{matrix} \begin{Bmatrix} \\ \\ \end{Bmatrix} \overbrace{\left[\begin{array}{c|c} E & F \\ \hline G & H \end{array} \right]}^{\textstyle r \quad (n-r)} \begin{matrix} \\ \end{matrix} \} \, m \qquad \text{(A-11)}$$

$$\underbrace{\phantom{\left[\begin{array}{c|c} E & F \\ \hline G & H \end{array} \right]}}_{n}$$

Similarly, subdivide B into four smaller matrices

$$B = \begin{matrix} r \\ (n-r) \end{matrix} \begin{Bmatrix} \\ \\ \end{Bmatrix} \overbrace{\left[\begin{array}{c|c} L & M \\ \hline N & P \end{array} \right]}^{\textstyle s \quad (p-s)} \begin{matrix} \\ \end{matrix} \} \, n \qquad \text{(A-12)}$$

$$\underbrace{\phantom{\left[\begin{array}{c|c} L & M \\ \hline N & P \end{array} \right]}}_{p}$$

Then the product AB can be calculated as follows.

$$\left[\begin{array}{c|c} E & F \\ \hline G & H \end{array} \right] \left[\begin{array}{c|c} L & M \\ \hline N & P \end{array} \right] = \left[\begin{array}{c|c} EL + FN & EM + FP \\ \hline GL + HN & GM + HP \end{array} \right] \qquad \text{(A-13)}$$

The reader should check that each of the eight products satisfies the conformability requirement for multiplication of matrices (and then that each of the four sums satisfies the conformability requirement for addition). In the individual multiplications, no product involves a sum of n products of pairs of elements; either r or $(n-r)$ products are required, but never n.

The following example illustrates. Let

$$A = \begin{bmatrix} 1 & 2 & 3 \\ 4 & 5 & 6 \\ 7 & 0 & 0 \end{bmatrix} \qquad B = \begin{bmatrix} 1 & 1 & 1 & 1 \\ 2 & 2 & 3 & 1 \\ 1 & 1 & 2 & 1 \end{bmatrix}$$

Suppose we partition A as follows:

$$A = \left[\begin{array}{cc|c} 1 & 2 & 3 \\ 4 & 5 & 6 \\ \hline 7 & 0 & 0 \end{array} \right]$$

That is,

$$E = \begin{bmatrix} 1 & 2 \\ 4 & 5 \end{bmatrix}, \qquad F = \begin{bmatrix} 3 \\ 6 \end{bmatrix}, \qquad G = [7 \quad 0], \qquad \text{and} \qquad H = [0]$$

Then, B *must* be partitioned between rows 2 and 3 to allow the submatrix multiplication. The column partition in B is arbitrary. Suppose

$$B = \begin{bmatrix} 1 & 1 & | & 1 & 1 \\ 2 & 2 & | & 3 & 1 \\ \hline 1 & 1 & | & 2 & 1 \end{bmatrix}$$

That is,

$$L = \begin{bmatrix} 1 & 1 \\ 2 & 2 \end{bmatrix}, \qquad M = \begin{bmatrix} 1 & 1 \\ 3 & 1 \end{bmatrix}, \qquad N = [1 \quad 1], \qquad \text{and} \qquad P = [2 \quad 1]$$

Then, finding AB as in Eq. (A-13), we have

$$AB = \left[\begin{array}{c|c} \begin{bmatrix} 1 & 2 \\ 4 & 5 \end{bmatrix}\begin{bmatrix} 1 & 1 \\ 2 & 2 \end{bmatrix} + \begin{bmatrix} 3 \\ 6 \end{bmatrix}[1 \quad 1] & \begin{bmatrix} 1 & 2 \\ 4 & 5 \end{bmatrix}\begin{bmatrix} 1 & 1 \\ 3 & 1 \end{bmatrix} + \begin{bmatrix} 3 \\ 6 \end{bmatrix}[2 \quad 1] \\ \hline [7 \quad 0]\begin{bmatrix} 1 & 1 \\ 2 & 2 \end{bmatrix} + [0][1 \quad 1] & [7 \quad 0]\begin{bmatrix} 1 & 1 \\ 3 & 1 \end{bmatrix} + [0][2 \quad 1] \end{array} \right]$$

$$= \begin{bmatrix} 8 & 8 & | & 13 & 6 \\ 20 & 20 & | & 31 & 15 \\ \hline 7 & 7 & | & 7 & 7 \end{bmatrix}$$

This can be easily checked by ordinary matrix multiplication, without any partitioning.

The Inverse of a Partitioned Matrix

We now explore the potential usefulness of partitioned matrix multiplication when an inverse matrix is to be found. Consider again the matrix A given in Eq. (A-11), above, only now let $m = n$, so that A is square. Furthermore, let $q = r$, so that both E and H are square submatrices. That is, we have

$$A = \begin{matrix} q \\ n-q \end{matrix} \begin{Bmatrix} \overbrace{\begin{bmatrix} E & | & F \\ \hline G & | & H \end{bmatrix}}^{\displaystyle q \quad n-q} \end{Bmatrix} \begin{matrix} \\ n \end{matrix} \qquad \qquad \text{(A-14)}$$

Notice in particular that both E and H are square matrices, of order q and $n - q$, respectively. Thus, A^{-1}, if it exists (meaning, if $|A| \neq 0$) will be an $n \times n$ matrix, R (for reciprocal), which can be thought of as made up of four submatrices of the same dimensions as those in A. That is,

$$R = \begin{matrix} & \overbrace{q}^{\ } & \overbrace{n-q}^{\ } \\ q\ \{ & \\ n-q\ \{ & \end{matrix} \underbrace{\left[\begin{array}{c|c} S & T \\ \hline U & V \end{array} \right]}_{n} \begin{matrix} \\ \end{matrix} \Big\} n$$

By the definition of an inverse, $AR = I$, and since I will also be of order n, we can think of it as also partitioned in the same way, namely

$$I = \begin{matrix} & \overbrace{q}^{\ } & \overbrace{n-q}^{\ } \\ q\ \{ & \\ n-q\ \{ & \end{matrix} \underbrace{\left[\begin{array}{c|c} I & 0 \\ \hline 0 & I \end{array} \right]}_{n} \begin{matrix} \\ \end{matrix} \Big\} n$$

Thus the $n \times n$ matrix equation $AR = I$, or

$$\left[\begin{array}{c|c} E & F \\ \hline G & H \end{array} \right] \left[\begin{array}{c|c} S & T \\ \hline U & V \end{array} \right] = \left[\begin{array}{c|c} I & 0 \\ \hline 0 & I \end{array} \right]$$

can be looked at as compactly summarizing the four smaller matrix equations

$$\begin{array}{ll} \textbf{1}\ \ ES + FU = I & \textbf{3}\ \ GS + HU = 0 \\ \textbf{2}\ \ ET + FV = 0 & \textbf{4}\ \ GT + HV = I \end{array}$$

(The reader should be clear that all of these statements are dimensionally correct. That is, that conformability requirements are met for the eight multiplications, for the four additions, and for the four equalities.)

Our object now is to show that the (presently unknown) elements (submatrices) of the inverse matrix—S, T, U, and V—can be found as algebraic expressions of the four (known) submatrices in A—E, F, G, and H. While the algebra may appear involved, the results are of practical importance, as we shall see. Assume that E^{-1} can be found. Then from **1**—premultiplying both sides by E^{-1} and rearranging

$$S = E^{-1}(I - FU) \tag{A-15}$$

Putting this into **3** gives $GE^{-1}(I - FU) + HU = 0$. Removing parentheses and rearranging, $-GE^{-1}FU + HU = -GE^{-1}$, or $(H - GE^{-1}F)U = -GE^{-1}$ so that, finally

$$U = -(H - GE^{-1}F)^{-1}GE^{-1} \tag{A-16}$$

The important point is that all of the elements in U, the $(n-q) \times q$ submatrix in the inverse, have been found in terms of the known submatrices E, F, G, and H. It is true that in the process two inverses, E^{-1} and $(H - GE^{-1}F)^{-1}$ must be found; but it is worth noting that these are inverses of $q \times q$ and $(n-q) \times (n-q)$ matrices respectively. Thus if A is a 5×5 matrix (i.e., $n = 5$), we could let $q = 2$ and $n - q = 3$, and therefore the inverses required would be for the smaller matrices of size 2×2 and 3×3. The very important point, as we are about to see, is that these two smaller inverses are the *only* inverses that we need to find. Knowing U, from Eq. (A-16), we can substitute back into (A-15) and find S, another submatrix in the inverse. Additional matrix operations are necessary—two multiplications and one subtraction—but no new inverses are needed.

Consider next 2 and 4. From 2, using E^{-1} again,

$$T = -E^{-1}FV \qquad \text{(A-17)}$$

Putting this into 4, $-GE^{-1}FV + HV = I$, or $(H - GE^{-1}F)V = I$, that is,

$$V = (H - GE^{-1}F)^{-1} \qquad \text{(A-18)}$$

But we already have found $(H - GE^{-1}F)^{-1}$ in solving for U in Eq. (A-16). Thus V is known, and putting this result into Eq. (A-17) defines T in terms of known submatrices.

Therefore all of the elements in the $n \times n$ inverse matrix R have been determined in a sequential procedure that circumvents the necessity of finding the $n \times n$ inverse directly. It requires, instead, inverses of two smaller matrices and some additional matrix algebra. One can equally well begin with the assumption that H^{-1} can be found (recall that in the partitioning of A in Eq. (A-14) both E and H are square submatrices). The interested reader may wish to derive the facts that, from 1 and 3, above, $S = (E - FH^{-1}G)^{-1}$ and $U = -H^{-1}G(E - FH^{-1}G)^{-1}$. Similarly, from 2 and 4, $T = -(E - FH^{-1}G)^{-1}FH^{-1}$ and $V = H^{-1}(I - GT)$. Again, all four submatrices in the partitioned inverse R have been found in terms of the inverses of two smaller matrices—here H^{-1} and $(E - FH^{-1}G)^{-1}$ instead of E^{-1} and $(H - GE^{-1}F)^{-1}$, as before.

For inverses of large matrices, this may be an efficient computational procedure. In addition, careful partitioning can simplify the technique even further in some cases. For example, if A can be partitioned into $\left[\begin{array}{c|c} I & F \\ \hline 0 & H \end{array} \right]$, then the reader should check that

$$A^{-1} = \left[\begin{array}{c|c} I & -FH^{-1} \\ \hline 0 & H^{-1} \end{array} \right]$$

In this case, only one smaller inverse, H^{-1}, needs to be found.

A-8 | VECTOR GEOMETRY

Consider again Eqs. (A-1):

$$x_1 + 2x_2 = 10$$
$$2x_1 - 2x_2 = 8$$

with coefficient matrix $A = \begin{bmatrix} 1 & 2 \\ 2 & -2 \end{bmatrix}$. Consider the individual columns of A; denote the first column by A_1, that is, $A_1 = \begin{bmatrix} 1 \\ 2 \end{bmatrix}$, and let $A_2 = \begin{bmatrix} 2 \\ -2 \end{bmatrix}$, the second column. Then, recalling the definition of multiplication of a matrix by a scalar, we see that Eqs. (A-1) can also be written (where $B = \begin{bmatrix} 10 \\ 8 \end{bmatrix}$, as before):

$$A_1 x_1 + A_2 x_2 = B$$

that is

$$\begin{bmatrix} 1 \\ 2 \end{bmatrix} x_1 + \begin{bmatrix} 2 \\ -2 \end{bmatrix} x_2 = \begin{bmatrix} 10 \\ 8 \end{bmatrix}$$

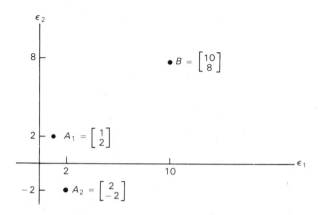

FIGURE A-4 Vector-space locations of A_1, A_2, and B.

Vector Addition and Multiplication by a Scalar

Suppose that we define a new kind of geometric space—termed vector space, as opposed to solution space. Given a pair of perpendicular axes (like those used for x_1 and x_2 in solution space), measure the size of the first element in a given 2×1 column vector along the horizontal axis and the size of the second element in the vector along the vertical axis. Denote the axes by ε_1 and ε_2, for "first element" and "second element" in each column vector. In this geometry, we would represent A_1, A_2, and B as in Fig. A-4. To make the locations in vector space more vivid, it is customary to connect the coordinate points to the origin, and to put on an arrowhead, as in Fig. A-5. Three-element vectors would be represented as arrows emanating from the origin of three-dimensional vector space, and so on, although higher dimensions are not easily visualized.

It is useful to consider the geometric representations, in vector space, of the operations of addition and multiplication by a scalar. Since a column vector is just a matrix whose second dimension is unity, the rules of matrix addition apply. Consider A_1 and A_2, above; the sum $S = A_1 + A_2$ will be the 2×1 column vector

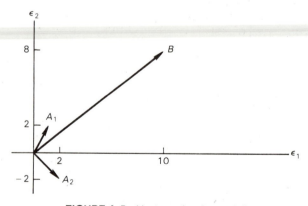

FIGURE A-5 Vectors A_1, A_2, and B.

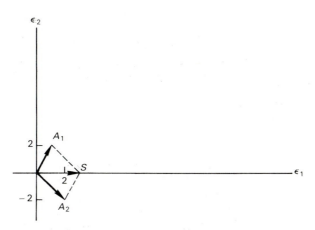

FIGURE A-6 Geometry of vector addition.

$\begin{bmatrix} 3 \\ 0 \end{bmatrix}$, by the element-by-element rule for matrix addition. Clearly, $S = \begin{bmatrix} 3 \\ 0 \end{bmatrix}$ can be shown as in Fig. A-6, above. Since order of addition is immaterial, S can be thought of as $A_1 + A_2$ or $A_2 + A_1$. Algebraically this is trivial, but geometrically the first sum can be visualized as beginning at the endpoint of A_1 and counting two to the right and two down, that is, "attaching" the A_2 vector at that point; the second sum, on the other hand, begins with the endpoint of A_2 and then moves over one and up two, that is, draws the vector A_1 from A_2. The reader should be convinced that these two alternative ways of viewing addition of two vectors produce a parallelogram, and that the resulting sum, S, is the diagonal of the parallelogram, beginning at the origin.[10]

Multiplication of a vector by a scalar is even more straightforward. Consider $P = 2A_1 = 2 \begin{bmatrix} 1 \\ 2 \end{bmatrix} = \begin{bmatrix} 2 \\ 4 \end{bmatrix}$. Again, $P = \begin{bmatrix} 2 \\ 4 \end{bmatrix}$ can be shown in the same two-dimensional vector space (Fig. A-7). The arrow, A_1, is just stretched to twice its former length; the vector P is on the same line from the origin (often termed a

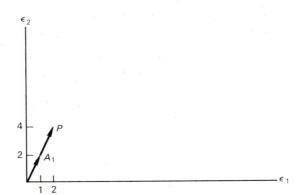

FIGURE A-7 Geometry of multiplication of a vector by a scalar.

[10] This is the same as the "parallelogram of forces" concept in elementary physics.

ray) as is A_1, but it has twice the length of A_1. Similarly, $(1/3)A_1$ would shrink the vector A_1 to $1/3$ its former length, $(-2)A_1$ would double the length *and* rotate the vector 180 degrees, that is, flip it over, through the origin, and so on. All scalar multiplications of a vector generate vectors that lie on the same line through the origin, either pointing in the same direction as A_1 or in the opposite direction (if the scalar is a negative number); such vectors are termed collinear, since they lie on the same line.

Linear Combinations

In an expression like $3A_1 + 4A_2 = A_3$, where A_1 and A_2 (and therefore also A_3) are column vectors with the same number of elements, A_3 is called a *linear combination* of A_1 and A_2. More generally, given m column vectors A_i ($i = 1, \cdots, m$) of n elements each and given m known numbers (scalars) c_i, the vector B, given below

$$c_1 A_1 + c_2 A_2 + \cdots + c_m A_m = B$$

is a linear combination of the vectors A_1 through A_m. More compactly, $\sum_{i=1}^{m} c_i A_i = B$.

We now see that the second matrix form of the original equation system (A-1), namely

$$A_1 x_1 + A_2 x_2 = B$$

or, specifically

$$\begin{bmatrix} 1 \\ 2 \end{bmatrix} x_1 + \begin{bmatrix} 2 \\ -2 \end{bmatrix} x_2 = \begin{bmatrix} 10 \\ 8 \end{bmatrix}$$

is in linear combination form. In fact, finding x_1 and x_2 consists of finding the scalars, x_1 and x_2, in the linear combination of $\begin{bmatrix} 1 \\ 2 \end{bmatrix}$ and $\begin{bmatrix} 2 \\ -2 \end{bmatrix}$ that will produce $\begin{bmatrix} 10 \\ 8 \end{bmatrix}$. We have investigated the geometry of the two algebraic operations that are involved, vector addition and multiplication by a scalar. The problem of solving the equations for x_1 and x_2 is precisely that of finding the amounts by which to stretch or to shrink A_1 and A_2 so that, when the resulting (stretched or shrunk) vectors are added, the vector $B = \begin{bmatrix} 10 \\ 8 \end{bmatrix}$ results. We are restricted to movement in the directions defined by A_1 and A_2; the reader should visualize in Fig. A-5 (perhaps with a ruler) that if we extend A_1 quite a bit (six times its present length, to be exact) and then, at that point, add something parallel to but longer than A_2 (twice A_2, in fact), we will come out at exactly the point $B = \begin{bmatrix} 10 \\ 8 \end{bmatrix}$. That is, B is the diagonal of the parallelogram, included between the adjacent sides represented by $6A_1 = \begin{bmatrix} 6 \\ 12 \end{bmatrix}$ and $2A_2 = \begin{bmatrix} 4 \\ -4 \end{bmatrix}$.

A_1 and A_2, in effect, define directions, or axes, with respect to which the point B is to be located. Ordinarily, and in particular in all of the two-dimensional solution-space or vector-space pictures we have used, the axes have been represented as perpendicular (also known as *orthogonal*) to one another. Given such coordinate axes *and* given a unit of length which is defined as a unit measure along each axis, we define the location of any point in such space by the distance (number of unit measures) along each axis. However, if we have a pair of nonperpendicular axes (i.e., directions), we could define the location of any point in that two-dimensional space relative to these axes, provided that (1) the axes are not parallel (i.e., that they define two distinct directions) and (2) we have a length that is understood to be a unit measure along each.

Recalling the geometry of multiplication of a vector by a scalar, we realize that a statement like $6A_1 = 6\begin{bmatrix} 1 \\ 2 \end{bmatrix} = \begin{bmatrix} 6 \\ 12 \end{bmatrix}$ is simply locating a point six times as far out along the direction given by A_1 as was the original endpoint $\begin{bmatrix} 1 \\ 2 \end{bmatrix}$. That is, the length of the vector A_1 serves as one unit of measure along the direction given by A_1; similarly, $2A_2$ defines a point that is two units along the direction given by A_2, where the length A_2 serves as the unit measure along that axis.[11] Thus, solving the Eqs. (A-1) for x_1 and x_2 is, in vector-space terms, finding the coordinates of the right-hand side vector, B, in terms of the coordinate system defined by the directions and the lengths of A_1 and A_2. (This logic extends to higher-order systems; for three linear equations in three unknowns, the vector space is three-dimensional, and the columns of the 3×3 coefficient matrix A provide the axes with respect to which the 3×1 vector B is to be located, using $\|A_1\|$, $\|A_2\|$, and $\|A_3\|$ as unit lengths along the three axes.)

This geometric approach is instructive when we turn to cases (A-2) and (A-3), for both of which $A = \begin{bmatrix} 1 & 2 \\ 2 & 4 \end{bmatrix}$, that is, $A_1 = \begin{bmatrix} 1 \\ 2 \end{bmatrix}$ and $A_2 = \begin{bmatrix} 2 \\ 4 \end{bmatrix}$, that is, $A_2 = 2A_1$. Geometrically, the two vectors define only *one* direction in two-dimensional vector space (Fig. A-8). If, as in the case of $A_1 = \begin{bmatrix} 1 \\ 2 \end{bmatrix}$ and $A_2 = \begin{bmatrix} 2 \\ -2 \end{bmatrix}$, the two vectors are *not* collinear, that is, when they define two distinct directions, they are said to *span* two-dimensional vector space. They are also said to define a *basis* for that space, which is to say that they indicate a set of axes; they are therefore defined as *basic* (i.e., providing a basis) vectors. That is, they provide a set of two distinct axes with respect to which the location of *any* other point in that space can be defined. Given unit measures of length along these two axes, any other point in that space can be located *uniquely*. When the two vectors are collinear, as with $\begin{bmatrix} 1 \\ 2 \end{bmatrix}$ and $\begin{bmatrix} 2 \\ 4 \end{bmatrix}$, they do not span two-dimensional vector space, which is to say that they do not provide a set of two distinct axes. Thus, all other points in that space may be divided into two classes: (1) those that lie on the line defined by A_1 (or A_2) and (2) those that do not lie on this line.

This is precisely what differentiates equation sets (A-2) and (A-3), in which B has the values $\begin{bmatrix} 10 \\ 20 \end{bmatrix}$ and $\begin{bmatrix} 10 \\ 30 \end{bmatrix}$, respectively. We add this right-hand-side

---

[11]More formally, the length, or *norm*, of a vector such as A_1, denoted $\|A_i\|$, is derived by application of the Pythagorean theorem, that is, $\|A_1\| = \sqrt{(1)^2 + (2)^2} = \sqrt{5}$. Thus the unit of measure along the direction provided by a particular vector is given by the norm of that vector.

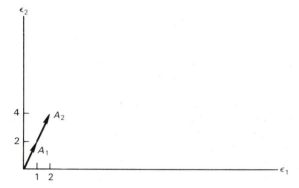

FIGURE A-8 Vector-space representation of the columns of *A* in Eqs. (A-2) and (A-3).

vector to the vector space picture given in Fig. A-8, above. In the case of the equations in (A-2), B lies on the line defined by both A_1 and A_2; thus the location of B can be expressed in terms of this one direction and the units of measure provided by the lengths $\|A_1\|$ and $\|A_2\|$. Geometrically, it is clear that some multiple of A_1 (not necessarily a whole number) *or* some other multiple of A_2 will serve to define the location of B. In particular, $10A_1 = B$ and $5A_2 = B$, so both of the following linear combinations A_1 and A_2 express B: $10A_1 + 0A_2$ or $0A_1 + 5A_2$; that is, both $x_1 = 10$, $x_2 = 0$, and $x_1 = 0$, $x_2 = 5$ are solutions to Eqs. (A-2). There are, of course, other possibilities (infinitely many, in fact)—$20A_1 +$

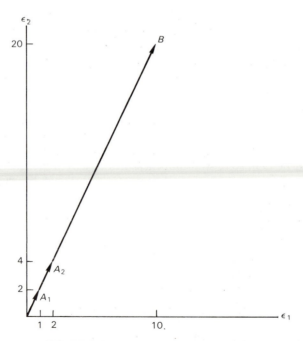

FIGURE A-9 A_1, A_2, and B from Eqs. (A-2).

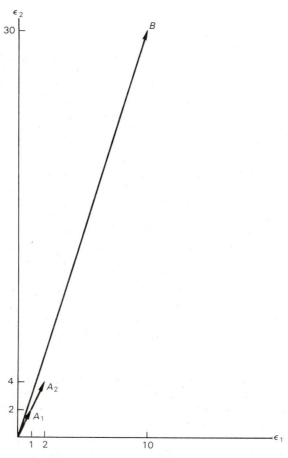

FIGURE A-10 A_1, A_2, and B from Eqs. (A-3).

$(-5)A_2 = B$, $2A_1 + 4A_2 = B$, and so on (Fig. A-9).

With Eqs. (A-3), the vector space picture shows why it is impossible to express $B = \begin{bmatrix} 10 \\ 30 \end{bmatrix}$ as any linear combination of $A_1 = \begin{bmatrix} 1 \\ 2 \end{bmatrix}$ and $A_2 = \begin{bmatrix} 2 \\ 4 \end{bmatrix}$, since B is not on the single line defined by these two column vectors, and no amount of stretching or shrinking (multiplication by a scalar) of A_1 and A_2 can ever define any points other than those on that line (Fig. A-10).

Linear Dependence and Independence

The three situations illustrated by Eqs. (A-1) through (A-3), and the geometric differences underlying them (in vector space), are distinguished nicely by the notions of linear dependence and linear independence. The idea is simple, especially when we can visualize the situation in vector space; it will be illustrated by reference again to the columns in the A matrices of Eqs. (A-1) through (A-3). In the case of Eqs. (A-1), A_1 and A_2 are said to be *linearly independent*. Geometrically, this is because in vector space they do not lie on the same line (are not collinear)—that is, they have some nonzero angle between them. Somewhat formally, this property can be represented by the following fact: The only way in which the origin—that is, the vector $\begin{bmatrix} 0 \\ 0 \end{bmatrix}$—can be represented as linear combination of A_1 and A_2 is by multiplying both by zero. No other shrinking or stretching of A_1 and A_2, when then summed, can possibly represent $\begin{bmatrix} 0 \\ 0 \end{bmatrix}$. In Eqs. (A-2) and A-3), A_1 and A_2 are termed *linearly dependent*, since they lie on the same line. Again, more formally, this is because there are many different linear combinations of A_1 and A_2 (including $0A_1 + 0A_2$) that will generate the vector $\begin{bmatrix} 0 \\ 0 \end{bmatrix}$. For example, $2A_1 + (-1)A_2 = 0$, $6A_1 + (-3)A_2 = 0$, $(-4)A_1 + 2A_2 = 0$, and so on. Furthermore, in Eqs. (A-2), B and A_1 are *linearly dependent* (as are B and A_2); in Eqs. (A-3), B and A_1 are *linearly independent* (as are B and A_2).

In general, consider $A_1, A_2, \cdots, A_n$, each one an m-element column vector. If there are scalars $x_1, x_2, \cdots, x_n$ which are *not all zero* such that the origin can be expressed as a linear combination of the A's, that is, such that

$$x_1 A_1 + x_2 A_2 + \cdots + x_n A_n = 0 \qquad \text{(A-19)}$$

then the vectors $A_1, A_2, \cdots, A_n$ are said to be linearly dependent. On the other hand, if the only scalars for which Eq. (A-19) holds are $x_1 = 0, x_2 = 0, \cdots, x_n = 0$, then the vectors $A_1, A_2, \cdots, A_n$ are said to be linearly independent. This can also be thought of as follows: If a vector, A_n, can be expressed as a linear combination of vectors $A_1, A_2, \cdots, A_{n-1}$, then all the vectors $A_1, A_2, \cdots, A_n$ are linearly *dependent*. The demonstration follows directly from the definitions of a linear combination and linear dependence. If A_n is a linear combination of $A_1, A_2, \cdots, A_{n-1}$,

$$x_1 A_1 + x_2 A_2 + \cdots + x_{n-1} A_{n-1} = A_n \qquad \text{(A-20)}$$

and all x_i $(i = 1, \cdots, n-1)$ cannot be zero, since there would be no point in forming a linear combination of vectors in which each A_i was multiplied by zero.[12] But if Eq. (A-20) holds, then by rearrangement,

$$x_1 A_1 + x_2 A_2 + \cdots + x_{n-1} A_{n-1} + (-1) A_n = 0$$

and we find that the set of vectors $A_1, A_2, \cdots, A_{n-1}, A_n$ satisfies the definition of a linearly dependent set, since not all the x_i $(i = 1, \cdots, n-1)$ are zero and, in addition, the scalar multiplying A_n, namely x_n, is -1 (i.e., also $x_n \neq 0$).

This second way of looking at linear dependence is useful when we are dealing with vector space of more than two dimensions. For example, in the easily visualized case of three-element column vectors, that is, three-dimensional vector space, examples of three linearly dependent vectors would be (1) three vectors lying along the same line or (2) lying in the same plane, but not on the same line. These are shown in Figs. A-11 and A-12. The first case—three

---

[12] Except as a (trivial) way to generate the null vector. We assume that we are dealing with an A_n which is not the null vector.

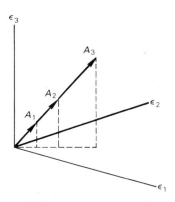

FIGURE A-11 Three collinear vectors in three-dimensional vector space.

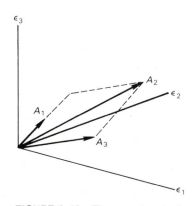

FIGURE A-12 Three vectors in the same plane in three-dimensional vector space.

FIGURE A-13 Two-dimensional vector subspace containing A_1, A_2, and A_3.

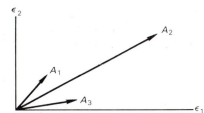

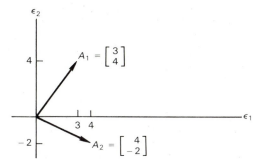

FIGURE A-14 A pair of linearly independent vectors in two-dimensional vector space.

parallel vectors lying on the same line—is an obvious generalization of the 2×2 case that was illustrated by the two columns of A in Eq. (A-2) or (A-3). The second case, however, has no counterpart in two-dimensional vector space.[13] Looking at the plane that contains all three vectors, we know that any of these vectors can be expressed as a linear combination of the other two, since any two of them span the two-dimensional space in which all three lie. For example, assume that $2A_1 + A_3 = A_2$. (The figure was drawn so that this actually is the

[13] Two-dimensional space defines a plane, and has one-dimensional subspaces (lines). Three-dimensional space has both one-dimensional (lines) and two-dimensional (planes) subspaces. Although it is not possible to visualize, the definition of linear dependence is satisfied by a set of n vectors in n-dimensional vector space if all of them are contained in a subspace of one, two,$\cdots$, or $(n-1)$ dimensions.

case.) Then A_1, A_2, and A_3 are linearly dependent; $2A_1 + (-1)A_2 + A_3 = 0$ (Fig. A-13).

Finally, it follows from these algebraic and geometric considerations that more than two vectors in two-dimensional vector space, more than three in three-dimensional vector space, and so on, are necessarily linearly dependent. In Fig. A-14, no matter where a third vector were to be drawn, it clearly could be described as a linear combination of the existing two, since they already span the two-dimensional space; hence all three would be linearly dependent. Thus, the maximum number of linearly independent vectors in n-dimensional vector space is n.

A-9 │ SYSTEMS OF LINEAR EQUATIONS

"Square" Systems (Number of Equations = Number of Unknowns)

The notions of linear dependence and independence make it possible to develop a simple rule for distinguishing consistent from inconsistent linear equation systems—Eqs. (A-1) and (A-2) from Eq. (A-3)—and further to differentiate unique solutions—Eqs. (A-1)—from nonunique solutions—Eqs. (A-2) —in the consistent case. Returning to the matrix representation of an n-equation, n-variable linear equation system, $AX = B$, the *augmented matrix* of this system is the $n \times (n + 1)$ matrix consisting of all the columns of A plus the column B, that is, the matrix $[A \vdots B]$, where the vertical dotted line *partitions* the matrix into two logical parts—the original $n \times n$ matrix A and the added $n \times 1$ right-hand column vector B. We now need one further concept from matrix algebra.

Rank of a Matrix   The rank of a matrix A, generally denoted $\rho(A)$, is defined to be the number of linearly independent columns in the matrix.

This is rather more subtle than it may appear at first glance. If A is a square $n \times n$ matrix, we know that $\rho(A) \leq n$. The matrix A has only n columns, and we have seen in small-dimensional cases that the maximum number of linearly independent vectors (that is, columns) in n-dimensional space is n. If A is an $m \times n$ matrix, with $m > n$ (e.g., two columns of three elements each), we have seen, considering vectors A_1, A_2, and A_3 in pairs in Figs. A-11 and A-12, that the number of linearly independent columns can be n or less. Finally, if A is an $m \times n$ matrix with $m < n$, the number of linearly independent columns is m or less (as illustrated by the 3 two-element vectors A_1, A_2, and B in Figs. A-9 and A-10). Therefore, the *maximum* number of possible linearly independent columns in A is the *smaller* of the two dimensions of A.

We now make use of the augmented matrix. For square linear equation systems—involving n variables and n equations—when $\rho(A) = n$, this means that the columns of A, the coefficient matrix, are linearly independent and hence span the relevant n-dimensional vector space. Thus, *any* other vector B (the right-hand-side vector of the equation system) can be expressed as a linear combination of the column vectors in A; hence B is linearly dependent on the columns of A and hence the ranks of A and the augmented matrix $[A \vdots B]$ are

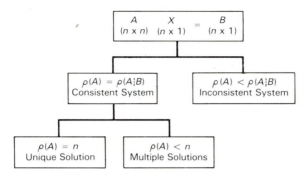

FIGURE A-15 Rules of rank for $n \times n$ systems of linear equations.

the same, namely n.[14] Thus $\rho(A) = \rho(A \vdots B)$ simply states that B can be expressed as a linear combination of the columns in A, and hence says that the equation system involving A and B is a *consistent* one. Comparison of the ranks of the coefficient and augmented matrices is thus the *consistency test* for linear equation systems.

Suppose, however, that $\rho(A) < n$. This is the case illustrated, for example, in Figs. A-8 (where $n = 2$), A-11 (where $n = 3$), and A-12 (where $n = 3$); the ranks are 1, 1, and 2, respectively. Then, adding B to A (to form an augmented matrix for the equation system) produces a matrix—$[A \vdots B]$—with a rank either equal to that of A (if B is a linear combination of the columns of A) or with a rank one larger than that of A (if the columns of A are linearly dependent and B is independent of them). If $\rho(A) = \rho(A \vdots B) < n$, then the equation system is consistent but does not have a *unique* solution (as in Fig. A-9). On the other hand, if $\rho(A) \neq \rho(A \vdots B)$, which necessarily means that $\rho(A) < \rho(A \vdots B)$, then the equation system is inconsistent, since column vector B is linearly independent of the columns of A and hence cannot be expressed as a linear combination of them, as the equation system requires (Fig. A-10).

All of these considerations extend to $n \times n$ systems of linear equations of any size. The consistency test is whether or not $\rho(A) = \rho(A \vdots B)$. The uniqueness test, on the other hand, is whether or not $\rho(A) = n$. Figure A-15 summarizes the situation for n equations in n unknowns.

Recalling the fact that the determinant of a matrix is zero if any two (or more) columns—or rows—of the matrix are proportional, we see that for an $n \times n$ matrix A, if $|A| \neq 0$, then $\rho(A) = n$, and similarly, if $|A| = 0$, $\rho(A) < n$. This is consistent with our earlier exploration of the inverse; if $|A| \neq 0$, then A^{-1} exists, and if A^{-1} exists, then a unique solution to the equation system $AX = B$ can be found—as with Eqs. (A-1). However, by attaching B to the columns of A in the augmented matrix $[A \vdots B]$ and then introducing the concept of the rank of a matrix, the cases illustrated by Eqs. (A-2) and (A-3) can be distinguished.

[14]Since $[A \vdots B]$ has the dimensions $n \times (n + 1)$, we know that the rank cannot exceed the smaller dimension, namely n. But we know that A itself has rank n, and adding a column, B, to a matrix, A, cannot *reduce* its rank.

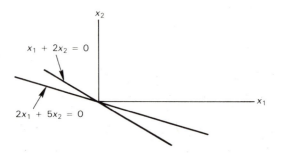

FIGURE A-16   Equations (A-21) in solution space.

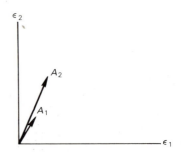

FIGURE A-17   Equations (A-21) in vector space.

Homogeneous Equations   A special case that occurs in some input-output situations is when, in the linear equation system $AX = B$, all right-hand-side elements are equal to zero; this is termed a set of *homogeneous* equations. (When $B \neq 0$, the equations are *nonhomogeneous*.) Clearly, *any* homogenous equations have the solution $x_1 = 0$, $x_2 = 0, \cdots, x_n = 0$. This not particularly interesting result is called the trivial solution to a set of homogeneous equations. If A^{-1} exists, then $X = A^{-1}B = A^{-1}0 = 0$, and the trivial solution is the *only* solution. A 2×2 illustration is:

$$\text{(a)} \qquad x_1 + 2x_2 = 0$$
$$\text{(b)} \qquad 2x_1 + 5x_2 = 0 \tag{A-21}$$

for which $A^{-1} = \begin{bmatrix} 5 & -2 \\ -2 & 1 \end{bmatrix}$ and hence whose unique solution is $\begin{bmatrix} x_1 \\ x_2 \end{bmatrix}$ $= \begin{bmatrix} 5 & -2 \\ -2 & 1 \end{bmatrix} \begin{bmatrix} 0 \\ 0 \end{bmatrix} = \begin{bmatrix} 0 \\ 0 \end{bmatrix}$. The solution-space picture is in Fig. A-16. Figure A-17 represents the same system in vector space. In this case it is clear that the only scalars, x_1 and x_2, for which $x_1 A_1 + x_2 A_2 = \begin{bmatrix} 0 \\ 0 \end{bmatrix}$ are $x_1 = 0$ and $x_2 = 0$.[15]

On the other hand, consider

$$\text{(a)} \qquad x_1 + 2x_2 = 0$$
$$\text{(b)} \qquad 2x_1 + 4x_2 = 0 \tag{A-22}$$

for which $|A| = 0$, since the columns of A are linearly dependent. The picture in solution space is in Fig. A-18, below. Since the second equation is just twice the first, both represent the same line. In this case, along with the trivial solution $x_1 = 0$, $x_2 = 0$, we see that there are infinitely many nonzero solutions—all points lying on the line $x_1 + 2x_2 = 0$, that is, all points for which $x_2 = (-1/2)x_1$, such as $x_1 = 2$, $x_2 = -1$; $x_1 = 10$, $x_2 = -5$; and so on. Figure A-19 represents the system in vector space, and, as we have already seen, *any* other point on this line—including B, the origin—can be expressed in infinitely many linear combinations of A_1 and A_2.

---

[15] This is, in fact, precisely the definition of linear independence of A_1 and A_2; the only way of expressing the origin in a linear combination of linearly *independent* columns is by weighting each column by zero.

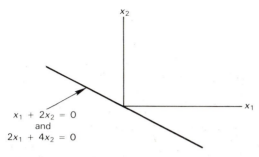

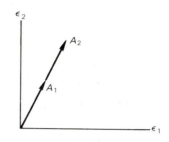

FIGURE A-18 Equations (A-22) in solution space.

FIGURE A-19 Equations (A-22) in vector space.

These observations suggest a general rule, which is that for *nontrivial* solutions to a homogeneous linear equation system it is necessary that the coefficient matrix be singular (i.e., that the columns of A be linearly dependent or that $\rho[A] < n$). Note that homogeneous equations are always consistent; $\rho(A) = \rho(A|B)$ since $B = 0$, and adding a column of zeros to the A matrix leaves the rank unchanged. Thus the only question to be asked of homogeneous equations is whether or not their only solution is the trivial one $X = 0$ and this depends on whether or not $|A| = 0$.

"Nonsquare" Systems (Number of Equations ≠ Number of Unknowns)

The input-output models that we examine in this text will usually be $n \times n$ (square) systems of linear equations; hence the development thus far has completely equipped us to evaluate the kinds of solutions to be expected. However, in some advanced applications—for example, in the commodity-by-industry model (Chapter 5) and when the input-output equations are embedded in, say, a linear programming optimization model—nonsquare systems of linear equations result. While a completely general discussion of solution possibilities for such systems involves definitions of generalized inverses for nonsquare matrices, the terminology that we have at hand makes it possible for us to explore such equation systems. Thus, for completeness, we examine the nonsquare cases in this subsection; it can be omitted without loss of continuity. Denoting the number of equations by m and the number of variables by n, there may be either more equations than variables ($m > n$) or fewer equations than variables ($m < n$). In these terms, we have been dealing with the $m = n$ case up to now.

More Equations than Variables (m > n) An example of this case would be three linear equations in two unknowns. In $AX = B$ terms, A is a 3×2 matrix, X is a 2×1 column vector, and B is a 3×1 column vector. In solution space (with x_1 and x_2 on the axes) the three lines may (1) intersect in one unique point, in which case any two equations (lines) would be adequate to define the unique point and any one of the equations could be regarded as redundant, (2) be parallel, in which case there is no solution satisfying more than one equation at a time, (3) be coincident, in which case there is an infinite number of solutions,

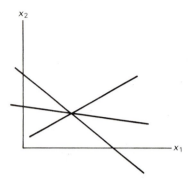

FIGURE A-20   Three-equation, two-variable system with a unique solution.

or (4) intersect in two or more points, in which case there is no solution satisfying all equations at the same time. Figures A-20 through A-23 illustrate.

Examining the ranks of the coefficient and augmented matrices, these situations correspond to: (1) $\rho(A) = \rho(A|B) = 2$, where $(m - n = 3 - 2)$ represents the number of redundant equations in the system, (2) $\rho(A) = 1$, $\rho(A|B) = 2$, an inconsistent set of parallel equations (3) $\rho(A) = 1$, $\rho(A|B) = 1$, a consistent set of completely identical equations, and (4) $\rho(A) = 2$, $\rho(A|B) = 3$, an inconsistent set of equations in which—in solution space—some pairs of equations intersect in particular points, but all three do not intersect in a unique point.

Thus, with more linear equations than unknowns, we find either that the system is consistent, in which case some of the equations are redundant and can be ignored (Figs. A-20 and A-22) or that the system is inconsistent and no solution can be found to simultaneously satisfy all equations (Figs. A-21 and A-23). In general, then, in the $m > n$ case—more equations than unknowns—the system is overdetermined; there are too many requirements being made on the variables. In the one instance in which a unique solution *is* possible, this is only because some of the equations $(m - n$ in number) are redundant and can be ignored; in that case we are back to the situation of the same number of equations as unknowns—the "square" case explored earlier.

Fewer Equations than Variables (m < n)   In the opposite case, with fewer equations than variables, the system is underdetermined; too few requirements are being made on the variables. In two-dimensional solution space there would

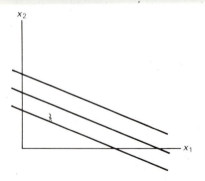

FIGURE A-21   Three-equation, two-variable system with a no solution.

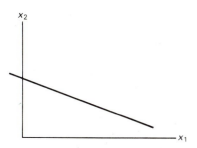

FIGURE A-22 Three-equation, two-variable system with an infinite number of solutions.

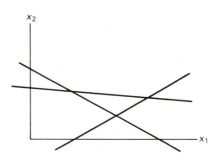

FIGURE A-23 Three-equation, two-variable system with no common solution.

be only one line for two variables to satisfy. In the case of three variables, the solution-space picture would be either one plane (the $m = 1$ case), or two planes ($m = 2$), which would intersect—provided they were not parallel or identical—in a single line. This latter would be a case in which $\rho(A) = 2$, $\rho(A|B) = 2$. Thus, in general, there will be infinite numbers of solutions in the $m < n$, underdetermined case. This is because the rank of the $m \times n$ coefficient matrix will never exceed the smaller dimension, m. But since the rank of a matrix is the number of its linearly independent columns, this means that the m-element columns in A in the $m < n$ case are necessarily linearly dependent; B is also an m-element column vector. Thus B can be expressed as a linear combination of various sets of m columns from the total of n; since columns are associated with x's, this means that there are multiple (nonunique) solutions to the equation set.

For example, consider the following 2×3 system:

$$\text{(a)} \qquad x_1 + 2x_2 + 3x_3 = 3$$

$$\text{(b)} \qquad 2x_1 + 5x_2 + \ x_3 = 5 \tag{A-23}$$

or $\begin{bmatrix} 1 & 2 & 3 \\ 2 & 5 & 1 \end{bmatrix} \begin{bmatrix} x_1 \\ x_2 \\ x_3 \end{bmatrix} = \begin{bmatrix} 3 \\ 5 \end{bmatrix}$. In vector space, we recognize that A_1, A_2, and A_3, the columns of the coefficient matrix, are linearly dependent, since no more than two vectors can be linearly independent in two-dimensional vector space. Thus B may be expressed as a linear combination of A_1 and A_2 or A_2 and A_3 or A_1 and A_3, since all three *pairs* of vectors form a distinct set of axes, with respect to which *any* other 2×1 vector may be expressed. Figure A-24 illustrates.

Note that when A_1 and A_2 are used we are, in essence, giving A_3 a weight of zero in the linear combination; that is, we are looking for the values of x_1 and x_2 in the linear combination $x_1 A_1 + x_2 A_2 + 0 A_3 = B$. Similarly, using A_2 and A_3 or A_1 and A_3 involves forming the linear combinations $0 A_1 + x_2 A_2 + x_3 A_3 = B$ and $x_1 A_1 + 0 A_2 + x_3 A_3 = B$, respectively. Thus, in each case, one of the variables (x's) has been set equal to zero, leaving then a set of two linear equations in only two unknowns. The procedure of discarding "extra" variables—by setting them equal to zero—in an $m < n$ set of linear equations is known as finding *basic* solutions, since the sets of linearly independent columns used in the various linear combinations are bases, that is, they are *basic* vectors.

In exploring basic solutions, the notion of a *partitioned* matrix is useful. (Partitioning was discussed in section A-7, above.) A partition, as its name implies, is a division set up between a pair of rows and/or a pair of columns, usually for the purpose of separating a matrix into two or more submatrices which have particular meanings in terms of the system that the matrix represents. For example, if we consider the pair of vectors A_1 and A_2 as the basis with respect to which we wish to express B, we could write Eqs. (A-23) as

$$\begin{bmatrix} 1 & 2 & \vdots & 3 \\ 2 & 5 & \vdots & 1 \end{bmatrix} \begin{bmatrix} x_1 \\ x_2 \\ \text{---} \\ x_3 \end{bmatrix} = \begin{bmatrix} 3 \\ 5 \end{bmatrix}$$

where the dashed vertical line in A serves to isolate the basic vectors (the two on the left) from the nonbasic one (on the right), and the dashed horizontal line in X reminds us that basic variables are those above it and the nonbasic variable (which is set equal to zero) lies below it. Essentially, the partitions are simply reminders of logical divisions in the matrices.

In addition, however, if matrices in an arithmetic operation are properly partitioned, so that the resulting submatrices are conformable for a particular algebraic operation, then that operation can be carried out on the individual submatrices. For example, in the equation system

$$\begin{bmatrix} 1 & 2 & \vdots & 3 \\ 2 & 5 & \vdots & 1 \end{bmatrix} \begin{bmatrix} x_1 \\ x_2 \\ \text{---} \\ x_3 \end{bmatrix} = \begin{bmatrix} 3 \\ 5 \end{bmatrix}$$

define A_{I} to be $\begin{bmatrix} 1 & 2 \\ 2 & 5 \end{bmatrix}$ and $A_{\mathrm{II}} = \begin{bmatrix} 3 \\ 1 \end{bmatrix}$; also let $X_{\mathrm{I}} = \begin{bmatrix} x_1 \\ x_2 \end{bmatrix}$ and $X_{\mathrm{II}} = [x_3]$ and, as before, $B = \begin{bmatrix} 3 \\ 5 \end{bmatrix}$, so that the system is $[A_{\mathrm{I}} \vdots A_{\mathrm{II}}] \begin{bmatrix} X_{\mathrm{I}} \\ \text{---} \\ X_{\mathrm{II}} \end{bmatrix} = B$. Then, because the partitionings have been made so that the individual multiplications are possible, this matrix multiplication can be carried out as follows:

$$\underset{(2\times 2)\,(2\times 1)}{A_{\mathrm{I}} \quad X_{\mathrm{I}}} + \underset{(2\times 1)\,(1\times 1)}{A_{\mathrm{II}} \quad X_{\mathrm{II}}} = \underset{(2\times 1)}{B}$$

Now, for basic solutions, the "extra" variable (or variables, in larger systems) in X_{II} are set equal to zero, so that the remaining system is $A_{\mathrm{I}} X_{\mathrm{I}} = B$. Provided that A_{I} has an inverse, which it will as long as its columns are linearly independent, then the associated basic solution is $X_{\mathrm{I}} = A_{\mathrm{I}}^{-1} B$. In the example, this is

$$\begin{bmatrix} x_1 \\ x_2 \end{bmatrix} = \begin{bmatrix} 1 & 2 \\ 2 & 5 \end{bmatrix}^{-1} \begin{bmatrix} 3 \\ 5 \end{bmatrix} = \begin{bmatrix} 5 & -2 \\ -2 & 1 \end{bmatrix} \begin{bmatrix} 3 \\ 5 \end{bmatrix} = \begin{bmatrix} 5 \\ -1 \end{bmatrix};$$

the complete basic solution is thus: $x_1 = 5$, $x_2 = -1$, $x_3 = 0$.

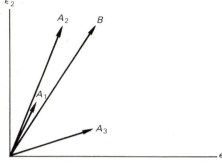

FIGURE A-24 Equations (A-23) in vector space.

This is only one basic solution to the equation set. *Any* set of linearly independent columns may be selected to act as the basis vectors. Thus, adopting the subscript B for the basic elements in the system and NB for the nonbasic ones (where I and II were used previously), we could also select A_2 and A_3 or A_1 and A_3 and represent the system $[A_B \ \vdots \ A_{NB}] \begin{bmatrix} X_B \\ ---- \\ X_{NB} \end{bmatrix} = B$ as $[A_2 \quad A_3 \ \vdots \ A_1]$ $\begin{bmatrix} x_2 \\ x_3 \\ --- \\ x_1 \end{bmatrix} = B$ or $[A_1 \quad A_3 \ \vdots \ A_2] \begin{bmatrix} x_1 \\ x_3 \\ -- \\ x_2 \end{bmatrix} = B$. Setting $X_{NB} = 0$, these lead, respectively, to the following additional basic solutions ($X_B = A_B^{-1}B$):

$$\begin{bmatrix} x_2 \\ x_3 \end{bmatrix} = \begin{bmatrix} 2 & 3 \\ 5 & 1 \end{bmatrix}^{-1} \begin{bmatrix} 3 \\ 5 \end{bmatrix} = \begin{bmatrix} -\dfrac{1}{13} & \dfrac{3}{13} \\ \dfrac{5}{13} & -\dfrac{2}{13} \end{bmatrix} \begin{bmatrix} 3 \\ 5 \end{bmatrix} = \begin{bmatrix} \dfrac{12}{13} \\ \dfrac{5}{13} \end{bmatrix}$$

$$\begin{bmatrix} x_1 \\ x_3 \end{bmatrix} = \begin{bmatrix} 1 & 3 \\ 2 & 1 \end{bmatrix}^{-1} \begin{bmatrix} 3 \\ 5 \end{bmatrix} = \begin{bmatrix} -\dfrac{1}{5} & \dfrac{3}{5} \\ \dfrac{2}{5} & -\dfrac{1}{5} \end{bmatrix} \begin{bmatrix} 3 \\ 5 \end{bmatrix} = \begin{bmatrix} \dfrac{12}{5} \\ \dfrac{1}{5} \end{bmatrix}$$

That is, the other complete basic solutions are: $x_1 = 0$, $x_2 = 12/13$, $x_3 = 5/13$, and $x_1 = 12/5$, $x_2 = 0$, $x_3 = 1/5$.

Since basic solutions involve selection of linearly independent sets of columns from among those in the coefficient matrix A (so that A_B will be nonsingular and hence have an inverse), the maximum possible number of basic solutions is given by the combinatorial formula $C_m^n = \dfrac{n!}{m!(n-m)!}$, which is the total number of ways of selecting m items (columns to be in the basis, A_B) from n (the total number of columns in A). This is only a maximum possible number; some selections of columns from A may lead to a singular A_B, if those columns happen to be linearly dependent. This was not the case in Eqs. (A-23); all $C_2^3 = 3$ possible basic solutions could be found.

Consider, however, another 2×3 system:

$$x_1 + 2x_2 + 3x_3 = 3$$

$$2x_1 + 5x_2 + 6x_3 = 5 \tag{A-24}$$

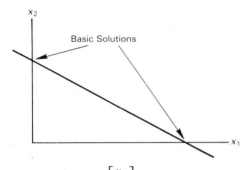

FIGURE A-25 One linear equation in two variables (solution space).

or $\begin{bmatrix} 1 & 2 & 3 \\ 2 & 5 & 6 \end{bmatrix} \begin{bmatrix} x_1 \\ x_2 \\ x_3 \end{bmatrix} = \begin{bmatrix} 3 \\ 5 \end{bmatrix}$. The three possible basic matrices are, as before,

$[A_1 \quad A_2]$, $[A_2 \quad A_3]$, and $[A_1 \quad A_3]$. Here, these are $\begin{bmatrix} 1 & 2 \\ 2 & 5 \end{bmatrix}$, $\begin{bmatrix} 2 & 3 \\ 5 & 6 \end{bmatrix}$, and

$\begin{bmatrix} 1 & 3 \\ 2 & 6 \end{bmatrix}$. In the third matrix, the columns are proportional and hence linearly dependent—the determinant is zero and no inverse exists—and therefore they do not form a basis for two-dimensional vector space. Thus for this particular pair of linear equations in three unknowns, only two basic solutions exist:

$$\begin{bmatrix} x_1 \\ x_2 \end{bmatrix} = \begin{bmatrix} 1 & 2 \\ 2 & 5 \end{bmatrix}^{-1} \begin{bmatrix} 3 \\ 5 \end{bmatrix} = \begin{bmatrix} 5 & 2 \\ -2 & 1 \end{bmatrix} \begin{bmatrix} 3 \\ 5 \end{bmatrix} = \begin{bmatrix} 5 \\ -1 \end{bmatrix}$$

and

$$\begin{bmatrix} x_2 \\ x_3 \end{bmatrix} = \begin{bmatrix} 2 & 3 \\ 5 & 6 \end{bmatrix}^{-1} \begin{bmatrix} 3 \\ 5 \end{bmatrix} = \begin{bmatrix} -2 & 1 \\ \dfrac{5}{3} & -\dfrac{2}{3} \end{bmatrix} \begin{bmatrix} 3 \\ 5 \end{bmatrix} = \begin{bmatrix} -1 \\ \dfrac{5}{3} \end{bmatrix}$$

That is, $x_1 = 5$, $x_2 = -1$, $x_3 = 0$, and $x_1 = 0$, $x_2 = -1$, $x_3 = 5/3$ are the only basic solutions.

Clearly, a system of fewer linear equations than variables will have infinitely many other solutions as well. Again, the solution-space picture for $m = 1$, $n = 2$ is a single straight line, as in Fig. A-25.[16] Basic solutions occur when one of the variables is set equal to zero; geometrically, this is where the line intersects an axis. There are infinitely many nonbasic solutions elsewhere along the line. For the $m = 2$, $n = 3$ case, the reader may visualize two planes intersecting in a line in three-dimensional solution space. Basic solutions are located at the points where that line intersects the three planes representing $x_1 = 0$ (the plane defined by the x_2 and x_3 axes), $x_2 = 0$, and $x_3 = 0$ (both similarly defined). Points elsewhere along the line are solutions—but not basic ones—to the 2×3 equation system. A basic solution in the $m < n$ case involves setting $(n - m)$ variables equal to zero and finding the solution to the resulting $m \times m$ square system. In the examples discussed, $n - m = 1$, so in each case only one variable has been set equal to zero for basic solutions. For example, with three equations and seven variables, basic solutions would require that four $(7 - 3)$ variables be set equal to zero and the resulting 3×3 linear equation system solved.

---

[16] Except for the rather special case in which the line is parallel to one of the axes.

appendix
B

The U.S. National Input-Output Tables (1947-1977)

B-1 | INTRODUCTION

In this appendix we present aggregated versions of the U.S. national input-output tables for the years 1947, 1958, 1963, 1967, 1972, and 1977. Since the late 1950s the Bureau of Economic Analysis (BEA, formerly the Office of Business Economics) of the U.S. Department of Commerce has periodically compiled national input-output tables for the United States as a part of the national accounts. Benchmark survey-based tables have been compiled for the years 1958, 1963, 1967, 1972, and 1977.[1] A table for 1947 prepared originally by the Bureau of Labor Statistics (BLS) was reworked by Vacarra et al. (1970) to conform with the industry classification and other conventions of the subsequent tables. The original tables were developed at various levels of aggregation (the more recent ones—1963, 1967, 1972, and 1977—at 85-, 365-, and 496-sector classifications). The tables presented here are 23- and 7-sector aggregations of the benchmark tables and the BLS 1947 tables. All but the 1972 and 1977 benchmark tables were previously published at the 23-sector level in the *Historical Statistics of the U.S.* (U.S. Department of Commerce 1975).

The 1972 and 1977 tables presented here are based on Ritz (1979), Ritz et al. (1979) and *Survey of Current Business* (1984) and were reworked to conform as closely as possible with the industry classification and other conventions of the

---

[1]These have been published in Vacarra et al. (1970), *The Survey of Current Business* (1965a, 1965b, 1969, 1974, 1984), and Ritz (1979).

previous tables, although some significant differences remain.[2] The 1972 and
1977 tables, as originally published, were prepared using the commodity-by-
industry conventions described in Chapter 5. Finally, we include the commodity-
by-industry make and use tables for 1972 and 1977 at the 23- and 7-sector levels
of aggregation.

The aggregation codes for the 85 BEA sectors to the 23 sectors adopted
here as well as the 23- to 7-sector code are given in Table B-1. The total output
vectors for all tables (in current dollars) are given in Table B-2.

TABLE B-1   INPUT-OUTPUT SECTOR AGGREGATION CODES

7-Sector Aggregation	23-Sector Aggregation	85-Sector Aggregation Industry Numbers*	Related SIC Codes (1975 edition)
1. Agriculture	Agriculture, Forestry, and Fishing	1–4	01–09 (except 0722)
2. Mining	Metal Mining	5, 6	10
	Petroleum and Natural Gas Mining	8	13 (except 138)
	Other Mining	7, 9, 10	11, 12, 14
3. Construction	Construction	11, 12	15–17, 138, 656†
4. Manufacturing	Food, Feed, and Tobacco Products	14, 15	20, 21
	Textile Products and Apparel	16–19	22, 23, 3992
	Wood Products and Furniture	20–23	24, 25
	Paper, Printing, and Publishing	24–26	26, 27
	Chemicals and Chemical Products	27–30	28 (except 28195)
	Petroleum and Coal Products	31	29
	Rubber, Plastics, and Leather	32–34	30, 31
	Stone, Clay, and Glass Products	35, 36	32
	Primary and Fabricated Metals	37–42	33, 34, 28195
	Machinery, Except Electrical	43–52	35
	Electrical Equipment and Supplies	53–58	36
	Transport Equipment and Ordnance	59–61, 13	37, 19
	Other Manufacturing	62–64, 82	38, 39
5. Transportation and Trade	Transportation and Trade	65, 69	40–47, 50, 52–59, 7396
6. Services	Electric, Gas, and Sanitary Services	68	49
	Other Services	66, 67, 70–77, 81	48, 60–89 (except 7396, 6561†, 0722)
7. Other	Government Enterprises	78, 79	———
	Scrap and Secondhand Goods	83	———

*The detailed sectoral definitions are given in Ritz et al. (1979).
†Split between sectors 5 and 21 of the 23-sector classification.

[2] For the 1972 table the Bureau of Economic Analysis (BEA) adopted the 1972 Standard
Industrial Classification. This classification is revised considerably from the classifications used in the
earlier tables (Ritz 1979). In addition, the commodity-by-industry system of accounts (as detailed in
Chapter 5) was adopted for the first time in the preparation of the 1972 table, resulting in much
more accurate representation of secondary production in the economy, but compromising compatibil-
ity with earlier tables. BEA is in the process of developing commodity-by-industry versions of the
1963 and 1967 tables. Scrap and secondhand goods appear only as a secondary product in the 1972
and 1977 tables; hence this sector is not present in the industry-by-industry tables in this Appendix.

TABLE B-2 TOTAL OUTPUT VECTORS (23-SECTOR AGGREGATION) (MILLIONS OF DOLLARS)

Total Industry Outputs	1947	1958	1963	1967	1972	1977
1 Agriculture, Forestry, & Fishing	46858	51960	56690	63097	83956	129663
2 Metal Mining	1322	2532	2925	3362	3502	5356
3 Petroleum & Natural Gas Mining	4441	10852	12265	15031	17820	49083
4 Other Mining	4619	4936	5352	6538	9064	23592
5 Construction	29331	69291	85313	103280	165998	264334
6 Food, Feed, & Tobacco Products	50785	71109	81688	97391	127545	202053
7 Textile Products & Apparel	24496	29341	37025	46356	58771	87237
8 Wood Products & Furniture	8856	13513	16908	21200	32994	55671
9 Paper, Printing, & Publishing	13517	26565	33856	44529	57593	101544
10 Chemicals & Chemical Products	10701	23889	33236	44999	54565	112483
11 Petroleum & Coal Products	8108	17997	21837	26975	31440	98895
12 Rubber, Plastics, & Leather	7288	10883	14241	19069	26251	47022
13 Stone, Clay, & Glass Products	4141	9805	12469	14808	20853	34613
14 Primary & Fabricated Metals	26459	48612	62698	87906	106340	188385
15 Machinery, Except Electrical	12346	24165	33762	53593	63901	118665
16 Electrical Equipment & Supplies	9457	20694	32142	46759	53311	89020
17 Transport Equipment & Ordnance	16399	43715	63935	82831	102164	174581
18 Other Manufacturing	5451	11879	15575	22288	25527	44814
19 Transportation & Trade	76644	129332	159794	216165	291163	510639
20 Electric, Gas, & Sanitary Services	6878	20289	29660	37321	50148	105596
21 Other Services	74376	178536	237685	335588	562970	974237
22 Government Enterprises	3485	8889	13100	17337	156533	246512
23 Scrap & Secondhand Goods	606	1394	1518	1991	0	0

B-2 | DIRECT REQUIREMENTS TABLES (23-SECTOR AGGREGATION)

TABLE B-3 DIRECT REQUIREMENTS: 1947

Sector	1	2	3	4	5	6	7	8	9	10	11
1	.3146	.0000	.0000	.0000	.0031	.4154	.0913	.0493	.0005	.0083	.0000
2	.0000	.0983	.0000	.0006	.0000	.0000	.0000	.0000	.0000	.0030	.0001
3	.0000	.0000	.0124	.0000	.0003	.0000	.0000	.0000	.0000	.0024	.4884
4	.0010	.0030	.0000	.1338	.0092	.0013	.0015	.0009	.0061	.0243	.0036
5	.0121	.0008	.0018	.0013	.0002	.0018	.0017	.0019	.0032	.0025	.0017
6	.0542	.0000	.0000	.0002	.0004	.1509	.0061	.0033	.0046	.0975	.0028
7	.0024	.0000	.0016	.0004	.0006	.0044	.3839	.0350	.0081	.0048	.0002
8	.0032	.0166	.0014	.0136	.0843	.0025	.0017	.1785	.0214	.0053	.0020
9	.0001	.0000	.0074	.0048	.0058	.0159	.0091	.0128	.2793	.0439	.0200
10	.0134	.0159	.0142	.0167	.0212	.0075	.0384	.0167	.0207	.1845	.0229
11	.0111	.0061	.0063	.0078	.0202	.0024	.0028	.0097	.0087	.0228	.0931
12	.0030	.0000	.0023	.0011	.0026	.0013	.0049	.0094	.0048	.0066	.0022
13	.0006	.0015	.0043	.0028	.0568	.0050	.0005	.0073	.0015	.0106	.0048
14	.0025	.0144	.0180	.0255	.1569	.0129	.0024	.0490	.0088	.0495	.0197
15	.0016	.0098	.0133	.0312	.0107	.0012	.0017	.0128	.0075	.0037	.0012
16	.0004	.0000	.0047	.0030	.0170	.0003	.0003	.0020	.0017	.0031	.0011
17	.0020	.0008	.0023	.0061	.0008	.0004	.0009	.0034	.0012	.0017	.0016
18	.0001	.0000	.0009	.0006	.0022	.0002	.0089	.0054	.0042	.0031	.0007
19	.0558	.0840	.0349	.0197	.1324	.0420	.0447	.0797	.0630	.0634	.0834
20	.0012	.0257	.0038	.0167	.0012	.0035	.0047	.0055	.0073	.0105	.0094
21	.0624	.0552	.1385	.0392	.0622	.0255	.0243	.0484	.0543	.0714	.0429
22	.0001	.0008	.0007	.0006	.0000	.0005	.0010	.0011	.0043	.0030	.0026
23	.0000	.0000	.0000	.0000	.0011	.0020	.0009	.0000	.0180	.0010	.0000

TABLE B-4 DIRECT REQUIREMENTS: 1958

Sector	1	2	3	4	5	6	7	8	9	10	11
1	.2849	.0000	.0000	.0000	.0034	.3160	.0512	.0739	.0000	.0015	.0000
2	.0000	.1252	.0000	.0004	.0000	.0000	.0000	.0000	.0000	.0047	.0002
3	.0000	.0000	.0223	.0002	.0000	.0000	.0000	.0000	.0000	.0010	.5163
4	.0020	.0028	.0000	.1070	.0109	.0008	.0006	.0003	.0047	.0194	.0039
5	.0118	.0008	.0004	.0010	.0001	.0033	.0005	.0013	.0037	.0015	.0014
6	.0577	.0000	.0000	.0000	.0002	.1651	.0013	.0021	.0029	.0170	.0006
7	.0020	.0008	.0002	.0004	.0001	.0021	.4078	.0209	.0048	.0022	.0002
8	.0020	.0028	.0006	.0038	.0608	.0016	.0007	.2290	.0255	.0255	.0002
9	.0011	.0004	.0006	.0059	.0058	.0215	.0110	.0175	.2887	.0320	.0051
10	.0233	.0217	.0050	.0162	.0218	.0080	.0585	.0191	.0250	.2253	.0329
11	.0186	.0075	.0048	.0164	.0196	.0040	.0013	.0066	.0059	.0332	.0690
12	.0037	.0016	.0029	.0111	.0054	.0022	.0077	.0154	.0073	.0095	.0004
13	.0006	.0028	.0004	.0219	.0693	.0086	.0010	.0115	.0021	.0093	.0021
14	.0023	.0336	.0066	.0221	.1552	.0260	.0016	.0518	.0078	.0350	.0177
15	.0039	.0229	.0133	.0504	.0140	.0002	.0025	.0056	.0041	.0072	.0002
16	.0006	.0032	.0042	.0032	.0255	.0005	.0001	.0019	.0012	.0010	.0004
17	.0016	.0016	.0008	.0051	.0001	.0000	.0001	.0010	.0010	.0000	.0000
18	.0002	.0004	.0004	.0014	.0051	.0009	.0123	.0050	.0056	.0037	.0008
19	.0547	.0857	.0384	.0517	.1219	.0729	.0549	.0884	.0577	.0590	.0607
20	.0051	.0186	.0072	.0259	.0025	.0051	.0064	.0063	.0099	.0152	.0146
21	.0784	.0679	.1790	.0458	.0590	.0484	.0360	.0434	.0797	.0892	.0389
22	.0002	.0008	.0004	.0012	.0002	.0010	.0015	.0010	.0044	.0031	.0021
23	.0000	.0004	.0101	.0020	.0012	.0000	.0011	.0002	.0064	.0002	.0002

12	13	14	15	16	17	18	19	20	21	22	23
.0086	.0000	.0000	.0000	.0000	.0000	.0033	.0002	.0000	.0275	.0043	.0000
.0000	.0022	.0402	.0000	.0005	.0000	.0002	.0000	.0000	.0001	.0000	.0000
.0000	.0000	.0000	.0000	.0000	.0000	.0000	.0001	.0282	.0007	.0000	.0000
.0030	.0787	.0218	.0015	.0013	.0012	.0092	.0066	.0545	.0014	.0072	.0000
.0036	.0060	.0040	.0028	.0023	.0030	.0029	.0194	.0315	.0535	.1443	.0000
.0611	.0005	.0004	.0000	.0000	.0000	.0073	.0031	.0001	.0211	.0000	.0495
.0803	.0113	.0019	.0016	.0034	.0118	.0198	.0012	.0003	.0019	.0009	.0314
.0051	.0082	.0072	.0062	.0189	.0080	.0294	.0007	.0003	.0017	.0006	.0182
.0254	.0555	.0093	.0093	.0181	.0051	.0314	.0136	.0009	.0418	.0095	.0462
.0718	.0275	.0149	.0073	.0226	.0124	.0268	.0026	.0013	.0057	.0052	.0248
.0054	.0121	.0113	.0047	.0045	.0034	.0050	.0165	.0238	.0033	.0060	.0017
.1763	.0070	.0033	.0212	.0200	.0404	.0352	.0033	.0001	.0027	.0023	.0264
.0043	.0799	.0094	.0062	.0201	.0106	.0081	.0015	.0020	.0008	.0011	.0050
.0169	.0273	.2791	.2023	.1768	.1829	.0950	.0057	.0172	.0027	.0055	.3845
.0036	.0087	.0186	.0967	.0345	.0489	.0152	.0015	.0003	.0040	.0014	.0594
.0023	.0060	.0103	.0423	.1064	.0190	.0172	.0020	.0026	.0051	.0020	.0627
.0021	.0029	.0027	.0067	.0038	.2259	.0015	.0088	.0015	.0115	.0023	.1386
.0092	.0014	.0024	.0044	.0062	.0065	.0748	.0015	.0003	.0092	.0029	.0264
.0536	.0993	.0721	.0445	.0510	.0310	.0635	.0472	.0314	.0571	.1073	.0066
.0071	.0285	.0136	.0068	.0067	.0048	.0046	.0089	.1114	.0086	.0201	.0000
.0399	.0449	.0268	.0357	.0442	.0251	.0488	.1209	.0315	.1272	.0350	.0017
.0019	.0024	.0011	.0015	.0033	.0019	.0018	.0105	.1550	.0117	.0017	.0000
.0010	.0027	.0498	.0028	.0002	.0000	.0006	.0000	.0000	.0000	.0000	.0000

12	13	14	15	16	17	18	19	20	21	22	23
.0049	.0004	.0000	.0001	.0000	.0000	.0013	.0015	.0000	.0129	.0702	.0000
.0000	.0013	.0386	.0000	.0005	.0000	.0001	.0000	.0001	.0001	.0002	.0000
.0000	.0000	.0000	.0000	.0000	.0000	.0000	.0000	.0575	.0007	.0022	.0000
.0025	.0621	.0123	.0007	.0002	.0005	.0003		.0269	.0004	.0142	.0000
.0006	.0004	.0030	.0012	.0010	.0024	.0014	.0156	.0272	.0408	.1357	.0000
.0193	.0006	.0002	.0000	.0000	.0000	.0017	.0049	.0000	.0132	.0292	.0022
.0705	.0021	.0017	.0013	.0016	.0077	.0165	.0013	.0001	.0039	.0007	.0660
.0040	.0075	.0037	.0029	.0099	.0046	.0107	.0016	.0001	.0000	.0000	.0000
.0173	.0437	.0074	.0048	.0137	.0043	.1324	.0090	.0011	.0387	.0096	.0574
.1286	.0393	.0141	.0041	.0160	.0068	.0298	.0026	.0006	.0071	.0030	.0000
.0019	.0094	.0060	.0045	.0019	.0024	.0022	.0174	.0121	.0047	.0053	.0072
.1304	.0089	.0040	.0118	.0167	.0203	.0273	.0040	.0004	.0037	.0008	.0050
.0077	.1100	.0105	.0074	.0157	.0095	.0093	.0018	.0012	.0013	.0013	.0000
.0146	.0180	.2945	.1747	.1382	.1401	.0828	.0029	.0111	.0018	.0030	.2561
.0033	.0033	.0274	.1154	.0275	.0461	.0176	.0030	.0006	.0073	.0002	.1033
.0028	.0045	.0111	.0509	.1270	.0384	.0336	.0026	.0008	.0099	.0002	.0725
.0018	.0003	.0069	.0264	.0163	.2386	.0201	.0066	.0001	.0227	.0025	.1191
.0066	.0035	.0044	.0067	.0151	.0121	.0514	.0040	.0011	.0124	.0056	.0488
.0515	.0851	.0688	.0530	.0551	.0455	.0615	.0390	.0302	.0420	.1018	.0603
.0081	.0299	.0170	.0056	.0055	.0050	.0039	.0160	.1666	.0086	.0505	.0000
.0532	.0502	.0357	.0540	.0650	.0361	.0612	.1450	.0266	.1393	.0475	.0022
.0018	.0023	.0013	.0013	.0026	.0015	.0016	.0165	.1452	.0105	.0013	.0000
.0003	.0035	.0210	.0014	.0003	.0005	.0004	.0008	.0000	.0007	.0000	.0000

TABLE B-5 DIRECT REQUIREMENTS: 1963

Sector	1	2	3	4	5	6	7	8	9	10	11
1	.3005	.0000	.0000	.0000	.0038	.2917	.0459	.0642	.0000	.0017	.0000
2	.0000	.1101	.0000	.0013	.0000	.0000	.0000	.0000	.0000	.0051	.0000
3	.0000	.0000	.0242	.0000	.0000	.0000	.0000	.0000	.0000	.0010	.4494
4	.0023	.0062	.0000	.0873	.0086	.0006	.0005	.0003	.0043	.0184	.0041
5	.0100	.0027	.0309	.0052	.0003	.0019	.0015	.0026	.0025	.0041	.0160
6	.0641	.0000	.0000	.0000	.0003	.1794	.0015	.0001	.0040	.0206	.0011
7	.0037	.0000	.0002	.0000	.0024	.0020	.4122	.0228	.0048	.0011	.0002
8	.0020	.0041	.0000	.0032	.0564	.0012	.0004	.2443	.0252	.0020	.0002
9	.0021	.0003	.0002	.0017	.0034	.0327	.0106	.0082	.2675	.0267	.0075
10	.0277	.0263	.0086	.0174	.0167	.0079	.0664	.0182	.0361	.2059	.0305
11	.0205	.0062	.0052	.0149	.0195	.0026	.0013	.0034	.0054	.0401	.0743
12	.0027	.0058	.0013	.0194	.0073	.0031	.0079	.0217	.0080	.0131	.0002
13	.0008	.0017	.0033	.0222	.0750	.0095	.0013	.0089	.0017	.0072	.0025
14	.0047	.0195	.0050	.0196	.1406	.0253	.0010	.0602	.0090	.0356	.0090
15	.0043	.0379	.0053	.0559	.0175	.0006	.0028	.0038	.0032	.0058	.0003
16	.0013	.0007	.0082	.0065	.0250	.0001	.0001	.0015	.0002	.0011	.0000
17	.0008	.0024	.0002	.0062	.0007	.0002	.0001	.0005	.0004	.0001	.0000
18	.0001	.0010	.0007	.0004	.0055	.0008	.0127	.0041	.0074	.0040	.0006
19	.0493	.0701	.0347	.0458	.1147	.0631	.0502	.0600	.0505	.0561	.0625
20	.0053	.0229	.0115	.0305	.0034	.0062	.0062	.0073	.0115	.0213	.0179
21	.0787	.0851	.2095	.0581	.0637	.0512	.0337	.0470	.0813	.0867	.0549
22	.0002	.0014	.0007	.0015	.0008	.0011	.0019	.0010	.0061	.0020	.0007
23	.0001	.0021	.0000	.0013	.0004	.0000	.0012	.0000	.0071	.0012	.0008

TABLE B-6 DIRECT REQUIREMENTS: 1967

Sector	1	2	3	4	5	6	7	8	9	10	11
1	.2939	.0000	.0000	.0000	.0025	.2927	.0346	.0531	.0000	.0027	.0000
2	.0000	.0952	.0000	.0014	.0000	.0000	.0000	.0000	.0000	.0026	.0000
3	.0000	.0000	.0249	.0002	.0000	.0000	.0000	.0000	.0000	.0011	.4284
4	.0022	.0051	.0000	.0818	.0090	.0005	.0004	.0004	.0035	.0179	.0027
5	.0096	.0137	.0317	.0076	.0003	.0027	.0020	.0044	.0050	.0061	.0135
6	.0596	.0000	.0000	.0000	.0000	.1693	.0015	.0003	.0030	.0139	.0011
7	.0032	.0006	.0003	.0047	.0027	.0015	.4089	.0241	.0079	.0021	.0001
8	.0019	.0042	.0000	.0035	.0535	.0013	.0006	.2209	.0272	.0015	.0000
9	.0026	.0003	.0001	.0040	.0029	.0331	.0087	.0102	.2518	.0262	.0060
10	.0388	.0232	.0115	.0191	.0143	.0090	.0711	.0179	.0332	.2158	.0269
11	.0176	.0030	.0022	.0171	.0196	.0023	.0011	.0056	.0039	.0449	.0679
12	.0034	.0068	.0023	.0098	.0073	.0076	.0070	.0191	.0097	.0154	.0022
13	.0005	.0012	.0055	.0200	.0690	.0103	.0021	.0093	.0008	.0067	.0022
14	.0030	.0300	.0153	.0307	.1471	.0250	.0017	.0567	.0138	.0338	.0057
15	.0051	.0351	.0184	.0340	.0178	.0026	.0036	.0065	.0045	.0096	.0033
16	.0009	.0009	.0114	.0026	.0243	.0001	.0004	.0017	.0006	.0008	.0004
17	.0006	.0024	.0000	.0002	.0000	.0000	.0001	.0021	.0001	.0007	.0001
18	.0002	.0006	.0011	.0005	.0052	.0009	.0047	.0046	.0077	.0031	.0011
19	.0657	.0637	.0214	.0310	.1049	.0613	.0423	.0648	.0515	.0512	.0627
20	.0048	.0265	.0114	.0006	.0007	.0066	.0071	.0085	.0115	.0197	.0171
21	.0830	.0946	.1920	.0927	.0758	.0588	.0387	.0467	.0852	.1164	.0642
22	.0001	.0009	.0004	.0008	.0006	.0010	.0016	.0009	.0068	.0016	.0006
23	.0000	.0042	.0057	.0032	.0001	.0000	.0008	.0000	.0054	.0015	.0004

12	13	14	15	16	17	18	19	20	21	22	23
.0040	.0006	.0000	.0000	.0000	.0000	.0012	.0016	.0000	.0117	.0488	.0000
.0000	.0014	.0331	.0000	.0002	.0000	.0000	.0000	.0001	.0001	.0000	.0000
.0000	.0000	.0000	.0000	.0000	.0000	.0002	.0657	.0003	.0030	.0000	
.0015	.0758	.0094	.0004	.0002	.0003	.0004	.0001	.0214	.0002	.0115	.0000
.0022	.0045	.0041	.0018	.0012	.0017	.0017	.0097	.0300	.0365	.1030	.0000
.0170	.0003	.0002	.0002	.0000	.0000	.0017	.0054	.0001	.0112	.0163	.0059
.0612	.0052	.0020	.0014	.0018	.0100	.0157	.0013	.0003	.0013	.0023	.0685
.0054	.0093	.0037	.0027	.0075	.0046	.0124	.0012	.0001	.0002	.0000	.0000
.0204	.0261	.0076	.0038	.0120	.0012	.1320	.0104	.0008	.0355	.0044	.0896
.1598	.0326	.0191	.0053	.0147	.0059	.0361	.0031	.0019	.0073	.0070	.0000
.0020	.0096	.0051	.0038	.0034	.0023	.0023	.0182	.0075	.0051	.0055	.0066
.1146	.0133	.0041	.0135	.0213	.0181	.0335	.0034	.0002	.0028	.0012	.0138
.0070	.1061	.0045	.0075	.0153	.0082	.0082	.0013	.0000	.0013	.0015	.0000
.0173	.0231	.2949	.1758	.1296	.1459	.0803	.0046	.0025	.0017	.0011	.2451
.0023	.0087	.0240	.1415	.0316	.0513	.0109	.0027	.0001	.0041	.0002	.0705
.0019	.0033	.0094	.0558	.1427	.0370	.0394	.0030	.0009	.0056	.0021	.0685
.0028	.0007	.0088	.0226	.0176	.2597	.0101	.0051	.0001	.0041	.0015	.1318
.0131	.0038	.0044	.0075	.0141	.0108	.0626	.0041	.0008	.0107	.0016	.0257
.0467	.0758	.0595	.0425	.0452	.0360	.0464	.0453	.0248	.0392	.1126	.0514
.0090	.0338	.0184	.0063	.0063	.0048	.0046	.0145	.1864	.0115	.0584	.0000
.0492	.0512	.0392	.0501	.0584	.0396	.0662	.1336	.0378	.1477	.0623	.0000
.0018	.0018	.0010	.0015	.0016	.0013	.0021	.0170	.1470	.0126	.0011	.0000
.0003	.0013	.0207	.0015	.0000	.0007	.0008	.0000	.0000	.0001	.0000	.0000

12	13	14	15	16	17	18	19	20	21	22	23
.0007	.0000	.0000	.0000	.0000	.0000	.0009	.0009	.0000	.0090	.0226	.0000
.0000	.0015	.0297	.0000	.0002	.0000	.0001	.0000	.0000	.0000	.0000	.0000
.0000	.0000	.0000	.0000	.0000	.0000	.0001	.0675	.0005	.0000	.0000	.0000
.0016	.0637	.0088	.0002	.0002	.0003	.0004	.0001	.0240	.0003	.0084	.0000
.0030	.0088	.0054	.0031	.0030	.0026	.0028	.0085	.0305	.0274	.1022	.0000
.0141	.0004	.0001	.0001	.0000	.0000	.0014	.0049	.0001	.0113	.0070	.0050
.0607	.0057	.0012	.0011	.0014	.0106	.0161	.0020	.0005	.0013	.0014	.0362
.0052	.0059	.0042	.0026	.0079	.0069	.0089	.0012	.0000	.0002	.0000	.0000
.0217	.0333	.0073	.0049	.0116	.0028	.1209	.0097	.0012	.0340	.0043	.0648
.1542	.0261	.0144	.0028	.0143	.0072	.0311	.0031	.0016	.0078	.0095	.0000
.0014	.0075	.0030	.0039	.0021	.0025	.0019	.0156	.0074	.0049	.0081	.0060
.0995	.0147	.0046	.0106	.0163	.0147	.0277	.0048	.0006	.0043	.0025	.0070
.0055	.1028	.0041	.0072	.0149	.0068	.0061	.0016	.0000	.0014	.0004	.0000
.0228	.0219	.2926	.1688	.1118	.1479	.0845	.0052	.0021	.0064	.0014	.2953
.0080	.0162	.0324	.1259	.0272	.0513	.0118	.0035	.0010	.0060	.0019	.0542
.0013	.0033	.0101	.0647	.1630	.0327	.0363	.0026	.0020	.0051	.0014	.0482
.0037	.0010	.0079	.0183	.0161	.2247	.0080	.0047	.0001	.0046	.0010	.0844
.0096	.0050	.0036	.0060	.0112	.0099	.0638	.0044	.0008	.0104	.0017	.0176
.0512	.0787	.0582	.0433	.0394	.0358	.0448	.0530	.0205	.0426	.0831	.0291
.0095	.0334	.0179	.0058	.0067	.0049	.0045	.0128	.1846	.0097	.0731	.0000
.0618	.0680	.0460	.0656	.0716	.0523	.0718	.1419	.0268	.1530	.0803	.0055
.0015	.0016	.0008	.0011	.0013	.0011	.0016	.0182	.1503	.0109	.0013	.0000
.0008	.0007	.0200	.0011	.0001	.0026	.0000	.0001	.0000	.0001	.0000	.0000

TABLE B-7 DIRECT INDUSTRY-BY-INDUSTRY REQUIREMENTS
(INDUSTRY-BASED TECHNOLOGY): 1972

Sector	1	2	3	4	5	6	7	8	9	10	11
1	.3148	.0000	.0000	.0000	.0019	.2936	.0219	.0539	.0007	.0023	.0001
2	.0000	.0816	.0000	.0002	.0000	.0000	.0000	.0000	.0001	.0036	.0000
3	.0004	.0005	.0335	.0007	.0005	.0001	.0001	.0003	.0002	.0017	.4773
4	.0018	.0036	.0001	.0820	.0087	.0005	.0006	.0014	.0023	.0119	.0041
5	.0069	.0140	.0412	.0082	.0003	.0019	.0013	.0031	.0060	.0071	.0173
6	.0632	.0003	.0003	.0002	.0004	.1799	.0014	.0013	.0034	.0108	.0015
7	.0027	.0012	.0001	.0023	.0049	.0009	.4138	.0241	.0067	.0012	.0004
8	.0017	.0038	.0000	.0042	.0603	.0009	.0018	.2370	.0281	.0012	.0002
9	.0051	.0056	.0046	.0063	.0052	.0348	.0139	.0111	.2519	.0268	.0075
10	.0376	.0271	.0062	.0119	.0123	.0063	.0759	.0141	.0277	.2076	.0287
11	.0148	.0115	.0038	.0196	.0188	.0024	.0044	.0093	.0065	.0156	.0727
12	.0045	.0164	.0003	.0084	.0093	.0091	.0120	.0222	.0106	.0206	.0019
13	.0004	.0054	.0005	.0045	.0628	.0134	.0021	.0115	.0015	.0071	.0030
14	.0031	.0476	.0122	.0346	.1233	.0310	.0021	.0668	.0091	.0288	.0123
15	.0063	.0298	.0168	.0533	.0227	.0020	.0049	.0067	.0049	.0091	.0017
16	.0008	.0046	.0075	.0042	.0250	.0004	.0010	.0020	.0009	.0010	.0002
17	.0016	.0117	.0008	.0042	.0022	.0005	.0007	.0022	.0011	.0007	.0002
18	.0006	.0027	.0011	.0019	.0058	.0005	.0092	.0029	.0067	.0028	.0009
19	.0515	.0433	.0111	.0401	.1014	.0654	.0552	.0759	.0733	.0639	.0650
20	.0066	.0392	.0114	.0270	.0012	.0061	.0079	.0084	.0124	.0242	.0184
21	.0903	.1251	.1874	.0895	.0726	.0571	.0467	.0519	.0992	.1342	.0418
22	.0020	.0095	.0031	.0063	.0019	.0029	.0039	.0034	.0112	.0068	.0048
23	.0000	.0000	.0000	.0000	.0000	.0000	.0000	.0000	.0000	.0000	.0000

TABLE B-8 DIRECT INDUSTRY-BY-INDUSTRY REQUIREMENTS
(INDUSTRY-BASED TECHNOLOGY): 1977

Sector	1	2	3	4	5	6	7	8	9	10	11
1	.2472	.0001	.0001	.0002	.0026	.2787	.0268	.0687	.0003	.0037	.0000
2	.0000	.0875	.0000	.0001	.0000	.0000	.0000	.0000	.0000	.0058	.0000
3	.0012	.0022	.0472	.0015	.0010	.0003	.0005	.0006	.0009	.0177	.6084
4	.0017	.0064	.0001	.1149	.0080	.0007	.0011	.0003	.0035	.0165	.0025
5	.0107	.0065	.0554	.0072	.0011	.0044	.0041	.0058	.0067	.0078	.0083
6	.0860	.0003	.0001	.0002	.0002	.1738	.0007	.0008	.0028	.0113	.0005
7	.0028	.0007	.0003	.0020	.0058	.0006	.3698	.0210	.0087	.0043	.0006
8	.0015	.0055	.0000	.0031	.0707	.0005	.0005	.2455	.0264	.0009	.0003
9	.0042	.0023	.0027	.0039	.0052	.0351	.0112	.0086	.2588	.0245	.0057
10	.0542	.0289	.0077	.0146	.0132	.0103	.0910	.0157	.0344	.2490	.0322
11	.0296	.0226	.0055	.0232	.0270	.0043	.0109	.0099	.0164	.0355	.0767
12	.0052	.0160	.0005	.0083	.0115	.0099	.0143	.0184	.0124	.0172	.0016
13	.0007	.0044	.0004	.0044	.0602	.0146	.0016	.0066	.0013	.0063	.0020
14	.0027	.0525	.0152	.0245	.1228	.0331	.0022	.0595	.0101	.0324	.0061
15	.0071	.0562	.0137	.0629	.0214	.0019	.0055	.0074	.0064	.0094	.0017
16	.0032	.0060	.0055	.0067	.0273	.0004	.0011	.0021	.0012	.0010	.0002
17	.0024	.0104	.0006	.0036	.0027	.0005	.0006	.0022	.0013	.0007	.0011
18	.0006	.0027	.0009	.0015	.0052	.0005	.0077	.0016	.0066	.0025	.0004
19	.0576	.0520	.0118	.0372	.1095	.0734	.0503	.0702	.0745	.0739	.0488
20	.0108	.0638	.0132	.0291	.0027	.0090	.0114	.0109	.0180	.0351	.0219
21	.0898	.0678	.1236	.0708	.0771	.0629	.0482	.0470	.0791	.0938	.0320
22	.0029	.0114	.0028	.0056	.0025	.0041	.0053	.0039	.0129	.0075	.0043
23	.0000	.0000	.0000	.0000	.0000	.0000	.0000	.0000	.0000	.0000	.0000

12	13	14	15	16	17	18	19	20	21	22	23
.0006	.0006	.0004	.0002	.0002	.0002	.0011	.0005	.0017	.0053	.0001	.0000
.0000	.0022	.0344	.0000	.0001	.0000	.0000	.0000	.0000	.0000	.0000	.0000
.0001	.0004	.0002	.0002	.0001	.0001	.0002	.0006	.0752	.0001	.0001	.0000
.0023	.0527	.0087	.0003	.0003	.0004	.0009	.0000	.0452	.0001	.0020	.0000
.0042	.0076	.0065	.0025	.0023	.0021	.0034	.0107	.0357	.0261	.0171	.0000
.0178	.0007	.0006	.0007	.0008	.0006	.0023	.0011	.0002	.0294	.0001	.0000
.0543	.0035	.0023	.0015	.0019	.0159	.0159	.0010	.0002	.0024	.0004	.0000
.0045	.0097	.0052	.0027	.0085	.0131	.0034	.0002	.0000	.0002	.0000	.0000
.0251	.0313	.0119	.0070	.0138	.0047	.0323	.0107	.0030	.0123	.0013	.0000
.1455	.0298	.0180	.0045	.0143	.0065	.0303	.0008	.0024	.0051	.0019	.0000
.0074	.0091	.0046	.0050	.0027	.0024	.0056	.0138	.0266	.0036	.0019	.0000
.0798	.0153	.0073	.0133	.0184	.0199	.0329	.0031	.0010	.0037	.0003	.0000
.0054	.1050	.0061	.0050	.0129	.0110	.0067	.0004	.0009	.0012	.0001	.0000
.0251	.0180	.3204	.1623	.1213	.1636	.0955	.0018	.0006	.0025	.0003	.0000
.0089	.0075	.0286	.1288	.0187	.0398	.0087	.0018	.0025	.0038	.0004	.0000
.0017	.0029	.0108	.0489	.1242	.0398	.0268	.0011	.0021	.0039	.0004	.0000
.0016	.0010	.0064	.0082	.0033	.1852	.0024	.0052	.0003	.0106	.0006	.0000
.0059	.0037	.0030	.0051	.0075	.0054	.0536	.0010	.0007	.0057	.0002	.0000
.0614	.1055	.0723	.0479	.0438	.0598	.0586	.0556	.0177	.0223	.0072	.0000
.0116	.0298	.0189	.0065	.0069	.0049	.0060	.0114	.1946	.0086	.0093	.0000
.0717	.0626	.0451	.0626	.0867	.0491	.1091	.1472	.0502	.1706	.0141	.0000
.0044	.0075	.0053	.0031	.0034	.0029	.0043	.0074	.0350	.0086	.0019	.0000
.0000	.0000	.0000	.0000	.0000	.0000	.0000	.0000	.0000	.0000	.0000	.0000

12	13	14	15	16	17	18	19	20	21	22	23
.0002	.0001	.0000	.0000	.0000	.0000	.0006	.0013	.0001	.0051	.0007	.0000
.0000	.0004	.0299	.0000	.0001	.0000	.0000	.0000	.0000	.0000	.0000	.0000
.0020	.0016	.0011	.0004	.0003	.0003	.0004	.0014	.1306	.0004	.0004	.0000
.0025	.0572	.0185	.0003	.0004	.0004	.0011	.0000	.0565	.0001	.0048	.0000
.0056	.0145	.0126	.0045	.0047	.0028	.0044	.0141	.0352	.0291	.0202	.0000
.0121	.0008	.0006	.0003	.0003	.0002	.0018	.0008	.0001	.0277	.0020	.0000
.0450	.0044	.0013	.0012	.0014	.0176	.0164	.0008	.0001	.0022	.0003	.0000
.0034	.0085	.0031	.0021	.0060	.0084	.0106	.0009	.0006	.0002	.0000	.0000
.0253	.0277	.0088	.0075	.0142	.0039	.0327	.0124	.0016	.0136	.0014	.0000
.1886	.0347	.0221	.0050	.0177	.0072	.0424	.0010	.0042	.0070	.0011	.0000
.0231	.0201	.0097	.0049	.0046	.0036	.0088	.0259	.0733	.0052	.0042	.0000
.0758	.0059	.0071	.0164	.0308	.0308	.0328	.0040	.0006	.0033	.0003	.0000
.0078	.1158	.0059	.0060	.0121	.0104	.0069	.0005	.0006	.0013	.0003	.0000
.0217	.0222	.3206	.1620	.1215	.1648	.0807	.0027	.0017	.0042	.0003	.0000
.0078	.0113	.0259	.1385	.0179	.0413	.0105	.0026	.0063	.0038	.0010	.0000
.0018	.0023	.0091	.0451	.1392	.0403	.0339	.0013	.0019	.0049	.0012	.0000
.0012	.0032	.0068	.0096	.0042	.2196	.0021	.0048	.0004	.0060	.0006	.0000
.0039	.0025	.0024	.0039	.0072	.0049	.0468	.0020	.0012	.0056	.0004	.0000
.0572	.0931	.0754	.0612	.0640	.0493	.0675	.0603	.0317	.0247	.0093	.0000
.0162	.0439	.0263	.0083	.0093	.0066	.0077	.0143	.1747	.0112	.0124	.0000
.0640	.0579	.0393	.0522	.0725	.0430	.0964	.1633	.0283	.1592	.0115	.0000
.0053	.0088	.0056	.0036	.0049	.0031	.0052	.0075	.0260	.0082	.0032	.0000
.0000	.0000	.0000	.0000	.0000	.0000	.0000	.0000	.0000	.0000	.0000	.0000

B-3 | TOTAL REQUIREMENTS MATRICES (23-SECTOR AGGREGATION)

TABLE B-9 Total Requirements: 1947

Sector	1	2	3	4	5	6	7	8	9	10	11
1	1.532	.011	.015	.010	.030	.757	.249	.118	.026	.121	.020
2	.001	1.111	.002	.004	.012	.002	.002	.005	.003	.009	.003
3	.012	.008	1.019	.008	.019	.010	.008	.012	.011	.024	.552
4	.006	.010	.004	1.160	.029	.008	.010	.010	.016	.044	.013
5	.030	.012	.015	.009	1.016	.022	.016	.016	.017	.020	.019
6	.107	.007	.009	.007	.015	1.234	.042	.023	.021	.158	.017
7	.010	.003	.006	.005	.014	.016	1.630	.076	.026	.018	.007
8	.011	.026	.006	.023	.112	.012	.009	1.224	.042	.017	.010
9	.018	.013	.027	.019	.038	.042	.038	.041	1.407	.099	.057
10	.032	.027	.024	.030	.045	.031	.088	.040	.046	1.243	.049
11	.024	.013	.012	.015	.036	.018	.015	.022	.021	.041	1.115
12	.008	.003	.006	.005	.011	.008	.014	.019	.013	.015	.009
13	.005	.004	.007	.006	.069	.010	.005	.014	.006	.019	.012
14	.027	.040	.045	.070	.267	.045	.030	.112	.058	.118	.069
15	.006	.015	.019	.044	.026	.007	.008	.024	.019	.014	.015
16	.004	.003	.009	.009	.028	.004	.004	.008	.009	.010	.009
17	.008	.005	.008	.013	.011	.008	.007	.012	.012	.010	.010
18	.003	.002	.004	.003	.007	.003	.018	.011	.010	.008	.005
19	.120	.120	.064	.049	.206	.125	.119	.147	.126	.140	.153
20	.007	.036	.009	.026	.015	.011	.014	.015	.018	.024	.021
21	.142	.100	.182	.074	.139	.122	.099	.118	.125	.160	.182
22	.005	.009	.005	.007	.007	.006	.007	.007	.012	.012	.011
23	.002	.002	.003	.004	.015	.006	.004	.007	.028	.009	.005

TABLE B-10 Total Requirements: 1958

Sector	1	2	3	4	5	6	7	8	9	10	11
1	1.451	.007	.008	.007	.022	.555	.135	.151	.017	.025	.009
2	.002	1.147	.001	.004	.012	.003	.002	.006	.002	.011	.003
3	.020	.010	1.029	.017	.019	.014	.010	.012	.011	.032	.575
4	.007	.008	.002	1.126	.025	.007	.007	.007	.012	.033	.009
5	.029	.011	.013	.010	1.013	.022	.013	.015	.018	.016	.015
6	.106	.005	.005	.004	.008	1.241	.019	.019	.012	.034	.007
7	.009	.005	.005	.006	.010	.011	1.695	.053	.019	.011	.005
8	.008	.007	.003	.009	.085	.009	.006	1.302	.050	.009	.004
9	.022	.015	.019	.024	.037	.056	.050	.053	1.427	.079	.028
10	.054	.040	.014	.035	.051	.041	.143	.055	.058	1.308	.058
11	.036	.016	.010	.026	.033	.024	.015	.021	.017	.054	1.084
12	.010	.006	.006	.019	.015	.010	.021	.029	.017	.019	.006
13	.007	.007	.003	.032	.086	.017	.007	.022	.008	.019	.007
14	.029	.077	.030	.069	.262	.066	.028	.118	.043	.088	.054
15	.012	.036	.022	.071	.033	.010	.012	.018	.014	.021	.016
16	.006	.011	.012	.013	.040	.007	.006	.010	.009	.009	.010
17	.011	.010	.012	.016	.013	.009	.008	.011	.012	.010	.011
18	.005	.004	.005	.006	.012	.006	.026	.012	.014	.010	.006
19	.118	.128	.065	.092	.191	.156	.137	.167	.120	.123	.120
20	.018	.034	.015	.044	.022	.021	.024	.023	.026	.036	.033
21	.180	.133	.237	.103	.149	.171	.139	.139	.177	.192	.208
22	.007	.010	.006	.011	.009	.009	.011	.010	.014	.014	.012
23	.001	.003	.011	.004	.008	.002	.003	.004	.011	.003	.008

12	13	14	15	16	17	18	19	20	21	22	23
.115	.019	.017	.015	.019	.023	.037	.015	.010	.074	.017	.068
.003	.006	.066	.016	.015	.018	.009	.001	.003	.002	.003	.031
.010	.014	.014	.009	.009	.009	.009	.012	.051	.007	.009	.011
.014	.108	.044	.016	.018	.019	.022	.012	.078	.008	.017	.026
.018	.020	.017	.014	.015	.016	.016	.033	.069	.070	.155	.015
.115	.013	.015	.011	.014	.017	.027	.011	.006	.038	.007	.081
.165	.027	.014	.013	.018	.041	.049	.006	.004	.009	.006	.074
.016	.020	.022	.018	.035	.023	.047	.007	.011	.014	.020	.042
.069	.102	.040	.036	.052	.035	.070	.034	.017	.077	.028	.102
.126	.051	.040	.028	.049	.044	.054	.010	.013	.019	.017	.069
.018	.025	.026	.016	.017	.017	.016	.023	.037	.012	.017	.021
1.220	.014	.014	.036	.034	.072	.052	.007	.004	.008	.006	.056
.011	1.092	.019	.015	.031	.023	.015	.005	.009	.008	.013	.021
.062	.077	1.468	.359	.323	.392	.183	.029	.060	.041	.057	.678
.011	.020	.042	1.122	.055	.085	.028	.006	.008	.011	.008	.102
.008	.013	.027	.061	1.129	.040	.028	.006	.008	.011	.008	.092
.009	.011	.023	.018	.014	1.301	.009	.016	.007	.021	.008	.194
.017	.005	.009	.009	.012	.014	1.085	.004	.003	.013	.006	.037
.124	.155	.148	.108	.120	.110	.125	1.079	.090	.106	.157	.123
.018	.044	.031	.019	.020	.020	.015	.015	1.135	.016	.028	.021
.115	.109	.093	.092	.108	.092	.112	.164	.086	1.187	.087	.092
.009	.013	.010	.008	.011	.009	.008	.016	.179	.018	1.009	.008
.006	.009	.074	.022	.018	.021	.011	.002	.003	.004	.004	1.036

12	13	14	15	16	17	18	19	20	21	22	23
.040	.011	.008	.008	.010	.010	.016	.015	.026	.036	.126	.018
.004	.005	.065	.015	.013	.014	.008	.001	.002	.002	.003	.022
.010	.015	.012	.008	.007	.008	.008	.014	.084	.008	.016	.012
.011	.084	.025	.009	.008	.009	.008	.003	.042	.004	.023	.011
.012	.012	.015	.012	.012	.013	.014	.029	.064	.055	.150	.012
.038	.007	.005	.005	.006	.006	.010	.012	.011	.024	.048	.009
.142	.010	.012	.010	.012	.027	.041	.006	.003	.012	.006	.124
.011	.017	.011	.010	.020	.014	.026	.006	.007	.009	.015	.012
.056	.087	.034	.029	.046	.032	.219	.029	.016	.075	.032	.117
.212	.071	.039	.025	.043	.035	.068	.012	.011	.023	.021	.038
.016	.021	.017	.013	.011	.012	.013	.024	.023	.012	.019	.020
1.157	.017	.012	.023	.029	.039	.042	.008	.004	.010	.006	.023
.016	1.130	.022	.018	.027	.023	.019	.006	.010	.009	.017	.015
.053	.054	1.469	.324	.263	.315	.168	.024	.046	.040	.055	.481
.013	.016	.058	1.150	.051	.086	.036	.009	.009	.017	.010	.152
.009	.012	.029	.077	1.158	.072	.051	.009	.007	.020	.009	.112
.010	.009	.026	.051	.036	1.328	.039	.017	.006	.039	.011	.177
.014	.009	.013	.015	.024	.024	1.062	.009	.006	.019	.011	.064
.113	.138	.142	.115	.117	.120	.127	1.069	.088	.085	.162	.159
.024	.053	.040	.022	.022	.023	.020	.027	1.218	.019	.072	.023
.142	.125	.117	.130	.145	.121	.153	.200	.098	1.207	.128	.112
.010	.015	.012	.009	.011	.010	.010	.024	.180	.018	1.016	.010
.002	.006	.032	.009	.007	.008	.006	.002	.002	.002	.002	1.012

TABLE B-11 Total Requirements: 1963

Sector	1	2	3	4	5	6	7	8	9	10	11
1	1.486	.007	.009	.007	.021	.534	.125	.136	.016	.025	.010
2	.002	1.126	.001	.004	.009	.003	.002	.005	.002	.011	.002
3	.020	.010	1.032	.015	.017	.012	.010	.009	.010	.033	.506
4	.007	.011	.003	1.102	.022	.007	.007	.006	.010	.030	.009
5	.026	.014	.045	.016	1.013	.019	.014	.015	.015	.019	.046
6	.122	.005	.006	.005	.007	1.266	.021	.016	.014	.039	.008
7	.013	.004	.003	.006	.013	.012	1.707	.059	.018	.008	.003
8	.008	.009	.005	.008	.080	.009	.006	1.328	.049	.009	.006
9	.026	.015	.018	.016	.028	.074	.047	.033	1.385	.065	.030
10	.064	.047	.020	.039	.045	.045	.160	.057	.076	1.279	.057
11	.041	.014	.011	.024	.032	.023	.017	.016	.016	.062	1.092
12	.009	.012	.005	.029	.018	.010	.022	.038	.018	.024	.005
13	.007	.006	.009	.031	.090	.018	.007	.017	.007	.015	.011
14	.033	.059	.027	.067	.240	.065	.027	.133	.043	.086	.040
15	.012	.055	.011	.078	.035	.009	.011	.014	.011	.017	.009
16	.007	.008	.015	.017	.038	.005	.005	.008	.006	.008	.010
17	.005	.009	.004	.015	.010	.005	.004	.006	.006	.005	.004
18	.004	.005	.006	.005	.012	.006	.027	.011	.015	.010	.006
19	.112	.108	.065	.083	.173	.140	.127	.124	.104	.114	.120
20	.021	.041	.023	.052	.025	.025	.026	.025	.031	.047	.042
21	.188	.153	.280	.119	.151	.175	.135	.137	.176	.188	.236
22	.008	.012	.009	.013	.010	.010	.012	.010	.017	.015	.013
23	.001	.004	.001	.003	.006	.002	.003	.003	.011	.004	.002

TABLE B-12 Total Requirements: 1967

Sector	1	2	3	4	5	6	7	8	9	10	11
1	1.467	.006	.007	.006	.015	.521	.093	.108	.013	.022	.007
2	.001	1.108	.002	.004	.008	.002	.002	.004	.002	.007	.002
3	.018	.008	1.031	.015	.015	.011	.009	.009	.008	.035	.478
4	.007	.010	.003	1.094	.020	.006	.006	.006	.009	.029	.007
5	.025	.025	.043	.018	1.012	.019	.014	.016	.017	.022	.041
6	.111	.005	.005	.004	.006	1.246	.015	.013	.011	.028	.007
7	.012	.005	.004	.013	.013	.011	1.698	.059	.025	.011	.004
8	.007	.009	.005	.008	.074	.008	.005	1.288	.050	.008	.005
9	.027	.015	.018	.021	.027	.074	.040	.035	1.356	.065	.027
10	.085	.043	.024	.039	.040	.054	.170	.055	.071	1.296	.054
11	.037	.010	.008	.026	.030	.021	.016	.017	.014	.069	1.082
12	.011	.013	.007	.016	.017	.018	.020	.033	.020	.028	.009
13	.006	.006	.011	.028	.083	.018	.008	.017	.005	.015	.011
14	.032	.078	.052	.076	.248	.067	.030	.126	.053	.088	.046
15	.015	.052	.029	.050	.038	.014	.014	.020	.015	.025	.021
16	.006	.010	.021	.011	.039	.006	.006	.009	.007	.009	.013
17	.004	.008	.005	.005	.008	.004	.003	.008	.004	.006	.004
18	.005	.005	.006	.005	.012	.006	.021	.011	.015	.010	.006
19	.137	.102	.053	.066	.163	.147	.112	.128	.105	.111	.112
20	.020	.045	.023	.048	.020	.025	.027	.026	.030	.045	.039
21	.207	.170	.265	.163	.172	.195	.149	.140	.186	.242	.235
22	.009	.012	.008	.012	.009	.011	.011	.010	.018	.014	.012
23	.001	.007	.007	.005	.006	.002	.003	.003	.009	.005	.004

12	13	14	15	16	17	18	19	20	21	22	23
.035	.010	.008	.007	.008	.009	.016	.013	.020	.032	.089	.019
.004	.005	.055	.013	.010	.013	.007	.001	.001	.001	.002	.017
.011	.014	.010	.008	.007	.007	.008	.013	.093	.008	.017	.011
.010	.098	.019	.007	.007	.008	.007	.002	.034	.003	.018	.009
.014	.017	.016	.012	.011	.012	.013	.022	.066	.049	.116	.011
.036	.007	.006	.005	.006	.005	.011	.012	.008	.021	.031	.014
.122	.016	.013	.011	.012	.032	.040	.005	.004	.006	.008	.131
.013	.019	.011	.010	.017	.014	.028	.005	.006	.007	.011	.012
.059	.055	.033	.026	.040	.024	.213	.028	.013	.066	.021	.152
.250	.063	.048	.030	.044	.037	.082	.013	.014	.022	.023	.046
.019	.021	.016	.012	.012	.012	.013	.024	.017	.012	.017	.019
1.138	.024	.013	.026	.035	.037	.050	.007	.004	.007	.006	.033
.014	1.125	.012	.016	.025	.019	.016	.005	.008	.008	.014	.010
.058	.062	1.465	.334	.253	.335	.162	.021	.027	.026	.038	.456
.011	.023	.052	1.184	.056	.098	.026	.007	.007	.010	.008	.116
.008	.010	.026	.086	1.178	.073	.057	.007	.007	.012	.009	.106
.008	.006	.027	.046	.036	1.363	.022	.009	.003	.009	.006	.194
.022	.009	.012	.016	.023	.023	1.075	.008	.004	.016	.006	.040
.104	.124	.122	.099	.099	.103	.105	1.071	.081	.073	.160	.136
.029	.061	.044	.025	.024	.025	.024	.026	1.251	.024	.083	.025
.139	.126	.120	.127	.136	.127	.158	.188	.122	1.213	.139	.108
.011	.016	.012	.010	.010	.010	.011	.025	.187	.021	1.018	.010
.003	.003	.031	.009	.006	.008	.006	.001	.001	.001	.001	1.011

12	13	14	15	16	17	18	19	20	21	22	23
.023	.007	.006	.005	.006	.007	.012	.010	.011	.026	.043	.011
.003	.004	.048	.010	.008	.011	.006	.001	.001	.001	.001	.016
.010	.012	.008	.007	.006	.006	.007	.011	.094	.007	.015	.008
.010	.082	.017	.006	.006	.006	.006	.002	.036	.003	.015	.007
.015	.021	.017	.013	.013	.014	.014	.019	.065	.038	.115	.011
.028	.006	.004	.004	.005	.005	.008	.011	.005	.020	.015	.010
.119	.017	.009	.009	.010	.031	.039	.006	.004	.006	.006	.071
.012	.014	.012	.009	.017	.017	.022	.005	.006	.006	.010	.010
.058	.066	.030	.026	.037	.026	.192	.027	.012	.063	.020	.109
.242	.055	.039	.023	.040	.034	.072	.013	.014	.023	.025	.032
.018	.018	.012	.011	.009	.010	.011	.021	.017	.011	.018	.014
1.120	.024	.013	.021	.028	.029	.042	.009	.005	.009	.008	.020
.012	1.120	.011	.015	.024	.016	.012	.005	.008	.006	.011	.008
.069	.065	1.465	.316	.226	.323	.167	.023	.030	.034	.039	.497
.021	.031	.064	1.165	.052	.095	.029	.009	.010	.013	.010	.095
.008	.011	.028	.098	1.206	.066	.054	.007	.009	.012	.009	.079
.009	.006	.022	.036	.031	1.300	.017	.009	.002	.009	.004	.121
.017	.011	.010	.013	.019	.020	1.075	.008	.004	.016	.006	.028
.107	.127	.118	.097	.090	.098	.100	1.080	.068	.076	.126	.099
.029	.059	.042	.023	.023	.024	.022	.024	1.251	.021	.100	.022
.167	.157	.135	.153	.159	.150	.169	.202	.111	1.223	.155	.105
.011	.016	.012	.009	.009	.009	.011	.026	.191	.019	1.021	.008
.003	.003	.030	.008	.005	.010	.005	.001	.001	.001	.001	1.011

TABLE B-13 TOTAL INDUSTRY-BY-INDUSTRY REQUIREMENTS (INDUSTRY-BASED TECHNOLOGY): 1972

Sector	1	2	3	4	5	6	7	8	9	10	11
1	1.517	.008	.008	.006	.016	.548	.066	.115	.015	.020	.008
2	.002	1.093	.002	.004	.009	.003	.002	.006	.002	.008	.002
3	.018	.016	1.041	.019	.017	.012	.012	.014	.011	.021	.541
4	.006	.010	.003	1.094	.018	.006	.006	.008	.007	.021	.009
5	.022	.027	.052	.019	1.012	.017	.013	.015	.019	.022	.051
6	.127	.011	.011	.008	.010	1.271	.018	.019	.016	.029	.012
7	.011	.008	.003	.008	.017	.010	1.712	.061	.022	.009	.005
8	.007	.010	.006	.010	.085	.008	.008	1.316	.052	.008	.006
9	.027	.021	.015	.019	.025	.074	.048	.035	1.349	.058	.025
10	.082	.051	.015	.027	.037	.049	.179	.051	.060	1.279	.052
11	.031	.021	.009	.029	.029	.019	.017	.022	.016	.029	1.087
12	.014	.026	.004	.015	.020	.021	.031	.039	.022	.034	.008
13	.006	.011	.006	.009	.076	.022	.008	.021	.006	.014	.009
14	.032	.108	.042	.088	.220	.078	.031	.150	.041	.076	.053
15	.017	.046	.025	.073	.040	.014	.016	.021	.014	.022	.019
16	.006	.013	.014	.013	.036	.005	.006	.009	.005	.007	.010
17	.008	.021	.006	.010	.009	.007	.006	.009	.006	.007	.006
18	.004	.006	.004	.005	.010	.004	.020	.008	.012	.007	.004
19	.117	.085	.036	.075	.162	.149	.137	.150	.133	.121	.109
20	.023	.064	.021	.046	.019	.026	.030	.028	.031	.050	.041
21	.229	.222	.262	.166	.173	.210	.182	.165	.218	.267	.226
22	.009	.017	.007	.012	.009	.011	.013	.011	.021	.016	.013
23	.000	.000	.000	.000	.000	.000	.000	.000	.000	.000	.000

TABLE B-14 TOTAL INDUSTRY-BY-INDUSTRY REQUIREMENTS (INDUSTRY-BASED TECHNOLOGY): 1977

Sector	1	2	3	4	5	6	7	8	9	10	11
1	1.389	.006	.005	.005	.019	.473	.066	.133	.013	.021	.006
2	.002	1.100	.002	.003	.008	.003	.003	.005	.002	.012	.002
3	.049	.048	1.063	.036	.038	.032	.038	.030	.035	.082	.712
4	.009	.020	.004	1.137	.022	.010	.011	.009	.012	.034	.010
5	.031	.023	.067	.020	1.019	.026	.022	.023	.023	.030	.060
6	.154	.008	.007	.007	.010	1.269	.018	.022	.014	.029	.009
7	.011	.006	.003	.007	.018	.009	1.594	.050	.025	.015	.005
8	.008	.013	.008	.008	.099	.008	.006	1.330	.051	.008	.008
9	.029	.016	.011	.016	.026	.076	.042	.030	1.363	.058	.021
10	.118	.062	.020	.037	.048	.072	.216	.064	.082	1.359	.065
11	.061	.046	.015	.041	.049	.038	.041	.034	.040	.071	1.102
12	.016	.026	.005	.016	.023	.023	.033	.034	.025	.031	.008
13	.008	.010	.007	.010	.074	.026	.008	.015	.006	.015	.009
14	.039	.127	.049	.078	.224	.086	.035	.140	.047	.092	.053
15	.020	.083	.023	.090	.041	.016	.019	.023	.018	.027	.021
16	.010	.017	.012	.017	.040	.008	.007	.010	.007	.008	.010
17	.008	.019	.004	.009	.010	.007	.005	.008	.006	.006	.005
18	.004	.006	.003	.004	.009	.004	.016	.005	.012	.007	.004
19	.133	.104	.040	.078	.178	.167	.132	.148	.143	.149	.098
20	.037	.102	.025	.052	.029	.038	.043	.037	.045	.076	.052
21	.224	.153	.183	.143	.181	.215	.174	.156	.192	.227	.192
22	.011	.020	.007	.012	.010	.014	.016	.012	.023	.018	.012
23	.000	.000	.000	.000	.000	.000	.000	.000	.000	.000	.000

12	13	14	15	16	17	18	19	20	21	22	23
.023	.009	.008	.007	.008	.010	.012	.007	.008	.031	.001	.000
.003	.005	.057	.012	.009	.013	.007	.001	.001	.001	.000	.000
.012	.015	.012	.009	.007	.008	.009	.011	.118	.006	.003	.000
.009	.069	.019	.006	.006	.007	.006	.002	.063	.002	.003	.000
.016	.020	.020	.013	.013	.014	.015	.019	.056	.035	.019	.000
.036	.009	.009	.009	.010	.009	.014	.010	.006	.048	.001	.000
.105	.013	.011	.009	.011	.042	.037	.004	.003	.008	.001	.000
.012	.019	.015	.010	.018	.027	.011	.003	.006	.005	.002	.000
.057	.058	.035	.025	.035	.026	.061	.021	.012	.026	.003	.000
.221	.056	.047	.025	.038	.036	.063	.007	.012	.016	.004	.000
.019	.020	.015	.013	.010	.011	.014	.019	.041	.008	.003	.000
1.098	.025	.019	.024	.030	.037	.045	.006	.005	.008	.001	.000
.012	1.121	.014	.012	.021	.021	.013	.003	.007	.006	.002	.000
.069	.054	1.510	.305	.228	.340	.176	.014	.026	.025	.006	.000
.020	.020	.057	1.163	.036	.073	.022	.005	.014	.010	.002	.000
.007	.008	.025	.071	1.149	.067	.038	.004	.008	.009	.001	.000
.007	.006	.017	.018	.010	1.235	.009	.010	.004	.017	.001	.000
.011	.007	.008	.010	.012	.011	1.061	.003	.003	.008	.001	.000
.119	.157	.144	.103	.094	.134	.109	1.075	.048	.049	.013	.000
.032	.054	.047	.024	.023	.025	.022	.020	1.251	.017	.013	.000
.188	.159	.153	.153	.179	.157	.209	.206	.136	1.240	.025	.000
.012	.015	.014	.010	.010	.011	.011	.011	.047	.013	1.003	.000
.000	.000	.000	.000	.000	.000	.000	.000	.000	.000	.000	1.000

12	13	14	15	16	17	18	19	20	21	22	23
.018	.007	.006	.005	.007	.008	.011	.008	.004	.026	.003	.000
.004	.003	.050	.010	.008	.012	.006	.001	.001	.001	.000	.000
.049	.044	.035	.020	.021	.023	.025	.029	.238	.014	.008	.000
.015	.082	.039	.011	.011	.014	.010	.003	.081	.004	.007	.000
.023	.032	.032	.019	.020	.020	.019	.026	.064	.040	.023	.000
.028	.009	.008	.007	.009	.008	.012	.010	.005	.044	.004	.000
.083	.013	.008	.008	.010	.044	.035	.004	.003	.007	.001	.000
.011	.019	.012	.009	.015	.021	.021	.005	.008	.006	.002	.000
.059	.054	.030	.026	.037	.025	.062	.025	.011	.029	.004	.000
.299	.071	.062	.034	.056	.052	.091	.012	.023	.022	.004	.000
.053	.045	.035	.021	.022	.024	.027	.037	.108	.015	.008	.000
1.094	.014	.019	.030	.046	.054	.046	.008	.006	.008	.001	.000
.016	1.136	.015	.014	.021	.022	.014	.004	.007	.006	.002	.000
.071	.067	1.515	.310	.236	.361	.158	.019	.037	.028	.008	.000
.022	.029	.058	1.177	.037	.080	.025	.008	.024	.010	.003	.000
.008	.009	.024	.069	1.170	.071	.048	.005	.010	.010	.003	.000
.006	.009	.017	.020	.012	1.289	.008	.009	.004	.011	.001	.000
.008	.006	.007	.008	.012	.011	1.053	.004	.004	.008	.001	.000
.127	.152	.157	.127	.128	.134	.126	1.086	.075	.055	.018	.000
.049	.078	.066	.033	.034	.037	.031	.026	1.229	.023	.017	.000
.179	.153	.142	.140	.167	.150	.193	.230	.119	1.225	.025	.000
.014	.017	.015	.011	.012	.012	.013	.012	.036	.013	1.004	.000
.000	.000	.000	.000	.000	.000	.000	.000	.000	.000	.000	1.000

B-4 | SEVEN-SECTOR AGGREGATIONS

TABLE B-15   U.S. NATIONAL INPUT-OUTPUT TABLES: 1947 (MILLIONS OF DOLLARS)

Sector	Interindustry Transactions							Final Demands	Total Outputs
	1	2	3	4	5	6	7		
1 Agriculture	14741	0	92	23946	16	2048	15	6000	46858
2 Mining	47	810	277	6602	513	732	25	1376	10382
3 Construction	568	15	7	509	1489	4197	503	22043	29331
4 Manufacturing	4435	952	11132	70687	4743	8643	668	96744	198004
5 Trade & Transportation	2617	357	3884	10734	3617	4461	378	50596	76644
6 Services	2981	997	1860	8300	9951	11083	193	45889	81254
7 Other	5	7	32	2065	803	1938	6	765	4091

Sector	Direct Requirements						
	1	2	3	4	5	6	7
1 Agriculture	.3146	.0000	.0031	.1209	.0002	.0252	.0037
2 Mining	.0010	.0780	.0094	.0333	.0067	.0090	.0061
3 Construction	.0121	.0014	.0002	.0026	.0194	.0517	.1230
4 Manufacturing	.0946	.0917	.3795	.3570	.0619	.1064	.1633
5 Trade & Transportation	.0558	.0344	.1324	.0542	.0472	.0549	.0924
6 Services	.0636	.0960	.0634	.0419	.1298	.1364	.0472
7 Other	.0001	.0007	.0011	.0104	.0105	.0239	.0015

Sector	Total Requirements						
	1	2	3	4	5	6	7
1 Agriculture	1.5141	.0410	.1290	.2978	.0362	.0935	.0782
2 Mining	.0144	1.0940	.0379	.0629	.0160	.0235	.0243
3 Construction	.0300	.0122	1.0170	.0199	.0332	.0701	.1350
4 Manufacturing	.2804	.2012	.6724	1.6592	.1648	.2760	.3847
5 Trade & Transportation	.1186	.0641	.1986	.1266	1.0781	.1043	.1507
6 Services	.1472	.1454	.1516	.1312	.1779	1.2035	.1149
7 Other	.0079	.0070	.0139	.0219	.0173	.0328	1.0100

TABLE B-16 U.S. NATIONAL INPUT-OUTPUT TABLES: 1958 (MILLIONS OF DOLLARS)

Sector	Interindustry Transactions							Final Demands	Total Outputs
	1	2	3	4	5	6	7		
1 Agriculture	14806	0	237	25078	190	2304	624	8721	51960
2 Mining	102	1097	756	13349	37	1913	148	918	18320
3 Construction	613	11	8	752	2024	7842	1206	56835	69291
4 Manufacturing	6109	1461	26543	131228	7977	23258	1575	154016	352167
5 Trade & Transportation	2842	889	8446	21906	5041	8117	989	81102	129332
6 Services	4338	2593	4261	21040	20817	30327	874	114575	198825
7 Other	10	133	100	1974	2237	4940	12	877	10283

Direct Requirements

Sector	1	2	3	4	5	6	7
1 Agriculture	.2849	.0000	.0034	.0712	.0015	.0116	.0607
2 Mining	.0020	.0599	.0109	.0379	.0003	.0096	.0144
3 Construction	.0118	.0006	.0001	.0021	.0156	.0394	.1173
4 Manufacturing	.1176	.0797	.3831	.3726	.0617	.1170	.1532
5 Trade & Transportation	.0547	.0485	.1219	.0622	.0390	.0408	.0962
6 Services	.0835	.1415	.0615	.0597	.1610	.1525	.0850
7 Other	.0002	.0073	.0014	.0056	.0173	.0248	.0012

Total Requirements

Sector	1	2	3	4	5	6	7
1 Agriculture	1.4365	.0250	.0782	.1736	.0258	.0526	.1304
2 Mining	.0192	1.0744	.0419	.0711	.0106	.0258	.0357
3 Construction	.0283	.0129	1.0139	.0168	.0293	.0553	.1311
4 Manufacturing	.3388	.2008	.6934	1.6961	.1773	.2938	.4071
5 Trade & Transportation	.1174	.0810	.1888	.1346	1.0698	.0862	.1614
6 Services	.1939	.2140	.1744	.1770	.2246	1.2340	.1891
7 Other	.0092	.0157	.0133	.0168	.0252	.0341	1.0114

TABLE B-17   U.S. NATIONAL INPUT-OUTPUT TABLES: 1963 (MILLIONS OF DOLLARS)

Sector	Interindustry Transactions							Final Demands	Total Outputs
	1	2	3	4	5	6	7		
1 Agriculture	17034	0	326	26752	260	2771	639	8908	56690
2 Mining	128	1111	737	14637	46	2727	189	967	20542
3 Construction	567	415	25	1400	1556	9556	1349	70445	85313
4 Manufacturing	7649	1675	31588	179025	10172	22015	1687	205561	459372
5 Trade & Transportation	2795	876	9789	24220	7244	10052	1553	103265	159794
6 Services	4762	3501	5725	28828	23669	44491	1581	154788	267345
7 Other	15	33	102	2555	2726	7371	14	1802	14618

Sector	Direct Requirements						
	1	2	3	4	5	6	7
1 Agriculture	.3005	.0000	.0038	.0582	.0016	.0104	.0437
2 Mining	.0023	.0541	.0086	.0319	.0003	.0102	.0129
3 Construction	.0100	.0202	.0003	.0030	.0097	.0357	.0923
4 Manufacturing	.1349	.0815	.3703	.3897	.0637	.0823	.1154
5 Trade & Transportation	.0493	.0426	.1147	.0527	.0453	.0376	.1062
6 Services	.0840	.1704	.0671	.0628	.1481	.1664	.1082
7 Other	.0003	.0016	.0012	.0056	.0171	.0276	.0010

Sector	Total Requirements						
	1	2	3	4	5	6	7
1 Agriculture	1.4654	.0225	.0659	.1481	.0209	.0400	.0942
2 Mining	.0190	1.0676	.0344	.0610	.0087	.0221	.0282
3 Construction	.0255	.0333	1.0130	.0172	.0212	.0503	.1048
4 Manufacturing	.3828	.2122	.6783	1.7299	.1637	.2254	.3238
5 Trade & Transportation	.1099	.0758	.1726	.1170	1.0717	.0748	.1573
6 Services	.2033	.2541	.1786	.1820	.2116	1.2473	.2072
7 Other	.0101	.0113	.0129	.0168	.0251	.0371	1.0114

TABLE B-18 U.S. NATIONAL INPUT-OUTPUT TABLES: 1967 (MILLIONS OF DOLLARS)

Sector	Interindustry Transactions							Final Demands	Total Outputs
	1	2	3	4	5	6	7		
1 Agriculture	18542	0	263	31390	196	3014	392	9300	63097
2 Mining	138	1256	930	17280	42	3686	145	1454	24931
3 Construction	603	572	30	2560	1833	10328	1771	85583	103280
4 Manufacturing	8679	2343	37563	232248	13705	33431	1938	278797	608704
5 Trade & Transportation	4144	738	10839	30981	11447	15050	1498	141468	216165
6 Services	5539	4258	7898	44695	33428	62483	2671	211937	372909
7 Other	9	135	80	3371	3947	9310	23	2453	19328

Direct Requirements

Sector	1	2	3	4	5	6	7
1 Agriculture	.2939	.0000	.0025	.0516	.0009	.0081	.0203
2 Mining	.0022	.0504	.0090	.0284	.0002	.0099	.0075
3 Construction	.0096	.0229	.0003	.0042	.0085	.0277	.0916
4 Manufacturing	.1376	.0940	.3637	.3815	.0634	.0896	.1003
5 Trade & Transportation	.0657	.0296	.1049	.0509	.0530	.0404	.0775
6 Services	.0878	.1708	.0765	.0734	.1546	.1676	.1382
7 Other	.0001	.0054	.0008	.0055	.0183	.0250	.0012

Total Requirements

Sector	1	2	3	4	5	6	7
1 Agriculture	1.4474	.0206	.0546	.1277	.0167	.0323	.0531
2 Mining	.0175	1.0632	.0316	.0538	.0079	.0206	.0201
3 Construction	.0240	.0346	1.0122	.0177	.0188	.0402	.1024
4 Manufacturing	.3860	.2328	.6592	1.7075	.1635	.2288	.2858
5 Trade & Transportation	.1345	.0632	.1617	.1142	1.0799	.0758	.1238
6 Services	.2192	.2582	.1955	.2007	.2245	1.2525	.2352
7 Other	.0104	.0147	.0125	.0169	.0263	.0341	1.0111

TABLE B-19   U.S. NATIONAL INPUT-OUTPUT TABLES
(INDUSTRY-BY-INDUSTRY; INDUSTRY-BASED TECHNOLOGY): 1972 (MILLIONS OF DOLLARS)

Sector								Final Demands	Total Outputs
	Interindustry Transactions								
	1	*2*	*3*	*4*	*5*	*6*	*7*		
1 Agriculture	26369	10	468	41263	183	2944	23	12696	83956
2 Mining	158	1649	1498	22417	73	6113	314	−1837	30386
3 Construction	583	858	47	3244	3125	16464	2672	139005	165998
4 Manufacturing	12046	2866	58441	285096	12286	49841	1249	339430	761255
5 Trade & Transportation	4323	710	16833	48238	16196	13429	1126	190308	291163
6 Services	8123	5196	12133	59466	46106	113905	3827	364363	613118
7 Other	189	216	471	5892	2218	5785	118	141646	156533

Direct Requirements

Sector	*1*	*2*	*3*	*4*	*5*	*6*	*7*
1 Agriculture	.3141	.0003	.0028	.0542	.0006	.0048	.0001
2 Mining	.0019	.0543	.0090	.0294	.0002	.0100	.0020
3 Construction	.0069	.0282	.0003	.0043	.0107	.0269	.0171
4 Manufacturing	.1435	.0943	.3521	.3745	.0422	.0813	.0080
5 Trade & Transportation	.0515	.0234	.1014	.0634	.0556	.0219	.0072
6 Services	.0967	.1710	.0731	.0781	.1583	.1858	.0244
7 Other	.0022	.0071	.0028	.0077	.0076	.0094	.0008

Total Requirements

Sector	*1*	*2*	*3*	*4*	*5*	*6*	*7*
1 Agriculture	1.4911	.0204	.0549	.1349	.0118	.0247	.0030
2 Mining	.0181	1.0676	.0313	.0552	.0065	.0199	.0037
3 Construction	.0205	.0391	1.0113	.0172	.0185	.0364	.0185
4 Manufacturing	.3960	.2255	.6227	1.6847	.1160	.1973	.0303
5 Trade & Transportation	.1163	.0531	.1587	.1287	1.0748	.0485	.0128
6 Services	.2437	.2625	.1948	.2163	.2249	1.2673	.0382
7 Other	.0098	.0124	.0111	.0168	.0113	.0142	1.0015

TABLE B-20 U.S. National Input-Output Tables
(Industry-by-Industry, Industry-Based Technology): 1977 (millions of dollars)

Sector	Interindustry Transactions							Final Demands	Total Outputs
	1	2	3	4	5	6	7		
1 Agriculture	31930	29	934	63714	733	4745	172	27405	129663
2 Mining	275	5566	2397	77704	372	19794	1217	−29295	78031
3 Construction	1383	2923	303	8706	7182	32058	4971	206809	264334
4 Manufacturing	26198	7425	98337	517408	30714	93117	3301	578483	1354983
5 Trade & Transportation	7463	1726	28970	88262	30795	27283	2274	323867	510639
6 Services	13056	9875	20934	101615	90507	188910	6226	648710	1079832
7 Other	355	292	844	10375	4050	9521	492	220583	246512

Sector	Direct Requirements						
	1	2	3	4	5	6	7
1 Agriculture	.2463	.0004	.0035	.0470	.0014	.0044	.0007
2 Mining	.0021	.0713	.0091	.0573	.0007	.0183	.0049
3 Construction	.0107	.0375	.0011	.0064	.0141	.0297	.0202
4 Manufacturing	.2020	.0952	.3720	.3819	.0601	.0862	.0134
5 Trade & Transportation	.0576	.0221	.1096	.0651	.0603	.0253	.0092
6 Services	.1007	.1265	.0792	.0750	.1772	.1749	.0253
7 Other	.0027	.0037	.0032	.0077	.0079	.0088	.0020

Sector	Total Requirements						
	1	2	3	4	5	6	7
1 Agriculture	1.3608	.0170	.0491	.1097	.0139	.0213	.0042
2 Mining	.0404	1.0963	.0567	.1119	.0163	.0389	.0092
3 Construction	.0289	.0500	1.0172	.0253	.0250	.0415	.0224
4 Manufacturing	.5162	.2391	.6841	1.7307	.1637	.2191	.0456
5 Trade & Transportation	.1303	.0549	.1762	.1384	1.0867	.0562	.0172
6 Services	.2503	.2088	.2127	.2206	.2553	1.2570	.0426
7 Other	.0112	.0084	.0121	.0171	.0123	.0136	1.0030

B-5 | COMMODITY-BY-INDUSTRY TABLES

TABLE B-21   23-Sector Use Matrix: Commodities by Industries: 1972
(MILLIONS OF DOLLARS)

Commodity / Industry	1	2	3	4	5	6	7	8	9	10	11
1	26328	0	0	0	264	37009	1286	1744	29	111	2
2	0	286	0	2	0	0	0	0	3	199	0
3	0	0	596	0	0	0	0	0	0	69	14981
4	136	12	1	757	1407	50	16	44	124	603	123
5	583	49	735	74	47	237	78	103	345	388	543
6	5399	0	5	1	50	23403	70	40	188	563	44
7	226	1	2	18	803	96	24663	797	354	46	12
8	147	13	0	38	10143	97	94	7952	1629	60	6
9	242	1	4	30	479	4288	705	300	14502	1266	205
10	3322	99	116	112	2067	791	4507	467	1656	11976	936
11	1180	38	66	177	3131	289	127	302	329	512	2332
12	377	59	5	78	1516	1203	644	751	603	1122	55
13	24	19	8	29	10706	1747	115	384	76	377	93
14	240	146	216	292	20937	4010	51	2223	326	1520	391
15	557	105	312	507	3600	211	285	193	264	492	51
16	56	9	132	24	4095	7	36	36	8	19	3
17	125	31	6	21	68	15	3	41	5	3	2
18	30	7	14	13	870	23	536	67	338	90	24
19	4379	152	200	367	17052	8445	3284	2538	4267	3529	2070
20	645	160	235	285	219	900	536	323	829	1526	638
21	7774	449	3423	832	12350	7462	2811	1756	5857	7509	1347
22	18	9	17	13	61	133	110	35	471	108	37
23	3	51	1	45	26	70	65	14	300	62	0

TABLE B-22   23-Sector Make Matrix: Industries by Commodities: 1972
(MILLIONS OF DOLLARS)

Industry / Commodity	1	2	3	4	5	6	7	8	9	10	11
1	81265	0	0	0	0	2396	0	133	0	0	0
2	0	3501	0	1	0	0	0	0	0	0	0
3	0	0	16685	0	0	0	0	0	0	0	837
4	0	1	0	8676	0	0	0	0	0	259	43
5	0	0	0	0	165998	0	0	0	0	0	0
6	5	0	0	0	0	127287	0	0	2	175	5
7	0	0	0	0	0	0	58380	16	52	56	0
8	0	0	0	0	0	0	25	32586	41	6	0
9	0	0	0	0	0	5	78	66	43525	98	0
10	0	0	12	0	0	158	464	0	41	53021	64
11	0	0	0	27	0	3	2	0	5	1663	29668
12	0	0	0	0	0	5	167	47	69	267	6
13	0	0	0	139	0	0	13	8	28	22	32
14	0	0	0	0	0	0	33	136	165	248	4
15	0	0	0	0	0	0	6	36	14	42	0
16	0	0	0	0	0	0	8	27	6	34	0
17	0	0	0	0	0	0	36	32	1	24	0
18	0	0	0	0	0	0	26	79	126	195	0
19	0	0	0	0	0	0	0	0	0	0	0
20	0	0	33	0	0	0	0	0	0	59	6
21	0	0	0	0	0	0	0	0	0	0	0
22	0	0	0	0	0	0	0	0	0	17	0
23	0	0	0	0	0	0	0	0	0	0	0

12	13	14	15	16	17	18	19	20	21	22	23
6	10	36	7	8	9	25	135	87	2680	18	0
0	45	3659	0	5	0	0	0	0	0	0	0
0	0	0	0	0	0	0	31	3686	0	0	0
43	1107	932	15	7	38	20	1	2308	30	313	0
111	158	692	161	124	218	86	3125	1790	14674	2672	0
461	12	28	41	35	49	55	313	8	16894	8	0
1429	68	129	81	91	1622	400	278	10	1356	68	0
112	200	529	158	446	1332	78	41	0	72	0	0
596	609	820	299	598	290	744	2154	95	4713	147	0
3991	645	1994	278	779	636	785	225	118	2926	308	0
76	167	425	322	124	229	123	4153	1370	1989	300	0
2184	319	745	868	1019	2095	872	957	51	2149	40	0
138	2237	636	314	696	1130	170	108	5	670	13	0
632	350	34208	10437	6564	17005	2469	502	21	1299	40	0
228	148	2672	8543	796	3781	171	513	128	2084	61	0
26	49	734	3029	6908	3966	668	322	106	2172	67	0
22	6	72	250	4	19054	11	1519	12	5996	89	0
125	66	216	262	345	467	1430	226	34	3211	27	0
1631	2227	7719	3096	2361	6181	1513	16402	897	12692	1140	0
349	724	2329	485	424	583	178	3860	11382	5662	1704	0
1930	1338	4919	4098	4738	5144	2854	43935	2583	98443	2263	0
43	27	140	89	91	133	63	1375	176	3839	51	0
23	47	1991	166	77	147	46	12	0	63	0	0

12	13	14	15	16	17	18	19	20	21	22	23
0	0	0	0	0	0	0	97	0	65	0	0
0	0	0	0	0	0	0	0	0	0	0	0
0	0	0	0	0	0	0	0	298	0	0	0
0	85	0	0	0	0	0	0	0	0	0	0
0	0	0	0	0	0	0	0	0	0	0	0
17	0	32	6	0	0	0	0	0	0	0	16
130	4	2	1	0	3	51	0	0	0	0	76
74	43	93	24	29	18	55	0	0	0	0	0
164	90	111	105	44	0	141	0	0	12955	0	211
478	52	41	29	5	4	196	0	0	0	0	0
14	47	1	0	0	0	0	0	0	0	0	10
25206	101	86	106	6	79	89	0	0	0	0	17
68	20388	45	35	37	30	8	0	0	0	0	0
126	42	102965	1174	344	319	141	0	21	1	0	621
54	65	1218	59840	1221	1098	222	0	0	0	0	85
49	32	756	1206	50201	477	404	0	0	0	0	111
44	16	809	980	726	99094	192	0	0	0	0	210
200	44	114	211	361	130	23423	0	0	590	0	28
0	0	0	0	0	0	0	291036	0	81	0	46
0	0	21	0	0	0	0	0	50029	0	0	0
0	0	0	0	0	0	0	0	0	562970	0	0
0	10	0	0	0	0	0	3721	8035	435	144315	0
0	0	0	0	0	0	0	0	0	0	0	0

TABLE B-23 SEVEN-SECTOR USE AND MAKE MATRICES: 1972 (MILLIONS OF DOLLARS)

Commodity/ Industry	Use Matrix: Commodities by Industries							Final Demand	Total Commodity Output
	1	2	3	4	5	6	7		
1 Agriculture	26328	0	264	40282	135	2767	18	11476	81270
2 Mining	136	1654	1407	22083	32	6024	313	−2574	29075
3 Construction	583	858	47	3244	3125	16464	2672	139005	165998
4 Manufacturing	11925	2754	58465	285070	11311	47489	1168	331804	749986
5 Trade & Transportation	4379	719	17052	48861	16402	13589	1140	192712	294854
6 Services	8419	5384	12569	61587	47795	118070	3967	377689	635480
7 Other	21	136	87	4488	1387	4078	51	135498	145746
Total Industry Output	83956	30386	165998	761255	291163	613118	156533		

TABLE B-24 23-SECTOR USE MATRIX: COMMODITIES BY INDUSTRIES: 1977 (MILLIONS OF DOLLARS)

Commodity/ Industry	1	2	3	4	5	6	7	8	9	10	11
1	31868	0	2	6	658	55692	2334	3802	22	400	0
2	0	470	0	0	0	0	0	0	3	652	0
3	0	0	2302	0	0	0	0	0	0	1819	60050
4	163	32	0	2757	2044	117	40	10	334	1667	227
5	1383	35	2718	170	304	883	355	320	678	876	818
6	11358	1	5	1	10	35854	22	36	248	1184	35
7	283	1	11	41	1435	73	32587	1146	776	141	20
8	196	29	0	71	18901	83	15	13894	2691	67	23
9	302	2	16	51	836	6939	808	394	26482	2503	501
10	7735	168	410	349	3575	2131	8629	939	3770	31139	3361
11	3554	116	259	547	7218	773	463	520	1509	2254	7754
12	664	88	22	198	3024	2062	1176	1042	1253	1878	150
13	75	23	18	80	16376	3034	123	365	95	663	197
14	291	276	757	550	33183	6836	75	3353	640	3512	595
15	946	313	698	1560	5414	310	458	365	593	1003	167
16	408	25	270	133	7233	17	49	73	22	35	7
17	292	46	5	48	132	8	5	50	15	7	102
18	24	12	36	27	1234	55	638	51	628	142	27
19	7514	277	578	877	29238	14941	4421	3941	7602	8352	4851
20	1623	397	750	797	834	2108	1147	702	2116	4543	2378
21	11924	372	6214	1710	20877	13013	4308	2683	8224	10802	3244
22	59	13	19	28	166	376	266	85	956	195	99
23	0	15	0	35	29	0	78	0	508	40	0

TABLE B-23 (*Continued*)

Industry / Commodity	Make Matrix: Industries by Commodities							Total Industry Output
	1	2	3	4	5	6	7	
1 Agriculture	81265	0	0	2529	97	65	0	83956
2 Mining	0	28864	0	1224	0	298	0	30386
3 Construction	0	0	165998	0	0	0	0	165998
4 Manufacturing	5	178	0	746120	0	13567	1385	761255
5 Trade & Transportation	0	0	0	0	291036	81	46	291163
6 Services	0	33	0	86	0	612999	0	613118
7 Other	0	0	0	27	3721	8470	144315	156533
Total Commodity Output	81270	29075	165998	749986	294854	635480	145746	

12	13	14	15	16	17	18	19	20	21	22	23
0	4	3	1	2	2	27	643	7	4471	163	0
0	13	5655	0	10	0	1	0	0	0	0	0
53	0	27	0	0	0	0	79	13148	0	0	0
49	1984	3498	30	16	54	34	4	6065	22	1202	0
263	502	2365	535	417	497	197	7182	3712	28346	4971	0
540	21	21	17	11	9	71	399	5	27483	491	0
2023	130	92	114	84	3059	706	399	4	2066	77	0
144	287	484	203	508	1419	465	450	59	180	0	0
1089	921	1000	686	1081	392	1360	4843	112	10373	305	0
9809	1292	4397	556	1654	1227	2048	305	321	7239	268	0
527	633	1608	572	322	562	284	13851	8099	4829	1061	0
3687	193	1292	1977	2842	5540	1516	2116	61	3269	75	0
355	4123	1078	708	1090	1827	306	243	9	1298	64	0
956	728	60695	19490	10988	29249	3675	1289	156	3871	65	0
338	392	4217	17099	1290	6769	392	1350	701	3618	255	0
56	56	1012	5236	12964	6857	1539	637	201	4803	295	0
28	82	82	589	56	38621	13	2414	28	5733	150	0
128	69	248	354	532	714	2195	987	130	5532	95	0
2708	3235	14176	7322	5743	8677	3050	30999	3163	24170	2289	0
875	1765	5756	1141	963	1333	399	8494	21426	12628	3548	0
3085	2052	7590	6347	6612	7686	4425	85435	3064	158907	2912	0
107	63	242	192	236	277	138	2187	332	5562	366	0
3	43	3551	104	55	217	0	48	0	224	1	0

TABLE B-25　23-SECTOR MAKE MATRIX: INDUSTRIES BY COMMODITIES: 1977 (MILLIONS OF DOLLARS)

Industry / Commodity	1	2	3	4	5	6	7	8	9	10	11
1	125829	0	0	0	0	3617	0	102	0	0	0
2	0	5344	0	12	0	0	0	0	0	0	0
3	0	4	43385	2	0	0	0	0	0	62	3264
4	0	11	1	22550	0	0	0	0	0	823	31
5	0	0	0	0	264334	0	0	0	0	0	0
6	9	0	0	0	0	201365	10	5	57	402	0
7	0	0	0	0	0	4	85177	99	163	1281	6
8	0	0	0	0	0	0	49	54752	82	76	3
9	0	0	0	0	0	20	159	96	81189	243	3
10	0	0	50	141	0	615	429	7	148	108075	1200
11	0	0	0	44	0	0	5	1	16	7135	91504
12	0	0	0	2	0	30	235	72	128	528	4
13	0	0	0	201	0	0	25	34	69	153	55
14	0	0	0	3	0	8	38	180	406	709	2
15	0	0	0	0	0	9	27	91	87	236	1
16	0	0	0	0	0	0	38	74	55	106	0
17	0	0	0	0	0	0	51	110	50	26	10
18	0	0	0	0	0	9	68	80	128	456	1
19	34	0	0	0	0	0	0	0	0	0	0
20	0	0	86	0	0	0	0	0	0	143	30
21	0	0	0	0	0	0	0	0	0	0	0
22	0	0	0	0	0	0	0	0	0	41	0
23	0	0	0	0	0	0	0	0	0	0	0

TABLE B-26　SEVEN-SECTOR USE AND MAKE MATRICES: 1977 (MILLIONS OF DOLLARS)

Commodity / Industry	Use Matrix: Commodities by Industries							Final Demand	Total Commodity Output
	1	2	3	4	5	6	7		
1 Agriculture	31868	8	658	62286	643	4478	163	25768	125872
2 Mining	163	5562	2044	76342	82	19234	1202	−32792	71837
3 Construction	1383	2923	304	8706	7182	32058	4971	206809	264334
4 Manufacturing	26128	7261	98570	518309	29283	90180	3200	568803	1341733
5 Trade & Transportation	7514	1732	29238	89017	30999	27333	2289	326312	514435
6 Services	13546	10241	21711	105296	93930	196026	6460	673188	1120398
7 Other	59	109	195	7827	2235	6118	367	208475	225385
Total Industry Output	129663	78031	264334	1354983	510639	1079832	246512		

Industry / Commodity	Make Matrix: Industries by Commodities							Total Industry Output
	1	2	3	4	5	6	7	
1 Agriculture	125829	0	0	3720	15	100	0	129663
2 Mining	0	71311	0	4414	0	2307	0	78031
3 Construction	0	0	264334	0	0	0	0	264334
4 Manufacturing	9	441	0	1333361	0	18991	2182	1354983
5 Trade & Transportation	34	0	0	0	509271	1266	68	510639
6 Services	0	86	0	173	0	1079519	54	1079832
7 Other	0	0	0	66	5150	18215	223081	246512
Total Commodity Output	125872	71837	264334	1341733	514435	1120398	225385	

12	13	14	15	16	17	18	19	20	21	22	23
0	0	0	0	0	0	0	15	0	100	0	0
0	0	0	0	0	0	0	0	0	0	0	0
0	8	0	52	0	0	0	0	2307	0	0	0
0	174	0	0	0	0	0	0	0	0	0	0
0	0	0	0	0	0	0	0	0	0	0	0
60	0	76	22	3	0	15	0	0	1	0	27
177	53	25	43	8	8	137	0	0	1	0	54
87	82	210	75	79	45	105	0	0	3	0	23
437	28	273	204	145	7	346	0	0	18136	0	259
572	130	159	182	164	13	531	0	0	1	0	65
18	112	40	10	0	0	2	0	0	0	0	9
45134	99	214	243	74	120	139	0	0	1	0	0
88	33680	80	77	72	30	48	0	0	1	0	0
283	204	181938	1817	679	770	295	0	44	4	0	1005
150	41	1955	112302	1612	1549	453	0	0	3	0	151
119	63	1063	1796	84017	980	490	0	0	2	0	216
72	58	1847	1979	1149	168658	246	0	0	0	0	323
232	69	276	334	623	137	41560	0	0	793	0	49
0	0	0	0	0	0	0	509271	1264	2	0	68
0	0	0	0	0	0	0	0	105282	0	54	0
0	0	0	0	0	0	0	0	0	974237	0	0
0	25	0	0	0	0	0	5150	13559	4656	223081	0
0	0	0	0	0	0	0	0	0	0	0	0

| REFERENCES

RITZ, PHILIP. "The Input-Output Structure of the U.S. Economy: 1972." *Survey of Current Business* 59, no. 2 (February 1979): 34–72.

RITZ, PHILIP, EUGENE ROBERTS, and PAULA YOUNG. "Dollar Value Tables for the 1972 Input-Output Study." *Survey of Current Business* 59, no. 3 (April 1979): 51–72.

Survey of Current Business. "The Transactions Table of the 1958 Input-Output Study and Revised Direct and Total Requirements Data," 45, no. 9 (September 1965a): 33–56.

———. "Additional Industry Detail for the 1958 Input-Output Study," 45, no. 10 (October 1965b): 7–28.

———. "The Input-Output Structure of the U.S. Economy: 1963," 49, no. 11 (November 1969): 16–47.

———. "The Input-Output Structure of the U.S. Economy: 1967," 54, no. 2 (February 1974): 24–56.

———. "The Input-Output Structure of the U.S. Economy: 1977," 64, no. 5 (May 1984): 42–84.

U.S. DEPARTMENT OF COMMERCE. *Historical Statistics of the United States.* Washington, D.C.: U.S. Government Printing Office, 1975.

VACARRA, BEATRICE, ARLENE SHAPIRO, and NANCY SIMON. "The Input-Output Structure of the U.S. Economy: 1947." U.S. Department of Commerce, Office of Business Economics, March 1970. Mimeo.

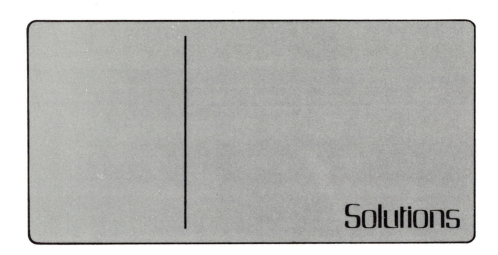

Solutions

Chapter 2

2-1

a Since $X = Zi + Y$, we find Y as $X - Zi$. Here $Y = \begin{bmatrix} 150 \\ 120 \end{bmatrix}$.

b **(1)** Here $A = Z(\hat{X})^{-1} = \begin{bmatrix} 0.500 & 0.438 \\ 0.320 & 0.450 \end{bmatrix}$. Using the first five terms in the power-series approximation to the Leontief inverse, with $Y^{new} = \begin{bmatrix} 200 \\ 100 \end{bmatrix}$, $X^{new} = (I + A + A^2 + A^3 + A^4)Y^{new} = Y^{new} + AY^{new} + A^2Y^{new} + A^3Y^{new} + A^4Y^{new} =$

$$\begin{bmatrix} 200 \\ 100 \end{bmatrix} + \begin{bmatrix} 144 \\ 109 \end{bmatrix} + \begin{bmatrix} 120 \\ 95 \end{bmatrix} + \begin{bmatrix} 101 \\ 81 \end{bmatrix} + \begin{bmatrix} 86 \\ 69 \end{bmatrix} = \begin{bmatrix} 651 \\ 454 \end{bmatrix}.$$

(2) The Leontief inverse for this problem is $(I - A)^{-1} = \begin{bmatrix} 4.074 & 3.241 \\ 2.370 & 3.704 \end{bmatrix}$. In conjunction with $Y^{new} = \begin{bmatrix} 200 \\ 100 \end{bmatrix}$, we find $X^{new} = \begin{bmatrix} 1139 \\ 844 \end{bmatrix}$.

2-2

a For this problem, $A = \begin{bmatrix} 0.35 & 0 & 0 \\ 0.05 & 0.5 & 0.15 \\ 0.20 & 0.3 & 0.55 \end{bmatrix}$ and so

$$(I - A)^{-1} = \begin{bmatrix} 1.538 & 0 & 0 \\ 0.449 & 2.500 & 0.833 \\ 0.983 & 1.667 & 2.778 \end{bmatrix}.$$

b Given $Y^{t+1} = \begin{bmatrix} 1300 \\ 100 \\ 200 \end{bmatrix}$, $X^{t+1} = \begin{bmatrix} 2000 \\ 1000 \\ 2000 \end{bmatrix}$.

c From year t data, $Y^t = \begin{bmatrix} 650 \\ 50 \\ 100 \end{bmatrix}$. Year $t + 1$ final demands are double those in year t, and similarly, outputs in year $t + 1$ are double those in year t. This illustrates the linearity in the input-output model. If all final demands are multiplied by a factor of k, all total outputs will also be multiplied by the same factor of k.

2-3   The transactions matrix for the model in problem 2-1, with households in-

cluded as sector 3, is $Z = \begin{bmatrix} 500 & 350 & 90 \\ 320 & 360 & 50 \\ 100 & 60 & 40 \end{bmatrix}$. In conjunction with $X = \begin{bmatrix} 1000 \\ 800 \\ 300 \end{bmatrix}$,

we find $A = \begin{bmatrix} 0.500 & 0.438 & 0.300 \\ 0.320 & 0.450 & 0.167 \\ 0.100 & 0.075 & 0.133 \end{bmatrix}$ and therefore $(I - A)^{-1}$

$= \begin{bmatrix} 5.820 & 5.036 & 2.983 \\ 3.686 & 5.057 & 2.248 \\ 0.990 & 1.019 & 1.693 \end{bmatrix}$. With the new final-demand vector $Y^{new} = \begin{bmatrix} 200 \\ 100 \\ 0 \end{bmatrix}$, we

find $X^{new} = \begin{bmatrix} 1668 \\ 1243 \\ 300 \end{bmatrix}$. In particular, $X_1^{new} = 1668$ and $X_2^{new} = 1243$. In the model

that was open with respect to households (problem 2-1), the same final demands generated on $X_1^{new} = 1139$ and $X_2^{new} = 844$. The increases in both X_1^{new} and X_2^{new} reflect the increased economic activity caused by including households in the model.

2-4

a $Z = \begin{bmatrix} 2.50 & 5.00 & 2.50 \\ 2.50 & 5.00 & 2.50 \\ 30.00 & 30.00 & 15.00 \end{bmatrix}$ and $Y = \begin{bmatrix} 35.00 \\ 40.00 \\ 25.00 \end{bmatrix}$, all in units of \$100,000. Therefore

$X = \begin{bmatrix} 50 \\ 50 \\ 100 \end{bmatrix}$ and $A = \begin{bmatrix} 0.050 & 0.200 & 0.025 \\ 0.050 & 0.100 & 0.025 \\ 0.600 & 0.600 & 0.150 \end{bmatrix}$.

To satisfy the Hawkins-Simon conditions in this three-sector example, we need to check that in $(I - A)$, (1) all three first-order principal minors are positive, (2) all three second-order principal minors are positive, and (3) the third-order principal minor, which is just the determinant of $(I - A)$, is also positive. Here these values are (1) 0.950, 0.900, and 0.850, (2) 0.845, 0.750, and 0.793, and (3) 0.68675. Thus the Hawkins-Simon conditions are satisfied, since all determinants are positive.

b $(I - A)^{-1} = \begin{bmatrix} 1.092 & 0.269 & 0.040 \\ 0.084 & 1.154 & 0.036 \\ 0.830 & 1.005 & 1.230 \end{bmatrix}$.

c   With $Y^{new} = \begin{bmatrix} 26.250 \\ 38.000 \\ 22.500 \end{bmatrix}$, $X^{new} = \begin{bmatrix} 39.805 \\ 46.868 \\ 87.652 \end{bmatrix}$.

d   Since $Z^{new} = A\hat{X}^{new}$, we find $Z^{new} = \begin{bmatrix} 1.990 & 9.374 & 2.191 \\ 1.990 & 4.687 & 2.191 \\ 23.883 & 28.121 & 13.148 \end{bmatrix}$. The value-

added vector is the difference between the column sums of Z^{new} and the elements in X^{new}. Here this is $[\, 11.942 \quad 4.687 \quad 70.122 \,]$. The intermediate output vector is

made up of the row sums of Z^{new}; here, this is $\begin{bmatrix} 13.555 \\ 8.868 \\ 65.152 \end{bmatrix}$.

2-5

a In millions of dollars, $Z = \begin{bmatrix} 2 & 8 \\ 6 & 4 \end{bmatrix}$.

b $A = \begin{bmatrix} 0.067 & 0.267 \\ 0.200 & 0.133 \end{bmatrix}$. Since $1 - a_{11} = 0.933$, $1 - a_{22} = 0.867$, and $|I - A| = 0.7556$, the Hawkins-Simon conditions are satisfied for this A matrix.

c $(I - A)^{-1} = \begin{bmatrix} 1.147 & 0.353 \\ 0.265 & 1.235 \end{bmatrix}$ and $Y^{new} = \begin{bmatrix} 15 \\ 18 \end{bmatrix}$, so $X^{new} = \begin{bmatrix} 23.559 \\ 26.206 \end{bmatrix}$. Interindustry activity needed to support this final demand is found as $Z^{new} = A\hat{X}^{new}$
$= \begin{bmatrix} 1.571 & 6.988 \\ 4.712 & 3.494 \end{bmatrix}$.

2-6

a The row vector of value-added elements is $\begin{bmatrix} 10 & 11 \end{bmatrix}$; the final-demand vector is $Y = \begin{bmatrix} 12 \\ 9 \end{bmatrix}$. $A = \begin{bmatrix} 0.300 & 0.133 \\ 0.200 & 0.133 \end{bmatrix}$; $1 - a_{11} = 0.7$, $1 - a_{22} = 0.867$, and $|I - A| = 0.580$, so the Hawkins-Simon conditions are met.

b For $r = 4$, $\tilde{X} = \begin{bmatrix} 19.795 \\ 14.846 \end{bmatrix}$; for $r = 5$, $\tilde{X} = \begin{bmatrix} 19.918 \\ 14.939 \end{bmatrix}$. Since $X = \begin{bmatrix} 20 \\ 15 \end{bmatrix}$, both values in $\tilde{X}$ are within 0.2 of the corresponding elements in X when $r = 5$.

c With $c_1 = 0.5c_2$ and $r = 5$, $C_r = 6.5c_2$; this is the cost of the round-by-round method. The cost using the inverse is $C_e + C_f = 21c_2$. Hence, in this case, the round-by-round method is cheaper.

d For the round-by-round method, the total cost would be $4C_r = 26c_2$. For the method that uses the Leontief inverse, the total cost would be $C_e + 4C_f = 24c_2$. In this case, the use of the exact inverse is cheaper.

e For the round-by-round method, the cost for m final-demand vectors will be $mC_r = 6.5mc_2$; for the method using the Leontief inverse, the cost will be $20c_2 + mc_2$. Equating these two total-cost expressions, $m = 3.636$; therefore, for $m < 4$, the round-by-round method is cheaper, and for $m \geq 4$, the exact method is cheaper.

2-7

a Consider partitioning $(I - A)$ as follows:

$$(I - A) = \left[\begin{array}{ccc|cc} 1.0 & -0.1 & -0.3 & -0.2 & -0.2 \\ -0.1 & 0.9 & -0.1 & 0 & 0 \\ \hline -0.2 & 0 & 0.9 & -0.3 & -0.1 \\ -0.3 & 0 & 0 & 0.9 & -0.3 \\ -0.3 & -0.2 & -0.1 & -0.1 & 0.8 \end{array} \right] = \left[\begin{array}{c|c} E & F \\ \hline G & H \end{array} \right]$$

Further, partition H as follows:

$$H = \left[\begin{array}{cc|c} 0.9 & -0.3 & -0.1 \\ 0 & 0.9 & -0.3 \\ \hline -0.1 & -0.1 & 0.8 \end{array} \right] = \left[\begin{array}{c|c} H_1 & H_2 \\ \hline H_3 & H_4 \end{array} \right]$$

Let $(I - A)^{-1} = \left[\begin{array}{c|c} S & T \\ \hline U & V \end{array} \right]$, where matrices in similar positions in $(I - A)$ and $(I - A)^{-1}$ have the same dimensions. From the results on the inverse of a partitioned matrix (section A-7 of Appendix A), we find that we need E^{-1} and H^{-1}, the inverses of a 2×2 and a 3×3 matrix. Therefore, to find H^{-1} we again use the results on the inverse of a partitioned matrix, where H is partitioned as above. This requires that H_1^{-1} and H_4^{-1} be found; since these are 2×2 and 1×1

matrices, respectively, this is easily done. Here, then,

$$H^{-1} = \begin{bmatrix} 1.144 & .415 & | & .299 \\ .050 & 1.177 & | & .448 \\ \hline .149 & .199 & | 1.343 \end{bmatrix}$$

This, in conjunction with E^{-1}, F, and G, allows us to find

$$S = \begin{bmatrix} 1.566 & .332 \\ .253 & 1.172 \end{bmatrix} \qquad T = \begin{bmatrix} .638 & .640 & .711 \\ .231 & .150 & .148 \end{bmatrix}$$

$$U = \begin{bmatrix} .708 & .217 \\ .802 & .270 \\ .839 & .478 \end{bmatrix} \qquad V = \begin{bmatrix} 1.441 & .707 & .622 \\ .388 & 1.509 & .815 \\ .525 & .554 & 1.733 \end{bmatrix}$$

and therefore

$$(I - A)^{-1} = \begin{bmatrix} 1.566 & .332 & | & .638 & .640 & .711 \\ .253 & 1.172 & | & .231 & .150 & .148 \\ \hline .708 & .217 & |1.441 & .707 & .622 \\ .802 & .270 & | & .388 & 1.509 & .815 \\ .839 & .478 & | & .525 & .554 & 1.733 \end{bmatrix}$$

b   In this problem we used the method of partitioning repeatedly on subpartitions of the original four partitions of $(I - A)$, sometimes called a recursive application of the method. We can in theory invert an infinitely large matrix by recursively partitioning it into smaller and smaller submatrices.

2-8

a   For this problem, we find that $A = \begin{bmatrix} 0.200 & 0.067 \\ 0.300 & 0.267 \end{bmatrix}$ and therefore that $(I - A)^{-1} = \begin{bmatrix} 1.294 & 0.118 \\ 0.529 & 1.412 \end{bmatrix}$. The new final-demand vector, reflecting the cutback in government spending, will be $Y^{new} = \begin{bmatrix} 49.50 \\ 156.75 \end{bmatrix}$ and hence $X^{new} = \begin{bmatrix} 82.50 \\ 247.50 \end{bmatrix}$.

b   Value added in the two sectors is $(100 - 50)$ and $(300 - 100)$, respectively. Therefore, the revenue from a value-added tax would be $(0.12)(50) + (0.14)(200) = \$34.00$. The money saved through decreased spending, as in part **a**, is $10.50 + 33.25 = \$43.75$. Therefore, the money saved through reduced government spending is more than the revenue gained through the value-added tax.

2-9

a   After arranging all the data properly, it can be found that

$$Z = \begin{bmatrix} 140 & 350 \\ 800 & 50 \end{bmatrix} \qquad Y = \begin{bmatrix} 510 \\ 150 \end{bmatrix} \qquad X = \begin{bmatrix} 1000 \\ 1000 \end{bmatrix}$$

and therefore $A = \begin{bmatrix} 0.14 & 0.35 \\ 0.80 & 0.05 \end{bmatrix}$.

b   Here $(I - A) = \begin{bmatrix} 0.86 & -0.35 \\ -0.80 & 0.95 \end{bmatrix}$. Therefore, $(1 - a_{11}) = 0.86 > 0$, $(1 - a_{22}) = 0.95 > 0$, and $|I - A| = 0.537 > 0$ and the Hawkins-Simon conditions are met.

c   Since $Y^{new} = \begin{bmatrix} 400 \\ 200 \end{bmatrix}$ and $(I - A)^{-1} = \begin{bmatrix} 1.769 & 0.652 \\ 1.490 & 1.601 \end{bmatrix}$, we find that $X^{new} = \begin{bmatrix} 838.0 \\ 916.2 \end{bmatrix}$.

d   The demand for sector 1 output also declined, from 510 to 400, and this caused a decrease in sector 1's use of sector 2's product as an input.

2-10   Since $Y = X - Zi$, we find here that $Y = \begin{bmatrix} 5 \\ 7 \\ 12 \end{bmatrix}$. $(I - A)$

$$= \begin{bmatrix} 0.864 & -0.444 & -0.194 \\ -0.091 & 0.778 & -0.161 \\ -0.318 & -0.167 & 0.710 \end{bmatrix}$$ and $|I - A| = 0.351 \ (\neq 0)$, so $(I - A)^{-1}$ exists.

Using the power-series approximation, after A^{11} we find $\tilde{X} = \begin{bmatrix} 21.846 \\ 17.900 \\ 30.819 \end{bmatrix}$; after

$A^{12}, \tilde{X} = \begin{bmatrix} 21.900 \\ 17.935 \\ 30.882 \end{bmatrix}$; and after $A^{13}, \tilde{X} = \begin{bmatrix} 21.934 \\ 17.957 \\ 30.923 \end{bmatrix}$. Since $X = \begin{bmatrix} 22 \\ 18 \\ 31 \end{bmatrix}$, the highest

power of A needed for all three elements in $\tilde{X}$ to be within 0.1 of their actual value is 13. After A^{11}, $\tilde{X}_2$ is within 0.1 of its true value, but $\tilde{X}_1$ and $\tilde{X}_3$ are not. After A^{12}, both $\tilde{X}_1$ and $\tilde{X}_2$ are within 0.1 of their true values, but $\tilde{X}_3$ still is not. Only after A^{13} are all three elements in $\tilde{X}$ within 0.1 of their true values.

2-11

a   For this problem, A is

.228	.179	.191	.074	.005	.025	.004	.022
.040	.155	.149	.086	.016	.033	.004	.013
.003	.001	.000	.010	.027	.001	.007	.002
.027	.023	.003	.223	.021	.020	.004	.014
.116	.099	.180	.066	.142	.155	.103	.092
.057	.001	.014	.030	.001	.073	.002	.042
.013	.000	.004	.000	.011	.000	.323	.165
.141	.042	.065	.026	.067	.039	.109	.288

and $(I - A)^{-1}$ is

1.339	.296	.312	.172	.034	.058	.030	.067
.089	1.214	.209	.153	.038	.057	.025	.051
.013	.009	1.011	.019	.034	.008	.018	.013
.065	.056	.034	1.306	.038	.041	.021	.041
.265	.215	.320	.174	1.207	.230	.229	.240
.100	.029	.045	.059	.011	1.089	.018	.074
.109	.049	.068	.035	.054	.030	1.547	.372
.321	.162	.210	.117	.135	.103	.269	1.506

b   The new final-demand vector (transposed to make it easier to present), is

$$[Y^{new}]' = [\,5192.2 \quad 25049.7 \quad 39348.0 \quad 22625.0 \quad 110056.8 \quad -653.0$$
$$8327.0 \quad 82996.0\,].$$

In conjunction with $(I - A)^{-1}$, found in part **a**, the new total-output vector, also transposed, is

$$[X^{new}]' = [\,39997.912 \quad 51180.823 \quad 45454.986 \quad 40403.944 \quad 177755.656$$
$$11181.953 \quad 54928.717 \quad 158686.876\,]$$

Chapter 3

3-1 Here $P = \begin{bmatrix} 0.60 \\ 0.90 \\ 0.75 \end{bmatrix}$; using the A matrix from problem 2-2, we find that $A^R = \hat{P}A$

$$= \begin{bmatrix} .210 & 0 & 0 \\ .045 & .450 & .135 \\ .150 & .225 & .413 \end{bmatrix}. \text{ Therefore } (I - A^R)^{-1} = \begin{bmatrix} 1.266 & 0 & 0 \\ .202 & 2.007 & .461 \\ .401 & .769 & 1.879 \end{bmatrix} \text{ and,}$$

with $Y^{new} = \begin{bmatrix} 1300 \\ 100 \\ 200 \end{bmatrix}$, $X^{new} = \begin{bmatrix} 1645.570 \\ 555.346 \\ 973.257 \end{bmatrix}$.

3-2 Here $A^{LL} = \begin{bmatrix} .110 & .130 \\ .164 & .026 \end{bmatrix}$, $A^{LM} = \begin{bmatrix} .056 & .070 \\ .130 & .070 \end{bmatrix}$, $A^{ML} = \begin{bmatrix} .137 & .156 \\ .192 & .182 \end{bmatrix}$, and

$A^{MM} = \begin{bmatrix} .093 & .125 \\ .093 & .078 \end{bmatrix}$, so that the full A matrix for the two-region interregional

model is $A = \begin{bmatrix} .110 & .130 & .056 & .070 \\ .164 & .026 & .130 & .070 \\ .137 & .156 & .093 & .125 \\ .192 & .182 & .093 & .078 \end{bmatrix}$ and

$$(I - A)^{-1} = \begin{bmatrix} 1.205 & .202 & .115 & .123 \\ .263 & 1.116 & .189 & .131 \\ .273 & .262 & 1.177 & .200 \\ .330 & .289 & .179 & 1.156 \end{bmatrix}. \text{ With } \Delta Y = \begin{bmatrix} 280 \\ 360 \\ 0 \\ 0 \end{bmatrix}, \text{ we find that}$$

$$\Delta X = \begin{bmatrix} 409.98 \\ 475.67 \\ 170.62 \\ 196.24 \end{bmatrix}.$$

3-3 Here $A^L = \begin{bmatrix} .364 & .385 \\ .545 & .077 \end{bmatrix}$, $A^M = \begin{bmatrix} .214 & .450 \\ .500 & .450 \end{bmatrix}$, $\hat{C}^{LL} = \begin{bmatrix} .417 & 0 \\ 0 & .500 \end{bmatrix}$, $\hat{C}^{LM}$

$= \begin{bmatrix} .462 & 0 \\ 0 & .615 \end{bmatrix}$, $\hat{C}^{ML} = \begin{bmatrix} .583 & 0 \\ 0 & .500 \end{bmatrix}$, and $\hat{C}^{MM} = \begin{bmatrix} .538 & 0 \\ 0 & .385 \end{bmatrix}$. Thus,

$$A = \begin{bmatrix} .364 & .385 & .000 & .000 \\ .545 & .077 & .000 & .000 \\ .000 & .000 & .214 & .450 \\ .000 & .000 & .500 & .450 \end{bmatrix}, \quad C = \begin{bmatrix} .417 & .000 & .462 & .000 \\ .000 & .500 & .000 & .615 \\ .583 & .000 & .538 & .000 \\ .000 & .500 & .000 & .385 \end{bmatrix},$$

and $(I - CA)^{-1}C = \begin{bmatrix} .971 & .566 & 1.024 & .524 \\ .882 & 1.197 & .889 & 1.251 \\ 1.297 & .714 & 1.264 & .677 \\ .663 & 1.010 & .673 & .854 \end{bmatrix}$. With $Y^{new} = \begin{bmatrix} 50 \\ 50 \\ 60 \\ 40 \end{bmatrix}$, we

find $X^{new} = (I - CA)^{-1}CY^{new} = \begin{bmatrix} 148.78 \\ 214.54 \\ 191.72 \\ 161.77 \end{bmatrix}$.

3-4

a $A^A = \begin{bmatrix} .333 & .333 \\ .167 & .333 \end{bmatrix}$, $A^B = \begin{bmatrix} .583 & .571 \\ .083 & .286 \end{bmatrix}$, $A^C = \begin{bmatrix} .50 & 0 \\ .25 & 0 \end{bmatrix}$.

b $A^N = \begin{bmatrix} .500 & .500 \\ .125 & .300 \end{bmatrix}$.

c Because we do not have origin-destination data on shipments of each good.

d Using A^N, $(I - A^N)^{-1} = \begin{bmatrix} 2.435 & 1.739 \\ 0.435 & 1.739 \end{bmatrix}$; with $Y^{new} = \begin{bmatrix} 5000 \\ 4500 \end{bmatrix}$, we find X^{new} $= \begin{bmatrix} 20000 \\ 10000 \end{bmatrix}$.

e The original gross outputs were $X = \begin{bmatrix} 2000 \\ 1000 \end{bmatrix}$. Also, the original final-demand vector was $Y = \begin{bmatrix} 500 \\ 450 \end{bmatrix}$. Thus, from the linearity of the input-output model, when final demands are multiplied by a factor of 10, gross outputs are also multiplied by a factor of 10.

3-5

a $Y^N = \begin{bmatrix} 1453353 \\ 111595 \\ 2186205 \end{bmatrix}$ and $Y^S = \begin{bmatrix} 1663741 \\ 76675 \\ 3612485 \end{bmatrix}$. $A^{NN} = \begin{bmatrix} .076 & .005 & .157 \\ 0 & .003 & .055 \\ .094 & .053 & .619 \end{bmatrix}$,

$A^{NS} = \begin{bmatrix} .002 & 0 & .012 \\ 0 & 0 & .002 \\ .012 & .005 & .107 \end{bmatrix}$, $A^{SN} = \begin{bmatrix} .002 & 0 & .009 \\ 0 & 0 & .001 \\ .020 & .011 & .185 \end{bmatrix}$,

and $A^{SS} = \begin{bmatrix} .069 & .005 & .116 \\ 0 & .005 & .046 \\ .086 & .048 & .580 \end{bmatrix}$.

b For this two-region interregional model, $A = \begin{bmatrix} A^{NN} & | & A^{NS} \\ --- & + & --- \\ A^{SN} & | & A^{SS} \end{bmatrix}$. Given the reduced total outputs in construction and manufacturing in the two regions, the new total-output vector (transposed) is

$[X^{new}]' = [\, 3633382 \quad 743965 \quad 10384473 \quad 3697202 \quad 766751 \quad 13004947 \,]$.

The corresponding final demands are found by subtracting the row sums of the new Z matrix from the new total outputs. That is, $Y^{new} = X^{new} - (AX^{new})$. Here, $[Y^{new}]' = [\, 1556842 \quad 144617 \quad 2132819 \quad 1835571 \quad 144444 \quad 3107061 \,]$; specifically, $Y^{N,new} = \begin{bmatrix} 1556842 \\ 144617 \\ 2132819 \end{bmatrix}$ and $Y^{S,new} = \begin{bmatrix} 1835571 \\ 144444 \\ 3107061 \end{bmatrix}$.

c $[Y^{new}]' = [\, 1453353 \quad 111595 \quad 1858274 \quad 1663741 \quad 76675 \quad 3612485 \,]$. Using the full two-region interregional model, we have $(I - A)^{-1}$ is

1.145	.038	.567	.028	.012	.188
.020	1.014	.180	.007	.004	.054
.348	.183	3.128	.124	.058	.875
.033	.016	.219	1.111	.024	.365
.011	.006	.075	.014	1.012	.135
.215	.112	1.500	.284	.147	2.868

and so $[X^{new}]' = [\, 3447445 \quad 684913 \quad 9875755 \quad 3625440 \quad 742265 \quad 13957983 \,]$. In particular, then, $[X^{N,new}] = \begin{bmatrix} 3447445 \\ 684913 \\ 9875755 \end{bmatrix}$.

d Using A^{NN} from part **a**, we find $(I - A^{NN})^{-1} = \begin{bmatrix} 1.131 & .031 & .468 \\ .016 & 1.011 & .152 \\ .282 & .149 & 2.760 \end{bmatrix}$.

In conjunction with $Y^{N,new} = \begin{bmatrix} 1453353 \\ 111595 \\ 1858274 \end{bmatrix}$, we find $X^{N,new} = \begin{bmatrix} 2517159 \\ 417336 \\ 5554462 \end{bmatrix}$. Com-

pared with the results in part **c**, we conclude that interregional linkages are very important in this economy. The outputs found using region N alone are 26, 39, and 44 percent below their values found using the full two-region interregional model.

3-6 With $[\Delta Y]' = [\Delta Y^E \mid \Delta Y^C \mid \Delta Y^S] =$

$$[0 \quad 0 \quad 0 \quad 0 \quad 0 \mid 0 \quad 0 \quad 0 \quad 0 \quad 0 \mid 0 \quad 0 \quad 100 \quad 50 \quad 25],$$

we find

$$\Delta X = [\,0.750 \quad 1.125 \quad 23.300 \quad 13.200 \quad 8.225 \mid 3.525 \quad 5.375 \quad 38.175$$

$$20.475 \quad 13.400 \mid 4.825 \quad 4.650 \quad 96.450 \quad 68.125 \quad 25.600\,]$$

3-7 With $[\Delta Y]' = [\Delta Y^C \mid \Delta Y^N \mid \Delta Y^S]$ as above, in problem 3-6, we find

$$\Delta X = [\,0.550 \quad 0 \quad 13.225 \quad 0.850 \quad 3.075 \mid 0.200 \quad 0 \quad 3.625 \quad 1.425$$

$$0.450 \mid 3.725 \quad 0.525 \quad 181.650 \quad 56.100 \quad 42.825\,]$$

Chapter 4

4-1 In each case, we want the column sums of the appropriate Leontief inverse.

Problem	Output Multipliers							
2-1	6.444	6.944						
2-2	2.970	4.167	3.611					
2-4	1.356	2.940	1.930					
2-5	1.412	1.588						
2-6	1.839	1.437						
2-7	4.168	2.470	3.223	3.559	4.030			
2-8	1.824	1.529						
2-9	3.259	2.253						
2-10	2.573	3.373	2.877					
2-11	2.301	2.031	2.209	2.035	1.551	1.616	2.156	2.364

4-2 Using problem 2-2 as an example, the row vector of output multipliers is $O = [\,2.970 \quad 4.167 \quad 3.611\,]$. In conjunction with the final-demand vector used in that problem, namely $Y^{t+1} = \begin{bmatrix} 1300 \\ 100 \\ 200 \end{bmatrix}$, we find $[O][Y^{t+1}] = 5000$. In the solution to problem 2-2, we had $X^{t+1} = \begin{bmatrix} 2000 \\ 1000 \\ 2000 \end{bmatrix}$, and the sum of these elements is 5000; that is, $i'X^{t+1} = 5000$.

4-3 Output multipliers for the three-sector model, closed with respect to households, are $O = [\,10.496 \quad 11.112 \quad 6.924\,]$. The type I income multipliers require that we have the labor-input coefficients, which are $a_{31} = 0.100$ and $a_{32} = 0.075$, along

with the Leontief inverse of the model that is open with respect to households. This
was $(I - A)^{-1} = \begin{bmatrix} 4.074 & 3.241 \\ 2.370 & 3.704 \end{bmatrix}$. Then $H_1 = (0.1)(4.074) + (0.075)(2.370) =$
0.5852 and $H_2 = (0.1)(3.241) + (0.075)(3.704) = 0.6019$ and $Y_1 = 0.5852/0.1 =$
5.852 and $Y_2 = 0.6019/0.075 = 8.205$. The type II income multipliers can be found
as the first two elements in the bottom row of the Leontief inverse of the model
closed with respect to households. These are $\overline{Y}_1 = 0.990$ and $\overline{Y}_2 = 1.019$. For both
sectors, the ratio of the type II to the type I multiplier is 1.69.

4-4   The larger effect is in sector 1. The difference, for \$100 in exogenous demand, is
\$29.50.

4-5

a   Concentrate on stimulating export demand for the product of sector 1; it has the
larger output multiplier.

b   Knowing $a_{31} = 0.1$ and $a_{32} = 0.18$, we can find $H_1 = 0.4451$ and $H_2 = 0.3534$.
Thus, converting output effects to income earned per dollar of new final demand
for each of the sectors does not change the ranking; stimulation of export demand
for the output of sector 1 is still more beneficial.

4-6

a $O^{LL} = [\,1.468 \quad 1.318\,]$ and $O^{MM} = [\,1.356 \quad 1.356\,]$.

b $O^L = [\,2.071 \quad 1.869\,]$ and $O^M = [\,1.660 \quad 1.610\,]$.

c $O^{\cdot L} = [\,1.478 \quad 0.593 \quad 0.464 \quad 1.405\,]$ and
$O^{\cdot M} = [\,1.292 \quad 0.368 \quad 0.323 \quad 1.287\,]$.

4-7

a   Sector 1 in region L; output multipliers for sectors 1 and 2 in region M are equal.

b   Sector 1 in region L.

c   In region L.

d   Still region L.

4-8

a $O^{LL} = [\,1.853 \quad 1.753\,]$ and $O^{MM} = [\,1.937 \quad 1.531\,]$.

b $O^L = [\,3.813 \quad 3.477\,]$ and $O^M = [\,3.850 \quad 3.306\,]$.

c $O^{\cdot L} = [\,2.268 \quad 1.545 \quad 1.270 \quad 2.207\,]$ and
$O^{\cdot M} = [\,2.288 \quad 1.562 \quad 1.201 \quad 2.105\,]$.

d   Sector 1 in region L; sector 2 in region M.

e   Sector 1 in region M.

f   In region L.

g   Still in region L.

4-9   We now want the Leontief inverse matrices for each of the three regions. These are
found to be: $(I - A^A)^{-1} = \begin{bmatrix} 1.714 & 0.857 \\ 0.429 & 1.714 \end{bmatrix}$, $(I - A^B)^{-1} = \begin{bmatrix} 1.667 & 2.286 \\ 0.333 & 2.857 \end{bmatrix}$, and
$(I - A^C)^{-1} = \begin{bmatrix} 1.0 & 0 \\ 0.5 & 2 \end{bmatrix}$. The largest column sum is associated with sector 2 in
region B; that is, with walnuts.

Chapter 5

5-1

a $X = Vi = \begin{bmatrix} 30 \\ 30 \end{bmatrix}$, $Q = (i'V)' = \begin{bmatrix} 20 \\ 30 \\ 10 \end{bmatrix}$, $W = X - i'U = [\,23 \quad 15\,]$, $E = X - Ui$

$= \begin{bmatrix} 12 \\ 21 \\ 5 \end{bmatrix}$, and $B = U(\hat{X})^{-1} = \begin{bmatrix} 0.100 & 0.167 \\ 0.067 & 0.233 \\ 0.067 & 0.100 \end{bmatrix}$.

b $\quad D = V(\hat{Q})^{-1} = \begin{bmatrix} 0.750 & 0.167 & 1 \\ 0.250 & 0.833 & 0 \end{bmatrix}; \; (I - DB)^{-1}D = \begin{bmatrix} 1.021 & 0.555 & 1.220 \\ 0.435 & 1.149 & 0.129 \end{bmatrix}.$

5-2

a $\quad B = U(\hat{X})^{-1} = \begin{bmatrix} 0.083 & 0.250 \\ 0.250 & 0.500 \end{bmatrix}.$

b $\quad D = V(\hat{Q})^{-1} = \begin{bmatrix} 1.0 & 0.2 \\ 0 & 0.8 \end{bmatrix}; \; C = V'(\hat{X})^{-1} = \begin{bmatrix} 0.833 & 0 \\ 0.167 & 1 \end{bmatrix}.$ Therefore,

$(I - DB)^{-1}D = \begin{bmatrix} 1.333 & 0.889 \\ 0.444 & 1.630 \end{bmatrix}$ and $(I - C^{-1}B)^{-1}C^{-1} = \begin{bmatrix} 1.412 & 0.706 \\ 0.235 & 2.118 \end{bmatrix}.$

Under an industry-based technology assumption, $\Delta X = \begin{bmatrix} 12.44 \\ 10.81 \end{bmatrix}$; under a com-

modity-based technology assumption, $\Delta X = \begin{bmatrix} 12 \\ 12 \end{bmatrix}.$ These are different because the
accounting of secondary production is different for each of the two assumptions.

5-3 Since V is nonsquare, C will be nonsquare and hence no unique C^{-1} exists. We
therefore cannot use the mixed-technology assumption requiring computation of
C^{-1}; that is, we cannot find $(I - C^{-1}B)^{-1}C^{-1}$ or $R(I - BR)^{-1}$ where $R = [C_1^{-1}(I - \langle D_2' \rangle) + D_2]$. We can use the industry-based technology assumption, as in

problem 5-1, with $T(I - BT)^{-1}$, where $T = \begin{bmatrix} 0.333 & 0.333 & 1.333 \\ 0.667 & 0.667 & -0.333 \end{bmatrix}$ and

$T(I - BT)^{-1} = \begin{bmatrix} 0.685 & 0.685 & 1.476 \\ 0.949 & 0.949 & -0.264 \end{bmatrix}.$

5-4 For $V_1 = \begin{bmatrix} 10 & 0 \\ 0 & 2 \end{bmatrix}$ and $V_2 = \begin{bmatrix} 0 & 2 \\ 0 & 6 \end{bmatrix}, \; X_1 = V_1 i = \begin{bmatrix} 10 \\ 2 \end{bmatrix}, \; Q = i'V = \begin{bmatrix} 10 \\ 10 \end{bmatrix}, \; C_1 = $

$V_1'(\hat{X}_1)^{-1} = \begin{bmatrix} 1 & 0 \\ 0 & 1 \end{bmatrix}, \; D_2 = V_2(\hat{Q})^{-1} = \begin{bmatrix} 0 & 0.2 \\ 0 & 0.6 \end{bmatrix}, \; C_1^{-1} = \begin{bmatrix} 1 & 0 \\ 0 & 1 \end{bmatrix},$

$R = C_1^{-1}(I - \langle D_2' \rangle) + D_2 = \begin{bmatrix} 1 & 0.2 \\ 0 & 0.8 \end{bmatrix}, \; R(I - BR)^{-1} = \begin{bmatrix} 1.333 & 0.889 \\ 0.444 & 1.630 \end{bmatrix}, \; Q_1 = $

$i'V_1 = \begin{bmatrix} 10 \\ 2 \end{bmatrix}, \; D_1 = V_1(\hat{Q}_1)^{-1} = \begin{bmatrix} 1 & 0 \\ 0 & 1 \end{bmatrix}, \; C_2 = V_2'(\hat{X})^{-1} = \begin{bmatrix} 0 & 0 \\ 0.167 & 0.750 \end{bmatrix},$

$T = (I + D_1 C_2 - \langle C_2' i \rangle)^{-1}D_1 = \begin{bmatrix} 1.2 & 0 \\ -0.2 & 1 \end{bmatrix}, \; T(I - BT)^{-1} = \begin{bmatrix} 1.412 & 0.706 \\ 0.235 & 2.118 \end{bmatrix}.$

5-5

Run Number			X′						X′i
1	2.31	1.84	1.12	1.60	2.88	1.43	2.26	2.82	16.26
2	2.48	3.33	1.13	1.61	2.87	2.28	2.87		16.56
3	4.85	3.14	1.15	1.58	2.20	2.62			15.54
4	4.78	3.11	3.86	1.58	2.29				15.62
5	4.73	5.51	3.91	1.57					15.72
6	6.15	5.44	3.94						15.53

5-6 $\quad S = \begin{bmatrix} 1 & 1 & 0 & 0 & 0 & 0 & 0 \\ 0 & 0 & 1 & 1 & 0 & 0 & 0 \\ 0 & 0 & 0 & 0 & 1 & 1 & 1 \end{bmatrix}; \; Z^* = SZS' = \begin{bmatrix} 29086 & 67789 & 9749 \\ 16303 & 379950 & 97181 \\ 19091 & 144757 & 225286 \end{bmatrix}$

$X^* = SX = \begin{bmatrix} 110345 \\ 915984 \\ 1076080 \end{bmatrix}; \quad A^* = Z^*(\hat{X}^*)^{-1} = \begin{bmatrix} .264 & .074 & .009 \\ .148 & .415 & .090 \\ .173 & .158 & .209 \end{bmatrix}$

$$(I - A^*)^{-1} = \begin{bmatrix} 1.404 & .188 & .038 \\ .415 & 1.819 & .212 \\ .390 & .405 & 1.315 \end{bmatrix}; \qquad \tilde{X}^* = \begin{bmatrix} 701.6 \\ 702.4 \\ 702.1 \end{bmatrix}$$

$$\tilde{X} = (I - A)^{-1} \Delta Y = \begin{bmatrix} 184.5 \\ 123.1 \\ 117.2 \\ 372.2 \\ 165.1 \\ 262.7 \\ 111.0 \end{bmatrix}$$

$$F = (A^*S - SA)\Delta Y = \begin{bmatrix} 19.030 \\ 12.380 \\ 7.597 \end{bmatrix}$$

$$i'F = 39.007$$

$$T = \tilde{X}^* - S\tilde{X} = \begin{bmatrix} 394.0 \\ 213.0 \\ 163.2 \end{bmatrix}$$

$$i'T = 770.2$$

5-7

$$B = U(\hat{X})^{-1} = \begin{bmatrix} .314 & .000 & .002 & .053 & .000 & .005 & .000 \\ .002 & .054 & .008 & .029 & .000 & .010 & .002 \\ .007 & .028 & .000 & .004 & .011 & .027 & .017 \\ .142 & .091 & .352 & .374 & .039 & .077 & .007 \\ .052 & .024 & .103 & .064 & .056 & .022 & .007 \\ .100 & .177 & .076 & .081 & .164 & .193 & .025 \\ .000 & .004 & .001 & .006 & .005 & .007 & .000 \end{bmatrix}$$

$$D = V(\hat{Q})^{-1} = \begin{bmatrix} 1.000 & .000 & .000 & .003 & .000 & .000 & .000 \\ .000 & .993 & .000 & .002 & .000 & .000 & .000 \\ .000 & .000 & 1.000 & .000 & .000 & .000 & .000 \\ .000 & .006 & .000 & .995 & .000 & .021 & .010 \\ .000 & .000 & .000 & .000 & .987 & .000 & .000 \\ .000 & .001 & .000 & .000 & .000 & .965 & .000 \\ .000 & .000 & .000 & .000 & .013 & .013 & .990 \end{bmatrix}$$

$$C = V'(\hat{X})^{-1} = \begin{bmatrix} .968 & .000 & .000 & .000 & .000 & .000 & .000 \\ .000 & .950 & .000 & .000 & .000 & .000 & .000 \\ .000 & .000 & 1.000 & .000 & .000 & .000 & .000 \\ .030 & .040 & .000 & .980 & .000 & .000 & .000 \\ .001 & .000 & .000 & .000 & 1.000 & .000 & .024 \\ .001 & .010 & .000 & .018 & .000 & 1.000 & .054 \\ .000 & .000 & .000 & .002 & .000 & .000 & .922 \end{bmatrix}$$

$$C^{-1} = \begin{bmatrix} 1.033 & .000 & .000 & .000 & .000 & .000 & .000 \\ .000 & 1.053 & .000 & .000 & .000 & .000 & .000 \\ .000 & .000 & 1.000 & .000 & .000 & .000 & .000 \\ -.032 & -.043 & .000 & 1.020 & .000 & .000 & .000 \\ -.001 & .000 & .000 & .000 & 1.000 & .000 & -.026 \\ .000 & -.010 & .000 & -.018 & .000 & 1.000 & -.059 \\ .000 & .000 & .000 & -.002 & .000 & .000 & 1.085 \end{bmatrix}$$

$$\alpha = (I - DB)^{-1}D = \begin{bmatrix} 1.491 & .021 & .055 & .139 & .012 & .027 & .004 \\ .018 & 1.060 & .031 & .057 & .006 & .021 & .004 \\ .021 & .039 & 1.011 & .017 & .019 & .036 & .019 \\ .396 & .234 & .623 & 1.678 & .115 & .227 & .046 \\ .116 & .054 & .159 & .129 & 1.061 & .050 & .014 \\ .244 & .263 & .195 & .217 & .223 & 1.228 & .040 \\ .010 & .012 & .011 & .017 & .024 & .027 & .992 \end{bmatrix}$$

$$\beta = (I - C^{-1}B)^{-1}C^{-1} = \begin{bmatrix} 1.558 & .015 & .055 & .141 & .011 & .025 & .001 \\ .017 & 1.125 & .032 & .058 & .006 & .021 & .003 \\ .021 & .040 & 1.011 & .017 & .019 & .037 & .017 \\ .340 & .156 & .636 & 1.725 & .112 & .193 & .018 \\ .116 & .050 & .162 & .133 & 1.076 & .049 & -.017 \\ .247 & .261 & .191 & .192 & .231 & 1.274 & -.038 \\ .004 & .008 & .006 & .010 & .008 & .010 & 1.085 \end{bmatrix}$$

$$\text{MAD} = \frac{1}{49} \sum_{i=1}^{7} \sum_{j=1}^{7} |\alpha_{ij} - \beta_{ij}| = .0161$$

Chapter 6

6-1

a (1) $\tilde{Q} = \begin{bmatrix} 0 & 0 & 0 \\ 0 & .708 & 0 \end{bmatrix}$, (2) $D = \begin{bmatrix} 0 & .667 & 0 \\ .050 & .033 & .050 \end{bmatrix}$, (3) $\varepsilon = D(I - A)^{-1}$

$+ \tilde{Q} = \begin{bmatrix} .077 & .769 & .077 \\ .058 & .785 & .115 \end{bmatrix}$. Since there is only one primary energy sector (oil) in

this problem, and the secondary energy sector (refined petroleum) receives all its energy input from oil, the rows of total energy coefficients should be identical in order to satisfy the conditions of energy conservation. They are not, in ε, in this example, illustrating one of the weaknesses of Method I for computing total energy coefficients.

b Here $X^* = \begin{bmatrix} 20 \\ 20 \\ 20 \end{bmatrix}$ and $F^* = \begin{bmatrix} 20 & 0 & 0 \\ 0 & 20 & 0 \end{bmatrix}$. We find $A^* = \begin{bmatrix} 0 & 1 & 0 \\ .05 & .05 & .05 \\ 0 & 0 & 0 \end{bmatrix}$ and

$(I - A^*)^{-1} = \begin{bmatrix} 1.056 & 1.111 & .056 \\ .056 & 1.111 & .056 \\ 0 & 0 & 1.0 \end{bmatrix}$. $\alpha = \hat{F}^*(\hat{X}^*)^{-1}(I - A^*)^{-1}$

$= \begin{bmatrix} 1.056 & 1.111 & .056 \\ .056 & 1.111 & .056 \end{bmatrix}$; yes, this model does obey the conditions of energy conservation.

6-2

a Here $(I - A)^{-1} = \begin{bmatrix} 1.02 & .04 \\ .07 & 1.09 \end{bmatrix}$ and $D = \begin{bmatrix} .2 & .3 \\ .1 & .4 \end{bmatrix}$, so the total energy require-

ments matrix is found as $\varepsilon = D(I - A)^{-1} = \begin{bmatrix} .22 & .34 \\ .13 & .44 \end{bmatrix}$.

b $\Delta Y = \begin{bmatrix} 106 \\ 14 \end{bmatrix}$, so the net increase in energy requirements is given by

$\varepsilon[\Delta Y] = \begin{bmatrix} 28.08 \\ 19.94 \end{bmatrix}$. The direct energy requirements are given by $D[\Delta Y] = \begin{bmatrix} 25.40 \\ 16.20 \end{bmatrix}$;

the indirect energy requirements are therefore $\begin{bmatrix} 28.08 \\ 19.94 \end{bmatrix} - \begin{bmatrix} 25.40 \\ 16.20 \end{bmatrix} = \begin{bmatrix} 2.68 \\ 3.74 \end{bmatrix}$.

c With $D = \begin{bmatrix} .2 & .3 \\ .1 & .3 \end{bmatrix}$, we find $\varepsilon = \begin{bmatrix} .22 & .34 \\ .12 & .33 \end{bmatrix}$. Direct energy requirements are

now $D[\Delta Y] = \begin{bmatrix} 25.40 \\ 14.80 \end{bmatrix}$, so the change from the direct requirements found in part

b is $\begin{bmatrix} 0 \\ 1.4 \end{bmatrix}$. Similarly, total energy requirements associated with the same final

demand are $\varepsilon[\Delta Y] = \begin{bmatrix} 28.08 \\ 17.34 \end{bmatrix}$, and the difference from the part **b** result is $\begin{bmatrix} 0 \\ 2.6 \end{bmatrix}$.

6-3

a $E = \begin{bmatrix} 12 & 4 & 25 \\ 15 & 2 & 7 \end{bmatrix}$.

b $D = E(\hat{X})^{-1} = \begin{bmatrix} 1.2 & .2 & 2.5 \\ 1.5 & .1 & .7 \end{bmatrix}$, since $X = \begin{bmatrix} 10 \\ 20 \\ 10 \end{bmatrix}$.

c $\varepsilon = D(I - A)^{-1} + \tilde{Q} = \begin{bmatrix} 4.52 & 2.53 & 4.69 \\ 3.53 & 1.71 & 2.12 \end{bmatrix}$ and with $Y = \begin{bmatrix} 2 \\ 14 \\ 18 \end{bmatrix}$, we find X

$= \begin{bmatrix} 128.90 \\ 69.21 \end{bmatrix}$.

6-4

a $\alpha \hat{X}^* = \alpha Z^* + \hat{F}^*$ and $Z^* = A^* \hat{X}^*$, so $\alpha \hat{X}^* = \alpha A^* \hat{X}^* + \hat{F}^*$. Rearranging, $\alpha(I - A^*)\hat{X}^* = \hat{F}^*$ or $\alpha = F^*(\hat{X}^*)^{-1}(I - A^*)^{-1}$.

b The first matrix satisfies the energy conservation conditions, since $\alpha_{\text{ref. pet}} + \alpha_{\text{elec.}} = \alpha_{\text{crude}} = [.6 \quad .5 \quad .3]$. The second matrix does not satisfy the energy conservation conditions, since $\alpha_{\text{ref. pet.}} + \alpha_{\text{elec.}} = [.6 \quad .2 \quad .2] \neq \alpha_{\text{crude}}$.

6-5

a $F = Ei + E_y = \begin{bmatrix} 40 \\ 40 \end{bmatrix}$.

b Here $A = \begin{bmatrix} 0 & .25 & 0 \\ .5 & .13 & .25 \\ 0 & 0 & 0 \end{bmatrix}$ and $(I - A)^{-1} = \begin{bmatrix} 1.17 & .33 & .08 \\ .67 & 1.33 & .33 \\ 0 & 0 & 1 \end{bmatrix}$. Also, $D = E(\hat{X})^{-1} = \begin{bmatrix} 0 & 1 & 0 \\ .5 & .13 & .75 \end{bmatrix}$ and $\tilde{Q} = \begin{bmatrix} 0 & 0 & 0 \\ 0 & 4.6 & 0 \end{bmatrix}$, so $\varepsilon = D(I - A)^{-1} + \tilde{Q}$

$= \begin{bmatrix} .67 & 1.33 & .33 \\ .67 & 4.83 & .83 \end{bmatrix}$. For the hybrid units calculations, $Z^* = \begin{bmatrix} 0 & 40 & 0 \\ 5 & 5 & 15 \\ 0 & 0 & 0 \end{bmatrix}$,

$X^* = \begin{bmatrix} 40 \\ 40 \\ 20 \end{bmatrix}$, $A^* = \begin{bmatrix} 0 & 1 & 0 \\ .13 & .13 & .75 \\ 0 & 0 & 0 \end{bmatrix}$, and $F^* = \begin{bmatrix} 40 & 0 & 0 \\ 0 & 40 & 0 \end{bmatrix}$, so $\alpha = \hat{F}^*(\hat{X}^*)^{-1}(I - A^*)^{-1} = \begin{bmatrix} 1.167 & 1.333 & 1.0 \\ .167 & 1.333 & 1.0 \end{bmatrix}$.

Chapter 7

7-1

a $A = \begin{bmatrix} .1 & .3 \\ .5 & .1 \end{bmatrix}$ and so $(I - A)^{-1} = \begin{bmatrix} 1.364 & .455 \\ .758 & 1.364 \end{bmatrix}$. Forming $D = \begin{bmatrix} u \\ v \\ w \end{bmatrix}$, we find

$D(I - A)^{-1} = \begin{bmatrix} .288 & .318 \\ .576 & .636 \\ .652 & .773 \\ .500 & .500 \\ .652 & .773 \end{bmatrix}$. The four candidate projects are represented by the

following final-demand change vectors: $\Delta Y = \begin{matrix} & \text{Projects} \\ & \begin{matrix} 1 & 2 & 3 & 4 \end{matrix} \\ & \begin{bmatrix} 3 & 4.5 & 6 & 3 \\ 3 & 5.0 & 4 & 7 \end{bmatrix} \end{matrix}$. Total allo-

cated budget is given by $i'[\Delta Y] = [6 \quad 9.5 \quad 10 \quad 10]$; that is, all four candidate projects satisfy the budget constraint. Then $\Delta X^* = D(I - A)^{-1}\Delta Y$

$$= \begin{bmatrix} 1.8 & 3.0 & 3.0 & 3.1 \\ 3.6 & 6.1 & 6.0 & 6.2 \\ 4.3 & 7.2 & 7.0 & 7.4 \\ 3.0 & 5.0 & 5.0 & 5.0 \\ 4.3 & 7.2 & 7.0 & 7.4 \end{bmatrix}.$$ Project 4, using 3.1×10^{15} Btus of oil, exceeds the 3.0

limit.

b Project 2 should be chosen, since it maximizes employment, among the three feasible projects (from the bottom row of ΔX^*).

7-2 Parts **a**, **b**, and **c** of this question can be answered simultaneously by finding $X^* = D(I - A)^{-1}Y^{new}$. Here $A = \begin{bmatrix} .1 & .2 \\ .3 & .4 \end{bmatrix}$ and $(I - A)^{-1} = \begin{bmatrix} 1.250 & .417 \\ .625 & 1.875 \end{bmatrix}$.

Following the same order in D as in the text in Table 7-2, we can form D as D

$$= \begin{bmatrix} .050 & .200 \\ .100 & 0 \\ \hline 3 & 5 \\ 1 & 2 \\ \hline .002 & .002 \end{bmatrix}.$$ (It should be clear that one could list first the emissions, then the

energy consumption, then employment; any other order would be equally accept-

able.) In the present case, $X^* = \begin{bmatrix} 12.708 \\ 2.917 \\ 368.750 \\ 141.667 \\ .171 \end{bmatrix}$. That is, $u^* = \begin{bmatrix} 12.708 \\ 2.917 \end{bmatrix}$ represents

12,708,000 tons of coal and 2,917,000 barrels of oil that will be consumed in production next year; $v^* = \begin{bmatrix} 368.750 \\ 141.667 \end{bmatrix}$ indicates that 368,750,000 pounds of SO_2 and 141,667,000 pounds of NO_x will be emitted because of that production; and $w^* = [0.171]$ represents the fact that 171,000 workers will be employed. Total output is found as $X^{new} = (I - A)^{-1}Y^{new} = \begin{bmatrix} 29.167 \\ 56.250 \end{bmatrix}$; that is, $X_1^{new} = \$29,167,000$ and $X_2^{new} = \$56,250,000$.

7-3 $(I - A)^{-1} = \begin{bmatrix} 1.247 & .598 & .839 \\ .857 & 2.494 & 1.665 \\ 0 & 0 & 1.110 \end{bmatrix}$, $D = \begin{bmatrix} 4.20 & 7.00 & 9.10 \\ 7.60 & 2.60 & 0.50 \\ .73 & .33 & .63 \end{bmatrix}$, and ΔY

$$= \begin{bmatrix} 2 & 4 & 2 & 2 \\ 2 & 0 & 0 & 2 \\ 2 & 2 & 4 & 3 \end{bmatrix},$$ with, as usual, one column in ΔY for each of the projects.

a Then $\Delta X^* = D(I - A)^{-1}\Delta Y = \begin{bmatrix} 112.986 & 95.527 & 123.618 & 138.270 \\ 67.980 & 69.341 & 68.440 & 79.236 \\ 8.628 & 8.496 & 9.832 & 10.490 \end{bmatrix}$. Then

Project 4 contributes most to gross regional product, since $i'[\Delta Y] = [6 \quad 6 \quad 6 \quad 7]$.

b Project 4 also consumes the most energy (79.236×10^6 bbls of oil).

c Project 4 also contributes the most to regional employment (10.490×10^6 workers).

7-4 From problem 2-9, $A = \begin{bmatrix} .14 & .35 \\ .80 & .05 \end{bmatrix}$. Let $D = \begin{bmatrix} v \\ \hline w \end{bmatrix} = \begin{bmatrix} .3 & .5 \\ \hline .005 & .070 \end{bmatrix}$. Then

$D(I - A)^{-1} = \begin{bmatrix} 1.276 & .996 \\ .113 & .115 \end{bmatrix}$. Therefore, for $Y^{new} = \begin{bmatrix} 1 \\ 0 \end{bmatrix}$, $X^* = \begin{bmatrix} 1.276 \\ .113 \end{bmatrix}$, meaning that for each new dollar's worth of final demand for the output of sector 1, there will be 1.276 pounds of pollutant emitted and 0.113 new workers. Similarly, with $Y^{new} = \begin{bmatrix} 0 \\ 1 \end{bmatrix}$, we find $X^* = \begin{bmatrix} .996 \\ \hline .115 \end{bmatrix}$, meaning that for each new dollar's worth of final demand for the output of sector 2, there will be 0.996 pounds of pollutant emitted and 0.115 new workers. Thus, there would not be a conflict between unions and environmentalists; each dollar's worth of new demand for sector 2 generates less pollution and also generates more employment (notice that this is true despite the fact that sector 2's direct-pollution coefficient per dollar of output is larger than sector 1's direct-pollution coefficient).

Chapter 8

8-1

a

	Lilliput (L)	Brobdingnag (B)	Houyhnhnm (H)
Value Added (W)	[15 7]	[27 6]	[77.14 46.03]
Intermediate Inputs (V)	[5 8]	[8 9]	[22.86 68.97]
Final Demands (Y)	$\begin{bmatrix} 13 \\ 9 \end{bmatrix}$	$\begin{bmatrix} 24 \\ 9 \end{bmatrix}$	$\begin{bmatrix} 49.33 \\ 73.84 \end{bmatrix}$
Intermediate Outputs (U)	$\begin{bmatrix} 7 \\ 6 \end{bmatrix}$	$\begin{bmatrix} 11 \\ 6 \end{bmatrix}$	$\begin{bmatrix} 50.67 \\ 41.16 \end{bmatrix}$

b The true technical coefficients matrices are: $A^L = \begin{bmatrix} .050 & .400 \\ .200 & .133 \end{bmatrix}$ and $A^B = \begin{bmatrix} .200 & .267 \\ .029 & .313 \end{bmatrix}$. After three RAS iterations, the L estimate of the A^B matrix is $^L A^B = \begin{bmatrix} .086 & .532 \\ .141 & .073 \end{bmatrix}$; the mean absolute deviation (MAD) between $^L A^B$ and A^B is 0.188. Similarly, after two RAS iterations, the B estimate of A^L is $^B A^L = \begin{bmatrix} .208 & .194 \\ .042 & .339 \end{bmatrix}$, with a MAD of 0.182. Therefore, the Brobdingnagian economist does slightly better.

c The two Houyhnhnm estimates are $^H A^L = \begin{bmatrix} .208 & .194 \\ .042 & .339 \end{bmatrix}$ and $^H A^B = \begin{bmatrix} .200 & .207 \\ .029 & .313 \end{bmatrix}$, after two iterations and no iterations of the RAS procedure, respectively (since $A^H = A^B$). The error, as measured by MAD, is 0.182 in the first case and 0.0 in the second case.

d The true impact is found from $\Delta X^L = (I - A^L)^{-1} \begin{bmatrix} 100 \\ 150 \end{bmatrix} = \begin{bmatrix} 1.166 & .538 \\ .219 & 1.278 \end{bmatrix} \times \begin{bmatrix} 100 \\ 150 \end{bmatrix} = \begin{bmatrix} 197.3 \\ 218.6 \end{bmatrix}$. The estimate provided from $(I - {}^H A^L)^{-1} = \begin{bmatrix} 1.283 & .377 \\ .081 & 1.537 \end{bmatrix}$, in conjunction with the same new final-demand vector, is $\Delta^H X^L = \begin{bmatrix} 184.9 \\ 238.6 \end{bmatrix}$. The mean absolute deviation between these two vectors is $\frac{1}{2}(12.4 + 20.0) = 16.20$.

8-2

a

	Lilliput (L)	Brobdingnag (B)	Houyhnhnm (H)
Value Added (W)	[11 6 4]	[21 4 14]	[60.5 33.0 22.0]
Intermediate Inputs (V)	[9 9 8]	[14 11 16]	[49.5 49.5 44.0]
Final Demands (Y)	$\begin{bmatrix} 7 \\ 8 \\ 6 \end{bmatrix}$	$\begin{bmatrix} 16 \\ 8 \\ 15 \end{bmatrix}$	$\begin{bmatrix} 38.5 \\ 44.0 \\ 33.0 \end{bmatrix}$
Intermediate Outputs (U)	$\begin{bmatrix} 13 \\ 7 \\ 6 \end{bmatrix}$	$\begin{bmatrix} 19 \\ 7 \\ 15 \end{bmatrix}$	$\begin{bmatrix} 71.5 \\ 38.5 \\ 33.0 \end{bmatrix}$

b   For these three-sector economies we find

$$A^L = \begin{bmatrix} .050 & .400 & .500 \\ .200 & .133 & .083 \\ .200 & .067 & .083 \end{bmatrix} \quad \text{and} \quad A^B = \begin{bmatrix} .200 & .267 & .267 \\ .029 & .333 & .033 \\ .171 & .133 & .233 \end{bmatrix}$$

Similarly, after three RAS iterations in each case, we find

$$^B A^L = \begin{bmatrix} .265 & .201 & .396 \\ .051 & .340 & .067 \\ .134 & .059 & .205 \end{bmatrix} \quad \text{and} \quad ^L A^B = \begin{bmatrix} .034 & .462 & .366 \\ .106 & .122 & .048 \\ .261 & .150 & .119 \end{bmatrix}$$

The mean absolute deviation for the L estimate of B is 0.109, while the MAD for the B estimate of L is 0.121.

c   The two Houyhnhnm estimates are $^H A^L = \begin{bmatrix} .050 & .400 & .500 \\ .200 & .133 & .083 \\ .200 & .067 & .083 \end{bmatrix}$ and $^H A^B$

$= \begin{bmatrix} .034 & .462 & .366 \\ .106 & .122 & .048 \\ .261 & .150 & .119 \end{bmatrix}$, after no and three iterations, respectively. (Note in this

case that $A^H = A^L$.) The error, as measured by MAD, is 0.0 in the first case and 0.109 in the second case.

8-3

a   The cost of (1), using the exact inverse, is $c_1 + c_2$; with $c_2 = 10c_1$, this cost is $11c_1$. With $m = 4$, the cost of using the round-by-round approximation, method (2), is $4c_1$. Thus use method (2), the round-by-round approximation, in this case.

b   Since the RAS procedure converges to within a tolerance of 0.01 in two iterations, the cost of the RAS estimate of region 2's coefficients matrix is $2c_1$. Then utilizing it in a round-by-round application, with $m = 4$, gives a total cost of $6c_1$.

c

RAS Tolerance	Number of Iterations	RAS Cost	Impact Analysis Cost	Total Cost
0.01	2	$2c_1$	$4c_1$	$6c_1$
0.001	2	$2c_1$	$4c_1$	$6c_1$
0.0001	3	$3c_1$	$4c_1$	$7c_1$
0.00001	3	$3c_1$	$4c_1$	$7c_1$
0.000001	4	$4c_1$	$4c_1$	$8c_1$

Therefore, the maximum affordable tolerance is 0.00001.

Chapter 9

9-1 The $\vec{A}$ and $(I - \vec{A})^{-1}$ matrices for each of the years 1947, 1958, 1963, 1967, 1972, and 1977 are shown below. The row sums of each $(I - \vec{A})^{-1}$ matrix are given in the Total Forward Linkages table in the answer to problem 9-2, below. The column sums of the $(I - \vec{A})^{-1}$ are shown here, with each of the tables.

1947

$$\vec{A}$$

$$\begin{bmatrix} .315 & .000 & .002 & .511 & .000 & .044 & .000 \\ .005 & .078 & .027 & .636 & .049 & .071 & .002 \\ .019 & .001 & .000 & .017 & .051 & .143 & .017 \\ .022 & .005 & .056 & .357 & .024 & .044 & .003 \\ .034 & .005 & .051 & .140 & .047 & .058 & .005 \\ .037 & .012 & .023 & .102 & .122 & .136 & .002 \\ .001 & .002 & .008 & .505 & .196 & .474 & .001 \end{bmatrix}$$

$$(I - \vec{A})^{-1}$$

$$\begin{bmatrix} 1.514 & .009 & .081 & 1.258 & .059 & .162 & .007 \\ .065 & 1.094 & .107 & 1.199 & .118 & .184 & .010 \\ .048 & .004 & 1.017 & .134 & .087 & .194 & .019 \\ .066 & .011 & .100 & 1.659 & .064 & .113 & .008 \\ .073 & .009 & .076 & .327 & 1.078 & .111 & .008 \\ .085 & .019 & .055 & .320 & .168 & 1.203 & .006 \\ .090 & .018 & .100 & 1.059 & .325 & .652 & 1.010 \end{bmatrix}$$

$$[\,1.941 \quad 1.163 \quad 1.535 \quad 5.957 \quad 1.899 \quad 2.620 \quad 1.067\,]$$

1958

$$\vec{A}$$

$$\begin{bmatrix} .285 & .000 & .005 & .483 & .004 & .044 & .012 \\ .006 & .060 & .041 & .729 & .002 & .104 & .008 \\ .009 & .000 & .000 & .011 & .029 & .113 & .017 \\ .017 & .004 & .075 & .373 & .023 & .066 & .004 \\ .022 & .007 & .065 & .169 & .039 & .063 & .008 \\ .022 & .013 & .021 & .106 & .105 & .153 & .004 \\ .001 & .013 & .010 & .192 & .218 & .480 & .001 \end{bmatrix}$$

$$(I - \vec{A})^{-1}$$

$$\begin{bmatrix} 1.437 & .009 & .104 & 1.176 & .064 & .201 & .026 \\ .054 & 1.074 & .159 & 1.366 & .074 & .280 & .020 \\ .021 & .003 & 1.014 & .085 & .055 & .159 & .019 \\ .050 & .010 & .136 & 1.696 & .065 & .166 & .012 \\ .047 & .011 & .101 & .366 & 1.070 & .132 & .013 \\ .051 & .020 & .061 & .314 & .146 & 1.234 & .010 \\ .047 & .028 & .090 & .576 & .317 & .660 & 1.011 \end{bmatrix}$$

$$[\,1.706 \quad 1.156 \quad 1.665 \quad 5.580 \quad 1.792 \quad 2.831 \quad 1.111\,]$$

1963

$$\vec{A}$$

$$
\begin{bmatrix}
.300 & .000 & .006 & .472 & .005 & .049 & .011 \\
.006 & .054 & .036 & .713 & .002 & .133 & .009 \\
.007 & .005 & .000 & .016 & .018 & .112 & .016 \\
.017 & .004 & .069 & .390 & .022 & .048 & .004 \\
.017 & .005 & .061 & .152 & .045 & .063 & .010 \\
.018 & .013 & .021 & .108 & .089 & .166 & .006 \\
.001 & .002 & .007 & .175 & .186 & .504 & .001
\end{bmatrix}
$$

$$(I - \vec{A})^{-1}$$

$$
\begin{bmatrix}
1.465 & .008 & .099 & 1.200 & .059 & .189 & .024 \\
.052 & 1.068 & .143 & 1.364 & .068 & .288 & .020 \\
.017 & .008 & 1.013 & .093 & .040 & .158 & .018 \\
.047 & .009 & .126 & 1.730 & .057 & .131 & .010 \\
.039 & .010 & .092 & .336 & 1.072 & .125 & .014 \\
.043 & .020 & .057 & .313 & .126 & 1.247 & .011 \\
.039 & .016 & .076 & .528 & .274 & .678 & 1.011
\end{bmatrix}
$$

$$[\,1.703 \quad 1.138 \quad 1.606 \quad 5.564 \quad 1.696 \quad 2.816 \quad 1.110\,]$$

1967

$$\vec{A}$$

$$
\begin{bmatrix}
.294 & .000 & .004 & .497 & .003 & .048 & .006 \\
.006 & .050 & .037 & .693 & .002 & .148 & .006 \\
.006 & .006 & .000 & .025 & .018 & .100 & .017 \\
.014 & .004 & .062 & .382 & .023 & .055 & .003 \\
.019 & .003 & .050 & .143 & .053 & .070 & .007 \\
.015 & .011 & .021 & .120 & .090 & .168 & .007 \\
.000 & .007 & .004 & .174 & .204 & .482 & .001
\end{bmatrix}
$$

$$(I - \vec{A})^{-1}$$

$$
\begin{bmatrix}
1.447 & .008 & .089 & 1.232 & .057 & .191 & .016 \\
.044 & 1.063 & .131 & 1.312 & .068 & .308 & .016 \\
.015 & .008 & 1.012 & .104 & .039 & .145 & .019 \\
.040 & .010 & .112 & 1.707 & .058 & .140 & .009 \\
.039 & .007 & .077 & .322 & 1.080 & .131 & .011 \\
.037 & .017 & .054 & .328 & .130 & 1.253 & .012 \\
.034 & .019 & .067 & .532 & .294 & .658 & 1.011
\end{bmatrix}
$$

$$[\,1.657 \quad 1.133 \quad 1.542 \quad 5.537 \quad 1.727 \quad 2.826 \quad 1.094\,]$$

1972

$$\vec{A}$$

$$
\begin{bmatrix}
.314 & .000 & .006 & .491 & .002 & .035 & .000 \\
.005 & .054 & .049 & .738 & .002 & .201 & .010 \\
.004 & .005 & .000 & .020 & .019 & .099 & .016 \\
.016 & .004 & .077 & .375 & .016 & .065 & .002 \\
.015 & .002 & .058 & .166 & .056 & .046 & .004 \\
.013 & .008 & .020 & .097 & .075 & .186 & .016 \\
.001 & .001 & .003 & .038 & .014 & .037 & .001
\end{bmatrix}
$$

$$(I - \vec{A})^{-1}$$

$$
\begin{bmatrix}
1.491 & .007 & .109 & 1.223 & .041 & .180 & .006 \\
.050 & 1.068 & .171 & 1.384 & .062 & .402 & .019 \\
.010 & .007 & 1.011 & .079 & .033 & .134 & .017 \\
.044 & .009 & .136 & 1.685 & .044 & .159 & .006 \\
.034 & .006 & .091 & .337 & 1.075 & .102 & .007 \\
.033 & .013 & .053 & .269 & .107 & 1.267 & .010 \\
.005 & .002 & .012 & .082 & .021 & .055 & 1.002
\end{bmatrix}
$$

$$
\begin{bmatrix}
1.667 & 1.112 & 1.583 & 5.059 & 1.383 & 2.299 & 1.067
\end{bmatrix}
$$

1977

$$\vec{A}$$

$$
\begin{bmatrix}
.246 & .000 & .007 & .491 & .006 & .037 & .001 \\
.004 & .071 & .031 & .996 & .005 & .254 & .016 \\
.005 & .011 & .001 & .033 & .027 & .121 & .019 \\
.019 & .006 & .073 & .382 & .023 & .069 & .002 \\
.015 & .003 & .057 & .173 & .060 & .053 & .005 \\
.012 & .009 & .019 & .094 & .084 & .175 & .006 \\
.001 & .001 & .003 & .042 & .016 & .039 & .002
\end{bmatrix}
$$

$$(I - \vec{A})^{-1}$$

$$
\begin{bmatrix}
1.361 & .010 & .100 & 1.147 & .055 & .178 & .008 \\
.067 & 1.096 & .192 & 1.944 & .107 & .538 & .029 \\
.014 & .015 & 1.017 & .130 & .048 & .170 & .021 \\
.049 & .014 & .134 & 1.731 & .062 & .175 & .008 \\
.033 & .008 & .091 & .367 & 1.087 & .119 & .008 \\
.030 & .015 & .052 & .277 & .121 & 1.257 & .010 \\
.006 & .003 & .013 & .094 & .026 & .059 & 1.003
\end{bmatrix}
$$

$$
\begin{bmatrix}
1.560 & 1.161 & 1.599 & 5.690 & 1.506 & 2.496 & 1.087
\end{bmatrix}
$$

9-2

DIRECT BACKWARD LINKAGES

				Sectors			
	1	2	3	4	5	6	7
1947	.542	.302	.589	.620	.276	.407	.437
1958	.555	.338	.582	.611	.296	.396	.528
1963	.581	.371	.566	.604	.286	.370	.480
1967	.597	.373	.558	.596	.299	.368	.437
1972	.617	.379	.542	.612	.275	.340	.060
1977	.622	.357	.578	.640	.322	.348	.076

DIRECT FORWARD LINKAGES

1947	.872	.867	.248	.511	.340	.435	1.187
1958	.832	.950	.180	.563	.373	.424	.915
1963	.843	.953	.174	.553	.354	.421	.877
1967	.853	.942	.171	.542	.346	.432	.873
1972	.848	1.059	.163	.555	.347	.405	.095
1977	.788	1.377	.217	.574	.366	.399	.104

TOTAL BACKWARD LINKAGES

1947	2.113	1.565	2.220	2.319	1.524	1.804	1.898
1958	2.143	1.624	2.204	2.286	1.563	1.782	2.066
1963	2.216	1.677	2.156	2.272	1.523	1.697	1.927
1967	2.239	1.687	2.127	2.238	1.538	1.684	1.832
1972	2.295	1.681	2.085	2.254	1.464	1.608	1.108
1977	2.338	1.675	2.208	2.354	1.573	1.648	1.144

TOTAL FORWARD LINKAGES

1947	3.091	2.777	1.503	2.021	1.681	1.855	3.254
1958	3.017	3.027	1.356	2.136	1.741	1.835	2.729
1963	3.045	3.003	1.346	2.111	1.688	1.817	2.622
1967	3.041	2.943	1.343	2.076	1.667	1.831	2.615
1972	3.057	3.156	1.291	2.083	1.652	1.752	1.179
1977	2.859	3.973	1.415	2.173	1.713	1.762	1.204

9-3 If we reorder sectors, as in Eq. (9-30) in the text, so that those with exogenously specified final demands are first (here this is only sector 3) and those with exogenously specified total outputs are second (here this is sectors 1, 2, and 4), we have the following submatrices: $P = [.864]$ $Q = [.105 \quad .025 \quad .124]$

$$R = \begin{bmatrix} -.213 \\ -.168 \\ -.219 \end{bmatrix} \text{ and } S = \begin{bmatrix} -.832 & .155 & .212 \\ .194 & -.807 & .115 \\ .178 & .101 & -.814 \end{bmatrix}. \text{ Thus}$$

$$M = \begin{bmatrix} .874 & 0 & 0 & 0 \\ -.213 & -1.0 & 0 & 0 \\ -.168 & 0 & -1.0 & 0 \\ -2.19 & 0 & 0 & -1.0 \end{bmatrix} \text{ and}$$

$$N = \begin{bmatrix} 1.0 & .105 & .025 & .124 \\ 0 & -.832 & .155 & .212 \\ 0 & .194 & -.807 & .115 \\ 0 & .178 & .101 & -.814 \end{bmatrix}. \text{ It follows that}$$

$$M^{-1} = \begin{bmatrix} 1.144 & 0 & 0 & 0 \\ -.244 & -1.0 & 0 & 0 \\ -.192 & 0 & -1.0 & 0 \\ -.251 & 0 & 0 & -1.0 \end{bmatrix} \text{ and}$$

$$M^{-1}N = \begin{bmatrix} 1.144 & .120 & .029 & .142 \\ -.244 & .806 & -.161 & -.242 \\ -.192 & -.214 & .802 & -.139 \\ -.251 & -.204 & -.107 & .783 \end{bmatrix}$$

from which we find that, with $\left[-\dfrac{\overline{Y}}{\overline{X}} \right] = \begin{bmatrix} 2050 \\ \overline{4558} \\ 5665 \\ 5079 \end{bmatrix}$, $\left[-\dfrac{X}{Y} \right] = \begin{bmatrix} 3775.756 \\ \overline{1033.197} \\ 2468.991 \\ 1923.926 \end{bmatrix}$. That is,

total output of sector 3 will be 3775.756, and amounts of sector 1, 2, and 4 production available for final demand are 1033.197, 2468.991, and 1923.926, respectively.

9-4

a $A = \begin{bmatrix} .500 & .438 \\ .320 & .450 \end{bmatrix}$, $(I-A)^{-1} = \begin{bmatrix} 4.074 & 3.241 \\ 2.370 & 3.704 \end{bmatrix}$, and $\Delta Y = \begin{bmatrix} 0.9 \\ 63.0 \end{bmatrix}$, so ΔX

$= \begin{bmatrix} 207.833 \\ 235.467 \end{bmatrix}$.

b We now have $A = \begin{bmatrix} .500 & .438 & .001 \\ .320 & .450 & .070 \\ .020 & .050 & .150 \end{bmatrix}$ and

$(I-A)^{-1} = \begin{bmatrix} 4.130 & 3.310 & .277 \\ 2.433 & 3.782 & .314 \\ .240 & .300 & 1.201 \end{bmatrix}$. In conjunction now with $\Delta Y = \begin{bmatrix} 0.9 \\ 63.0 \\ 135.0 \end{bmatrix}$

we find $\Delta X = \begin{bmatrix} 249.710 \\ 282.911 \\ 181.341 \end{bmatrix}$.

9-5 Here $B^{-1} = \begin{bmatrix} 0 & 10 \\ 10 & 0 \end{bmatrix}$ and $Q = \begin{bmatrix} 0 & 5 \\ 5 & 0 \end{bmatrix}$. Solving the characteristic equation $|Q - I| = 0$, we find $\lambda_{max} = c = 5$.

9-6 With $Q = \begin{bmatrix} 1 & .1 \\ 10 & 1 \end{bmatrix}$, we find $\lambda_{max} = 2$.

9-7

a Here $Q = \begin{bmatrix} 10 & -2 \\ -3 & 7 \end{bmatrix}$ and $\lambda_{max} = 11.37$.

b With $B = \begin{bmatrix} .1 & 0 \\ .1 & .1 \end{bmatrix}$, we find $Q = \begin{bmatrix} 10 & -2 \\ -12 & 9 \end{bmatrix}$ and $\lambda_{max} = 14.42$.

Name Index

Subject Index

A

Absorption matrix (*see* Use matrix)
Aggregation:
    sectoral, example of, 176–178
    spatial, example of, 182–189
Aggregation bias, measures of,
    178–182

B

Balanced regional input-output
    model:
    numerical example, 88–89
    structure of, 85–88
Best practice firms, 275
Biproportional nonsurvey methods
    (*see* RAS technique)
Business establishment product
    accounts, example of,
    150–151

C

Columns-only approach for survey-
    based tables, 306–308

Commodity-by-industry approach
    in input-output models,
    139–174, 189–196
Commodity-by-industry energy
    accounts, 210–211
Completely closed model, 30
Consumption coefficients, household:
    average, 52
    defined, 26
    marginal, 52

D

Direct input coefficients (*see* Techni-
    cal coefficients)
Dynamic input-output models,
    340–351
    difference equations in, 341
    differential equations in, $341n$
    turnpike growth in, 350–351

E

Ecological coefficients, 241–243, 254
Ecological commodities, 240–243
Ecological inputs, 241–243, 284